Ina Coolbrith

Ina Coolbrith
Librarian and Laureate of California

Josephine DeWitt Rhodehamel

Raymund Francis Wood

Brigham Young University Press

LCN: 78-84093
ISBN: 0-8425-1445-7
Brigham Young University Press, Provo, Utah 84601
Printed in the United States of America
1973 2.5M   8074

For Margaret Ann Wood and Harry Ernest Rhodehamel

Contents

List of Illustrations

Foreword

One man's maxim is another man's cliché. But even the hoariest of clichés usually bears in its heart a solid grain of truth, like the piece of grit underlying all the nacreous layers of a pearl. The maxim/cliché which best applies to the career of Ina Coolbrith is the one which prescribes an unhappy childhood as essential to a writer's success.

Certainly, as coauthors Rhodehamel and Wood make clear in this excellent biography, Ina Coolbrith had far from the happiest of childhoods. And her adulthood, as well, was beset with more than its share of downs, as well as ups. These vicissitudes taught her much about life, love and death, just as the axiom suggests. The results may be seen in her poetry. Her writing was but an extension of her being. Thus it was a key to her reactions to the alternating current of victories and defeats which made up her career.

Was Ina Coolbrith's life a tragic one? It is difficult to say, since tragedy, like beauty, lies in the eye of the beholder. She was bruised by adversity; but is not everyone? She had loved ones taken by death, but that is the fate of all of us, hod carriers and poets alike. What gave a peculiar and pathetic, if not exactly tragic, cast to the career of the California poetess was a series of searing humiliations. She managed to hide most of them from the public but the price of their seclusion was a high one in psychological terms. Ina thought that she had successfully repressed the dark side of her past. But it leaked out between the lines of her gloomier poems, which offer such a striking contrast with her bright, summery verse of birds and flowers. In London, George Meredith noted this and wrote: "In touch with every human emotion; she has suffered; an echo of sadness rings in her work."

So reticent was Miss Coolbrith about her origins, youth and young adulthood, and so respected was her reserve by those fond of her, like Gertrude Atherton (who, accordingly, did not even mention her in *Adventures of a Novelist*), that most Californians have no idea that she was born Josephine Donna Smith in 1841. Her father, Don Carlos Smith, died that very year. She was the niece of the founder of The Church of Jesus Christ of Latter-day Saints, Joseph Smith, later martyred in Nauvoo, Illinois.

Ina's mother had fled from Missouri bigotry to Illinois, only to face new mobs there. Later she married a non-Mormon printer and lived with him in St. Louis, attempting to forget, forever, the trauma of Nauvoo. Thus she exacted a sworn pledge from her little girl to banish from her heart and mind all consciousness of her Mormon birth and upbringing. Technically, California's first poet laureate was a fallen-away Saint, a jack Mormon. But her apostasy was not of her own doing but forced upon her by the fears of her persecuted mother. Ina never adopted another faith, although she was a highly ethical and moral person, even religious in a sense, though not sectarian. But she loved nature more, and it helped her to honestly confront the dark side of life which constantly pulled her from a feeling of joy to one of sorrow.

Shortly after Josephine Donna Smith married she suffered a second painful humiliation. Her husband, in an unwarranted fit of jealousy and suspicion, attempted to kill her. She divorced him, lost her only child, and suffered deep psychological wounds from the double trauma. But these blows were far from the last.

When Ina Coolbrith (for she now assumed this name to hide her identity) later had to decide between a purely literary career, for which she showed such great promise, and a mundane occupation which would guarantee her a steady income, she compromised. To support her dependent niece and nephew, she became Oakland's first city librarian and relegated her writing to a part-time activity. Then came the next crushing defeat. She made the mistake of replying with candor to a prying newspaperman doing an exposé of the creaking public library. The library board was as politically sensitive as it was personally and professionally insensitive and fired her from her post.

When friends, the newspapers, the public and various sympathetic organizations tried to rally to the support of the librarian with almost

20 years of hard work behind her, they hurt Ina more. Since she was basically a private person, they only made matters worse by spreading her name over the front pages. Ina Coolbrith did not waste time lamenting the injustice of her dismissal. But she was again humiliated and was disturbed profoundly by the realization that her sacrifice for her kin had brought her more mortification. She wrote, "What a wickedness my whole life has been forced to be, against its truer self."

As a young girl, she had taken to the literary life like a spaniel to water, publishing poems in her teens and holding her own with the likes of Bret Harte and Charles Warren Stoddard as a writer of the 1860s. Her poetry, sentimental and naive at first, grew to be mature and perceptive, full of imagery and insight. It was difficult to return to these promising beginnings after the long years of librarianship, but return she did during the 1890s. She shut out of her mind the cruel action of the library board just as she had walled off her Mormonism and her disastrous marriage. She traveled, she wrote. She returned to librarianship eventually. But, above all, she encouraged others to read and to write. Just as Jack London had come to her library for recognition, guidance and inspiration, others now came to her home as it became a genuine literary salon.

At last, late in life, wider recognition came when, in 1915, she was chosen the first Poet Laureate of California by virtual acclamation of her fellow-authors in a Congress of Writers and Journalists. The California Legislature made it official four years later by joint resolution.

This biography is a labor of love but not an uncritical work; it is no blind paean, no eulogy. The coauthors are fair, critical of Miss Coolbrith's aloofness and vanity, and as objective as sympathetic but honest partisans can be. They have no doubt (nor does this writer) that she was badly used by Fate. Their narrative succeeds well in portraying this pioneer poet and real person, rather than the shadowy creature of legend which most of us have accepted. Though chock-full of biographical detail, it is an interesting, colorful and anecdotal narrative. In short, this work by authors Rhodehamel and Wood is both a reference tool, with its splendid bibliographical appendices, and a volume which is highly readable. Rarely does the oft-cited "definitive biography" really exist, but the term is appropriate for this book.

We owe the coauthors a debt of gratitude for restoring Ina Coolbrith to her rightful place in the gallery of great westerners. She was the first of a long line of talented women who created a literary and poetic tradition in an anti-intellectual and "strictly business" West. The authors claim that she was more proud of her career in librarianship than of her poetry. Perhaps so. But she will not be remembered as a librarian but as a writer, a poet whose verse holds up remarkably well when compared to that of most of her peers, like Henry Meade Bland or Joaquin Miller.

In truth, Ina Coolbrith deserves best to be remembered as a literary catalyst, a force for culture in the raw, pioneer West. It was said of her, as she grew old, that "Her hair was sixty, but her eyes were twenty." For all of her reserve, she kept this spark, this youthful spirit, until her death. And she drew creative people, both the recognized (Sterling, London, Mary Austin, Gertrude Atherton, Isadora Duncan) and the unknown, to her as if by some kind of mysterious magnetism or gravitational pull. It is in this role of "evangelizer" of culture that Ina Coolbrith will be longest remembered.

Richard H. Dillon
Mill Valley, California

Acknowledgments

When Ina Coolbrith was named California Poet Laureate in 1915, she accepted a wreath of laurel "with deep gratitude and deeper humility." Her words come back to us as we begin this list of acknowledgments of our indebtedness for friendly cooperation from a large number of libraries, societies, publishers, governmental agencies, and individuals. Without such generous help through several years of preparation this publication would have been impossible. To all whom we are about to name we owe our profound thanks.

Among library resources we found the largest and most varied collection of Coolbrith papers in the Bancroft Library of the University of California in Berkeley. Here are correspondence, scrapbooks, manuscripts, pictures, etc., associated directly with Miss Coolbrith, as well as a quantity of related material in a library rich in the sources of her period in California letters. Our thanks go to Dr. James E. Skipper, University Librarian, and to Dr. James D. Hart, Director, Bancroft Library. We are grateful to the staff of the Bancroft Library, especially to Mr. Robert Becker and Dr. John Barr Tompkins, as well as Mrs. Julia H. Macleod, now retired, and the late Mrs. Helen Harding Bretnor, for gracious assistance over several years. In the General Library we were aided by the use of materials in the Document and Map Departments. To Miss Audrey Phillips of the General Reference Department and Mrs. Anne Reed of the Newspaper Department go our special thanks.

Second only to the Bancroft Library for volume of material in its collection of Coolbrith papers is the Henry E. Huntington Library in San Marino. For the use of these materials we express our gratitude to Mr. Robert O. Dougan, Librarian, and to Miss Mary Isabel Fry of Readers' Service.

We appreciate our access to the varied resources of the California State Library. To Mrs. Carma Leigh, State Librarian, Mr. Allan R. Ottley, Librarian, and Mrs. Joan P. Dugdale, Reference Librarian, of the California Section, Miss Charlotte Harris of the Reference Section, all in Sacramento, and to Mr. Richard Dillon, Librarian, Sutro Branch, San Francisco, goes our sincere appreciation for many favors.

In the Oakland Public Library, where Miss Coolbrith herself was the first city librarian, are many mementos, scrapbooks, letters, and pictures. Here, too, are the *Minutes* of the Board of the Oakland Library Association and of the Oakland Board of Library Directors during the years of Miss Coolbrith's employment. We want to express our thanks to Mr. William Brett, Librarian, and to members of his staff for their patience and courtesy. To Mrs. Frances Buxton, Librarian of the California Room; Miss Harriet Feldman, Fine Arts Librarian; Mrs. Mary Sawyer, Sociology Division Librarian, and Miss Virginia Smith of the Literature Division go our thanks for many kindnesses. We wish to record here our appreciation to former staff members, now retired: Miss Leona Alexander, Reference Librarian; Dr. Peter Thomas Conmy, Librarian; Miss Marguerite Rodgers, Art Librarian; and Miss Helen Willits, California Room; all of Oakland, California.

In the Bender Room of the Mills College Library in Oakland there is a collection of letters to Albert Bender from Miss Coolbrith during her last years, also some manuscripts of individual poems. We want to thank Miss Flora Elizabeth Reynolds, Librarian, and Mrs. Mary Manning Cook, Reference Librarian in charge of the Bender Room, for permission to use these items. To the late Mrs. Evelyn Steele Little, former Librarian of Mills, we express our gratitude for use of Coolbrith items in the Bender Room several years ago.

We wish to thank Mr. Carl S. Dentzel, Director, Southwest Museum in Los Angeles, for use of Miss Coolbrith's letters to Charles Fletcher Lummis. We appreciate the kindness of Mrs. Gladys Hansen of the Department of Rare Books and Special Collections in the San Francisco Public Library, in verifying a Coolbrith manuscript in that department. To Mr. William W. Whitney, Director, Mr. James de T. Abajian, Librarian, and Mr. M. K. Swingle, Assistant Librarian, California Historical Society in San Francisco, we are grateful for reference assistance and for the use of Coolbrith letters in the Society's files. Mrs. Helen S. Giffen, Director, Society of California Pioneers in San Francisco, graciously permitted use of Coolbrith correspondence on file in the library of that society. For permission to use the family papers of Mrs. Ina Graham, a grandniece of Miss Coolbrith, we are particularly grateful. For assistance in locating some out-of-print anthologies we are under obligation to the Reference Department of the Library of Congress. We are indebted to the Los Angeles Public Library and the Powell Library of the University of California in Los Angeles for use of the files of the *Los Angeles Star*.

Of special help to us in our search for material on Miss Coolbrith's Mormon background are several libraries in Salt Lake City. We appreciate the kindness of Mr. John James, Librarian, and Mrs. Karen Hackleman, Reference Librarian, of the Utah Historical Society. In two official libraries of The Church of Jesus Christ of Latter-day Saints, the Genealogical Society Library, Mr. Delbert E. Roach, Librarian, and the Church Historian's Office, Mr. Earl E. Olson, Librarian, we found answers to specific questions, and are grateful. We also acknowledge help from the LDS Genealogical Research Library in Oakland, Mrs. Pearl A. Sparks, Librarian.

We have quoted from some of the materials mentioned above and acknowledge our appreciation here. By permission of the Bancroft Library, University of California, Berkeley, we are quoting one letter by Ina Coolbrith in full, and excerpts from a number of other letters to and from her, also a passage from one letter in the Gertrude Atherton papers. Reproduced by permission of the Huntington Library, San Marino, California, are brief passages from several items, four letters from Ina Coolbrith, and nine from other correspondents. We are permitted by the California State Library to quote brief passages from letters in the Coolbrith papers on file in the California Section. With the permission of the Oakland Public Library we have quoted from letters and miscellaneous items as well as the *Minutes* of the boards of the Oakland Library Association and the Oakland Free Library. Mills College Library grants us permission to quote briefly from four of Miss Coolbrith's letters in the Bender Room. We are also allowed to quote passages from three letters in the library of the Southwest Museum in Los Angeles. The California Historical Society in San Francisco permits the quotation of two letters by Ina Coolbrith in their files.

For permission to quote copyrighted passages in books and periodicals we acknowledge our sincere gratitude. Quotation of a sentence from George W. Beattie's *Heritage of the Valley* (Pasadena, 1939) has been permitted by Biobooks of Oakland, California. Ina Coolbrith's poem, "In the Library," has been reprinted with permission from *Library Journal*, December 1891, published by the R. R. Bowker Company (a Xerox com-

Joyce Backus of San Francisco for a quotation from her thesis, "History of the San Francisco Mercantile Library Association" (University of California, 1931), and to Mr. Carlton Waldo Kendall of Oakland for permission to use a sentence from his article, "California's Pioneer Poetess," in the *Overland Monthly* for August 1929. We thank Dr. Lionel Stevenson of Duke University for his courtesy in granting us the right to reprint in full his essay, "The Mind of Ina Coolbrith," in the *Overland Monthly* of May 1930, also for permitting our brief quotation from his article, "Ina Coolbrith, *Wings of Sunset*," in the *Saturday Review of Literature*, 26 April 1930. Mrs. Ina Graham of Berkeley has given us permission to quote from the manuscript of Miss Coolbrith's unpublished poem, "Twenty-two," also to quote most of Jack London's letter to Ina Coolbrith, dated 13 December 1906, as well as his inscription in an autograph album belonging to Miss Coolbrith. To Mrs. Louis A. Sanchez of Oakland we are obliged for an excerpt from a letter of Mrs. Ina L. Cook to Mrs. Nellie van De Grift Sanchez.

Our picture credits are as follows: To Mr. Ansel Adams, Carmel, California, for the right to reproduce his portrait of Ina Coolbrith made in 1925; to Mr. Morley Baer, Berkeley, for permission to reprint (in this book only) his photograph of 15-17 Macondray Lane, San Francisco; to the Bancroft Library, University of California, Berkeley, for courtesy in permitting reproduction of the following pictures in their collection: portraits by Bianca Conti of Ina Coolbrith and Carl Seyfforth, Ina Coolbrith and Charles Fletcher Lummis in 1925 by Harry Noyes Pratt, Francis Bret Harte, Charles Warren Stoddard, Gertrude Franklin Atherton, Senator James Duval Phelan, Albert Bender, and the view of Los Angeles in 1853, from a drawing by Charles Kopple in the *Pacific Railroad Reports*, volume five; to the Oakland Public Library for the right to reproduce pictures of the following: Ina Coolbrith as a child, Ina Coolbrith photographs of 1870, 1894, 1895, 1923 and 1925, Henry Frank Peterson, Josephine Clifford McCrackin, John Henry Carmany, and views of the Oakland Free Library, 1878-1902, Ina Coolbrith's home in Oakland, and Ina Coolbrith Branch, Oakland Free Library; to the Preston Player Collection at Knox College, Galesburg, Illinois, for permitting reproduction of the original painting of *Nauvoo by the Miss. River;* to Mrs. Ina Graham of Berkeley for permission to reproduce pictures of the following: Ina Coolbrith about the time of her marriage, Miss Coolbrith's mother, her sister, Ina Lillian Peterson as a child, Miss Coolbrith's home at 1067 Broadway, San Francisco, and two interior views of her home at 1604 Taylor Street, San Francisco; to Mrs. Alice Bashford Wallace of Sidney, British Columbia, for her courtesy in permitting our use of the following: two details from a group portrait of the Congress of Authors and

Journalists, 2 July 1915, portraits of Joaquin Miller and of Herbert Bashford, also the manuscript of Ina Coolbrith's poem, "When the Grass Shall Cover Me." The sketch of the Oakland Free Library, 1878-1902, first appeared in the *Oakland Tribune Yearbook, 1887*, was copied by Jerry Ferguson for the Oakland Library, and is here reproduced through the courtesy of Mr. William Knowland, publisher of the *Oakland Tribune*.

We are obliged to several public offices for their aid in our search for information, among them the following: the County Clerk and Recorder of Hancock County, Carthage, Illinois; the Los Angeles County District Court; Los Angeles County Recorder; Mountain View Cemetery Association, Oakland; Oakland City Clerk and Oakland Park Department; St. Louis County Recorder, Clayton, Missouri; St. Louis (City) Bureau of Vital Statistics; and the San Francisco Recreation and Park Department.

In addition to those listed above, the following persons have aided us in a variety of ways; some knew Miss Coolbrith personally, and they and each of the others mentioned supplied us with needed information on many points: Mrs. Carol Ives Alderson, City Librarian, Ashland, Oregon; Mrs. Aldrich Barton, Oakland, California; Miss Clara Breed, City Librarian, San Diego, California; Mr. Robert Brownell, Associate Registrar, University of California, Berkeley; Mr. Ferdinand Burgdorff, Pebble Beach, California; Mr. and Mrs. Robert Carmany, Walnut Grove, California; Mrs. Alden Crow, Junior League of San Francisco; Miss Anna De Martini, San Francisco; Mr. Daniel Gilson, Historiographer, Bohemian Club, San Francisco; Mrs. Edith Googins, Librarian, Scarborough, Maine; Mr. Kenneth L. Graham, Secretary, Board of Publication, Reorganized Church of Jesus Christ of Latter Day Saints, Independence, Missouri; Mr. and Mrs. C. Dewey Hale, Nauvoo Restoration Association, Nauvoo, Illinois; Mrs. Philip S. Haring, College Curator, Knox College, Galesburg, Illinois; Mr. and Mrs. William Harlan, Benicia, California; Dr. Ray Held, Assistant Dean, School of Librarianship, University of California, Berkeley; Miss Joyce Jansen, San Francisco; Mr. Henry Kirk, Oakland; the late Mrs. Eunice Mitchell Lehmer, Berkeley; Mrs. Dorothy Shaw Libbey, Scarborough, Maine; Dr. T. Edgar Lyon, Historian, Nauvoo Restoration, Inc., Salt Lake City, Utah; Mrs. Frances McFall, Berkeley; Miss Juanita Miller, Oakland; Mr. Louis M. Nourse, City Librarian, St. Louis, Missouri; Mrs. Irene D. Paden, Alameda, California; Mrs. Annaleone D. Patton, Berkeley; Mr. Louis J. Rasmussen, San Francisco Historic Records, Colma, California; Mr. John S. Richards, Carmel, California; Miss Amy Rinehart, Oakland; Miss Millie Robbins, *San Francisco Chronicle;* Mr. Robert L. Rose, Librarian, Bohemian Club, San Francisco; Mr. Jesse Winter Smith, San Jose, California; Mr. Roy A. Smith, Joseph Smith Historical Center, Nauvoo, Illinois; Mrs. Delpha Stevens de

Timofeev, Librarian, Ina Coolbrith Branch, Oakland Free Library; Mrs. Alice Bashford Wallace, Sidney, B. C., Canada.

We are especially indebted to Mrs. Ina Graham, Berkeley, a grand-niece of Ina Coolbrith. Mrs. Graham has not only put her files of family papers at our disposal, but has made copies of letters of particular interest, has permitted reproduction of several of these as well as valuable family photographs, and finally has read the entire manuscript and made meticulous notes that have prevented a number of errors. Her cooperation and patience over several years are gratefully acknowledged.

The authors wish likewise to record their gratitude for the special and personal cooperation of Mrs. Margaret Ann Wood and Mr. Harry Ernest Rhodehamel, without whose understanding and encouragement this endeavor might not have been realized. Though we note assistance from many sources, we state that we are wholly responsible for the text and for any errors or omissions.

We are deeply appreciative of the expert advice of Mrs. Gail W. Bell, Senior Editor, Scholarly Publications, Brigham Young University Press, and of her suggestions for improvement in phrasing, her concern for accuracy, and her cheerful cooperation at all times.

Josephine DeWitt Rhodehamel
Raymund Francis Wood

Prologue:
The Crossing
of the
Mountains

On a chilly autumn day in 1851 the quiet of a mountain pass was broken by the growing din of a train of covered wagons, winding west. The pass was the lowest and easiest in the Sierra Nevada range, and the seventeen dilapidated wagons were the first to roll that way, breaking trail through low sagebrush and bunchgrass.

Ahead of the caravan jogged a tired pony carrying a man and a child. Picturesque in leather jacket and moccasins, his long black hair in two braids with bright cord entwined, Jim Beckwourth, a mulatto, was mountain man, self-made Crow chief, and teller of outrageous tales. To the blonde, gray-eyed girl, ten-year-old Ina Smith, sitting ahead of him, he was the most romantic person she had ever seen. His dark face, his attire, and the stories of his own exploits had bewitched the weary little traveler from St. Louis. To be riding with so wondrous a being was exciting beyond telling. And now another honor would soon be hers.

She had ridden with Jim Beckwourth that she might be the first white child to enter California by the pass he had just discovered. The thought that she should have been singled out from all the children in the caravan was joy almost too great to bear. It stiffened her tired backbone and put an extra shine in the dark gray of her eyes. They reached the summit and stopped to wait for the wagons. The worn vehicles jolted and halted and jolted on again with maddening slowness as the oxen faltered through the sage. Ina found it hard to look at the poor beasts, so near their destination and as near the end of their endurance after seven months of toil and hunger.

Jim slid off the saddleless pony and lifted the girl down. Ina looked around her, puzzled by the appearance of this pass. She had expected and feared a rocky canyon and perhaps snow. But the land was rolling hill country. Mile-high, as they were, there were no towering peaks about them. The highest and most imposing elevation was a long, wooded mountain a few miles south of the pass. It lay in remote dignity, its slopes darkening, as a cloud crossed the sun. A gust of autumn wind, cold and tangy with the scent of pine from the mountain, struck Ina's face. The girl shivered. She did not know that her mere passing this way was to give that peak her name in years to come.

Jim called her attention to the valley below them. Though cloud shadows lay around them, the valley was illuminated by a shaft of sunlight. It was small and level and perfect, a gem in a sober setting. Fed by Sierra streams, the southern end was still green in spite of frosts that touched it every morning. To the north the valley floor was colored by the muted gray-green of sage. In the center, like an island in a lake, rose a small, pointed butte that had a rosy translucence in the sun. And beyond, their color intensified by the thunderheads above them, were the distant blue mountains. The picture before her was like a promise, the girl thought, like the Promised Land in the Bible. Ina's eyes were bright with anticipation, Jim's with pride of possession, and with love, too. For he loved this little valley with more tenderness than he had ever loved his women. He stood still, looking out, then turned to the girl. This was the moment for which he was waiting.

"There, little girl," he said quietly, hiding the swagger. "There is California. There is your kingdom."[1]

Part One
Nauvoo to the Western Sea
1841 to 1861

1
Roads
to
Nauvoo

There are thorns in the smoothest of pathways.

Ina Coolbrith, from
"Sorrow Is Better than Laughter" (1892)

New England Ancestry

The child who was to grow up and become California's first poet laureate, and to become known throughout the English-speaking world as Ina Coolbrith, the Poetess of the Golden Gate, was born on 10 March 1841, in Nauvoo (formerly Commerce), Illinois, and was named Josephine Donna Smith.[1] She was the youngest of three, all girls, the children of Agnes Moulton (née Coolbrith) and Don Carlos Smith. Josephine Donna's middle name honored her father, but her first name was a reminder of the Josephs in her family; both of her grandfathers were named Joseph, and so was her uncle, Joseph Smith, the Prophet of The Church of Jesus Christ of Latter-day Saints. Despite the importance of the name Joseph in their family, Agnes and Don Carlos seldom, if ever, called their youngest child Josephine, but always Ina, a pet name, or diminutive, derived from Josephine; and so from her earliest recollection the little girl believed her first name was Ina, and she herself never used any other.[2]

Her grandparents were New Englanders, as were also their forebears. It is a coincidence that all four of her grandparents were born and reared not far from each other, in an area extending from Topsfield, Massachusetts, northwest to Gilsum, New Hampshire, then northeast to Scarborough on the coast of Maine. Yet the two couples, the Smiths and the Coolbriths, never knew each other.

These four persons were born in the same decade, the mid 1770s and the early 1780s, a critical decade in the history of their country. Indeed, the very day that the Declaration of Independence was read aloud in the town square in Philadelphia, Lucy Mack Smith, Ina's paternal grandmother, drew her first breath in a New Hampshire farmhouse.[3] Restless, driven, and driving, she became the most articulate of the four grandparents. Between the hurried comings and goings recorded in her reminiscences, the story of Ina Smith's beginnings emerges, as disconnected as a bag of quilt pieces, waiting to be put together. If the words, "Life, Liberty, and the Pursuit of Happiness," read aloud in Philadelphia on Lucy Mack's birthday were to thrill the citizens who heard them, and stir all the colonies to action, their intent was to be an unconscious force in the lives of Lucy, her children, and her children's children. The search for these three inalienable rights took them down many a desperate road, roads sodden with rain or rough and frozen, and took them panting, running for dear life, seeking cover in all weathers. It was seldom a conscious pursuit of happiness, but always a search for liberty, and often a frantic race for life. This was the road to Nauvoo.

The Family of Joseph Smith, the Prophet

The road to Nauvoo really began in Tunbridge, Vermont, where in 1796 twenty-year-old Lucy Mack married a farmer of twenty-four, Joseph Smith. Lucy's mother, Lydia Gates, was a Connecticut schoolteacher. Lucy's father, Solomon Mack, who had been a soldier in the Indian wars with Major Robert Rogers, had inherited some wealth but lost it all in a series of unfortunate speculations.[4] Lucy's farmer husband was an unsettled man. The frequent moves he made from one locality to another, now in Vermont, now in New Hampshire, were motivated by the hope of economic improvement as he and Lucy reared their family of eleven children. Even after the children were grown, Joseph and Lucy were unable to put down roots. From voluntary wanderers they became refugees, compelled to flee from the enemies of their son's religion.

All but three of their children lived to maturity and marriage. Their fourth child, Joseph, became the founder of a new religious movement, his earliest and consistently most loyal followers being his parents and his brothers and sisters. The youngest son was Don Carlos, father of Ina. He was born in Norwich, Vermont, 25 March 1816, when his brother Joseph, whom he came to adore, was thirteen.[5] Don Carlos was a baby when his father went west from Vermont to Palmyra, New York, in search of better farming land, to be followed soon by Lucy and her children. Here in Palmyra, in this family named Smith, occurred the incident that was to affect the destiny of thousands yet to come, to cause

4

persecutions and migrations, to build cities and even a commonwealth, to create a culture within a culture, and a history within a history.

During the 1820s, when the Smith family was building a log farm-house near Palmyra, people everywhere in the country were being stirred by religious revivals. New ideas were shaking old complacencies in city and village. As preachers held camp meetings, groups were converted en masse, born anew in their old beliefs or embracing new faiths. All were tossed and driven, some won over by fear, some by pleading of prayer and hymn, while others were still tormented by doubts. The Smith family joined the Presbyterian church; all but adolescent Joseph. Tortured by indecision and self-analysis, he finally reported to his astonished parents that he had had a vision in which he was told to join none of the churches he knew. From time to time he declared that new visions had appeared to him, the cumulative effect of which was to convince him and his father and mother that he, Joseph, was chosen of God to be the Prophet and founder of a new church. He said that an angel called Moroni appeared before him and directed him to a spot on the Smith farm where he unearthed a set of golden plates, mysteriously inscribed. The sensational story of this discovery and the ultimate printing of the Book of Mormon are too well known to be repeated here."

What follows is the story of an enthusiast who believed himself called to lead a people. Joseph was now growing into a tall, well-built man, sure of himself in a group. The inner conviction of his mission added a glow to the large dark gray eyes and an eagerness to a mouth at once strong and sweet, the lower lip full, the upper, a perfect Cupid's bow. The eyebrows were straight and distinct under a high forehead. His nose was strongly aquiline as was his mother's. Joseph was twenty-seven when the Book of Mormon was printed and The Church of Jesus Christ of Lat-ter-day Saints was organized in Fayette, New York. The farmers round-about were not impressed. They considered the golden plates the pro-duct of Smith's imagination, and guffawed at the idea that he, a country boy, could have translated the plates or written the Book of Mormon. Derision soon gave way to downright hostility. The atmosphere became unsafe for both Joseph's new church and his family, for by this time Joseph was married to his beloved Emma Hale.

About this time, December 1830, Joseph Smith had a visitor from Ohio, Sidney Rigdon, a Campbellite minister who had read the Book of Mor-mon and was converted to the new faith. He and Joseph had long dis-cussions not only of doctrine but of practical steps for the church to take. A little group of Rigdon's friends, converts like himself, were liv-ing in Kirtland, Ohio, a hamlet about twenty-five miles east of Cleve-land, and Rigdon believed the place ideal for church headquarters.

Near the latter part of January 1831, therefore, Joseph and Emma, with Sidney Rigdon and Edward Partridge, started for Kirtland by sleigh, reaching the place about the first of February. They were warmly greeted by the Saints there, especially Newel K. Whitney and his wife, in whose home Joseph and Emma were guests. Joseph was urged to invite the rest of his family to join him in Kirtland.[7] It was because of this that the Mormon church as a growing institution had its real start in Kirtland, Ohio. From here the missionaries went out, north, east, south, and west, and even across the Atlantic. And to the same little Ohio town converts came streaming, from Maine and Massachusetts, from Canada and England. During the spring Joseph's parents came by boat from Buffalo. With them were their children and a number of church members who had decided to move west.[8] Mother Smith's heart was full, now that her family was about her again. Her two older, married sons, Hyrum and Joseph, were there with their families. So was her oldest daughter, Sophronia, the wife of Calvin Stoddard. The next daughter, Catherine, had married Wilkins Salisbury in January, and was beginning a new home in Kirtland. Still living at home were the unmarried children, Samuel, William, Don Carlos, and the little girl Lucy. Lucy was ten and Don Carlos fifteen when they arrived in Kirtland.

In Kirtland, the Saints, as they came to be called, set about building homes, planning a city to be dominated by a temple, and developing farms. Hopes were high, and missionaries were going out to bring the gospel to New Englander and western settler alike. Some had gone as far as the Kaw River in Kansas to convert the Pawnees. Journeying with some of these missionaries through Missouri, Joseph was entranced with the beauty of the flower-decked prairie, the rolling hills and the timbered banks of meandering streams. Here, too, they would come! Here they would build cities peopled by Saints. In Missouri would be the new Zion.

The place eventually selected for Mormon settlement was called Far West, and was located near Independence, on the Missouri-Kansas border. Another sight that stirred Joseph's imagination was a promontory in a bend of the Grand River. Here he found a great rock which he declared was revealed to him as the altar of Adam. He gave the place a strangely poetic and foreign name, Adam-ondi-Ahman, but the place was to come and go before map makers could pin it to any map. Joseph's interest in a new Zion farther west was increased by a sudden show of violence against him at Hiram, near Kirtland. Out of the night a mob appeared, dragged him from his house, stripped him and tarred him. He had previously known scoffing and ridicule, but not manhandling. Joseph recovered from his injuries, but the memory of them remained, and he determined to remove his followers, as soon as it was feasible, to the great open prairies of western Missouri. For the present the building went on in Kirtland. A schoolhouse was erected, and plans were under way for laying the foundation of a temple. New convers streamed in. And still the missionaries went abroad in the land to seek more and more followers.

Agnes Coolbrith of Maine

Two of these missionaries, Samuel Harrison Smith and Orson Hyde, headed for New England in February 1832.[9] For, though they did not know it, one of the roads to Kirtland, and thence to Nauvoo, ran through Boston. In this story of Ina Coolbrith the winding road from Boston to Nauvoo is an important one. Samuel and Orson carried copies of the Book of Mormon with them. The book had gone ahead of them, to Boston at least. Friends and relatives of two of the Saints, Martin Harris and Thomas Marsh, had heard about the golden plates. Some had actually read the Book of Mormon. There was intense excitement in this little group when they learned that Samuel, brother of Joseph Smith, was coming to Boston to preach.[10] Among these devotees was Mrs. Augusta Cobb, a boardinghouse keeper. Living in her home were two young women who had come to Boston recently, one from Andover, Massachusetts, the other all the way from Maine. Mary Bailey from Andover was a village girl in her twenties. So was Agnes Moulton Coolbrith who had come down by boat from Scarborough, on the Maine coast.

Agnes's Scottish ancestors had settled in Scarborough in the middle seventeenth century. The men were woodsmen and farmers, carpenters and shipbuilders. In 1776 they had put down their axes and hoes and hammers to join the Colonial armies. And when the war was over, they had come back to Scarborough to rear families and build churches and schools. A close community feeling held families in Scarborough for generations.[11] The family named Coolbrith, or Coolbroth (as Agnes's father, Joseph, spelled the name) was no exception. Agnes's mother, Mary Foss of nearby Pepperellborough (now Saco), was born in 1783; she was three years her husband's junior. Of their eight children, all born in Scarborough, Agnes Moulton was their third, arriving 11 July 1811.[12] With her two elder sisters, Charlotte and Catherine, she came to know the pleasures and the drudgery of life in the small New England community in the 1820s, growing up on the Coolbroth homestead, where the Dunstan River meanders through the marshes to the Atlantic. While Scarborough, with its widely scattered homes, may have been long established, and even smug in its self-sufficiency, life there was scarcely more comfortable than in any of the pioneer towns developing in New York and farther west.

The girls learned the frontier skills of carding and spinning and weaving wool, and making the goods into the warm clothing demanded by Maine winters. They may have grown flax and prepared it for sturdy homespun sheets and other household linens, or for linsey-woolsey garments. But the fabrics that most delighted them were the calicos and sprigged muslins and dimities that came in bolts from the new mills in Massachusetts. Needlework was not only a necessary skill; it was a source of pleasure as well. The girls must have enjoyed quilting parties as well as skating, sleighing, and maple sugar boiling. Whether or not they went to neighborhood dances, they certainly attended church, where they joined in congregational hymn singing. Her love of singing and her skill with the needle Agnes took with her when she went to Boston to make her way in the world. Boston, in 1832, was a city to make a village girl gasp. The closely built houses, the churches with their great steeples, the streets full of people hurrying on a thousand errands, all amazed Agnes. Boston, with its growing mills and other opportunities for employment, was attracting the children of many farmers and craftsmen of New England. Agnes might have worked as a seamstress, mill worker, shop assistant, or domestic help. Fortunately, at Mrs. Cobb's boardinghouse she found Mary Bailey, another girl as lonely and as homesick as herself. Both girls went together to Old South Church where they were soon singing in the choir.[13]

The unrest that had brought them to Boston was characteristic of the New England of the period. That province of America, hitherto self-satisfied and tradition-bound, was being swept by revolutions and movements, economic, social, literary, political, and religious. It was the age of the abolitionists and transcendentalists, both movements stirring old complacencies. This was the time when church and state were finally divorced, and the Congregationalists lost their political control. Even that sect was torn apart, giving rise to a strong Unitarian movement. Religious ties were being loosened, and religions themselves liberalized. Reformers, educators, and revivalists were attracting wide audiences.

In June 1832 two young, inexperienced, and footsore evangelists, Samuel Smith and Orson Hyde, walked into Boston after a long journey from Kirtland, Ohio. Since the religious climate of the city was receptive to change, the preachers were somewhat successful, and they had organized a small band of their church before the year was over. They had gone directly to the home of Mrs. Augusta Cobb, who had already read the Book of Mormon and who was almost as breathless with anticipation as were two of her boarders, Mary Bailey and Agnes Coolbrith. Samuel and Orson did not fill any large halls in the city, but the small groups who came to hear were deeply moved by the earnestness of the young men.[14]

8

This new religion, though stemming from the mysterious golden plates, seemed to the girls to come straight out of the New Testament. It seemed based on community living, the brotherhood of man, and helping one another. It seemed warm and friendly. Agnes thought of the Old South Church. Without Mary she could never have been happy with the cold formality of worship there. With Mrs. Cobb the girls attended every meeting held by the young preachers. They were strongly affected. The long, sweet summer evenings were given over to soul-searching and mental anguish. To join the Saints in the West would mean departure from all that was familiar and dear. They might never see their families again. But the pull of the unknown was strong and romantic.

So too, it must be admitted, was the physical attraction of the young missionaries. Mary made her decision before June was out, and was baptized by Samuel. Agnes also was baptized early in July, shortly before Samuel and Orson left Boston to preach in other cities. The new church in Ohio now seemed all the more attractive to the girls, and they decided to go west. They made their preparations and left in the summer of 1833.[15] Their journey was made in company with other converts, in a train of large covered wagons, with whole families and many unattached young people like themselves. All were taking advantage of this opportunity to move west and improve their economic conditions, as well as to build the foundations of a new Zion on earth.

2
Kirtland
to
Nauvoo

Far away, and strange . . . Seem the dark, troubled years.

Ina Coolbrith, from
"Memorial Poem" (1881)

Life in Kirtland, Ohio

The new converts were welcomed in Kirtland. Agnes and Mary became boarders in the Smith home.[1] The household was dominated, nominally, by the church's patriarch himself, Joseph Smith, a work-worn farmer now in his sixties. Actually it was his wife, Lucy, "Mother Smith" to the Saints, who some felt ruled the household as well as many church activities. Forever about the business of her Father in heaven and her son, the Prophet, on earth, she had a hand in the feeding, clothing, housing, and schooling of the converts. Agnes and Mary were soon busy weaving and sewing and mending for the men who were building the temple. The girls felt they were needed in this new community.

Mary Bailey did not remain long in Mother Smith's home. She and Samuel were married soon after she reached Kirtland, and the young couple found living quarters of their own. William Smith also married that summer, leaving only Don Carlos and Lucy at home. And Don Carlos was frequently away, spending long hours with his brother Joseph, learning the trade of a printer.[2] Carlos was seventeen that summer, and he was wildly happy in his new occupation. His talk was all of the stick and ems, forms and makeready, and his long fingers were always smudged with ink. He was a tall lad, well on the way to the six feet four inches he was to reach, blue-eyed and fair-haired. He was fanatically loyal to his father and to his brother, whom he believed to be divinely

11

inspired, and he had been fearless in running dangerous errands when necessary.

Every time the bashful Carlos came home he seemed to have grown an inch. Agnes had to look up to him more and more. She was a little thing, with small neat features, dark eyes, dark, tidy hair, and always self-possessed.[3] When near her, Carlos felt awkward and he stumbled for words. It was strange; he was never at a loss for words with anyone else. Agnes sensed his feeling for her, but dismissed the idea, being fully aware of the five-year difference in their ages. But when he was gone she missed him. She missed his willing helpfulness about the house. She missed his smile. Without knowing it they had become good companions. She realized that with no man she had met did she feel the same sense of security as with this teen-age lad. With Don Carlos this new emotion was sudden and intense and unchanging. With Agnes it was a gradually ripening love founded on companionship. They were married 30 July 1835.[4] He was nineteen and his bride twenty-four. Like Carlos's brothers and sisters they soon had their own home and like the others they were blessed with children, all three of them girls. The first was Agnes Charlotte, born the next year, on 1 August 1836.[5]

While Don Carlos was a printer, his brother Joseph was engaged in a variety of occupations from farming to innkeeping, from land speculation to banking. It was Joseph's banking experiment that brought about the downfall of Kirtland as Mormon headquarters, and the temporary loss of leadership among his followers. Opened without state sanction in the fall of 1836 his bank was dissolved the following spring, at the beginning of the great panic of 1837. Joseph left for Missouri where a new Zion was already building. Meanwhile the Kirtland temple was completed and dedicated. But Joseph's political ambitions had turned many of his own people and their gentile neighbors against him. Only the members of his family and some followers who were faithful to him turned their eyes and steps to the west. Some of these left for Far West, Missouri, the year Joseph departed. The remainder, including a well-organized group calling themselves the Kirtland Company, left in the summer of 1838.[6]

At this time members of the Smith family were being hounded by creditors. The old patriarch was threatened with imprisonment and had to go into hiding in New Portage. Carlos brought his wife and daughter to Norton, near by, to await the family exodus to Missouri. He had a reason for bringing Agnes to a place of safety; she was in the last month of pregnancy. On 23 April 1838, she gave birth to their second daughter, Sophronia, in the home of friends in Norton.[7] With Sophronia only two weeks old the Smith family began the long trip to Missouri, first by canal boat and then by wagon. The overland journey was filled with discomfort and pain. Camping and riding in the rain the little party found few shelters. In one poor hut, Catherine Salisbury, Don Carlos's sister, was seized with labor pains and gave birth to a tiny daughter.[8]

Reaching Far West in July, the family, along with the Kirtland Company, was welcomed warmly, and homes were found for them, chiefly cabins bought from local gentiles. Don Carlos took his wife and two little girls to Millport, a village three miles west of the Grand River.[9] After suffering and deprivations of all kinds the Saints had finally reached the new Zion. Independence Day that year, 1838, had a special significance for them and they made a gala day of it. They laid out the lines for a new temple in the center of Far West. All hearts were filled with optimism. The Mormons, several thousand of them, were swarming into the little settlements around Far West. In a triangle of land between the Grand and Missouri rivers, northeast of Independence, were Liberty and DeWitt, Far West and Gallatin, Millport, and Marrowbone. And three miles north of Millport, across the river, was the imaginary city-to-be, Adam-ondi-Ahman.[10]

Ordeal in Missouri

The remainder of the year 1838 was a black one in the annals of the Saints. The sect had already known ridicule and persecution. Joseph Smith had been tarred and feathered, his companions beaten, their lives threatened. The history of Far West had been one of persecution ever since its first Mormon settlement in 1832. Now the newcomers from Kirtland, still weary from the long journey, found themselves surrounded by enemies. July was really the only peaceful month that the Saints experienced in Missouri. On 6 August an election took place. The Mormons were ordered not to vote. They voted, and violence occurred. In the small skirmish that followed several men were killed.

The incident was the spark that set off a riot. Homes were burned, families driven out, and men hunted as the Indians before them had been hunted. Women and children hid in the wood, creeping through the night to whatever haven they might find. If a husband were absent on business for the community, his wife and children were particularly vulnerable, for the mobs were made up of cowards who preferred to attack the defenseless. Scarcity of housing and economic necessity compelled the Saints to scatter themselves in the villages in the vicinity of Far West. Many families therefore were isolated from the group as a whole. Agnes, Don Carlos, and their children lived in Millport. Samuel and Mary and their two little girls had settled in a hamlet bearing the plebeian name of Marrowbone.

13

Here, in October, Mary's son Samuel was born. When the baby was three days old, his father went to Far West to get a team and wagon, leaving his wife in the care of sister Saints. Not long after he left, a mob swept through the community, shooting, firing houses, driving out the terrified Saints. Mary's cabin was no exception. Weak as she was, she was ordered out. Lying on a feather bed in the road, her babies with her, she watched her house burn to the ground. Somehow a wagon and team were found, and an eleven-year-old boy volunteered to drive. Her bed was loaded into the vehicle, and, weak with fright after her recent ordeal, she and her infant son started for Far West, her two little girls riding with the driver. A drizzle started and soon a steady rain was pelting the exposed mother and child. After they had reached the half-way point, the refugees were met by Samuel. Enraged almost to tears, he took his little family to his mother's home. There the chilled and speechless Mary was wrapped in blankets, given wine, and prayed for.[11]

The Smith family and all their neighbors were horrified at this outrage. These atrocities could not go on. The High Council of Adam-ondi-Ahman was called together, and four elders, including Don Carlos and his cousin George Smith, were appointed to go out of the state to obtain money "to buy out the mobbers in Missouri." Carlos knew that his absence would leave his family exposed. Mary's experience was still fresh in their minds. Agnes trembled at the thought of being alone among the savage Missourians, but agreed that aid must be sought at once.[12] Before the month was over the two young men were on their way. They traveled by wagon, by boat, and on foot, on a fifteen-hundred-mile journey that took them into Kentucky and Tennessee. While away, Don Carlos wrote his wife frequently, but she could not answer for he was always on the move. Carlos was gone three months. They were three terror-ridden months for the Saints. Agnes never knew when the dreaded knock would be heard on her door. She dared not undress at night and could not sleep. If ever she had been given to self-pity, this was the time to indulge in it. She thought of Carlos on his disheartening journey. She thought of poor, sick Mary.

Then, the night of 18 October, she heard the sound she feared. Her little girls were asleep in her bed and she was lying, wide-eyed, heart thumping, beside them. She jumped up as she heard running feet and rough shouts, increasing in volume, until she could hear oaths rolling out above the din. Her door was jerked open, and a crowd of drunken men lurched in. Before she could open her mouth to scream or question she was ordered out of the house. Grabbing her babies and the blankets from her bed, she darted out. At first she hid in a haymow, then, in sudden panic that it might catch fire, she rushed outside. Running, stumbling, carrying the six-month-old child in one arm, the two-year-old astride her hip, she found the road. It was lighted suddenly by a flare from her burning cabin. Hers had been the first one set on fire. Other homes were soon burning, their occupants coming from every direction, panting and sobbing. On the road they headed toward the nearest refuge, Adam-ondi-Ahman, three miles north, where Lyman Wight, a fellow churchman and local militiaman, lived.[13]

They ran into a biting north wind that tore at them savagely. A storm had started the day before and the ground was covered with several inches of snow. To the over-burdened woman, the road seemed endless, as one in a nightmare. Near its end was the river to be crossed. Agnes and her husband had forded the Grand here, and she knew where the road went down the embankment and where it climbed the other side But she had never crossed it at night. And she had never waded it. She was not prepared for the depth and chill of the water. The shock took her breath. But her very fright and her concern for her young ones took her into the icy water that came to her waist. Bracing herself against the current, she got across. She scrambled up the bank, and managed to reach Lyman Wight's house. Drenched and shaking, she gasped out her story.

Wight was a fearless Saint and an officer in the local militia. That night, as it happened, his superior officer, General Parks, was present in Wight's house. Such barbarism as this night's business was more than the General could stomach. He gave Wight permission to call up troops to protect the Mormons from future outrages. The story is short, involved, and bitter, with perfidy on the part of the state. The Saints were no match for their enemies in any way—in a fair fight on the field of battle, in civil settlement of differences, or in coping with mob violence that was spreading like an underground fire. Outrage followed outrage: Governor Boggs's "extermination order," the siege of Adam-ondi-Ahman and Far West, the fiendish massacre at Haun's Mill, and finally the arrest, exhibition, and imprisonment of Joseph and Hyrum Smith and other leaders—all well-documented incidents in the history of Mormon persecution in Missouri.[14] The Mormons were beaten and homeless. Deprived of food, shelter, and transportation, they were commanded to leave the state, which they proceeded to prepare for under the direction of Brigham Young and Heber Kimball.

Exodus from Missouri

While these blows were falling on his family and friends, Don Carlos and his cousin were absent, their lives too in frequent danger. His journal reveals his courage, though the writing is an unhappy recital of en-

15

counters with Mormon-haters, and of nearly freezing to death. But worse than anything he experienced was a spectacle he and George witnessed on the banks of the Mississippi. While at Columbus, in Hickman County, Kentucky, they saw the last of the Cherokee Indians waiting to cross the river and continue their long "trail of tears." Men, women, and children had been driven on a death march from their homes to a barren land in the cold of winter. Filled with compassion for these miserable victims of man's greed, he thought of his own loved ones, little dreaming that his small family had had to flee for their lives and were themselves destitute this winter day.[15]

When he returned on Christmas Day to find his people terrorized and disorganized, he joined with other men in a plan to effect the exodus from Missouri as quickly as possible. They agreed to leave and to take their families, but first they presented their enemies with a petition for aid in leaving. Mobs had destroyed their food, clothing and shelter, and had stolen their wagons and animals. How could they go? Ordered to leave, they were helpless. They secured some aid, and the men signed a covenant of mutual assistance, agreeing that no individual among them would be abandoned or allowed to suffer if the group could help. In their utmost need they were putting into practice the religion they preached.[16]

It was not until February 1839 that Don Carlos got out of Missouri with his family and his father's family. With Joseph and Hyrum still in jail, he assumed responsibility for his parents. They headed east in two conveyances, an ox-drawn wagon and a buggy. It was a dreary ordeal of mud and rain and snow and sleet, day after day, camping sometimes in the open, sometimes finding shelter in a miserable shed.[17] They reached Quincy, Illinois, in the latter part of the month. Shocked by Missourian barbarism, Illinois citizens vied with each other in giving asylum to the refugees who were flocking from across the Mississippi. Don Carlos and his family settled near Macomb in McDonough County.[18]

His brothers were released from prison in April and came at once to Quincy. Joseph looked around for a home for his followers, and discovered Commerce. It was a sorry collection of shacks on the riverbank, but had a promising townsite rising behind it. At the time it was marshy and probably unhealthy, but Joseph knew that by draining the swamp and building on higher ground he could make the place habitable.[19] Actually the site was a superb one, on the east shore of the Mississippi, not far north of the Iowa-Missouri boundary. Imagine a semicircle of land in a wide bend of the great river. Here the Mississippi is more than a mile in width as it curves around the gently curving halfcircle. Joseph walked up the slope from the river. Standing on top of the rise, he let his imagination begin to build a new city. This would be the new Zion. They would call it *Nauvoo,* "the beautiful." Here, at the top, would be the temple, situated equidistant from the river to the north, the west, and the south. Here, among the hospitable citizens of Illinois, they would begin again. He was young and possessed of an optimism that was naive in view of his past experiences.

3
Birth
and Death
in Nauvoo

Ah, God! and yet we know
It was no dream in those days, long ago!
It was no dream.

Ina Coolbrith, from
"Memorial Poem" (1881)

Birth of Ina Coolbrith; Death of Her Father

Don Carlos Smith joined his brother in Nauvoo and began with other men in the Church to prepare the land and buildings for use. He did not send for his family until he had a place for them. First, however, he was busy remodeling a room for use as a printing shop. The ground floor of a two-story building, already there when the land was acquired by Joseph Smith, it was little better than a cellar. A small spring seeped through the floor and the room was never dry.[1] Here, nevertheless, Don Carlos and his partner, Ebenezer Robinson, cleaned the type that had been buried during the Missouri troubles, and, in November 1839, issued the first number of a new newspaper, *Times and Seasons.* Their printing was interrupted again and again by the chills and fevers of the Saints whom Don Carlos visited, healing many, he said, "by the laying on of hands."[2]

In spite of illness the work of building a new city went ahead. Wide, straight streets were laid out, in the manner of Mormon towns, with Main Street eighty-two feet wide, running north and south, and beginning and ending on the banks of the same curving river. Houses were built, industry invited, farmlands fenced, gardens planted, and fields sown. Late in the summer of 1839 Agnes and her children came to Nauvoo, making a home for the little family in the rooms above the printing shop. As places were provided, more and more of the Saints came in

19

from the surrounding country. In 1840 all of the members of the Smith family lived near each other, so that in September Joseph, the old Patriarch, could bless each of his children as they gathered around his deathbed.[3]

In December that year a report of the grievances suffered by the Latter-day Saints in Missouri from 1831 through 1838 was presented to a joint session of the two houses of Congress. This was in the form of a petition offered on 21 December 1840 by Elias Higbee and Robert B. Thompson of Nauvoo. The land from which the Mormons had been driven by force had been purchased by them from the general government. The petitioners now prayed "Congress to provide a remedy." The document recounts Mormon transactions and gentile atrocities in detail, including the massacre at Haun's Mill and putting the torch to Agnes Smith's cabin. By placing all the facts before Congress, the Saints hoped for some restitution of financial losses at least. Old debts should be paid, they believed, though their new city of Nauvoo was apparently flourishing. Its citizens, represented by John C. Bennett, were congratulated that same December by Abraham Lincoln, a member of the Illinois legislature, on their new charters—charters for city, university, and militia. These documents authorized the building of an unusually self-sufficient and independent city-state. Don Carlos was elected to the city council and also served as an officer of the Nauvoo Legion. The new year dawned as a hopeful one for the Saints. Here they felt safe. With the full sanction of the friendly state of Illinois they could govern themselves. They could build homes and schools for their families. They could build a new temple.[4]

Both Agnes and her friend Mary were pregnant again. As the two women relaxed together over their sewing, they talked of better times to come for themselves and their new babies. These young ones would enjoy a childhood free from terror. Only six short years ago the two friends had sat sewing while the Kirtland Temple was building. Now, in a few months, a new temple would be begun in Nauvoo, grander in scale than that in the Ohio town. Already Nauvoo was assuming the character of a quiet, orderly town where strangers noticed no saloons or brothels. It would be a good place in which to rear children.

Mary's baby was born on 25 January 1841, but the mother's strength was not equal to her travail. She was gone as the child's first cry was heard. And tiny Lucy, the newborn, followed her mother within the week.[5] Agnes's sorrow was tinged with resentment. She had always been ready to put herself completely in the hands of her Lord, to accept all as a trial of her faith. But Mary! Mary, her dearest friend, dearer than any of her own sisters, dearer than any of her sisters in the Church. How

20

could she accept this loss? As her own time approached, she was apprehensive. The bright promise of spring had lost its luster. The days were heavy as February wore on, heavy, like her own body.

Winter was still on the land when Agnes went to bed for the birth of her third child. Her daughter was born on 10 March 1841, a pretty baby with a pale gold fluff on her head, and with strangely dark gray eyes that had a knowing look in them before they could focus. She was named Josephine Donna Smith. And Don Carlos, proud of his new small daughter, was equally proud of the decent city he had helped build for her.[6]

The baby, growing to resemble her young father in looks and disposition, was never to remember him. Late in July, when her mother and sisters were ill, her father nursed them and caught a cold. The cold became pneumonia. Don Carlos died on Sunday, 7 August 1841, aged twenty-five years. His big frame had received one blow too many. From the time he was fourteen he had assumed the responsibilities of a man. There were times when he was afraid, as when surrounded by Mormon-damning gentiles, but he never once gave in to his fears. In the few references to him in the histories of his church and its members, in his letters and his journal, it is apparent that he never ran away from obligation or danger. He was a singularly courageous and sensible man, and so young at his death that his brother Joseph spoke tenderly of him as a "child," a "lovely, a good-natured, a kind-hearted and . . . upright child," adding, "and where his soul goes let mine go also."[7]

The community was stunned. They had taken advantage of his gentle disposition, his generosity of time and effort, his inability to say no. Responsibilities were pressed upon him: member of the city council, editor of *Times and Seasons,* officer in the Nauvoo Legion, and president of the Church's high priesthood. He had accepted frequent mission assignments which required him to be away from his family. When at home in Nauvoo his care of the sick had taxed his own strength beyond its limit. He was buried on 9 August, with full military honors. His obituary, in the next issue of *Times and Seasons,* written by his partner Ebenezer Robinson, who could not find enough adjectives of praise for his dead co-worker, was followed by a long, flowery tribute in verse by Eliza R. Snow.[8]

Agnes's expression of grief was unrecorded. But words can only hint at the shock and the loneliness and the loss of security. When on his mission, he had written to her with affection. She was his "Beloved," his "Dear Companion." In his last letter, shortly before she joined him in Nauvoo, he had written, with a youthful rush of sentiment, "you are entwined around my heart, with ties that are stronger than death, and

21

time cannot sever them. Deprived of your society, and that of my prattling babes, life would be irksome . . . . From your husband, who will ever remain devoted and affectionate, both in time and in eternity, Don C. Smith."[9] The memory of these endearments and many others came rushing over her. Agnes dared not dwell on them, for her three small girls needed a calm and cheerful mother, now most of all. There was immediate economic stress. She had no income aside from her share of the profits from the little paper, *Times and Seasons*. Her husband had been owner and publisher as well as editor. The printing shop and the press, property of the widow, brought in scarcely enough for her family's subsistence. Editor Robinson, realizing her need, suggested that provisions would be accepted in lieu of local payments, and that distant subscribers should be prompt in sending money.[10]

Nauvoo, meanwhile, was growing rapidly and, for a brief period, excelled Chicago in size. The temple had been begun in April 1841. Prosperity and peace were becoming a reality instead of a dream. But Agnes's world was being broken to bits. Two years later her second child, Sophronia, then five years old, caught scarlet fever and died on 3 October 1843. Her eldest, Agnes Charlotte, was eight, and already had a vivid personality enticingly enhanced by coal black hair and gray eyes so dark they seemed black. Little Josephine, called Ina by her mother, at two-and-a-half was as fair-haired as her sister was dark. To provide for these two, her whole family now, was Agnes's single purpose. Her burden, however, was easier because it was shared by the sisters and brothers who made up that cooperative community, Nauvoo.[11]

While Agnes was enduring personal loss and adjusting herself to widowhood, the Saints were to experience their greatest calamity. Joseph and Hyrum Smith were murdered on 27 June 1844, while imprisoned in the jail at Carthage, Illinois. The event was the climax of a growing animosity to the Mormons, based on envy, on rumors of polygamy, and particularly upon Joseph's rashness in destroying the types of a printing press that had opposed him. His flaunting of the freedom of the press brought indictment from the state, and imprisonment while awaiting trial. He and his brother were shot by a cowardly mob. Another brother, Samuel, who had ridden to their rescue, but arrived too late, died soon after from shock and supreme exertion.[12]

Nauvoo by the Mississippi River. About 1848; artist unknown. Reproduced from the original painting at Knox College, Gallesburg, Illinois, through the courtesy of the Preston Player Collection, Knox College.

The Saints were beside themselves with grief and terror. They knew that the assassination of their leaders was now a signal to their enemies who were increasing in numbers. Their peace was shattered. This city, too, would have to be abandoned. And so it was, within two years. But meanwhile the work on the temple went on, and the structure was completed in September 1845. It was consecrated in a three-day convention that began on 5 October. Here, in the sacred building, Agnes was "sealed" to Don Carlos for eternity, and her two small daughters, Agnes and Ina, were "endowed."[13]

Now in Nauvoo, as previously in Kirtland and in Far West, the gentiles moved in to take a city ready to their hands, ordering the residents to be out by spring, 1846. Brigham Young had assumed leadership after the death of Joseph Smith, and had decided that the Latter-day Saints could live in peace only by moving so far to the west that they would never be pursued. They would go a thousand miles, across the plains and the mountains. They would create a new city, a new temple, and a new country. They began to build wagons and to prepare in every way for the westward journey. They were forced to sacrifice well-built houses and most of their possessions. They were compelled to turn their backs on their fair, young city, and the shining limestone temple that crowned the small acropolis. They must now cross the wide Mississippi and make their way over the wilderness miles beyond it.

Departure from Nauvoo; Remarriage of Ina's Mother

Under Brigham Young's direction the exodus of the Saints was well planned. The migration was to take place in easy stages, with a settlement called Winter Quarters established near the present Omaha, Nebraska, where the travelers would rest, plant crops, and replenish both vitality and food supplies for the rest of the journey. A vanguard of Saints would go ahead and choose a permanent site for a city, put up shelters, and start field cultivation. On 10 January 1846 the first teams crossed the river on flatboats. Then, as if in answer to prayer, the river was frozen in February, and departure was easier. All spring and summer a stream of wagons was ferried across, ready to begin the long overland trek.[14]

That spring Agnes wrote to her husband's cousin, George A. Smith, who had started overland, "If there was a Carlos or Joseph or Hyrum then how quickly I would be there." She assured him that she loved the Church and would love to be with her brethren. "But, alas," she wrote, "there is an aching void I seem never able to fill." With a tone of finality she told him that she had sold the old printing shop for seventy dollars, and that she had removed her dead into Emma's garden.[15]

24

Both Agnes and Emma decided to remain in Nauvoo. So, too, did Mother Smith and her daughter and son-in-law, Lucy and Arthur Milliken. Mary Bailey's daughter, Mary, kept her grandmother company. The restless old woman had become an invalid. She would be a refugee no longer. Her ties were here, near the graves of her husband and martyred sons. She was not reconciled to Brigham Young's leadership. She, with a few others, became the nucleus of the Reorganized Church of Jesus Christ of Latter-day Saints. Mother Smith's last years, until her death in 1855, were spent with her daughter-in-law, Emma, and Emma's second husband, Major Lewis C. Bidamon.[16]

Major Bidamon was one of the "new citizens" of Nauvoo, newcomers who were outraged by the actions of the Mormons' enemies. During the violence that took place in the summer and autumn of 1846, the new citizens took sides with the Mormons against the mobs who were running rampant in the streets. Another new citizen was William Pickett, from St. Louis, formerly a lawyer in Mobile, Alabama, but at this time foreman of the printing office of the *Missouri Republican*, later the *St. Louis Republican*. This was one of several Missouri newspapers that had castigated Governor Boggs for his infamous "extermination order." Sympathetic with the victims of mob cruelty, the paper was now concerned with the new Mormon troubles in Nauvoo, and sent reporters to get eyewitness stories. Whether William Pickett came in this capacity, or in some other, we do not know.[17] We do know that he was there at the close of summer in 1846, and, outraged by what he saw, participated in the violent street fighting that took place in August and September. One day he saw a gun in the hands of a gentile. He recognized it as the property of a Mormon farmer who had been mobbed shortly before. Pickett was always a man of action, and he snatched the gun away. He was arrested but not jailed. On 7 September the few remaining Saints were given sixty days to evacuate the city. But the mob could not wait. A week later it ransacked houses, shoved Mormons into the river in profane baptisms, and ran through the temple, shouting, and ringing bells.[18]

This behavior was so repugnant to Pickett that, if he had ever had any notion of settling in Nauvoo, he was now anxious to leave. He had come to know Agnes Smith during these troubled times, and his affection for her was matched by her appreciation of his concern for the few Saints remaining in Nauvoo. This mutual affection ripened into love, and he persuaded her to marry him and come away with him to St. Louis where he could give her and the two little girls a home in a civilized society.[19] They left by river boat in September. As the boat moved slowly out to turn south, Agnes looked back. Nauvoo, "the beautiful," they had called it. It was still lovely. It had not been destroyed. But it had been looted of all that was dear to her, physically and spiritually. The temple shining in the sun was like a gravestone, and the city, to her, a graveyard. She turned to her new husband as they walked slowly toward the prow of the boat, looking south to where their future lay. As they talked of that future, William extracted from his wife a promise that she was to keep as long as she lived, and her children after her.

The St. Louis Years

The promise troubled her as she made it while still in the sight of Nauvoo. But as they neared St. Louis, and the city's skyline took shape ahead of them, her pledge seemed only natural and easy. Her pledge was that she was to enter this new life with William Pickett with her past forgotten and forever hidden. She agreed never to speak of her membership in the Church of the Saints, or of her marriage to a brother of the Prophet. This agreement was not made to bolster William's ego, but to ensure freedom forever from the kind of persecution that had followed the Mormons all their days. William had been as shocked by the rawness and the savagery running through the streets of Nauvoo as he had been at stories of rape and murder of Mormons in Missouri eight years before. He wished to make sure that no threat of this horror would ever touch his wife again.[20]

For Agnes, St. Louis was a gateway, as it was the Gateway City to the West. The children were excited by the river journey and by the variety of craft they met coming upstream: great barges and flatboats loaded with cargo, rafts of all sizes, and steamboats like their own. Their first sight of the city was of smoke that hovered over it like a thin blanket. As they drew nearer, they thought the city must have more boats than houses; there were hundreds moored along the riverfront docks, or moving in or out of their places. As their steamer docked and they left its moving deck for the solid boards of the wharf, they were bewildered and frightened by the din. In 1847 St. Louis was a city of some 60,000—a city rising abruptly from the river along its west bank. It was a city of movement; transportation was its life. At that time river traffic, on both the Mississippi and the Missouri, was the most important factor in its economy. The city was no longer a supply base for trappers and mountain men, but many migrants and settlers still came through on their way to the Southwest or to the Oregon Country, and it would soon be swarming with travelers to the gold fields of California.

The Picketts were not moving on. They would rest for a while, make a home, give the girls a chance to go to school. William Pickett was a "college man," and would want these advantages for his family. Though there was no public library in St. Louis at this time, the Mercantile Li-

26

brary had started only the year before. Pickett had brought his own "library" to the house they had rented, chiefly law books, but also a set of Shakespeare, a volume of Pope and a well-worn one of Byron, a Bible, and a Greek Testament. The poetry meant little to the girls now, but would be important to Ina a few years later.[21]

The year 1847 was a placid one for Agnes. In December she became the mother of twin boys. William was proud, and gave in playfully to his wife's whim to name them for the two men in her life. They were named William, Junior, and Don Carlos Pickett.[22] The little boys were spoiled and adored by their sisters, especially by eleven-year-old Agnes Charlotte who watched her mother closely in handling and changing them. To Ina, only six, they were better than dolls, but she was too little to be allowed any responsibility with them.

Until the spring of 1849 this was a happy period. The girls' mother, respecting her husband's wish, never spoke of the horror she had known recently. She wanted to forget it. It would be years before she could discuss any of it, even in her own family circle. So, bottling up the nightmare of her past, she went about her household tasks with a bright cheerfulness that was strange to her daughters. In time they took this gaiety for granted, and their own fears lessened, and their sleep became less haunted. In later years Ina was to remark that her earliest memory was of death, of "the blood-stained couch of death." This was poetic license. Actually her first memory of this kind was of the funeral of her five-year-old sister Sophronia, when she, Ina, was two-and-a-half.[23] Perhaps the keening of the Saints when her uncles, Joseph and Hyrum, were killed, left an impression, too, on her mind. But now the tensions were disappearing, the fears vanishing. Life was easier in a city big enough to take them in without questioning. William Pickett's employment was secure and gave him a certain amount of prestige.

Then one night in May 1849 the *White Cloud,* one of the ships moored at a riverfront wharf, burst into flames. For fear of danger to the wharves and the boats alongside, the burning ship was cut from its moorings, and sent adrift down the river. But the flames spread, and the *White Cloud* set one boat after another on fire. Before the fire was brought under control, much of the dock area and fifteen square blocks of the city were burned. Many boats and more than four hundred buildings were lost. All members of the Pickett family were probably beyond the edge of the burned area, for, in the family history of disasters which did occur to them, there is no mention of the St. Louis fire, the largest fire in the United States up to that time.[24]

Nor is there mention in the Pickett annals of the great cholera epidemic that took more than four thousand St. Louis lives in 1849. In fact the disease was at its height when the fire broke out. It was one of the worst such epidemics in the medical history of the country. The two greatest calamities in the history of the city took place in the same year and occurred during the short period the Pickett-Smith family was there.[25]

Even so, another fever, not of fire or of disease, caught hold of them a year or two later, the fever we call the *Westward Movement*. St. Louis faces west. The Missouri River was an enticing highway into the north and west. Roads were leading out across the state. And soon a railway would be starting west from St. Louis. Men with families began to look in that direction and consider moving on. Several parties had gone into the Oregon country or to California. The journey would be a serious undertaking. It had to be well planned. The year that the Mormons were driven from Nauvoo, the year that Agnes and William were married and had come to St. Louis, was the very year the Donner Party went its tragic way through snow and starvation. The Donner agony frightened the timid, but it supported the insistence of the cautious that the journey could be made without loss if proper plans and procedures were followed.

With the discovery of gold in California in 1848 excitement had increased. In the streets of St. Louis the talk was all of "going west." Every day the Mississippi boats landed strangers bound for St. Joseph by way of the Missouri or turned others loose to secure animals and provisions to start the overland trek by crossing the state to Independence. There were several guidebooks in print but none proved more attractive to migrants than a slim booklet put together by Joseph Ware and published in St. Louis in 1849. The book was on display wherever supplies were sold, and it was bought eagerly by restless men who liked its brevity. They did not know that the book was lacking in detailed description or personal adventure because its author had never set foot on the emigrant's trail himself. Young Ware had pored over Fremont's journal and other Western diaries and guides, and had compiled his own, helping himself freely to the best in each.[26]

William Pickett read his fellow townsman's publication with interest, but curbed his own excitement. The guide seemed sensible enough, he reasoned, if you paid attention to it and started after the grass was up with a party large enough for protection, but small enough to have feed and water for all. Pickett considered his future in the West. A man might strike it rich if he went directly to the mines, but he himself might do better if he put out his lawyer's shingle, or got a job as a printer in San Francisco or some other of the mushrooming cities of California. What could he lose? The more he thought about it and talked about it in the printing office, the more his excitement and determination to go increased. He was boyishly eager when he finally dared suggest the venture to Agnes. His fever was contagious. Together they pored over the little guidebook. In April and May 1849 they had both read all the letters sent to the *Republican* by its correspondent, "California," and printed in Pickett's own office. These were eye-witness descriptions of both Independence and St. Joseph as outfitting posts for the emigrants, giving practical information on costs of equipment and animals. Late in the fall of 1850 William and Agnes made plans and what preparations they could. By the time the first flowers would be up the following spring, they would be on their way west.[27]

4
Overland
to
California

Men and beasts alike in utter stress,
Through weary miles and miles
And days of tears and smiles.

Ina Coolbrith, from
"Portolá Speaks" (1926)

Over the Prairie

The following March, in 1851, Ina celebrated her tenth birthday and began the long journey westward with her family.[1] She tried to be as reserved as her sister, who would be fifteen in midsummer, but the prancing twins expressed her real feelings, when they all went aboard the crowded Missouri River boat that was to take them to St. Joseph. This Western outpost was like nothing the Pickett family had known. It was a sprawling, brawling place that frightened the timid. William had been advised to travel light to St. Joseph and buy his supplies there. The essential covered wagon and his oxen were his costliest investment. He bought a tent and a few tools, and a supply of powder and lead for his gun. He followed his guidebook recommendations for food and other necessary items. Bedding and cooking utensils they had brought with them. And William carried his few precious books to stow in the corners of the wagon. He took his time equipping his outfit, bargaining, getting the best for his money. Whether he settled his family in one of the crude rooming houses of the place or pitched his new tent on the edge of the town, among others awaiting the long journey, is not known. Much as the family may have fretted in this camp of gamblers and swindlers, they were forced to stay until the grass was up to provide food for the bulls.[2]

The day had come at last, crisp, sparkling, blue of sky, fragrant with the moist earth and new grass. By 1851 the road was clearly defined.

31

Striking straight west from St. Joseph, heading for the valley of the Little Blue River on the way to the dreaded Platte crossings, the Pickett family enjoyed the novelty of miles and miles of green prairie with grass and water enough for their plodding animals. When the children grew tired and sore from the jolting wagon ride, they walked and gathered wild flowers new to them, keeping in sight of their own schooner, but out of the dust. To these and other children, sleeping and eating out-of-doors was a delight in this early stretch of the overland trail. And infecting all the young people in the caravan was the secretly delicious thrill of a possible encounter with Indians. This was Pawnee country, but so far, no redskins had appeared.

The trail was little traveled in 1851.[3] It was later said to have been a good year for the crossing. There was less sickness, and the grass and water supplies were unusually abundant. There was even less Indian trouble in 1851 than in some other years. Sometimes when the caravan had stopped for the night, Ina could not sleep. She would hear the voices of the men around the campfire, carried distinctly through the prairie's night air, as they talked of possible Indian attack. She snuggled closer to her sister, shivering with fright. She lost her fears when the sun came up, warm and reassuring, but she told Agnes Charlotte what the men had said and the two girls kept the information to themselves.

They soon forgot their fears of Indians when the caravan entered the valley of the Little Blue. Here the grass was lush and flower-starred. For several days the road followed the river, a fresh stream of good water, almost to its source, not far from the great Platte. Reaching the Platte, the wagons turned west to follow the wide river as far as the junction of its north and south forks. Emigrant parties crossed the South Platte at different places: some at the junction, others a few days' ride away near the present Brule, Nebraska, still others farther upstream, near the mouth of Lodgepole Creek. Which crossing the Pickett family and their party chose is not known. But the most frequently used ford was that near Brule, and it is reasonable to assume that William turned his oxen into the stream at this point. This was the moment the girls dreaded most. They were breathless when their stepfather started across, heading his animals downstream to make an oblique crossing and thus reduce the force of the current. He knew that he must keep his oxen moving, for a stalled wagon or a hesitant team could be sucked down by the quicksands. However tense with fear the children may have been, their father got them safely across.

Leaving the South Platte the caravans turned north across the prairie, reaching the North Platte at Ash Hollow. This was a happy camping place, wooded, and rich in grass. Here most of the families stayed long enough to rest their animals. Here the women washed and baked, and the men repaired gear. Here in the evenings the young people found the campfire an invitation to singing and talking. As tensions were eased, someone's cherished fiddle would be taken out and tuned, and there would be dancing in the circle of wagons, the crisp night air filled with rollicking tunes. The high wagons around the fire had a protective look about them. No one saw the schooners' grotesque shadows moving wildly on the grass outside the ring. For the moment no one felt the miles of thick darkness in the wider periphery of the camp's single fire. The brief layover at Ash Hollow renewed ambition to be on with the journey. Guidebooks were pulled out. Fort Laramie was only one hundred-fifty miles away. The caravans turned west to wind along the southern bank of the North Platte, day after day, often without sufficient feed and water for the stock, and always without good fuel for cooking, except the prairie variety, the dried dung of the buffalo. The monotony of the road was broken by such natural monuments as Court House Rock and Chimney Rock and Scott's Bluff.

To the Crest of the Rockies

At Scott's Bluff Ina had her first glimpse of the Rocky Mountains. Her stepfather and the other men in the party consulted their guidebooks again. Yes, that would be Laramie Peak in the forefront of the range. Ina had grown used to the muted green of endless prairie stretches. Now there, at last, were the mountains! Always ahead of her, the mountains. Their calm and dignity and massiveness increased imperceptibly as the wagons crept nearer, and day succeeded day. Their color delighted her. Violet in early morning and at sundown, their snow crests were painted the color of fire. In the heat haze of noon they shimmered cool against the sky. And in an afternoon thunder shower, their beauty was exciting. Through the clean, washed air they were a blue too vivid to name, sprawled against the billowing thunderheads and the slate-gray sky. Ina buried these pictures in her memory, not even seeking any expression for something to be forever a part of her.

Laramie Peak meant something else to the men; before they could come abreast of the mountains they would reach Fort Laramie. They might get supplies, and certainly advice, and news of feed and Indians, and maybe some idea as to the number of people on the road ahead of them. At last the travelers saw a lone settlement in the vast landscape. As they drew nearer, they made out a stockade and a group of buildings on a bluff. This was Fort Laramie. In 1851 there was not a tree in sight except a fringe of willows along the Laramie River at the base of the bluff. But even more refreshing than trees to the sight of the emigrants who had left the States behind at St. Joseph was the American flag flying from a pole set on the roof of the blockhouse that served as a gateway and lookout to the adobe stockade. When they were only a mile from the fort, they crossed the Laramie River by toll bridge. Beyond the fort rose the Black Hills, and, beyond them, the higher Rockies. If the Pickett family tarried at the fort to replenish supplies, they did not record the fact. But we can well imagine that their spirits rose when certain rumors they had heard were confirmed. There would be no Indian attack. This very year a treaty had been made with the Plains Indians to permit (for a price) white families to travel westward. The emigrants were warned, however, that the going would become increasingly more rugged as the trail twisted through the Black Hills, on its way to the North Platte crossing.

Over rocky terrain, across numerous mountain streams and a few grassy vales blessed by the weary emigrants for the sake of their more weary animals, the wagons climbed and jolted to a stop at the ford, some eighty miles beyond Fort Laramie. Here the North Platte was swift and cold. It could be crossed by ferry, or fording, or swimming. Once across, the emigrants bade farewell to the Platte, whose monotonous banks the caravans had trailed for seemingly endless weeks. The wagons were dragged by tired animals through clumps of sagebrush on the plateau until they came to the Sweetwater River which they crossed near Independence Rock. The country was rough, but there were both water and grass, and the scenery was spectacular enough to make one forget a few of the troubles. At Devil's Gate the river was forced through a narrow defile that sent it leaping and surging, and compelled the wagons to make a wide detour. The next eighty or ninety miles along the Sweetwater were easier, camping was better, and the climb was not too steep.

So gradual, indeed, was the ascent that when South Pass was reached, three hundred miles beyond Fort Laramie, the travelers were scarcely aware that they were crossing the backbone of the mountains. When the party reached the next stream, Pacific Creek, they were excited to discover it flowing west. They had topped the crest of the Rockies! For better or worse, there was no turning back now.

Lost in the Nevada Desert

West of the Rockies they were, but not over them. Fearful times were ahead. Following Pacific Creek to the junction with Dry Sandy Creek, they struck off on Sublette's Cutoff, heading west for the Green River. Here was a sandy waste, wild and waterless, hard going for man and beast under the blazing sun. Some families attempted to lighten their wagonloads by throwing away goods and provisions. Some lost oxen on this trying stretch. The animals that got through became crazed when they smelled the water of the Green. Getting down the steep bank of this river with the lumbering schooners was an engineering problem that called for cooperation and ingenuity. Once down to the icy waters of the Green, people and wagons crossed by ferries. As always, the travel-worn animals were compelled to swim, the weakest of them unable to push through the current.

The fate of these poor creatures was an agony to Ina, and the beauty of the Green River and its canyon was spoiled for her by the sight of the struggling, drowning oxen. The memory was to haunt her forever. Her sorrow, here in the strange majesty of mountain and river, found no words, but it groped for them. The groping for expression of her thoughts on this journey was the early stirring of a sleeping talent. "On the plains and in the mountains," she later said, "I had my first desire to write."

Continuing on the Sublette Cutoff beyond the Green, the wagons were pulled and pushed to the top of a ridge that overlooked a valley of surprising beauty. The upper end of Bear River Valley lies high in the mountains, nearly 7,000 feet in elevation. Here at this altitude the summers are short. When the late snows are gone, grass and flowers spring up quickly in a thick covering that is watered frequently by summer showers. The slopes rising from the meadowland are wooded with pine and aspen and mountain mahogany, but the floor of the wide, level valley following the meandering Bear is lush with wild hay. The Pickett family may have reached this small Eden early in July. Ina and her sister were entranced. Wild shrubs were in bloom, serviceberry, and choke-cherry with its musty-sweet fragrance. The currants had replaced their small blossoms with luscious fruit, yellow or black. Springy patches of watercress choking the streams were raided by the greens-starved travel-ers. Ina had never tasted anything as good as the cress with some of her mother's camp bread. And for dessert, wild strawberries. Strange new flowers delighted the girls; small, fragrant sweet williams, pink and white; dwarf penstamon, bright, bright blue; gilias, scarlet or pink or spotted, with honey in their tiny horns; and mariposa lilies swaying on slender stems. As she watched them, Ina may have thought how like white butterflies the blossoms seemed to float in air. Years later she was to write a sonnet that may have been conceived here in Bear Valley.

The party could have stayed here forever. But they knew that there were several hundred miles between them and the Sierra Nevada which must be climbed as the Rockies had been. They followed the course of the Bear north, but downstream, leaving it when it turned west and south

35

not far from Soda or Beer Springs. Here was a novelty all the guidebooks described. Numerous springs, large and small, of highly carbonated water dotted a somewhat arid mountain-rimmed plateau. The water was cold and sparkling and was left with regret.

A few miles west of the soda springs was the parting of the ways for Oregon or California. The traveler might go on to Fort Hall and turn south for California at that place. But by 1851 most of the wagons were turned onto the trail known as Hudspeth's Cutoff, to meet at the Raft River those who had preferred to go by way of Fort Hall. This leg of the journey presented the most difficult mountain going the party had experienced. They crossed sagebrush land and wooded slopes and weird rocky terrain where there was no visible road. Here, until they had followed the Little Goose Creek into what is now Nevada, they were forced into back-breaking maneuvering of the great schooners. Sometimes the men unloaded the wagons and pulled them up the mountainsides with ropes. Again, going down, they had to tie whole trees to the rear axles to serve as brakes and to prevent the vehicles from going end over end. It was an exhausting, terrifying experience, for men and oxen, for women and children.

The Pickett family had come this far without too much trouble. They had left these badlands behind, and had come out onto the mile-high sage lands that would take them toward the Humboldt River. It was late July when they crossed the alkali, and knew thirst and dust and watched the terrible suffering of their animals. Here they saw the bones of oxen that had lain down and died in their tracks. They saw abandoned wagons and precious household goods brought thus far with difficulty. Amid this desolation, somewhere in the vicinity of Carson Sink, the Pickett family and their party lost their way. They were dazed and frantic. An Indian showed up and offered to guide them as far as the Truckee River. Afraid of treachery, they hesitated. But they knew they could die here in the desert like the animals on the trail if they had no guide. So they put their trust in him. For days they followed him. He led them out of the alkali dust toward the clear, roaring mountain river, the Truckee. Before they reached the stream he advised the men to unyoke the oxen to prevent a stampede to the water. This was done and the thirsty beasts rushed as fast as their feeble legs would take them. The families forded the river here, and again Ina was filled with anguish as she saw some of the weakened oxen drown in the swift and icy current.

Ina Coolbrith (Josephine Donna Smith) about Eleven Years of Age. Courtesy of the Oakland Free Library.

Entry by Beckwourth Pass

The Truckee River was the end and the beginning for William and his friends. They made camp on the north bank of the stream for a few days, resting from their desert ordeal. Haggard, unkempt, their wagon covers dirty and torn, their poor beasts more dead than alive, the men rested uneasily. Ahead of them towered the Sierra. It was late in the season. September would be here soon, and perhaps snow. In the back of their minds there was always the thought of the Donner Party who were caught by the snows of 1846 not many miles from this pleasant spot on the Truckee. Near their camp they had found a sick man in a hastily made shelter of branches, his untethered pony standing near. He had thrown back his blanket and was tossing in a fever. The women brought him water and put cold wet towels on his head. As his fever subsided and he was given food, he told them weakly who he was and why he was here. He said his name was James Beckwourth, that he had found a good shortcut over the mountains and had made a road of it for the folks coming to California.[4]

"But, now, it's no use," he said weakly, "I'm gonna die right here. I've already made my will. I'll never live to see the wagons on my road." But the women nursed him back to health.

"Bless them!" he exclaimed, "in a few days we'll start out. Down at Bidwell's Bar they've got a perfect mania for this road. And Mayor Miles in Marysville says he'll pay me what I've put out on it. Says it'll be worth ten thousand dollars to the city." To the drivers in the train Jim Beckwourth described his road. He said he had worked on it all summer, and then had gone to the Truckee to bring the emigrants over. He told them that this would be the shortest, easiest way across the Sierra. He thought it was the lowest pass over the entire range. It had no canyons, no steep grades, no badlands of any kind; just a gradual climb through the sagebrush, and his men had grubbed out the worst of that.[5]

"You'll be the first folks to come over my road. You're mighty lucky," he finished, remembering that he was lucky, too, that they found him. He'd have been dead by now, he was sure. Three or four days later Beckwourth said that he thought he was able to travel. They could start in the morning. After supper the children gathered around him, timid, but fascinated by his stories and his garb. Bright yarn was braided into his black hair. As he talked he smiled at the youngsters, and they watched the play of the firelight on his dark face, and the flash of white teeth. He reached into one of the big side pockets of his beaded deerskin jacket and pulled out a small paper bag of candies which he passed to the little ones around him. Ina thought he was the

38

most wonderful man she had ever seen. For all their weariness, excitement kept the children and their elders talking far into the night. The men questioned Beckwourth, and his stories of the wonders and wealth of California rekindled their ambitions. They would leave next morning if Beckwourth would show them the way. They needed a guide, and Beckwourth needed them, for they would prove the practicality of his road.

Next morning the party was on its way to the pass. Three days' hard riding through the sagebrush brought them to it. Beckwourth rode slowly ahead of the column of seventeen worn and creaking schooners. When near the pass, he turned back and rode alongside the Pickett wagon. He asked Mrs. Pickett if her younger daughter would like to ride with him over the pass. She would then be the first white child to do so. Ina's heart pounded and she could hardly talk for happiness. Beckwourth put her ahead of him on his pony and it was not long before they reached the highest point on the journey, Beckwourth Pass. This place in the mountains is slightly less than a mile above sea level. It is indeed the easiest and lowest pass in the Sierra, and a natural gateway to the Feather River country from the east. At the pass Beckwourth dismounted and helped the girl off the horse. An autumn wind had come up, stinging their faces, whipping their clothes. Storm clouds were gathering, darkening all the landscape except the valley lying to the west below them. The sun lighted it as if on purpose for this moment. Jim pointed to the glowing valley lying against a range of blue.

"There, little girl," he said, "there is California! There is your kingdom!"[6]

Ina's response to Jim Beckwourth's exclamation is unrecorded, but in her heart she believed the mountain man. Some day she would receive a crown, but not of gold; a crown put into her hand, not one placed on her head. Jim, thinking of his road, and Ina, daydreaming of the promised land before her, waited for the caravan to reach the top. Here the oxen were halted for a rest, and the surprised and relieved emigrants climbed down to have a look at this broad pass which was actually the crest of the Sierra. This was the top. They had made it! There would be no Donner Party repetition for them. This late August day was Thanksgiving Day for half a hundred souls. They faced the next step with confidence.

5
The
Glittering
Lure

Gold! Gold! The glittering lure that beckoned them!

Ina Coolbrith, from
"The Gold Seekers" (1896)

From Spanish Ranch to Marysville

James Beckwourth's store lay some fifteen miles ahead. "Store and hotel combined," he said.[1] He could put them up there while they made plans for reaching the gold fields. The travelers decided to find a camp for the night and make for Beckwourth's place the next day. Another day's riding brought them to the mountain man's trading post. Here William and Agnes decided to go on to Spanish Ranch as soon as possible. Some form of permanent shelter must be found before winter caught them. Spanish Ranch boasted a hotel and excellent pasture. It was a miners' pack station, furnishing animals and provisions for trips to the gold camps on the Feather and Yuba rivers. Here Agnes and her children could remain while William would go "to see the elephant" with his own eyes.[2] Taking leave of their host and guide, to whom they felt deeply indebted, the Picketts climbed into their wagon and urged their tired animals forward once more. In the next fifty miles they lost about two thousand feet of altitude, coming finally to Bradley's Ranch, the beginning of the settlement later called Quincy. They followed Spanish Creek for eight or ten miles, over rocks and through brush where there was no road at all, until they reached Spanish Ranch.

The children were excited about the prospect of living on a California ranch. Whatever they may have imagined, the reality was an abrupt and noisy surprise. They came first to an immense pole-fenced corral, dusty, and foul with manure. The place was clamorous with profanity, and alive with men and mules, neither species accepting gracefully the requirements of pack-saddle fitting. Nearby were smaller, mucky pens crowded with cattle. Beyond the corral, and separated from it by a narrow dusty lane, was a row of unpainted buildings, the "hotel," barns, and a slaughterhouse. A thickly wooded slope rose back of the buildings, its height and density minimizing the size of the structures. The tall pines and cedars swayed in serene aloofness to the blotch at their feet where once a gentle mountain meadow had lain. It was a rough, loud place, settled two years before by Mexicans who carried on the pack station, pastured horses and mules for the men at the mines, and butchered beef for the camps along the river, some of the meat going as far as Marysville, eighty miles away.[3]

Marysville, indeed, was the destination of the other travelers in Pickett's wagon train. They were glad to go on with Beckwourth, thereby helping him accomplish his summer's goal, to bring an emigrant train from the Truckee River to Marysville by way of his road. His friend the mayor and other townsmen congratulated him for his success and found places for the tired emigrants to camp for the night. The next day would be soon enough to make permanent plans of the newcomers, and to discuss compensation for Beckwourth's road building. This was the evening of 31 August 1851.

That night the bustling town of Marysville was almost destroyed by fire. The disaster was overwhelming. All energies of local officials went to help those who were burned out, and to begin rebuilding as soon as possible. Beckwourth's road was out of the question as far as town support was concerned. He was never compensated for the work and money he had put into it, and he concluded, morosely, that if he ever built another road from which he would derive no benefit, it would be because he had nothing better to do.[4]

Back at Spanish Ranch William Pickett saw his family settled in the primitive accommodations the "hotel" provided. At least it would be a shelter while he was away on a brief prospecting expedition. A group of miners were outfitting pack mules at the Ranch for a trip to the Gibsonville Ridge, about twenty-five miles south of the present Quincy, and Pickett decided to join them. In this area, known later as the Gibsonville mining district, there were a number of quartz diggings and prospects. William did not stay long, as it was late in the season and he had no equipment. But he did stake his claim at mile-high Howland Flat, halfway between Port Wine and Whiskey Diggings. He named his claim the Ina Ledge. He decided to return and take his family to Marysville for the winter.[5]

42

Waiting for their father to come back from prospecting, the children relaxed and rested from the long overland journey. They ran and played among the trees in the brief autumn sunlight. Here they were sheltered by the pines, yet the wind was in the tops of the trees, swaying them, making music, bearing their aroma to the children. And it brought them the scent of woodsmoke that drifted powder blue against the blue black pines. These wild smells and home smells made them shiver with delight. Ina heard music other than the humming in the trees. For the first time she heard bits of Spanish talk and song that made no sense at all to her but pleased her ears. As usual she looked after her little brothers, obeying her mother's stern orders to stay out of the woods and not go near the corrals or the slaughterhouse. Sometimes she helped her sister and mother with household tasks.

Agnes spent her days at Spanish Ranch in going over their poor belongings, mending, and making repairs that had gone neglected on the long journey. As they mended, the girls chattered about the future, but their mother's thoughts drifted back. They slipped back to a day in Boston when a Maine girl in her twenties had said Yes to a Mormon missionary and had started on the rough path that had had no return. Now, at forty, in a lonely Sierra valley, across the continent from home, she waited impatiently for William's return. She was eager to be back among people. She could endure shared hardship, but not this isolation. There was a happy reunion when William rode back into camp a few weeks later. He was dog weary, but all the way back he had been thinking about what they must do now. Before he reached Spanish Ranch, he had made up his mind. There was only one sensible course. He must see his family comfortably settled, in a less isolated place, before he would go into the mines again. Marysville, of course, was his choice. After he had found a house for them, he could make a few prospecting trips into the gold country east of there.

Agnes fell in gratefully with his proposal. But how would they go? They had sold their teams as soon as they reached Spanish Ranch. There seemed to be only one answer, to go horseback or on foot. In the end they rented pack mules for their bedding and clothing, their food and utensils, and William's precious books. The little boys, soon to be four years old, rode donkeys. All the others, greenhorn mountaineers indeed, walked every step of the way, up, over the mountain, and down, eighty miles or more. The most direct way from Spanish Ranch, at an altitude of about thirty-five hundred feet, would have been southwest, up to the summit near the present Buck's Lake, then down the gradual but rugged descent along the ridges between the north and middle forks of the Feather River. It was a never forgotten ordeal for the girls and their

43

mother. Ina's shoes gave out and the soles of her feet were soon sore and bleeding. Her mother bandaged them, but the little girl went the rest of the way in agony.[6]

When the family reached Marysville, they were surprised at its extent. They were surprised, too, at the hundreds of tents in sight. The recent fire had destroyed a great many wooden structures, and Pickett must have had difficulty in renting a place for his wife and children. On a rise, however, away from the business center, he found a small vacant cabin which he was able to rent. Satisfied that they were under a roof, he hurried off to the mines near Grass Valley, on the South Fork of the Feather River, expecting to be back within the month.[7]

The Forest near the Mines

Like St. Louis, Marysville was a river city, dependent on riverboats for its contact with the outer world. Lying where the Feather and the Yuba rivers unite, Marysville's new streets ran down to the landing. There boats, bound for Sacramento and San Francisco, were docked. As St. Louis had been the home port to trappers and mountain men, so Marysville was "the city" to prospectors in the quartz mining country to the north and east. But there the resemblance to St. Louis stopped. The Missouri city had had a long history when William Pickett and his Mormon refugee family had made it their home. Marysville was brand-new. This was one of California's "boomtowns," legally not yet a year old. It had changed quickly from a tent city to one of permanent structures of brick and timber, though the recent fire had given it a setback.[8]

As a gateway to the mines the place had attracted merchants, doctors, dentists, craftsmen of many skills, as well as hotel, saloon, and stable keepers. Marysville had its newspapers, too. Two names important in the literary annals of the state are associated with journalism in this city, Stephen Massett (Jeems Pipes of Pipesville) and John Rollin Ridge ("Yellow Bird"). Though Ina Smith came to know both these men as colleagues in later years, she did not know them there. Her stepfather, however, as a printer working at his trade while not at the mines, may have known them both.[9]

This was a winter Ina never forgot, a winter of heavy rains and floods. Her stepfather was marooned in the diggings by exceptionally heavy snows and was not able to return until May. Fortunately the little cabin was on higher ground than the business area. Though water lapped against the walls of the house, it did not rise to floor level. A boat, however, was tied to the step railing for three days and nights, in case of need. Agnes and her children had one protector, Old Thompson, a Virginia ex-slave, whose tent laundry in the neighborhood had gone down in

44

the flood. They gave him shelter, and he did what he could to aid them.[10] All winter and spring they were ill with chills and fever. And all winter and spring they were on short rations, as was William himself while snowbound. Ten-year-old Ina was the only one able to go on errands. She had to be "the middleman," she said, as her sister Agnes Charlotte was now fifteen, and considered herself quite a young lady. Actually errands away from home in those rough times were occasionally dangerous for unprotected young women, and Agnes was right not to let her young daughter out alone, though ten-year-old Ina might be sent on a similar errand without too much fear for her safety. But even a simple trip to the grocery was not without its physical perils. One time Ina started to the store, walking carefully on a narrow levee between a ditch and a flooded field, when the softened soil caved in and she fell into the ditch. Fortunately Old Thompson was at hand and he pulled her out.[11]

The winter of 1851-1852 was one of unrelieved misery, increased by worry about the stepfather. Word of him must have come to them, for the plight of those snowed in was well known, and rescue parties were sent out with supplies for those stranded. With the scarcity of food, prices went up. One man reported that the supplies he could carry on his back would cost as much as a hundred dollars. When Agnes was well enough, she sewed for certain women of the town, "better left unnamed," she later said. Thus she provided what little food they had. They all survived, and the little boys were not sick.[12]

William's return in May was hailed with tears of joy and relief. In spite of the winter's hardships for all of them, he was not discouraged about his gold mine prospects. He proposed to go back to his claim for the summer and take his family with him. The mild, dry air of the foothills would restore their dampened health and spirits. This time they would ride. He was going with a party of men who had claims in the Gibsonville district near his own. They had pooled their cash for drills and powder, and engaged mules for pack and saddle animals for the summer.

For Ina, eleven in March, the summer of 1852 was an adventurous one. She saw the claim her stepfather had named for her. The Ina Ledge, near Howland Flat, was in mile-high country where the air was heady with the scent of sun-warmed pine needles. There were oaks on the grassy slopes and willows along the little stream at the bottom of Gold Canyon, near which the Pickett family may have made their camp. Ina and her little brothers watched the men at work or played among the rocks or under the oaks. Her only fear was of rattlesnakes. Because of her father's warning about them, she seldom ventured any distance from the camp or from the mining operation where he was working.

One afternoon she and the twins wandered into the woods near the camp. The tent was actually out of sight, but she could hear her mother and sister talking. The little boys were running ahead of her, climbing rocks, watching squirrels and chipmunks, picking up shiny stones, shouting at each new find. Ina called them.

"Let's go back," she said, "it will soon be suppertime." She waited for them, suddenly aware that she did not hear any of the familiar camp chatter and clatter. She gave a hand to each of the boys and the three started back on the run. As they hurried along, Ina began to see rocks and trees she had not noticed before. They stopped. She listened. The forest was strangely quiet.

She saw now that evening was coming on and that even the birds seemed silent. In sudden terror she knew that she was lost, lost in a forest with unknown wild animals. She remembered hearing the men speak of bears and lions in these mountains, as well as snakes. Her panic was contagious, and both Willie and Don began to cry. It was getting dark and they were hungry and they wanted their mamma. Ina tried to comfort them. She said that they would sit down under this big tree and soon their father would come along and take them back to camp. With an arm about each she drew comfort from their very nearness and warmth. The little boys cried themselves to sleep, and slipped down, putting their heads in her lap. Their sister was afraid to call. She was afraid she would waken the birds and they in turn would warn the larger animals of the woods. She could not sleep. Gradually her fear subsided. She remembered what her mother had said about God watching over those who trusted Him. She would trust God to keep them safe. She thought of her mother, bustling about, getting supper. But it was past suppertime. By now her mother would be worried. And feeling sorry for her mother, she finally relaxed into sleep.[13]

Her mother, meantime, looked up from her fire to see William coming into the camp alone.

"Are Ina and the boys coming along?" she asked.

"The children? Aren't they here in camp?"

"No," Agnes said, "they were going down to the other mine with you. They left just after dinner." Then, suddenly realizing what had happened, she screamed in fright. "Oh, they're lost, lost!" She started for the woods, but her husband begged her to stay in camp. He would get some of the men and they would find the youngsters in no time. Pickett told the men what had happened. All of them, including "Sailor Dick," a big fellow who was a favorite of Willie and Don, started out, noisy and excited. All night long they tramped through the brush, stumbling,

46

slipping on the uneven ground, calling, and stopping to listen. There was no response.

Ina awoke with sun in her eyes. The boys were still asleep, their faces tear-stained and dirty. Sunshine, voices! She heard men talking and striding through the woods, breaking twigs as they walked, coming nearer. The children got up, stiff and wobbly, just as the shrubs parted, and Sailor Dick appeared.

"Here they are!" he shouted. He was a giant of a man, and he gathered all three children into his arms. The twins' father and the other men came up and carried the children back to camp. Ina, in a still sleepy voice, said, "We didn't see any snakes at all. But is Mother all right?"

Flood in Marysville; Fire in San Francisco

With the coming of frost, the Pickett family returned to Marysville. The summer's work had been strenuous for William, and his takings were slim. He was discouraged. Perhaps this was not his line of work after all. He had other skills. He might do better to follow them. He would not let the claim go; he would go back for another try at it, maybe next summer. The local weathermen were prophesying another bad winter; snow in the hills and lots of rain in the valley. When they reached Marysville, Pickett rented a place on Third Street, near the post office, and went to work as a printer on one of the several newspapers in the city, which one we do not know. Here he could be with his family. There would be no repetition of the horrors of last winter.[14]

The rain began early in November, and before the month was out the rivers were as high as they had been the winter before. Then the rains let up and the water level subsided. There was more rain in December, and on New Year's Eve the water raced through the streets of Marysville again, flooding First Street and the plaza, covering floors of buildings with six to ten inches of water. The hotel where a New Year's ball was to take place was surrounded by water, but the guests came in boats and greeted the New Year, 1853, cheerfully in their flooded city. The surrounding country was under water. Boats were the only means of transportation and communication. Though the flood was higher this year than last, the loss of livestock and goods was not as great, for there had been time enough to get animals to higher ground, and move belongings to higher shelves or second stories.[15] Whether the Pickett place on Third Street was flooded or not, we do not know. William, however, continued through the winter, spring, and summer, working at his trade. He was listed in the first Marysville city directory, published in August 1853, and was probably in town until about that time. But he did not feel compelled to remain another winter in what seemed to be a

47

disaster area. Before another rainy season began, he and his family took the steamboat for Sacramento and on to San Francisco. [16]

Here another boomtown was growing. Among the ships crowding San Francisco Bay, many had been abandoned by their crews who rushed off to the mines. Some of the nearest vessels had even been converted into commercial establishments where they stood at anchor, the edge of the Bay being filled, and the fill paved or planked. Up from the Bay, on the lower hills, along miserable roads, dwelling houses were in all stages of construction, for San Francisco was going through one of its regular rebuilding periods. Houses were hastily put up, built of redwood brought by barges across the Bay from the *Contra Costa,* and fires swept the city repeatedly.[17] Pickett must have been enthusiastic about his prospects here, for almost at once he went into debt to build a house of his own in the Mission district.[18] At the same time he secured employment as a printer for the *Bulletin,* and shortly after opened a law office.[19]

After suffering through a hot summer in Marysville, the Pickett family were met by brisk winds off the Pacific, refreshed by them and by the cool fogs of San Francisco. For them all, this was their first sight of the Pacific Ocean, a thrilling first for any midlander, and even for one who, like Agnes, had known the Maine coast as a girl. For the children, the dunes, the vivid beach asters and sand verbenas, the waves casting an occasional shell upon the sand were all wonders. Years later Ina recalled those brief months in the young city, when she wrote, after the fire of 1906,

> In olden days, a child, I trod thy sands,
>   Thy sands unbuilded, rank with brush and briar
> And blossom—chased the sea-foam on thy strands,
>   Young City of my love and my desire.
> I saw thy barren hills against the skies . . .[20]

To William Pickett this town of some thirty thousand people was the liveliest place on earth, San Francisco of the fifties, where a man could make a fortune or lose it in a day or a night. And while there were beginning to be schools and churches, even a library, that would attract a man with a family, these institutions were little felt in 1853. "It was a wooden city," said Horace Davis, "men only, no women or children, but men of every sort." Precisely because there were men of every sort, not all were attracted to the numerous gambling dens, brothels, saloons, and cheap auction houses. There were theaters, but they were expensive; so a group of young men decided to form a library association: *The Mercantile Library Association* they called it. Davis, with a temporary job as a lumber surveyor on the dock, was persuaded to be the Association's librarian. It is doubtful if the Pickett family were in San Francisco long enough to be aware of this little library, a library that was later to play an important part in Ina's life, just as its early librarian, Horace Davis, later a president of the University of California, was to be one of her many friends.[21]

The Pickett family's sojourn in San Francisco in the fifties was cut short by a catastrophe. Very soon after they had settled in their new home, their house was robbed, and the thief put a match to it to hide the crime. The senseless incident turned them against the city, but they remained long enough for William to pay his debt on a house no longer there, and to provide some funds for a future move. Fortunately Pickett's books, brought with care over plain and mountain, were not destroyed; they had been on the shelves of his law office. He would continue to practice, but not in San Francisco. Los Angeles and the Mormon settlement at San Bernardino now attracted him. They took passage on one of the coastal steamers, and soon Agnes and her husband, the Smith girls, and the twin Pickett boys found themselves in an environment as new to them as a foreign country.[22]

6
Los Angeles in the Fifties

In the balm and the blossoming.

Ina Coolbrith, from
"In Blossom Time" (1868)

Los Angeles, a Mexican Pueblo

The little Mexican town with the lovely name, *El Pueblo de Nuestra Señora la Reina de los Angeles,* actually had been foreign country less than ten years before the Pickett family arrived in 1855. In the midfifties, when the pueblo's low, brea-roofed adobes first came into Ina's gaze, it was more Mexican than American. The speech was Spanish, and Spanish the singing and the guitar strumming and the fiestas.[1]

If the Picketts came in the spring, they found a blossoming valley cut by two main watercourses: the Los Angeles River, its banks thick with cottonwoods and alders, and the Arroyo Seco, a dry stream bed until heavy rains would make it a torrent. Orchards and vineyards surrounded the village, watered by a meandering *zanja,* and beyond the fields were wild flower gardens; early in the spring the cool, yellow mustard, tall enough for children's games of hide-and-seek, and also the gaudy poppy and its companion, the blue lupine. But if the newcomers arrived in early autumn, they found a parched land. The pueblo, surrounded by its fields and orchards, was a struggling oasis, the *zanja* its lifeline. All around lay the desert, the hills to the northeast gray with dusty chapparal and cactus, the plain to the west spreading hot and empty to straw colored hills, beyond which boomed the Pacific, the crash of its waves unheard in the pueblo. Southward, at the end of the river's course, the ocean could be glimpsed as a thin, bright line of horizon.

51

The village lay close to the hills. Its first settlement was around the plaza, as were all the Mexican pueblos. The pioneers who came north built homes similar to those they left, long and low adobe houses, with columned arcades across the front. But these hastily erected houses were different in one respect. Instead of tile or wattle roofs, a local water-proof building material was used, brea from the asphalt pits. The dwellings were flat topped, mostly one-story, with plain posts supporting arcade roofs. They were built side by side, presenting to the streets continuous shaded porches. Their stark façades were unrelieved by either loving craftsmanship or the patina of time and planting. Some were white-washed, but most were the color of the soil from which they were formed. The unglazed windows were wooden barred; the floors were of packed earth. Many of the yards at the rear of the buildings were enclosed by adobe walls and used as corrals for saddle horses. Gardens were scarce, as water had to be carried by hand from the *zanja*. Drinking water was even more precious. It was hauled from the river by the waterman who charged fifty cents a bucket. Some people, who remembered Los Angeles "in the adobe age," remembered no trees at all. Others recalled the pepper trees they glimpsed now and then through courtyard doors left ajar. In spite of the labor of carrying water, some of the women kept the struggling pepper trees alive in their patios, so that a few years later these graceful trees became a characteristic sight in an otherwise drab little town that baked in the summer sun.[2]

There were also some trees in the yard of the new schoolhouse out at Second and Spring streets. Here a determined young schoolmaster endeavored with the grudging aid of the water man to keep alive a dozen black locusts bought by the school trustees. This was the city's first public school building, a kiln-dried brick structure of two rooms, one for boys and one for girls. The construction was completed in February, and the building was opened for use on 19 March 1855, just nine days after Ina Smith's fourteenth birthday. She was enrolled with Miss Louisa Hayes, the teacher in charge of the girls' department. The boys' teacher was William A. Wallace. Here Ina had three years of classroom education, the last, if not the only, formal schooling she received. She herself said, "The very little I had, I got from home study at night, and reading."[3]

Los Angeles in 1853, as It Looked when Ina Coolbrith Came with Her Family Two Years Later. From the drawing by Charles Koppel for the **Pacific Railroad Reports,** volume 5 (Washington, 1855-1861). Courtesy of the Bancroft Library, University of California, Berkeley.

The Pickett Family and Their Friends

When the Pickett family arrived in the midfifties, the population of Los Angeles was about two thousand, half Mexican, half Indian. The American families were very few indeed, though more than the half dozen Ina was later to remember. A number of wealthy Yankees, like Abel Stearns and Benjamin Wilson, had taken Californian brides, and they served as a social and commercial liaison between their compatriots and the colonial families. Living in the pueblo, or on nearby ranchos granted by Spain and by Mexico, were the Carillos, the Lugos, the Verdugos, the Picos, the Sepulvedas, the Bandinis, the Figueroas, and others whose names remain on maps of the region.

While the American colony was small, William Pickett found it made up of adventurers like himself. He began the practice of law at once, finding himself at home among the members of his own profession. His law library, brought across the plains, was the first and best in a region that was thick with lawyers. As money lenders flourished in a community of the landed poor, so men of the law grew numerous and prosperous among clients who sought help to retain what they could of their diminishing ranchos. Pickett soon became known as an able attorney. He was never timid. In 1858, it is told, he rented an office in San Bernardino where there were no justice court chambers. He permitted the use of his office for such purposes, but if the trial did not proceed to his liking he was known to order the court—judge and jury, prisoner and attorney— out of his office. Pickett was no more eccentric than many of his colleagues in the frontier courtroom of Southern California. Of all his acquaintances in the pueblo, none were more daring or spirited than the tribe of lawyers. Pickett knew them all: Judge Benjamin Hayes, Ezra Drown, E. J. C. Kewen, A. J. King, William H. Peterson, and Horace Rolfe, among others.[4]

Horace Rolfe was the youngest. He began his reading of law in Pickett's San Bernardino office, and in later years became a judge, and a compiler of San Bernardino history materials. William Peterson was a little older and already established in numerous civic responsibilities. Son of a Swedish sea captain (Peter Peterson, a naturalized American citizen of Philadelphia), he had come west by way of service as a wagon master in the Mexican War, arriving in Los Angeles in 1852 when he was twenty-six. His talents were varied, and all put to use. If, as a peace officer, he could capture a notorious bandit, one Garcia, who had "two six-shooters and a sixteen-inch Bowie knife on his person," Peterson could also preach the funeral sermon for Sheriff Barton. He later tracked down and captured Barton's murderer. Orator, Master Mason, city attorney, school trustee, state legislator, Peterson was to become William Pickett's son-in-law.[5]

Another attorney friend of William Pickett was Andrew J. King who led a tumultuous career that progressed from under-sheriff to judge by way of newspaper editorship. Two others, both colorful personalities, Ezra Drown and Judge Hayes, were said to be hard drinkers, and if court had to be suspended on that account from time to time, they were nevertheless popular and highly respected. Lawyer Drown was a Midwesterner who had come to Los Angeles by way of the Isthmus, experiencing a shocking tragedy on the way. Off the coast of Baja California the ship caught fire and could not be saved. Those who could swim reached shore. Ezra Drown, an excellent swimmer, put his wife on a floating bit of wreckage, got his boy and girl on the beach, and was within a few strokes of saving their mother, when a crazed fellow passenger pushed her into the sea. She went down before her husband's eyes, just beyond his grasp. He became active in the life of the pueblo and was a favorite public speaker who expressed his strong Union convictions during the sixties.[6]

His colleague, Judge Benjamin Hayes, did not share his views. The judge came from Baltimore and was a Southerner at heart, yet he did not allow his personal sympathies to interfere with his decisions in court. Though of Secessionist leanings, his benign, bearded face might have been that of Uncle Sam himself. He was a man of action, mixing in many of the affairs of the pueblo, and very nearly getting himself assassinated. He possessed unusual ability and perception. He was the author of many legal articles in the Spanish edition of the *Los Angeles Star, La Estrella*. At heart he was an antiquarian, or, at least, a man who recognized in contemporary events the stuff of which future local history might be written. He clipped, dated, and classified thousands of Los Angeles newspaper items, assembling a collection that was ultimately pasted into more than a hundred scrapbooks, now a priceless source of information on the old pueblo.[7]

While Judge Hayes was discreet in voicing his views, his young colleague, Colonel Edward John Case Kewen, was not. There was no more outspoken Secessionist in Southern California than Colonel Kewen. His reckless use of words landed him in Alcatraz Prison as a traitor in the sixties, though his stay was brief, and his was the unique experience of going directly from Alcatraz to the State Assembly as a popular representative of his district.[8] Ed Kewen was an engaging rascal. Like the other attorney friends of Pickett, he too came briefly into Ina Smith's life. It is not surprising. Kewen was everywhere. He was electric. When the Pickett family knew him he was a rangy man, dark of hair and beard, quick of speech and temper, and as quick to smile. He was a story-book hero in the making. He might have been the prototype of all Hollywood's hot-headed Southerners, or Westerners, quick on the draw, or some splendidly mistaken defender of manifest destiny marching to Nicaragua with Walker himself. In time he became all these. He stumped for Breckenridge and Lane, capturing his audience as much with his witty handling of hecklers as with his oratory, heavy with classical references. Barely old enough to vote, he became California's first Attorney-General and was subsequently elected to other political offices.[9]

Ed and his wife Jennie lived in a house given them by Jennie's father, Dr. Thomas J. White, whose residence it had been. It is a distinguished house, *El Molino Viejo,* occupied as a private dwelling in San Marino until a few years ago when it was acquired by the California Historical Society. It is still "full of charm and physical hazards," as a former occupant once remarked. This was the old mill built about 1800 by the San Gabriel Mission fathers, then abandoned. Dr. White remodelled the place into a dwelling that became the setting for some of the area's most enjoyable social affairs. Ed and Jennie made further changes without altering its basic lines and character, planted trees, shrubs and flowers, and built a small fountain. To Ina Smith and her sister, as well as to many others who were guests of the Whites or Kewens, it was a small paradise, and undoubtedly influenced some of Ina's verse writing.[10]

Ina sometimes walked in the garden with the doctor, a thoughtful, white-haired man not yet out of his fifties. There was a bond between the teen-age girl and the older man. He too had lived in St. Louis. He too had crossed the plains. And he, like Ina, loved the stars, the fragrant garden paths, and the birds splashing in the little fountain. Here, on her rare visits to the old mill, was intellectual and aesthetic nourishment for a girl poet from the dusty pueblo.[11] Dr. White had been the first Speaker of the State Assembly when it met in San Jose. He had practiced medicine in Sacramento, turning his own home into a hospital without fee during an epidemic, and had later practiced in San Francisco. When he settled in Los Angeles, he spent some years as postmaster, continuing his medical service and running a drug store at the same time. But his interests turned more and more toward horticulture and he was soon producing excellent citrus fruits and grapes.[12]

These were the friends of William Pickett and his family. Pickett must have known both Harris Newmark and Horace Bell, though neither of them remembered him when they wrote their memoirs. He knew Editor Hamilton of the *Los Angeles Star* and was acquainted with a number of military men. When it came time to take sides for the North or the South, Pickett showed his loyalty to the Union by joining the National

Guard. He was living in Los Angeles at this time, only a few steps from one of the pueblo's guard camps, presumably that stationed at the quartermaster's headquarters at Second and Spring streets, across the street from the schoolhouse. Here he came to know Captain Davidson and perhaps even the Captain's superior officer, Major Carleton, who was destined to save the Southwest for the Union.[13]

Ina, the Young Poet

In the half-decade before Fort Sumpter was shelled, the Smith girls were enjoying the social life of the pueblo. They went to cotillions and danced in the homes of Americans and Mexicans alike. Ina was said to have opened a ball, leading the grand march on the arm of Don Pio Pico, California's last Mexican governor. These were happy days for the girls; Agnes, just turned twenty, dark haired and lovely; Ina in her teens, with a wealth of curling fair hair framing a face in which dark gray eyes glowed so brilliantly they seemed black.[14]

Enjoying family, school, and social life, Ina was unaware of the sordid character of Los Angeles in the fifties. The murders, the lynchings, the debauching and enslaving of the Indians, the cheating of the Mexicans by American moneylenders, the cruel sports, were all there, but beyond her horizon. Los Angeles was a shockingly brutal environment in which to rear a gentle girl poet. Experimenting in verse writing in those days, only once did she use local violence as a subject for her pen.

For Ina Smith, little more than a child, life was all sparkle and rapture. She breathed deeply the scent of orange blossoms in the springtime air. And every morning, while the hills lay in misty shadow at sunrise, the mourning dove's haunting call lent further enchantment to each new day's beginning. The clear air, the blossom scent, the distant cooing quickened her pulse and set rhythms and rhymes going in her brain as she walked to school. Here, one day, she wrote her first composition in verse, surprising Miss Hayes, and perhaps herself. She said it was easier that way. Out-of-doors she joined in the children's games where the school yard, partly shaded by its struggling locust trees, was continued by vacant land sloping steeply up the cactus-covered hillside. Often at recess, the children, running at play, would tumble into the prickles, and their games would end abruptly in tears or howls.[15]

At home, going about household tasks, Ina would be composing rhymes and concentrating on imagery so remote from dishwashing and sweeping that her stepfather would smile and say, "What is the matter with that girl?" She found verse making an exciting discipline and a satisfying means of expressing her thoughts and daydreams. She was her own teacher and critic, influenced by the volumes of Byron and Shake-

57

speare that had crossed the plains with her. Local verse appearing now and then in the *Los Angeles Star* and the *Southern Vineyard* may have encouraged her to compete. She may have borrowed books from Dr. White or have read Ed Kewen's romantic little volume *Idealina,* published two years before the author went to Nicaragua with William Walker.[16]

Her earliest exercises in prosody were the sentimental outpourings of a midnineteenth-century girl. She was fifteen when she first saw any of her rhymes in print. Her first published poem, "My Childhood's Home," appeared in the *Los Angeles Star* of 30 August 1856. When she wrote these verses, she idealized scenes she may have remembered from her St. Louis days, but she placed the ivy-covered cottage "far away o'er ocean's white foam." As distant and as stereotyped too was the setting of the next of the girl's rhymed compositions to be printed in the *Star,* memorial lines to "Ally," "child-angel," sleeping where "the white lily from her tomb springeth." Her writing in this vein was suggested by the trite memorial verses that brought a little comfort to families for the all too frequent loss of their children by disease in American pioneer communities. But Ina's juvenilia, though exercises in conventionally picturesque subjects, had a freshness of expression now and then, and were deeply sincere. Lyric form came to her easily and her rhymes were not forced.[17]

Dropping these gentle themes abruptly a few weeks later, she turned to crime as the subject of her next published verse, for the new year opened with an event that shocked even Los Angeles, accustomed as the pueblo was to its daily homicide. In January 1857 the county sheriff, James Barton, and three members of his posse were shot from ambush and killed. Although Barton was a gunman himself, inclined to draw first, then ask questions when too late—a man who considered all Indians and Sonorans his legitimate prey—his murder frightened the community. Even young Ina turned from romantic musing to ask for avengers for the dead man. The *Star* published her call, which may or may not have been in incitement to lynching. That a period of lawlessness followed and that the alleged murderer of Barton was lynched when caught the next year were perhaps only coincidental. "Judge Lynch" was a powerful personality in the pueblo, and it is unlikely that he would have been persuaded or deterred by a bit of newspaper verse, however provocative.[18]

Ina in Love

Ina's call for "revenge on their murders" was her only public affairs' composition to be printed in the *Star*. The teen-age girl preferred to write of more conventional dying, of friendship and memory, and to carry on a girlishly daring newspaper flirtation or two. In April, Sheriff Barton forgotten, she was daydreaming love lyrics to a Marysville poet whom she may have met when she was a child. Her "Lines to the Unknown" were printed in the *Star* in May and copied by the *Marysville Herald*. Childlike and uninhibited, she flattered the young man as an "unknown, yet loved one," and brought a rhymed reply, signed M**TB*R in the *Marysville Express*. He praised both the singer and the song, but reminded the "Gifted Child" that her unknown one existed only in her imagination, and that the mere man whom she professed to adore was made of clay, and that the eyes she flattered probably had a squint. His epistle and the editorial comment, in the *Express,* that the author of "Lines to the Unknown" and her subject "should not long be separated" were copied by the *Star.*[19]

Ina's answer, "To M**tb*r," penned shortly after, contained a reference to a boy she had known in Marysville. Looking back, she idealized a lad who had died, and she tried to fuse his personality with that of the man Montbar (the real name of her "Unknown"). Sixteen years old and in love with the idea of love, she indulged in a flood of sweet and mournful memories and put them on paper with a freedom from restraint that was sheer bathos. She undoubtedly reveled in her daring, too, for these verses were not intended for any secret diary but would be spread upon a printed page and sent up and down the state. Twice during the summer Montbar wrote lyric letters to the Los Angeles poet, one a trite little piece, the other a flowery address to his "angel by the sea." In July 1857 two more of Ina's compositions appeared in the *Star.* Both of them were melancholy, self-pitying. They expressed an adolescent's lightning shift from joy to despair. Her lines "To Nelly" were written to wish another girl happiness. For herself she said,

> But a sorrow dwells in my young heart—
>   Its shade is on my brow,
> And the memory of the past is all
>   That's left to cheer me now.[21]

During the weeks after the lines to Nelly appeared, Ina was worlds away, embroidering word fancies to a young man named *******.[22] Montbar counted the asterisks and penned a sentimental reply "To Ina of Los Angeles." Seven asterisks could spell Montbar. But the object of her dreaming lines was not the Marysville poet, nor indeed any poet. She was begging an obviously worldly man to leave his "transient pleasures" for a moment "to bestow a thought" on her. Ina's pretty face was pensive as she asked,

Have I been remembered, where light forms were gliding,
In all their fairy beauty, before thy sight,
Where dark eyes flashed, through jetty fringes hiding
Their wildering glances, their bewitching light;
Where snowy brows, by long black ringlets shaded,
And smiling lips were whispering soft and low—
In scenes like these, hath not every mem'ry faded,
Of her afar—and the days of long ago?

Even last week was long ago to an adolescent girl in love. And if her love were absent anywhere in this part of New Spain, there was reason for blonde Ina's fear of the magic of dark eyes and black hair. She had seen their effect on the American men of Los Angeles.

We can guess that *******, whoever he was, must have been a traveling man of sorts. Seven asterisks *could* spell Carsley. Robert Carsley was a young man who followed a carefree avocation that took him to San Francisco and elsewhere with a troop of minstrel players. He participated in the first such show in Los Angeles. Ina Smith may have seen him "playing the bones." His cleverness, his spontaneity, his nonchalance in the limelight must have attracted her. She was an exceptionally pretty girl, vivacious and popular. For all her melancholy verse writing there was nothing melancholy in her behavior. Spanish songs came readily to her lips by now, their phrases accented by her guitar. She was fond of dancing, her honey colored curls bobbing, her full skirts flying. Of course she was attractive to Robert Carsley, a man several years her senior, as she was to other men, indeed to many men throughout her life.[23] Bob Carsley did not spend all his time on the road. He had a business in Los Angeles that kept him hard at work most of the time. He and Daniel B. Lindsay were partners in the Salamander Iron Works. Bringing to the southern city the experience of several years in Sacramento and San Francisco, the partners were prepared to make anything in iron from heavy doors and shutters to delicately wrought balcony railings and cemetery enclosures.[24]

Agnes and William Pickett found that something as substantial as the Salamander Iron Works carried its own weight when Robert Carsley asked for Ina's hand. Early in 1858 they had moved to San Bernardino where William was to practice law for two years. The girls were as popular in San Bernardino as they were in Los Angeles. Through all the years, long after they had left, their neighbors remembered them, especially the impulsive Ina and how she "ran in and out their houses, her warm, rich personality gladdening all about her."[25] At that time she was in love with life, in love with love, in love with Bob Carsley.

60

Both girls became engaged during the winter, Agnes Charlotte to the eminently eligible bachelor, William Peterson, ten years her senior and already prominent in Los Angeles civic affairs, and Ina, not yet seventeen, to Robert Carsley, handsome, engaging, temperamental. Agnes and William were married on 3 March 1858, just a week before Ina's seventeenth birthday. The new Mrs. Peterson and her husband went to live in an adobe casa on Fort Street, later Broadway, in Los Angeles.[26] With romance in the air all about her, Ina's verse writing at this time was limited to sentimental bits, all related to home and family. During the later months of 1857 she had published "My Ideal Home," "We Miss Thee at Home," and "One on Earth, and One in Heaven," and in April 1858 a memorial poem to a child, "Little Elsie." Her thoughts all winter and spring were of her coming marriage to Robert.[27]

7
Marriage and Divorce

Love beckons, the ready heart follows,
How fleet to the summons, how fleet!

Ina Coolbrith, from
"Summons" (1871)

Ina's Marriage to Robert Carsley

Ina's domestic interests were expressed romantically when she wrote "My Ideal Home," imagining a vine-covered cottage in a fragrant vale, with birds and flowers and a tinkling fountain in the garden. Her lines might have described the setting for her wedding in San Gabriel, the region's most pleasant garden spot in the 1850s. No land was ever fairer to a girl in love than was California's Southland to Ina Smith on her seventeenth birthday, 10 March 1858. She wanted to sing.

> To sing and shout in the fields about
> In the balm and the blossoming!
> Sing loud, O bird in the tree;
> O bird, sing loud in the sky,
> And honey-bees, blacken the clover beds—
> There is none of you glad as I.[1]

She did not put these sentiments on paper that spring. But they were in her. At no other time in her life could she know such rapture, such careless abandon to the beauties of springtime. And she was loved!

> For O but the world is fair, is fair—
> And O but the world is sweet!

her heart sang.

63

The home of Dr. D. F. Hall near San Gabriel Mission provided the setting for the wedding of Josephine Smith and Robert B. Carsley, both giving Los Angeles as their official place of residence. Also from Los Angeles came the Reverend T. O. Ellis, ordained minister of the Methodist Episcopal Church South, to perform the ceremony, on 21 April 1858. Witnesses were D. F. Hall of San Gabriel Mission and William Horn of El Monte. It is likely that Ina's family from San Bernardino and her sister and brother-in-law from Los Angeles were also present.[2]

Perhaps the rapture of her wedding day prompted these lines:

> The leaves laugh low in the wind,
>   Laugh low with the wind at play;
> And the odorous call of the flowers all
>   Entices my soul away![3]

Three days later the editor of the *Star* congratulated his leading literary contributor in words befitting the regard with which he held her,

Cupid, the sly archer, has been winging his shafts pretty freely of late, in this locality. Among his conquests, as will be seen elsewhere to-day, we find enrolled our young friend, and highly esteemed correspondent, Miss Josephine Smith, whose compositions, over the signature of "Ina," have frequently delighted our readers. Entering now on the serious duties of life, we may be permitted to wish her all felicity, and that her future may be as happy as her past has been bright and full of promise.[4]

Before going to Los Angeles, Ina and Bob Carsley may have visited her friends, Dr. White and his wife, and Ed and Jennie Kewen, at *El Molino Viejo.* They may even have spent their honeymoon in that small paradise. Perhaps, while here, Ina had time to read Ed's florid *Idealina,* verses published in San Francisco five years before under the pseudonym of Harry Quillem. As Ina held the slender volume, with its neat binding of half morocco and marbled paper sides, she was awed that a man who could draw a gun so quickly could also pen sentiments of the most romantic sort, fairly drenched in grandiose classical allusions.[5]

Young Mrs. Carsley and her husband returned to Los Angeles to settle in one of the little adobes on a treeless street, baking in the spring sun. They lived near Bob's shop, which was moved that year to roomy quarters on New High Street in the rear of Temple's Block.[6] They were not far from Agnes and William Peterson's adobe on Fort Street (Broadway of today); Ina probably found her sister's home a haven of advice on matters domestic. It was a placid place, for William was easy-going, mature, and sure of himself in his home and his community. But Ina would never have changed places with her sister. Her Bob was charming and witty. There could be no denying, however, that he was unpredictable—the artistic temperament, her family said. But then, she was temperamental, too. That was part of their attraction for each other. They were both, moreover, somewhat spoiled by flattery. In the feeble limelight of the pueblo, praise of them had been extravagant and premature.

Robert was proud of his wife, proud of his own success in capturing the prettiest and cleverest girl in town. But with the appearance of her next verse in print, there may have been a prick of jealousy. Ever since Ina had read Ed Kewen's *Idealina*, she had thought about the dual nature of the man. On 4 May she wrote some lines "To 'Harry Quillem,'" in which she urged him to leave his sword and take up his harp once more. The poem was answered ten days later by "Harry Quillem" who said that the harp was no longer his, but should be passed to Ina. Both lyrics were published in the *Star* in May.[7] This poetic correspondence was purely objective and open, a question and an answer by practitioners of the same art. But the exchange of rhymed epistles left out Bob. Did he express his disapproval? Ina's verse appeared less frequently in the *Star*, and it reverted to her earlier style and subject matter, some of it mournful in tone, "Ida Lee," a song, in July, "One More Loved One Had Departed" in August, and "Little Fred" in October.[8] The next year only one of her compositions appeared in the *Star*, "How I Came to Be a Poet," written early in May.

This poem she originally sent to the *California Home Journal* in San Francisco. "How I Came to Be a Poet" was copied by the *Star* in June. It was a long, flowery avowal that love, and love alone, could have made her a poet. A chaste female poet could place the blame on Cupid's darts, which, she said,

> Transfixed my poor unguarded heart,
> When startled, as the heart and brain
> Thrilled to the intoxicating flame
> (Which seemed half rapture and half pain!)

So she wrote in May—an ecstatic paean to love, one year after her marriage.[9]

This was the last of her poems to appear in the Los Angeles paper for more than two years. She had not ceased to write; she had found a preferred outlet for her verse. She began to send contributions to the

65

California Home Journal, a family Sunday paper which was edited from 1858 to 1861 by Joseph C. Duncan of San Francisco.[10] The editor, himself a poet and a man with a classical education, prefaced each poem from her with such a genuinely appreciative comment that she continued to contribute. Duncan may have believed that he "discovered" Ina. He gave her front-page space, sent her verses to the Atlantic Coast papers on exchange, and liked to say that she had won national recognition before she was twenty. In later years Ina was to know Duncan and his daughter Isadora, the dancer. At this time the verse she was sending the *Home Journal* was all sentimental. Some of her writing suggested the influence of Longfellow or Poe, though the editor, remarking on the similarity, hastened to assure the reader that Ina had been moved "without any effort at vulgar imitation, to emulate the strain." Among the contributions she sent were "Doubting," "Bring Music," "Stanzas" (a lover lost at sea), "A Moonlight Search for the Fairies," "Leonore," "The Sleeping Maid," "To May," "Embroidery," and "In the Night; To My Mother." This last contribution was written for her mother's fiftieth birthday, 11 July 1861. It is one of her earliest autobiographical poems, with a hint of the trouble at Nauvoo, and references to her mother's hardships, to her "father—loved—yet never known," to the cemetery where he and her sister were buried. In the poem there is even a suggestion of her own discontent at this time, 1861, for "she would like to forgive all, forget all, and be a child again."[11]

Carsley, the Ironmonger

While Ina was creating these poetic fancies, her husband was making changes in his business on New High Street. In May 1859, the month she wrote "How I Came to Be a Poet," Robert Carsley began litigation to dissolve his partnership with Daniel Lindsay. The suit was successful, and Robert became the sole owner of the Salamander Iron Works.[12] He was apparently doing well enough to be given some important commissions, for during the summer of 1860 he built, in his own shop, an iron casing for the jail in San Bernardino. This was made of sheets of metal one-fourth-inch thick fastened to flat bars by screws. The *Star's* praises were glowing, "It is the most secure prison possible, as no attempt can be made to break jail without alarming everybody in the neighborhood. . . . The establishment weighs over six tons and is the heaviest piece of

---

Ina Coolbrith (Josephine Smith Carsley) about the Time of Her Marriage to Robert B. Carsley, Los Angeles, April 1858. Courtesy of Mrs. Ina Cook Graham, Berkeley, California.

iron work yet completed here. . . . It will cost about $2,000. The work has been executed in a manner highly creditable to Mr. Carsley." The plates, bars, and screws were hauled to San Bernardino and set in place in July.[13]

That the most orderly small town to spring up in Southern California should have come to this requirement seems a distortion of justice. The peace-loving founders of San Bernardino had needed no jail, had even stated that they could conduct their differences without courts of law. But the Saints had left, family by family, returning to Salt Lake City whither they were summoned by Brigham Young to defend Zion in a possible Utah War. San Bernardino came into the hands of church apostates and outsiders, and it was not long before conditions, civil and criminal, were no better in San Bernardino than elsewhere in Southern California.

Though Robert, builder of jails, wrought less delicately than his wife, and though the clang of iron on iron was in her ears all day, Ina did some writing. Yet other events of 1860 took her time and attention. In January her sister's son Henry was born.[14] In February, one of her half-brothers, William, was seriously injured in a hunting accident.[15] And some time that spring Ina's parents moved back to Los Angeles after their stay in San Bernardino, for in April 1860 William Pickett "of this city" was elected to the Los Angeles city school board, and acted as its secretary.[16] Ina's occupation with domestic duties in her own home, and with some assistance to her mother and sister, still left her some time for verse writing.

Little by little the character of the old pueblo was changing. When the census was taken in 1860, a total of 4,385 souls was recorded.[17] By this time there were two public schools; and, when funds for teachers' salaries gave out, public indignation was great.[18] The plaza was fenced. Trees were planted, and were irrigated by water "raised from the zanja." No one protested the waste of the precious element.[19] Street lights were installed the latter part of the year, oil lamps on posts.[20] Several of the city's institutions had their start just before the sixties: orphanages, lodges, a college, even a free reading room.

It was in 1860 that Dr. White deeded his property, *El Molino Viejo*, to his daughter and her husband, Fannie and Ed Kewen, an important step in the preservation of one of California's most storied landmarks. It was this year too that one of Kewen's most notorious scrapes occurred. One April day in court he and an opposing attorney, one Sims, punctuated their arguments with more than usual force. Sims in a fit of temper threw a water glass at Kewen. Ed immediately answered with his inkstand, and Sims followed promptly with the water pitcher. This had to

68

stop somewhere, so Kewen drew his gun and fired. More than the dignity of the court was hurt, however; the bullet lodged in the leg of a Mexican bystander. Los Angeles was changing in some ways, but it was still the toughest town in the West.[21]

A Jealous Rage

During 1861 none of Ina's poems graced the *Star* until the end of the year, when a poignant "In Memoriam" appeared, like a rush of tears held back too long. For this was the year of events Ina tried to forget, events "too sensational to print," she later said. Of her deepest grief nothing definite is known, so securely did she lock the door on this episode of her life.

Just as this was the year of decision in the conflict in Ina Carsley's heart, so it was in the nation at large. The firing on Fort Sumter across the continent on 12 April had its echoes in Los Angeles. Newspapers took sides. The *News* supported Lincoln, the *Star* Jeff Davis. Secessionist sympathizers were numerous in Southern California. Every patriotic demonstration brought trouble in San Bernardino, San Gabriel, and El Monte, as well as in Los Angeles itself. Guard units came into action. Camp Drum was established by the United States Army with barracks and guardhouse in Wilmington and headquarters in Los Angeles, for the discipline of those who were too ardent in their support of the Southern cause. For the irrepressible Ed Kewen, Camp Drum was a stepping stone to Alcatraz the following year. Under directions from Major, later General, James H. Carleton, the camp was commanded by Captain John W. Davidson. In October Union soldiers were brought into Los Angeles, setting up camps in the pueblo, Camp Fitzgerald on Spring Street and Camp Latham on Main. Volunteering for service in the Los Angeles units were such men as Abel Stearns, J. J. Warner, and Ezra Drown. William Pickett joined too, and spent part of his time in the camp which was only a stone's throw from his own house.[22]

Pickett's house had become the temporary home of his stepdaughter, for Robert was absent part of that fall with a company of minstrel players. He returned 12 October from an engagement in San Francisco. He went at once to the Pickett residence to take his wife home. But he came in anger too deep to control. All the long, tiresome voyage from San Francisco he had brooded over imagined infidelities of his wife. Ina and her mother were alone in the house. In a fit of jealousy he reviled her, ordered her home, and threatened her life. Calling her a whore, accusing her of affairs in Holcomb Valley, he rushed about the house looking for whatever weapons he could find. He was weak with rage, and Ina and her mother took away and hid the kitchen knife and the

69

scissors that he found. Attempting to drag his wife away, he begged her to kill him or he would kill her. Mrs. Pickett tried to reason with him, urging him to leave because her husband would soon be home. She was afraid there would be bloodshed. Bob stormed at his mother-in-law with vile epithets, but did leave with a promise not to return that day.[23]

He did not stay away long. He came back in the afternoon, waving a six-shooter, and tried to gain entry into the house. Mrs. Pickett had locked the doors and windows, but Bob found one window unlocked and was climbing in when the ubiquitous Ed Kewen drove by. Summoned frantically by the women, Kewen stopped and tried some of his famous oratory on the hysterical man. Carsley replied with a storm of abuse that shocked Kewen into a sharp rebuke. He told Bob that only a rowdy would annoy two helpless females in such a fashion.

"Why," he said angrily, "this is behavior unbecoming a dog!" There was only one course open to an honorable man, said Lawyer Kewen, his stern look piercing Bob and subduing him temporarily. He must challenge the man who had dishonored his name. The idea of a duel startled Bob and he promised to go away. Ed Kewen rode off, confident that he had settled the argument. But Bob stayed on, railing at his wife the rest of the afternoon.

When the twins came in from hunting that evening, they heard their sister crying. Bob grabbed a rifle from one of the boys, but Mrs. Pickett took it from her distracted son-in-law and hid it as she had hidden the other weapons. She and Willie hurried over to the guard camp for help. The very sight of Captain Davidson threw Carsley into a new frenzy, and accusing his wife of intimacy with the Captain and another officer, he dragged Ina out of the house and toward the street, a pistol in one hand.

Just then, to the relief and fear of everyone, the twins' father came in. Taking in the scene, his immediate reaction was to dash to the camp for a gun. There was an exchange of shots in the growing dark. Carsley aimed at his wife as she ran toward her mother near one of the guard tents. His shot went wild and tore through the tent, narrowly missing both women. But Pickett's aim was calm and sure. He wounded Bob in the hand.[24] This action put an end to the young man's insane torment of his wife, but it was the final humiliation. Pickett probably saved his stepdaughter's life, but both Ina and her mother had prayed that reason and not bloodshed would bring Bob out of his madness.

The Decree of Divorce

In the days that followed Bob Carsley's wild accusations, and the wounding of his hand that had to be amputated, Ina remained with her parents. What her husband might yet do filled her with physical terror. What he had already done hurt her spirit beyond recovery. Ina and her parents talked the matter over with Lawyer Kewen who had been a witness to Bob's behavior. Ed Kewen advised an immediate divorce. On 10 December, Ina wrote "Josephine D. Carsley" on papers to be served on her husband. Two days later, A. J. King, Deputy Sheriff, looking for the husband, found him sitting on the steps of the Pickett residence, shouting derisively at the women indoors. When King handed him the subpoena, he turned on the sheriff in rage. King arrested him and took him to jail.

Ina's brooding on her own troubles was interrupted by two events of deep concern to her, a birth and a death. Her sister Agnes's first daughter, Mary Charlotte, was born on 28 November.[25] On 17 December Ed Kewen's father-in-law, Dr. Thomas J. White, died suddenly. As citizen and social leader he would be missed by the American community. And as a rare personality in the raw West he would be missed by Ina Carsley to whom he was a gentle, white-haired old man nearing sixty. She recalled her walks and talks with him in the garden at *El Molino Viejo* as they watched the stars come out in the darkening sky above them.

When she heard the news that day, Ina forgot her own troubles enough to sit down and write a memorial poem for him. She too knew loss, not only loss of lover but loss of love, in circumstances of overwhelming shame. She sensed in the Kewen family's bereavement an ennobling quality. Ina immersed herself in their grief and, in her own highly emotional state, wrote nearly a hundred lines of blank verse,

> Oh, Earth, Earth, Earth, how sad thy destiny!
> One joy—a thousand sorrows! One bright day
>   Of spotless sunshine, and a month of clouds.

Her own suffering crept in there. Then she wrote on, remembering Dr. White,

>   All things
> Serve to recall his memory. The walks
> He loved. The trees he planted. Flowers and books
> And songs, in which he most delighted. All
> Things have a language, and converse of him
> Continually.

Ending with a flourish of angelic harps she signed her tribute with three asterisks and sent it to the *Star.* "In Memoriam" appeared in the next issue of the paper beside a long obituary item. Editorial comment was a compliment for her poem as the best composition from her "gifted pen," but did not mention her name. The next week the *Star* revealed the author with extravagant praise as "a young lady whose contributions to the literature of California have already obtained an almost world-wide reputation, 'INA.' "[26] Ina's brief reentry into creative writing was a beneficial release of tension for her and gave her heart to go through her next ordeal, the public accusation of her husband. And the *Star's* praise salved her injured ego.

Robert Carsley contested his wife's suit for divorce and petitioned for postponement until his lawyer could come from San Francisco. In the meantime, he talked to his friends and finally came to Kewen, hopeless and apologetic. Kewen's insistence on a duel had tormented Bob and he did go looking for the man who had started rumors against Ina. His search was fruitless; no one had heard anything of the sort. There were no grounds whatsoever for his loud and unprintable accusations of his wife and her family. Talking to Kewen, his bluster gone, the stump of his wrist hurting, he admitted that the only thing left for his wife to do now was to divorce him to maintain her own honor.

The divorce proceedings took place on 26 December 1861, in the Los Angeles District Court, Judge Benjamin B. Hayes presiding. E. J. C. Kewen appeared as counsel for the complainant, and the defendant in person for himself. Statements by Ina's witnesses were recorded by Ezra Drown. Those testifying for her were her mother, her stepbrothers, and A. J. King. Her counsel also reported what he had seen when he stopped by the house, putting on record some of the four-letter words he had heard Carsley use. Kewen also said that Carsley had come to him later, admitting that he could find no evidence against his wife, and that he would like to see her in person and ask her forgiveness, but that she should now go through with the divorce in order to clear herself. On 30 December Judge Hayes officially decreed "That the bonds of matrimony heretofore existing between Josephine D. Carsley and Robert B. Carsley, be and the same are hereby dissolved, annulled, rendered void and of no effect, and the said Josephine D. Carsley, by virtue hereof, is forever free from all marital relationship with the said Robert B. Carsley, as if such relationship had never existed between said parties; and is hereby entitled at her will and pleasure to marry again as though the said Robert B. Carsley was *dead*."[27]

Ina's Grief

"As though Robert B. Carsley was *dead!*" The phraseology shocked Ina. Her gloom was matched by the dark winter days, the little adobe house dim in the lamplight. The last day of the year a heavy rain began, beating hard against the mud walls, pouring noisily into the rain barrel off the brea roof. The storm continued for two weeks, turning the rivers into dangerous torrents and flooding all the area. Ed Kewen, crossing the San Gabriel River on horseback, nearly drowned. There was some loss of property and livestock, but not as much as in the previous winter which had been a lesson in survival.[28] During these dismal days Ina took stock of her situation. The publicity given the nightmare she had just experienced had added to her anguish. She must leave this place if possible. She must forget Bob, his love and his insults, must shut out the haunting picture of Bob's shattered hand, the hand that had caressed her, and had fired a gun at her!

In addition to the ruin of her love, there was another, a deeper wound, from which she sought the healing that only time and a new environment could bring. Her marriage and divorce had been common knowledge through the press and the courts. But the birth and loss of her baby received scant if any notice in the papers, and the preservation of vital statistics was not yet an official concern of the little town. Ina, in her desire to forget her tragedy in Los Angeles, never discussed the events outside her own family, so the true story of her child died with her. Whether boy or girl, whether born before or after the divorce, the length of the child's brief life—all these make up one of the unsolved mysteries of this narrative. The members of her family who knew the details were not there to answer when the story was told after the poet's death.[29]

When her short poem, "The Mother's Grief," appeared in the *Californian* on 25 March 1865, in San Francisco, no one in the Bay city suspected that it might be a personal experience. If this poem were indeed autobiographical, then her baby boy lived long enough to play in the sun and to delight his mother with his endearing ways. When Ina pasted this poem in her scrapbook years later, she snipped away her name printed at the bottom, as though to forestall any association of ideas in the casual reader who might see "Ina" linked with the mother. In only one other published poem did she mention her child, "Rebuke," which appeared in the *Overland* for February 1869.[30] Years later she was in the habit of saying that her biography was not needed; it was all in her poems. Was her baby there too?

The imagery and restraint that characterize the poignant lines of "The Mother's Grief" create a sense of recent loss, yet the poem may have been composed any time before the spring of 1865. She told her grief in these simple words:

73

So fair the sun rose, yester-morn,
  The mountain cliffs adorning!
The golden tassels of the corn
  Danced in the breath of morning;
The cool, clear stream that runs before,
  Such happy words was saying;
And in the open cottage door
  My pretty babe was playing.
Aslant the sill a sunbeam lay:
  I laughed, in careless pleasure,
To see his little hand essay
  To grasp the shining treasure .

To-day no shafts of golden flame
  Across the sill are lying;
To-day I call my baby's name,
  And hear no lisped replying:
To-day—ah, baby mine, to-day—
  God holds thee in His keeping!
And yet I weep, as one pale ray
  Breaks in upon thy sleeping;
I weep to see its shining bands
  Reach, with a fond endeavor,
To where the little restless hands
  Are crossed in rest forever![31]

Part Two City of Mists and of Dreams 1862 to 1874

8
Literary
San Francisco
in the Sixties

Fair on your hills, my City,

❋ ❋ ❋ ❋ ❋

City of mists and of dreams!

Ina Coolbrith, from
"To San Francisco" (ca. 1922)

Decision to Go to San Francisco

"Only twenty, and my world turned to dust," brooded Ina Carsley as the new year, 1862, dawned.[1] A divorced woman! Her marriage had been a failure, and it had nearly cost her her life. Already she was beginning to feel the social ostracism often accorded the divorcée. When those she thought her friends crossed the street to avoid speaking to her, she was deeply hurt. She must have felt trapped in the little town, sensitive to criticism, reluctant to get out. She had an outgoing personality and could not endure the life of a recluse. She believed that she should go away, take another name, and try to be a writer. San Francisco seemed the obvious choice to her and to her family with whom she discussed her future. As they talked, Ina's mother and stepfather questioned the need for Ina to go alone. Would not a move to San Francisco offer advantages to the Pickett family as a whole? William would have agreed for the sake of his sons, who would be fifteen that year and were eager to go to work. San Francisco, now a city of sixty thousand, could offer opportunities for employment for all of them. William, however, would leave Los Angeles with mixed feelings. He had had a short but gratifying legal career, had made loyal friends, and had accepted civic and military responsibilities. But on the other hand Pickett was always a restless man; he never stayed long in one place. He was ready to move on again, to leave the Southland and try

77

his fortune once more in the brisk climate of San Francisco. There he could resume his practice of law or obtain work as a printer. The hardest wrench for all of them would be to leave the rest of their family, Agnes and William Peterson and the two babies, Henry, now a toddler, and Mary Charlotte, a few months old. Nevertheless the decision was made. They would embark as soon as they could on one of the regular coastal boats.

Ina Carsley, therefore, did not come to San Francisco alone in 1862.[2] She came as the grown daughter in her family of five persons. All during the voyage she had been trying to think of her future in the city, trying to forget the dark happenings of late 1861. As they approached the Golden Gate near the end of the journey, the boys endeavored to recall San Francisco as they had known it eight or nine years before. They remembered little but the dunes and the wind and the beach. Now, as the boat steamed past the treeless Presidio with its scattering of military buildings, turned at the Gate and entered the quiet waters of San Francisco Bay, they remembered the hills—the many hills of San Francisco. As the boat moved along, the boys saw that some of the hills were islands in the Bay. Their father pointed them out. The nearest and smallest was Alcatraz, where there was already a federal prison. Others were Angel Island and Goat Island (now Yerba Buena Island). The boat steamed slowly along, following the curving lines of the waterfront, to dock at one of the wharves at the eastern edge of the city. On their way they passed Telegraph Hill, with its signal house at the top, one of the steepest of the city's elevations, already scarred by blasting on the east side, but still grassy elsewhere, with a scattering of cottages reached by incredibly steep and winding wooden stairs. William pointed out the hill beyond Telegraph; Russian Hill he said it was. He had been told that some Russian sailors had been buried there long before. There was some kind of romance connected with it, he said, about a Russian officer and a Spanish girl at the Presidio—he did not recall the story.[3] As the boat moved into its place beside the wharf, Agnes and William could see that San Francisco was no longer the little "wooden city" they had remembered.

When the family came down the gangplank onto the Embarkadero, the adults were surprised at the changes made in a few years; and surprised, too, at the bustle and noise. Streets were paved, some with cobblestones. The place was taking on an urban look. San Francisco had learned its lessons from the fires of the fifties and had begun to build its business houses of brick and stone, several stories high. Streets and grades were an incessant problem. As the city spread over its numerous hills, more and more streets were cut, not following the con-

78

tours, but climbing directly up and over. As streets were constructed, some existing houses were left high on embankments, easy victims of the next earthquake. Building was going on continuously: shops, hotels, roads, and dwellings. A building "boom" was on. It was said that the year after the Picketts came, in 1863 alone, twelve hundred new homes were built, the North Beach and Mission Street Railroad completed, the Cliff House road finished, the Oakland Long Wharf built, and the San Francisco waterfront transferred from private to state control.[4]

San Francisco was a city of many faces, many voices. It still attracted men (and by now more women) of every sort, as Horace Davis had said. As the metropolis of a state that had taken millions in gold from the earth, it soon became an important financial center and one of the locations for a United States mint. The city lured bankers, investors, speculators. As the gambling dens and parlors had flourished in the fifties with gold dust as money in some cases, now in the sixties banks and financial houses of many kinds were flourishing. A city where fortunes could be made or lost overnight attracted not only the rich and the would-be rich but also their hangers-on and enemies. It brought professional men, laborers, skilled and unskilled, merchants, hotel keepers, politicians; it brought actors, lecturers, musicians, painters, and writers. It brought journalists for its many newspapers, prose writers, and even poets.

It has been said that "London is a man's town," and "Paris is a woman's town." Charles Warren Stoddard, a young poet living in San Francisco when Ina Carsley came in 1862, would have said that "San Francisco is a poet's town." The city seemed articulate. This could have attracted Ina. Already there when she came to try her fortune were Francis Bret Harte, Charles Warren Stoddard, Edward Rowland Sill, Charles Henry Webb, and many others who expressed themselves in verse as well as prose. William Keith, the painter, was there too, with a studio in the Mercantile Library building. Soon to come—and as quickly to go—were Joaquin Miller (calling himself by his proper name of Cincinnatus Hiner Miller) and his wife Minnie Myrtle, Samuel Clemens, Adah Isaacs Menken, Ambrose Bierce, and others who found the literary climate invigorating.[5] San Francisco took music and drama, art and literature to its heart with an exuberance that was joyfully uninhibited. Its reception of Edwin Booth, Charles Kean, Adah Isaacs Menken, Lola Montez, and its own Lotta Crabtree, is well known. Its enthusiasm for Adelina Patti, Emma Nevada, and Camilla Urso was extravagant. The Great Music Festival with which it opened the decade of the seventies lasted five exciting days, unexcelled as a spectacle before or since in San Francisco, with the possible exception of the Panama-Pacific International Exposition in 1915. And this had been arranged as a benefit for a library, to give the Mercantile Library a push in the right direction.[6] It was a city that could keep fifteen vociferous newspapers flourishing, could publish a weekly literary magazine, and launch a mature and sophisticated literary monthly, unsurpassed by any Atlantic Coast publication. It was a city where an anonymously compiled anthology of innocent verse could start a conflict that raged like a forest fire from the Sierra to the sea. This city was a magnet to Ina Carsley, melancholy young divorcée, recently bereft of her only child, reticent, beautiful—and a poet, though a minor one, as she would always be the first to acknowledge.

Beginning a New Life

She came to her new environment under a new name, Ina Donna Coolbrith, retaining only the "Donna" of the names she was given at birth. Her mother's maiden name of "Coolbrith" suited her fancy. She would never use Carsley again. And Smith? What poet would allow herself to be Miss Smith? Besides, her mother's secret pledge to William Pickett, never to reveal her connections with the family of the Mormon prophet, was still honored by Ina and would be so honored all her life. She decided to continue using Ina as her *nom de plume* if any of her verses should find acceptance in the *Golden Era*. The pen-names in this ten-year-old literary weekly amused her: Yellow Bird, Dogberry, Squibob, Minnie Myrtle, Old Block, Bret, and Pip Pepperpod. The magazine was more like a newspaper in format, and she read it eagerly every week. Soon after she and the Picketts had arrived in San Francisco she caught sight of an item in the *Era* that was of intense interest to all the family. Colonel E. J. C. Kewen had come up to the city aboard the *Senator*, but not to make any social calls on old friends. He was accompanied by Union Army officers and was conveyed directly to Alcatraz on a charge of disloyalty.[7] William Pickett had been afraid that their Secessionist friend would get into this kind of trouble, but he was sure that the Colonel's persuasive tongue would get him out. And indeed Kewen was soon released to assume his duties as a State Legislator. Ina continued her perusal of the *Era* for its verse contributions, hoping that her work would one day be among them. She may not have been aware that many of those who wrote for it were beginners like herself, and that this periodical was a workshop for their apprenticeship.

The city held many other attractions for her. Here she was to enjoy her first theater, to see Shakespeare for the first time. She had an opportunity to see Charles Kean as Lear and Hamlet in the fall of 1864.[8]

Earlier that same autumn, Stephen Massett, as Jeems Pipes of Pipes-ville, an always popular entertainer, came to town. He gave a travelogue called "Drifting About," winning his audience by sitting down and conversing with them.[9] Another attraction was the Mercantile Library which Ina discovered one day. She saw shelves upon shelves filled with books. She did not know that there were so many books in all the world. She said later, years later, that no other library, no matter how large, ever seemed as big and important to her as this one.[10] As she browsed through its new-found riches, she would have stared in open-mouthed wonder to think that someday she would be the Librarian of the Mercantile Library of San Francisco.

But reading was a leisure time activity. She knew that she must find employment as her stepfather and half-brothers had done. William Pickett did not reestablish his law office, but went to work as a printer as soon as he reached the city. His son William was eager to learn the trade and began his apprenticeship. When the *Californian* began in 1864, both Williams were employed there, the father as foreman and his son as a compositor.[11] The paper was one of the best printed in early day San Francisco, and some credit for its good format may be due to both the Picketts. Don had found employment with a "wine and bitters shop," Mercado and Scully, but was soon to begin work as a book clerk for Hubert Howe Bancroft.[12] Ina herself was employed as a teacher of English in the primary grades, by Professor John Mibiele, principal of the French College at the corner of Mason and Jackson Streets, where she was occupied from ten to three every day. At home she performed the usual tasks of a woman, dishwashing, scrubbing, and helping her mother as much as possible with all the household duties for a family of five and two Spanish boys who boarded with them.[13]

Where the family lived when they first came to San Francisco we do not know. The first address for them in a city directory is given as 1302 Taylor Street, between Washington and Jackson Streets. Here they lived until 1873, and here Ina Coolbrith was to spend her happiest and most creative years. That was why Russian Hill as a residential area always had a strong appeal for her.[14]

Here, in odd moments between teaching and home duties, she continued to write. She sent nothing to the *Golden Era* or any other San Francisco paper until the new year. But as "Ina" she was already known to San Francisco readers, for the *Home Journal*, published for three years by Joseph Charles Duncan, father of Isadora Duncan, had printed her contributions and had praised them extravagantly. Unfortunately for Ina at this time, Duncan was no longer publishing the *Journal*. He was a versatile man who had made and lost fortunes in several businesses. He was an art connoisseur who had now opened an import house on Sacramento Street where he sold paintings, sculptures, rare porcelains, and other unique treasures to the wealthy men who were building and furnishing fine homes. He was a man of taste and erudition, and both his advice and art objects were in demand.[15]

Ina's only poem published in 1862 was one she sent to the *Los Angeles Star* where it was printed in November over the name *Ina*. This poem, entitled "Unrest," written in September, is the anguished cry of a soul, weary and haunted by the past, begging for sleep through a long and wakeful night. Lonely, and often depressed when she first came to San Francisco, Ina must have endured a period of sleepless nights filled with the worries that always loom fantastically in the darkness. Physically weary and longing for oblivion for a few hours each night, she fretted about the minutiae of her job, and about her position as a divorced woman, she questioned her ability as a writer now that she was here in the city of writers, and above all she missed her sister and needed her comfort. Beyond all these worries she was haunted by memories of last year, and the twin deaths she had mourned; of her love and her child. These unendurable nights found some release when she tried to put her emotions on paper:

> So many woes my Heart hath known,
> So true a child, am I of suffering,
> That, judging time to be, by time that's flown,
> I dare not dream what coming years may bring.
> Through all my life have pain and passion wove
> Their subtle net-work: by the grave of Love
> I've knelt, and shed no tear! My soul hath borne,
> Unmoved, the shafts of enmity and scorn
> From an unpitying world! . . .
>   Ah, my God!
> I'm weary, weary, would that I might sleep![16]

Always reserved, she was slow to make new friends and to find her own place in this new environment. One of her first friends was Mary Tingley, a woman about her own age, who also wanted to write. They met at Duncan's Bazaar on Sacramento Street. Joseph Duncan presented Ina as the girl whose poems he had published in the *Journal*. Mary had read the verses as they had appeared from week to week and had been so impressed by them that she thought her own attempts of no merit. She had lived in San Francisco since the early fifties. She was the daughter of a local judge and later became the wife of Senator James Henry Lawrence. Mary had written a story or two and had made a collection of local newspaper verse which she later turned over to Frank Harte, as she called Bret Harte. She knew him and Charles Stoddard well. Mary and Ina became friends there at Duncan's Bazaar; their friendship lasted for sixty-five years.[17]

Besides Miss Tingley, Ina knew few others at that time. When Cincinnatus Hiner Miller and his bride Minnie Myrtle came to San Francisco on their honeymoon in 1863, she did not meet them. She did not know Samuel Clemens at that time, except as a humorist in the press and on the lecture platform. Whether or not she saw Adah Isaacs Menken in her performance of *Mazeppa* that magnetized and scandalized the population that year is not known. But Ina followed the sketches and stories and poems in the *Golden Era*. She may have been puzzled, yet stirred, by the serious, unconventional verse of Adah Menken. Ina, who believed that a poem should be singable, but not singsong, continued to write in her own style, trying always to avoid the trite in expression. She finally sent some lyrics of her own to the *Era*, "June," and "December," which were published in those months in 1863, her first in that periodical.[18]

In the last issue of the year, next to the column reporting "the irresistible Menken's" success in "Black-Eyed Susan" at Maguire's Opera House and describing also the Christmas night performance of "Aurora Floyd" at the new Metropolitan Theatre, opened for the first time that night, was a long composition of twenty-one stanzas, by Ina, "Christmas Eve, 1863." Thomas Starr King's influence was apparent in this poem. She compared her own comfort by the fireside with the scenes taking place at that moment on the battlefields of the East. She wrote bitterly,

> Yet we sing of the splendor of battle,
> "The pomp and glory of war!"
> Oh, God! could those battle fields open,
> And *show* what their trophies *are*.[19]

While her sympathies were with the Union, her verse was never strongly partisan. She was appalled by war itself, by the shedding of brothers' blood. She was stirred by Starr King's eloquence, and had been attending his lectures and church services since coming to the city. At one of these, in November 1862, she heard of Bret Harte for the first time.[20] This was at a benefit for the Ladies' Patriotic Fund, when Thomas Starr King read "The Goddess," which he said was by his friend, Francis Bret Harte of this city. Starr King was the conscience of wartime San Francisco. He spent his frail body in the interest of the

Sanitary Fund to aid the wounded and imprisoned. When he died of diphtheria on 4 March 1864, at the youthful age of forty, the city mourned its loss. To all three poets, Ina, Charlie Stoddard, and Bret Harte, it was the loss of a personal friend. The next day the *Golden Era* printed Stoddard's "Dirge" and Harte's "Relieving Guard," in memory of King, and a week later, Ina's "Starr King."[21] These three were brought close to each other that month by their common loss, the three who would one day be so happily en rapport that they would be nick-named "The Golden Gate Trinity." The memory of Starr King was the bond now; Ina, as a listener, had been thrilled by the oratory and swayed by the ideas; Stoddard had been prodded out of the silly mask of "Pip Pepperpod" and told to use his real name; and Harte had been given the very criticism and praise that could come only from one of the best friends he ever had.

Contributions to *The Californian*

That same spring, 1864, a new literary weekly appeared in San Francisco, *The Californian*, published by Charles Henry Webb, alias "John Paul," alias "Inigo." Webb was editor as well as publisher, but was assisted by Bret Harte. From the first it was a sparkling paper in format and content, printing sketches by "Bret" and a witty column by "Inigo." Not long after the first issue appeared, Ina sent in some graceful but anonymous verses called "Cupid Kissed Me." Webb liked the poem, and so did Harte when he saw it. But Webb hesitated. He did not want to print it without knowing its authorship. Finally, however, he did use it, still unsigned, in one of the August issues.[22] Soon Webb learned, to his surprise and pleasure, that the anonymous poet was Miss Ina, the stepdaughter of his printing room foreman, William Pickett. Shortly after Webb's acquaintance with Ina, the two were walking together down Montgomery Street. A handsome young man with "side whiskers" was coming toward them. He was Francis Bret Harte. As Webb presented him to Miss Coolbrith, he said, "Frank, here's Ina. Be good to her!" Harte obeyed this injunction to the letter, and was ever her good friend and sympathetic editor.[23] She continued to send her verse to *The Californian*, and three more poems signed "Ina" appeared that year, "Mists," "A Lost Day," and one which Harte did not like. This was "Fragment from an Unfinished Poem." Harte argued that *The Californian*'s readers would say that if a poet knew how to write a poem

---

Charles Warren Stoddard. Courtesy of the Bancroft Library, University of California, Berkeley.

she should know how to finish it. As far as Ina was concerned, it was finished, though called a fragment; a single fleeting impression of some of the loveliness—and the tragedy—she had known as a girl in Los Angeles. It was a fragment out of her life. Had she rounded out her verses she felt she would have spoiled their spontaneity.[24]

Charles Warren Stoddard was another contributor to *The Californian*, now using his full name. That fall he attended classes at the College of California in Oakland, but found regular classwork so difficult and distasteful that he had what amounted to a nervous breakdown and went to Hawaii to visit his married sister Sara Makee and to recuperate.[25] Ina had come to know Stoddard, who was two years her junior, for she later said she had known Charlie always. And always the handsome boy was charming and unstable, but she loved him and excused him, not as a sweetheart might, but as an older sister might love a spoiled young brother.

In February and March, 1865, Ina made a trial of her prose style in what promised to be a regular feature in *The Californian*, her "Meg Merrilliana," informal essays signed "Meg Merrill."[26] The same periodical published lyrics of hers during those two months also, the first one in February, "In the Pouts." This was the first of her poems signed by her full name, Ina D. Coolbrith. In a March number her lyric "The Mother's Grief" appeared on the front page, also signed in full.[27] National events of this spring, however, crowded out the personal. The war had come to an end. Lincoln was assassinated. San Francisco, in the midst of celebrating the end of hostilities, mourned the death of the President, its papers black bordered, its authors writing memorials in verse and prose. Ina's poem to Lincoln, "The Blossom of the South," was not published in *The Californian*, but a memorial poem by Harte did appear. In June *The Californian* published her poem "Hereafter."[28]

The year 1865 had another significance for literary San Francisco and for Ina. This was the year of *Outcroppings*, an innocent little anthology of California verse, out in time for Christmas giving, a small quarto in gilt and purple, to sell for one dollar.[29] Published by Anton Roman and compiled anonymously by Bret Harte (who acknowledged use of Mary Tingley's clippings), the small volume caused a literary civil war in the state. Said Charles Henry Webb in *The Californian*, "The population of California is now divided into two classes; those who contributed to *Outcroppings* and those who did not. The latter have decidedly the advantage, as far as numbers are concerned. Merit, I think, is pretty evenly divided."[30] The miners and others in the foothills looked for some of their favorite authors and favorite verses, and not finding them, blasted the pretty little book as a fraud and a poor excuse for something representative of the California poets. They regarded Harte as a coward for neither putting his name on the title page as compiler nor including any of his own verse. The din of this literary war was deafening. Frank Harte was amused by the fuss created by his first publication and found it excellent for sales.[31]

The miners even resented the inclusion of women poets, not from masculine chauvinism only, but because they thought the volume lacking in the toughness that had gone into the real fiber of the state. Webb, in his review of the book, said gallantly, "If *Outcroppings* be anything like a fair expression of the poetic development of California, the manifest superiority which the female exhibits over the masculine poet is something worthy of notice. Two or three poems by Mrs. Lawson and one or two by Ina Coolbrith are not only remarkable for California but are worthy of an older civilization."[32] *Outcroppings* brought Ina Coolbrith her first important national recognition, for the *Nation*, in reviewing the book, chose "The Mother's Grief" as "veritable and fine" and said "Miss Coolbrith is one of the real poets among the many poetic masqueraders in the volume; Emilie Lawson is another."[33] Ina's four contributions to the volume, "Cupid Kissed Me," "The Mother's Grief," "A Lost Day," and "In the Pouts," had all appeared in *The Californian*. Many of the contributors to *Outcroppings* were Ina's friends, or soon became so: Emilie Lawson, Charles Henry Webb, Charles Stoddard, W. A. Kendall, James F. Bowman, Benjamin P. Avery, Joseph C. Duncan, and John Rollin Ridge ("Yellow Bird").

Ina always acknowledged her debt to Yellow Bird, the handsome Cherokee poet and journalist, for she said he was one of the first authors to encourage her to develop her talent.[34] Ridge is best known today for his potboiler, *The Life and Adventures of Joaquin Murieta*, a piece of fiction that later gave rise to a number of serious biographies of a legendary villain.[35] Yellow Bird's own life, as a member of the Cherokee family involved in the Ross-Ridge feud, was as melodramatic as Joaquin's story, and a good deal more interesting. Ridge himself came to California as a fugitive from justice, became a newspaperman, and a favorite among the pioneer poets. He was an early contributor to the *Golden Era*, and was, of course, represented in *Outcroppings*.

Among the vast majority not included in *Outcroppings* was May Wentworth (Mrs. Mary Doliver), author of children's stories. She had contributed verse now and then to the *Golden Era*, and was easily persuaded to take advantage of the current furious interest in California poets and to compile a bigger, if not better, anthology of her own. The material was readily collected, for there was no problem of selection; May Wentworth's idea was to include as many poets as possible. It was a thick volume, and the very weight, inclusiveness, and mediocrity of May Wentworth's *Poetry of the Pacific* put an end to the war over the poets. Bret Harte was not among the contributors, probably because he asked to be omitted, not because May Wentworth would have slighted anyone. Ina Coolbrith was represented by three contributions, "Love in Little," "Sunset," and "Fragment from an Unfinished Poem," which Harte had rejected for *Outcroppings*.[36]

In 1866 Charles Henry Webb returned to New York, and readers missed his jaunty "Inigoings" in *The Californian*. James F. Bowman became the new editor, an erudite journalist and lecturer in his mid-thirties. In his hand *The Californian* flared brightly, but went out suddenly a year later.[37] Ina was a favored contributor during those few months when the weekly printed her "Sunset," "A Poet's Grave on Lone Mountain," "The Sweetest Sound," "Love in Little," and "Heliotrope."[38] She was a favorite in the Bowman home as well, her beauty and her reserve the first attraction. Here, in the stimulating conversations led by her host, Jimmy Bowman, slight, dark, intense, and brilliant, whether in his cups or out, her reserve relaxed, her old spontaneity returned, her wit sparkled. With the friendly Bowmans Ina learned to find her place in the literary society of San Francisco and to charm her writing friends as she had charmed her neighbors in San Bernardino and Los Angeles ten years before. In 1867, after *The Californian* ceased publication, Ina sent lyrics to eastern periodicals. *Galaxy* published "At Peace," "Who Knoweth?" and "Wearisome"; and *Harper's Weekly*, "Today's Singing."

Toward the end of 1866, a war correspondent, age twenty-four, came to San Francisco to begin his literary career, a young man with surprisingly blue eyes and yellow curling hair, Ambrose Bierce, not yet wholly bitter, though his war reporting was a good start.[39] Bierce too found this raw Western city provocative to the creative impulses, and at the same time providing a market for the product created. There was a flourishing journalism; there were publishers and sellers of books, all pioneers and all lively. In 1867 Harte published two volumes of short stories and sketches.[40] Stoddard, back from the islands, brought out his first book that year, his *Poems*, beautifully printed and bound.[41] Its reception was far from kind, and the sensitive young man was so hurt that he resolved never to publish verse again.[42] He turned to prose, which from him was also a form of poetry. The next year saw the publication of Edward Rowland Sill's *The Hermitage, and Other Poems*, and a posthumous volume of Yellow Bird's *Poems*.[43]

San Francisco was a poetic city in those days, Charlie Stoddard said, musing about it a score of years later. And the poets found Ina Coolbrith's drawing room in the Pickett home on Taylor Street near Washington a pleasant mecca. They began to gather there after the publication of *Outcroppings* and while *The Californian* was flourishing. Stoddard thought back, dreamily, and wrote:

In the rosy retrospect, the writer of these lines sees a cosy interior, in a quiet house, on a hill, in San Francisco. There was always a kind of twilight in that place, and a faint odor of fresh violets, and an atmosphere of peace. It was a poet's corner in a city which was far more poetical then than it is now, and far more poetical than it will ever be again. There were little Parian busts on the mantel, delicate pictures upon the walls, rich volumes with autograph inscriptions everywhere; through the curtained windows one saw a marble Cupid wrestling with a marble swan in a shower of sparkling spray—but this was in the garden opposite. If the lawn was limited on the other side of the street, the exquisite atmosphere of the small salon—it was a salon in the best sense of the word—was most attractive. Here Bret Harte chatted with the hostess over the table of contents of the forthcoming *Overland Monthly;* here the genial "John Paul," Charles Henry Webb, discussed the prospects of his *Californian;* and here Joaquin Miller, fresh from the glorious fields of Oregon, his earnest eyes fixed upon London in dreaming of future fame, met the gracious lady who was the pearl of all her tribe.

Ina D. Coolbrith, although a native of Illinois, and of New England parentage, passed her childhood and early youth in Los Angeles, California, when that old Spanish settlement was worthy of the name. She might easily have been mistaken for a daughter of Spain; the dark eyes, the luxuriant dark hair, the pure olive skin flushed with the ripe glow of the pomegranates; even the rich contralto voice, the mellifluous tongue and the well-worn guitar were hers—everything, in fact, save only the stiletto and the cigarette. Those were halcyon days: she was singing her full-throated songs— perhaps too often touched with a gentle melancholy, but this also is Spanish and semi-tropical—and the world was listening to catch the far-off strain from California. She was a constant contributor to the *Overland Monthly,* and she frequently appeared in *The Californian,* the *Galaxy, Harper's,* and other leading periodicals. Her muse was speedily and cordially recognized in the best quarters, and, in later years when on a flying visit to the Atlantic sea-board, Whittier and many another master-singer welcomed her fraternally. . . . "

9
Golden Gate Trinity

There is a poetic divinity—
Number One of the "Overland Trinity"—
Who uses the muses
Pretty much as she chooses—
This dark-eyed, young Sapphic divinity.

Bret Harte

(Quoted by Ina Coolbrith in 1919)

The *Overland Monthly*

Charlie Stoddard's "rosy retrospect" is kaleidoscopic in its dreamy interlapping of chronologically separate events. After Charles Henry Webb had gone east, and James Bowman had sought other fields, and *The Californian* was a completed file, the prospects for a literary monthly were discussed in Ina's drawing room. Anton Roman, the bookseller who had published *Outcroppings,* was willing to undertake the monthly, if Harte would assume editorship and if he would widen the scope to include articles of general interest. Though a bookman himself, Roman felt that a purely literary magazine might write itself out or become ingrown, but he knew that the past and future of the state of California and the whole Pacific coastal region could provide unlimited subject matter for a monthly of nationwide appeal. To be sure Bret and Charlie and Ina's contributions must grace the pages of the new magazine, but Roman was practical enough to call on Noah Brooks and others to help balance the subject content.[1]

The year was 1868, an exhilarating one for Ina, though it was marred for her by her sister's troubles in Los Angeles. Her brother-in-law, William Peterson, then a state assemblyman from Los Angeles County, died suddenly on 11 May, at the age of forty-two years.[2] His widow, Agnes, was left with four small children, from eight to three years of age.[3] Then in June the second living child (the couple had lost two

91

babies) died. This was Mary Charlotte, whose birth had seemed to her Aunt Ina the only sunny spot in the dark months of late 1861. Ina wrote a memorial poem for her little niece, calling it "Heart of Our Hearts."[4]

In July the first issue of the *Overland Monthly* was out, a substantial magazine with the heft and appearance too reminiscent of the *Atlantic Monthly*, some thought. But the angry bear on the overland railway tracks belonged to the West. The journal was a sensation, east and west, though all contributions were unsigned. Bret and Charlie and Ina contributed lyrics, Ina's "Longing" appearing first, an uninhibited expression of the frustation of a young teacher who wanted time to write and time to live,

> O foolish wisdom sought in books!
>   O aimless fret of household tasks!
> O chains that bind the hand and mind—
>   A fuller life my spirit asks!

> ✿ ✿ ✿

> For Eden's life within me stirs,
>   And scorns the shackles that I wear;
> The man-life grand—pure soul, strong hand,
>   The limb of steel, the heart of air!

> And I could kiss with longing wild,
>   Earth's dear brown bosom, loved so much
> A grass-blade fanned across my hand
>   Would thrill me like a lover's touch.

This was universal, not Californian. Charlie and Bret contributed local pieces; Stoddard, "In the Sierra," and Harte, "San Francisco From the Sea."[5]

One afternoon, 6 July, after the first *Overland Monthly* had appeared, Ina was at work on a lyric for the next issue. The words came to her with a rush, singing themselves, still in the mood of "Longing,"

> It's O my heart, my heart,
>   To be out in the sun and sing—
> To sing and shout in the fields about
>   In the balm and the blossoming!

There were five more stanzas, lilting and fresh. "In Blossom Time" she

called it. The ink was scarcely dry when a messenger came to her door
with a note from Harte saying that the first form was ready for the
poem and asking her to send it back by the bearer. Excited, half afraid,
she folded the sheet and handed it to the boy with a smile, asking him
to be sure to give it directly to Mr. Harte himself. Closing the door, she
turned to the room, half singing the lines to herself,

> Sing loud, O bird in the tree;
>   O bird, sing loud in the sky,
> And honey-bees, blacken the clover-beds—
>   There are none of you glad as I.

Was it too spontaneous? Was it too personal? Perhaps she should have
put more time on it. Frank was fastidious. He had been known to spend
an evening on a paragraph of prose.[6] And if the scansion of a line were
short, he would notice it.[7] She was always glad to have his advice. But
shrugging off her uneasiness, she sat down, beginning to relax as the
tension of composition lessened. Harte's letter was still in her hand, and,
laughing to herself, she picked up a pencil and jotted down a bit of
doggerel on the back of the editor's note,

> O bliss of a patient heart
>   To sit on a stool "to hum"
> And wait in a desperate sort of way
>   For ideas that never come.
>
> Or to try for three long hours
>   With temper and pulse serene
> To alter a line in a "pome" to shine
>   In the Overland magazine.[8]

She expected an acknowledgment the next day. But none came.
There was no word the following day, or the next. If he did not like
a poem he said so and suggested alterations or a substitution. Was this
one so hopelessly bad that he dared not tell her? Her anxiety building
up, she finally wrote him a biting note that demanded an answer. She
was answered on 22 July by a very contrite editor, stung by her note
which he said he found among his papers like a little asp that had not
been there very long for it was still quite lively. He had been in Santa
Cruz for two weeks. Her poem was his most sensitive contribution.
There was nothing wrong with it. It was already in type and would
soon be in print.[9]

Ina must have felt as contrite as the editor, but incidents like this were to be repeated again and again throughout her life. She was to subject herself to unnecessary periods of self-torment brought on by waiting for an answer to a letter she had written. "What have I done to lose your friendship?" she would mourn. "Of what sins of omission or commission am I guilty?" And her correspondent, devoted as always, may have been out of town, or overwhelmed with business or personal matters, or simply careless of time, and would hasten to reassure her.[10] After the incident of the "little asp," however, Bret Harte was careful to acknowledge Ina's notes and to keep her fully informed of his attitude toward her contributions. He suggested the title of her next lyric, "Siesta," for the September issue, and she readily adopted the slight changes he proposed.[11]

By August they were on the best of terms, and Harte proposed her name as author of the annual poem to be read at the Admission Day program of the Corporate Society of Pioneers. This eighteenth Admission Day anniversary was also the Society's eighteenth annual program. Bret Harte had written the poem for the fourteenth celebration, and her old friend, Ed Kewen, had been the orator of the day at the fourth yearly affair. So, in keeping with a tradition of self-praise for the young city and the younger state, she wrote some lines on "The City by the Golden Gate," which she did not see fit, later on, to include in her first book. The poem was read by one Master Lucio M. Tewksbury. The Society paid her fifty dollars for the poem—five newly minted gold coins put one by one into her hands by Harte.[12]

Ina continued to write for the *Overland*. Each issue of the first volume contained one of her lyrics. In addition to those mentioned above there appeared "October" in the October issue, "December" in the December issue, and in November her well-known "When the Grass Shall Cover Me." The hint of self-pity in this short lyric was dignified by her honest statement of the common human need for understanding and for an enfolding tenderness, even if these two needs could never be met until she would be "holden close to Earth's warm bosom." There was more than pathos here; there was the sense of a real and tragic experience that her Los Angeles friends would understand. Those who knew her in San Francisco probably thought it pure invention, a sweet if solemn fancy.[13]

The "Golden Gate Trinity" (Harte - Stoddard - Coolbrith)

Of the seventeen lyrics in Volume One of the *Overland Monthly*, all but one were by the three friends, Ina and Charlie and their editor. There was some good-natured criticism of the exclusiveness of the small circle of poets who had access to the magazine. But the general public was unable to criticize, for the authorship of all contributions remained anonymous until the table of contents was published in December.[14] The welfare of the young periodical gave the three poets an *esprit de corps* that soon brought them a corporate nickname, the "Golden Gate Trinity."[15] They were said to have had the three keys to the *Overland* office and to have enjoyed a Bohemian camaraderie that seems out of character with at least two of the Trinity, the editor himself, a married man living in San Rafael with a wife and sons to whom he gave much of his time, and the young woman whose school commitments kept her busy.[16] While mentally stimulating, the relationship was not romantic. Charlie and Frank (as she called Harte in those days) were like brothers to her and the latter always "unfailingly kind and helpful" as editor and critic.[17] Ina Coolbrith's small "salon" was often the scene of fervid literary talk and nimble repartee. One of the pastimes of the Golden Gate Trinity was the extemporaneous making of limericks. Ina recalled two of these years later at a dinner in New York, remarking that it was strange that these things should stick in her memory and more important things slip away.[18] Bret Harte one day, she said, was in a mood of depression from some criticism or other, perhaps of "The Luck of Roaring Camp," and Ina cheered him with her spontaneous,

> There was a young writer named Francis
> Who concocted such lurid romances
>   That his publishers said,
>   "You will strike this firm dead
> If you don't put a curb on your fancies."

To this Frank made immediate and gallant reply,

> There is a poetic divinity—
> Number One of the "Overland Trinity"—
>   Who uses the Muses
>   Pretty much as she chooses—
> This dark-eyed, young Sapphic divinity.

During the merriment of one of these limerick contests, perhaps, Ina snipped a lock from Frank's brown hair which she kept with the small packet of his notes to her during the sixties.[19]

There was work as well as play, and sometimes hectic activity when Harte was close to a deadline. On these occasions, Ina recalled long after, all who were intimately involved with the fortunes of their magazine sometimes appeared at the printing shop to set type and perform other

last minute jobs.[20] This could not have happened often, however, for Roman was no amateur publisher. He published and carried a stock of books by local authors, and sold them in his own bookshop. He was the publisher of *Outcroppings*, of Stoddard's *Poems*, Hittell's *Resources of California*, May Wentworth's *Fairy Tales*, and a number of other volumes which he advertised in the *Overland*.[21] If the contributors were on hand in the printing office when the *Overland* was going through the press, it was probably more to watch than to aid. They left the work to skilled craftsmen. Ina, daughter and stepdaughter of printers, felt at home, but it is unlikely that her fingers were often occupied with typecase or stick. Usually Ina sent her poems to Harte by messenger.[22] But sometimes she walked down to the *Overland* office, at first on Montgomery Street, in Roman's bookstore, and later on Clay Street, where she became acquainted with other contributors. Here she met Mark Twain and Ambrose Bierce. In the Clay Street office, in 1869, Ina first saw Josephine Clifford, a woman two years her senior.[23]

Josephine Clifford, a slim, dark-eyed widow, was employed as Bret Harte's secretary. Daughter of a German countess and a Prussian army officer, she came to America as a girl. Like her mother she married an army officer, Lieutenant Clifford. Living in Washington, she met the generals and the presidents; Grant and Sherman, Sheridan and Meade. She knew President Lincoln and his successor. At the close of the Civil War she went to the Southwest territories where her husband served under General Carleton. There she knew Kit Carson and others prominent in the Indian wars. While on this assignment Lieutenant Clifford went insane and died shortly afterward.[24] His widow came to San Francisco where she hoped to make a living as a writer, if, as she said, she could stop crying long enough. Some of her prose sketches began to appear in the *Overland* in 1869. Her descriptions of life as an army wife in the Indian wars are vivid and authentic. Like Ina, Josephine Clifford was reticent about her brief, tragic marriage, and could neither speak nor write of it for years. "And Mr. Harte," she said, "did not urge it. He knew the sore spot in my heart and respected my wish to hide it."

The editor was at home in the "elegant surroundings" of the *Overland* office. It was here that Josephine Clifford, then the newest writer for the monthly, "became acquainted with the other writers, some of whom were younger in years" than herself. "Ina Coolbrith, the star always, beautiful in form and figure as she was brilliant in mind; Charles War-

---

Francis Bret Harte. Courtesy of the Bancroft Library, University of California, Berkeley.

ren Stoddard, a beardless youth, a poet born, loved by all other writers of that day. . . . " Mrs. Clifford, recalling those days, went on:

> From the day that Miss Coolbrith, the slender, graceful girl, whose face held an expression too serious for her years, was presented to me, the more mature woman, her dark eyes haunted me, for I could not understand the shadow in their depths. It was in the Clay Street office of the *Overland Monthly*, to which I still felt a stranger, as I felt to Bret Harte who introduced us; and I learned then of the friendship that had already bound the three together, Ina Coolbrith, Charles Warren Stoddard, and Bret Harte—the Golden Gate Trinity. . . .[25]

Ina and Jo, as she was later called, had much in common; each the secret of a troubled past she wanted to forget, each a literary friendship with Stoddard, Harte, Bierce, and Miller, then later Herman Scheffauer; finally each lost her possessions by separate fires from which were snatched two thin packets of Bret Harte letters, one to Miss Coolbrith, one to Mrs. Clifford.[26] Josephine Clifford was able to put her own experience on paper, to marry again, to participate effectively in the conservation movements dear to her, and to continue to write. Ina allowed her youthful tragedies to affect all her years. She brooded over the inadequacies of her personal life, and feared another marriage, or any involvement deep enough to give herself to another. So she expressed herself in carefully constructed and polished lyrics, more restrained as time went on, often melancholy, and too few in number. In 1869 she contributed eight lyrics to the *Overland Monthly*: "Under the Christmas Snow," "Rebuke," "My 'Cloth of Gold,'" "To-day," "Fulfillment," "The Coming," "I Cannot Count My Life a Loss," and "Ungathered."[27]

10
A Wreath
of
Laurel

For him I pluck the laurel crown!
It ripened in the western breeze,
Where Saucelito's hills look down
Upon the golden seas.

Ina Coolbrith, from
"With a Wreath of Laurel" (1870)

San Francisco's Mercantile Library

San Francisco began the new decade with enthusiasm.[1] When the census was taken in 1870, the population was found to be nearly one hundred fifty thousand.[2] The city had undergone building booms and depressions, and now was in the beginning of a new surge upward. This was the decade when many of the Nob Hill mansions were built, their size and style a reflection in wood and masonry of both the wealth and the taste of their owners. Transportation was improving, local and interurban, with horsecars, steam railways, and ferries.[3]

Suburbia was already attracting San Francisco businessmen, for real estate speculation as well as homes away from the fog and the noise of the city. Trans-Bay communities like San Rafael, across the Golden Gate and north on the Marin County shoreline of the Bay, among the laurels and wild lilacs at the foot of Mount Tamalpais, lured some. Bret and Anna Harte lived there in the sixties, next door to Amelia Ransome Neville, social chronicler of the period.[4] Others preferred Oakland, across the Bay to the east, a sprawling young city itself with comfortable homes in wide lawns shaded by great, twisted live oaks, where the residence area was gradually spreading north and east as far as the newly chartered University of California and beyond. There Edward Rowland Sill went to teach English in the high school, and later Edwin Markham became principal of an elementary school.[5]

99

At this time San Franciscans were beginning to develop country estates, southward, down the peninsula, or they went to San Jose or Santa Cruz for the weekend. But the city itself was the cultural center. In February 1870 the most elaborate community festival ever celebrated in San Francisco took place. While it was inspired by a popular violinist, Camilla Urso, the week-long event, beginning on Washington's Birthday, was actually a benefit affair for the Mercantile Library. Accustomed as we are today to the meager and reluctant appropriations for libraries, we read descriptions of this citywide affair, planned for library support, with something like awe. Imagine an auditorium to seat fifteen thousand, alive with bird song from hundreds of cages suspended in the rafters. Imagine a grand ball, lighted by fifteen hundred gas jets, each festooned with flowers. Imagine, indeed, five days of this, for library purposes! San Franciscans knew how to turn their customary enthusiasm for the arts, musical or literary, into pure pleasure for themselves.[6]

A Poet's Moods

Though her city greeted the new decade with a light heart, Ina Coolbrith did not. She would be twenty-nine that spring and she stopped to survey her position. She looked in only one direction, however, and that was the way she had come. In the midst of the New Year revels she was thinking, "Why should I celebrate? What do I owe the years? They have brought me nothing but dead hopes and mocked desires." Meditating she tried to shake off the bitter mood. Yes, there had been satisfactions, some peace of mind, but not happiness. There would always be her delight in little, transient things, a wild bird's trill, the wind in the grass, the texture of a poppy's petal. There was the painful joy of making a poem. And there were long hours of talk with her friends, informal, easy, and intellectually stimulating. But true contentment, pure happiness, these were not hers. Would they ever be hers? This New Year's Eve she was thinking back, remembering her "mocked desires," remembering the ways of the baby she had lost and of whom she could not speak to her friends. Miserable and hopeless, she was musing of

> the tender voice—
> Sweet as a throstle's after April rain—
> That may not sing again.[7]

She was able to shake off the mood only by putting it into rhyme and meter on paper,

100

What do I owe the years, that I should greet
    Their bitter, and not sweet,
With wine, and wit, and laughter? Rather thrust
    The wine-cup to the dust!
What have they brought to me, these many years?
    Silence and bitter tears.[8]

"The Years" she called the three candid stanzas. She took them to the *Overland* office after the holiday. Frank might use them in his February issue. Out in the street, in daylight, among people, her usual calm and cheerfulness returned. Her thoughts were once more occupied with the present or the immediate future. Could she have known what this decade was to hold for her, she would not have walked so blithely.

In the office Harte handed her the January issue of the magazine, pointing out her own contribution, "La Flor del Salvador," and showing her the review he had written, following her urging, of a small volume of verses by one Cincinnatus Hiner Miller of Oregon.[9] The subject matter was Californian; *Joaquin et al.*, the title poem about a legendary outlaw whose praises Miller sang extravagantly.[10] Ina read the review and smiled wryly at the editor's manner of conceding to her request of a few weeks before by urging the would-be poet to learn to control his galloping steeds. Miller had sent the book first to Stoddard, to whom he had written occasionally since the days of the *Golden Era,* asking him to see that the editorial powers would give it some notice in the *Overland.* Harte was scornful, but both Ina and Charlie put in a tender-hearted plea, and the editor relented but did not retreat from his position.[11]

The Trinity had heated discussions from time to time as new books came in for review. None was more controversial than Harriet Beecher Stowe's *Lady Byron Vindicated,* published that year.[12] Even the memory of it, half a century later, would put anger in Ina's voice and eyes, "I don't know of anything that was not my business that ever made me more indignant." Harte reviewed it at length in the April issue.[13] The review pleased Ina. She wished she could speak her mind as effectively. A poem, perhaps, but what good would it do? Yes, she would write one about Byron and put into it some of the tender feeling she had had for him from the time she used to dig out the shabby volume of his poems packed among the family belongings in the overland wagon and transported by his imagery, forget for a while the weariness and the dust. She would like to send an answer to England to prove that not all American writers agreed with Mrs. Stowe.

Her bitter New Year's lament found a place in the February *Over-*

land." Nearly every issue that year carried one of her contributions, several of them nostalgic for the Los Angeles days. One of them, "If Only," was a daydreaming fancy that might even suggest Robert Carsley, legally dead to her. Was it a desire to see, in dreams at least, Bob's face, to hear Bob's voice? If so, the bitterness was softened. But no reader who opened his July *Overland* to this unsigned lyric would have suspected that it came out of its author's own experience. During the spring her contributions, "Not Yet," "Dead," and "While Lilies Bud and Blow," were printed.¹⁵ Late in July Ina received a rejection note from the editor. She had written a lyric about the Golden Gate, entitled "Two Pictures," in two parts, "Morning," and "Evening." Bret Harte wrote her a brief note, saying that some friends of "the late lamented Pollock" might think that her poem was suggested by the lines,

> The day grows late
> And the fogs come in at the Golden Gate

in, as Harte wrote, "that sloppy 'Evening' of his which neither you nor I could suffer."¹⁶ Ina could see the resemblance herself, when she read over her own lines at the beginning of the second part,

> The day grows wan and cold;
> In through the Gate of Gold
> The restless vapors glide
> Like ghosts upon the tide.¹⁷

He asked her to bring in something else, and she later complied with "An Answer," four brief stanzas suggestive of Los Angeles, which were printed in the August number. The September issue contained "With a Wreath of Laurel," and the November, "A Hope."¹⁸

A Wreath for Byron's Grave

As it happened, Ina was not at home when the messenger brought Frank's note about "Two Pictures." That very day, 28 July, was an eventful one in her life, a day set aside to satisfy a personal whim of hers. Had she dreamed of the international consequences of her simple and spontaneous action, she would have dismissed the idea as absurd. C. H. Miller was in town, down from the Oregon woods to "see the poets," and later to journey to London. In the absence of Stoddard and the preoccupation of Harte with thoughts of a business change, Ina introduced the visitor to the local authors she knew. She took advantage of Miller's presence and his coming voyage to begin her answer to Harriet Beecher Stowe's insult to the memory of Byron.[19]

That day, therefore, she and Hiner Miller took the ferry to Sausalito to gather bay leaves for a wreath for Byron's tomb. The notion came to her as Miller talked of his plans to visit Byron's burial place before going on to London. He was to take the train for New York on 29 July, and he would carry the wreath in his luggage.[20] Ina knew a place where the gathering would be easy. The laurels on those steep, sun-drenched slopes lean far out toward the Bay, most of the foliage beyond reach on their contorted branches. But Ina and Miller found suitable leafy clusters for the making of a wreath. As they rode back to the city, tired but radiant from their outing, breathing in the heady fragrance of the branches in their arms, she was already fashioning in her mind the rhythms of a song to go with them. This would be her answer.

As she went about, helping her mother in the preparation of supper that evening, the lines were already forming in her thoughts. She would have them ready when the wreath was complete. The words sang themselves to her as she set the table, absent-minded, elated,

> I weave and strive to weave a tone,
>   A touch, that, somehow, when it lies
> Upon his sacred dust, alone,
>   Beneath the English skies,
>
> The sunshine of the arch it knew,
>   The calm that wrapped its native hill,
> The love that wreathed its glossy hue,
>   May breathe around it still!

The spicy aroma of the bay boughs scented the flat. By the time Miller arrived from his hotel with his valise the eleven stanzas were ready, as sweet as the day that had produced them. Ina had written them out in her strong, sloping hand, underscoring twice each word in the title, "With a Wreath of Laurel," and signed with a flourish to the C in her name.

Her fingers were deft with the laurel. As she twined the wreath, she brought up the subject that had bothered her during Miller's visit to the city. Discussing the Oregonian's coming literary pilgrimages, Ina asked:

> "And how do you expect to climb Parnassus and be crowned of the gods with such a name as Cincinnatus Hiner? Miller is bad enough, but—"

103

"It's my name," he responded, "what can I do?"

"Why not take that of Joaquin?" Ina suggested. "It will identify you with your first little song venture and be sure to attract attention."

"By Jove!" He was enthusiastic. "I'll do it!"[21]

Ina smiled as she looked up from the wreath. Her look took in the quiet, conventionally dressed man sitting across from her, as she recalled later, "in no way distinguished from sane people by the cut of his hair or clothes." She suggested that he might adopt a garb to go with the new name, boots, perhaps, and a wide-brimmed hat. He might let his hair grow long, in the fashion affected by the old Indian scouts. It was only an idea. She shrugged as she fastened the wreath inside the lining of Miller's valise. But she could see that the notion caught on and that he was already musing about the addition to his wardrobe somewhere along the line on his way East.[22]

Ina was sorry to see him go. And Miller, eager as he was to tackle the literary lions in their own dens, was reluctant to leave. He confessed that this month was the brightest spot in his life so far. When he had come early in the month, he went directly to Charlie Stoddard's lodgings. But Stoddard was leaving the next day for Tahiti and would not be there to show Miller the city and present him to its authors. He had brought Miller to see Ina Coolbrith in the Pickett home on Taylor Street. Hiner Miller was awed. "Divinely tall and most divinely fair," he whispered to Stoddard.[23]

Together the two poets, Ina and Miller, "did the city." Ina was twenty-nine, poised, beautiful, her light brown hair in ringlets above the clear forehead and the shining dark gray eyes. The Oregonian, more than three years her senior, was tall and good-looking, with thick blond hair and blue eyes, a bit diffident in this sophisticated *milieu*, not yet the "splendid *poseur*" he was to become. Together they made the rounds of the newspaper offices. Ina introduced Miller to Editor Benjamin Parke Avery of the *Bulletin*, and later took him round to the office of the *Alta* to meet John S. Hittell. They called on her friends and visited points of interest in the Bay Area. On 22 July they both went to Edouart and Cobb's photographic parlor on Kearny Street to have their portraits made to send to Charlie in his island paradise. Miller wrote

---

Joaquin Miller. Photograph by Taber of San Francisco. Courtesy of Mrs. Alice Bashford Wallace, Sidney, B.C., Canada.

a few sketches, wrote a long letter on foolscap paper to Stoddard, and dreamed away many hours, loath to leave the beautiful Bay.[24]

After his departure the first letter Hiner wrote was addressed to Ina Coolbrith. It was signed Joaquin Miller, as were all subsequent letters from him to her.[25] In one of those letters, perhaps, he told the story of what happened to the laurel wreath she wove and the poem she wrote to accompany it. It is a story that has been told since by others in England and the United States. In Ina Coolbrith's own words, many years later, this is what occurred:

> I wrote my "With a Wreath of Laurel" and made a wreath of laurel which I sent by Joaquin to the poet's grave in Hucknall Torkard Church. Joaquin faithfully deposited it there, but some enemies of Byron objected; his friends took it up and the dispute grew violent. The King of Greece took up the fight, added *another* wreath, and placed both under glass to preserve them—and attention being called to the ruinous condition of the church which was almost falling down, Byron's adherents caused it to be *restored,* and it is now in splendid condition. A fund is being raised to *keep it so.* All this from my little wreath.[26]

The poem itself appeared in the September issue of the *Overland Monthly,* unsigned of course, and with no mention of the story behind it.[27]

O winds, that ripple the long grass!
O winds, that kiss the jeweled sea!
Grow still and lingering as you pass
Above this laurel-tree.

Great Shasta knew you in the cloud
That turbans his white brow; the sweet,
Cool rivers; and the woods that bowed
Before your pinions fleet.

With meadow scents your breath is rife;
With redwood odors, and with pine:
Now pause, and thrill with twofold life
Each spicy leaf I twine.

The laurel grows upon the hill
That looks across the western sea.
O wind, within the boughs be still,
O sun, shine tenderly,

And bird, sing soft about your nest:
    I twine a wreath for other lands,
A grave! nor wife nor child has blest
    With touch of loving hands.

Where eyes are closed, divine and young,
    Dusked in a night no morn may break,
And hushed the poet's lips that sung,
    The songs none else may wake:

Unfelt the venomed arrow-thrust,
    Unheard the lips that hiss disgrace,
While the sad heart is dust, and dust
    The beautiful, sad face!

For him I pluck the laurel crown!
    It ripened in the western breeze,
Where Saucelito's hills look down
    Upon the golden seas;

And sunlight lingered in its leaves
    From dawn until the scarce dimmed sky
Changed to the light of stars; and waves
    Sang to it constantly.

I weave, and strive to weave a tone,
    A touch, that somehow, when it lies
Upon his sacred dust, alone,
    Beneath the English skies,

The sunshine of the arch it knew,
    The calm that wrapt its native hill,
The love that wreathed its glossy hue,
    May breathe around it still!

11
The
University
Poet

Change follows upon change
Swift as the hours.

Ina Coolbrith, from
"Memorial Poem" (1881)

Departure of Bret Harte for Boston

In January 1871 Charlie Stoddard, free from all routine, was alternately relaxing or starving on his South Sea isle, writing his *Idyls*.[1] At the same time Bret Harte was preparing to turn his back on California to accept an attractive offer with the *Atlantic Monthly* in Boston.[2] The Golden Gate Trinity was thus scattered, and its beloved creation the *Overland Monthly* had become the editorial concern of W. C. Bartlett, though it was still owned by John H. Carmany who had bought it from Anton Roman in 1869.[3]

On the last day of January Bret Harte paid his formal farewell call on Ina Coolbrith in her Taylor Street home. He and Anna and the boys were to take the overland train on Thursday next.[4] He talked of his own prospects in the East. He was elated—ten thousand dollars a year to write for the *Atlantic Monthly!*[5] Though only in its fifteenth year, this was already the country's leading literary journal. Christened by Oliver Wendell Holmes, it was launched under the editorship of James Russell Lowell, who remained with the periodical until 1861. That year James Thomas Fields became editor and held the position for a decade. Now William Dean Howells, a year younger than Harte himself, had just begun his first year as editor and had summoned, among other contributors, the West's most promising writer.[6]

109

Bret Harte believed that his coming association with the *Atlantic Monthly* would give him an *entrée* into the publishing world that would help Ina, too. He said he would show her verses to his friend and publisher, Osgood. James Osgood, Harte's own age, was one of the publishers of the *Atlantic*. What could be more promising? Osgood would be sure to give Harte an opinion on bringing out a volume of Ina's verse. She was as enthusiastic about the idea as Frank was. After all, his presence in Boston would make his errand a natural and easy one. She knew that his prestige would be its own recommendation for anything of hers he might offer. She had made a little collection of clips of her verse, about thirty of the poems she thought best. They had all appeared in the *Golden Era, The Californian,* and the *Overland Monthly*. She slipped them into an envelope which she handed him, saying, "Take good care of these and send them back to me."[7]

Bret Harte's departure left a vacant place in her daily living that no one else could fill. His advice had always been friendly, his knowledge of prosody sure, his poetic feeling strong. His approval bolstered her whenever she was unsure of a word or a line or the idea she was trying to express. Contrary to a notion some of her friends had, that both Stoddard and Harte brought their work to her for criticism and correction, the reverse was true. The first editor of the *Overland* was a competent literary critic. He was candid and he was kind. Ina was never associated with him editorially but only with his corps of contributors. She often found it necessary in the years to come to defend him against his detractors. While it was true, as she said, that when Harte left California he passed out of her life entirely, she once remarked, with some vehemence:

> I bear witness that he was one of the most genial, unselfish, kind, unaffected, and *non*-conceited of all the writers I have known.[8]

Although nothing came of Harte's farewell agreement with Ina to put her little envelope of lyrics into the hands of a Boston publisher, a reader can find no word of hers in print or in her letters about what some of her friends regarded as a broken promise.[9]

Ina's Many Friends

With Harte and Stoddard gone, with Ambrose Bierce and Joaquin in England, Ina Coolbrith still had many literary associates left in San

---

Josephine Clifford McCrackin. Courtesy of the Oakland Free Library.

Francisco. But the carefree camaraderie of the Trinity was over. Those had been her three happiest and most creative years. She too hoped to go East and on to Europe, but she was destined to spend most of her life in California, to be so intimately en rapport with its natural and cultural setting, that she alone of the Trinity would become her state's troubadour.

There were many friends. She need not have been lonely. Three associates of the sixties were still in the city, Mary Tingley, Josephine Clifford, and Alice Kingsbury, all of them writers. Alice Kingsbury also had a brief stage experience. All lived to old age, their friendship undiminished, their letters commiserating each other on the woes of waning years.[10] She first heard of Alice Kingsbury from Charlie Stoddard as he called on his way home from Maguire's Theatre one evening, where he had just seen *Fanchon*, with Alice Kingsbury in the lead role.

"Why!" exclaimed Charlie, "that little English actress *is* Fanchon." Alice Kingsbury varied her stage career by writing verse and stories for children. Later she married, became Mrs. W. W. Cooley, and reared a family of twelve.[11] "Jo" Clifford, Mrs. Jackson McCrackin, Ina's other literary friend, moved to the Santa Cruz Mountains where she and her husband built and planted a beautiful estate which they named Monte Paraiso. She and Ina kept in touch by letter. Mary Tingley married Senator Lawrence and lived in the city most of her life, active with club work.[12]

There were many others. Ina Coolbrith often visited the homes of William and Lydia Morrow and of James and Margaret Bowman. The actor and distinguished entomologist, Henry Edwards, and his wife Minnie, were close friends of hers too, as were William Keith the painter, and John Muir, the latter deeply worried that a woman as attractive as Ina Coolbrith should remain unmarried. She knew Benjamin P. Avery, who had been state printer in the early sixties, one time editor of the *Bulletin*, editor of the *Overland Monthly* in 1874, and later United States Ambassador to China where he was to die in Peking.[13] Both the Hittell brothers and their families were her friends: John Shertzer Hittell, editor of the *Alta*, popular public speaker, and author of *The Resources of California, A History of San Francisco*, and many other books on a wide variety of subjects; and his younger brother, Theodore, author-to-be of a standard reference book in all California libraries, his big, four-volume history of the state.[14] Gatherings at the home of Theodore Hittell and his wife were brilliant and stimulating. Years after, Mary Austin was to describe an evening there, dropping the names of those present to emphasize the distinction of the company:

112

John Muir, William Keith, Ina Coolbrith, Charles Warren Stoddard, and others.[15]

Lydia and William Morrow, younger than Ina Coolbrith, were staunch friends always. W. C. Morrow was the author of *The Ape, the Idiot, and Other People; Blood Money; Lentala of the South Seas,* and other works.[16] He has left a charming word portrait of Ina Coolbrith as he first saw her when, as a young journalist, he called at her home to request a poem for a small literary magazine he and some friends were planning. He waited for her in the drawing room, self-assured. When she came in, she presented such a superb picture that he said his courage vanished. He remembered only her appearance and her ready consent to give him some verses, not what she said. She wore a loose morning gown, open at the throat, of a rich Persian pattern that complemented her olive complexion. Her brown hair (he thought it was very black) was arranged with what he called a "careless grace." Her eyes, he said, were "bluish-grey . . . darkling mysteriously under finely pencilled black brows." She had "a queenliness of pose and carriage that had the pliancy of physical perfection in every contour; and a general maturity of look that far surpassed in impressiveness the ripening which years alone may bring. The young man felt before her a keen sense of youthful inadequacy" . . . but the "impressiveness of that picture remains with the man as one of the most dramatic pictures that a lifelong experience with the dramatic has stored in his memory."[17]

The Bowmans were among her first San Francisco acquaintances. Margaret Bowman was a beautiful and charming woman who loved to have a house full of people. Her husband, James, was a brilliant conversationalist, an art critic, an Anglo-Saxon scholar, a poet and a satirist. Friends flocked to his home for talk at pleasantly prolonged Sunday morning breakfasts, or for talk-filled evenings. He was a small man, frail in body, dark, intense. His gifts as a poet were frustrated by poor health and the daily demands of his work as a journalist. It was when James Bowman was editor of the short-lived *Californian* that he and his wife first came to know Ina Coolbrith, then a young woman of twenty-three. From 1864 and after she was a frequent guest in their home, listening to and engaging in the talk that sparkled about her. Miss Coolbrith's poetry and, indeed, her ideas about life and religion may show the influence of James Bowman. Or it may be that her own similar beliefs were reinforced by his. He despised bigotry. He was not bound by narrow creeds. She said of him,

> Careless of church or shrine,
> Blessing or ban;

His prayer the common good,
His faith the brotherhood
Of man with man.

At his death in 1882 she wrote one of the most poignant of her memorial poems, "Unbound," using trimeter and dimeter lines with masculine endings to produce a staccato expression of grief. In one of the eleven stanzas she wrote,

Eloquent eye and lip,
Peerless companionship,
    Passed from the earth.
Friend of the many years,
Well for thee fall my tears,
    Knowing thy worth.[18]

Another friend of this period was John Henry Carmany, successor to Anton Roman as owner and publisher of the *Overland Monthly*. He bought the periodical in 1869, at the close of the second volume in June of that year, and owned it through December 1875—to the end of the fifteenth volume. He was unable to keep Harte as editor after 1870, though he offered a high salary and many inducements. In the six and one-half years of his ownership Carmany had a succession of editors, beginning with W. C. Bartlett. Because of the turnover in the position of editor, Miss Coolbrith found that it was easier to deal directly with the publisher in sending her contributions to the magazine. Carmany kept all the manuscripts she sent him for publication, and it was through his extraordinary care in preserving them that these now exist in the Bancroft Library at the University of California in Berkeley. Miss Coolbrith's own manuscripts, first drafts of her poems, were lost in the San Francisco fire of 1906.[19]

Ina Coolbrith's Commencement Ode, University of California

Under William C. Bartlett the policies of the *Overland* were to change somewhat. The new editor wanted to broaden the scope of the journal's appeal. All contributions were now signed. It was no longer necessary for the reader to refer to the index for the author of a piece. Seven of Ina's lyrics appeared in the magazine in the year 1871; the first one to bear her signature was "An Emblem" in the February issue. Most of her contributions to that year's *Overland* expressed her growing pessimism: "Just for a Day," "An Emblem," "Sometime," "In Adversity," and especially the cold mustiness of "Oblivion," the best

114

of the five. Two were nostalgic and were happier, "Summons," lovely and full of love, and "From Year to Year," expressing a mood of hope."[20]

Her most ambitious piece of writing that year, however, did not appear in the *Overland*, although it should have been printed there in spite of its length. When she was asked to write the commencement ode for the University of California, she was aware that she would be the first woman anywhere to be so honored. She took the whole of her adopted state for her subject. She sang a paean of love for the young and still unspoiled land and sea and sky of California. It was indeed a young state, its twenty-first year of statehood not yet complete. Young—"tawny of limb"—she said. There were no acres of dun-colored roofs, no lines of "little boxes on the hillside," no creeping blight of smog, no "high-rises" shutting out the old vistas, no mad and tangled freeways, no practicing bombers to drown the song of meadowlarks. She could sing the three simplicities of beauty, peace, and freedom; all these, to her, were the meaning and the purpose of her adopted state. The commencement ode, read in Oakland when that city was like a park of live oaks, praised a sylvan paradise. And such it was in many ways in 1871.

She herself did not read the ode. Like Bret Harte she did not consider it seemly to read one's own verse in public. She would be present. She would rise, if asked to do so. But she found it more comfortable to ask a local orator or actor to read her "poems of occasion."

The commencement exercises of the University of California, now in its third year, took place at 10:30 in the morning, Wednesday, 19 July 1871, in the college Music Hall on the oak-shaded campus at Fourteenth and Franklin Streets in Oakland. Five young men, the Class of '71, were given their diplomas that day by the University's first president, the Reverend Henry Durant.[21] Orations were delivered by each of the graduates, but the chief address was given by Governor Henry H. Haight, who had signed the University Charter on 23 March 1868.[22] Coeducation was a new-fangled notion. So far, since the beginning of the College of California (the University's predecessor) in 1865, no young women had graduated, though, after October 1870, women were admitted as students.[23] And when the Reverend Horatio Stebbins, pastor of the Unitarian Church in San Francisco, rose to read Ina Coolbrith's ode, he acknowledged, in a humorous vein, that coeducation had now arrived. He said:

I beseech you to look with pity and compassion on me, as the last of the giant race soon to pass away. The University is now open to your sons and daughters alike, and soon the woman who writes the poem will herself read it, and then the wind from her

115

rustling garments, as she comes on the stage, will brush away the insignificant insects who now people it. But she who has written the verse I am about to read still clings to the old traditions and womanly instincts, and has conferred on a man the honor of reading it publicly to you. I read you a poem of sentiment, entitled, 'California.' "[24]

The poem was not short; it required ten minutes of reading. But it had a lively singing pace that was well suited to the best of the dramatic reading of the period. Sensuous, emotional, with now and then a reference to a familiar place, it held the interest of those in the small auditorium. Though Mount Tamalpais was visible from Fourteenth Street in Oakland, the Golden Gate was not. But five miles north, out on the new campus in Berkeley, where building was already underway, the westward view might have called forth her imagery in the closing lines of her ode:

Lo, I looked

And saw . . . saw the Gate
Burn in the sunset; the thin thread of mist
Creep white across the Saucelito hills;
Till the day darkened down the ocean rim,
The sunset purple slipped from Tamalpais,
And bay and sky were bright with sudden stars.[25]

Almost prophetically Ina Coolbrith had made of her words a picture that was to be spread before many a student in years to come, as he hurried home to supper after a late class or an afternoon of study, the Golden Gate unbridged, the long slope of Tamalpais beyond the darkening bay, and, in the foreground, the dark pines on the western edge of the Berkeley campus.

12
The Bohemian Club

The sparkling jest, the laughing lip,
The royal, genial fellowship—
Of these thy wealth, Bohemia.

Ina Coolbrith, from "Bohemia" (1893)

Bohemian Club Beginnings

When Ambrose Bierce read a copy of Ina's commencement ode, "California," he declared it was too long and added immediately that that was only an afterthought; while he was reading it, he did not think it too long. He was extravagant in his praise, remarking that, with Joaquin Miller and Sill away, no one west of the Rocky Mountains could have written a better ode; then, with a characteristic thrust at feminism, he said that if, for every ten thousand Susan B. Anthonys,[1] there could be one Ina Coolbrith, the world would be a better place.[2]

The poem was long, and it was seldom reprinted outside of Miss Coolbrith's own collections. The *San Francisco Examiner* made a full-page decorative feature of it one Sunday in 1895, and Paul Elder included it in his *California the Beautiful* in 1911. Seven years later the Book Club of California, with printer John Henry Nash, made the poem into a handsome folio.[3] In the ode, too, there was a seed of pageantry. This was realized by the girls of Dominican College in San Rafael in 1916, when they accompanied the singing words with music and dance in an oak-shaded glade, in the presence of the author. The pageant was repeated many years and many student generations later.[4]

All this is ahead of the story. In 1872 a new era of pageantry, unknown and unsuspected, was conceived. That year the Bohemian Club came into being, an event of great importance in the San Francisco

117

circle of arts and letters. In the years to follow, the Club's members would create and produce plays and pageants in their Bohemian Grove in Sonoma County. From its organization on 23 February 1872, to the present, its membership is a roster of the leading male authors, artists, musicians, and actors of the Bay Area.[5] An exclusive club it is, and could be accused of intellectual snobbery and male chauvinism by the ineligible. It is strictly masculine, its club rooms a true sanctuary not to be disturbed by the invasion of women, however clever or charming, except by invitation to special programs.

It began with the congenial group of creative writers and artists meeting in their homes or studios for a late sandwich and a glass of beer, and endless, lively conversation. They were often joined by newspapermen, finished with their jobs for the day, and the conversations were recharged and prolonged. The *Annals* of the Club relate how they often met for Sunday noontime breakfasts in the home of James and Margaret Bowman, sitting around the table for hours, talking, or listening to Charlie Stoddard at the piano. After they were gone, Mrs. Bowman would find her white tablecloth profusely, if unconsciously, decorated with sketches and scribblings of all kinds, so attractive that she hated to launder them. It is related that she decided to starch the linen heavily and supply her guests with indelible pencils. Her scheme was a failure. It only inhibited the artists at her table.[6]

It was not long before the men decided to organize a club, to increase their membership, find permanent headquarters and a name, write a constitution and collect dues. The association was to be open to professional journalists, artists, actors, essayists, poets, novelists, playwrights, and musicians. At first they agreed to deny membership to owners of newspapers or any others who were wealthy or in positions of authority, but soon removed this ban. After heated arguments they finally agreed on Bohemian Club for their name—though some contended the name was not respectable enough—and chose for their *insigne* a jaunty owl encircled by a motto that read, "Weaving spiders come not here."

They rented a large hall by the month and furnished it with castoff chairs and tables. Ina Coolbrith and Margaret Bowman set to work with enthusiasm to make the curtains for those modest first quarters of the Bohemian Club. The members were ready to hold their first entertainment or "High Jinks" on 13 April, a Saturday afternoon, and they invited as guests their wives or lady friends, among whom were Margaret and Ina. The High Jinks was usually literary in its inspiration: the William Shakespeare Jinks or a Tennyson night. While all the active members were men, the club gave honorary memberships to a

118

few women. Mrs. Margaret Bowman, their hostess at many a Sunday breakfast, was one of the first. Mrs. Sarah Lippincott, an author, Mrs. D. P. Bowers, an actress, and Miss Ina Coolbrith, a poet, were others. The Club's distinguished roll of honorary members later included a few presidents and even a king. This type of authority would not bother them. But they were still wary of local publishers and business men. While Benjamin Parke Avery, the editor of the *Overland Monthly* that year, was one of the organizers of the Club, the owner of the magazine, John Henry Carmany, who ran a wide variety of publishing enterprises, was not among the charter members. Although the old Golden Gate Trinity were all members, only Charlie Stoddard enjoyed full participation in this Bohemia. Bret Harte was away in Krefeld, Germany, and he never attended a Jinks, high or low. Ina Coolbrith was made an honorary member in May 1874.[7] But she was always aware that she did not enjoy all the privileges of the Club, and never more so than on a day many years later when she was persuaded by a woman friend to enter the Club uninvited—to the consternation of the men present and to her own chagrin.[8]

The Club's first president was Thomas ("Tommy") Newcomb, and one of its founders was handsome, portly Henry Edwards, an English actor. He was an amateur entomologist, and the guests in his home were fascinated by the insect collections that decorated his library. Ina was a guest of Harry and Minnie Edwards from time to time, as she was at home with William and Lydia Morrow, Jimmy and Margaret Bowman, and Judge John H. and Elizabeth Boalt. Indeed the Club's membership included many of her literary friends besides Morrow, Bowman, Stoddard, and Harte. There were Colonel John C. Cremony, Joaquin Miller, Daniel O'Connell, George Bromley, Mark Twain, Clay M. Greene, and Edward Robeson Taylor. And there were William Keith and Edwin Booth and Luther Burbank. In the years to come there would be other Bohemians who were dear to her, James Duval Phelan, Albert Bender, Herman Whitaker, Jack London, and most loved of all, George Sterling.[9] Ina Coolbrith was present at many a High Jinks, and wrote occasional poems for them. Throughout her life the Bohemian Club was to play an important role in her activities. The Club was an ever present help in time of trouble. Its members were loyal of heart and hand, as she emphasized in her poem, "Bohemia."

New Home Responsibilities

Ina Coolbrith followed her commencement ode with other verse. The first three issues of the *Overland Monthly* in 1872 contained lyrics of hers, all three slight and light-hearted; "At the Hill's Base"; a nostalgic piece named, strangely enough, "Le Chemin de l'Ecole"; and "The Brook." Her contribution to the May issue of the magazine, "An Ending," was an expression of utter weariness and discouragement that she later excluded from her published collections.[10] "I toil my task, I nothing ask," she complained. Perhaps a change in the household that spring was responsible for the desolate outlook. The change was brought about by Joaquin Miller, back from England, his literary career well launched.

Late in 1871 Miller had been notified by Oregon authorities that his half-breed daughter, thirteen or fourteen years of age, was in need of care. Miller came to San Francisco with the girl late in December, and shortly after New Year's Day, 1872, he talked over his predicament with Ina and Mrs. Pickett. They agreed to give the girl a home until he could provide a place of his own for her. So Miller's natural daughter, Calle Shasta, a dark, frightened teen-ager, from what her father had called "the wilds of Oregon" when he himself came to San Francisco two short years before, found herself in a home in the city. It is believed that she was not a stranger to the domestic ways of her father's people, for George and Lischen Miller, Joaquin's brother and sister-in-law in Eugene, Oregon, may have given her a home. Or her grandparents, Huling and Margaret Miller, may have helped provide for her as they did for her half-brothers, the children of Joaquin and Minnie Dyer Miller.[11]

Now, in the Pickett household, the girl was among strangers indeed. Her father, carefree, was off to the tropics or the East, according to whatever whim should prompt him. He sent money for the child's care, and Ina assumed the responsibility. She wanted to help him, and envious as she may have been of his freedom, she turned her attention to the girl, Callie, as she called her, and gave her not only shelter and food, but love. Calle Shasta Miller went to school while in San Francisco, where her strange beauty was conspicuous and she was thought to be Spanish. Callie adored her benefactor and lived with her until she was grown.[12]

Though at times weary and discouraged Ina Coolbrith published three more lyrics in the Overland that year: "Love Song," which was later set to music; "Loneliness," gently nostalgic; and "A Perfect Day," a poem as happy as its title.[13] She wrote it as though there was not a cloud in the sky. Then early in the year 1873 a cloud appeared, small at first, but increasing as spring advanced. Ina's older sister, Agnes Peterson in Los Angeles, had been sick and was not regaining her health. Ina and Mrs. Pickett were alarmed. Agnes was now alone with two children, the only survivors of her six. Her husband had died in May 1868, in the midst of an active life. He had just completed his term as Democratic Assemblyman from Los Angeles County and had come home from

Sacramento. His death at forty-two had been a sharp blow to his wife and four children. He was followed in July by his eldest daughter, Mary Charlotte. Then on Washington's Birthday, 1871, seven-year-old Willie died.[14] When the often-bereaved widow was taken ill in 1873 she had the comfort and care of her thirteen-year-old son, Henry Frank, and a daughter, Ina Lillian, not yet ten. Agnes and her boy and girl remained in the little adobe house on Broadway where she and William had lived since their marriage. Though now shadowed by grief, her life had held security and much happiness while her husband lived. Ina had often compared the tranquillity of her sister's marriage with the brevity and bitterness of her own. Ina's lyric, "Two," published that March in the *Overland* seemed to be inspired by such a comparison:

> To one all blessed knowledge was revealed,
>> And love made clear the way:
> One thirsted, asked, and still was answered nay.

> To one, a glad, brief day, that slumber sealed
>> And kept inviolate:
> To one, long years, that only knew to wait.[15]

Before this poem came out, the *Overland* had published "Christmas Eve, 1872" in January 1873, and "After the Winter Rain," in February. The latter ended blithely:

> Sing, heart!—for thee again
>> Joy comes with the morrow.[16]

For all her singing, however, joy did not come with the morrow. By summer Agnes's condition was much worse. She begged her mother to come to her if possible. When Mrs. Pickett reached Los Angeles, she found her daughter's condition very serious. She could not give her the day and night care required and keep a household of four going at the same time. She persuaded Agnes to come with her to San Francisco where she and Ina could relieve each other in the nursing. She therefore wrote Ina immediately, for she knew that the flat on Taylor Street would not be large enough for all of them. She urged Ina to have her brothers find a larger house. When she was assured that a place had been found on Folsom Street, she and the children made their preparations to leave Los Angeles.[17] Transportation in those days was by boat, and the voyage to San Francisco was always tiring and sometimes perilous. This journey was rough, as the boat headed into a coastal storm, and

121

the passengers stayed on deck all night. The children were frightened and clung to their grandmother, a small wiry woman whose faith was as strong as her enduring body. With her arms about them she prayed that they and the children's sick mother might all come through safely.[18]

The months that followed were heartbreaking for Ina and her mother who could see that Agnes would not recover. Yet there must have been many hours that Ina cherished. The sisters had been separated for ten years, and now they talked over the Los Angeles days, the good times and the tragic ones. It was good to be able to speak freely to one who was intimate to all her personal joys and sorrows. Ina published one poem in the *Overland* during the summer, her "Marah," an answer to those who fretted because her verse was becoming too melancholy to please them. They liked her joyful, carefree lyrics and urged her to write more in that vein. "Marah" is gently sarcastic but ends in bitterness:

> I cannot sit in the shadow
> Forever, and sing of the sun.[19]

She sent nothing else to the *Overland Monthly* until autumn. Exhausted by care and anxiety for her sitser, she wrote little at this time, but she used poems she had already composed for the September, October, and November contributions, "Sea Shell," "A Fancy," and "'One Touch of Nature.'" The December poem, "Withheld," was, from internal evidence, written during the autumn of 1873.[20] It is a cry of protest against the long, hard confinement of the last half of the year. She was probably as gentle and patient a nurse as her sister could have hoped for, but the long hours of sickroom duties, cooking and housekeeping for a greatly enlarged household (there were now nine persons at home) taxed Ina's spirit and her own health. The dejection expressed in this lyric is evidence of Ina's depleted inner resources.

With the beginning of the new year, Agnes was no better. 29 January 1874, brought her release from pain forever.[21] To Agnes Pickett, exhausted with overwork and anxiety, the death of her eldest daughter was a harsh blow. Her child was only thirty-seven! Yet how long ago was that year of her birth in Kirtland. This daughter, who had known mob violence in Missouri, massacre in Nauvoo, the long trek across the plains, and finally peace in a Mexican village was now taken from her.

Ina Coolbrith's Sister, Agnes Smith Peterson, in Los Angeles, March 1858. Courtesy of Mrs. Ina Cook Graham, Berkeley, California.

Agnes Pickett turned to comfort her stunned grandchildren. She would give them the love that overflowed her heart as she recalled all her daughter's days and ways.

Ina herself was ill from fatigue. She went about the work that had to be done, then accompanied her sister's body to Los Angeles for burial beside William and the four children. As often in the past, her thoughts took form poetically. The rhythms and rhymes came easily. "It must be sweet," thought Ina, "to be released from care." It may have been at this time that her superb sonnet "Beside the Dead" came into being. It applied to her sister as to no one else. If the words came to her then, she kept them to herself. They were an intimate expression of her own grief and her own weariness. Not until two years later did she permit their publication.

> It must be sweet, O thou, my dead, to lie
> With hands that folded are from every task;
> Sealed with the seal of the great mystery,
> The lips that nothing answer, nothing ask.
> The life-long struggle ended; ended quite
> The weariness of patience, and of pain
> And the eyes closed to open not again
> On desolate dawn or dreariness of night.
> It must be sweet to slumber and forget;
> To have the poor tired heart so still at last:
> Done with all yearning, done with all regret,
> Doubt, fear, hope, sorrow, all forever past:
> Past all the hours, or slow of wing or fleet—
> It must be sweet, it must be very sweet![22]

Honorary Membership in the Bohemian Club

With the dawn of 1874 Ina Coolbrith though sick and weary, knew that she had to face and analyze the doubts that were tormenting her. She must have daydreamed of what a trip abroad would have meant to her. And she knew that her expenses could have been met easily, for San Francisco publishers would have welcomed her letters from any of the literary shrines she chose to visit. If she had been alone, there would have been no doubt. Her half-brothers were still at home but would not remain long. They were twenty-six and would soon want to marry and have their own places.

The whereabouts of the twins' father, William Pickett, at this time, is one of the unsolved mysteries of this narrative. His name does not appear in San Francisco directories after 1870, when he lived with his wife and sons at 1302 Taylor Street.[23] William, Junior, was employed in 1874 as a compositor by the *New Age,* but it is doubtful that his father was still employed as a printer with any San Francisco publication.[24] Members of the family have said that he "seemed to have disappeared," or that he may have returned to Los Angeles, or, perhaps, have gone prospecting.[25] His sons, Don and William, Junior, were engaged in prospecting and mining in the Southwest and in northern Mexico for thirty years, but no evidence has been found that their father went with them on any of these expeditions.[26] The family in the 1870s still had a ledger for the Ina Mine, but it was blank, and was later used by Joaquin Miller for verse writing.[27] The Ina Mine in Plumas County was sold for taxes in 1904.[28]

In 1874, therefore, Ina's mother and her deceased sister's children were dependent on her alone. An occasional poem in the *Overland* would not support them. She received twenty dollars for each poem published by Carmany.[29] Regular employment was necessary. Her friends were disturbed, for they knew that, great as the physical and emotional strain of the last few months had been, her financial worries must have been proportionately serious. Many of her friends were members of the newly formed Bohemian Club, and they organized a "complimentary testimonial" for Ina Coolbrith, which took place at Platt's Hall on Thursday evening, 15 January 1874.[30] With Henry Edwards as master of ceremonies, the program of poetry reading and music was said by the *Alta* to be "a pecuniary and artistic success." The night was cold and rainy. Not many ventured out, but all seats had been sold in advance, and over six hundred dollars had been realized. Ina, with characteristic modesty, did not appear, but sent an appreciative letter which was read by Harry Edwards.[31]

The Bohemians' tribute to a fellow craftsman in need gave them a feeling of achievement in their first public affair. They reviewed Ina Coolbrith's accomplishments. They knew that she would have been one of them but for her sex. In May they elected her an honorary member of the Club.[32] She and Margaret Bowman were initiated the same evening at what the members called a *Ladies' Jinks.* She had gone with her friends the Bowmans and "Tommy" Newcomb, who was president at the time. George Bromley was the master of ceremonies and conducted the initiation. Miss Coolbrith, recalling the program years later, said that " 'Uncle George' had put on an inimitable performance." He told Margaret and Ina that they were elected as honorary members because they had made the Club's curtains. Ina's skill with a needle was sincerely appreciated by the all-male membership, but her skill with a rhyme made her truly one of them.[33]

Miss Coolbrith's verse during the spring and summer that year betrayed the turbulence in her soul. This was the theme of her religious lyrics, "How Looked the Earth?" and "Question and Answer," in the January and March issues of the *Overland*.[34] But the May issue carried a vivacious pagan piece, "Respite," that delighted the reviewers of the monthly—the "one small gem in a heap of lumber in the *Overland*," remarked the *Call*.[35] She pleased her readers when she "sang of the sun." But the cloud of doubt above her was dark and real. She wrote of "Hope" and proved to herself that there was no hope, only

> . . . lagging length of days
> That once were fleet! . . . [36]

Then, in July, her "Song of the Summer Wind" seemed to scatter the doubts that had plagued her.[37]

Her writing of this period is intensely subjective. She was writing letters to herself, to help her make up her own mind. The August issue of the *Overland* appeared with her "Prayer for Strength," in which she prayed that she would never seek personal gain at the expense of another.[38] "Another" could be her mother or Henry or little Ina. She had made her decision, though she alone knew that this plea was a decision. She would seek a position. She would give up all thoughts of a literary career in the East and abroad. She would devote the immediate future to providing for her aging mother and the two orphans left in her charge. As if in answer to her "Prayer for Strength," the opportunity came. The Oakland Library Association was looking for a librarian.[39] Her friends on both sides of the Bay urged that she should be appointed and they urged her at the same time to accept.

Part
Three
The
Librarian
1874
to 1899

13
Oakland in the Seventies

And light on her feet she was, when with a light heart for the moment she would dance some Spanish fandango.

Ina L. Cook, from
Wasp-News Letter (1928)

The Oakland Library Association

It is an irony of urban development that Oakland, California, born on the edge of Rancho San Antonio, and known in the 1870s as the Athens of the Pacific, should have sold its birthright for a country schoolhouse. This primitive structure and three wooden wharves extending into the mud flats of the Estuary were accepted by the town's Trustees on 12 May 1852, in exchange for the town's waterfront. The audacious trader, in cavalier disregard of the Peralta family,[1] heirs to the rancho, was Horace Carpentier, a New York lawyer. His ambition and the gullibility of a few villagers were to cost the city of Oakland fifty years of litigation and millions of dollars. Schools, libraries, or a university might have been built with what was spent in the courts on the notorious *Oakland v. Carpentier*, and *Oakland v. Oakland Waterfront Company* cases.[2]

Yet, in spite of this unusual financial drain on a growing city, Oakland became known for its schools, its library, even its university. Here, on 23 March 1868, the University of California received its charter, written by State Assemblyman John W. Dwinelle.[3] The young university, guided by its first president, the Reverend Henry Durant, had grown out of the College of California, which in turn had emerged from the College School, started in a rented room on Broadway, in 1853, by the same Durant.[4] During the seventies and the eighties Oakland was the

129

seat of Mills College and St. Mary's College, Mrs. Blake's Seminary, a military academy, and a public astronomical observatory, as well as a high school, several elementary schools, and a public library.

When the Rogers Free Library Act was approved on 18 March 1878, Oakland lost no time. On 1 June the Board of Trustees of the Oakland Free Library held their first meeting, and in November the library was opened to the public.[5] Oakland was the second city in the state to take advantage of the new act, following by only a few weeks the north coast city of Eureka. Before this legislation was drafted, two California cities had already created tax-supported public libraries: Marysville in the late 1850s and Los Angeles in the early 1870s. Oakland, however, was an early and eager participant in the free library movement, and Ina Coolbrith was the city's first librarian. She was prouder of that distinction, she was later to say, than of being the state's first woman writer.[6]

Back of the Oakland Free Library lay ten years of library history. On 5 March 1868, less than three weeks before the university was chartered, a group of Oakland citizens met in Shattuck and Hillegass Hall for the purpose of organizing a public library association. Dr. Samuel Merritt, physician, businessman, and civic leader was elected chairman; and Fred M. Campbell, city school superintendent, secretary. Dr. Merritt asked immediately for pledges for a building; and, before the meeting was over, his request had brought a response of some six thousand dollars, one thousand of which was pledged by one man, H. D. Bacon. A lot on the southeast corner of Twelfth and Washington streets, given by Edward Tompkins, was vacant and ready for a building.[7] The group met again in April 1868, when it adopted a constitution that gave it a name, the Oakland Library Association. Dues were set at six dollars a year plus a two dollar initiation fee; a life membership was fifty dollars. The list of charter members included many names important in East Bay history; Sessions, Glascock, DeFremery, Harmon, Shattuck, Armes, Pardee, Shafter, Hobart, Dwinelle, Durant, McChesney, Hardy, Campbell, Stratton, Kirkham, and Bacon, among others.[8]

When the Association met in May, they had a library building plan to scrutinize. This was a plan for a two-story structure, with two street-level stores fronting on Twelfth Street, and with library rooms above, entered by a broad stairway leading from the Washington Street vestibule. Reading rooms, a chess room, and a "Ladies' Parlor," with additional space for a committee room and for janitor's supplies, made up the second floor of the building. A note of pride crept into the secretary's *Minutes* when he wrote, "While the style of the architecture is not perhaps sufficiently pronounced or distinctive to be called Grecian, it may yet be denominated classic."[9]

130

Until the building was ready for occupancy, the library was housed in two different locations on Broadway: the Holmes Building at Eighth Street and later in rooms at Eleventh Street.[10] At this time, and even before the organization of the Library Association, there was a Reading Room Association with a room for newspapers and magazines at Eleventh and Washington. This was a popular place, open in the summer months from seven in the morning to ten at night, and opening an hour later on winter mornings. The reading rooms later came under library administration and were the beginning of the branch library system.[11]

During this first year the Library Association found that a paid employee with regular hours and duties was necessary. A man who could buy, process, lend, and shelve books was sought. C. H. Phelps, a poet, was hired in March 1869, and paid fifty dollars a month.[12] He served for two years and was followed by L. H. Fairchild whose special contribution was a catalog which he was requested to have "written up at an expense not to exceed $12.50."[13] His successor was Miss L. C. Willard who served until 4 September 1874. Four days later the directors met to select a new librarian. They had several applications to study. They voted, giving four votes to Miss Laura Merritt, and five to Miss Ina Coolbrith, the San Francisco poet. Her salary was to be eighty dollars a month.[14]

The affairs of the Association were, at this time, far from prosperous. Their building had cost them three thousand dollars. They found that books, salary, maintenance, and taxes added up to far more than the desultory income from members' dues. It had even been necessary to take more than one bank loan. The Association could see no way out of their dilemma. All at once someone had a daring idea. Could this have been one of Dr. Merritt's less spectacular imaginings? It was decided to ask the City Council for a site on the City Hall grounds, two blocks north, at the end of Washington Street. The building could then be moved, and the valuable lot at Twelfth Street sold to pay the debts! This was the business on hand the very day Ina Coolbrith was appointed, 8 September 1874.[15] City business was simpler in those days. The Association found a sympathetic Council. The mayor, at that time, was the Reverend Henry Durant, retired president of the University of California. He was, moreover, a member of the Library Association. The answer was Yes.[16]

Within the month the lot was sold for $12,500, the debt was paid, and the building was moved. That is, the top floor was moved.[17] The ground floor stores may have been sold with the lot. Whatever happened, the simple little building with its classic pretensions was reduced to one story when it was placed on a foundation just west of the tall, ornate City Hall. The latter stood at the head of Washington Street—the view from its front steps taking in the length of the street. Perhaps, someday, the larger building or the authority it represented might take its humble neighbor under its wing, at least financially. There was already talk of state legislation to encourage free libraries.

The little building was open to the members of the Association again on 29 September 1874, with two hundred dollars worth of new books ready to circulate, and with Miss Coolbrith on hand to greet the readers.[18] A tall woman, reserved, beautiful, her quiet smile belying the shining eyes and the curling brown hair piled high, she was, on this memorable 29 September, to experience the first day of a long career in librarianship.

Johnny Muir, Matchmaker

The time required for the removal and new placement of the small structure had been a blessing to Ina Coolbrith, for it gave her more than two weeks to find an Oakland home for her family and to move their possessions. She found consideration and helpfulness from the directors of the Association. There were four women on the board that year, one of them a writer, Jeanne (Mrs. Ezra) Carr. One of the directors was the city superintendent of schools, Fred Campbell; another, a school principal, J. B. McChesney; and still another, a bibliophile with a fine, large library of his own, W. W. Crane, Junior. They were reasonable people, elated to have her among them.[19]

Knowing that her hours would be long and her home responsibilities demanding, Miss Coolbrith preferred to live near the library. With her brothers' aid she found a cottage on the north side of Fifteenth Street, number 564, between Jefferson and Clay.[20] William and Don took charge of the moving, saw her and their mother, the two children and Calle Shasta established, and then returned to make their home in the city. They would soon be twenty-seven and both were employed there, William as a printing compositor, like his father, and Don as a book clerk for Bancroft.[21]

The path to work was a short one; a few steps to Clay, south one short block, and around the corner to the library. The building was open from nine in the morning to nine at night, six days a week. Miss Coolbrith had little time to become familiar with the looks of her new city. Beyond the City Hall, in the gore made by the meeting of San Pablo Avenue with Fourteenth Street at Broadway, was in a small park with trees and benches, its lawn crossed by a gravel path from Fourteenth to Fifteenth. This park or plaza was the town's center. A small bandstand, with a conical roof, stood in the center of the park; and on summer evenings there was music that attracted young people and their elders, whether out walking, or driving along Fourteenth in their carriages.[22] One block east on this same street was the old campus of the University of California. It covered about seven-and-a-half acres, or four blocks; Franklin to Harrison, Fourteenth to Twelfth, a fenced area of trees and lawn; but the school buildings were no longer used by college students, since they were now attending classes in Berkeley.[23]

On these grounds, some of the old live oaks that gave the city its name may have been standing in the seventies. Old timers then, who had seen the region before the settlers came to build and lay out streets, said it was a vast plain sloping gently from the hills to the Bay which curved around it and cut into it in a number of sloughs. The plain was fed by several streams, dotted with fine live oaks, and carpeted with wild oats, poppies, and lupine. "Muy bonita," thought Sergeant Luis Maria Peralta, when he first caught sight of the land granted to him by the King of Spain in 1820, a rancho with room enough for his cattle, and for his four sons and their cattle.[24] Eleven leagues long it was, from San Leandro Creek to the *cerrito* on the north. Room enough! A few years later came the Yankee Carpentier, and to him the area meant business, and was his for the grabbing. To him, Spanish land grants and their *diseños* were mere scraps of paper. Here was real estate, American style. He saw commercial value, not the grass, rippling under the wind. He valued the oak trees, however, and urged the builders on the lots he sold to spare them if possible.

Now, in the seventies, it was a city of homes and schools, its population a little above ten thousand.[25] San Franciscans liked the climate, and many of them moved across the Bay, built tall, roomy frame houses, planted gardens, fenced their large yards, and enjoyed commuting to the city by ferry. The handsomest of the homes at this time stood in a narrow swathe a few blocks either side of Fourteenth, running west from Lake Merritt to Adeline Street, where DeFremery Park began. One of the most pretentious of them all was the great Victorian mansion built by William Cameron for his bride, Alice, daughter of the pioneer Dr. John Marsh. It was for many years the home of Josiah Stanford, and it was the center of Oakland society. It stands today among the great weeping willows on the west bank of the lake. Situated diagonally across the street from the present central library, the mansion was for many years the city's historical museum.[26] Ina Coolbrith herself, in the eighties and nineties, occupied a two-story Victorian house a few blocks west on Webster Street between Fifteenth and Sixteenth.[27]

133

Like San Francisco in the sixties, Oakland in the seventies attracted poets and other writers. Edward Rowland Sill came to teach in Oakland High School in 1871 and remained three years. The autumn that Ina Coolbrith began her library duties, Sill accepted a chair in the English Department of the University of California.[28] The next decade was to bring Joaquin Miller to make a permanent home in the Oakland hills, to write, to plant trees, and build monuments.[29] Later came Edwin Markham, who served as principal of Tompkins School, and lived in an East Oakland cottage where he wrote his celebrated "Man With the Hoe."[30]

Another of Ina Coolbrith's writer friends, John Muir, lived briefly in Oakland while he was editing and preparing for publication the manuscript of what would be two heavy, illustrated volumes on the beauties of California. He called this period of his life his "strange Oakland epoch."[31] While he was living here he was courting Louise Strenzel of Martinez. He called on Miss Coolbrith and her mother frequently at this time. Ina's single state saddened him, but his one attempt at matchmaking brought a rebuff that put an end to all such endeavors. She "rhymed him," as she sometimes threatened to do anyone who vexed her. Her lines "To John Muir," all seventy-five of them, are among the most amusing and spirited of her very few attempts at nonsense verse; these are about one Mr. Brown, a schoolmaster, who seems to have been a pedant and a prig:

> Up from her catalogues she sprung,
> And this the song she wildly sung:
> O Johnny Muir! O Johnny Muir!
> How could you leave your mountains pure,
> Your meadow-breadths, and forests free,
> A wily matchmaker to be?
> And sail across the solemn Bay
> All on the sacred Sabbath day,
> My blood to chill, profane my ears
> With such most monstrous, mad ideas.
> Could you have gone clean off the haft
> Of reason—as you Scotch say, "daft"?
> Or were you moved by pitying fate
> A fancied grief to palliate
> And find me some appropriate
> As well as a congenial mate?

✿ ✿ ✿

Sail him across the placid Bay
And sun him in the smiles of MAY;
Or tow him up to Martin-ez,
There to abide with fair Louise;

   ❁   ❁   ❁

Or clasp him to your pitying breast,
And bear him to some glacial nest,
There tuck him in and let him rest.
But O of this I pray there be
No more, John, 'an thou lovest me! '

   ❁   ❁   ❁

Or if you smile, or if you frown
I DO NOT WANT YOUR MR. BROWN.[32]

At Home on Fifteenth Street

The bantering mood of these mocking measures is a token of a new relaxation for a brief period, a reaction, now that time had partially healed mind and body after the tension of the past year. At the close of this first year in Oakland, the household was smaller than in San Francisco, financial worries had lessened, and the children were old enough to help in many ways. Little Ina was eleven on 8 December 1874, a pretty child with black hair and dark eyes like her grandmother. She was alert, sensitive, and fond of poetry, writing verses herself once in a while, but hiding them from her aunt. Her brother Henry was almost fifteen; his birthday would be at the end of January. He was blond and blue-eyed, a handsome lad.[33] Callie was a little older than Henry. All three were assuming more and more responsibility. Callie helped Mrs. Pickett with household tasks, becoming indeed a maid of all work.[34] Ina Peterson was still in school, but she and Henry helped their aunt in the library from time to time. They were both fond of books too, and though they could receive no pay they found this kind of work a pleasure.

Shortly after Ina moved to Oakland, the Bohemian Club surprised her with another "testimonial" affair. This was the auction of an album or portfolio of a large number of paintings, drawings, and sketches which were raffled off individually, the proceeds from this sale going to her.[35] She had little time for verse writing this autumn, her one published composition being a lyric in the November *Overland Monthly*, "Unto the Day," a light, fragile thing with not a hint of melancholy in it.[36] It is a love poem. Was it autobiographical in any way? She was known to have had many suitors, and it was equally well known that she rejected them all.[37]

Nevertheless, this period of her life, the first few years of her librarianship, had a kind of glow upon it. She was in her best years—thirty-three when she took the position. She enjoyed her work in spite of the long hours, and she found the new, daily encounters stimulating. One of her new friends was Mrs. Benton, wife of a local physician, who invited her to spend Christmas with her family and her other guests, the Sills. When Ina told her mother, Mrs. Pickett's eyes filled with tears. "O, Ina," she said, "I am afraid it will be the last Christmas we shall be together, and I wanted you here with me and the children." Ina had not the heart to disappoint her, and she declined the invitation.[38]

As it happened, Mrs. Pickett lived to spend two more Christmases in the Fifteenth Street cottage. To young Ina Peterson these two years were happy ones. Speaking of her aunt years later, she recalled, "She had a beautiful, strong voice, yet with a minor cadence, sweet and plaintive. One of my earliest pleasures was to listen when on some summer evening she would take her guitar and sing in a rich contralto old English and Scotch ballads, or some lively Spanish air. 'Allan Percy,' I remember, was one of my favorites, and others were, 'If I Had But a Thousand a Year, Gaffer Gray,' and 'Oft in the Stilly Night.' And light on her feet she was, when with a light heart for the moment she would dance some Spanish fandango . . . Then she was one of the prettiest sights I have ever seen, and most adorable."[39] During those rare evenings in the family circle Ina would sometimes relate forgotten incidents of the Los Angeles days. She recalled, for Ina and Henry, the glamor of that evening when she, still in her teens, had led the grand march at a ball on the arm of ex-Governor Pio Pico.[40] She held her young hearers spellbound with her dramatic stories of their father's bravery when he was under-sheriff of Los Angeles County. They asked her to tell over and over how Bill Peterson, in disguise and speaking perfect Spanish, tracked down Pancho Danielo, leader of the gang that had waylaid and killed Sheriff Barton and his posse in 1857; and how he had captured the outlaw in a game of cards in a San Jose gambling den, in classic Western movie style. The young people were entranced. Little Ina never forgot the stories, or her aunt's charm, during those evenings. Dipping into the past became contagious, and Mrs. Pickett was persuaded by her grandchildren to recite once more some of her own ex-

136

periences during the dreadful days in Far West and Nauvoo. As she talked, the grandmother became more and more animated, her dark eyes brilliant, as she recalled the drama and terror. The stories filled the children with awe and admiration for their small, brave grandmother and for the grandfather who had died so long ago, so young. Those were evenings to be cherished in memory.[41]

Her Mother's Death

When January of 1875 came, Ina Coolbrith did not suspect that this would be the old *Overland's* last year, though her friend the publisher, John Henry Carmany, may have discussed the possibility with her. During the year to come she sent him seven pieces which appeared in as many issues of the magazine. One she already had on hand. She may have written it shortly after the death of her sister two years before. This was her sonnet, "Beside the Dead," which appeared in the May issue.[42] She had put it away, for a while, to let time soften for her the poem's acute inspiration. Now it could be turned into type and she could read it from the printed page without tears.

While this sonnet was the best of her work to appear during 1875, it was not part of the year's mood. The other lyrics are slight, reflecting a release from tension, and with one exception there is not more than a hint of gloom in any of them. Indeed one of her most joyous pieces was written this spring, her "Meadow Larks," published in the June magazine. In March "Discipline" appeared, and in August, "Ownership." The October issue carried her slight and merry "In Time of Storm," and in November there was a longer composition that failed to express clearly the author's meaning. The editor at the time, Walt Fisher, chose its title from three she suggested, "Wisdom," "Folly," and "Regret." Ina could not decide. Fisher chose the last named. When she selected this for inclusion in her second collection, she used still another title, "Freedom." The lines concerned a personal decision of some kind, disguised as a bird set free. What or whom did she give up or send from her? She was not satisfied with the writing.[43]

"Believe me," she pencilled on the back of the manuscript, in a note to John Carmany, "I am sorry the verses are not better."[44] John Carmany had called at the library to see her about this poem, not for content, but as copy, which he as a printer needed at once. But she was ill at home and could not see him. She mailed him the manuscript in time for the November issue. Unable to see her in Oakland, the publisher must have gone back to the city disappointed. He had a number of matters on his mind. One was to break the news to her that this would be the last volume of the *Overland* that he would publish. He still needed

138

a Bret Harte, or a Benjamin Avery. He wanted a contribution from Ina for the December issue, something special. It would be fitting that the last issue of volume fifteen would contain a poem of hers, as the first issue of volume one had. Her name had given the *Overland* a continuity. Well, so had he, he may have mused. He had published it since before Harte's departure, but he had not found Harte's genius in any successor.

These things were on his mind when he came to the library that fall day. But in the back of his mind there was still more. He wanted to tell Ina how much these five years of their association as contributor and publisher had meant to him. The end of the magazine must not mean the end of their friendship. He had other enterprises, mostly publishing, in San Francisco, but nothing else like the *Overland Monthly*.[45] They were business publications. None of them needed a Bret Harte. And he was sure that he could see no way of publishing a poem of Ina's in any of them! But, as a printer, he could tell her that, if at any time she would like a poem, any poem, set up in type, he would do it for her.[46] And if she could get her scattered poems together, he would like to print them for her in a book.

As he returned to the city, frustrated, he knew that there would be another occasion when he could talk over some of these things with her. Oakland looked good to him. What about a farm out east of there some time? He could have orchards in the Fruitvale district, near the hills. He and his brother Cyrus talked about it once in a while; their one wish was to get away from the financial district and onto a farm.[47] He would soon be forty-two. And he had money enough. Why stay? These imaginings are pure speculation. But they all occurred to John Carmany, whether on that one autumn day or not. And they were all discussed with Ina Coolbrith from time to time.

When she knew that the December issue would be the last, she set to meditating about it. Then, in November, came the news of the death of Benjamin Parke Avery, on 8 November, in Peking.[48] He was a dear friend of hers, as well as of John Carmany. Her "In Memoriam" for this third editor of the *Overland* would be from both of them, and bring to a sad close the volume and the file.[49]

Near the end of the year Ina received a letter from Harry Edwards, enclosing a clipping from a Brisbane, Australia, newspaper, "to let you know that you are heard of in the Antipodes."[50] Not long after, while thumbing Whittier's new anthology, *Songs of Three Centuries*, she found her own poem, "When the Grass Shall Cover Me." But instead of her own name at the top, there appeared the word UNKNOWN.[51] She smiled briefly and a little bitterly. Here were persuasions for a col-

lection of her own poems. She hoped to collect them and have them dedicated to her mother when they were published. Whittier's anthology was put out by James R. Osgood and Company in Boston. She thought of Bret's promise, nearly five years before, to give Mr. Osgood her poems. But nothing had come of it. She knew that she should get the pieces together. Yet the long hours at the library, and her work and weariness at home, made her procrastinate.

Now and then the Library Association arranged for a lecture by a prominent speaker. This was a fund-raising device used from the beginning of the organization. In March 1876 John Muir was the lecturer. Of course the library was closed for the occasion. Ina must have urged her mother to come too. Her niece and nephew needed no persuasion. He was their favorite of all the callers at their house. So delighted with the lecture were the members of the Association that they regretted taking the receipts, and voted to give Muir half of the profits.[52]

With the passing of the *Overland Monthly*, only one of Ina Coolbrith's poems appeared in print during 1876, and that in a newspaper. This was her long commencement ode, "From Living Waters," read at the University of California's campus in Berkeley on 7 June. Harry Edwards read it for her.[53] This time there were no quips about coeducation, for among the graduates of the class of '76 were two young women, the first to receive the bachelor's degree from the University, Elizabeth Bragg and Sarah Shuey. That year's class was the largest in the history of the institution, a total of thirty graduates. There was no classroom on the new campus large enough for all the guests, so the exercises were held in the grove. Many brought picnic lunches and spent the entire day.[54]

Mrs. Pickett was pleased about this new triumph for her daughter. It saddened her that Ina was writing little now, and she feared that the drudgery of the two jobs would destroy the urge to create. She herself was beginning to find even light tasks beyond her strength. She was gradually slipping away, as her daughter wept to see. Ina thought back over the long years and the ways in which her mother's strength had been tested; the cold night she crossed the Grand River carrying her two children, her young widowhood, the long trek overland, the flood in Marysville, her aid when Robert Carsley threatened them both, her voyage to Los Angeles alone to bring back with her the sick daughter

---

Ina Coolbrith's Mother, Agnes Coolbrith Smith Pickett. Courtesy of Mrs. Ina Cook Graham, Berkeley, California.

141

and two frightened children, the selfless care for Agnes, and the hurt of losing her eldest daughter.

Agnes Coolbrith Pickett spent Christmas Day in bed that year, Ina and the grandchildren near her. The next day she died.[55] Funeral services were held in the cottage at one o'clock in the afternoon of 27 December, with the Reverend Laurentine Hamilton speaking. The friends who gathered there saw that the rooms had been decorated with sprays of autumn leaves, collected perhaps by the children. Pallbearers who came to take the slight burden to Mountain View Cemetery were friends of hers as they were of her daughter: Harry Edwards, John H. Carmany, John Muir, William Keith, and two Library Association directors, Fred M. Campbell, and E. P. Flint.[56]

In her room that night Ina sought the solace of her pen and wrote eight stanzas, more to express her own grief than to memorialize her mother. "When Spring Shall Come," she titled the poem. It was not published for more than five years. As she wrote, on this darkest night of the year, she believed that she would never know spring or robin or sunshine again, but could only say:

> Wail, winter wind, and work your will!
>   For me no spring shall come again,
> To weave its tender miracle
>   Of beauty upon field and plain.
>
> For I would leave the fairest clime
>   God ever decked for mortal eyes,
> Shut from the lapse of earthly time,
>   Shut from the lapse of earthly skies;
>
> Nor miss the dark, nor miss the day,
>   Nor flowering of the pleasant land—
> Could I but hear her voice, and lay
>   My hand once more in her dear hand![57]

14
A
Free
Library

*Oakland established one of the
first public libraries in the state and
I was its librarian.*

Paraphrased from a remark made
by Ina Coolbrith in 1925

The Oakland Library Association's Gift to the City

"The City Hall's on fire!"

The cry rang out all over town that night, 25 August 1877. Firemen sought to save the hall but could not. It burned to the ground. The alarm brought Library Association members from every direction. Principal McChesney of the high school "worked with might and main to save the Library," said one spectator, a girl at the time. The little building was very close to the burning City Hall, but a miracle, or bibliophily at work, kept it unscorched.[1]

That year and the next, members of the Association, not as an organization but as individuals, were working for the passage of state legislation to enable cities to organize tax-supported public libraries. The members knew that their small book collection, and even the building that housed it, would be a starter for library service in Oakland, once such an enabling act could be passed.

The Board agreed on this subject, as it did on all that concerned the library. It was a congenial group of thirteen members, meeting the first Monday of every month. It was governed by a constitution that provided for the management of business by a number of committees, Book, Finance, and Lecture being the most important. All decisions and policies were made by these committees. The librarian was employed to keep the books in order, to lend them, and to keep records of registra-

143

tion and circulation. At first there was no thought of delegating responsibility of book selection to her. The Book Committee made up lists which they sometimes asked the librarian to check for duplicates, and the Committee placed the orders, preferably with local firms, Hardy in Oakland or Bancroft in San Francisco. The librarian's salary was eighty-five dollars a month at this time.[2] Miss Coolbrith was present at Board meetings, where she read her monthly statistical reports which were always recorded in full in the *Minutes*. The Board secretary was usually a school teacher, whose handwriting was expected to be clear and legible. Sometimes, in the absence of the secretary, the librarian wrote down the proceedings in the big ledger. Ina did this so well that she was regarded as an unofficial assistant secretary.[3]

She made occasional recommendations for book purchase. She was particularly interested in the use of the library by students from Oakland High School, two blocks away, and by some of the university students who lived near by.[4] The Board of Directors considered giving free student memberships, but made no decision.[5] The free library idea was in the air, and they believed the matter would soon be out of their hands. The Association was not self-supporting. Its capital was dwindling. It still sponsored an occasional public lecture to raise funds. In June 1877 the Board seriously debated "the propriety or impropriety of asking Col. Robert Ingersoll to lecture."[6] No decision was recorded in the *Minutes*. There was no debate, however, when the question of buying an important book came up, such as what they called the "Alameda Yearbook," in reality, Halley's *Centennial Year Book of Alameda County,* out in December, and available at Hardy's.[7] The Board hoped that their money would last as long as their library was needed.

It did. In fact, there was money enough to pay for remodeling the building when the time came. The "time" was 18 March 1878. That was the day the Rogers Free Library Act was ratified by the State Legislature, an act to establish free public libraries and reading rooms.[8] The Board lost no time. Exactly two weeks later on 1 April, its monthly meeting day, it drafted a resolution to be submitted to the membership as a whole, proposing that the Oakland Library Association donate its books, building, and other property to the city.[9] The resolution was adopted by the membership two weeks later, only one member dissenting. The property thus to be turned over included the library building, between four and five thousand books, and two thousand dollars in money. This amount could be used for any necessary changes.[10] According to the Rogers Act, when a library was to be donated to the city, the governing body had to be composed of a number of trustees appointed by the Common Council equal in number to those elected by the donors.[11]

144

The Association members on the new Board included two from the Free Reading Room Association and five from the library organization. The Association Directors agreed to empower the president and vice-president, J. Preston Moore and O. H. Burnham, to transfer all property and sign necessary papers.[12]

The Beginning of the Oakland Free Library

By the end of May the transfer had taken place, the old Association had been dissolved, and a new Board had taken office. This first Board of Trustees of the Oakland Free Library elected the following officers from the fourteen members who composed the Board: J. Preston Moore, president; W. W. Crane, Junior, vice-president, Fred M. Campbell, corresponding secretary, Joseph B. McChesney, recording secretary, and Galen M. Fisher, treasurer. They held their first meeting on 1 June, requested the librarian not to lend any more books for a while, and appointed a committee to draft an ordinance of acceptance by the city, which was to be presented at the next Council meeting.[13]

Following these legal provisions, the rest of the business went ahead. The building was to be remodeled by raising it and making a reading room of the lower floor, that is, a room for newspapers and magazines, to take the place of the old reading room at Eleventh and Washington Streets. The second floor would house the library proper. A reading room would be opened at the Point in West Oakland, and another in East Oakland at the same time.[14] On 24 August a set of *Rules and Regulations of the Oakland Free Library* was adopted. This provided that the library would be open every day, except Sundays and holidays, from nine to nine, and the reading room from eight to ten, opening an hour earlier during the summer. All residents over fourteen years of age would be entitled to borrow books, no more than two at a time.[15] In September two new encyclopedias, the *American,* and the *Britannica,* as well as two hundred dollars' worth of new books for circulation, were ordered, in addition to new furniture, all to be on hand when the remodeling was completed.[16] On 18 October the Board of Trustees unanimously elected Miss Ina Coolbrith to the position of City Librarian, and ordered that a warrant be drawn for salary due her since 1 October.[17] Her pay was still eighty-five dollars monthly. The alterations were now complete. New carpeting was put down, and extra help hired to get the books on the shelves as soon as possible, ready for the opening.[18]

A formal opening of the library and central reading room took place on the evening of 7 November 1878. Board Vice-president, W. W. Crane, Junior, gave an address, and he was followed by three local preachers, the Reverends D. D. McLean, John Thompson, and Galen Fisher, each speaking briefly.[19] Miss Coolbrith was on hand to greet the visitors, to register borrowers, to charge out books, and to answer questions—the cheerful confusion of a typical opening night in a new library—with a noteworthy difference, this was one of the first free city library openings in California.

The rooms were fresh and inviting, smelling of new paint and fresh wallpaper. Gaslight fixtures illuminated the new chairs and tables, some of which were for chess and checkers in the ground floor reading room, and a big pot-bellied stove heated the place. Up the stairway was the library itself, with books on open shelves, except the reference collection shelved back of the railing which enclosed the librarian's desk and work area. At one end of the floor was a smaller room without books, fitted as a "retiring and conversation room for the ladies."[20] Off this room was an 1878 version of a powder room, where, above the washstand hung a fine, oval, walnut-framed mirror, now in the California Room in the present library building near Lake Merritt. This glass, long ago, often reflected Ina Coolbrith's lovely face as she pinned back a stubborn curl or adjusted an earring.[21]

Miss Coolbrith, for the present, had no assistance, except a janitor, for a twelve-hour day. The building may have been closed for the noon and evening meals, but that is doubtful. A strong tradition of service that required branch librarians forty and fifty years later to "eat on the job," so the readers could remain throughout the day, must have had early roots. It is reasonable to assume, however, that Henry or young Ina took turns at noon and evening relief.[23] Indeed the need for assistance was apparent within the month. Transformation from private to public library increased business. The next month the Trustees voted to pay the librarian $175 a month for herself and any needed assistance, but the following month they made their own appointments and allotment of the payroll.[24] A first assistant librarian was to be appointed at a salary of $40, and a second assistant at $30 a month. The chief librarian's salary would remain at $85, the janitor's at $40, and the curators of West and East Oakland reading rooms at $60, their curatorship including janitorial work. This made a total central library payroll of $195. At the January 1879 Trustees' meeting, Henry Peterson was elected first assistant and Ina Peterson second assistant. Henry was nineteen that month, and his sister fifteen in December. Henry had helped his aunt for most of the

---

Oakland Free Library, 1878-1902, Fourteenth Street, between Washington and Clay Streets. From the drawing by Jerry Ferguson in the Oakland Free Library; based on a sketch in the Oakland Tribune Yearbook, 1887. Courtesy of the Library and of Mr. William Knowland, publisher, Oakland Tribune.

146

four years since she came to the position, and his sister after school and on Saturdays. Miss Coolbrith was glad to see them employed full time and financially compensated at last. Her niece had finished the eighth grade in June 1878. Young Ina had wanted to go on to high school, but she was needed to help in both library and home. Now, realizing that high school would be denied her, she resolved to make the library her school.[25]

Both Miss Coolbrith and the Trustees knew that a catalog was an immediate necessity. In December they had authorized an edition of one thousand copies which could be sold at twenty-five cents each.[26] The work would have to be done along with routine duties. Already so many people were coming in that circulation had to be limited to one book at a time. By midsummer the catalog was completed, "with a vast amount of labor thoroughly and well done by the librarian in addition to her other duties, at no additional cost," said the Trustees admiringly.[27]

There was progress along other lines too. A tax of four cents on each one hundred dollars had been levied for library purposes by the City Council.[28] This would mean between eleven and twelve thousand dollars for the year 1879-1880. And, in a burst of optimism, the Trustees authorized the enterprising young first assistant to procure a horse and carriage to collect the overdue books.[29] Trustees became alarmed about the physical condition of the books. These were showing wear and tear from use by the general public, and a program of binding was begun, and also "casting aside" when necessary.[30] The librarian urged the curators to retain all files of local newspapers for future binding, and to keep complete runs of other periodicals for the same treatment. It was not long before an inventory was taken. And one of the first acts of the next year, 1880, was increase of the assistant librarians' salaries by ten dollars a month each.[31]

In April 1880 new library legislation was passed in Sacramento. This act repealed that of 1878 and enacted a substitute.[32] The new law was derided, as the idea of some meddlesome politician, by Col. John P. Irish's *Oakland Times*.[33] It provided that, in cities of less than one hundred thousand population, a library board of five members was to be elected.[34] In the meantime, until the next city election, the new Trustees would be appointed by the Council. The newly appointed board of five (replacing an unwieldy but more democratic group of fourteen) included two men from the old Board. They appointed a committee to study their powers and duties under the new law.[35]

This committee consulted several lawyers and came up with the unexpected notion that the Board could not employ women or minors. The

148

men agreed to retain the present employees and to consult the city attorney at once.[36] They were relieved by his decision "that 'sex is no test of citizenship,' 'that the office of Librarian and Assistant Librarian are not elective offices,' and that 'there is no legal objection to appointing a woman as Librarian.' "[37] Hearing this the library Board proceeded to elect the same employees.[38] This was a true vote of confidence. This Board delegated the responsibility of book selection to Miss Coolbrith, saying that the "Librarian is to furnish the Book Committee with lists of books she may consider desirable" in her examination of book catalogs and book review magazines.[39]

In July 1881 the Library Board presented its first annual report to the City Council. It seems to have been prepared by Miss Coolbrith, in whose hand it appeared in full in the Board *Minutes* of that month. It began with a history of the old Association, gave an account of the transfer, and proceeded to the last year's activities, showing that the collection now amounted to 8,108 books, that there were 5,050 borrowers, and that the year's circulation had been 94,859. The report stated that the daily attendance was large, and that "one of its most gratifying features is the number of pupils of the Grammar and High Schools and Students generally to whom the library offers facilities for information of inestimable value."[40] "The library was advancing in usefulness." The Board was pleased and appreciative. On 13 September they adopted a new pay scale for employees; $100 a month to the librarian, $60 monthly each to the three reading room curators and to the first assistant librarian who was also to act as assistant secretary to the Board. The second assistant, Ina Peterson, would receive $45 a month. The new scale went into effect in October.[41]

Ina Coolbrith as Librarian

Miss Coolbrith enjoyed being a reader's adviser, especially with the student group. High school students flocked in after school. One of them recalled, many years after, how the librarian always welcomed them, sitting at her desk, smiling slightly, her arms before her on the desk, as though she had all the time in the world for each and every one of her young visitors.[42] She recommended sources for assignments, but most of all she enjoyed guiding their general reading. Here she was, without a high school diploma, without a bachelor's degree, without any sort of certificate of librarianship, the embodiment of the ideal in her profession; one who likes people and books, and likes to get them together.

Her beauty too attracted them all, girls and boys. They remembered it. And they never forgot her smile.[43] Amy Rinehart remembered it. So did other students, Georgia Loring (later Mrs. Bamford), Isadora Dun-

149

can, and Henry Kirk, and so, later, did Jack London, "just a little kid";
and so too did Mary Austin, as a girl, seeking advice on placing her
first manuscript." Isadora Duncan in particular was to write later:
"There was a public library in Oakland, where we then lived, but no
matter how many miles we were from it, I ran or danced or skipped
there and back. The librarian was a very wonderful and beautiful woman, a poetess of California, Ina Coolbrith. She encouraged my reading, and I thought she always looked pleased when I asked for fine books.
She had very beautiful eyes that glowed with burning fire and passion."
Isadora Duncan confided that she thought her father, who sometimes
accompanied her, must have been secretly in love with the librarian.[45]

Henry Kirk also remembered his first sight of Ina Coolbrith when
he was a student recalling it in later life as if it were yesterday:

> She was a marvelously handsome woman; none of her pictures
> do her justice. A magnificent woman. She sat in her chair as though
> on a throne. I thought she was austere. The first book I took out
> was a life of Mary Stuart. She opened it to the frontispiece, looked
> at the portrait, and said, "Humpf! She was not so beautiful." Years
> later I came to know her in her house on Russian Hill, and remem-
> ber her by the fireplace, pouring tea. She was a wonderfully en-
> tertaining, lively conversationalist.[46]

Jack London would never forget how he found that library one day—
the most important thing that ever happened to him, he later said—how
he had rushed in with his bundle of newspapers under his arm. He
recalled too that he felt compelled to write her a letter about it, years
later, something like this:

> The old Oakland library days! Do you know, you were the first
> one who ever complimented me on my choice of reading matter?
> Nobody at home bothered their heads over what I read. I was an
> eager, thirsty, hungry little kid—and one day at the library I drew
> out a volume on Pizarro in Peru (I was 10 years old). You got the
> book and stamped it for me; and as you handed it to me you praised
> me for reading books of that nature. Proud! If you only knew how
> proud your words made me! For I thought a great deal of you. You
> were a goddess to me. I didn't know you were a poet, or that you
> had ever done such a wonderful thing as write a line. . . . But I
> stood greatly in awe of you—worshipful awe. In those days I named
> by adjectives, and I named you "Noble"—that is the feeling I got
> for you. . . . I have never seen you since those library days, yet
> the memory picture I retain of you is as vivid as any I possess.

150

When I hear your name mentioned or think of you, up at once flashes that memory picture, and with it its connotation, and its connotation is "Noble." Often and often the mere word "noble" recalls you to my mind.[47]

Mary Austin would have agreed with Jack London, for she afterwards wrote:

I found her at the Oakland Library, where she was employed, a tall, slow woman, wearing an expression I was to front later in my glass, which I think she must have acquired crossing the plains as a child, the look of one accustomed to uninhibited space and wide horizons. She had a low, pleasant voice; now and then a faint smile swam to the surface of her look, and passed without the slightest riffle of a laugh; and she was entirely kind and matter of fact with me. She told me how to prepare my manuscripts and advised me to see the *Overland* editor.[48]

Even the unknown, those who never made a name for themselves in the literary world, used to frequent the Oakland Library just to see Miss Coolbrith. One of these, in later years a school teacher in a nun's habit, confided, "Why, we used to come to the library just to look at her—she was so beautiful!"[49] Another who could not forget, though years had passed, asked, "Where is the librarian who was here thirty years ago? Her hair was sixty but her eyes were twenty. She was one of your local poets." When told that he was referring to Miss Coolbrith, he said, "Coolbrith, that was the name. She gave me a book of Homer, and she gave it with a smile. I have been away from here for thirty years, but I have always remembered her—her smile."[50]

15
A
Perfect
Day

Read my riddle clearly,
You will understand!
Ina Coolbrith, from
"A Riddle" (ca. 1881)

John Henry Carmany

For the task of helping Ina Coolbrith select her poems for publication in a single volume, John Henry Carmany had two important sources, his file of the fifteen volumes of the *Overland Monthly*,[1] and all the separate sheets of manuscript poems he had received from her as contributions when he was publisher of the magazine. This sheaf of loose manuscripts included a few which he had not published, and three that were never published at any time. After the book, which he entitled *A Perfect Day*, appeared in 1881, the printer put together all the manuscript sheets, along with a frontispiece portrait, a title page and a table of contents, into a neat portfolio. This was done with such unusual care that one might suspect that his regard for the poet was more than respect, more than friendship, even more than affection.[2]

Was Carmany in love with her? And did she return his love? The three unpublished lyrics in this portfolio were love poems, tender, deeply sincere, but they seemed to be somewhat platonic. They were birthday poems, all written to one man who was unnamed. They were written on 24 May 1877, 1878, and 1879; even the hour of composition of two of them was noted—"at 1 p.m." They were intimate, personal; it is easy to see why she did not want them published. But she gave them to Carmany, and even asked him to set one up in type for her. Who was the man to whom they were addressed? Not John Carmany. They were composed for a younger man, a man who would outlive her. The date alone was proof that they were not for Carmany; he was born 28 November 1833.[3] Here was a mystery for the reader of the little portfolio, one which makes the reader of today feel like an intruder, like reading someone's personal mail.

Any matchmaker of that day, especially John Muir, would have considered the successful San Francisco printer most eligible as a husband for the poet-librarian. John Henry Carmany was born of Pennsylvania-Dutch stock in Lebanon County, Pennsylvania. He learned the printing trade as a young man, and with his brothers, Cyrus and Ringgold, and his sister Mary, came to California. He was in San Francisco in the fifties, having made two trips to Mexico, and returned to engage in printing. He had many interests: mining, farming, and the stock market. He wrote a little; a few essays on industry and finance, and a short story or two, but no poetry. In the 1860's he was the proprietor of the *Stock Circular,* and other publications.[4]

He had made money from these enterprises, and he could afford to take a chance with the *Overland Monthly.* He bought it from Anton Roman in 1869, and began his publication with volume three, in July of that year. His brief association with Bret Harte was one of the most stimulating and exasperating experiences of his life. It is well known that he offered Harte many inducements to remain as editor, but was unable to outdo the attractive offers coming from Chicago and Boston in late 1870. Harte was followed by three other editors in four years: W. C. Bartlett, Benjamin P. Avery, and Walter M. Fisher. But Bret Harte's touch was not there. The *Overland* ceased publication with the close of volume fifteen.[5] Carmany, however, never lost interest in it, and when its revival was proposed he was again ready to give his support. He was honestly anxious to keep alive, if possible, the West's most important literary monthly, through which, from first issue to last, ran the bright thread of Ina Coolbrith's lyrics, giving the periodical a unique continuity.

Ina Coolbrith's First Book, *A Perfect Day*

Ina Coolbrith had hoped to collect her scattered poems for publication while her mother was living. After her mother's death, the poet's ambition drooped. But Carmany brought it to life again. He wrote to Bret Harte in Krefeld, Germany, in 1879, to ask if he still had the clippings Ina had given him eight years before. Harte replied that he had

---

John Henry Carmany. Courtesy of the Oakland Free Library.

154

left them with the publisher, Osgood, who had never returned them to him.[6] So, together, Ina and John assembled all they could find. She had her own first drafts as well as clippings of most of them, which she had saved to put into her scrapbook. And of course she too had her files of the *Overland Monthly* where most of her poems had appeared. The compilation was not difficult. Of the sixty-three final selections, forty-six came from the *Overland*. Miss Coolbrith and the printer agreed, as Edward Rowland Sill had urged, that the two University of California commencement odes should be part of the volume.[7] A few others were lyrics from the old *Golden Era, The Californian, Galaxy,* the *Alta,* and *Harper's Weekly,* before the days of the *Overland*. They chose to call her book *A Perfect Day,* from its lead poem, and to publish it as an "author's special subscription edition," copyrighted under her name and printed by John H. Carmany and Company.[8]

As a printer John Carmany put his best workmanship into this little book. Severe restraint of design, good paper, and ten-point type, wide margins and judicious spacing were factors governing the work. The binding selected was that of beveled boards covered with pebbled cloth in dark red, with a gilt title. He decided to issue it in two formats, a trade edition to sell for two dollars, and a limited, large-paper edition of fifty copies, with red line borders, priced at ten dollars. The book came out in March 1881, planned perhaps to coincide with the author's fortieth birthday. Ina's only regret was that she could not have placed it in her mother's living hands; she could only dedicate it to her mother's memory.[9]

Ina's friends were jubilant. Sill wrote to her to tell her that he had sent a review of her book to the *Atlantic Monthly*.[10] It was reviewed in many other periodicals from which friends sent clippings. Bierce, in tardy praise, said it was "a pleasant rill of song in a desert cursed by fantastic mirages."[11] Ina mailed an inscribed copy to Stoddard, then in San Francisco, who praised her extravagantly in a letter to "Beloved Ina." "I know of no living poetess in either England or America," he wrote her, "who is your superior and but few who approach you in beauty of sentiment—richness of melody and delicacy of expression; with all the old love. . . ." Before she put this letter away in a desk drawer, she drew out a minute, tissue-wrapped packet and placed it inside the envelope. She never lost this letter. It survived the San Francisco fire. It is among the Coolbrith papers in the Bancroft Library, and, if the reader were to unfold the fragile little packet, he would find a dark-brown curl and a memo which the girl Ina wrote, "Charlie Stoddard's hair, 1869."[12]

The stimulation of the last year or so, in actually getting a collection of her poems into print, produced a new urge to write, though she still had little time for doing so. She went about her work at home, feeling and thinking lyrics but not getting them on paper. She was persuaded to write the "Memorial Poem," that year of 1881, for the Grand Army of the Republic. It was read by Miss Nellie Holbrook, at services held in a large tent in the San Francisco Odd Fellows Cemetery, where the old soldiers, school children, and friends had gathered after decorating the graves with flowers and little flags. The principal address was given by her friend, Judge Boalt, a popular speaker.[13] Near the end of the year, one more lyric of Ina's was published, "Be Happy, Happy, Little Maid."[14]

Puzzles in Poetry

About this time there appeared a short, rhymed letter, which she named "A Riddle." It was never published but was set in type, as it appears in one of Ina Coolbrith's scrapbooks. She, and perhaps one other, knew the answer. Could the other one have been John Carmany? Carmany never married. In the 1880s he moved to Oakland and bought a farm east of town which he shared with his bachelor brother Cyrus. Of the three brothers and the sister, only Ringgold Carmany married. This brother had children and grandchildren and great-grandchildren. And told by his descendants today is a family legend about Great-uncle John and the beautiful woman poet. Yes, the two were interested in each other; they were fond of each other; they might have married had it not been for Great-aunt Mary who thought that, because Ina's friends were all literary people, Ina was too "fast" for her brother John.[15] So there may have been no romance, or if there were, it was as discreetly hidden as were the other secrets in Ina Coolbrith's life.

It is Ringgold Carmany's grandson who cherishes today a book that is a strong but long-mute proof of John's love for Ina. This is the printer's own copy of A Perfect Day. Taking one of the large-paper copies of the volume, he made it into the most beautiful book he ever owned. In this edition, each page of the text has a red line border. An equal number of pages, otherwise blank, were printed with the same red borders, and each of these was hand-decorated superbly with a floral design in watercolor. This enhancement gives the volume a rich quality; yet each painting is restrained and quiet enough to brighten the text, not rob interest from it. He had the large book bound with black morocco, with quiet, gold-tooled borders on the cover, and with endleaves of crimson watered silk. Centered in the inside of the front cover was a sepia print of Ina's photograph taken in 1870, an oval in a flat, blind-tooled leather frame. Completing the volume was Ina Coolbrith's full-page autograph verse inscription on the front flyleaf. She wrote

157

this in the book on her birthday in 1893, though she had composed it in January of that year. At that time she was in deep despair, and her writing reflects it. Had he not known the reason for her mood, he might have been disappointed in what she wrote. She spoke of the contents of the volume as,

> These children mine, one day
> When I am passed away,
> From the visible world, and all that in it is,
> My truest witnesses,
> With simple words to breathe
> Of one at rest beneath
> The sod, no longer green,
> Of what she was . . . alas, and might have been!

If she were indulging in self-pity, it may have been because of blows she had borne alone; or it may have been because at an earlier date she had decided not to be Mrs. Carmany. The inscription was not for him; she was talking to herself.[16]

"A Riddle," which Ina wrote at about the same time *A Perfect Day* was published, is even more baffling:

> Two hearts in your bosom
> Alternate command—
> Read my riddle clearly,
> You will understand!
>
> Each hath separate dwellers,
> Each is leal and true,
> Yet the far is even
> Nearest unto you.
>
> One heart says you love me,
> But the other: "Nay,
> My own love is drifting
> Farther day by day!"
>
> One heart thrusts me from you,
> One still holds me fast,
> Will my own, I wonder,
> Let me go at last?

All my soul is open—
  All my heart is read;
Nothing that is spoken
  Would I have unsaid.

But each thought that thrills me
  Looking from your eyes,
Straightway brings another
  That the first denies.

Not till blade and blossom
  Grow above my rest,
Will you know me truly—
  Will you love me best.[17]

John Carmany set this song in type for her. Did Ina expect him to read it clearly and to understand?

Three Birthday Poems, May 24

The "Riddle" leaves one wondering. So do the three birthday poems, dated 24 May, written to an anonymous loved one. Ina Coolbrith had the 1878 birthday poem set in type. At about the same time and by the same printer (apparently Carmany) "A Riddle," and a translation from Horace, entitled only "Written for °°°," were printed for her at her request. Her name was not printed at the bottom, but when she pasted the birthday lyric and the translation in her scrapbook, she signed them both. She also dated the lines from Horace, "May 24, 1878," as though they too were a birthday gift. Did she translate this for a student, taking his prose and putting it into verse? Were the birthday poems, then, for a student who frequented the library?[18]

On the same scrapbook page with these two poems, and on the adjacent page, appear three pieces of nonsense verse making, all unsigned, source not given, and in a typeface wholly unlike anything else in the scrapbook. One is the epistle "To John Muir," mentioned earlier. The other two are student verse, one "Dreams and Reality, (Mostly Reality)" and the other "Enter June. (College Verses Written for °°)." Who wrote the college verse? Was he the lad for whom the Horace translation was rhymed? If so, the significant date in May was *his* birthday. Who was the student? After all, was the establishment of his identity necessary in unraveling and reweaving the fabric of our poet's long life? Probably not.[19]

159

Then one day, years after we first read the three baffling birthday poems, we found at the very end of the second of Ina Coolbrith's two heavy scrapbooks, a loose piece of paper torn from the Knave's page of the Oakland *Tribune,* undated, but sometime in the 1920s, the source not given, but obvious from type and style. It was a fragment of a letter to the Knave about an obscure little volume of college verse picked up at a book auction, *College Verses,* compiled by the Berkeleyan Stock Company and published in San Francisco in 1882.[20] The Knave's correspondent found contributions by Milicent Shinn and others of interest, but he was surprised to see two, "Dreams and Reality" and "Enter June," by a prominent California Supreme Court Justice. Who would have suspected his Honor, Justice Frederick William Henshaw, '79, of such frivolities?

The scrap from the Knave's page was the clue. Frederick Henshaw, born in Ottawa, Illinois, in 1858, had lived in Oakland since he was five years old. As a high school boy he was part of Belle Osbourne's "crowd," and later married a chum of hers, one of the pretty and vivacious Tubbs sisters. Fred and Belle were classmates in the Oakland High School, where she, by her own admission, had a light-hearted attitude toward her lessons. When their teacher, Edward Rowland Sill, discovered that Belle allowed Fred Henshaw to do her algebra and Frank Bonney her French, the instructor was exasperated, and she was "sent home in disgrace," as she related in her delightful book, *This Life I've Loved,* by Isobel Field.[21] The biographical sketches of Frederick Henshaw are devoid of such pleasant anecdotes; they dwell instead on his career in a dignified profession. But all the sketches, including the obituary notices in the *New York Times* and the *San Francisco Chronicle* in June 1929, have one thing in common. None give the month and day of his birth. And since his ashes were scattered over the San Francisco Bay, there are no cemetery records.[22] Having gone this far in what was, perhaps, a pointless pursuit of information, we could not stop. There was one more local source, the office of the Registrar of the University of California. The Registrar does not give information from the records in answer to questions, but will confirm a date that is known. When the office was asked if Frederick William Henshaw of the class of 1879 was born 24 May 1858, the expected confirmation came. The date was 24 May.

What does it matter, after all the years? Why probe? Why pry into the feelings of a sensitive and unhappy woman? To satisfy the curiosity aroused by an enigma, using a reference librarian's methods, is not reason enough. But, if it is to know the heart of the woman whom circumstances made Oakland's first librarian, the search may be forgiven. All

160

three unpublished poems are singularly poignant. They might have been written by a teacher to a favorite pupil or a mother to her son. This is the briefest of them:

To————— —————
A Birthday Poem
God bless thee, dear!
Make glad the year
    To-day beginning.
Make all days glad, indeed,
And all thy strivings speed
    To gracious winning!

God love thee, dear!
Earth-ways make clear
    To heaven above thee . . .
Love thee, as I love thee!
Dearer thou could'st not be!
Better, belovéd, He
    Only can love thee!²³
24 May, 1 P.M., 1878.

As a mother her son, she may have cared for him, this student who made the library his second home, from high school days through college and after. He was a handsome, brown-eyed lad whose family, prominent in Oakland, lived on Washington Street at that time, only a few steps away from the little library.²⁴ There he came on sunny afternoons or rainy winter evenings, spending long hours, reading, studying, asking advice on school assignments, perhaps even helping polish the two pieces of verse that were published over his name. For her his presence brightened the room when, as she said at the time,

The night shuts down with falling rain,
    That drapes the world in double pall;
The loud blast battles with the pane,
    And fierce and far the breakers call.

When too as she could add,

Down the long room, grown weird and grim,
    Strange shadows hover, waveringly;
I move among the folios dim,
    And count the hours till I am free.

"Free," she asked, "and for what?"

> Free to recross the threshold dark
> Of the four walls I name my home;
> To change of toil; then, sleepless, mark
> The long slow hours till dawn shall come.

And, smiling at the boy absorbed in his book,

> O my one friend—unfailing, sure,
> Through life's young years! How far indeed
> The way, the barriers how secure
> That hold thee from my earnest need!

> From this thy dear abiding place
> What undreamed mysteries divide—[25]

✿   ✿   ✿

That "one friend," reading in the flickering gaslight that winter night, was Fred Henshaw. Ina Coolbrith's own son, had he lived, would have been a little younger. All her long life she encouraged young people. Fred Henshaw was one of many. They came to her for guidance, sympathy, friendship. If they were ill or in need, she appealed to her friends for aid for them. Jack London was a baby when Frederick Henshaw graduated from college, but in a few years Jack would be coming into this library, and Ina Coolbrith would try to draw him out. He was a reticent boy. She was quoted as saying, "All he wanted from the Library was books and to know if they were good."[26] So it was with George Sterling, whom she had known from his boyhood to his death.

"The first time I saw George," she said, "he was shinning up a tree."[27] She loved him as a poet and a friend and was deeply grieved when he took his own life. The last poem she wrote was for George Sterling.[28] She was to outlive Herman Scheffauer, another young poet, also a suicide.[29] She asked for help for Clark Ashton Smith, a gifted writer, sick with tuberculosis.[30] Most dearly loved of all was "the boy, Carl," to whom her posthumous book, *Wings of Sunset*, was dedicated. He was Carl Gunderson, born in San Francisco, a young musician and writer, who used two pseudonyms, Ulv Youff and Carl Seyfforth, who died before her.[31] But others too found her presence inspiring, nourishing; all her "Charlies," Stoddard, Keeler, Phillips, and Lummis. To Torrey Connor and her daughter, June Nahl, she was their "Santa Ina," and almost worshipped as such; to Derrick and Eunice Lehmer, she

162

was a "mountain of strength."[32] She also encouraged Ruth Harwood, and many another gifted poet, woman or man.[33]

The friendship, then, of the librarian for the young, promising reader, Frederick Henshaw, was not unusual. If her feeling for him was love, well, through all the long years she loved many a young follower of "the Gleam."

Revival of the *Overland Monthly*

Not long after the publication of *A Perfect Day* there was talk of reviving the *Overland Monthly*. Anton Roman, first publisher of the old *Overland* in 1868, had started a new venture in January 1880, a periodical which he called the *Californian, a Western Monthly*. After a year he sold it to Charles Phelps, the poet who had been the first librarian employed by the Oakland Library Association back in 1869. Phelps remained editor and publisher until late in 1882 when he sold the monthly to Warren Cheney of the California Publishing Company. At this time John Carmany gave Cheney the right to use the title of *Overland Monthly* if he cared to do so. For the rest of the year Cheney did use it in combination, calling his magazine the *Californian and Overland Monthly*. This was a cumbersome title, so, with Carmany in hearty agreement, Cheney decided to begin the new year of 1883 with a revived *Overland Monthly*, dropping *Californian* from the name and closing the file with the December issue. He employed Miss Milicent Shinn, a recent graduate of the University of California, as editor, and decided to begin the new *Overland Monthly* in January 1883 as volume one, number one, of a new series.

No ship ever had a more impressive launching, or debutante a more brilliant coming-out party, than the *Overland Monthly*, Second Series. The party was a formal dinner given by Irving M. Scott, San Francisco civic leader and capitalist. The invitations received by fifty guests read:

Mr. and Mrs. Irving M. Scott
desiring to celebrate the revival of the
Overland Monthly
request your presence at dinner
at their residence
507 Harrison Street
Friday December twenty-second, 1882
at half-past five o'clock

Though several sent regrets, forty-three people were seated at the long I-shaped table; six at the head, seven at the foot, and fifteen on each side. As the guests moved into the long room and admired the center-piece, a large bear fashioned of violets, one was heard to pun, *sotto voce*, "A bear inviolate!"

All the guests were contributors to the old *Overland*, except Judge Boalt, who said he represented the readers. John Carmany sat at the head of the table, at the right of Mrs. Scott. The host, half way down one side, had Miss Shinn on his right and Miss Coolbrith on his left; at her left sat Warren Cheney, the publisher. There were many distinguished guests; the LeConte brothers, Martin Kellogg, William Keith, W. C. Bartlett, Theodore Hittell, and Edward Rowland Sill, among others. There were toasts and long responses from many of them. Ina Coolbrith's poem, "Our Poets," was read by Professor John Murray. The most interesting of all these talks was the last, that by John Henry Carmany who had faith in "our new editress," and was full of optimism. When he spoke he gave a full and spirited history of his relations with Bret Harte on the old magazine, how painstaking the author was, how hard it was to get copy out of him (apologizing for using the word "copy" to describe a literary creation), with what ease Harte had produced "Dickens in Camp," which Carmany read in full, what a sensation "The Heathen Chinee" had been, how he had tried to lure Harte on a lecture tour to capitalize on this "sensation." He told what he knew of that strange dinner in Chicago, where Harte was the guest of honor but did not come, and why there were five hundred dollars under each of the dinner plates! The money was there to persuade Harte to bring the *Overland* to Chicago, but the gesture was wasted. Carmany's talk was a highlight. He brought with him some of Harte's manuscripts which were of great interest to all present. A full account of the proceedings, with speeches quoted, and with Miss Coolbrith's poem, was printed on the front page of the *San Francisco Daily Report* of 26 December, the official city and county newspaper, where it appeared as a report of an event of singular civic importance. This account was copied by the *Overland Monthly* as a sixteen-page supplement to its February 1883 issue.[34]

Uninvited to the party was Ambrose Bierce, who wrote caustically of the affair, even criticizing the California wines served as evidence of frugality. When Ina's poem, "Our Poets," appeared in the February *Overland*, he praised it, but said it was a wonder she did not write a dirge, because "our poets" were all dead or ought to be.[36] He promptly named the periodical *The Warmed-Overland Monthly*.[37]

Miss Coolbrith published a lyric entitled "Unattained" in the first issue of the new *Overland*, and another, "February," in the March *Century Magazine*.[38] Bierce, perhaps smarting from having been ignored at the *Overland* dinner, turned on Ina's "Unattained" with such sarcasm that she did not permit it to be printed again. The verses, Bierce said, were "marred by this dainty writer's tiresome lugubriousness. Having in mind the whole body of Miss Coolbrith's works for the last fifteen years, we are compelled to ask—when is she going to 'attain'? If never, is it not about time for her to remove her pretty lace handkerchief from her pretty brown eyes and put it comfortably in her pocket?"[39]

On the last day of March a memorial service was held for a beloved Oakland clergyman, the Reverend Laurentine Hamilton (for whom Mount Hamilton is named), who had died the spring before. The principal address was given by the Reverend Horatio Stebbins of San Francisco, and other eulogies were spoken by W. C. Bartlett and Professor Joseph LeConte. A memorial poem had been written for this occasion by Miss Coolbrith, who asked Joshua Barker, a former library trustee, to read it.[40] This poem was the last of her verse writing for months. What happened at the Oakland Library in April was far from lyrical.

16
An Elected
Board of
Library Directors

They fetter feet and hands; they give
Me bitter, thankless tasks to do.

Ina Coolbrith, from
"Withheld" (1873)

A New Library Board

In April 1883 the Municipal Library Act of 1880 struck Oakland with the force of a cyclone. At the city elections, held earlier that spring, the voters elected, for the first time, a Board of Library Directors. The Board of five took office on 3 April. There were no lawyers, doctors, or teachers on the new Board. The two incumbents, O. H. Burnham, and Charles W. Kellogg, were businessmen, one the owner of a planing mill, the other a bookkeeper. The three new members were Wilbur Walker, a lumberyard salesman, Emory M. Long, and Eugene A. Trefethen, both railroad office clerks.[1] At the 3 April meeting Charles Kellogg was elected president, and most of the time was spent in explaining procedures to the new men. The new regime really began with the June meeting. After that, for many months, reporters from papers on both sides of the Bay did not miss any of Oakland's Library Board meetings. They were to coin a new word, *trefethenization*.[2] Even Bierce, sharp master of invective, would never be more explicit than when calling Trefethen "an illiterate blackguard."[3] In June, Oakland citizens from the mayor to the most retiring reader would protest. In July Colonel John P. Irish's *Sunday Morning Times* would end a long article with the remark that three upstarts had wrecked the Oakland Free Library.[4]

The first piece of new business at the June Board meeting was proposed by Director Trefethen. He said that he had learned that the

167

second assistant librarian, Miss Ina Peterson, was a relative of the librarian, and he proposed that she be dismissed. Both Burnham and Kellogg protested, and President Kellogg asked the Secretary to read a letter that was handed to him. The letter was from Miss Coolbrith, who had learned of Trefethen's proposal. It contained a strong defense of her niece's proficiency, her knowledge of books, and her helpfulness to the users of the library. Miss Coolbrith urged that they retain her, as it would be impossible to replace her immediately with anyone with similar qualifications.[5] President Kellogg was incensed.

"I don't like things sprung on the Board," he said. "I don't believe in dismissing anyone without cause, and I am not prepared to vote." The new trio had their way, and Ina Peterson was dismissed. Trefethen then nominated Mrs. J. L. Plummer for the position.

"Who is she?" asked Burnham.

"A widow," said Trefethen, "and a sister of mine." Burnham asked Long if he knew her, and Long said he did not. Turning to Wilbur Walker, Burnham put the same question.

"I'm acquainted with her," Walker responded.

"Do you know what her qualifications are?" persisted Burnham.

"No, but I have confidence in Mr. Trefethen." The vote was taken to appoint Mrs. Plummer, and passed with three "ayes," and a "no," the President not voting. Burnham then moved that a third assistant be elected. This was seconded by Kellogg. Burnham immediately spoke up, "I would like to nominate Mrs. Morgan for the position. She's a relative of Director Long."

Long stated indignantly that the lady did not want the position. The frivolity shocked President Kellogg who declared the nomination out of order. He then presented his resignation which he had written previously. He said that he had been with the library Board for many years and that it was never run by a "ring," as it now seemed to be. His resignation was refused, but he said he would absent himself from future meetings. He kept his word.

Sometime during the month of June, A. M. Long, the Secretary of the Board, learned that an annual report was expected at the end of the fiscal year. He called a special meeting near the end of the month. This was an illegal act, as only the president could call a special meeting. The three new members came as summoned and proceeded then and there to draft the *Annual Report*.[6]

The whole town was disturbed by the dismissal of Miss Peterson. Petitions were circulated and signed in time for the next Board meeting which took place on the eve of Independence Day with a premature display of fireworks. The small committee room, opening off the library reading room, was crowded. Amid the confusion the routine business went forward haltingly, every step bringing objection from Burnham. President Kellogg was absent. Burnham objected to the special meeting of the week before as illegal; to Trefethen, as Chairman of the Book Committee, ordering books without checking with the librarian for duplicates; to the proposal that the *Rules and Regulations* be rewritten; to accepting President Kellogg's resignation; and finally to appointing Wilbur Walker in Kellogg's place. Every motion passed over his objection. The room was becoming more and more crowded, and Burnham prevailed upon the unwilling trio to move to a larger room where there was space enough to hold the interested listeners. They moved into the main reading room, and, as soon as they were settled for business once more, Director Burnham rose.

"Gentlemen," he said, and paused, then went on, speaking clearly and slowly, "I move that we all resign and request the Council to name a new board of educated gentlemen." The *Minutes* do not record the reaction of the visitors, of course. But they indicate that Director Burnham's sarcasm was ignored. The visitors came to hear the communications, including the petition which many of them had signed. These were all read and incorporated in full in the *Minutes* in Henry Peterson's neat handwriting, every name precisely as signed. The first letter was from Mayor Martin, a full page, urging the Board to rescind its former action and reinstate Miss Peterson to the position she had filled efficiently and agreeably. The second letter, making the same request eloquently, came from members of the disbanded Oakland Library Association. Signers to this communication looked like a roster of the city's most important citizens: George W. Armes (father of William Dallam Armes); H. D. Bacon (Bacon Hall, University of California); Edson Adams; Judge John H. Boalt (Boalt Hall of Law); William C. Bartlett; W. W. Crane, Jr.; Governor Perkins; Anthony Chabot (Chabot Observatory); Hiram Tubbs; A. K. P. Harmon (Harmon Gymnasium); Fred Campbell, high school principal; W. B. Hardy, the book dealer; J. K. McLean and Galen Fisher, prominent clergymen, and many others. Following the reading of these impressive names, the Secretary read a petition of regular library users, signed by one hundred twenty-three persons who had known and been served by Ina Peterson. The three new Board members were not impressed; and, when Director Burnham offered a resolution to the effect that the previous action of the Board concerning Miss Peterson be rescinded and that she be reinstated, Trefethen objected, and Long moved that the meeting adjourn.[7]

It soon becomes apparent to a reader of the old *Minutes* that the new Board wanted to run the library, about which they knew nothing, in their own way. They appointed a friend of the trio, Columbus Brier, to take Kellogg's place, and they rewrote the *Rules and Regulations* in such a way that the library seemed to exist for the benefit of the Board. It took them all summer to award the binding contract, a matter of routine business usually handled at the meeting at which the bids were opened. They initiated embarrassing and absurd economies, such as discontinuing gas illumination and putting kerosene lamps into use in the central library. They cut the newspaper subscription lists and wrote begging letters to publishers all over the country requesting that the Oakland Free Library be put on their free mailing lists. They ignored Fred Campbell's request that the library subscribe to Bancroft's new *History of California*, just announced. They were pleased to say that they had cut expenses everywhere, including the amount spent for books. Instead of allowing two thousand dollars a year for books, the Board was glad to get the amount down below five hundred dollars. And what happened to that hastily written *Annual Report?* Somehow it got lost on its way to the City Treasurer. None of the trio could find it. The Board even stooped to book censorship, when, near the end of their term, they ordered the novels of Emile Zola and DeFoe's *Moll Flanders* removed from the library shelves.[8]

To Colonel Irish, in the *Times*, the Board's behavior was shabby. "Instead of an intelligent, liberal and wise administration of the trust," he wrote, "we see the welfare and prosperity of the library imperiled by petty self-seeking and the despicable political methods of the small ward politician. The dignified expression of the opinions of the founders of the library, and of all competent to judge of its affairs, is treated with contempt by a set of men who consider the office of librarian of no more account and requiring no greater attainments than that of a janitor."[9] If Trefethen's "self-seeking" included the thought of securing Miss Coolbrith's position for his sister, no such daring notion came out in an open Board meeting. There was gossip, however, of such an intention. And it was obvious that he was trying to goad Miss Coolbrith into resigning.[10]

A New Catalog

The goad was a catalog. Trefethen was Chairman of the Book Committee and regarded the catalog as that committee's responsibility. He proposed that the new edition pay for itself by the use of interleaved advertisements. Director Brier felt that that should be considered very carefully. To be sure, a revised edition was needed. No one was more aware of this than Miss Coolbrith, who had compiled the 1879 catalog.[11] The Committee had its own ideas and in November decided that

170

the Oakland library should adopt immediately the classification scheme in use in the San Francisco Public Library which had opened four years before. Miss Coolbrith was "instructed" to visit the San Francisco library, investigate the system, and give her recommendations to the Board at its December meeting.

Miss Coolbrith, accordingly, called on F. B. Perkins, San Francisco City Librarian, and reported by letter to the Board at its December 4 meeting. She wrote:

> . . . Our library is so small, as you are aware, that to attempt to follow literally the Catalogue or classification of much larger Libraries, would be not only absurd but impractical, & yet, in order to number & place the Books as you desire, some such system must be followed as closely as possible.

She went on to describe in brief the classification used in the San Francisco Public Library, and closed with,

> I do not know if I make my meaning clear to you, but if not, I can do no better than to refer you to Mr. F. B. Perkins of the San Fran— Public Library, "Rational Classification of Literature for Shelving and Cataloguing Books," which I propose following unless the Board otherwise decides & instructs, as nearly as possible.
> With this is a copy of the work alluded to.
> Respectfully submitted
I. D. Coolbrith[12]

It will be remembered that library service techniques were new in the country. Melvil Dewey's decimal classification was still in its first edition of 1876, a booklet of forty-two pages. Up to this year, 1884, when Dewey organized the first school of library economy in the country, there had been no formal education in this field.[13] There were no professional catalogers for small libraries as we know them today. Each librarian classified, in his own way, the books in his charge. Young Joseph Rowell was working out his own classification for the library of the University of California in Berkeley, and his scheme was in use for many years; even today some sections of the collection remain under the system he devised. Librarian Perkins was doing likewise for the new public library in San Francisco; and Ina Coolbrith, who had compiled one catalog, was ready to reclassify and prepare another for publication. The card catalog, taken for granted today, was little known; typewriters were not in general use. It was a progressive library that had a printed catalog instead of having to depend wholly on that in the librarian's head.

On 8 January 1884, Miss Coolbrith received her instructions to begin work on the new catalog. She agreed to begin at once if some additional assistance were given her. She insisted that she could not perform her regular and imperative duties and at the same time reclassify the collection and prepare a catalog for the printer. She was promised help. In March, though no additional help had been provided, Secretary Long came storming into the Board meeting, insisting that practically nothing had been done toward the new catalog.[14] The usual reporters were present, and the publicity that followed humiliated and angered Miss Coolbrith. She discussed the matter by letter with Librarian Perkins of San Francisco, mentioning, probably, that the drawer of the very table at which Mr. Long sat when he made his accusation was full of her work which she had done in addition to her regular duties. Perkins commented, "About classifying and cataloguing the books while the library is used in the ordinary way, I may say this: I should not myself undertake the work, except on the condition of being entirely relieved from all other library work, during the time used in such cataloguing: and rather than undertake both, I should leave."[15]

The San Francisco librarian went further. He wrote to the Oakland Library Board saying that the cataloguing of their collection would take about a year. This letter was read and placed on file, as was also a long, explicit and indignant, yet tactful letter from Miss Coolbrith. She went into the background of the subject fully, then added:

As for my competency for the task assigned me, I can best reply, perhaps, by again quoting from Librarian Perkins—"The catalogue without errors has yet to be made"—and the one upon which I am engaged will doubtless contain its full share, but, while I have never presumed to any superior degree of excellence in my capacity as librarian, feeling myself, on the contrary, only a very beginner in a profession which finds me every day at fault and with something to learn, I can yet say with truth, that during my (nearly) ten years service in this library, during which period there have been numbered among its trustees, some of the clearest minds of the state . . . it is the first time, within my knowledge, that my competency to perform my work has been called in question.

. . . I have never sought to defy or disregard the orders or instructions of the board, nor do I offer this statement in any spirit of disrespect or defiance to any member thereof, but simply and solely in exercise of the right inherent to every human being, that of self-defense.[16]

172

Each month the Book Committee reported progress on the catalog, which Miss Coolbrith said, in June, might be completed by 1 November 1884. President Walker prepared the *Annual Report* which showed that there had been little money for books, and that the total book holdings had actually gone down, since the year's acquisition had not surpassed discards.[17]

Annoyances and interruptions plagued Miss Coolbrith, working toward an impossible deadline. Not the least of these was that the Fire Department built a bell tower next to the rear wall of the already shaky library. Whenever there was a fire, the quiet of the library would be shattered by the pealing of the great bell, and the building itself would creak and rattle.[18] Then, in August, for the first time in the history of this Board, the librarian was delegated one of her former responsibilities. She was requested to make up a purchase order of five hundred dollars' worth of books for circulation, the list to be ready by the September meeting. At the same time Director Brier was empowered to select three hundred dollars' worth of reference books.[19] Brier, who had always been friendly and reasonable in his dealings with Miss Coolbrith, undoubtedly turned to her for assistance in compiling his purchase list, knowing full well that the work on the catalog was to be completed by November.[20] Miss Coolbrith counted the months she would have to work under this Board. Four to the end of the year, and three after that. Would her health and her patience endure? She made a shrewd decision.

In September she requested a six months' leave of absence without pay. This was granted almost eagerly at a special Board meeting. Her leave would extend from 1 October 1884, to 1 April 1885. In the meantime the two assistant librarians, who were now receiving equal pay of fifty-five dollars a month would be paid seventy-five dollars a month during the Librarian's leave. Trefethen was thus able to increase his sister's pay without any objection. Miss Coolbrith reported that the catalog was nearly half completed and could be resumed when she returned.[21]

The trio was gleeful. Almost immediately after the librarian's departure, they advertised for a cataloger, and, after considering several applications, gave the work to one Charles Miel. He agreed to catalog the collection for four cents a volume in addition to supplies. He would start after the November elections (for reasons, he said, known to the Board) and expected to be through by 15 January, by devoting his full time to it. Both Peterson and Mrs. Plummer helped him. But, instead of the promised two months for completion, five months in all were required. On 7 April 1885, the Miel catalog was complete, with

173

author and subject cards, and a manuscript ready for the printer. A total of 12,181 works were classified and cataloged. Miel reported that he had had to go over the work done by Miss Coolbrith as it did not fit his system. He regretted that he had not used the Perkins scheme, which she had followed. Why not? That plan had been expressly ordered by the Board. If this little catalog, promptly printed and bound by the *Oakland Tribune* in a volume of two hundred-eight pages, was a monument to Walker, Long, and Trefethen, it was the only positive accomplishment of a singularly negative regime. They could always point with pride to this product of their frantic endeavor, the Miel *Catalogue*.[22]

17
A Leave
of
Absence

O my Earth, to know thee fully! I who love
thee, singly, wholly!

Ina Coolbrith, from
"From Living Waters" (1876)

A New Home in Oakland

The decision to request a leave of absence was not a hasty one in Miss Coolbrith's mind, though it may have seemed so to the Board of Library Directors. The idea may have occurred to her the previous December, when she wrote a poem in celebration of the one hundredth birthday of a cousin of her grandfather Coolbrith.[1] The aged relative was Jacob Milliken, son of Lemuel. Lemuel's sister, Rebecca, married George Coolbroth (as he spelled the name). Their son, Joseph, was Ina's grandfather. Ina's poem, from distant California, was happily received. It was published in a Portland, Maine, newspaper with a flattering comment.[2] Ina was urged to visit her mother's people in Scarborough. The idea grew in her mind. If she were to see her centenarian cousin, she could not put off the visit.

There was little time to think of such pleasures. Exasperating events in the library had kept her in turmoil. There had been, also, new decisions to make at home. Her niece was suddenly unemployed and was eager to take a new position. There were few library openings; so she considered secretarial work of some kind. The typewriter was coming into general use in business offices, and Ina Peterson, with her limited clerical experience, could see that skill in the operation of such a machine offered a solution for the immediate future. She enrolled in a business school and was soon employed as a typist in a San Francisco

175

office. She later opened her own office as a public stenographer, one of the first women to do so.[3]

Commuting to her new job in the city, the younger Ina still lived at home with her aunt and brother. But home was no longer the cottage on Fifteenth Street. Her aunt had recently purchased a larger house at 1261 Webster Street, between Fifteenth and Sixteenth.[4] It was a tall, two-storied, frame building, unpretentious but inviting, built in an L-shape, with a front porch inside the L. The east gable end, fronting the street, was graced with a lower floor bay window, topped with a wooden railing that served as a balcony for the double windows above. All windows, with double-hung sash, were in pairs, with shallow arched tops on each, and a half-circle arch above the pair. The house, with white painted exterior, was thus pleasing and restrained in ornament. It had none of the gingerbread characteristic of the period. Surrounding the yard was a neat picket fence, and across the sidewalk from the gate was an iron hitching post. In the garden, which lay along the south and west sides of the house, were palms, cedars, and a few deciduous trees, casually grouped. Dominating the rear yard was one of Oakland's great evergreen oaks. It was a simple home, but it had dignity and graciousness.[5]

The interior was spacious, with airy, high-ceilinged rooms. Here was privacy for each of the four adults with their varying tastes. Henry was now, in 1884, twenty-four years of age, and his sister would be twenty-one in December. Calle Shasta Miller was still a member of the household, having remained longer than the seven years most commentators gave her. At this time Mrs. Charlotte Perkins Stetson (later Mrs. Gilman) lived with her little daughter across Webster Street from Miss Coolbrith. Mrs. Stetson was a writer, a sociologist with outspoken views on the position of women in a male-dominated society, and was also a talented poet. As a guest in Miss Coolbrith's home she met other writers who were friends of her hostess. One of these was Joaquin Miller, whose daughter, Mrs. Stetson observed, was a maid in the house.[6]

Calle Shasta. Miss Coolbrith referred to her as "poor Indian Callie." She was a young woman at this time, about twenty-six. As a girl she was beautiful, according to several accounts, and had charmed a young Wells Fargo agent in San Francisco. The couple were married, but Callie became an alcoholic, and the marriage did not last. It is said that she reviled her father, who, she said, had given her his blood and

his name, and nothing else. According to some accounts she spent her last years at the Hights, her father's home, where she died about 1903 and where she was buried. Her mother, Amanda Brock, outlived her, dying at the age of seventy-five on the McCloud Indian Reservation in 1909. Though Miller acknowledged the girl as his daughter, he denied in public that Amanda Brock had ever been his wife. This was true, indeed, legally. But under the name of Sutatot she had been Miller's common-law wife when he lived among the Modocs as a young man. There Calle Shasta was born about 1858, her father being about twenty-one at the time and Sutatot a few years older.[7]

To return to 1884, one Sunday afternoon callers were present in Miss Coolbrith's drawing room. One of them was a small boy, uncomfortable in his ruffled white blouse, bored and fidgety. Miss Coolbrith suggested that he go out to the yard to play. His mother reminded him to be careful of his clothes, then resumed her conversation with her hostess. When the woman prepared to leave, she could not find the lad. Young Ina and Calle Shasta joined in the search. Finally the boy was discovered under the house. He refused to budge. His mother coaxed and bribed and threatened.

"I'll get him out," offered Calle Shasta. She went into the kitchen and came out with a carving knife. Everybody gasped.

"What do you mean?" screamed the mother. Calle Shasta smiled, and started to crawl under the house.

"You'd better come, or I'll cut your heart out," she called, and, putting the knife in her teeth, she neared the terrified boy. He saw the dark face and the glittering knife, and he was out before she could move another inch. Callie laughed, the two Inas suppressed their own amusement, but an indignant mother led away a trembling little boy in a very dusty Sunday blouse. He was probably to boast ever after about his narrow escape from scalping, or worse, by an Indian.[8]

Ina Peterson, secretly ambitious to be a writer, was interested in all the famous people who came to see her aunt. She longed to know them, too. Yet she was never included. Her aunt, unaccountably, seldom presented her to her guests. The niece, though hurt, was doubly careful not to intrude. But her ambiguous position was as embarrassing as it was wounding. It is hard to understand why the aunt, poised and sure of herself, should have been so thoughtless. Miss Coolbrith, preoccupied with private worries and frustrated because she found no time to write, was not aware of some of the problems of the sensitive, intelligent girl in her care. Young Ina bore a striking resemblance in features and in general expression to her lovely aunt. She might have been taken for a younger sister or a daughter. When, at fourteen, she had finished the

178

eighth grade at school, she took over most of the cooking and house-work. She even learned to make her own clothes and struggled by her-self with the intricate dress designs of the seventies and eighties. Self-conscious in her homemade clothing and aware of the limitations of her education, she was lonely and unhappy as a girl. But she decided to make the library her school. She began by reading all the novels, then went on to the classics, poetry, history, geography, and general literature. If there were gaps in her education, the condition was never apparent to those who knew her. She was sixteen when she was ap-pointed as an assistant in the library, and when she was suddenly dis-charged four years later, to make way for a Board member's sister, her knowledge of books and her able assistance to readers were asserted by her aunt, by the city's mayor, and by many loyal townspeople. The younger Ina was experimenting in verse writing at that time. In later years her lyrics, published in magazines, were to receive the praise of Bierce, Stoddard, and others. But, reserved and respectful of her aunt's distinction, she allowed herself to be overshadowed, was loyal, and loved her aunt dearly. It evidently did not occur to her to resent her aunt's interest in the work of other young writers, Mary Austin, for one.[9]

Journey to New England

Ina Coolbrith, in the meantime, was writing very little. Those were barren years for her. She had poems in her desk, among them "The Poet" and "Retrospect," which she might have sent to publishers, but she hesitated for personal reasons.[10] She composed two pieces dur-ing 1884, both for occasions. One was a tribute to Longfellow, which she read at a meeting of the Longfellow Memorial Society in the as-sembly room of North Hall at the University of California. It was pub-lished in the *Overland Monthly* for April.[11] The other, unpublished, was written in memory of W. W. Crane, Jr., who died that year.[12] Perhaps the muse would return when the poet was relieved of routine duties and would have a change of scene.

Miss Coolbrith added to her period of leave a few days of annual vacation, to which she was entitled, and left a week before 1 October. At the Sixteenth Street station she boarded an eastbound train on 23 September.[13] We do not know her itinerary or her schedule. Letters of this period did not find their way into the collections consulted. We do not know if this was the year she visited the Grand Canyon. But it probably was, since her poem on the Canyon was published before her next journey across the country. Unless she went on a special excursion, a few years later, she thus saw those "turrets and battlements" in the

179

fall of 1884. And, not content with the view from the South Rim, she took the zigzag trail, by mule-back to the river at the bottom of the chasm. Stirred by the forces that produced this phenomenon and filled with awe as she gazed up the sheer, silent walls, she must have labored for words to convey some of this force and some of her own emotions. The spectacle defied her as it has all poets and painters. No one can express it all. Each must stand where he is, humble and speechless, or try to convey what it is. She chose to represent what she felt at the river's edge, looking skyward. Not until eight years later did her lines "In the Grand Cañon" take form in type, and when the lyric appeared in *Lippincott's,* people said of her, "silent no longer."[14]

She did not have time to linger at the Canyon. She had an appointment to keep in Maine. She may have planned her journey in time to see the brilliant foliage of a New England autumn. We do know that she reached Scarborough, her mother's birthplace, early in October. She went at once to the old Coolbrith homestead, on Black Point Bay, south of Dunstan River and near the southern boundary of the present town of Scarborough.[15] The old house had been occupied by Rebecca Milliken (daughter of Squire Edward Milliken) and her husband George Coolbroth, Ina's great-grandparents. Here she found her centenarian cousin, living in his aunt's old farmhouse. The old man was a veteran of the War of 1812, and he still boasted of having voted for Thomas Jefferson for the second term.[16] Ina's visit was not too soon, for on 13 October, the old man passed away, aged one hundred years, nine months and nine days.[17] The poet must have lingered here for the funeral and for a prolonged getting acquainted with her mother's people, in particular, her mother's younger brother, Joseph Coolbrith, sixty-two that month.[18]

She spent much of October in Maine, going from Saco to Boston, Massachusetts, where she registered at the United States Hotel.[19] She visited John Greenleaf Whittier late in the month. At that time he shared the home of his cousins, the three daughters of Edmund Johnson in Danvers. As Miss Coolbrith waited in the drawing room for the Quaker poet to come in, she was tempted to run away, for she was filled with awe at the prospect of meeting the great man with whom she had carried on a correspondence ever since she had first called to his attention that she was the "Unknown" to whom he had credited her lyric "When the Grass Shall Cover Me." She found him a gentle, fatherly man who charmed her with his plain speech and his glowing eyes. She was to say later that no man she knew, except Edwin Booth, had finer, more expressive eyes. He told her that he knew her long poem, "California," by heart. He urged her to remain in Danvers and make

180

her home with him and his relatives. She demurred, still thinking of her obligation to her sister's son and daughter, but forgetting that the young people were capable of supporting themselves. If she had taken Whittier's advice, what course would her life have followed? One of the minor "ifs" of history, this would be pleasant but idle to contemplate. Whittier bade her goodbye at the end of the day with his blessing and a kiss. She later often spoke of her visit with the Quaker poet, continued to correspond with him until his death eight years later, and gave several Whittier programs in California.[20]

Other red-letter days during this long holiday were those on which she met Oliver Wendell Holmes and Edmund Clarence Stedman.[21] From the meeting with the latter grew a warm association that lasted as long as he lived. His letters were among her most carefully kept possessions and were in the handful that escaped the San Francisco fire of 1906. His language was flowery but sincere when he addressed her as "Sweet Singer," and "Hesperia," and "Sappho of the Western Sea." He later included several of her lyrics in his American Anthology.[22] She dedicated her Songs from the Golden Gate to him in 1895.[23] On her way west in the spring she may have stopped to see her old friends, the Sills, in Cuyahoga Falls, Ohio. If so, they introduced her to their friends among writers and teachers in the Cleveland area. One newspaper woman who met her there, must have been overwhelmed, for she described Miss Coolbrith in a feature article as a tall woman, "with hair, eyebrows and eyes as black as coal."[24]

Miss Coolbrith's holiday was not all play. She received regular reports from her nephew Henry Peterson relating to library matters in Oakland. She said she read some of these reports as she was sitting at the base of Bunker Hill Monument in Boston, and they made her blue. She told him she had seen Dr. William Poole of Chicago and that he was shocked at the small size of Oakland's staff and the long hours required of each employee. She dreaded going back to her position, but knew that it would be necessary for a while at least. Nevertheless she was considering a change. She was spending as much time as possible visiting Eastern libraries, and wrote that "the more acquaintance in the library world . . . the better it will be for me." She had investigated employment possibilities in Maine, but found the climate not worth the low pay. Boston and New York, though no better weatherwise, were full of interest for her. She prowled around the old bookshops of Boston even if they made her purse "ache with emptiness."[25] Nothing came of her hopes for a change of library employment. But she continued to observe library building plans and arrangements, new shelving facilities, catalogs. She even took time to learn the craft of book repair so she could instruct a helper in this practical branch of library economy when she returned to her own position.[26] Some Oakland people were afraid that she might not come back. Press notices about her in the *Boston Transcript* and in the New York papers were copied by Oakland dailies whose editors expressed an uneasiness that Oakland might lose its librarian as well as one of its leading women writers.[27] Refreshed in mind and body and spirit, though homesick, and tired of travel, she took her train for the West. At home she would face a new library board. Who would the members be? What surprise might await her in April 1885?

18
The Library in the Eighties

Dear Ina Coolbrith: Do you remember the small boy,
in short knee pants, to whom you gave the keys to the gates
of knowledge in the old days at the Oakland Library?
Affectionately thine,
Jack London, 1911.
(In Ina Coolbrith's autograph album)

Library Problems and Pleasures

The surprise was an agreeable one. After climbing the library stairs and going to her desk back of the familiar railing, Miss Coolbrith soon learned that the "ring" was no longer in control. Indeed the people had elected two experienced trustees who had been charter members of the old Library Association, men who had been on the Board when Miss Coolbrith was first appointed back in 1874. These were former Board President Charles W. Kellogg and J. B. McChesney. Of the other three, one was Judge John H. Boalt, whose wife, Elizabeth, had become her personal friend.[1] The others were R. H. Graham and Dr. S. H. Melvin. When the new Board met to organize on 10 April 1885, just three days after the final meeting of the outgoing officers, their first piece of new business was the acceptance of the voluntary resignation of Mrs. Plummer, who no doubt felt uneasy without her brother's support. Miss L. L. Marsh was appointed in her place.[2] In the next few months Librarian and Board took stock of their situation. Miss Coolbrith found that the files of *Atlantic Monthly, North American Review, Eclectic Magazine,* and *St. Nicholas,* for the last two years, being held for binding, had been sold in her absence.[3] The building needed attention at once, for it was beginning to be unsafe. A new brick foundation was put in at a cost of three-hundred-fifteen dollars, and the ever troublesome skylight was repaired. The building was closed for two weeks in June to permit cleaning and renovating where needed.[4]

183

With the coming of the new fiscal year in July the library faced a period of real austerity, for the City Council had cut the appropriation in half. The previous year's budget had been adequate, over eleven thousand dollars. For the year 1885-86 only five thousand eight-hundred-fifty dollars were granted.[5] The institution was able to keep open and to apologize for the lack of new books. Only one hundred thirty-nine volumes were added that year, but the staff repaired four thousand and sent some to the bindery. It was a year of penny-pinching. The librarian was authorized to use the money collected from fines to buy the works of local authors.[6] Judge Boalt was a member of the Book Committee, and probably received from her more than one imploring letter to resolve a book crisis, a title at a time.

One such crisis could be met by the purchase of the *Annual Statistician* for 1885-6, for example. "Every day," said Miss Coolbrith to Judge Boalt, "there are calls for certain information most readily and in some cases *only* to be found in its pages. The agent has been here about it until his and my combined patience is exhausted!—gone!!—no more!!!!— and now he tells me he leaves for the Arctic zone on Friday, & if he doesn't hear from me by Special tomorrow we can't get the book for several months. What am I to do? Pay for it out of the fines? It is $4.00." She probably got the book, for her request was sent by messenger who was instructed to bring back a yes or no in answer.[7] Not all her problems were fiscal, however. She felt free to relieve her feelings in little notes to the Judge when she needed sympathy in irritating situations. In September 1886 she was bothered by too many temperance books being forced on the library.

"If it would do any good," she wrote the Judge, "if it would reach and help the all-to-be-pitied-victims of drink, I should say fill the shelves with these books. But it doesn't. It is such a namby-pamby, boshy, imbecile, Sunday-School method of doing nothing."[8]

The latter half of the decade was a period of inconspicuous progress. Judge Boalt served only one term of two years, but his prestige and his awareness of the library's actual needs helped convince the Council that an adequate budget must be provided. The Judge's legal experience was an asset when the Board was asked to draft the library section of the new charter under consideration.[9] During this five-year period one new reading room was opened. This was the North Oakland at Thirty-fourth and Peralta Streets, and a set of encyclopedias was provided for it. Still none of the reading rooms circulated books. Their chief function was to provide newspapers and magazines, but a few reference books were on hand: a dictionary, a city directory, an atlas, and an encyclopedia. The curator was actually the custodian, as janitorial work was part of his duties. There was no attempt to give informational service. North Oakland was the third such reading room to be opened.[10]

Binding contracts were let to the lowest bidder, usually the Tribune Publishing Company in Oakland. Books were purchased from the local dealer giving the best discount; either Hardy in Oakland or Bancroft in San Francisco. Book selection by this time was recognized as the regular responsibility of the librarian, with nominal review and approval by the Book Committee of the Board.[11] The few books purchased for the reading rooms were chosen and ordered by the Reading Room Committee, still quite separate from selection for the library proper. Miss Coolbrith was particular to maintain bound files of periodicals and local newspapers, going back to procure early or missing numbers when necessary. She was also zealous in acquiring the current works of local authors, and it is owing in part to her care and knowledge that the present California Room in the Oakland Free Library has a good collection of the works of earlier authors of the state, often minor, but important in the local scene. Shy Mary Bamford, the daughter of Robert Louis Stevenson's physician, and Alice Cooley, once an actress with Edwin Booth and Charles Kean, were local authors whose books she sought at this time. She was scrupulous in maintaining high standards for the fiction collection, and when she reminded the Board that the "ring" had removed Zola's novels from the shelves, the books were replaced.[12]

It was about this time that Miss Coolbrith came to know the little boy whose name would one day head the list of local authors. He came in from the street, a newsboy of nine or ten, his papers under his arm. Jack London's discovery of the Oakland Library was the "second wonderful thing that had happened to him," he said later.[13] That day he was excited, eager, hungry for books, but too young for a library card. He got all his family to register, and, with cards enough, he was soon caught by the library habit. As a child Jack was in awe of Miss Coolbrith and was proud of her praise of his choice of books. "Noble," he thought, was the word that suited this grand lady.[14] Long after Ina Coolbrith had left her position in Oakland, Jack London kept on coming to the little library next door to the city hall. One of the staff members in the late nineties, young Mrs. Carrie Louderback, used to say that he was always a welcome sight as he came up the stairs, his arms full of books to be exchanged for a fresh supply. His effect on the circulation statistics was invigorating, for by that time he was driving up to the library in an express wagon to handle his cargo.[15]

185

During the late eighties, when Jack London was satisfying an early adolescent hunger for knowledge from books and life, another child, two years his junior, came dancing into the library almost daily, alone, or with members of her family, to take home volumes of Shakespeare, Dickens, and Thackeray as well as works of many another writer. This was slender, blithe little Dora Duncan, the child who was to become the great classical dancer, Isadora. She hated school-room routine, but loved the tottering library and all the wealth it contained. Sometimes she came with her father, Joseph Charles Duncan, who, though divorced from Dora's mother, occasionally came from Los Angeles to visit his little dancing daughter. Her father, who had made and lost several fortunes, as a publisher, as an art dealer, and as a banker, was again at a peak of prosperity. At this time he bought the family a large new home which was lost, of course, with the next downward sweep of Duncan's fortunes.[16] Dora discovered that her father was a poet and that one of his special interests was the art of ancient Greece. This may have influenced her own career as much as did her mother's love of music and of Shakespeare. She was delighted to learn that her father and the librarian were old friends. They could have shown the child a book that contained poems by both of them, published before the child was born. If Dora had turned through the pages of Bret Harte's little anthology, Outcroppings, to find her father's lyric, "The Intaglio," near the end, her joy of the moment would have been heightened and her appreciation of her father deepened. The poem is suffused with the light of sunset on the Parthenon.[17] Then and there, in the library, Miss Coolbrith and Joseph Duncan might have shown pictures of the Acropolis to the eager little girl, who would one day dance among the splendid columns of Athena's temple.

The three adults most important to Isadora Duncan in those years, mother, father, and librarian, were individually aware of the child's need for beauty, and each helped supply it. About Miss Coolbrith Isadora was later to say, "Afterwards I learnt that at one time my father had been very much in love with her. She was evidently the great passion of his life and it was probably by the invisible thread of circumstance that I was drawn to her."[18] Ina Coolbrith never forgot Joseph Duncan. As late as 1927 she spoke of him (in a conversation with Samuel Dickson) as a poet, musician, and connoisseur of art. She said that he was a gentle person, a dreamer, an idealist, and that he lived on in his children, especially Isadora. Her look and tone, even then, implied that there had been a romantic interest long before.[19]

The librarian's nephew, Henry Peterson, was still, in the late eighties, her first assistant, and one of his most important duties was to attend

Board meetings where he served as assistant to the Secretary of the Board. He was paid a small salary for this task, fifteen dollars added to his regular monthly pay of sixty dollars. He was later given the title of Assistant Secretary and served in that capacity for several years. He was faithful, meticulous, and well liked by succeeding boards, who found it easy and natural to consult with him about library matters, and to delegate some of the work relating to book orders and contracts, instead of doing so through the librarian. There was no friction on this account, for Henry handled such assignments well and tactfully. Toward the end of the decade the need for a new catalog was becoming acute. A supplement to the Miel list was prepared and it served adequately for a while. In the fall of 1889 work on a new catalog was begun with the appointment of two new assistants, Miss Lillie Cole and Miss Elizabeth Welton, to be paid salaries of forty dollars a month each. Their title was Assistant Cataloguer. Henry directed their work, and was authorized by the Board to purchase a catalog case, not to exceed five dollars in cost.[20]

The little building, with its increasing functions and staff, required constant attention. It was closed for two or more weeks every June for cleaning and repairs. This annual chore was like the good old spring and fall housecleaning. In the old library, where the carpeted floors were without benefit of vacuum cleaners, the problem of dust on books and furniture was serious. Covering all bookcases with cloth during the daily sweeping was considered, but given up as impractical. In 1888 the library exterior was given two coats of white paint, at a cost of one hundred ten dollars, so that it would not appear too shabby beside a newly repainted city hall. That year extra attention was paid to brightening the interior with new carpets, shelving, and lamps. By that time gaslights were used at the ends of alcoves, and a single arc light was suspended in the library and another one in the reading room downstairs. But kerosene lamps still lighted the tables used by students and general readers. The eighties were coming to a close. What changes would the new decade bring to the Oakland Free Library? Was there any hint of the depression to come?[21]

Tree-Planting Ceremony on Yerba Buena Island

While library hours were long and Miss Coolbrith was weary at the end of a day's work, her prestige as poet and librarian demanded her presence if not her participation in a variety of local affairs. She was a regular member of few clubs, however, for she had little free time, though she had been made an honorary member of a dozen organizations.[22] She was one of a numerous company active in observing

187

California's first Arbor Day on 26 November 1886. This was Joaquin Miller's famous tree-planting expedition to barren Yerba Buena Island in San Francisco Bay, midway between San Francisco and Oakland. Miller, always a planter of trees, conceived the idea in August and could not rest until the project was accomplished. With the permission of the United States Navy, financial assistance from James D. Fair and George Hearst, and a supply of seedlings from Adolph Sutro, he was ready to go to work. He had obtained school support, and school children from both sides of the Bay were given a holiday to help plant a forest. A program was planned, with Colonel John P. Irish, then editor of the *Alta Californian,* as the principal speaker. Old General Mariano Guadalupe Vallejo was also expected to speak.

The day was warm and sunny, and the sky unusually blue above the dry yellow grass on the steep island. Persons on the program, officials and special guests, came in a government boat, and the school children with their parents and teachers made the voyage in two crowded river steamers and two tugs. Between three and four thousand youngsters landed and started climbing the steep goat trails to the top, where the trees were to be planted in a huge Greek cross, extending down the slopes. General Vallejo could not make the climb; after all he was near his eightieth year. He handed his written speech to Fred Campbell who promised to read it for him. The program went on as planned, with Miller as master of ceremonies; then, just as Fred Campbell finished reading the General's speech, the old man appeared, riding a white horse led by Miller's friend, Harr Wagner. This may have been the last public appearance of California's most illustrious Mexican American. It seems singularly fitting, if so, for Vallejo's appearance to have been such a dramatic one at that place and time, though a little too suggestive, now, of a Hollywood finale in technicolor.

Adolph Sutro planted the first seedling, followed by Doña Conchita Ramirez, daughter of a man who had once pastured his goats on the island. Joaquin Miller recited a poem as he planted the third tree; then he handed the trowel to his daughter Calle Shasta to place the next seedling in the soil. Ina Coolbrith planted the fifth and General Vallejo the sixth of the tiny trees, before the children began their work in orderly fashion down the slopes. It was hot, dusty work, and everyone was tired, hungry and thirsty. Those who had brought picnic lunches were fortunate, but many had not thought to do so. They were not prepared to spend the day with hundreds of others on a desert island. When Miss Coolbrith was heard to remark that she was glad she had worn a cotton print dress, a spectator whispered to her neighbor, "She must be from New England; she calls 'calico,' 'print.'" One can imagine how irritating must have been the dry foxtails picked up in the hems of the full, trailing skirts worn by the ladies.[23]

The growth of the trees was watched with pleasure by ferryboat passengers as they glided past the island in years to come. But one day a fire ravished the young forest, partially destroying it. The work of three thousand children, however, was not lost for Yerba Buena Island was promptly replanted. Today the cameraman who photographs the great suspension bridge from the island to the city may find his picture softened by the intrusion of trailing eucalyptus branches. Joaquin Miller went on planting trees. The bare grounds of the Presidio in San Francisco inspired his next self-imposed task. Near the end of the year he bought eighty acres in the Contra Costa hills, planted a forest, and named the place *The Hights*, a spelling he insisted upon using.[24]

Ina Coolbrith in Print

In the latter half of the 1880s Ina Coolbrith wrote little verse, and most of it was written for an occasion or a person. Only about ten new pieces were published during the five-year period. The library's gain was a loss to those who watched for creations from her pen. "A pity," wrote Mabel Thomas, reference librarian in Oakland years later:

A pity to cage a bird with so rare a note, a bird who could sing only in the free air! In another way than she had planned and hoped, in a way whose greatness, she herself doubtless never recognized, the eighteen years given to service in the Oakland library were not 'fruitionless.' The beauty and the strength, which, had it been otherwise, might have been wrought into poetry, were not without some lasting impression on human lives.[25]

During this period she received praise from good sources for both the new and her earlier lyrics. Whittier was enthusiastic about her lines in memory of Helen Hunt Jackson, who died in August 1885, and Bierce wrote glowingly once more about his favorite of her sonnets, "Beside the Dead," after seeing it in Thomas Wentworth Higginson's anthology, *American Sonnets*.[26] Two small booklets of floral paintings, interleaved with a few of her nature poems, were published by artists for the holiday trade in 1886.[27] At the end of the decade Edmund Clarence Stedman, preparing his excellent *American Anthology*, wrote to "My dear Hesperia" about her lyrics which he intended to include.[28] At the same time Charles Warren Stoddard wrote a long article on Ina Coolbrith and her salon in San Francisco, creating a pleasant and often quoted word picture. His biographical tribute was followed by the quotation of twelve of her lyrics. This article appeared in the imposing *Magazine of Poetry*, new in 1889.[29] Miss Coolbrith's poem, written for the 1886 Christmas Jinks of the Bohemian Club, remembered the old days in San Francisco; "The Colonel's Toast," it was called. It recalled to her fellow Bohemians the favorite toast of one of their number, then five years dead, Colonel John C. Cremony, who used to raise his glass with the words, "May the Lord love us and not call for us too soon!" As a souvenir of the occasion Ina Coolbrith's sixteen lines were printed in an attractive folder with hand-lettered cover and text, a charming period piece, printed by Edward Bosqui.[30]

Other occasions she attended during this part of her life called forth poems. One was a "Welcome to the Grand Army," read by Alice Kingsbury Cooley, another "The Light in the Cottage at Stratford-on-Avon," read by Fred M. Campbell at an Athenian Club Social affair, and still another, her tribute to Julia Ward Howe, read by Mrs. S. W. Horton at the Ebell Club reception for Mrs. Howe.[31] The *Overland Monthly* had published Ina Coolbrith's memorial poem to Helen Hunt Jackson in September 1885, and during the rest of the decade the same periodical printed several more of her lyrics; her "Lines on Hearing Kelley's Music of 'Macbeth'" (inspired while listening to the composer playing this music on the piano in her home), "March (by the Pacific)," "A Birthday Rhyme," and her memorial lines, "Edward Rowland Sill," for the poet of her own age who died in February 1887.[32] *Century* published three lyrics during this period, "The Poet," "Retrospect," and "Frederick III of Germany."[33] As Ina saw the first two of these in print at last, she recalled the occasions of their creation. She had opened her window one spring night in 1880 and was transported by some flower scent to the Los Angeles of her childhood. In a rush of nostalgia she wrote a lyric of twenty lines, partly to keep her "from the burden of a longer one," she confided to John Carmany a few days later. "The Poet," too, recalled John, and her eyes softened as she remembered the October afternoon in 1877 when he wrote it down as she dictated it to him. She may have laughed to herself as she recalled their argument about the word "unclad," and how she changed it to "unveiled," and even later omitted the poem entirely from *A Perfect Day* to humor his sense of propriety. Unknown to her he treasured the verse as a souvenir of their afternoon together and gave it first place in his sheaf of her manuscript poems when he arranged them in a portfolio.[34]

19
Dawn
of the
Nineties

*I can but feel an abiding interest in an
institution that has claimed my care and labor
for so many years.*

Ina Coolbrith, from
Oakland Times (1892)

Improved Library Services

Oakland was growing. In 1890 its population was not far from fifty thousand.[1] But the small library building could only bulge as more books and services were added. One newspaper reported that the structure seemed to lean a little to the east.[2] The Board ordered great steel tie rods put in to prevent a catastrophe.[3] Some readers were afraid to come in. But the majority continued to come, for, in spite of reported lopsidedness, the library had suddenly become more attractive than ever.

Electric lights were installed in 1890.[4] While the new reading lights must have been far from standard light-metered illumination, their superiority to the old kerosene lamps was like the coming of a new age. No longer were the library alcoves "weird and grim," where "strange shadows hover, waveringly" and where the librarian moved "among the folios dim," as Miss Coolbrith wrote ten years before. The new lights were a blessing to students. And the staff carried out with enthusiasm the Board's order to dispose of all the old lamps, an enthusiasm that would be shared by anyone who had had to clean lamp chimneys.

The new lights alone were evidence of progress. But there was advancement along many lines in the early years of the new decade. The salary of the Assistant Secretary, Henry Peterson, was increased by twenty-five dollars, making his total pay amount to the same as that of the City Librarian, one hundred dollars a month.[5] For the first time a collection of new circulating books was purchased for one of the reading rooms, East Oakland.[6] This was the beginning of a branch library's functioning in Oakland. In July another reading room was opened, after the Board heard a petition from readers in the neighborhood of Twenty-third Avenue and East Fourteenth Street. The librarian ordered new circulating books for this reading room too, ready for the formal opening of the room on 8 July. The Board was invited to attend. Pleased, the members accepted and asked Peterson to "procure a suitable conveyance." This reading room was the beginning of the Twenty-third Avenue Branch Library, later housed in a Carnegie building.[7] On 22 December 1966, its name was changed to Ina D. Coolbrith Branch Library, appropriately named, since it did come into being during Miss Coolbrith's administration.[8]

Branch reading room, as a designation, was first used in the annual report of the Board for the fiscal year ending in June 1890. The report, an interesting and excellently written one, was prepared by the Assistant Secretary (Henry Peterson), and was included in the Board *Minutes* in full. It stated that the library had been open 280 days, and 1,258 borrowers used 70,102 volumes, or an average daily circulation of 251. The report indicated an awareness of the library as an educational institution, saying that its most important function was its reference work with students. The acute space problem and the need for a new building were stressed. Appended to the annual statement was a detailed description of the new library built and recently opened at Florence, Illinois. This was a large two-story structure built of granite at a cost of $12,000. Its style and floor plan seemed well suited to the needs of Oakland. The report stated, also, that the new catalog was not quite finished. The need for a permanent full-time cataloger was apparent to the Board as well as the librarian then; and Miss Coolbrith, asked to find and interview catalogers, had to report, as many a librarian has since, "all the cataloguers are employed by other libraries."[9]

About this time a new charging system went into use, one that was retained for many years.[10] This was the "Brown System," where each borrower was issued two library cards of his own, one of which could be used for fiction. Instead of a book-card, each volume had a pocket, held inside another pocket. When the book was borrowed, the reader's card was inserted into the loose pocket, which was removed, stamped, and filed under the date due. This created an extremely bulky circulation file. Its disadvantages for the reader were obvious, for he was limited to only two books at a time.[11] In 1890 two outstanding sets were purchased for the reference collection; John Muir's two magnificant folios, *Picturesque California,* with many plates and textual illustrations by California artists, the text by California authors; and the *Century Dictionary,* useful for many years to come. The library was now issuing a printed bulletin of recent accessions, monthly or quarterly, as the number of books received warranted. This publication was proposed and compiled by Henry Peterson.[12]

In December the Board received a letter from John Vance Cheney, then City Librarian of San Francisco, requesting the Oakland City Librarian and a Board member to come to a meeting to discuss plans for the reception and entertainment of the members of the American Library Association who would hold their annual convention in San Francisco in 1891.[13] So, on 20 December, Miss Coolbrith, Dr. Melvin, and Director Kellogg met with a group of librarians and trustees from San Francisco and Berkeley to make such plans and decide on committees.[14]

While 1890 seemed to be a year of progress in many ways for the library, it was marred in September by a personal quarrel between Henry Peterson and his aunt. The dispute might not have amounted to much if the incident had not leaked to one of the city papers. It was about cats, the fourteen cats that lived at 1267 Webster Street. Cats are newsworthy, especially in numbers. The *Tribune* account, copied and enlarged by the *Examiner,* the *Chronicle,* and the *Times,* said that the animals were everywhere; on the stairs, on the chairs; wherever Henry wanted to be, there sat a cat.[15] His aunt was especially fond of long-haired, white angoras, and she had owned some beautiful creatures through the years. Here, at 1267 Webster Street, had lived, had died, and was buried, the most beautiful and beloved of all Miss Coolbrith's cats, Calla, a gift of Mrs. Boalt in 1880, and so named by the judge, who admired the long, soft, white coat.[16] Calla's son was given the English translation of his mother's name, Beauty, and had her lovely characteristics.

Henry was a fastidious man. And dark wool fabric, whether navy blue serge, or black or gray broadcloth, is magnetic to white cat hairs. Henry, moreover, was courting Miss Elizabeth Welton, one of the assistant catalogers who had just completed her library assignment. His position at the library was one of considerable prestige, especially in her eyes, and undoubtedly in his own. His presence at work and at Board meetings required a well-groomed appearance. His exasperation with the ever present cat hairs wins our sympathy. Henry did not suggest that his aunt give up any of her pets. He simply moved out, taking his possessions to a lodging house on Nineteenth Street. He remained away from work for a few days, and Miss Coolbrith was alarmed when

193

she learned that he had given a letter of resignation to the Board. She talked to him, saying earnestly that neither she nor the Board could do without him. At her suggestion Dr. Melvin returned the letter to Henry and said nothing to the rest of the members of the Board about the matter. Henry resumed his duties and agreed with his aunt that their private quarrel should not affect their relations in public. The matter was settled and was soon forgotten by Henry. Early in December 1890 he and Elizabeth Welton were married and went to live in the cottage on Fifteenth Street where he had lived as a teen-ager with his aunt and sister.[17]

American Library Association Convention, 1891

Henry's new status as a married man was recognized by the Board in a pay raise. This amounted to twenty dollars a month, and the same amount was added to Miss Coolbrith's pay. Each therefore still received the same salary, one hundred twenty dollars a month. The increase followed a recommendation of the retiring Board in the spring that library pay scales be studied in relation to those of other city departments.[18] Peterson was also provided with a new desk and chair, and Miss Coolbrith with a revolving bookcase of oak.[19] It held the most frequently used reference books ready to grasp instantly by simply twirling the case with a finger. This practical but ungainly piece of furniture stood beside the library reference desk for many years.

A new Board took office in April. Two members had served the previous term, Dr. S. H. Melvin, an East Oakland druggist who was chosen president, and John A. McKinnon, a merchant tailor. The others were F. S. Osgood, also a druggist, who was made secretary, Dr. B. A. Rabe, a physician and surgeon, and Jeremiah Tyrrel, an insurance agent. Their occupations are of interest in view of subsequent events. Some Boards had had teachers or preachers, writers, a judge—but not this one.[20]

Two new positions were added to the staff in 1891, a messenger and a book mender.[21] An inventory was taken in time for inclusion of results in the annual report. It was found that the library's total book stock was 17,256, which included 747 bound magazines, 118 bound newspapers, 1,228 public documents, and 520 pamphlets.[22] Both state and federal publications were being added, including an up-to-date file of the *Patent Office Gazette*. In August Miss Coolbrith presented to the Board a special report she had compiled "drawing a comparison

---

Ina Coolbrith's Nephew, Henry Frank Peterson, about 1899, Librarian, Oakland Free Library, 1893-99. Courtesy of the Oakland Free Library.

between the Oakland Public Library and other libraries on the coast, showing the amount spent for books in proportion to the income, and urging the necessity of larger additions of books and a new building." This was read and placed on file without other comment recorded in the *Minutes* of 4 August. But the immediate reaction of the Board was to ask the assistant secretary to write an article for the newspapers asking for book donations.[23] More and more functions were being delegated to Peterson directly in Board meetings instead of going first to the librarian.

The important library event of the year 1891 was the meeting of the American Library Association in San Francisco in October, the sixteenth annual conference. Taking advantage of this event, the *Overland Monthly* published an informative, illustrated article on libraries of the Pacific coast, by F. H. Clark. This was the November issue, published in time for perusal by the delegates. The article was illustrated with views of the University of California Library in Berkeley, the new Mercantile Library building in San Francisco, and a Los Angeles Public Library interior. Portraits of library administrators included those of A. E. Whittaker, Mercantile Library; Horace Green, Mechanics Library; J. V. Cheney, San Francisco Public Library; Ina D. Coolbrith, Oakland Public Library; J. C. Rowell, University of California; E. H. Woodruff, Stanford University Library; also H. H. Bancroft and Adolph Sutro, owners of outstanding private libraries.[24]

According to F. H. Clark, author of this article, "The Oakland Free Library, as such, dates from 1878; it was a subscription library, maintained by an association, for ten years before. Its present librarian, the poet Ina D. Coolbrith, has been in charge since 1874. The library has about 15,700 volumes, of which 1,200 were purchased in the year ending June 30, 1891. The number of books issued for home use during the year was 79,003. This library has the distinction of owning a building. Although a small, unsubstantial wooden structure, it affords the library 'a local habitation' that counts for much more than a name. The main room, always fresh and tidy, is an attractive place, and the boys and girls of Oakland are at home within it." Appended to the article is a note from the editor (Miss Milicent Shinn) concerning Miss Coolbrith's portrait, an enlargement of the lovely 1870 photograph by Edouart and Cobb (taken when she and Joaquin Miller had gone merrily off to have their pictures taken to send to Charlie Stoddard in Tahiti). Miss Shinn wrote, "From an old photograph of years ago Miss Coolbrith writes that she has 'neither time nor inclination' to have a new one taken; and for nothing but the *Overland* would she consent to let even this one go into print. If we were able to give our readers a more recent picture of this chief poet of California they would see how little cause there is for want of 'inclination.' "[25]

While the library was closed one evening so that both Miss Coolbrith and Henry Peterson could attend one of the general sessions in San Francisco, the important day for both of them was Thursday, 15 October, when the American Library Association was entertained in Oakland and Berkeley. The Reverend Charles W. Wendte, Unitarian minister, was chairman of the local committee, and Henry Peterson secretary. Others on the committee included three Oakland Library Board members, Dr. Melvin, John McKinnon, and Dr. Rabe; Miss Coolbrith, J. B. McChesney, J. C. Rowell, and Professor Frank Soulé.[26] Of them all, Henry Peterson seemed to be the busiest, with newspaper publicity to prepare, letters to write, arrangements to make for meeting places, and for transportation. All this was on top of his newest domestic responsibilities. On 10 September he and Elizabeth became parents. Their new little daughter was named Ina Dorothy Peterson.[27] A very full schedule was planned for the forty-five ALA members who crossed the Bay from San Francisco on the one o'clock ferry. In the group were ALA President Samuel S. Greene, Librarians Cheney and Whittaker of the San Francisco Public and Mercantile Libraries, and Librarian Yonker of San Diego. Adolph Sutro also came. The youngest member in the party was Mary Eileen Ahern, just out of library school and attending her first professional conference.[28]

The librarians went directly to the university campus in Berkeley, taking the broad-gauge train from the ferry. They visited the University Library and Art Gallery, then boarded the new electric cars (first operated in May that year) for Oakland. They stopped at the Oakland Library, where, according to a contemporary account, "Miss Coolbrith received her guests in her delightful, entertaining way," assisted by Dr. B. A. Rabe. After a cable car ride to Piedmont Heights, the tired and hungry delegates arrived at the Starr King Hall of the Unitarian Church, Fourteenth and Castro Streets, in time for a hearty dinner at 5:30. During the social hour which followed, the visiting librarians were welcomed by Dr. Wendte, chairman of the reception committee, and pastor of the church; and, after presenting the City Librarian, Miss Coolbrith, he read a poem she had composed for the occasion, "In the Library."[29] Young Miss Ahern was entranced. Writing to Miss Coolbrith nearly a quarter of a century later, she recalled that evening. "I remember seeing you at that time," she wrote, "and being just out of school, untraveled and unknowing, the sight of a woman poet, even though my home at that time was in Indiana, thrilled my soul with pleasure!"[30]

197

The evening session was held in the church auditorium, the guests being reminded to take their wraps with them so that there would be no delay when leaving for the San Francisco train. The meeting, which began at 7:45, took up three topics, with formal talks followed by discussion on each: "Public Support of Public Libraries," by William F. Foster, Providence, Rhode Island, Librarian; "Impressions of Foreign Libraries," by Miss Mary S. Cutler, Vice-Director of the Library School at Albany, New York; and "State Library Associations," by Charles A. Cutter and Miss Harriet F. Green of the Boston Athenaeum. The reporters who were present liked Miss Cutler's talk especially for its lively use of anecdote and personal experience. This full program ended promptly at 9:30, for carriages were waiting to take the guests to the train which left shortly after ten o'clock.[31]

While Miss Coolbrith's verses, read by Dr. Wendte prior to the general session, stirred the librarians in the room with emotions they themselves had known, the author was never satisfied with the poem. She may have thought it trite or inadequate and so did not include it in the collection she published four years later. The poem appeared in the *Library Journal* in 1891, but seldom elsewhere. It was part of the mood of the evening, however, and it belongs in these pages.

In the Library

Who say these walls are lonely, these,
    They may not see the motley throng
That people it, as thick as bees
    The scented clover beds among.

They may not hear, when footfalls cease,
    And living voices, for awhile,
The speech, in many tongues and keys,
    Adown each shadowy aisle.

Here are the friends that ne'er betray;
    Companionship that never tires;
Here voices call from voiceless clay,
    And ashes dead renew their fires.

For death can touch the flesh alone;
    Immortal thought, from age to age
Lives on, and here, in varied tone,
    It speaks from many a page.

198

Here searching History waits—the deeds
  Of man and nations to rehearse;
Here clear-eyed Science walks and reads
  The secrets of the universe.

Here lands and seas, from pole to pole,
  The traveler spreads before the eye;
Here Faith unfolds her mystic scroll
  The questing soul to satisfy.

Here Homer chants heroic Troy,
  Here Dante strikes the harp of pain,
Here Shakespeare sounds the grief, the joy,
  The all of human life, the strain.

Alone and silent? Why, 'tis rife
  With form and sound! The hosts of thought
Are dwellers here; and thought is life.
  Without it earth and man were not.

To war and statecraft leave the bay—
  A greater crown to these belongs;
The rulers of the World are they
  Who make its books and songs.[32]

The sentiment, whatever Miss Coolbrith may have thought of its expression, did touch the listeners. Each of them must have recalled quiet evenings with quiet readers, each one absorbed in a lamp-lighted page. And back of the readers, rows and rows of book-filled shelves, rich and waiting. Each listener may have remembered, in hearing the simple meters, his own sense of muted ecstasy in this side of his calling, forgetting for the moment, the exactitudes of cataloging, or the pell-mell of clamoring students that brought another kind of excitement into the librarian's workday.

The East Bay day of the conference was over, a success in the minds of the guests and newspaper reporters, and a stimulating experience for librarians in Oakland and Berkeley. Whether or not the association accomplished its objective in bringing library awareness to the people in Oakland that year is open to question. The purpose of holding annual conferences in various cities throughout the country was exactly that. The ALA thereby hoped to make each local meeting place somewhat familiar with the importance, the functions and the problems of libraries, especially public libraries. Did this happen in Oakland? The events that followed the conference answered the question.

In San Francisco, the next morning, the annual business meeting was held, at which Dr. Linderfelt, librarian of the Milwaukee Public Library, was elected president for the next year, and Washington, D.C., was selected as the next meeting place. That evening, 16 October, association members attended a sumptuous banquet at the Palace Hotel, where, it was said, female librarians were present for the first time at an ALA dinner meeting. Postconference tours took the visitors south. They had lunch in the Big Basin redwoods, experienced dense fog in Santa Cruz, which "sent them shuddering to the cars," spent the night at Del Monte, and visited Carmel Mission before going on to Los Angeles. Members reported this the best conference in the association's entire fifteen years. They could also relate one of the tallest tales to come out of the West. Dr. William Frederick Poole, that revered gentleman in whose mind was born the idea of the magazine index that later became *The Reader's Guide to Periodical Literature*, while on a luncheon stop somewhere in Arizona, was attacked by a tarantula. Only a shot from a revolver loosened the monster's grip on the gentleman's ankle. The creature was reported to weigh six pounds, and its skin was said to have been tanned for the cover of a book in Dr. Poole's library.[33]

Library Financial Problems

Almost immediately after the pleasant hiatus of the ALA meeting in Oakland, the Library Board of that city was back in the familiar gloom of financial problems. While services were increasing, income was not. There had been trustees before who felt that the reading rooms scattered and weakened the central collection.[34] At its November meeting, therefore, this Board recommended a drastic step; to close all outside branches, and concentrate on building up the central collection. Books had not been added as needed, and circulation was going down. At first they proposed to close the reading rooms on 1 December, then decided to postpone the decision until the next meeting.[35] The Board felt that this was the only way to meet expenses. The suggestion got action. Petitions came in. The next Board meeting was packed with visitors who came to protest the closing of any of the reading rooms. Among them was City Councilman George J. Earl who stated that he might be able to get an additional two thousand dollars transferred to the library fund, and also see that the next annual appropriation be increased by the same amount. Two thousand dollars would not be enough, but the promise put off Board action on closing the reading rooms. Miss Coolbrith, at the Board's suggestion, prepared a list of

200

books most urgently needed, ready to purchase as soon as the promised funds were received. Assistant librarian Peterson was asked to have a periodical list ready for San Francisco News, the agency that gave a ten percent discount. By February 1892 the Board had received a communication from the City Council enclosing a resolution to the effect that the city treasury would not permit the transfer of two thousand dollars to the library fund. A special meeting was then called by the Board on 25 February to discuss the reading room closing. At this meeting there was a large delegation from the Twenty-third Avenue Reading Room, and, after lengthy discussion, the Board decided to defer closing until after the next tax levy would be made.[36]

Miss Coolbrith's report for February was accompanied by a letter describing a recent gift to the library of the large private collection that had belonged to W. W. Crane, Jr., and was presented by his widow, a close personal friend of the librarian. Crane had been a charter member of the old Library Association, and he was a member of the first Board of Directors of the Free Library. The collection presented was one of the most important gifts received by the library in many years. It was made up chiefly of the classics in English, French, and German, in good editions, with many of the volumes bound in morocco. The French and German portion of the gift became the nucleus of the foreign language collection in the library. The Board passed a resolution of thanks and suggested that the collection be shelved in a special section with a gift nameplate. At this time, too, a petition came to the Board from local music teachers and pupils to add music to the departments of the library, a request that was taken seriously, though it was impossible to comply at that time.[37]

Sometime that spring a young woman came into the library especially to see Ina Coolbrith. She had written some sketches and wanted advice about seeking publication. She knew who Ina Coolbrith was, for she had seen some of the issues of the *Overland Monthly*, also the volume of verse entitled *A Perfect Day*. The girl found the librarian entirely friendly and helpful. She told her visitor how to prepare a manuscript to submit to an editor and advised her to call on the *Overland* editor, Miss Shinn, as soon as she had her sketches in shape to present. Thus began Mary Austin's introduction to the writing profession. She was twenty-three that spring day when she brought her question to Miss Coolbrith. In later years the two came to know each other socially in the San Francisco home of Theodore Hittell and in those of other mutual friends. And Mary Austin secretly resolved to do as well as Ina Coolbrith, even to excel her one day as a writer.[38]

Late that summer Joaquin Miller fell to meditating on his long friendship with Ina Coolbrith and on what he considered the injustice of her confining work. Without her knowledge he wrote a long article about her which was published in the *San Francisco Call* in August under the headline, "California's Fair Poet. A Tribute to the Work and Worth of Ina D. Coolbrith." She was surprised, and certainly embarrassed, but amused and tolerant of his whims and fancies about her. He advanced the notion that she should be on the payroll of the University of California for having written two commencement poems in the 1870s. The post Miller visualized was not unlike that accepted many years later by Robert Frost; that of "poet in residence." Joaquin Miller deplored that his old friend was chained to a library desk where she would probably remain for the rest of her life, "dealing out books to children over a counter till she goes to her grave in the Oakland Library." The more he wrote, the more indignant he grew at the idea that a creative writer should be so restricted. Ina took the press story good-naturedly, as she did the many eccentricities of this truly loyal old friend.[39]

Miller's emotional outburst was followed shortly after by a more restrained tribute, some lines of verse, "To Ina Coolbrith," in the September *Overland Monthly*, written by a Washington state author, Ella Mae Higginson.[40] *Lippincott's* of the same month had just published Ina's lyric, "In the Grand Cañon," written some years before.[41] The poem evoked several press comments, one of which was headlined, "Silent No Longer."[42] The enthusiasm with which this one lyric was received only served to sharpen the pain the poet must have felt when she knew that she was no longer writing. She had composed one poem in the spring, but it was not published. It was in honor of "Uncle" George Bromley's seventy-fifth birthday in April, and was read by Daniel O'Connell at a Bohemian Club breakfast. There had been nothing else from her pen that year. The year before, she mused, there had been several lyrics. Aside from her "In the Library," and her "In Memoriam— John LeConte," her best pieces in 1891 had been her two Christmas songs, "The Day of Our Lord," and "Hymn of the Nativity." Each was used as a full-page newspaper feature, and the latter, printed with music, was sung in three churches on Christmas Day.[43] But this year of 1892, and especially this month of September, Ina Coolbrith's mind was filled with library matters instead of rhymes. On her way to Mrs. Howard's reception, early that month, she must have thought bitterly that business and social obligations were suffocating her creative gift. Mrs. Charles Webb Howard of Oakland had insisted on Miss Coolbrith's presence at this large, formal gathering in honor of educators of the Pacific Coast. Some of the other guests were Martin Kellogg, the Reverend S. H. Willey, Fred Campbell, David Starr Jordan, Mrs.

Jeanne Carr, John Stillman, Professor Lisser, William Keith, Mrs. Charlotte Perkins Stetson, John Muir, Joaquin Miller, among many others—a brilliant company." Afterward even the thought of this important function was soon forgotten in the rush of events at the library that fateful September 1892.

An Unfortunate Interview

That month Miss Coolbrith was shorthanded. Henry's vacation began on Thursday, 1 September, and he took his wife and infant daughter to Pleasanton. He had arranged for Dwight Strong, curator of the Central Reading Room, to take the minutes for him at the Board meeting to be held on the following Tuesday. Saturdays were always busy, and 3 September was no exception in that respect. Miss Coolbrith looked up from her work to greet a man who said he represented the *Oakland Times*. He apologized for interrupting her. He told her that he would like to have her opinion on the budget estimate for the coming year. She cheerfully granted the interview. She said, with complete candor, that she regretted the action of the Council in cutting the estimate. A little more than twenty-two thousand dollars had been requested, an amount that was to have provided five thousand dollars toward a building fund. The Council had reduced the estimate to thirteen thousand dollars, barely enough to meet expenses. She insisted that a new building was imperative, adding that this was the "worst public building in this city." This remark brought a question about the safety of the building.

"Yes, I consider the building very unsafe," she answered, and went on to say that it was so small and crowded that there was no space for new accessions. The reporter asked if the library was able to meet the demands for new books, and her answer was a negative one, elaborated by remarks on the need of school children for supplementary reading material not supplied by the school libraries. Asked about periodicals in the reading rooms, she said that magazine lists had had to be cut down in the interest of economy. His question about assistance brought forth her comparison of the Oakland Library with that in Los Angeles. She compared her situation, with two assistants and two boy pages, with the southern city whose population was only slightly more than that of Oakland. There the librarian had twenty assistants and needed more.[45]

Some women came to her with book requests, and she turned away from her questioner with a remark that she would like to see the library better housed and better provided for before she should "pass out of it." She had little time to think of her impromptu interview. Had she been too outspoken? But it was all true. Anyone could see that. Dismissing it from her mind, she gave all her attention to readers at her desk. When her day was over, she was tired enough to be reminded of Joaquin's silly prediction, that she would probably go to her grave right in the Oakland Library.

The next morning the Oakland Sunday *Times* lay on many a breakfast table in the city. A folded copy lay beside Mayor Chapman's plate when he came downstairs for his morning meal. The gentlemen on the City Council had their Sunday papers. There were copies in the hands of Doctors Melvin and Rabe, and of Directors McKinnon, Osgood, and Tyrrel. Miss Coolbrith opened her copy of the paper a little apprehensively. What had she said? Her remarks may have been too spontaneous and too blunt. She found the story and read it in full, from the headline to the modest statement that "the scribe withdrew." The report took most of a column. As she put down the paper, she felt a small twinge of uneasiness, but dismissed it, for she knew that her statement was honest.[46]

At the library, the next day, business went on as usual, though heavier for Henry's absence. Some of Miss Coolbrith's friends may have complimented her on her remarks to the *Times* reporter. They may have praised her for speaking out at last. It was time that the people of the city knew that the Council was to blame for the poor book fund and the shabby, shaky building. The next evening, Tuesday, 6 September, the Board members came into the library for their monthly meeting.[47] When the members came in, Dwight Strong, reading room curator, followed them upstairs, to take the minutes in Peterson's absence. The meeting was held, as usual, in the small room at the back of the general library reading room. The discussion was quiet, and shorter than usual. The men left in a body, as though they had an urgent appointment elsewhere. Dwight Strong acknowledged their thanks as they left, then resumed his duties in the first floor reading room. Miss Coolbrith may have thought it strange that none of the men had stopped to chat as they passed her desk. Not one of them had commented on the press story in the Sunday *Times*. She was puzzled, and a little hurt. It did not occur to her that her innocent remarks might have been too innocent—too naive, or that she could have been used in a political quarrel between the *Times* and the city administration. Taken by surprise, as she had been, and having spoken with her customary frankness when she talked to the reporter, she may have had no idea of the political consequences of her act, or of any embarrassment to the Library Board, an elected body, dependent on the City Council for all library funds.

204

20
Loss
of
Position

What have they brought to me these many years?
Silence and bitter tears.

Ina Coolbrith, from
"The Years" (1870)

Dismissal Without Cause

The headlines of the *Oakland Tribune* seemed to leer from every newsstand: "SUDDEN. INA D. COOLBRITH DISCHARGED." This was the evening edition on Tuesday, 27 September 1892. People who stopped to buy and read, perused the headlines, shocked and unbelieving, "Only Three Days Grace Given Her. No Direct Charges Made by the Trustees. History of the Disagreeable Outburst at the Libary" [sic]. If a thunderbolt had crashed through the roof of the Free Library it could have scarcely been a source of greater surprise than the message which the librarian, Miss Ina D. Coolbrith, received this morning from the Board of Library Trustees, curtly notifying her that her services as librarian will not be required after the 30th inst. . . ."[1] The text of the letter from the Trustees did not appear in the press story, but an account of their actions did.

The letter itself was in the morning mail at the library.[2] When Miss Coolbrith opened it, read it and reread it, she must have been weak with disbelief. She looked again; the date was 26 September. It was signed by all five members of the Board. Why? What was their reason? She read the letter once more, slowly:

OAKLAND, September 26th

Miss Ina D. Coolbrith, Librarian of Oakland Free Library: After a full and careful consideration of the subject, the undersigned

205

have unanimously but with reluctance arrived at the conclusion that the efficiency and usefulness of the library will be promoted by a change in the office of librarian. We, therefore, respectfully request you to file your resignation as librarian in the office of the secretary of the board, to take effect on the 30th inst.

Signed,

J. Tyrrel,
J. A. McKinnon,
F. S. Osgood,
B. A. Rabe,
S. H. Melvin.[3]

She decided to go to Secretary Osgood at once for an explanation. Slipping the letter into her reticule, she asked Miss Cole to take her place at the desk, as an urgent business matter had come up. As she put on her cloak and hat, it may have occurred to her to seek advice from a friend or two before calling on Osgood. She may have talked to Judge Boalt. Whatever friend she saw advised her to see Osgood immediately. That friend, moreover, felt obliged to bring the matter into the open. Within hours after Miss Coolbrith opened the letter, the *Tribune* was after the story.

Miss Coolbrith walked down to Osgood's Drug Store, then on Broadway near Eighth Street. Inside she found the Board secretary at his desk. He was expecting her. She asked him at once for the Board's reasons for requiring her resignation. Had she been negligent in her duties? Had she failed to carry out instructions from the Board? He was reticent, and he hedged. The Board was unanimous in their belief that this step was necessary for the good of the library. He trusted the other members of the Board, especially the two from the old Board. There was the matter of the strained relations between her and her nephew.

"Not in the library," she insisted. "You know that the matter was settled two years ago, and we agreed that it should never affect our work in the library." Miss Coolbrith was certain that this was not the true reason. She said that if she could not learn what the charges were, directly from the Board, she would demand a public hearing. She said, too, that the three-day notice was unnecessarily cruel. She should have been given time until the end of the year at least. Osgood, on the defensive against this articulate woman, jumped at her suggestion. It would be a kind of reprieve. He asked her if she had brought the letter with her.

"Yes," she said, "here it is." He recognized the envelope as the one he had addressed to her and mailed. Turning it over, he wrote on the back:

I am willing, if the majority are, that Miss Coolbrith remain until the end of the year.

Signed.   F. S. Osgood

He suggested that she have the other trustees sign the memorandum. All but Dr. Melvin did so, glad to mitigate, in some way, the unpleasant business.[4]

"Dr. Melvin did not sign it," Miss Coolbrith later told a *Tribune* reporter, "but I understand he will not oppose it. For some reason or other," she went on, "the doctor and Mr. McKinnon, who are the old members of the Board, have never been friendly to me. Why, I don't know and am sorry for it, although I can't help it."[5]

Before talking to the librarian at all, the reporter had gone to Osgood's Drug Store himself, and had found the druggist still at his desk. Miss Coolbrith had left shortly before. Secretary Osgood was more outspoken to the reporter than he had been to the lady. He said that he had acted in the matter on the information that had come to him from three other Board members, Dr. Rabe, Dr. Melvin, and Director Tyrrel. It was they who had said that Miss Coolbrith had disobeyed Board orders and had been neglectful of her duties. Dr. Melvin, said Osgood, related that the old Board had considered asking Miss Coolbrith to resign two years ago because of some difficulty with her nephew. The reporter asked Osgood if he had heard Miss Coolbrith's explanation, and the druggist replied that he had acted only on the "representation" of the other trustees, who had also commented that they could save her salary by letting her go. But the newspaperman pressed his point about Miss Coolbrith's side of the case, and asked if the Board was going to give her a hearing. Osgood said that she was probably entitled to one and that he supposed they would have to give it to her. The *Tribune* writer was not satisfied. He asked when the Board held the meeting at which the decision was made. And this is what the Board secretary told him.

"Three weeks ago. We had previously held a regular meeting in the usual place and adjourned to another place, where an executive session—a 'star chamber' session I suppose you would call it—at which the resolution was offered and carried unanimously to dismiss her. That was what the Board decided should be done and, of course, we had to carry out its wishes. It is very short notice, I admit. Only three days!"[6] The "star chamber" session, as Osgood frankly described it, took place on

207

Tuesday evening, two days after the appearance of Miss Coolbrith's statement to the *Times*. Was there any connection? The executive session, in some downtown back room, as one reporter said, amid the ever present cigar smoke, had left no minutes. Its only record, in writing, was the letter sent to Miss Coolbrith, with its hasty memo scribbled on the envelope. Hardly legal procedure!

The *Tribune* man hurried away to catch Dr. Rabe whose office was in the Blake Block on Washington Street, near Tenth. Dr. Rabe was in. He was disturbed by the appearance of a reporter and seemed to be astonished that there was any rumor abroad that the trustees had even considered discontinuing Miss Coolbrith's employment as librarian. He doubted if the Board had agreed to dismiss her and said that they had not taken any such action to his knowledge. The reporter brought him up with the rejoinder that the *Tribune* was aware that Miss Coolbrith's resignation was to take effect in three days. From then on Dr. Rabe was on the defensive. He said that the *Tribune* was wrong; that the resignation did not go into effect until the end of the year; that the librarian was not dismissed, but that her action should appear voluntary. He could give no specific reason for the Board's action. He spoke vaguely of personal observations and complaints, but did not explain what these were. He stated that the librarian had not been given a hearing because there were no charges against her, but the Board simply believed the library would get along better if Miss Coolbrith were out. He was uncomfortable. He ended with a plea that the reporter not "say anything about this."'

The newspaperman thanked Dr. Rabe and went to see Miss Coolbrith. He needed her statement to round out his report on the events. She was not at the library. Too agitated to remain at her desk, she had gone home. He found her there and learned that she was at a loss to explain the action of the Board. She believed that the trouble stemmed from the old disagreement she and Henry had had two years before and that the Board thought that the strained relationship still existed, and that this was their excuse for dismissal. She was told by one Board member, brutally, that, since the City Council wanted to cut the library appropriation, the Board had to reduce expenditures, and that they could do without her better than without Mr. Peterson, and thus they could save the amount of her salary. In answer to further questioning Miss Coolbrith said that she had never heard any expression of dissatisfaction with her work and that she had been faithful in the performance of her duties and in carrying out the wishes of the Board. She was told that morning that there had been complaints, but could learn neither their nature nor their source.

"There may have been some undercurrent working against me," she remarked. She told the *Tribune* representative that she had intended to resign in February anyway, then continued emphatically, "If the place were offered me now I would not under any circumstances take it! I am sick and tired of the constant trouble and annoyance connected with it." Her tone changed, "I would like to go out quietly, without publicity." The journalist had his story in time for the evening edition. He even wrote a touching introduction, relating the story of Ina Coolbrith having taken the position in the first place in order to rear and provide for her orphaned niece and nephew. The *Tribune* account was the first report, but it did not tell the whole story.[8]

For one thing the *Tribune* man saw only two members of the Board of Trustees, the two men near at hand. Two *Times* and *Enquirer* reporters later interviewed Dr. Melvin in East Oakland, president of the Board. They also questioned Director Tyrrel, the insurance agent. The opinion of the tailor, J. A. McKinnon, was not sought. To both reporters Dr. Melvin said that the action was taken for the good of the library. He told the *Times* man, furthermore, that "there were reasons why the Board took the action it did which he did not care to state."[9] To the *Enquirer* representative, on the other hand, he said that there had been numerous complaints against her management, mitigating his comments by adding that the Trustees "had done an unpleasant duty which was made more especially so as their ax had fallen on a woman. There is not the slightest breath of suspicion against her character."[10]

Tyrrel, when interviewed, expressed his conviction that Miss Coolbrith had been asked to resign solely for economic reasons; the Board could save her salary. He said that he had heard no complaints against her of any neglect of duty on her part, that the Board was not finding fault, but that the change was desired for the good of the library. Then he added, with a cold lack of compassion, "I do not see any reason for Miss Coolbrith having a hearing before the Board of Trustees. The Board has decided to get along without her, that is all the reason I have." So it was, in public employment, in the "Gay Nineties." The lack of a prepared statement from the directors, and glaring contradictions in their reasons for dismissal are evident. The men did agree, however, on one thing, "that Mr. Peterson had no knowledge of the affair, and if there was any blame, it should be on them."[11]

On 27 September, the day the news broke, Dr. Rabe kept an appointment. He attended the City Council meeting where he urged that the library rate be raised. The matter was discussed, then dropped. No action was taken. He left, disheartened, feeling that the Council, with the possible exception of Dr. George Pardee, was obviously against the library.[12] That day, too, Henry Peterson came home from his holiday in the country, rested, ready for work the next morning, wholly unaware of the library commotion.

Reactions of the Daily Press

The following morning the *Tribune*'s representative continued his private investigation. He learned from Secretary Osgood that the Board had no intention of calling a special meeting to rescind their resolution requesting the librarian's resignation. This could mean only one thing. If a special meeting were not called before the end of September, then the memo on the back of a flimsy envelope was the only guarantee Miss Coolbrith had that the Board would keep its promise to permit her to remain until the first of the year. As a document it had no validity, since it was not recorded in the minutes of a *bona fide* meeting of the Board as an official body. Osgood agreed, and he admitted that Peterson would thus be the librarian until the next regular board meeting on 4 October.

"It may be that we have called upon the wrong person to resign," he said, "it may be that Peterson is the one. . . . It may be necessary to remove him anyhow, ultimately. There is no telling," he added, as he dismissed the reporter.[13]

Leaving Osgood's, the man walked up to the library where he found Henry Peterson at his desk. The assistant librarian said that he had had no intimation of yesterday's events until he opened his *Tribune* in the evening, and that no one was more surprised than he. He hastened to deny, emphatically, that he had ever complained to the Board or accused Miss Coolbrith of neglect of duties or failure to execute Board orders. He added, with vehemence, that he had never said that either she or he would have to leave the library. When asked if he had been present at the Board meeting at which the decision had been made, he stated that he had left for his vacation a few days before and had arranged for Dwight Strong to take the minutes for him. On being asked about the so-called strained relations between himself and his aunt, he said there had been no trouble since the argument was settled two years before. The reporter reminded him that this was the reason for dismissal given by some of the trustees. Peterson remarked, "Well, two of them are members of the old Board."

"But," persisted the journalist, "the members who have assigned that as a reason for their action are new members." Peterson was baffled, "Well, I cannot explain it." He insisted that he had never tried to get his aunt out and himself in, though he admitted that, after eighteen years in the library, he had once said that he would someday be li-

210

brarian. When asked if he knew he would be librarian on 1 October, he said he had had no such notice, and all he knew about it was what he had read in the papers.

What he read in the papers the next few days was not flattering to himself. Newspapers had made much of the story of his aunt's caring for her orphaned nephew and niece and of her obtaining the position of library assistant for Henry. There was even a rumor that he had tried to have Miss Coolbrith fired two years before so that he himself might have her position. One newspaper went still further when it introduced a rather vicious piece of gossip that Henry had married a young woman who was obnoxious to his aunt. This story had no foundation. In fact Elizabeth Peterson named her little daughter "Ina" for her husband's aunt and sister. But the stories snowballed, adding a bit here and there, until an ugly rumor was built up—one that has endured to this very day—that Henry Peterson wanted his aunt dismissed so that he could be City Librarian.[14]

When questioned about him, Miss Coolbrith said with a shade of doubt that she hoped Henry had said nothing against her to bring about this unhappy situation.[15] She implied that there had been no unpleasantness between them for more than two years. And the Board emphatically exonerated Peterson. In spite of this, Henry was on the defensive. He said that if he had ever attempted to have his aunt dismissed he himself would have been fired promptly. He did not care to talk about the distressing subject. Of course he had always hoped to be City Librarian. "Not an unworthy ambition," he said. But he had expected, when that came about, that it would be "in a manner satisfactory to all concerned."[16] That was the kindest remark he made in the whole affair, according to newspaper accounts. His sin, if any, was thus one of omission rather than of commission. His attitude in the sorry incident was a negative one. He showed no indignation over the injustice to his aunt. He did not once come to her defense. He did not stand up to the Board. He did not resign in protest. He acquiesced. He excused himself. He took the Board's orders, deferentially, as always. He seemed to be happy when he was later made City Librarian and Clerk of the Board, and given a raise in pay. But was he happy? His promotion was possible only through his aunt's disgrace and loss of a position to which she had brought distinction.

Henry Peterson had a choice. So had his aunt nearly twenty years before. For her it was the choice of a promising literary career with travel and the association of other writers, or, the care of her sister's young orphaned children. It was a hard decision to make. This decision

211

she put into verse in "A Prayer for Strength," where she said, with deep feeling and no mawkish sentimentality,

> O soul! however sweet
> The goal to which I hasten with swift feet—
> If, just within my grasp,
> I reach, and joy to clasp,
> And find there one whose body I must make
> A footstool for that sake,
> Though ever and forever more denied,
> Grant me to turn aside!"

This was written in an agony of soul-searching after her sister's death. It was published in the *Overland Monthly* of August 1874, the month before she accepted appointment as librarian in Oakland in order to support the two left in her care. Did Henry know, when he perused the pages of *A Perfect Day*, by Ina D. Coolbrith, that these words were written for him when he was a teenage lad? This musing may be unfair to Henry Frank Peterson, Oakland's second City Librarian, a good administrator, conscientious, outgoing in personality, liked by public and staff. It may be unfair. But the regret remains, "ever and forevermore," that he did not speak out against the injustice to his aunt.

Miss Coolbrith's Resignation

The newspapers up and down the coast, from Seattle to San Diego, did speak out clearly against that injustice." An editorial in the *Oakland Times* denounced all "star chamber" proceedings as vicious and foolish, and in particular that of the Oakland Board of Library Trustees in "discharging from the public service, the *one* person who in the last eighteen years has, above all others, given tone and character to whatever there is good and useful in the Free Public Library." The editor ended his reprimand of the Board with "This *faux pas* ought to end all kinds of star chamber sessions in this city for a long time to come."¹⁹

It was not the Board, but the City Council, that brought the reproaches of the *Oakland Enquirer*. The Council was blamed for having cut the library appropriation in half, for having failed to provide the means for purchase of needed books, and for maintaining a building that, as a library, was a disgrace to the city. The paper declared that the reference collection was completely inadequate for the use of the students of the high school, that current books could not be bought to meet the demand of readers, and that the room was miserably understaffed. This diatribe against "the niggardly and careless methods" of the Council gave voice to the conviction that a public library is an "institution which, in all well-ordered cities, is as essential as water or light."[20]

The *Enquirer* writer was even more outspoken against the City Council than Miss Coolbrith had been in her interview published in the *Times* early in the month. The truth was that at this time, and perhaps at most times, the Oakland City Council was more concerned with paving and sewers than with any other aspect of municipal administration. They scarcely had time to lift their eyes and minds from those lowly strata to consider problems of schools or the library. They were more incensed over the apparently unlawful detention of a cow by the the City Poundmaster than the dismissal of the City Librarian. The Council listened to pleas from the Library Board for additional funds, and gave time to the public to protest suggestions that the reading rooms be closed. That elected body listened, and gave time, but took little action. Their minutes during those trying months were filled with motions on paving and sewering contracts.[21] Certainly a city needs paving; it needs sewage disposal. Perhaps that council did not believe that a city also needs a library. If that was their conviction, it was no different from that of an efficient and "well-read" Oakland City Manager who stated emphatically many years later, "The library, you know, is not necessary. The streets, the police, the fire department—these are necessary; not the library."[22]

If such a point of view had been taken for granted by the 1892 City Council, Miss Coolbrith's fighting remarks on 3 September could touch them in only one way—to anger them. And they could express their anger in only one way—to discharge her. That was how they dealt with the poundmaster who had violated the sacred right of private property, even though that "property" was roving the streets unattended.[23] Ina Coolbrith could not fight the City Council—the Oakland City Council. No city employee, even a department head, could talk to or about the City Council as she had. Moreover this department head was a woman. What did a woman know about the city's business? She could not even vote. The Council had no power to order Miss Coolbrith's dismissal, but they could suggest or insinuate in strong language. And such a suggestion to the Board would be treated as an order. Miss Coolbrith's friends may have pointed out to her that she had no choice. If she were to protest and demand a hearing, she would be discharged promptly. She had already stated her desire to retire in February. She would be wise to present her resignation to be effective 1 January 1893. That is what she did.

When the Board of Directors met on 4 October in the little room off the main library room, Miss Coolbrith sat at her desk, her head high, a quizzical smile on her lips. In the Board room, when the time came, Secretary Osgood cleared his throat and read a letter, Assistant Secretary Peterson taking it down dutifully for a permanent place in the big book of minutes. It was the librarian's letter of resignation. She said she tendered it under protest, since there had been no charges of incompetency on her part and that she was ignorant of the causes leading to the request for her resignation.[24] An embarrassed silence followed the reading of the letter. Then the insurance agent moved that the Librarian's resignation be accepted. The tailor seconded the motion. The *Minutes* record unanimous acceptance, but an *Enquirer* reporter who was present said there were two weak "ayes" and no "noes."[25]

If the Board seemed to rush through the action that was to bring them permanent dishonor, they immediately went headlong into another controversy. They voted, four to one, President Melvin dissenting, to close the North Oakland and Twenty-third Avenue branch reading rooms on 1 November.[26] Here was an invitation to trouble. Visitors at the Board meeting protested, but without effect. These citizens, and others from the two districts concerned, took the problem to the City Council on 18 October. At this session so much dissatisfaction against recent actions of the Board of Library Directors was expressed that the Council voted to transfer two thousand dollars from the general to the library fund so that the reading rooms could remain open. No details of the discussion which took place were recorded in the minutes of the City Council. There was thus no notice in writing about Miss Coolbrith's dismissal, although this incident must have been mentioned, since much of the time of the meeting was devoted to library affairs. The motion to transfer funds seemed to mollify the visitors in the Council chamber. Then, just before adjournment, the members of the Council had a change of heart. They decided to postpone the transfer of money until the next meeting.[27]

The Library Board, distressed about the severe criticisms of their recent actions, which were aired at the Council meeting, voted on 1 November to defer action on closing the reading rooms, especially since two thousand dollars would soon be transferred to the library fund. To this Board meeting Dr. Rabe came with a written speech which he prepared in answer to charges made against the Board at the Council meeting of the previous 18 October. At his request Secretary Osgood

Ina Coolbrith Branch, Oakland Free Library (Formerly Twenty-Third Avenue Branch). From the drawing by Thomas Fong, 1946, in Oakland Free Library. Courtesy of the Library.

read the speech aloud. Dr. Rabe had apparently written it for the information of the reporters present at this Board meeting. It was a review of Oakland library matters for the past three years, and also discussed recent library trends and library buildings. In it Dr. Rabe expressed a hope that Oakland would soon take substantial steps to improve plant and facilities in Oakland. Unfortunately the speech was not recorded in the *Minutes*. The meeting adjourned on a note of optimism because of expected temporary aid from the City Council, making it possible to keep the two reading rooms open.[28]

The "next meeting" at which the Council was to take action on the two thousand dollars, met without a quorum, and it was not until 14 November that the matter was brought up for action. A statement from the Library Board, to the effect that the reading rooms would remain open if the Council provided additional funds, was read. A motion to transfer the proposed amount, two thousand dollars, was made, then amended to read fourteen hundred dollars. This amount was voted transferred.[29]

A digression is made at this point to give some background for Oakland's fiscal problems in 1892. In the eighties and nineties California's economic structure was based on diversified agriculture, with wheat production in the lead. Gone were the days of the cattle ranches, the gold mines. Still to come were the myriad oil wells and heavy industry. While the country at large suffered an agricultural depression in 1887, California was to reach the peak of its real estate boom in that year. The boom subsided with some business failures and loss of personal fortunes, but the end of the eighties and the beginning of the nineties showed progress. Then the panic of 1893, followed by a year of killing frosts and three of drouth, crippled the economy of the state, with recovery delayed until about the turn of the century. Aside from money panics, lowered prices for agricultural products, and unemployment, each city had its unique problems.[30]

It was on the eve of this depression when Miss Coolbrith, in September 1892, compared the support of public libraries in Los Angeles and Oakland to the disadvantage of the latter. It is true that these two cities were, at the beginning of the nineties, similar in population and assessed valuation: about fifty thousand persons each, and about fifty million dollars in taxable property each. Los Angeles was adapting to a sudden influx of home seekers (who had found, to their pleasure, that one of the amenities of the place was a busy public library). The water problem of the southern city was not yet severe, but port troubles were. In Oakland the waterfront was a paramount concern at this time. Much of the waterfront land was claimed by private owners, and the city was engaged in costly litigation to recover it. During the same period the estuary that forms the southern edge of Oakland was dredged by the United States Army Engineers into a deep-water channel to connect San Leandro Bay with San Francisco Bay. While this was financed by the federal government, it had a drastic effect on the city's sewers, the outlets of which had to be replaced. The second step in the channeling was begun in 1892; so for years the City Council had been barely able to keep its head above sewer problems. These, and the waterfront recovery suit, were some of the reasons for the cut in the library budget that year. It is also likely that the Council was composed of men who were somewhat indifferent to cultural aspects of city life, or who believed that San Francisco libraries could fill the need, since many Oakland residents worked there.[31]

On 1 December Miss Coolbrith's successor was appointed, Henry Frank Peterson, to take office on the following New Year's Day. After the first of the year numerous changes were made. The reading rooms remained open. Some remodeling was done in the central building; also children of twelve were allowed to register as borrowers. In February Henry Peterson's title of Assistant Secretary was changed, and, as "Librarian and Clerk of the Board," his salary was increased to $145.00 a month. And so Librarian Peterson's administration began, and would continue for seven years, in the same shaky little building. But that is Henry Peterson's story, a story in which Ina Coolbrith took little part.[32]

The last day of the year 1892, Ina Coolbrith's last day as Oakland's City Librarian, was a Saturday, always a busy day in the institution. If Miss Coolbrith were tired and bitter, she had no time to express such a mood. She sat at her desk regally, like a queen on her throne, her dark gray eyes flashing, her warm smile ready for each person who came to bid God speed to one of California's first librarians—of a free public library—on the last day of her eighteen years of service to an officially ungrateful city.

21
Songs
from the
Golden Gate

California has a right to be proud of Ina Coolbrith.
It is too busy now. Sometime it will awaken from its dreams
of gold and gain and conquest to understand that here
was one who had been touched with the sacred fire.

Henry James, columnist, in *San Francisco Call* (1898)

Adjustment to Loss of Position

After the humiliation of the autumn of 1892, it would be many years before Ina Coolbrith could say, without constraint, "I am prouder of being the first public librarian in California than I am of being the first woman author, for I think the public libraries have been a greater help to the people. We worked for a law to create public libraries. Oakland established the first public library in the state and I was its librarian."[1]

Her honest pride can be shared by the Oakland of today,[2] a city now far removed from the quiet charm and dominant literary interests that gave it its old sobriquet of the Athens of the Pacific. Oakland citizens can say, "Ina Coolbrith was our first City Librarian," but their pride is soon chastened by remorse, when they remember that she was driven out by a pack of their own politicians. Miss Coolbrith's pride in her pioneer work in librarianship was nearly lost in bitterness. Injustice, ingratitude, and shame were her reward for conscientious service during eighteen of her best years, the years from age thirty-three to fifty-one. They were weary years, made up of long work days; eleven hours a day and six days a week.[3] The long hours made work an imprisonment that tired the body and stiffled her impulse to sing. This she resented with all her being.

"I was placed in prison," she said, "and fettered. I saw only the walls, or walked a path to and from the doors . . . and the bird forgets its notes and the wings their flight. . . ." She blamed herself; she believed that she had been guilty of blasphemy, "a blasphemy against the altar of the God of Mind and Melody. No one can realize in the least what a shell it is to me, because I know what it is and should have been; what a wickedness my whole life has been forced to be against its truer self."[4] In this mood she felt that she had made a mistake in entering the library, and that she should have developed her literary talents at any cost.

Some such thoughts as these may have come to her as she awoke on the first morning of the New Year, 1893. It would be some time before she could adjust herself to the meaning for her of her sudden freedom. She would have to recover from the state of shock brought on by the events of the past three months. While for years she had followed the same path, there would now be other paths open to her if she could find and follow them. It was imperative that one should lead to a livelihood, yet not compromise whatever she had left of a creative writing urge. She had begun to believe that her career as a lyric poet was over without having really existed. Most of what she had accomplished, she felt, had been in her girlhood.[5] The freshness, the spontaneity, the joyous singing, were over now. She was sure they could not be revived.

She was still in this pessimistic mood a week later, when John Carmany came to call, on Sunday, 8 January 1893. To cheer her he brought with him his copy of his special edition of her book, *A Perfect Day*. The watercolor plates he had commissioned were now finished, and the volume was ready for the binder. Together they went through the loose pages and she studied the charming paintings that would embellish the volume. She must have been moved deeply as she contemplated this evidence of Carmany's devotion, if not to her, at least to her book. It was a devotion that approached reverence for her poems. As she looked, the lyrics came back to her out of the past, the forgotten past. They seemed simple and innocent. The only reality was the recent galling experience at the library. Recovery from it would be slow and painful. John Carmany had come to solace her and beg a favor. He said that the book would not be complete until she had written an inscription on the flyleaf. He told her that he would bring the volume back when it was bound, and she could then write a poem in it for him. He may have hoped for a renewal of the close friendship they had known years before, when he had published her book. The drastic termination of her library obligations left her free to consider another career. He may have been hopeful that she might turn to him.

After John left, Ina moved about restlessly, hardly conscious that the words of her poem for him were taking place in her mind. The next morning the lines came to her with a self-pitying rush. She sat down and started to write, "Lines on the Flyleaf of My First Book." She paused, startled. Unconsciously she had indicated that there would be another. She continued to write, and wrote as though questioning, as though bewildered, then gave herself completely to her mood:

> Are these the songs I sung
> When life was young?
> Pale phantoms of the flowers
> Plucked in the morning hours,
> Mist-visions of the foam
> Of waves, that beat upon the shores of home
> In by-gone days! Like some beloved child
> To one, who from the wild,
> Sad tumult of the world returns again,
> Weary, and spent with pain,
> And sees—with eyes for tears that scarce can trace—
> The dear familiar face;
> So seem my songs to me,
> So may they be,
> These children mine, one day,
> When I am passed away,
> From the visible world, and all that in it is,
> My truest witnesses,
> With simple words to breathe
> Of one at rest beneath
> The sod, no longer green,
> Of what she was . . . alas, and might have been!

She signed the lines, dated them 9 January 1893, and sent them to Carmany.[6] What he thought of them we do not know. He may have expected some reference to himself, to their own friendship, instead of these melancholy musings. What did she mean by "alas, and might have been"? And might have been a poet of renown? And might have been Mrs. John Henry Carmany? He must have smiled ruefully. Then remembering her fondness for seeing her verses in type he had them set up for her. When he sent her the printed lines, he reminded her that he still expected her to transcribe them into his copy of her book when he received it from the binder. This she did on her birthday, 10 March, when he called, bringing the superbly bound book with him.[7]

Ina's emotional outburst in the lines she wrote for her old friend was good therapy for her. It broke the spell of hopelessness in which she had been caught. When she wrote the title for that inscription, she indicated, to herself at least, that she was now truly free to compile and publish her next book of verse. Carmany was only one of many friends who had come with sympathy and help and suggestions. Miss Coolbrith was soon deep in a series of activities, mostly literary. She was about to enter another productive period in her life. The years between 1892 and the end of the century were to bring her many satisfactions and a sense of achievement in new media. Except for a severe attack of pleurisy followed by pneumonia in 1895, she was singularly free from illness. She made the most of these years of physical well-being; she traveled a little, lectured, published the volume for which she is best known, accepted a new library position, and was the subject of critical acclaim and press interviews. She found that she could still sing, not always joyously, but always as occasion demanded. She had even responded that winter to the *Examiner's* usual request for a cover poem for its Christmas issue.[8] This was in the tradition of the year before when her cover song had been a hymn, liked well enough to be sung by the Christmas choirs of two churches in San Francisco and one in Oakland.[9] At the same time, the *Oakland Tribune* had featured one of her poems on a decorated holiday page.[10]

Two of these religious poems of hers were read the last day of January 1893, at a memorial program for Richard Realf, the poet who had come to Oakland to commit suicide.[11] It was a literary program held to raise funds for a monument at the dead poet's grave. Dr. William Wendte, the Unitarian minister, presided, and when he introduced Miss Coolbrith he presented her with a sprig of yew from Wordsworth's grave. Ina did not read her own contributions to the program, but asked David Leszinsky to do so. Numerous readings from their own works were given by local authors, and a biographical tribute to Realf was presented by Mrs. Ella Sterling Cummins.[12]

Mrs. Cummins had just completed her volume, *The Story of the Files*, to be published for sale at the World's Columbian Exposition in Chicago during the coming summer.[13] She was one of the "lady managers," and, under her direction, books of California authorship had been collected for exhibit in the California building at the Fair.[14] The monthly magazine *California Illustrated* published a large edition of its July issue for distribution there. And reprints of one page, Ina Coolbrith's

poem, "La Copa de Oro (California Poppy)," were given away.[15] The sonnet had been published in the 24 May 1893, *San Francisco Bulletin.* Often reprinted in later years, this lyric was declared by George Sterling to be the best poem written on the state's official flower.[16]

World's Columbian Exposition, Chicago.

Miss Coolbrith was urged to attend the fair. She had already been invited to participate in a program for the unveiling of a statue to Queen Isabella in the California building. Before her departure a testimonial affair in her honor was given by the Bohemian Club—an authors' evening. Held on 31 August 1893, the program was an expression of high regard for a fellow author, and a belated answer to one library Board member who had asked, petulantly, "What has she done?"[17] The evening was also a farewell party for Miss Coolbrith who would be leaving for Chicago next month. Poems were read by Joaquin Miller, Daniel O'Connell, and others. Miss Coolbrith was present but, modest as usual, she asked William Greer Harrison to read her message of appreciation.[18] This occasion inspired her poem "Bohemia," lines reminding the club of her gratitude for all its kindnesses.[19]

She left on 23 September, to spend October and November at the Exposition where she was a guest of honor at a number of literary affairs.[20] One was a special meeting of the Press League which she attended with Mrs. Winifred Black ("Annie Laurie") of the *San Francisco Examiner.* Miss Coolbrith spoke at this meeting in her customary casual manner. Miss Mary H. Krout, president of the league, in writing for the *Chicago Post* about the talk, said that, while Miss Coolbrith spoke "so diffidently of her achievements, depreciating the word 'literary' as applied to them, she is one of the few true poets of the continent. For many years librarian at Oakland, California, her life has been quiet and retired. But abroad she is a vogue. Englishmen of letters commend her highly and often, and even at home where prophet or poet hath but little honor, the praise of great men—notably Whittier—has fallen to her share, and she is perhaps the only woman—Gertrude Atherton excepted—whom Ambrose Bierce ever stops to eulogize." Miss Krout described Ina Coolbrith as "a tall, dignified woman with iron gray hair, gray eyes and almost faultless features."[21]

The California poet was present at the dedication of the "Pampas Palace," an ornate, Moorish-inspired booth in the California building, where a new statue of Queen Isabella was unveiled. A poem for the occasion was written and recited by Miss Coolbrith.[22] As she wandered through the grounds, day by day, she was entranced by the White City, and regretted that the handsome pavilions were only temporary.[23] Strolling one day through the Midway Plaisance, she came to an exhibit that disturbed her and haunted her always. There, in a log cabin, sat an Indian, under guard, Chief Rain-in-the-Face, the man advertised there as having killed Custer at the last stand. With crude barbarity, permitted by the United States government, the cabin had been hauled from Montana as the habitat for the exhibit of a man,

> There in the surging crowd
> Silent, and stern, and proud,
> . . . Rain-in-the-Face!

It was a shock to come suddenly upon this stark example of "man's inhumanity to man." The cabin walls were hung with relics of the battle of the Little Big Horn. So would a Roman soldier or a savage warrior have displayed his war trophies and his captive. Ina was repelled and bewildered. Why was he here? After all, she thought, this very land where Chicago and its White City stood was wrested from the Red Man. And if the prairies burned with fires of hate, she mused, they had been ignited by "the wrongs of the White Man's rule." She could see no decent reason to exhibit this man. Suppose Custer's widow were to walk into the place? Had the "exhibitors" thought of that? She could only wonder:

> And the throngs go up, go down,
> In the streets of the wonderful town;
> And jests of the merry tongue,
> And the dance, and the glad songs sung,
>   Ring through the sunlit space.
> And there, in the wild, free breeze,
> In the House of the Unhewn Trees,
>   In the beautiful Midway Place,
>   The captive sits apart,
>   Silent, and makes no sign.
>   But what is the word in your heart,
>   O man of a dying race?
>   What tale on your lips for mine,
>   O Rain-in-the-Face?[24]

"The Captive of the White City" was Ina Coolbrith's only spontaneous poem inspired by her visit to the World's Columbian Exposition. The Queen Isabella composition was written on request.

From Chicago Miss Coolbrith went directly to Maine where she visited friends and relatives in Portland and Biddeford. Homesick, or enjoying the contrast of a Maine winter with one in California, she sent the *San Francisco Examiner* a poem which was featured on a decorated page of the 1893 Christmas number. Here, looking out over

"The vast, unbroken silences of snow,"

she was remembering that in California

"In one swift month the poppy will lift up
Its golden cup."[25]

After a brief stay in Boston she went on to New York where she was the guest of honor at the annual reception for literary women given by the Author's Club at the Waldorf in January 1894.[26] And in February a large dinner party was given for her by the Edward Curtisses at the Murray Hill Hotel. One of the guests, Edmund Russell, stood up and read Miss Coolbrith's long ode, "California," to the surprise of the author and the delight of the others.[27] Like her acquaintances in Chicago, the people she met in New York were all urging her to bring out another volume of verse—an inclusive edition—up to date.

She remained in New York until March, returning to California by the southern route. The Mojave Desert was a brilliant expanse; from the train windows she saw "a carpet of bloom," she related, "stretching as far as the eye could reach, made up of every variety of color and tone and shade of color under the sun—more wonderful in combination and harmony than could ever come from the far-famed Persian looms."[28] The poet was home in time to attend a Congress of Literature held in San Francisco late in April. Mrs. Charlotte Perkins Stetson presided. Speakers included Charles H. Shinn, journalist, who described the California literature exhibits and lectures at the recent Chicago Fair, and John Vance Cheney, San Francisco City Librarian, whose paper was on the practical side of poetry. The next speaker, Miss Viona Woods, on the novel, disagreed with Librarian Cheney, saying that poetry was a thing of the past. On the program Miss Woods was followed by Miss Coolbrith in a reading from one of her own poems. She prefaced her reading with a wry comment, "If, as Miss Woods believes, the poet's time is past, I am glad my verse is brief."[29]

The next month, on 29 May 1894, Ina Coolbrith's niece, Ina Lillian Peterson, was married to a San Francisco attorney, Finlay Cook, son of Ronald and Mary Cook, natives of Scotland.[30] The young couple made their home in San Francisco. The poet was now alone in her large Oakland house. While she was alone, she could not have been lonely, for she had many callers. An amusing incident occurred one evening when Joaquin Miller brought Edmund Russell, artist and anthologist, to call. Russell was the man who had read Ina's "California" at the New York dinner party in February. Early in the year he had published a collection of verse of California writers. During the evening's conversation, Miller looked at his watch and found that he and his companion would have to leave at once in order to catch the San Francisco train. After a hurried "good-bye," they rushed out, pushed the front gate, and found it locked or stuck. There was no time to lose, so the men vaulted over the fence and dashed for their train. Once aboard, breathless, Miller recalled, between gasps, "Say, that gate opens in!"[31]

As the year 1894 drew to a close, Ina found little time for verse writing. The October *Century Magazine* printed a wistful lyric called "The Flight of Song," obviously suggested by the poet's own attempt to recapture the singing that once came to her so readily.[32] She wrote some lines which she read at the Emma Dawson testimonial in November.[33] And she composed a longer poem as a memorial to Celia Thaxter. This was published as an eight-page pamphlet, *The Singer of the Sea,* by the Century Club of San Francisco.[34] The booklet was printed for Christmas giving, as was also another, not much larger, containing some of Miss Coolbrith's flower sonnets illustrated in color with prints of wild flower sketches. *A Collection of California Wild Flowers* was an attractive little souvenir.[35]

Songs from the Golden Gate

Fully aware and a little frightened that her first two years of freedom from routine tasks had been nearly barren of literary inspiration, Ina Coolbrith spent the early part of 1895 preparing a book which she hoped to publish that year. She decided that, since *A Perfect Day* was out of print, she should include the best in that volume as well as later poems. Her final selection was cut severely to one hundred poems, sixty-two from *A Perfect Day,* and thirty-eight others. She changed the title of "In Memoriam—Hon. B. P. Avery" to "At Rest," and omitted one piece, "Discipline," which may have appeared trite to her. She was restrained in her choice of the more recent verse, omitting many that had a local or occasional interest. Some of these may be found only in her scrapbooks. The new collection, she decided, would include "The Poet," omitted from her first book, and the two best of her flower sonnets, "The Mariposa Lily" and "Copa de Oro." Three based on her travel experiences would find a place here, "In the Grand Cañon," "The Captive of the White City," and "Midwinter East and West." She would include "Helen Hunt Jackson," the lines that Whittier had praised ten

227

years before, and her sonnets to Edwin Booth and William Keith. The latter, always an enthusiast of hers, offered to illustrate her collection, and did so, with landscapes in the moods of four of her lyrics, "My 'Cloth of Gold,'" "At Set of Sun," "The Brook," and one of Keith's own favorites, "Meadow-larks." She planned to dedicate the volume to Edmund Clarence Stedman and to close it with a sonnet to her mother, "A Last Word." With a new portrait of herself for a frontispiece, she sent the manuscript to Houghton Mifflin Company in Boston, the publishers with the long tradition of interest in the works of American poets.

Her work on the book completed, Miss Coolbrith accepted an invitation early in July from Adeline Knapp, a Mill Valley author, to attend a picnic at Miss Knapp's rural place on the slope of Mount Tamalpais. Other guests included Charles Warren Stoddard, William Keith, Edwin Markham, and Charles Keeler and his wife. The talk was on the nature of art and literature, and was described by the *Call* in an amusing illustrated story, as "a modern holiday on Mt. Olympus."[36] It was a stimulating but relaxing day among the redwoods and the laurels. Miss Coolbrith seemed to be in the best of health and spirits. Then suddenly, with little warning, only a few weeks later, she was seized by a painful attack of pleurisy, followed by pneumonia, and was so seriously sick that a Eureka newspaper headlined a story, 27 July 1895, "INA COOLBRITH DYING."[37] Her brother William and his wife came from San Rafael to care for her. They were aided by two Oakland friends, Harriet Howe and Josephine Zeller. The newspapers up and down the coast published almost daily bulletins on her condition, and when she finally came through the long illness, her physician, Dr. Wheeler, suggested that a change of climate would be beneficial.[38]

She had recovered by the time her *Songs from the Golden Gate* came off the press late in October.[39] It was a small, dainty volume, a "sixteenmo," in a smooth, ivory cloth binding with gilt top and lettering. The frontispiece showed a pleasantly serious woman, a beautiful woman, with an intent clear-eyed look and a faintly smiling mouth. The eyes were dark, below straight, strong eyebrows, and the upper lip a nearly perfect Cupid's bow. The chin was rounded and the skin smooth. The ears were left bare by an upswept coiffure that piled brown curls high on the head and spilled curly bangs across the forehead. By now the brown hair had glints of gray. The portrait was a good likeness. The Keith reproductions were disappointing, for the black and white cuts scarcely hinted at the mood and colors of the originals. The books were

Ina Coolbrith, 1895. Courtesy of the Oakland Free Library.

bought eagerly by Ina's friends, who were delighted to see their old favorites as well as later verse; and they sent her clippings of the critics' comments in publications from Portland, Maine, to Los Angeles, from North Carolina to the state of Washington. She was showered by these cuttings from journals and she covered several scrapbook pages with them.[40] Most of the reviews were complimentary, some even flattering, but a few were cool, and that in the *New York Times* caustic.

All these comments were from United States journals. Not until nearly three years later was her book noticed in London. Then Albert Kinross, editor of the *London Outlook*, wrote an article of discovery about her, quoted her poems generously, and advertised his "find" in huge posters.[41] He was so enthusiastic that he hoped soon to arrange for an English edition of her verse.[42] The article was followed by a minor avalanche of press comments in England and this country. Ambrose Bierce was amused that London had discovered Ina Coolbrith.[43] And Henry James, a San Francisco journalist not to be confused with the novelist, concluded his remarks on British appreciation of the California poet in these words:

Miss Coolbrith, so far as has been my privilege to observe, does not attempt heroics. She is content with melody and lilt, with sentiment, tenderness, an appeal to the emotions. . . .

California has a right to be proud of Ina Coolbrith. It is too busy now. Sometime it will awaken from its dreams of gold and gain and conquest to understand that here was one who had been touched with the sacred fire. It does not realize this yet. . . . Let a Californian be successful and the shafts designed to wound will be hurled by those who had been his fellow citizens. . . . A Californian no sooner achieves eminence than he becomes a target. From this spirit Miss Coolbrith will not escape. Her hope is in recognition afar, and this is being realized.[44]

During 1895 Miss Coolbrith did a little writing in spite of her book and her illness. "Memory," published in a spring issue of *Scribner's Monthly*, was the most recent of her poems to be included in the *Songs*.[45] She wrote a piece for Oakland's Independence Day celebration, also a humorous bit of prose about Joaquin Miller's notorious handwriting, then, at the end of the year, "The Vision of Sir Francis Drake," which the *San Francisco Call* used in its Christmas number.[46] In November she followed her doctor's advice and went to Los Angeles, where she was a house guest of Mrs. Perry, a friend from childhood days.[47] In the southern city she was feted by friends and received by the Friday Morning Club.[48] While in the area she gave Charles Lummis a copy of her

230

new book, inscribing it with eight lines that proved his belief and hers, that there is only one race of mankind. She was outspoken and ahead of her time when she wrote "One,"

> Light of the suns and stars of heaven,
>   The sweet warm air, and the green earth sod,
> And birth and death unto all are given,
>   Children alike of the selfsame God.
> What matters the ebony locks or flaxen,
>   The skin of snow, or the skin of tan?
> Indian, Afric, Mongol, Saxon—
>   Within are the heart and soul of Man.[49]

Leaving Los Angeles she went further south, staying a short time at the Hotel del Coronado in San Diego, wishing she might remain longer to relax by the sea.[50]

Lectures on California Literature

Back in Oakland, after the holidays, she experimented with a new medium of self-expression, the lecture. Miss Coolbrith had always spoken in public with an easy naturalness, always extemporaneously and in connection with club or library activities. Accustomed though she was to reading verse in public, she had not attempted the formal address. Her first talk was given at the home of Mrs. Clinton Day, in Berkeley, on Friday afternoon, 20 March 1896. She chose the subject nearest her heart, and one that always appealed to her friends: "Reminiscences of Early California Writers."[51] As she made notes in preparation for her talk, she was vividly aware that some of these memories and anecdotes were going to be lost. Without considering ultimate publication, she began to assemble and keep her notes for future reference. She supposed that, if her talk in March proved popular, she might consider other lectures on what she knew of California letters. Perhaps she might give a course of lectures. There was a wealth of material in her mind, ready for sorting and transmitting.

Actually the talk in Berkeley was her only one for nearly a year. In January 1897 she spoke at the Century Club in San Francisco on "The Indian of Romance."[52] Then, with this experience behind her, she announced a course of four lectures to be given in Berkeley homes in March, for a fee: a dollar for the course or twenty-five cents for single admission. Her subjects were: "Celia Thaxter," "Early California Reminiscences," "Personal Reminiscences of Bret Harte," and "Some Rumanian Folk Songs."[53] In April she spoke at the Women's Congress in

San Francisco on "Poetry as a Factor in Education," and the next month at the Ebell Club in Oakland on "California's Early Distinguished Writers."[54] In November she gave two more addresses on California writers at Stiles Hall in Berkeley.[55] All her talks had been popular, and she was engaged to give a series of four at the Century Club in January 1898.[56]

Having been abandoned by the Muse, she feared, she was certainly not courting that goddess in those years. She was finding new stimuli in prose writing and in audience response. She continued, however, to write poems of occasion, such as "The Gold Seekers (in Memory of the Reverend Henry Durant)" which she herself recited at the Durant School graduation exercises for grade B-9 in June 1896.[57] Another was the humorous "A Paper for the Convention; or, The Attitude of the Muses toward Poems of Occasion." Her theme was that the poet who fell asleep while writing, and had only a blank page to present to the meeting, would be a welcome relief. This "paper," in the style of "Abou Ben Adam," was read at the convention of the Pacific Coast Women's Press Association in September 1896. The members were amused by her contribution, but when the group all took the train to the top of Mount Tamalpais for an outing in the mild autumn sunshine, she was begged to read her "California" to them.[58] If Adeline Knapp were present that day she would have tried to persuade Ina Coolbrith to use this poem as a text for a book of scenic views of California.[59] Miss Coolbrith wrote memorial lines for Kate Marshall Field in November of the same year. She also composed her usual Christmas poems for the Examiner, "The Crucifixion, Still" in 1896 and "Redemption" in 1897.[60]

During these years Ina Coolbrith was the subject of several newspaper and magazine accounts, the most important of which was a long article in the St. Louis Mirror, 6 July 1896. The author, Alexander de Menil, was interested in William Pickett's relationship to the poet, and mentioned the stepfather's connection with the old Missouri Republic and later with the San Francisco Bulletin. Most of the article, however, was devoted to Ina Coolbrith, and was copied by other periodicals, including the magazine Hesperian, and Leslie's Weekly. She was noticed in Munsey's that year, and was interviewed for the San Francisco Bulletin by Mrs. Fremont Older.[61]

In 1897 she had two brief holidays out of town; a week at Pacific Grove at the WCTU convention where she was on the program for readings of her own verse every evening.[62] The other was of a more frivolous nature. A young friend of hers, Annie Briggs, art student of William Keith, was queen of the Tacoma rose carnival in June. Miss Coolbrith was persuaded to attend and was accompanied on her journey by her Los Angeles friends, Mrs. Perry and the latter's daughter.[63]

All this was very agreeable, but the economic contribution was zero. Ina Coolbrith needed a regular income. The desultory receipts from lectures now and then could not be depended upon for the payment of taxes. And the sale of poetry would not fill the pantry shelves. An enthusiastic fan once gushed, "Oh, Miss Coolbrith, our whole family just lives on your poems!" "How nice," she smiled, "that is more than I was ever able to do."[64]

22
Librarian,
Mercantile
Library

Women are not cared for as numerously
as they were in the old days. . . . More and more
and in daily increasing numbers they are thrust into
the world to do its battles for themselves and others.

Ina Coolbrith, *San Francisco Call* (1898)

New Duties and Responsibilities

Miss Coolbrith's need for regular employment was urgent. She began
to look about for a library position in San Francisco, or perhaps in Los
Angeles. Her southern California friends reminded her of opportunities
in their part of the state. When the position of City Librarian in Los Angeles became vacant, Ina Coolbrith's name was proposed.[1] She had the
distinction of being endorsed by two of the state's most prominent educators, David Starr Jordan, president of Stanford University, and Joseph
LeConte of the University of California.[2] For whatever reason, perhaps
the technicality of a local residence requirement, Miss Coolbrith was
not appointed. At the end of the year 1897, however, H. R. Coleman
resigned as librarian of the Mercantile Library of San Francisco, and
Miss Ina D. Coolbrith was employed to fill the vacancy, though a mi-
nority of members grumbled because a woman was to manage the institution. Her duties began on Tuesday, 18 January 1898, after she had
completed her lecture series at the Century Club.[3]

She found herself in a library situation far different from that in Oakland. This was a subscription library that had served a limited membership for nearly a half a century. For a fee members enjoyed reference services, open-shelf reading rooms, borrowing privileges, and a chess
room. The building, at the corner of Golden Gate and Van Ness Avenues, was a handsome, three-story structure in the Italian Renaissance

235

style, a sharp contrast to Oakland's poor little rickety library. The book collection was much larger and richer than that in Oakland, nearly seventy-five thousand volumes at the time Miss Coolbrith became librarian. Among these were important reference sets in fields of science, history, literature, and art. A fine Shakespeare collection and important illustrated works, including the elephant folio of Audubon's *Birds of America,* were among the prized possessions of the Association. As the new librarian came to take charge, she must have recalled, from an early period thirty years before, her first awestruck sight of the Mercantile Library reading rooms then, in a building at the corner of Montgomery and Bush Streets—luxuriously furnished rooms, book-lined, floor to ceiling, with ladders on tracks to reach the top shelves.[4]

While Miss Coolbrith found the new building and collections even more impressive, she discovered that the number of books borrowed for home use was less than that in Oakland. The appropriation, too, was smaller, but there were no branch reading rooms to be maintained. The entire budget, small as it was, could thus be applied to one central collection and one building. The affairs of the Association were administered by a Board of fourteen, elected by the members. Like the budget, the staff was small. While the library was open day and evening, Miss Coolbrith found that she had only one full-time assistant, besides the janitor. Her assistant was Hawthorne Doxey, young son of William Doxey, the bookseller and publisher, whom she knew. William Doxey was also a member of the Board.[5] Until the Librarian could sell her house in Oakland, she commuted to and from the library, thus lengthening her day's work.

Her first assignment in the new position was a strange one. Her predecessor had not compiled an annual report for his last year's service, nor for the preceding year. Since the library reports were printed annually, Miss Coolbrith was asked to compile those for 1896 and 1897. Preparing these for the printer gave her immediate access to library and Board records, such as the treasurer's reports, so that she was soon familiar with the state of the library's health and was aware of its problems.[6] Of all the Board members, the Association's treasurer, T. R. Bannerman, proved most helpful to the new librarian, and most considerate of her needs. The matters of collecting the dues, making bank deposits, renewing contracts for periodicals, paying or "staving off" the gas and water "monsters," as well as selecting, ordering, processing books, and serving readers at the reference desk, were all in her province. Fiscal and personnel matters she took up with the treasurer. He valued her hurried little notes to him, and put them away. They may now be found in the Bancroft and Huntington libraries.

The librarian soon found that she needed more than one assistant. When Bannerman suggested employing a girl, she put in a plea for a middle-aged woman to help her.

"Young girls," she said, "I have had in my library work, a score of them. Dress, chit-chat, parties, beaus, 'marrying and giving in marriage!' It is the almost invariable result, that, just as you have them broken to harness, and going an even gait, some miserable masculine appears on the scene, and they come to you with a blush and tremble, and 'please ma'am, I'm going to be married.' They are off, and you have your work all over again with another.

"Now a *woman* has responsibility, and intelligence, and patience— if she be anything at all. They really do better work in the library than the generality of men, that is the reason for so many of the Eastern libraries employing them. The Sacramento library has never employed a man; neither has the Los Angeles, which, by the way, has a force of 26 ladies under Mrs. Wadleigh, and ranks the second in size and importance in the state."[7]

If this attitude seems to be female chauvinism, it is at least an expression of the thinking on the subject that was current in the 1890s. It was an attitude that created an image (not flattering to women) and a barrier, difficult to break for many decades, and discouraged from the profession many young men with the talents and aptitudes for good librarianship. Miss Coolbrith was relieved by some additional help, for which she expressed her gratitude, but she found later in the year that young Doxey tried her patience. Son of a Board member and prominent bookman Hawthorne Doxey may have found it galling to work under a woman administrator. Their differences concerned evening schedules. Each worked three evenings; nothing could have been fairer. It was essential that the schedule be regular, for the sake of the library as well as personal engagements. A clash came one day when the assistant had an unexpected guest and announced that he would not work that evening, thus compelling the librarian to miss an appointment with a prospective buyer for her Oakland house. Miss Coolbrith, vexed by the flaunting of her authority, came near resigning, but was talked out of it by Treasurer Bannerman.[8] She had been rehired after her six months' probation, evidence of the Board's confidence in her management of the library.[9]

In January 1899 the annual election of officers took place, and, in the absence of the recording secretary, the librarian took the minutes. She also sent official notices of election to the new officers. Bannerman was reelected treasurer; in the notice to him she enclosed a slip of paper with the words, "And may God have mercy on your soul!" This inspired him to write at the top of her letter:

'May God have mercy on your soul,' as
　　sure I say 'Amen'
And when the angel calls me hence,
　　I hope there will be then,
At least a quorum of the Board to
　　pass on my report
And give me as I pass away, their
　　voucher and support.

T. R. B.[10]

The year had been a busy one for the librarian, and a trying one in many respects. Her sympathy with the treasurer was well founded. The library, for all its apparent opulence, was often financially embarrassed, since its income was uncertain from year to year.[11] The librarian was compelled to handle many small problems on this account, or bother the treasurer. Thus fiscal matters—and personnel—formed the basis of their correspondence. Miss Coolbrith had not been able to sell her house in Oakland, and found it hard to meet possible buyers when she was in the city all day. She was beginning to feel the wear and tear of daily commuting and would be glad when she could settle in San Francisco, near her place of employment. More and more of her activities took place in the city with which she identified herself more truly than she ever had with Oakland.

Prose Writing

At this time, early in 1899, Miss Coolbrith was aware that her notes for talks on California's earlier writers were beginning to have some value of their own, not merely as aids to her own public speaking. She was becoming eager to expand them and to organize her material into some form for permanent use. She decided to begin systematic work on a history of California literature. The more she thought of the idea, the more she was convinced of the need for such a work. Mrs. Cummins' *Story of the Files* was of considerable value and interest, but Ina Coolbrith knew that her own personal comments would have their use, too. Besides, her friends, who heard her speak in public, were urging her to put all the anecdotes and other information in writing. She was thinking of this when she was offered a position as librarian of the Bohemian Club early in 1899. The pay and the responsibility would be less, but so would the hours of work at the library desk. She would have time to work on her book. Ina was tempted by the offer. She discussed the matter with Bannerman in February.[12] That month the Board had reelected her as librarian for the next six months. By the end of March she had made her decision. She resigned in April to accept the Bohemian Club offer.[13]

Her prose writing was absorbing more of her time and thought, though she did write some verse during her year at the Mercantile Library. She wrote "A Christmas Song," which was printed with music by Oscar Weil in the Christmas issue of the *San Francisco Call* in 1898.[14] The same month a quatrain of hers, "The California Year," was published in Charles Lummis' *Land of Sunshine*.[15] And her poem, "The Blood of a Nation," on the Spanish-American War, was included in an anthology of war poems published that year in San Francisco.[16] In June *Current Literature* published an article on how—physically—poets write their poems. Do they sit at a table or in a rocking chair, or do they lie abed? Miss Coolbrith was quoted as saying that she "writes them on her feet, going about her affairs until her poem is complete, and then writing it down exactly as she framed it in her mind."[17] That was the year, too, that Albert Kinross was "hard hit" by her poems, as he told her, and published his article in the *London Outlook*, creating a mild furor in English literary circles.

The furor was indeed mild in comparison with one that stirred San Francisco and the whole country in January 1899 with a noisy controversy that continued to reverberate for some time to come. This was Edwin Markham's "The Man With the Hoe," published by Bailey Millard with an editorial in the *San Francisco Examiner*.[18] Every reader was shocked by the poem, and every reader took a strong stand for or against Markham's articulation of the emotions that took hold of him when he first viewed Millet's great painting of the earthbound toiler in the mud—a painting that had created a similar stir when first exhibited thirty years before. Ina Coolbrith defended Markham hotly, first as a poet, second as a man of compassion for his fellowman. Only the year before her own attitude on certain acute social problems at the turn of the century had been expressed in print. She was deeply concerned about the plight of the working woman. This came out in her answer to the *San Francisco Call*, when the paper asked her, as one of the Bay Area's prominent citizens, how she would spend a million dollars if she had the opportunity. Among those similarly questioned and quoted were university presidents David Starr Jordan, of Stanford, and Martin Kellogg, of California, as well as other educators, businessmen, lawyers, club women, and clergymen. Ina Coolbrith was the only librarian questioned. Many of the answers suggested using the fund for educational and humanitarian needs. Miss Coolbrith combined both in a characteristic statement:

I would give the preference of its disposition to members of my own sex. Women are not cared for as numerously as they were in the old days, by the sons of men. More and more and in daily increasing numbers they are thrust into the world to do battle for themselves and others.

I would like to provide training schools in which girls and women wage-earners might be educated and thoroughly fitted for some occupation, that would insure their freedom from slavery.

I would connect therewith sick wards and medical attendance for those in need of such; temporary homes for the homeless and unemployed, and free intelligence offices, and, as woman does not live by bread alone any more than man, I would have in connection therewith libraries and reading rooms, lectures and music, that the mind and heart might be fed as well as the body, and life be endowed with its greatest humanizing and moral influences, hope and happiness.[19]

At the close of the summer of 1899 Miss Coolbrith moved to San Francisco, taking an apartment at 618 Golden Gate Avenue, very near the Mercantile Library.[20] She sold her house in August to William Kohler whom she reminded, after the business transactions were completed, that her beautiful white angora cat, Calla, lay buried beneath the old oak at the back of the yard.[21] Ina was happy to be in her own city once more, a city at once entrancing and ugly, her "city of mists and of dreams." In a city beautification campaign during the last year of the century she was asked her opinion, and her lengthy reply was published in the *Examiner*:

How best to beautify San Francisco? I should think they'd best tear it all down and begin over again.

Let us have finely paved streets and roads with lines of trees down either side. Take away those old rookeries facing the water front, and let us have a good front door and front yard to our city to begin with. Then there is that old, scarred, mutilated corpse of Telegraph Hill. What are we going to do with that?

These are things that impress a stranger first. If we are not going to raze Telegraph Hill completely away, so that not a suggestion of it shall remain to torture us, why not terrace it and beautify it? I for one plead for its preservation and restoration, as far as

240

may be, for it has the dearest historical associations of any point in the city.

We might borrow a lesson from Boston in one respect. There every little odd corner or waste place in the city, such as we give over to garbage and rubbish heaps, is planted with grass and flowers, with perhaps a tree. It is a great pity that a city as picturesquely situated as this didn't begin right. It might have been made beautiful—beautiful! What would not the old Romans have done with such a noble site as San Francisco? Wouldn't they have made the hills shine? And see what we have done with our seven hills."

Before the end of the year she wrote four more verse compositions, all slight, all for special occasions.[23] Her prose was demanding her thought. She looked to the new year and the beginning of the new century for the freedom to work on her new book, the literary history of her state.

Part Four
"Lost City"
1900
to 1913

23
On
Russian Hill
Again

Hill of desire and dream,
Youth's visions manifold
That still in beauty gleam
From the sweet days of old!

Ina Coolbrith, from
"From Russian Hill" (1915)

A Home on Russian Hill

Ina Coolbrith was restless as the new century dawned. Though advancing in years (she would be fifty-nine in March) and troubled with occasional attacks of rheumatism, she was filled with hope.[1] Now that she was back in the city where she felt most at home and employed on a part-time basis in congenial surroundings, she was strengthened by a conviction that she would soon complete her book. She was eager to settle where she could devote all her spare time to the project that was demanding a large share of her thoughts. After a brief stay at Van Ness and Golden Gate avenues, she moved out to 2913 Bush Street, to be near her friends Judge and Elizabeth Boalt who lived on Spruce Street.[2] This place was temporary, as was the next, to which she came early in 1901, 1200 Leavenworth Street.[3] While here she was ill for more than six months, and she knew that she would have to find a flat large enough for herself and a companion-housekeeper.[4]

In 1902 she settled in a place that met all her requirements.[5] It was on her beloved Russian Hill, only three blocks from the flat where she had lived with her mother a third of a century before, and to which Harte and Stoddard, Miller and Webb had trooped in the days of the "Golden Gate Trinity." Here, on her own "hill of memories," she would recall the old days and give them an immortality in the history she was preparing. She rented the upper flat in the house, a roomy place, with space for herself and Miss Zeller.[6] Josephine Zeller had come from Oakland to help move and to stay as housekeeper, nurse, and companion. She was older than Ina and deeply devoted to her.[7] She had cared for the poet during the severe illness in 1895, and Miss Coolbrith was confident that she was in good hands, and would be released from household tasks, to devote time to her duties as Bohemian Club librarian, as well as to continue her writing. Josie's affection developed into a fierce loyalty with the years. She kept the house neat and clean and gladly ran errands whenever Ina was bedridden with rheumatism, a condition that was becoming more frequent, each attack more prolonged than the previous one. But Ina's hilltop home consoled her somewhat. Her windows opened on enchanting vistas of Golden Gate and Bay and city. On a sunny day of north wind, Telegraph Hill seemed near enough to touch, and, beyond the Bay, the rimming hills of Marin and Alameda counties rose in sharp focus. On other days, she watched the fog creep in quietly, shrouding the familiar. And when the night was clear, the view was, as Ina herself said,

> Above, of stars a sea;
> Below, a sea of stars![8]

The new quarters were spacious, indeed, with even an extra bedroom that could be rented to a student. The small drawing room, which served also as a library and study, was soon crowded with the poet's treasures. The room was square, with ivory walls and dark woodwork, with windows on two sides. Against the chimney breast was a graceful white marble mantel; at the left of it stood an upright piano, and at the right were shelves, packed with books, many with their authors' inscriptions. Flying white birds decorated a dark Japanese screen that masked a doorway at the corner of the room between the bookcase and the wide desk. This latter was a handsome piece, built of walnut, beautifully waxed, with two ranks of drawers beneath the drop-leaf writing surface, with two shelves above it. On the shelves were photos of her colleagues, Stoddard, Mark Twain, and others. Above the big bookcase hung a fine framed engraving of Phillips' portrait of Lord Byron, and nearby, a group of small framed photographs, one of which was that of Whittier. A Keith landscape was among the paintings above the piano, and a gold-framed oval mirror graced the space above the mantel. In the room were more bookshelves, more Keith paintings, marble-topped occasional tables of carved walnut, vases, plaster figurines, Indian baskets. In front of the desk was a Navajo rug.[9]

The closed desk itself, with its many drawers, was where her most precious momentoes were stored. Here were the notes for her book, and here the small packets of letters from Harte, Stoddard, and Stedman. In a deep drawer at the bottom she kept her fat scrapbook, nearly filled with clippings, from her early poems printed in the *Los Angeles Star,* to her memorial poem for Joseph LeConte, in the September 1901 issue of the *University of California Magazine.* In case of fire, she laughingly told Robert Norman, the young law student who came to rent the small back bedroom—in case of fire—she would grab the things in the desk first. He understood, as he looked on with awe, when she took out the letters to show him, and let him browse through her bulky scrapbook. He was deeply impressed by the work she now had under way and was eager to read her narrative of events in which she had played an intimate part.

Bohemian Club Librarian

Before coming to her new home in 1902, Ina Coolbrith had finished several library related obligations. She was one of a group of librarians asked to help in the selection of plans for the new San Diego Public Library, soon to be constructed. This was in 1900.[10] The same year, as librarian of the Bohemian Club, she had edited a volume of Daniel O'Connell's verse which was published by Robertson as *Songs from Bohemia.*[11] The book was a success, as far as her fellow Bohemians were concerned. Several years later, 1904, she edited another book for the club. This was a collection of short speeches and toasts given from time to time by Henry H. Behr, a member of the California Academy of Sciences, as witty as he was learned. The volume, appropriately entitled *The Hoot of the Owl,* published by Robertson, was cherished by Behr's Bohemian peers.[12] The same year Robertson brought out another book of Miss Coolbrith's editing, printed by the Stanley-Taylor press, but slight in content. This was *A Voice from the Silence,* a book of sketches by Charles Nettleton, a theological student who died young. The volume was a souvenir for his friends, printed in trade and limited editions, the latter autographed by Ina Coolbrith, Edwin Markham, and Joaquin Miller.[13] She was not happy with either the compilation or the finished product of this effort.[14] It did not give her the sense of achievement that she experienced in editing the poems of O'Connell and the sketches of Behr.

This editorial work for the club broke the monotony of routine library work. For, no matter how casual the attitude or relaxed the atmosphere, a club library still requires a minimum of rules and records, and the latter must be kept in usable order for easy relations between reader and

librarian. A record of periodicals received and lent, and of books borrowed, must be kept. And the lending procedure must be simple enough for self-service during the hours when the part-time librarian is absent. A finding list is essential; perhaps even an elaborate catalog, that describes books with bibliographical exactness, may be desired by the bibliophiles among the members. Many of the books in the Bohemian Club were first editions with lengthy and witty autographed inscriptions. They were unique copies, and a detailed, descriptive catalog would have been in order. Books received by gift or purchase must be recorded, and letters relating to these and other subjects filed for future reference.

When the Board of Directors of the Bohemian Club named Ina Coolbrith Honorary Librarian in 1899, they specified her salary as fifty dollars a month, an amount that was doubled by private subscription after the fire of 1906.[15] This was for part-time employment. What her actual hours were we do not know. It is believed by members of the Bohemian Club that she continued to receive one hundred dollars monthly long after her days of active librarianship were past. Members of the club were magnanimous. And they were gallant. As one of their number says, "under the unwritten law that held among the members that no woman was 'talked about,' therefore no word other than the fact that she was the only woman having entree to the Club (after the fire) was ever mentioned."[16] The Bohemians regarded her honorary membership and librarianship as an honor to themselves. They revered her, and were truly appreciative of her abilities as poet, editor, and librarian—abilities that were enhanced by her wit, poise, and physical beauty.

Miss Coolbrith was often spoken of as the only woman member of the Bohemian Club. This was not strictly true, for, in the earlier days of the club's history, several other talented women were honored in the same way. But Ina Coolbrith and Margaret Bowman were the first women honorary members. This was not in recognition of any literary talents on their part. It was because the two women "made the curtains for the club's first quarters on Sacramento Street."[17] Years later, Ina recalled her initiation on 5 May 1874, saying that she first attended the club at a Ladies Jinks in company with Mr. and Mrs. James Bowman and Tommy Newcomb when Newcomb was president and "Uncle" George Bromley was master of ceremonies in the initiation performance.[18] When she be-

Corner of Ina Coolbrith's Drawing Room, 1604 Taylor Street, San Francisco, before the Earthquake and Fire of 1906. Courtesy of Mrs. Ina Cook Graham, Berkeley, California.

came librarian and the club rooms were at 130 Post Street, she was free to come and go in the performance of her duties. And being both sensible and discreet, she used a side door instead of the club's main entrance.[19]

During this period verse writing was of secondary importance to Ina Coolbrith, though she composed a number of pretty lyrics, "A Page of Herrick," "The Wind's Word," "Wood-call," and "Cactus Hedge."[20] The last named, reminiscent of her school days in Los Angeles, was set to music almost immediately.[21] Her more serious poems in these early years of the 1900s were, with the exception of "The Lot of Christ," all tributes to persons, "Paderewski," "Joseph LeConte," "William Keith, Artist," "Henry Holmes," "With the Laurel to Edmund Clarence Stedman on his Seventieth Birthday," and "Bret Harte."[22] With the sonnet to Stedman she sent a wreath of California bay leaves, as well as a spray of Sequoia sempervirens. He was touched by the tribute, and he praised her lyric as "strong, compact, high-phrased, showing your gift and art at their ripest."[23] When Stedman died in 1909, the poem was published in the *Atlantic Monthly*.[24] The tribute to Harte was written for the Bohemian Club Bret Harte Memorial Jinks and was published in the September 1902 issue of the *Overland*. Bret Harte's passing, in England, on 5 May 1902, was a deep sorrow for Ina Coolbrith. As she penned the lines in memory, she thought back to the early *Overland* days,

> I see him often, with the brown hair half
> Tossed from the leaning brow, the soft yet keen
> Gray eyes uplifted with a tear or laugh
>   From the pen-pictured scene.
>
> And hear the voice that read to me his dear
> Word-children—and I listen till I seem
> Back in the olden days; they are the near
>   And these but a dream.[25]

Bret Harte died on 5 May 1902. Only five days later, in San Francisco, occurred the death of Henry Frank Peterson, Ina Coolbrith's nephew.[26] Only forty-two years of age at his death, he was a victim of tuberculosis. By this time his aunt's rancor against him had lessened and finally disappeared. His critical illness saddened her, and she sent Henry her love whenever she wrote her niece who cared for her brother until his death. Henry's malady may have been upon him when he retired from his position as City Librarian on 30 June 1899. His small staff was devoted to him and gave him a fine leather purse as a parting gift, with a little presentation speech by Dwight Strong who had been with the library almost as long as Henry had and was a loyal personal friend of both Henry and his aunt. Another good friend was his brother-in-law, Finlay Cook, and, after Henry's divorce, the three, Finlay, Ina, and Henry, often went to the theater or a restaurant together. All three were interested in books. In fact it was a mutual interest in poetry that had attracted Ina Peterson and Finlay Cook in the first place. They found that when one started a quotation, the other could readily finish it. They were a devoted couple and included Henry in many of their outings.[27] When Henry was compelled to leave his position because of poor health, and became so ill he needed care, his sister came to his aid. She nursed him through his fatal illness. She herself contracted the disease and was told by her doctor to seek a drier climate than that of San Francisco. With her husband and child she moved to Menlo after the San Francisco fire, and spent some time in Arizona where she was restored to health and a very active life.[28] The devotion she gave her brother extended to his two daughters who were older than her own child.[29] Ina Coolbrith was devoted to all three of her grandnieces, and Mrs. Cook made it possible for them to see her often.

Miss Coolbrith also kept in touch with her two half-brothers who lived in San Francisco most of their lives. William had married Margaret Hayes, and, after her death, had married Margaret's sister Josephine, or Josie as she was called by her family.[29] Despite these two marriages William had no children. His twin brother, Don Carlos, who usually signed his name "Don C. Pickett," or simply "Your Brother" when writing Ina, remained a bachelor. He often made his home with William and Josie on Clay Street, San Francisco.[30] When away on business connected with his or his brother's mining interests, Don Carlos wrote regularly to his sister.[31] When one of the brothers suffered a bad case of blood poisoning in 1904, Ina spent all the time she could spare from her work to be with him.[32]

Stoddard's Novel, *For the Pleasure of his Company*

Though often ill, Ina was able to attend a number of interesting literary events in 1904 and 1905. One was a Sequoia Club reception for Gertrude Atherton in October 1904. This was Miss Coolbrith's first acquaintance with the novelist.[33] Another, in the same month, for Mary Austin, whose *Land of Little Rain* was then newly published, was given by the Pacific Coast Women's Press Association, in the Occidental Hotel. On this occasion Miss Coolbrith recited Mrs. Austin's poem, "The Young Men's Feet Are at the Door."[34] The following year the Press Association held its annual convention in May and gave a reception for Charles Warren Stoddard, by then a bearded, portly man, but gentle and debonair as always.[35]

Two months later Charlie read in *Sunset Magazine* Ina's brief lyric, "Wood-call," and was so moved that he wrote, in a little note she put away among her dearest treasures, "Ina dear, there has never been any doubt in my mind that you are the truest poet that ever glorified this coast."[36] She tucked the message in beside one from Edmund Clarence Stedman the year before, thanking her for the laurel wreath and sonnet. His closing words had put new heart in the aging woman writer: "Since you write better than ever, I hope you will still let your voice be heard, for it is not yet outrivalled on the Pacific Shore."[37] Shortly before she received Stedman's letter, she saw an anonymous compliment to her in the reader's letter column of the *San Francisco Bulletin*, gently sad, but gallant:

> I saw Ina Coolbrith on the street a few days ago for the first time in twenty-five years—and I could but be struck by the fine, strong face. I used to think that her eyes were as fine as any that ever shone, and I tried to get a good look at them, but the brow was shaded and I caught but a glimpse. This gifted woman should have lived anywhere but in California.[38]

These nostalgic words from one who "did but see her passing by" may have been penned by one of the many unknown readers whom she had served in the Oakland library. There were probably many more informal tributes to her as a woman and a writer, but they were ephemeral, lost in the air as speech, or, if put to paper, lost in the fire to come. More permanent were several notices that appeared in print in the early days of the new century. In 1900 she was one of a number of American poets whose biographies, portraits, and examples of verse appeared in the periodical *Current Literature*.[39] Appleton's *Annual Cyclopedia* for 1900 printed her portrait in its article on public libraries. She was the only woman librarian represented, but was erroneously described as the head of the San Francisco Public Library instead of the Bohemian Club.[40] In 1902, her friend, Laura Haines Loughead gave her three pages in the *Sunset Magazine*, and the following year George Wharton James wrote his first of several articles about her, four pages in the short-lived San Francisco periodical, *Impressions Quarterly*.[41] In preparing for this he called on her in her home at 1604 Taylor Street. It was James who told for the first time how Calle Shasta Miller had been reared by Ina Coolbrith. Indeed it had been in the company of Ina and Calle Shasta that James had first made the acquaintance of Joaquin Miller, before the turn of the century.[42] James's article appeared in the June 1903 issue of

Impressions Quarterly; and, in the *Atlantic Monthly* of June the next year, an article by Thomas Wentworth Higginson called attention to Miss Coolbrith's sonnet, "The Mariposa Lily."[43] Her flower poems were much admired and had been the inspiration for more than one pretty booklet of floral pictures in color. In 1904 she published a brief essay on "Some California Wild Flowers," and the same year she and John Muir were elected honorary members of the California Floral Society, an organization whose official botanist was Miss Alice Eastwood of the California Academy of Sciences.[44]

Ina Coolbrith took these press comments for granted. But in 1903 her appearance as a character in a novel did not please her. She liked neither the book, nor its treatment of the shadowy personnel who flitted through its pages, all of whom were known to her. She was especially annoyed because the fiction was by her dear friend Charlie Stoddard, who thereby proved that he did not know her as well as he thought he did. *For the Pleasure of his Company, an Affair of the Misty City, Thrice Told,* is a strange, autobiographical novel about Stoddard in the 1860s and 1870s, the young dilettante poet who lived on Folsom Street.[45] Among the persons moving in and out under fictional names were Charlie Stoddard himself, Minnie Myrtle Miller, James F. Bowman, Harry and Minnie Edwards, Constance Fletcher, and Ina Coolbrith. In the story Charlie is "Paul Clitheroe." Ina is "Elaine," and is pictured as a sweet but mournful young woman, worn out by the daily life at the library. She lives alone in a romantic vine-covered cottage in Oakland. The character "Elaine" is a lifeless person, wholly unlike the strong, vital, witty and sophisticated woman, Ina Coolbrith. As his dear friend for many years she must have resented "Paul Clitheroe's" obvious preference for two other females in the book to "Elaine." These were the sexy "Little Mama" and the outdoorswoman "Jack" or "Miss Juno." A key is needed to unmask the characters in this misty story. Ina Coolbrith had the key. Many years later, after most of the persons fictionalized were away or dead, she thoughtlessly gave the key to Edward F. O'Day, a prominent journalist in San Francisco, at his request, only to be upbraided in a letter from one of the persons in the story. The letter was from a woman who had married again, had moved to another city, and was afraid that the image of her in Stoddard's novel would shock her grown children.[46]

Manuscript of her Literary Recollections Almost Completed

By the spring of 1906 Ina Coolbrith was almost an invalid; her rheumatism kept her bedridden most of the time. She worried about her library responsibilities at the Bohemian Club, because, for long periods, she was unable to perform her part-time work there. It was even rumored that she had been dismissed, a baseless piece of gossip which she read in a local newspaper on 17 April 1906.[47] Her concern for this state of things, and for the financial loss if she should have to resign, was no help to her in trying to get well. In bed or out, however, she had frequent visitors. Usually she would hobble to an armchair, in her dressing gown, and receive her callers in her drawing room, surrounded by her books and pictures.

On Easter Sunday, 15 April 1906, a close relative, a son of one of Ina's cousins, Jesse Winter Smith, came to see her. He was at the time an engineering student at Stanford University. He was a grandson of Mary Bailey Smith, who as a young girl had been Ina's mother's dearest friend, and he was a devoted member of his mother's church and later served many years as an officer of the Mormon church in San Jose, California. Miss Coolbrith's young relative was not reticent about discussing her early connection with the Mormons. He knew why the break had been made when Ina's mother had married again. On that Easter Sunday he asked Ina why she herself had never revealed the relationship, now that her mother was gone. She told him that she had made a promise to her mother and had never asked to be released from it. She also told him that, for her own part, she was proud of her heritage, and added, "When I am gone, you may tell the world, if you care to do so."[48]

Her visitor asked her about the progress of her book and was surprised and pleased to see a nearly completed manuscript. Except for minor details, it was ready to offer to a publisher. Of course he was eager, like herself, to see the work in print, for much of the information it contained would otherwise be lost forever. She may have mentioned her age and afflictions as added reasons for the completion of this self-imposed and loving task. After all she had had her sixty-fifth birthday a month before. After the departure of "Cousin Jesse," as she called him, Ina put away the bulky manuscript, closed her desk, glanced around the pleasant room with all its cherished memories, and turned out the lights. Before making her way painfully to her bedroom, she stood a while before the window that looked out over the city—her city from her hill. It was a clear, still night. Below her the dark city was spangled with lights, and above her the stars were as bright.

"Night," she thought, "night, and the hill, to me!" Some lines of verse were forming in her mind. She would go over them. Someday, perhaps, she would write them down. A feeling of contentment came over her:

> Peace, that no shadow mars!
> Night and the hill to me!
> Below, a sea of stars!
> Above, of stars a sea![49]

24
Toppling Wall
and Ruined
Hearth

Gray wind-blown ashes, broken, toppling wall
And ruined hearth—are these thy funeral pyre?
Black desolation covering as a pall—
Is this the end—my love and my desire?

Ina Coolbrith, from
"San Francisco—April 18, 1906" (1906)

Earthquake and Fire, 1906

It is doubtful if Ina Coolbrith was asleep at five o'clock that fateful Wednesday morning, 18 April 1906. Suffering from the inflammatory rheumatism that now seemed chronic, she had found rest almost impossible. As she lay waiting for the daylight that she knew would bring little respite from the long night, she felt her bed suddenly seized by a savage, unseen force, and she was tossed and shaken painfully. The earthquake was of nearly a minute's duration, and was accompanied by a fearful din of shattering glass and the heavy thud and roll of falling stones and bricks. She called to Josie, and as soon as the quaking ceased, the two women prepared to leave the house for fear the chimneys might fall inward. Going through the rooms, they were dismayed by the havoc in their own home. Books had been thrown from the shelves, and vases, china, and small bric-a-brac lay shattered on the floor. As they joined their neighbors in the street and looked down over the already ruined city, they were stunned. Everywhere were toppled chimneys and collapsed brick or stone walls. Pavements were distorted and buckled, streetcar rails uprooted and bent, and there were tangles of wire and pipe. But most frightening of all were the scattered fires that they could see all over the city, west, south, and east. One by one most of them were put out. But south of Market Street, in the business district, fires were soon blazing out of control, spreading rapidly, devouring the

255

frame buildings, and consuming more slowly the large masonry structures in their path.[1]

The watching groups, huddled on Russian Hill, did not know that the earthquake had broken the water mains and that the city was without protection. When householders turned dazedly to do what they could to protect their own homes, many of which were of clapboard or shingle, they soon found that they had no water supply. Those who had cisterns filled tubs and buckets and waited, watching in horror as the fire spread. Another quake occurred shortly after eight o'clock, and a fire, starting in the neighborhood of McAllister Street and Van Ness Avenue not long after nine in the morning, burned, out of control until night, and destroyed the records in the already ruined city hall.[2] From the hill, in the afternoon, Ina and her neighbors could see the burning of Ralston's beautiful Palace Hotel; they could see that the shopping area and Chinatown would not escape. All night they watched, a night that was as bright as day, each family hopeful that their hill, or their block, or their own home would be spared.

By backfiring and dynamiting, firemen, householders, and soldiers tried but failed to prevent the progress of the fire north from Market along Powell. It was this fire that turned and destroyed the mansions on Nob Hill before dawn on Thursday. Not long after the flames had swept through the Fairmont Hotel, soldiers appeared on Russian Hill. They ordered the residents to evacuate the area and did not permit any householders with cisterns to remain and try to save their own homes. Numb with fear and despair, Ina and Josie, carrying their two frightened cats, Titian and Moona, and little else, joined their neighbors, the Stadtfelts, and made their way haltingly through heaps of rubble on the steep, distorted streets. The nearest open space of any size and safety was Fort Mason at North Beach on the Bay, more than a mile away from 1604 Taylor Street. Of course all walked, some dragging trunks and other luggage; there were no cars; no conveyance could get through.

Reaching Fort Mason, the two women found themselves among thousands of homeless people. The Stadtfelt family and Josie did all they could to make Ina comfortable. She was exhausted. It was probably here that they had their first opportunity to see the morning paper, the *Call-Chronicle-Examiner*, 19 April 1906.[3] The buildings of all three newspapers were gone, and this four-page news sheet was printed on the press of the *Tribune* in Oakland and rushed to the city by boat early that morning. From this the refugees learned of the extent of the fire, of the number of dead (estimated at five hundred at least), that the hospital was gone, and that the Mechanics Pavilion was being used as a temporary emergency station in its stead. They learned that the water

256

mains were destroyed by the quake and that the only means of fire fighting were to dynamite and backfire. They knew that the city was under military rule and learned from the newspaper that looters would be shot. They did not need a newspaper to tell them that by late afternoon the fire had reached Russian Hill, stormed it, and had laid it waste.

That night Ina and Josie lay on the ground, cuddling the two frightened cats, holding them tightly to keep them from bolting. They spent three nights and two days at Fort Mason, joining long breadlines, scanning the crowd for a familiar face in order to get word to Ina's niece or to friends in some undevastated area of the city. The fire had been halted at Van Ness Avenue by Saturday morning, 21 April. With few exceptions all the area east of that wide avenue was burned. Rain came on that night, too late to put out any flames, but dampening the still hot ashes, and adding discomfort to the refugees in the open. The rain stopped by morning, and then Ina spied a man she knew. He was Harr Wagner, the publisher, a friend of Joaquin Miller. He had come expressly to search for her among the crowds, and found her, chilled and miserable. He told her that Joaquin had tried to reach her, but had no pass, and had been forbidden to enter the city. Ina urged Wagner to notify Judge Boalt of her whereabouts, and, later that day she, Josie, Titian, and Moona were safe in the judge's house at 219 Spruce Street.[4]

In the meantime Miss Coolbrith's niece, Mrs. Cook, had been trying frantically to find her aunt. The Cook residence was outside the burned area. It was a small cottage which the family was preparing to leave in order to take up residence in Menlo. Their moving preparations were interrupted by the earthquake, and they found their home deluged with relatives who had lost their homes in the fire. The confusion about her must have added to Ina Cook's worry about her aunt. She was relieved and thankful to hear from Judge Boalt that Miss Coolbrith had been found and that she and Josie were expected to stay in his home until they could make arrangements for a place of their own. Shortly after this the Cook family moved to Menlo, a community in the warm, dry climate of the peninsula south of San Francisco. As soon as they were established in a house there, they invited their Aunt Ina to make her home with them.[5] She declined for two reasons: her work and her need for a dwelling place near her work. She knew that as soon as the Bohemian Club found temporary quarters she must begin the task of helping rehabilitate the lost library. And she knew that she must find a home of some kind nearby.

For Ina the devastation of the earthquake and fire was a crushing blow. "Imagine," she wrote to a friend, "your home with every article it contains swept from you, and you left with not so much as a comb or hair pin or common pin except what might be on your person!"[6] More serious was the loss of her manuscript and all the literary treasures accumulated during a rich and full life; the memory of that loss she must have tried to put from her.

When her new address became known, mail began to come to her. "For God's sake send me a line to say if you are alive and safe," wrote Harriet Howe, on the day after the earthquake, from Woodstock, New York.[7] And from South Biddeford, Maine, Ina's cousin Mary Huff begged her to come and live with them.[8] She received similar invitations from Mrs. Perry in Los Angeles and Mrs. Darling in Oakland.[9] Mrs. Boalt was planning to leave in July for an indefinite stay in Europe and she urged Ina and Josie to stay where they were until that time, then try to find a place to live in San Francisco. News trickled in, day by day. Alice Cooley had lost everything and was not insured.[10] The same was true of Mrs. Kip, Edmund Clarence Stedman's sister.[11] Gertrude Atherton took her own loss of home lightly—some clothes she was tired of, some manuscripts she could rewrite—her chief sorrow was that she had to stay in Oakland for a while.[12] William Keith's studio was burned, and his canvases, which had been taken to a place of supposed safety, were all destroyed when the fire reached that place.[13] Ina Coolbrith may not have known, or felt concern had she known, that the murals, which Arthur Mathews had just completed for installation in the new Oakland Free Library building at Fourteenth and Grove streets, were also destroyed by the fire, and that the artist later agreed to make a new set.[14] She grieved over the destruction of the Mercantile Library and its valuable collection. But she was even more deeply concerned about the loss of the Bohemian Club's library of rare California literary and pictorial treasures. That loss was intensified for her by the belief that her own position as librarian was gone, at least temporarily, in the flames. She had little hope of any other kind of employment.

"As soon as I can walk three blocks without being crippled for a week," she told Eleanor Davenport, "or write half a dozen pages without having to lie down, I shall try to find some kind of work to do, tho' what it will be, God knows, for no one seems to want an 'old woman' around."[15]

Soon after Miss Coolbrith arrived at the Boalt residence, Robert Norman, her former student roomer, came to see her. He brought with him her big scrapbook and the little box containing letters to her from Harte,

---

Part of Ina Coolbrith's Library Destroyed by the Fire of 1906. Courtesy of Mrs. Ina Cook Graham, Berkeley, California.

Stoddard, and Stedman.[16] It was all that he had saved. She could have hugged rescuer and rescued to her. But close to the joy of having these few momentoes was a pang for her lost manuscript. If she had it, she thought, she would have the prospect of some revenue for a time at least. Robert told her of the little he had been able to save from his own room. If he had been back to Russian Hill since 19 April, he could have reported the seemingly miraculous sparing of one lone house in their block on Taylor Street, the Sheppard home, at 1654, only a few doors away. It was spared because soldiers at the foot of the hill spied an American flag flying from a pole at the top of the house, rushed up, found tubs of water, and saved the house, although those on both sides were burning.[17] The boy might have known, too, and reported to her, of one row of cottages on the hill that the flames did not find. These were on a short, unpaved path, running from Taylor to Leavenworth, called Lincoln Street, later Macondray Lane. The owners of these houses had been overlooked by the soldiers, and were so busy fighting off the sparks from their roofs with water from their cisterns, that they did not know that every dweller on the hill was expected to leave.[18]

During May and June, Ina received a number of invitations and some small gifts of money and goods, usually presented with the utmost diplomacy to the proud and sensitive woman. Mrs. Boalt received a letter saying that Raphael Weill, of the White House department store, was giving away suits to the ladies who were burned out, and "would consider it an honor to fit Miss Coolbrith."[19] Mary Austin urged her, in poetic language, to come to Carmel, saying that Frank Powers of Pine Inn wanted her to be his guest there for a month. Mrs. Austin wrote, "You and I have never had an opportunity to become properly acquainted. Come and sit in my wickiup and write a poem, and we will walk by the sea and talk and talk."[20] Ina Coolbrith, always a practical woman, must have smiled wryly at this invitation, picturing her crippled self walking painfully along the beach. Her reaction was similar when she was told that there would be work for her in the Carmel library—at a salary of ten dollars a month—provided she did not disturb the incumbent! News of another library offer came in a very roundabout way. Mrs. Torrey Connor said that Charles Lummis, at that time Los Angeles City librarian, said that there was a position open for Miss Coolbrith in that library.[22] But she had no direct word from Lummis to that effect. In the meantime, Edmund Clarence Stedman was using all his influence and power to persuade John Vance Cheney, who had become librarian of the Newberry Library in Chicago, to make a place for Miss Coolbrith there, if possible. Stedman sent her a hundred dollars from what he called a special *authors' fund*. 1906 was a tragic year for him, too. He had lost his wife, his son, and his home that year, and he wrote to Ina, "Your motto and mine must be *Sursum Corda*. We must re-read Tennyson's 'Ulysses.' Even for you, reduced as you are to sheer personality and womanhood, what is essential is left, and before long, as the Bible says, all the other things shall be added also." He went on to tell her that Cheney had no place for Ina in his library, but had heard that Lummis had something in Los Angeles. Stedman was angry, and wrote, "I say frankly that Mr. Cheney has proved an ingrate concerning the first favor I ever asked of him."[23] And Ina mused, "I know, no one seems to want an old woman around."

Temporary Quarters, 15 Lincoln Street

As Mrs. Boalt was leaving soon for her European travels, Ina and Josie left the second week in July to stay for a while at 770 Seventeenth Street in Oakland.[24] Here Ina occupied a spare room and found a welcome for Titian and Moona. As soon as she was settled she tried to analyse her situation. She knew that she must find a permanent home of her own. The best house for her needs would be a double flat, so that the rent would pay taxes and give her some income when she was no longer able to work. But this was impossible. She was without funds. She knew that her one natural resource came through her pen. There had been a little coming in from time to time from the sale of her stock of *Songs from the Golden Gate*. But these were all burned, as were all her manuscript poems and her files of the *Golden Era*, the *Californian*, the *Overland Monthly*, and other periodicals that had published her verse. She wrote to James Gillis, librarian of the California State Library, to ask for a statement on the library's files of *Golden Era* and the *Californian*.[25] She may have been planning to rewrite her lost literary history of the state, as well as make copies of her own verse. Living frugally, on the pitiful sum of thirty cents a day, she hoarded what small savings she had and what she had been given after the fire, hoping to order another printing of her *Songs,* so that she could have a supply on hand.[26] During the exchange of letters between herself and the State Librarian, she complied with his request for a brief biography, answered his questions about pseudonyms of California writers, and gave an estimate of the size of her personal library, lost in the fire. She said that she had owned some three thousand volumes and many pamphlets.[27]

Shortly before Miss Coolbrith wrote to Gillis she had been in correspondence with George Wharton James of Pasadena who had ideas about a home fund for her. As early as June 1906, he had letterheads printed with "The Ina D. Coolbrith Home Fund Committee, Mrs. D. W. Lewis,

Chm."[28] He said that the Washington Heights Literary Circle would be the covering organization; he would have to keep his own name out of it if he wanted Lummis and others to cooperate.[29] His idea was to solicit authors' favorite sentiments in their own handwriting and to have these framed together with autographed photographs, all to be sold for the benefit of the home fund. He was excited about the prospects and asked her for plans for the type of three- or four-room house to be built for her on "Fellowship Heights" in Pasadena, and to revert to the committee at her death, so the house could go to some other needy author.[30] Ina Coolbrith was appalled. She must stop this man. The use of her name on the stationery without her permission made her an apparent object of charity. She was vexed by James's assumption that she wanted a small bungalow in Pasadena. Her letters, however, were tactful and appreciative of his sincere kindness in wanting to help her. To put him off a little, she told him that she had a lot in Corte Madera, Marin County, a recent gift of the Frank Pixley family.[31] This, at least, would divert his mind from a Pasadena building site, though she had no desire to live in isolated Corte Madera, either. She said that she planned to visit friends in Los Angeles during the fall and asked James to hold his plans in abeyance until they could have a frank talk on the subject.

Before Ina could leave for southern California, she had an accident in San Francisco that sent her to bed for more than a week. At the corner of Pine and California streets, she was knocked down by a runaway horse, but she was not trampled. She was saved by a man who grabbed the horse instantly. She had a cut on her forehead, numerous bruises, but no broken bones. The owner of the horse and buggy did not stop. He was a true forerunner of today's hit and run driver. Miss Coolbrith was taken to the ferry in a carriage, and she made her way home alone. Under the care of Dr. Cunningham she recovered in time to take the train for Los Angeles before the middle of August.[32]

She had already gone when a registered letter was brought to her door. The postman found no one at home and did not leave it that day, 10 August 1906, or three days later when he called again. The letter was returned to the sender, Miss Eleanor Davenport in San Francisco. It contained five hundred dollars from the Red Cross which Miss Davenport had obtained for a building site for Miss Coolbrith.[33] Learning that Miss Coolbrith had gone south, Miss Davenport wrote George W. James and asked him to see that the poet received her check. She told James something of a plan her club, the Spinners, had to benefit Ina Coolbrith. If the Red Cross money could buy a lot in San Francisco, and James's home fund could build the house, the Spinners would furnish it. The house would be Miss Coolbrith's as long as she lived, and afterward

262

go "to some other woman or man who has worthily upheld the standards of California literature." A lovely idea, it seemed to her.[34]

The Spinners Club was an organization of women writers, mostly amateur, and mostly young San Francisco society girls. They had made Ina Coolbrith, Gertrude Atherton, and a few other prominent writers honorary members. Their founder, and most talented active member, was Ednah Robinson Aiken, wife of Charles Aiken, the enterprising editor of the Southern Pacific's publication, *Sunset Magazine*. Mrs. Aiken had published several articles in the *Sunset* and was the author of several novels. She was especially interested in the arid Southwest and made it the subject of much of her writing. Eleanor Davenport was treasurer of the club and thus was stewardess of any benefit funds. Most of Miss Coolbrith's relations with the club were through Miss Davenport. Before Ina left for Los Angeles, the Spinners had met and discussed their plans for raising money. They agreed that it had to be a literary project. They decided to compile a book of stories by their members and give the royalties to Miss Coolbrith. They had already published a book of toasts, entitled *Prosit,* that had had a good local sale. But the proposed book was much more ambitious. Club members were ecstatic about the idea and went ahead with their plans. They hoped that Miss Coolbrith, too, would contribute something for the volume.[35]

Meanwhile, in Los Angeles, the object of their concern was the houseguest of the W. H. Perrys, her old time friends. She was entertained by them and was also a guest at the September and October monthly meetings of the Southern California Women's Press Association.[36] George Wharton James and his wife gave an informal reception for her.[37] She was in a happy mood that evening and told many stories of her early literary associations. One of the guests there was Irving Richman, a California historian, who told her many years later that he never forgot that evening and the stories she told.[38] While in Mrs. Perry's home and away from the scene of her recent ordeal, she wrote her poem on her beloved city, "San Francisco, April 18, 1906," and sent it to the new *Putnam's Magazine,* where it appeared in print in October 1906.[39] While she was still in Los Angeles, Edward F. O'Day published a sympathetic article in *Town Talk,* which he entitled "A Neglected Poet," and where he expressed his sorrow that California's favorite poet still "knew not where to lay her head."[40] In Oakland, Josie Zeller was so happy about the article that she went out and bought five copies of the magazine to send Ina, writing her at the same time, "Good for *Town Talk!* I think that there is someone on that paper that used his head without A. B.'s hand over him."[41] Did she mean Ambrose Bierce?

While in southern California, Ina had a good opportunity to explain her situation to James. She did not want her name used in connection with the fund. If he wanted to go on, she would be grateful, but she had to live in San Francisco, and preferably in the Russian Hill neighborhood, because, she said, that was the least expensive.[42] Moreover, she was still Bohemian Club librarian, and knew that when new quarters were found for the club, she would be expected to assist in the rehabilitation of the library.[43] Her own economic situation demanded that she remain in San Francisco. All during her stay in the South she had been ill, but had responded warmly to the hospitality spread before her. The weeks away from the Bay Area had given her a new perspective on her problems. She decided to rent a place in San Francisco as soon as possible. So, on her return to Oakland, she put the following sardonic and rather hopeless advertisement in a local newspaper:

> *Wanted* immediately—Some kind of shelter; rent less than $2000; can search no longer. Address: INA COOLBRITH, 770 Seventeenth, Oakland.[44]

The advertisement must have brought results, for, not long after, she and Josie were established on the ground floor of a tall, narrow, two-story house at 15 Lincoln Street on Russian Hill.[45] The little old house, cramped but picturesque, had been brought around the Horn many years before. The artist Giuseppi Cadenasso occupied the upper flat, number 17. This house, moreover, was one in that single row of hilltop dwellings that had survived the fire. The apartment had four tiny rooms, living room, dining room, bedroom, and kitchen. Ina occupied the front room, Josie the adjoining dining room, and the same law student, Robert Norman, came to rent the small bedroom.[46] This home was described a few months later by a San Jose friend, Mrs. Kate Kennedy, who visited her there, as "a little nest hanging upon the edge of a cliff" overlooking the city and the Bay. Into Ina's small sitting room were crowded a wide couch, four chairs, and a desk. A painting of California poppies lighted the wall; a dozen books on the desk comprised her library.[47] To Mrs. Boalt, writing from Vienna, Ina's abode on Lincoln Street was an

15-17 Lincoln Street (Now Macondray Lane), San Francisco; Formerly Home of Artist Giuseppi Cadenasso. Ina Coolbrith occupied the lower flat, number 15, from 1907 through 1909. Photograph, 1968, by Mr. Morley Baer, Berkeley, California. Reproduced with the permission of the photographer.

"unwholesome kennel," and she urged the poet to find a residence in the open spaces and fresh air of Hayward.[48] Number 15 Lincoln Street, now Macondray Lane, is second from the corner at Taylor, its situation being one of the last unspoiled streets of San Francisco. It is actually not a street, but is a rough and narrow brick and cobbled path of casual charm—a breathing space amid today's high-rise apartment houses. A short way down the hill from Macondray Lane today is Ina Coolbrith Park, a tiny resting place for the breathless who have climbed or descended the steep sidewalk. Here are native shrubs, winding paths and a bronze plaque in memory of the poet. The park is at the northeast corner of Taylor and Vallejo, and, though its area is only about a quarter of a city block, its location and association make it one of the city's "scenic highlights."[49]

Near the end of 1906, Ina received Jack London's impulsive letter, in which he said, "Often and often the mere word 'noble' recalls you to my mind . . . I am all iron these days, but I remember my childhood, and I remember you, and I have room in me yet, and softness, too, for memories."[50] She recalled Stedman's challenge, "Reduced as you are to sheer personality and womanhood, what is essential remains." Strengthened by these loyalties, she faced another year with a kind of tired courage mingled with skepticism.

25
The
Home
Funds

How weary are the ways
Unto our feet!
O lagging length of days
That once were fleet!

Ina Coolbrith, from
"Hope" (1874)

The Coolbrith Fund of the Spinners' Club

Several of Ina Coolbrith's literary friends, who had lost all in the recent fire, were soon comfortably housed in homes given them outright without any fanfare.[1] But Miss Coolbrith's own prominence was against her. Whatever happened to her or was done for her received wide publicity in Bay Area and Los Angeles newspapers. Over one hundred clippings on financial aid for her were pasted in her scrapbooks, some exaggerated, many completely false, the majority humiliating to a proud woman who did not ask to be supported but who wanted a chance to stand.[2] While her friends were quietly housed or had families who provided shelter, she became the unwitting victim of two organizations, each of which honestly wanted to help her. But both were carried away by two kinds of human vanity: the glory of an intimate association with a distinguished woman, who was even then almost as legendary as she was real, and the opportunity to create permanent benefit funds that would enhance their prestige for good deeds in their own communities. Both were possessed by an ideal, and both were amateurs in finance and fund raising. The result was that, out of all the turmoil, nothing was left for the immediate object of all their endeavors. Ina Coolbrith said bitterly that the fire had destroyed her home, her materials, and her means of livelihood. She was left with nothing but her name, and the "benefits" for her had taken even that away from her.[3]

The Spinners meant well, as George Wharton James meant well, but before their relations with Ina Coolbrith ceased, their projects had become as intricate as any web they might have spun. Their first proposal was sincere, if naive. In April 1906, a few days after the fire, a committee of the club came to Ina Coolbrith, at Mrs. Boalt's home, with a novel proposal. They said that the club had planned to bring out a book of stories by their members and give the profits to her. Of course she thanked them for their kind gesture. She did not tell them what she knew about books. She knew that to write a book, then have it published and put on sale, would bring no profits within a year. She probably thought little about it at the time. She said later that this proposition was the only one made her by the Spinners, and this visit was the only time she was consulted.[1] Her subsequent relations with the club were by correspondence with Eleanor Davenport, club treasurer.[5]

In early autumn, while Miss Coolbrith was in Los Angeles, and without her knowledge, the Spinners mailed two broadsides to their friends, to California newspapers, and to women's clubs all over the country. These announced the creation of a Coolbrith Fund, and the publication of a book for the Coolbrith Fund.[6] The poet's first knowledge of the announcements came from newspaper stories. She was so distressed by the use of her name that she begged the Spinners to change the fund name to the Spinners' Benefit Fund, and they complied willingly, though much of the damage was done.[7] The two circulars brought subscriptions for the forthcoming book and cash donations to be given by the Spinners directly to Miss Coolbrith. The Spinners were elated. Here they had the nucleus of a permanent fund. Miss Coolbrith would be the first beneficiary. When eight hundred dollars had been received in donations, the women decided to add two hundred dollars out of their treasury and buy a Western Pacific Railroad bond. Then, as additional funds came in, more bonds would be purchased, until the income from interest would provide for Miss Coolbrith for the rest of her life, and at her death would go to another worthy recipient. The pin that pricked the bubble was that no more funds were received. The interest would be five percent when the bond matured, fifty dollars a year, or four dollars, sixteen and two-thirds cents a month for Miss Coolbrith's annuity. This was what became of the money sent her for her immediate use. She learned about the state of the fund and her income from it during the summer of 1907. She did not keep it a secret. Her friends, especially those who thought they were helping her through the Spinners, were indignant. The *Examiner* journalist who wrote the story could not resist playing with the name of the club. He said that the Spinners' plans were woven of spun gold, and when they had a thousand dollars, they "spun it out of sight." The tone of the article was that of amused scorn of the well-meaning and talented young women and their financial naivete. To some of the members this was "yellow journalism." They were chagrined.[8]

Mrs. Gertrude Atherton, one of the indignant friends whose two-hun-dred-dollar gift had gone into the bond purchase, decided to talk to the club members about the income from the book to be out in October (eighteen months after the idea was first presented to Miss Coolbrith). She told Ina that she would "talk plain English. They are a lot of good, fussy women who got a real sensation out of their scheme, bustled about, felt important, and complimented one another upon being good and clever. They have made the worst bargain possible with the book, giving it to an amateur publisher and at ten percent!"[9] *The Spinners' Book of Fiction* was a more ambitious production than first planned. The club gave up the notion to publish members' stories and solicited those of prominent California writers instead. All those contributing, Gertrude Atherton, Mary Austin, Jack London, Isobel Strong, and others, did so with the understanding that all profits from the volume would go to Ina Coolbrith.[10] George Sterling sent a dedicatory poem, Mrs. Atherton a sequel to her *Rezanov,* Mrs. Austin a desert story, Charles Warren Stoddard a selection from his *For the Pleasure of His Company,* and Jack London an Alaskan Indian story. Some of the other authors were Eleanor Gates, Bailey Millard, W. C. Morrow, and Herman Whitaker. Paul Elder in San Francisco published the book, and the ty-pography was designed by John Henry Nash. Bound in coarse art linen, with color plates from paintings by California artists, it was an attractive gift book, to sell for two dollars.[11] The Spinners would receive twenty cents a copy as royalties, and it was their intention to invest all but ten percent of this in the permanent fund to buy more bonds. The ten percent would go to Miss Coolbrith, or two cents for each volume sold. Mrs. Atherton succeeded in talking them out of this penny-pinching. She urged them to turn over the royalties, small as they were, to their "beneficiary." The book was reviewed by Mrs. Anne Pratt Simpson, a Spinner, in the *San Francisco Sunday Call.* She prefaced her comments on the book with a history of the Spinners' Benefit Fund, the purchase of a good, safe bond, and now a book to add its profits to the fund. The article was actually an answer to the *Examiner* account that exposed the condition of Miss Coolbrith's "annuity." The poet was deeply humili-ated by the review, that spoke of her, though not by name, as being hopelessly and incurably ill, and living in poverty that was "final," what-ever was meant by that.[12]

Mrs. Atherton was so incensed by the Spinners' affair that she began

269

to make plans of her own for something of practical value to the poet. The results of her thinking will be described a few pages below. We are not quite through with the Spinners. The books sold, and Miss Coolbrith received over fifteen dollars in the next few months, in addition to her four dollars and a few cents each month. Then, during the summer of 1908, some of the members of the Spinners' Club were led to believe that Miss Coolbrith's friends might sue the club, and a really shocking article appeared in the *Call* on 3 September 1908. Miss Coolbrith was charged with having no appreciation of what the club had done for her. The story implied that none of the special donations for her had gone into the permanent fund but had been given to her directly. She was berated for not having taken the position in the Carmel library—no mention was made of the ten dollars monthly pay—and for not moving to Carmel where living would be cheaper.[13] The press story was a physical blow to her. She was literally prostrated by it. She suffered what she described as a slight stroke, with loss of eyesight for several weeks, in a local sanatorium under the care of Dr. Minora Kibbe.[14] She was unable to answer the club until November. Then she took the only dignified course left her. She resigned as honorary member and returned all moneys she had received from them, ninety dollars and eighty cents, during the two years and six months since the Spinners first told her of their plans to help her.[15] Her action brought new and startling headlines.[16]

The Spinners' story had an aftermath. Ina's friends could not get over the injustice and the indignity of the affair. Stoddard, bedfast with rheumatism, in a Monterey sanatorium, was appalled. He wrote, in what may have been his last letter to her, "God bless you, dear old friend, and deliver you out of the hands of this untrustworthy Trust."[17] Early in 1909, Herman Whitaker, one of the contributors of the *Spinners' Book of Fiction,* made himself a committee of one to canvass the other writers and get their consent to demand that the club turn over all profits from the book to the one for whom it was written. All but Richard Walton Tully and Miriam Michelson backed him in his plan. George Sterling agreed to go with Whitaker to face the Spinners, but backed out at the last minute, saying that he did not care to mix in a women's quarrel. Whitaker was exasperated. Ina was broken-hearted, she said, but begged Herman not to let George's change of mind affect their friendship. Whitaker made an appointment with Mrs. Regina Wilson, the club president, having kept her informed of what he was doing. The Spinners knew what to expect, and when he appeared, alone, before them, and read the contributors' letters, the members were glad to make some kind of amends for the whole unhappy affair. They wrote him a check for about eight hundred dollars, profits from the book. All Whitaker's mission was carried out with Miss Coolbrith's knowledge but with grudging consent and skepticism. He showed her the check, and immediately wrote out another one, payable to her, for an equivalent sum. He then banked the Spinners' check in his own account, so that Ina was not obliged to endorse that check. This final scene in a tragi-comic drama gave both Mrs. Boalt and Mrs. Atherton a good deal of satisfaction.[18]

The Home Fund of George Wharton James

The Spinners' fund was not the only one that failed. While all this was going on in San Francisco, a similar kind of agitation was taking place in literary circles in Pasadena. This was the aforementioned home fund which Ina said "was the plan that at the end of four years resulted in the loan to me of $1,365, all collected in my name, with a million wounds and a world of humiliation."[19] It had been the innocent inspiration of George Wharton James. James, enthusiastic, altruistic, egotistical, was given to causes and fads, but had many redeeming qualities, one of which was his awareness of the American Southwest, and his honest appreciation of the life and art of its first dwellers. When he took on Ina Coolbrith's housing problem, he said, "You know, darling girl, that I want to help in the way that is most satisfactory to you."[20]

Once he had started, there was no way to stop him. Gertrude Atherton's nickname for him was "Geewhillican."[21] His plan, not "what was most satisfactory to her," was to build an author's home in Pasadena or San Francisco, the house to belong to the Washington Heights Literary Circle, but to be occupied by Ina Coolbrith until her death. His method was to lecture before clubs on California literature, the "Golden Gate Trinity," "Ina Coolbrith, Poet," and other subjects, collecting silver offerings for his talks. His organization also solicited autographed books, photographs, and the like, from prominent American writers, to be sold for Miss Coolbrith's benefit. Edwin Markham, whom Lummis had visited and acquainted with the Spinners' fiasco, was said to have sent fifty of his autographed volumes, and two copies of "The Man with the Hoe" in his handwriting.[22] Another gift was a copy of *Liber Scriptorum*, the first book of the Author's Club, published in 1893, one of a limited edition of two hundred fifty copies, a collection of essays, stories, and poems by prominent American writers, each contribution signed by its author.[23] The varied materials assembled by James were on sale in his own home and in a Pasadena hotel. They were advertised by a circular distributed by the Literary Circle, but they did not sell readily. Miss Coolbrith suggested that San Francisco would have been a better place for the sale of material of that kind, and James later followed her advice.[24]

The poet's would-be benefactor was distressed that she did not want to live in Pasadena and went so far as to suggest that a house be built there, "furnished as for a bride," then sold so that she could build in San Francisco.[25] Of all the many news items on the home fund, most have a vague suggestion of future time. They had headings such as, "Will help build home for poetess of state," "A home for Ina Coolbrith," "Poetess to spend rest of life in Marin hills," "To have home," "To buy author home," "Benefits for Coolbrith fund," and similar heads. Money came into the fund by small trickles. A club voted five dollars in addition to a silver offering at one of James's lectures. An artist gave a percentage of his sales at an exhibition of his paintings. Such small contributions were collected by James over a period of many months. None of the newspaper accounts indicated that Miss Coolbrith actually had a house. One story, headed "Big subscription," related that, by August 1908, the Washington Heights Literary Circle had raised twelve thousand dollars for a home for their beneficiary. Miss Coolbrith seethed as she pasted this item in her scrapbook and wrote "Lie" in the margin.[26]

In November 1907 James brought the books and autographs to San Francisco, hoping to find them more salable. At first he placed them in the Palace Hotel, and, finding that of little use, had them transferred to Paul Elder's and Robertson's bookshops. If the material did not find buyers there, he suggested that Miss Coolbrith take them and try to sell them in her own home.[27] Ina made a trip to Pasadena in June 1908 to learn about the state of the "fund," and if she could depend on it for house construction. While there, she intended to have a frank talk with Mrs. Lewis, president of the Washington Heights Literary Circle, and to tell her that she wanted her name removed from the fund title. But Ina became ill during her stay and had to return to San Francisco at once. All her transactions, therefore, were carried on by letter. She requested a statement from the bank and asked that the name be changed from the "Ina D. Coolbrith Home Fund," to "Home Fund."[28]

Though collected in Miss Coolbrith's name, the fund was the property of the Literary Circle, to be used as the members thought best for the benefit of a needy writer. They decided to lend it to Ina Coolbrith. The amount was one thousand, three hundred sixty-five dollars. Miss Coolbrith agreed to borrow it, though she said that the money, collected in her name and with so much pain to her, should be rightfully hers.[29] She and James were very careful in the transfer arrangements. On the advice of an attorney she was to make a will, in the Circle's favor, for the

273

amount, in case she should die before the debt was paid. She, in turn, requested a complete list of all donors, for James's protection as well as her own, and suggested that he too make a will, saying, "Don't you think, George, that you had best make your 'will'? for I would be left in a bad position with regard to the 'Fund' in case you should be called before me." Then she added, "This is merely a suggestion in kind which seems not to have entered your thoughts, and *not* said in unkindness. I hope you are much better, but you know you are not a well man."[30]

Miss Coolbrith had previously commanded that her name be stricken from that of the fund. If it was not her own, she wanted it treated as the most impersonal of loans, even though James, in remorse perhaps, at the outcome of the unhappy affair, insisted that the bank bill him for the interest as long as the loan was out.[31] This borrowed sum, added to money received in December 1907, enabled her to buy a building site before the end of 1908.

An "Authors' Reading," Sponsored by Gertrude Atherton

In 1907, near the beginning of the year and again near the end, in time to observe two holidays, St. Valentine's Day and Thanksgiving Day, Ina Coolbrith was the recipient of two sums of money, given her without any embarrassing publicity. On 9 February the San Jose Women's Club sponsored an Ina Coolbrith Day, with a program of talks and music during that afternoon. The principal speaker was Judge John E. Richards. Henry Meade Bland of the English department of the San Jose Normal was also present. Miss Coolbrith's lyric, "Quest," set to music by a San Jose composer, Thomas V. Cator, was a solo number on the program. The special feature of this affair was the exhibit of a decorated booklet of manuscripts to be taken to Miss Coolbrith later in the month. It was a collection of prose and verse, written as tributes to the poet, attractively decorated and put together by a local artist, Mrs. Elva Sawyer Cureon. Contributors to the booklet were Joaquin Miller, William C. Morrow, Charles Warren Stoddard, Herbert Bashford, George Sterling, George Wharton James, Charles Keeler, and others of Ina's writing friends.[32]

After the program, Mrs. Kate M. Kennedy and other women in the club made arrangements to go with Mrs. William Morrow in San Francisco to call on Miss Coolbrith and present her with the booklet. Mrs. Morrow invited the women to be her guests on 14 February and she went with them to call on the poet at 15 Lincoln Street. Mrs. Kennedy was impressed by the limited size of the tiny living room, dominated by the wide couch that had become the bed of a near invalid. She was impressed too by the unlimited view of bay and city from the poet's windows. Ina Coolbrith was surprised and touched when the pretty booklet was presented to her and said there was never a sweeter Valentine sent. Left casually between the pages of the little book was a check from the club. Miss Coolbrith later thanked the women's club as a group for their program honoring her and for the gift made in person. She also wrote the individual contributors to thank them for their tributes to her. Stoddard's little poem, written from memory, was one he had composed on the ferry in 1863, on his way to classes in Brayton Hall on the old Oakland campus of the College of California (later the University of California). The lyric, "Twilight," was first published in the first issue of the old *Californian*.[33] The attractive "Valentine" is one of a number of sentimental items to be found among the Coolbrith papers in the Bancroft Library at the University of California in Berkeley. The incidents of the program, the gift booklet, and the check—all voluntary and unannounced—made a pleasant interlude amid Ina Coolbrith's troubled relations with the Spinners and the Washington Heights Circle.

In June 1907 the Houghton Mifflin Company published what was described as a new edition of *Songs from the Golden Gate*, actually the third impression. The author herself bought one thousand copies outright, half of them bound and the rest to be bound locally on demand. The cost to her was over three hundred seventy-five dollars, a large part of her small savings, but an investment as necessary to her morale as to supply her with a small source of income. The purchase enabled her to keep a stock of the books on hand to sell to those whose copies had been burned. Her *Songs*, promptly reviewed in the local press, sold for one dollar fifty cents a copy.[34]

In November of the same year Miss Coolbrith was pleased when her friend and fellow poet, Edward Robeson Taylor, won the race for mayor in the city elections. When she congratulated him, he remarked that the poets were having their innings, referring to former Mayor Phelan who had dabbled in verse making, though he tried to hide the fact for fear it would prejudice the voters.[35] On 20 November 1907, Miss Coolbrith was the guest of honor at a banquet held by the San Jose Short Story Club, where the toastmaster was Henry Meade Bland. Other speakers included Judge John E. Richards, Herbert Bashford, and George Wharton James. Miss Coolbrith talked about the old *Overland* days. It was on this occasion that she recalled how Bret Harte had come to the Pickett flat to persuade her to come for a walk up the hill where they could sit and talk over some contribution to the magazine and how she agreed to come if he would help her shell the peas for supper. Miss Coolbrith, always a lively and informal speaker, was at her best that evening in San Jose.[36]

This banquet came just a week before a San Francisco affair at the

275

Fairmont Hotel, also in her honor. The event was an Authors' Reading, a testimonial to Ina D. Coolbrith held on Thanksgiving Eve, 27 November 1907, at eight-thirty o'clock. It was arranged by the Bohemian Club, whose members stayed completely in the background. Patrons were San Francisco Women's clubs: the California Club, the Century Club, the Pacific Coast Women's Press Association, the Town and Country Club, the Spinners, the Sequoia Club, and the Art Association. Some of the women listed as patrons were Mrs. M. H. DeYoung, Mrs. David Starr Jordan, Mrs. William Keith, Mrs. Rudolph Spreckels, Mrs. Sigmund Stern, Mrs. Benjamin Ide Wheeler, Mrs. Virgil Williams, and others. The toastmistress, and the real instigator, was Mrs. Gertrude Atherton. This was her answer to the Spinners' pathetic venture.[37]

The program was opened by newly elected Mayor Taylor. Miss Coolbrith's "Hymn of the Nativity" was sung by a chorus. Three solos were given, also a number by the Bohemian Club Quartette. After Dr. Taylor's remarks, readings of varying lengths were given by thirteen other writers, Lucius Harwood Foote, George Sterling, Mrs. Fremont Older, Robert Howe Fletcher, Herman Whitaker, Herman Scheffauer, Warren Cheney, Charles K. Field, Charles Keeler, Gertrude Atherton, James Hopper, Luther Burbank and Joaquin Miller.[38] Another speaker, though not on the printed program, was the ubiquitous George Wharton James who rose to tell something of his "home fund," adding a note that was not appreciated by either Miss Coolbrith or Mrs. Atherton, though the latter said later and rather cruelly, "That's all right. Let Geewhilliken advertise himself. It's his only hope of arresting the most fleeting attention."[39]

Following the program a Keith painting was raffled off, a large landscape of the High Sierra, valued at twelve hundred dollars. It was won by a San Francisco attorney, C. T. Humphreys. The raffle committee was composed of university presidents Jordan and Wheeler, and former mayor Phelan.[40] Herman Whitaker appeared in his year-old tweeds, too poor to own a dress suit, he told Ina, laughingly, saying that he was "the solitary parti-colored man in a sea of black."[41] The affair was, like other Bohemian Club testimonials to the same poet, a social and financial success. As a result, a check for one thousand dollars was given to Miss Coolbrith by Mrs. Atherton, who reminded her that it was for her personal needs, whatever these were.[42]

The incidents that took place during the evening were related later on to Miss Coolbrith. She herself was not there! Her niece, who had come

---

Senator James Duval Phelan. Reproduced through the courtesy of the Bancroft Library, University of California, Berkeley.

up from Menlo to attend, must have been surprised and disappointed to find her aunt absent.[43] The poet may have planned to go, though her recent experience with Spinners and Literary Circle ladies may have made her shrink from anything that suggested a benefit. James Phelan had reserved a room for her at the Fairmont so that she could remain there the night after the program was over, and not be too fatigued. He said he would send a carriage for her. But she did not go. She was not well; she had "collapsed" in the street a few days before and had had to be helped home.[44] But the immediate reason was something that happened on the very afternon of 2 November. Her companion, Josie Zeller, out on an errand for her, had been thrown from a streetcar and painfully injured. Ina would not have left her for anything.[45]

Ina's next-door neighbor, Miss Anna DeMartini, thought there was another reason why the poet did not go. She said, years later, that Miss Coolbrith did not have the clothes for such an affair. She had been a long time getting on her feet after the fire; her clothes were all made for her by Miss Zeller. Such a reason to stay away seems unlikely, since she had attended a banquet in San Jose only a week before. Yet the more sophisticated setting and the social prominence of the patrons may have made her diffident about being in the limelight at the Fairmont. James Phelan called, told her about the room, and pleaded with her to go. Miss DeMartini, too, urged her, saying that, after all, the affair was for her. The neighbor remembered that Ina's eyes filled with tears, and she said she wanted to go, but . . . .[46]

26
A Home
of Her
Own

Tomorrow is not, yesterday is not,
Today alone is—and today is thine!

Ina Coolbrith, from
"Opportunity" (1909)

Purchase of a Lot on Russian Hill

Early in 1908 Ina Coolbrith decided to acquire a city lot as soon as possible, in order to invest the money she had received the previous December and to assure herself of a future San Francisco residence. To the one thousand dollars that came from the Fairmont event she added the five hundred dollars the Red Cross had given her in 1906, an amount she had kept intact for building. She had set her heart on a Russian Hill lot priced at twenty-five hundred dollars.[1] It occurred to her that the Red Cross might lend her a thousand dollars. This they were willing to do, but their security requirements were so unreasonable that the lady preferred to go to a bank for the loan.[2] During these transactions George Wharton James came to Livermore for a period of rest in a sanatorium.[3] While there he wrote to Professor and Mrs. Lemmon and other friends in the area, hoping that they might suggest some way by which a lot could be donated to Miss Coolbrith.[4] But the poet had gone ahead without consulting James. She bought a lot on Broadway between Taylor and Mason Streets, above the present Broadway tunnel. She wrote Mrs. Lewis, chairman of the Washington Heights Literary Circle, "This (securing a lot) I am doing with the use of what money has been raised for me to live on, and by my own further efforts. No fund or club is helping me in the least to the lot."[5] Miss Coolbrith was aware that the "home fund" could be applied to a dwelling only, not to land. Early in

279

March she requested from the American Bank and Trust Company in Pasadena a statement on the amount on deposit in the "Ina Coolbrith Home Fund," indicating that she had acquired the lot and was arranging to finance the construction of a house.[6]

Securing a piece of ground of her own was a declaration of independence from all well-wishing entanglements in the past or the future. In May she was able to confront James with a *fait accompli*. This she did with some flair on 6 May 1908, one of the most memorable days in the history of San Francisco. This was the day that President Roosevelt's "Great White Fleet" of sixteen battleships steamed through the Golden Gate to lie off Alcatraz Island in the Bay. Every window with a view of the Gate and the Bay, every vacant space on any city eminence, was crowded with eager spectators, thrilled by the sight of the great ships and their flags, bright in the sun. It was reported that fifty thousand people had flocked into the city from the hinterland, some from as far away as Reno and Salt Lake City. Among the thousands who came by train from San Jose were Professor Bland and his wife and the W. G. Kennedys. Miss Coolbrith had invited them to lunch with her at her hilltop cottage on Lincoln Street where they could watch in comfort as the battleships came in at high noon. Her other guests were George Wharton James from Livermore and his Berkeley friends, the botanist couple, John Gill Lemmon and his wife Sara, and also William and Lydia Morrow. Compared with James D. Phelan's dinner for Admiral Evans and his family, and prominent members of San Francisco "society," at the Fairmont, followed by Mayor Taylor's reception and ball for Secretary of the Navy Metcalf, and five thousand guests who danced until one o'clock in the morning, and compared with the band concerts in the parks that day and the parade the next, Miss Coolbrith's luncheon in her tiny house was a humble event. But it was momentous for her and for those with her. As they stepped out on her small porch to look about at the crowded hillsides, she could have pointed out her lot to them. It was within sight, two blocks south. Back indoors that afternoon she told her friends something of her plan for building. She wanted a two-story house with a flat on each floor, so that the rental of one unit would help pay taxes and the interest on the inevitable mortgage. Professor Bland was awed. He thought that if she could accomplish that she would be a very clever business woman.[7]

Between the acquisition of a piece of bare ground, and the breaking of it for a foundation, however, stretched a weary twelvemonth and more, beset with grief, illness and innumerable vexations. In January 1908 came the death of Edmund Clarence Stedman for whose sake, in April, Miss Coolbrith asked Bliss Perry to publish in the *Atlantic* the sonnet she had written for Stedman's seventieth birthday.[8] Perry did so in August.[9] During the summer she went to Pasadena to complete arrangements for closing and for borrowing the "home fund," and was taken sick, as related in the previous chapter. Then, in the fall, as also related the Spinners' cruel article brought serious illness to the poet and culminated in her resignation from the club. In the spring of 1909, after recovering from the blows of the previous year, she hoped to select a house plan and start building. In the midst of renewed enthusiasm, she received a message on 24 April that stunned her and minimized even her woes of 1908.

Death of Charles Warren Stoddard

The message came from Monterey. Charles Warren Stoddard had died of a heart attack at ten o'clock at night, Friday, 23 April 1909.[10] When the funeral services were held on Monday morning, the old mission church of San Carlos, where he loved to worship, was filled with his friends and neighbors of Carmel and Monterey, and a few mourners from the San Francisco Bay Area, including his brother Fred of Berkeley, Ina Coolbrith, George Sterling, and others from the city. Charlie's sister, Mrs. Sara Makee, was in Switzerland. All who were there were people who loved him for his gentleness and his humor. The parish priest, Father Mestress, who conducted the requiem mass, was a former student of Stoddard at the Catholic University of America in Washington, D. C. So, too, was the San Francisco priest, Father Stark, who gave a eulogy for the dead writer. Charlie's pallbearers were his fellow Bohemians, and the grave to which they bore his body was in the little San Carlos churchyard, within sound of the sea, but cypress-sheltered from its winds.[11]

During the simple service each of Charlie's friends sat wrapped in his own personal sense of loss. Ina Coolbrith mused on the long, long years she had known him, back to the early, happy days of the "Golden Gate Trinity," remembering him as he was when they were "little more than boy and girl together," thinking of the Shelley-like, almost girlish, beauty of his face. They had been good comrades through the years with never a shadow of misunderstanding, with never a change in their loyal trust and affection for each other.[12] He was her "life-long pal," she often said, and she was his "dearest Ina."[13] It is thought by some that he loved her and wanted to marry her, and that her rejection of his suit had sent him to the South Seas.[14] But she herself once said that, though women were always attracted to him, she did not believe he had ever fallen in love.[15] He knew, and he was puzzled, that he was not a marrying man. Ina loved him tenderly, but as an older sister might love a dear young brother. Stoddard was capable of deep and lasting friendships with both men and women, without, apparently, the emotional entanglements and jealousies that might have beset him. Now he was gone, and Ina, coming out of her reverie, felt left behind. George Sterling glanced at her. Her face, he thought, was that of a "sibyl of stone."[16] But she had lost one who was nearer than kin.

It was at Stoddard's funeral that Miss Coolbrith first met Charles Phillips, the young editor of the *Monitor,* a San Francisco Catholic periodical, the official organ of the Archdiocese.[17] He had been one of Stoddard's students in Washington, and was friend as well as disciple. Miss Coolbrith and Phillips agreed that day that Stoddard's poems should be collected and published. Charlie had brought out his one book of verse the summer he was twenty-four.[18] He had survived the criticism of that effort with a resolve never to publish another volume of poetry, though he sent a lyric to a magazine from time to time. Both Ina and Phillips knew that Stoddard must have had a good many poems in manuscript that he modestly kept out of the hands of printers. They both believed that the best memorial to him would be a collection of his poetical works, including the contents of the 1867 volume. The two also agreed that the collection should have a rather full biographical memoir. Phillips was stimulated by the idea, and Ina was heartened in finding an ally and possible co-worker in this young hero-worshipper she had just met. They knew that together, and with the aid of mutual friends, they could collect the material for such a publication. And, since both lived in San Francisco, they arranged to see each other in her home soon. Thus began an association as important to the sixty-eight-year-old woman as to the twenty-nine-year-old editor.

In July the first step toward a volume of Stoddard's verse was taken when his sister Sara arrived in San Francisco. On Friday, 16 July, she and Ina went to Monterey to take charge of Charlie's effects.[19] His books, papers, photographs, autographs (he had sought autographs with an almost boyish enthusiasm all his life), and the little effigies and trinkets of which he was fond—and of which he had once said, when funds were low, "Better to starve in the midst of my household gods than to part with them for the sake of prolonging this misery"—all these were sent to Miss Coolbrith's place in San Francisco at Mrs. Makee's earnest request.[20] She asked Ina to use her own judgment in going through the trunks and boxes, to retain whatever might be of use in a volume of verse or for a biography.[21] Though Ina had little space in her Lincoln Street flat to examine these things, and though she was involved in having a house built, she spent much of the summer at the depressing task, and answering letters from Charlie's friends, some of whom requested that their letters to Stoddard be returned to them or destroyed.[22] She found a photograph of Josephine McCrackin which she kept for herself (her own had been burned) after notifying "Jo" of her intention.[23] By September Ina's growing fears were confirmed. There were no verse manuscripts in any of the boxes. There must be other boxes in Monterey, she decided.

In the meantime Miss Coolbrith had discussed the matter of a volume of Stoddard's verse with A. M. Robertson, the San Francisco publisher who had printed the two Bohemian Club books she had edited. Robertson was anxious to publish a Stoddard collection. Mrs. Makee had gone to Boston to take care of the rest of her brother's possessions. At Ina's request she searched the boxes there and found none of her brother's verse, manuscript or printed. Miss Coolbrith and Robertson then went down to Monterey to try to solve the mystery. There, to their horror, they found that Stoddard had requested his landlady to burn his manuscripts in the fireplace, one after another, as he read them, lying in his sickbed, not long before he died. Such was the landlady's story. So, if there had been poems among the works destroyed, they were lost forever. A few might have been copied for friends. But which friends? As the full force of this loss struck them, the would-be editor and the publisher were filled with despair. To assemble any collected edition of Stoddard's verse now seemed hopeless. The two were deeply dejected as they rode back to the city.[24]

Mrs. Makee, in Boston, was preparing to return to Switzerland; so she stored most of her brother's possessions in a Cambridge warehouse, sent Charlie's scrapbooks and a manuscript journal to Ina, then sold the books to a man eager to buy them.[25] Her sale of the books infuriated friends of Stoddard, especially William Woodworth, in whose favor Stoddard had once made his will, though he afterward changed it to bequeath his possessions to his sister and brothers. Woodworth believed, rightly, that the books should have gone to the Bohemian Club. His anger stirred up a minor war among some of Charlie's friends that was not a credit to any of them.[26] Ina stayed out of it, but each one involved wrote to her with his grievances against the others. Sara Makee, overcome with remorse for her hasty sale of her brother's books, wrote Ina that what was left would go to her daughter, Ada, if anything happened to her. She said that if Charles Phillips, whom she had met at Ina's house when she was in San Francisco, planned to write a biography or a biographical introduction to a book of her brother's verse, she hoped Ina would supervise it, for she did not want it dominated by a Catholic point of view.[27] Sara Makee went on to Europe and was out of the scene of the unhappy turmoil she had unwittingly caused.[28] In San Francisco Ina Coolbrith and Charles Phillips discussed the tedious process of assembling Stoddard's scattered printed verse for the volume Ina was now determined to compile, disappointing though it might be. And the better she came to know Phillips, the more she came to believe that he, this new Charlie, was the man best fitted to write the biographical introduction.

At Home, 1067 Broadway

During the summer of 1909 the friendship between Ina Coolbrith and Charles Phillips grew. He aided her in the examination and sorting of Charlie's papers. Their mutual affection for Stoddard brought them into a blessed kind of rapport that extended into other matters of concern to each, such as his newspaper, an idea for a play he wanted to write, a lyric of hers in the May *Century,* the news of the death of Ina's Mill Valley friend, Adeline Knapp, and, finally, the plans for the new house.[29] He had been her guest at the Press Association's Ina Coolbrith Day program on 24 May, at which time she was elected vice-president of the club.[30] Miss Coolbrith knew that her club responsibilities would be light that year. And indeed they were, with the exception of a December program at which she gave an informal talk about her meeting with Whittier a quarter of a century before.[31] She expected all her time until January to be occupied with completing her house and moving into it.

The ground was broken that summer. And, as expected, by late December, Ina and Josie, and the cats Moona and Titian, were established in the new place at 1067 Broadway.[32] The lot was narrow, and the building occupied the full width of the strip of land, with access, through an inconspicuous tradesman's entrance, to the garden at the rear of the lot. The structure was tall, providing space for two large flats and an attic apartment. Miss Coolbrith had chosen a home design, popular at that time, that showed some faint influence of the Swiss chalet, with the hint of a second-story overhang, the simulated half-timbering in the gable of the attic dormer, the white-painted trim, and the window-boxes. These window boxes, hanging from the sills of the attic window and the second-story bays, were made for pots of the bright ivy geranium that thrives in the San Francisco fogs, but Miss Coolbrith did not bother to use plants in them. The narrow strip of soil between sidewalk and house allowed little room for planting of any kind. The main entrance, near

---

Ina Coolbrith's Home at 1067 Broadway, San Francisco, from 1910 through 1919. Courtesy of Mrs. Ina Cook Graham, Berkeley, California.

the left side of the buff-shingled façade, was recessed, to provide door-
ways to both flats.

After climbing the stairs to the second floor, Miss Coolbrith's callers
were ushered by Josie into a long, sparsely-furnished living room, well
lighted by the two deep, square bays. On sunny days, or when a fire
blazed in the grate, the room was cheerful. It faced north, but the buildings across the street shut off the view of the Bay. Miss Coolbrith's bedroom at the back of the house, however, looked out over Bay and city.
The interior architecture of the house was inspired by the Stickley
"craftsman" use of dark woodwork, heavy, dark beams, and a large tiled
fireplace flanked by glass-doored bookcases. Wide, wood-framed arches
opened from the hall and dining-room. The furnishings were austere,
and there never seemed enough chairs for visitors. There were some pictures on the walls, a few photographs on a graceful side table, vases with
flowers, and, on the mantel, an assortment of small bric-a-brac including plaster copies of a Venus de Milo and a seated Cupid. The one note
of luxury was a very large, mahogany-framed, pier glass, a rich piece of
Victorian craftsmanship given to Ina by Judge and Elizabeth Boalt.
Here, Ina Coolbrith, a gracious hostess, greeted her guests and poured
tea for them by her fireside, as many a friend remembered her. Here, in
the house she owned for the rest of her life, and where she lived with
Josie as a companion for ten years, the large living room became a new
literary salon.[33]

The Pacific Coast Women's Press Association

The poet, in her own home at last, must have felt that she was by
then entitled to a rest after the torment of the postfire years just past.
There is no mention, in her letters of that period, of employment in the
library of the Bohemian Club. It is known by members, however, that
"after the fire she undertook the difficult task of re-habilitating the library." As soon as the club had new quarters, at the corner of Post
and Leavenworth, she was at work part-time in the library on an upper
floor, entering and leaving by a side entrance, as she had done in her
first years as librarian for the Bohemian Club.[34] She continued to correspond with Sara Makee and with Stoddard's friends, William Woodworth and Burton Kline. Herman Whitaker and his wife, Gertrude
Atherton, Charles Phillips, and others called on her from time to time.[35]
She carried on a melancholy correspondence with Alice Kingsbury
Cooley, each complaining to the other that her age and poor health
denied her full enjoyment of a world still fresh and young and alluring.[36]
The Press Association, of which she was the vice-president from 1909
to 1910, was assuming more and more importance in her life. Although

286

she was an honorary member of at least nine other Bay Area clubs, the Pacific Coast Women's Press Association was the only one in which she was active, serving as officer, committee chairman, and frequent speaker.[37] The association was founded in 1890 by Mrs. Emilie Tracy Parkhurst of San Francisco, and its membership rolls included such names as Jessie Benton Fremont, Rose Hartwick Thorpe, Kate Douglas Wiggin, Jeanne C. Carr, Alice Kingsbury Cooley, Charlotte Perkins Gilman, Gertrude Atherton, Ruth Comfort Mitchell, and Josephine Clifford McCrackin.[38] The name indicates a rather wide membership, but during Miss Coolbrith's years in the club most of the women were in California, and the majority in the San Francisco Bay region.

On 16 May 1910, Ina Coolbrith was unanimously elected president of the Press Association for the year to come, July 1910 to May 1911.[39] When she accepted this honor, she assumed that she would have a year of presiding and program planning, and then could lean back and rest when the year's obligations were fulfilled. She asked Mrs. Augusta Borle, an Alameda teacher, to be her program chairman for the year, with meetings on the second and fourth Mondays of each month.[40] Ina and Gussie (as her friends called her) did not confine their programs to merely local literary topics, but ranged through music, art, travel, and current events, as well as literature. One of the most successful of all was the "Carmen Sylva Day," with Rumanian folklore, music, literature, and a talk by Leon Blum, a Rumanian living at the time in San Francisco.[41] One of the most controversial of all was a Browning program with Mrs. Frank Leslie, calling herself by then the Baroness de Bazus, as guest speaker. All Browning devotees in the room were dismayed by the candid, unflattering remarks by one who had known Browning and disliked him. She described him as gross, over fond of eating, and even faithless to the memory of his wife.[42] While in San Francisco Mrs. Leslie spent several hours with Ina Coolbrith, whom she had known only through the praises of Joaquin Miller and Iza Hardy, Joaquin's faithful sweetheart of his London days. Ina Coolbrith and Florence Leslie were reserved in each other's presence; Ina was awed by Florence's worldly successes, and Florence had, at first, an actual dislike of Ina, as she was later to admit in a letter to the poet. It was not long, however, during their short visit, that their mutual reserve fell away to be replaced by an honest liking for each other. Their shared concern for Joaquin Miller brought them together and kept them writing letters as long as Joaquin lived.[43] Of course Mrs. Leslie called on Joaquin while she was in San Francisco. They had had a romantic attachment for each other when they were much younger, when Miller wrote his *The One Fair Woman* for her. By 1910 they were both in their seventies, and the luxury-loving "baroness" must have found the poet's rustic surroundings somewhat less than romantic.[44]

In November that year Ina's friend, Alice Cooley, died.[45] Ina herself, feeling her own age as well as her sorrow, was ill and could not preside at the last club meeting of the month. She asked Mrs. Laura Pinney, vice-president, to do so in her place, and to read to the members the biographical memoir to little Alice Kingsbury Cooley which she had just written. This sketch, penned with feeling and some sentimentality, is a vivid picture of the popular young English woman who had acted with Booth, Barrett, and Kean in San Francisco, who married, bore twelve children, reared three step-children, and continued to write and paint up to the time of her death.[46] Ina did not know Alice Cooley in her acting days. She knew her in the 1880s in Oakland when she was buying Mrs. Cooley's little books for the library. This was about the time she published her own first book and was consulting with John Carmany. 1910, the year of Mrs. Cooley's death, was also that of Carmany's death, but no notice of his passing appears in Miss Coolbrith's papers. He was mentioned in none of her surviving letters, and she, who memorialized many of her friends in verse, apparently sang no dirge for him. Indeed the death of this prominent San Francisco publisher, the man who dared to carry on the *Overland Monthly* after Roman sold it, and who had faith in its revival in 1883, was little noticed in the press of the area. He died on 8 May 1910, in comparative obscurity, after a long illness, in the Berkeley home of his sister, Mary, who had persuaded him not to take a wife, and who survived him.[47]

The next spring, in 1911, Ina Coolbrith observed her seventieth birthday. It was a year of extraordinary activity for her. She began by inviting two personal friends to participate in the January programs of the club, Herman Whitaker and Herbert Bashford. Whitaker had just returned from one of his numerous trips to Mexico, and expressed his belief, in a talk on January 9, that there would be no revolution in Mexico, in spite of the poverty, the unemployment, and the increase of wealth in the hands of the few, which he acknowledged. Pancho Villa had begun to make an impression on his country, but had not yet impressed Whitaker.[48] Herbert Bashford, whose third play, "The Woman He Married," had just been produced, came on 23 January to talk on the drama.[49] At the close of this meeting Bashford asked leave to call on Miss Coolbrith and to bring his wife and daughter to meet

---

Herbert Bashford about 1910. Courtesy of Mrs. Alice Bashford Wallace, Sidney, B.C., Canada.

her. They came one evening early in March. Ina had known him since 1901 when, as Washington State Librarian, he had had an encounter with politics not unlike Ina's own Oakland library experience. Like her he was both poet and librarian, and was known unofficially as the poet laureate of the state of Washington. With his wife, the actress Kinnie Cole, and their small daughter Alice, he came to California, settling first in San Jose. In 1909 he accepted a position as literary critic with the *San Francisco Bulletin*. With his family, he then moved to Piedmont where he was a prominent figure in the Bay Area literary scene. There he was a neighbor of Herman Whitaker and of the artist Xavier Martinez, and was not far from Joaquin Miller who had long been a literary idol of his. Edwin Markham, too, was a family friend and made the Bashford home his headquarters when on lecture tours in the vicinity. Ina and Josie, as Ina said afterward, both "fell in love" with Alice Bashford, a pretty and vivacious school girl, gifted in music. Alice was not only the daughter of a poet; she was the godchild of two others, Ella Mae Higginson of Washington and Joaquin Miller.[50]

Herbert Bashford, as literary editor of the *Bulletin*, was highly interested in the next meeting of the Press Association, the Stoddard program. Members of the Bohemian Club had provided a Hawaiian setting for the afternoon.[51] Both Ina Coolbrith and Charles Phillips spoke, Ina, of course, on the old days, and Phillips on Stoddard as teacher, poet and friend.[52] The program, recalling the beginning days of the *Overland*, was so well received that Miss Coolbrith was persuaded to talk once more about the early writers—always her favorite theme—at the 10 April meeting of the club. Before that meeting took place, however, the California Writers' Club gave a party in honor of the poet's seventieth birthday.

The affair, held not on her birthday, 10 March, but on the first day of April, was a garden fête, with three hundred guests enjoying the natural wooded grounds surrounding the redwood cottage of William and Torrey Connor, on Harwood Drive in Oakland. The place was in Temescal Canyon, downhill from J. Ross Browne's imposing home, Pagoda Hill; nearby, on Harwood Drive, lived Mrs. Nellie Van de Grift Sanchez, historian, sister-in-law of Robert Louis Stevenson. A high redwood fence enclosed and sheltered the Connor grounds, its rigid lines softened by a tangle of native shrubs and trees. That April day sunshine warmed the large, clear areas where chairs were placed, and streamed in dappled light to the loam beneath twisted old live oaks. The occasion was more than a garden party, more than a septuagenarian's birthday celebration; it was a book shower for the poet who had lost her own books in 1906. The Writers' Club came into existence not long after the fire, and this collective gift of books was one of its most felicitous deeds. It was not planned as a surprise for the guest of honor, but Miss Coolbrith surprised the three hundred by bringing with her a stack of little folders, printed with her lyric, "In Blossom Time," each one signed by her in ink, one for each one present. Nothing she might have written to remember that sunny afternoon could have been as appropriate as those lilting lines out of her girlhood. Mrs. Connor, a contributor to several Western magazines, a favorite of Charles Lummis in his *Land of Sunshine* days and after, was a vivacious hostess. She was aided by her daughter, June, Mrs. Perham Nahl, whose golden-haired daughter, Mary Lee Nahl, became Miss Coolbrith's godchild. When the party was over, the poet stayed on as a weekend houseguest of the Connors. Torrey and June adored her and nicknamed her "Santa Ina." One of the guests who had been unable to come was Warren Cheney. He wrote to Miss Coolbrith from Sacramento, saying he had a copy of Stoddard's first book, the *Poems,* for the shower and would send it to her.[53]

A little more than a week after the book shower, on 10 April, Ina Coolbrith gave her talk on the early writers of the state. As in the 1890s her friends again urged her to get this material into writing and have it published before it was too late.[54] Henry Meade Bland congratulated her, "It is an epoch in one's life," he said, "to hear such a story."[55] And Mary Burbank, one of the older members of the club, remarked, "You can make us see those dear fellows as they lived. I knew C. H. Webb very well, and I thought I heard his voice this afternoon."[56] And State Librarian Gillis, having heard about this talk, "Early California Writers," requested a copy for the library. Miss Coolbrith thanked him for the courtesy but said she could not comply at the time as the material was part of a manuscript she intended to publish sooner or later.

"Should this never be done," she said, "I will see that you are furnished with a copy and if it should be you will have it, as a matter of course."[58] Her enthusiasm flared again. She could not replace the burned manuscript, but she may have planned a series of monographs. To do so would divert her from the nagging awareness that she was no longer writing verse. She had published a few lyrics in 1909, all slight, two in national magazines, one in *Sunset,* one in the *San Jose Notre Dame Quarterly,* and another in the *Oakland Tribune.* These were "Renewal," "Opportunity," "Evenfall at the Gate," "Harriet M. Skidmore," and "At Carmel."[59] In 1910 there were two slight pieces of local interest, "Santa Clara Valley" and "Woman," the latter written for the convention of the California Federation of Women's Clubs meeting in San Francisco.[60] In 1911 only one poem appeared, and that a quatrain, "Mt. Hamilton."[61]

291

It is ironic that the year 1911, when she was seventy and when her poetic output was most meager, was the year she was elected to the Poetry Society of America.[62] Her club work and some prose writing now seemed of first importance to her.

At the 24 April 1911 meeting, one of the members, Mrs. Isadore Lowenberg, a novelist, made a suggestion that excited the whole roomful. She proposed that the Pacific Coast Women's Press Association sponsor an authors' congress to meet in San Francisco in 1915. There would be a fair in the city that year, the Panama-Pacific International Exposition, for which plans were already being made by the city officials and the Chamber of Commerce. Mrs. Lowenberg's suggestion resulted in immediate action. The women agreed to present a request to the local fair committee at once. They voted that a committee of their own be appointed to serve for the next four years. Its initial action would be to draft a letter to the fair committee to request a place on the Exposition agenda for an authors' congress. If the request should be granted, the same committee would go on with all arrangements. The members urged Miss Coolbrith to serve as president of the committee, and Mrs. Lowenberg, who had had the idea, to be vice-president. Miss Coolbrith would select the other members to serve with her, and the women assured her that all she had to do was to delegate work. After all she was the member most actively associated with San Francisco's literary history. For that reason, her associates said, she must head the committee. Ina Coolbrith pondered. She was not young. She was not well. But, in the end, she decided to take the chairmanship. On Saturday evening, 29 April, she wrote the proposed letter to the proper authorities.[63] When the Association held its annual business meeting in May, Miss Coolbrith was asked to serve a second term as club president, but she declined, knowing that preparations for the authors' congress would demand all her time and energy in the coming months.[64]

Death of Joaquin Miller

When the Press Association met in the fall, its opening meeting was devoted to Gertrude Atherton, the writer and the woman. James D. Phelan and William C. Morrow spoke. And Miss Coolbrith was down in the program for an address. She said that the new president, Mrs. Martin, had meant that as a compliment to her. "I suspect she labors under the delusion," Miss Coolbrith laughed, "that I find it hard to relinquish the Chair of State, and in this way seeks to 'let me down easy.'" She went on to say that she had never made an "address" in her life, so would only say a few personal words about Mrs. Atherton. Most of her talks were extemporaneous, and therefore lost. This one, however,

292

was written out, yet it has the easy conversational style and sparkle of her most casual talk. From it one may learn that Miss Coolbrith did not know Mrs. Atherton until about 1905, and that the younger woman was responsible for the Fairmont Authors' Evening. It was this that produced a fund sufficient for an initial payment on Miss Coolbrith's lot, and on this account, she said, her lot was largely "Atherton ground." While she was speaking, she mentioned a request James Phelan had made of her when she was in the Bohemian Club library—to find what she could about the love story of Concepcion de Arguello for Mrs. Atherton who was in Monterey at the time. The material she collected and had sent to the novelist resulted in *Rezanov,* a California romance.[65]

Near the end of that month, September 1911, Edward F. O'Day called on Miss Coolbrith for an interview for his weekly, *Town Talk,* in which he was running a series of articles on local personalities.[66] What he wrote and published the last day of the month compensated, in some measure, for one issued by Henry Meade Bland in July, which had been an exaggerated comment on California's first literary period.[67] Bland's imagination led him to invent an unlikely conversation between Bret Harte and Ina Coolbrith concerning a review of Joaquin Miller's *Joaquin et al.,* in the *Overland.* But this slur against Harte was trifling compared with one against Ina herself in a feature article of a Sunday *Call* in November.[68] Bland showed a want of tact rather than actual malice, but his statement reopened old wounds. In an article on the homes of some of California's writers, he said that Ina Coolbrith's new house in San Francisco was built with funds collected by George Wharton James, and that the poet might have built at much less expense on any one of a number of free lots elsewhere in the state. Her friends were as annoyed as she was, one of them calling down a picturesque ancient curse upon the professor, another telling him, in a few short words, where he could go.[69]

Miss Coolbrith had barely recovered from Bland's careless barbs when she read another piece about herself that incensed her even more. She was sick in bed at the time, and she must have felt a kind of helpless rage. She had received in the mail a copy of the January 1912 *Out West,* George Wharton James's monthly. There she read a lively, attractively illustrated article on the literature of California, written by Mrs. Lannie Haynes Martin, a Pasadena newspaper woman.[70] In the pages were a number of errors relating to Bret Harte, Ina Coolbrith, and Joaquin Miller. Mrs. Martin was not happy when Miss Coolbrith pointed out the actual facts in each case. The author said that her information was based on a course of lectures given several years before by James.[71] One statement made by Mrs. Martin was that Joaquin Miller had denied that Ina Coolbrith had anything to do with giving him his pen-name. Ina wrote a long letter to Mrs. Martin and letters to both Miller and James.[72] To the latter she said, "You are, as you know, addicted to word painting. I wish you would not. I wish you would be content with the simple truth, however slim."[73] She scolded Joaquin for seeming to have forgotten the incident of the *nom de plume*, reminded him of his first use of it in a note to her, and told him that his mother spoke of it the last time Ina saw her. Miss Coolbrith solemnly pointed out that he and she were both very near the end of this and the beginning of a new life, and asked him to admit the truth in his mother's name.[74] Miller was contrite, "You say, Ina, I have my faith in you; who is Mrs. H. anyway?"[75] Joaquin was ill at this time, and forgetful. Ina was ill, too, and easily irritated. But she was right in saying that exaggerations and misstatements, if not corrected, come finally to be accepted as truth. This idea was emphasized by William Dallam Armes, a professor of English at the University of California, who urged her from time to time to get her own story into print, for soon fact and fiction could be hopelessly confused.[76] Of course Ina agreed with him. But illness, a wide correspondence, the urgency of obligations such as her responsibility for the coming writers' congress, or other emergencies, always combined to make her procrastinate.

The year 1912 was a gloomy one for our aging poet. She was bedfast much of the time. She envied her friend, Mrs. Games, who was traveling in Europe with Mrs. Leslie, saying that she was "miserably ill and unhappy."[77] To another she mourned the fact that she no longer had any real neighbors, like the kind and helpful DeMartini family who lived next door to her on Lincoln Street. Josie had been seriously ill twice during the year and she herself was too lame to get about.[78] This was the year that Ina's niece, Mrs. Cook, was obliged to go to Arizona for an indefinite time to seek some improvement in her health.[79] This was the year, too, of Charles Lummis's temporary blindness, an experience which, however, he did not regret, for, as he said, it was an education in another world.[80] This year also brought the death of Ina's beautiful Persian cat, Titian.[81] And all through the dreary year Ina had been troubled by Joaquin Miller's failing health. His wife, Abbie Leland Miller, and their daughter, Juanita, had come out from New York to take charge. He seemed to be happy in their presence, saying at one time, "Juanita is solid gold."[82] The women's care, however, was resented by all of Joaquin's old friends who thought that, with the coming of his family, he lost his freedom. He was "chaperoned," they said. This was resented especially by both Mrs. Leslie and Iza Hardy, who were writing to Ina from abroad for bulletins on Miller's condition.[83]

In November, Ina, whose portrait of Joaquin was lost in the 1906 fire, begged him to try and have his picture taken. He responded, in a surprisingly legible letter addressed to "My dear little girl of the days of gold," that a man on his back does not photograph well, but added, "I will do so if I live, and I *will* live." Ina was touched by the forced gaiety of his closing words, "I . . . eat well, sleep well and have little or no pain, am very stupid—like to rest and rest and rest. Love to you as of old, Your own Joaquin Miller."[84] He wrote to her a week later, stirred by some half-forgotten promise, to tell her that he had found the old back number of the *Galaxy* she had wanted, and was also sending a letter of interest to her. She had never had any trouble reading his notoriously bad hand, so she made this one out, too, written with the quill pen in the failing hand of a man unable to sit up in his bed. Written on 17 November 1912, but dated October, it may have been his last letter to her.[85]

The year 1912, nevertheless, was not wholly dismal for Miss Coolbrith. In September James D. Phelan gave a dinner party for Mrs. Atherton. The occasion may have been political, for Gertrude Atherton was becoming involved in Democratic party activities, and Phelan was being urged by his friends to run for the United States Senate. Both Mrs. Atherton and Miss Coolbrith are known to have endorsed him in print, though the latter called herself a "born and bred Republican."[86] Whatever the occasion for the dinner, Ina's illness compelled her to decline the invitation. She sent a poem, however, written to Mrs. Atherton and asked Phelan to read it aloud at the dinner. He did so, to the surprised pleasure of the novelist.[87] In June Miss Coolbrith also wrote a brief "Greeting" in verse to be read at the Press Association's breakfast meeting when that organization was host to other press associations from elsewhere in the state.[88] The "Greeting" appeared in print, but the lines to Mrs. Atherton did not. In June, also, appeared the "Coolbrith number" of the *Notre Dame Quarterly*, published by the College of Notre Dame in San Jose. Included were biographical and appreciative articles, a dozen of her lyrics, and even more verse tributes to her. The issue was well illustrated and was in every way highly complimentary to its subject. Charles Phillips, editor of the *San Francisco Monitor*, contributed both verse and prose to this number of the *Quarterly*.[89] He was becoming more than ever attached to Miss Coolbrith, idealizing her, inspired by her to fulfill his own literary ambitions in drama and verse and to prepare to teach English in a Catholic university. It was about this time that he left for a trip to Rome, and he asked Ina if he might store his piano in her flat during his absence and later.[90] She was overjoyed, for her own had been burned. She began to request her young friends who were studying music to come and play for her, and take her mind off her ills. Among these young musicians, over the next few years, were Alice Bashford, and a neighbor boy named Carl Gunderson.[91] Young Miss Bashford found the instrument woefully out of tune, but did her best. Miss Coolbrith preferred the music of Beethoven, and, as she listened, her dark gray eyes seemed to deepen to shining black. "Bright as lamps," the young musician thought, as her small, deft hands produced glorious sound in the poet's hilltop living room.[92]

As the year 1913 dawned, Joaquin Miller had grown very weak. His friends were sure that he was not receiving proper care. Ina wrote to Henry Meade Bland to urge him to get medical assistance. Bland, who had some personal ties with Miller, since Bland's daughter had married Miller's grandson, was often at the Hights, but Miss Coolbrith's appeal was ignored.[93] She wrote directly to Miller on 9 February, saying "Joaquin, you ought to have a *doctor*. You are not doing right by yourself or your friends, or the world, to go on this way. I have no doubt your wife and daughter are all devotion and care, but they should be under the direction of skilled medical advice. You should have massage to take the place of the exercise to which you are not equal, by some *man*. Juanita is not strong enough. A man should massage you and rub you with alcohol, and in a short time, with the proper tonics, you would be on your feet. Do this to oblige your old friends." With the letter, which was sent by friends, she enclosed a photograph of Joaquin which she had bought at the Emporium in San Francisco, and she begged him to put his name on the photo side, if he were strong enough, the last favor asked by one who had done Miller many a kindness.[94] Herman Whitaker was at the Hights on 15 February.

"Sick as he is, unable to speak," Whitaker told Ina, "it is the same old Joaquin. He was hot today, against the doctors (who had taken away his whiskey) and he nodded when I offered to go downstairs and kill a couple of them. It is pitiful to see him so weak and helpless."[95] Whitaker had seen him on Saturday. Joaquin Miller died two days later, on Monday, 17 February 1913, at age seventy-five.[96] The poet of the Sierra, flamboyant to the end, had asked that his body be burned on the funeral pyre he had built at the edge of the family burial plot. Both Juanita and her mother had agreed to the pagan rite, but the Oakland city health authorities did not. The body was cremated the next day, and services were held at the Hights.[97]

On 14 April, both Herbert Bashford and Ina Coolbrith paid their respects to Joaquin Miller's memory at a meeting of the Press Association.[98] Bashford gave a critical and biographical summary, and Miss Coolbrith a long, anecdote-filled account of her association with Joaquin,

296

beginning with the day he landed in San Francisco in 1870 "to see the poets." She said he was a good-looking, conventionally garbed man, in no way distinguished from other men by the cut of his hair or clothing. She related in her usual chatty way one amusing incident after another. She mentioned what she considered the true date of his birth, based on a notebook of his in her possession, a date disputed by Miller himself in his later years. Ina shrugged. Four years did not make much difference. She told how she had made a wreath for Byron's tomb, how Miller took it to England, and what happened. She described the way she came to suggest that he take a pen name instead of his own cumbersome Cincinnatus Hiner (not Heine). She said that she suggested *Joaquin*, taken from his little book, and hinted that long hair and Western garb would go well with such a name, and told with what enthusiasm her lightly-made proposals were accepted. She related the story of his appearance at her door, after his return from London, his long blond hair flowing from beneath a wide-brimmed hat, and recalled their conversation.

"What have you been doing?" she asked him.

"Lion hunting," was his reply, and she came back with, "Is that why you wear a mane?" He had come to invite her to go to the theater with him that evening. She said she would if he would visit a barber first. He agreed reluctantly and promised to come for her at seven. When he came in, Ina could see no sign of long hair.

"How nice you look, Joaquin," she remembered telling him. At the play they occupied a box. During an intermission Joaquin ran his fingers through his hair, shook out the long locks, and gave Ina a handful of hairpins. The house lights were on, and, she recalled laughingly, all eyes were upon them. These were some of the stories Ina brought out of the past and put into writing for that meeting on 14 April 1913.[99] When the poet went home, after the unusually stimulating and nostalgic meeting, she began to compose some rhyming lines for Joaquin, saying them over as she prepared to retire. In the next few weeks there were letters of comment on Joaquin's passing. Mrs. S. A. Darling said, "The true story of Joaquin will never be told; you, if anyone, could tell it and I think you will not."[100] And Lischen Miller, in Oregon, said she thought Joaquin owed more to Ina than to anyone else.[101]

It remained for the Bohemian Club to observe Joaquin Miller's death in a style fitting the poet's life. Ina Coolbrith was unable to attend, but she asked Herbert Bashford to try to locate "poor Indian Callie's grave." Mrs. Darling should know, she said, and added, "If ever I am able, it shall be marked." Though absent from the impressive memorial service the club held beside Joaquin's pyre on Sunday, 25 May, she expressed her own farewell in three long stanzas entitled "Vale, Joaquin!" which were read by Richard D. Hotaling. Professor William Dallam Armes, of the University of California English department, gave a simple but moving talk. Colonel John P. Irish gave a eulogy on his old friend, and then, after faggots had been placed on the pyre and set ablaze, he scattered the poet's ashes over the flames. The smoke from that symbolic fire drifted up like incense through the pines and eucalyptus trees that Joaquin had planted long before on a bare hillside he named *The Hights*, and that the city of Oakland has renamed *Joaquin Miller Park*.[103]

Part
Five
The
Laureate
1914
to 1928

27
The
Laureate

*I accept this laurel, with deep
gratitude and deeper humility.*

Ina Coolbrith, 30 June 1915

Organization of the Congress of Authors

Before Miss Coolbrith's "Vale, Joaquin," was read aloud at the
"Hights" on 25 May 1913 the author had composed her memorial lines
to Charles Warren Stoddard. The lyric was a long time taking form.
She had learned early in 1913 that a monument was to be placed above
Stoddard's grave in the mission cemetery in Monterey. When she was
satisfied with her verse, she sent it to the parish priest, Father Mestress,
asking him to have it read at the service, as she would be unable to attend.
She waited in vain for a reply from the clergyman. Puzzled, she wrote
to George Sterling who had been out of town, and he answered her a
month later, decrying Mestress, but giving no information.[1] Finally, in
June, she learned from Mrs. McCrackin in Santa Cruz that there actually was a cross over Charlie's grave, newly placed.[2] Ina complained of
her frustrations in the matter when she wrote to Iza Hardy who had
known Stoddard when he was in London in the 1870s.[3] With the letter
she enclosed a manuscript of the memorial lines, "At Anchor." It was
a very personal lyric which Ina had written for Charlie. She attempted
to make the words speak for him. In twenty lines of clear and carefully
limned imagery she pictured the tropical islands that he loved, the
"lift of emerald hills against the blue from blue," the "wash of waves
upon the coral reef," his "tawny Comrades," and their "soft-voweled

301

speech," and at the end a reference to his faith. Now he was at anchor, and he could himself have said the very words she gave him:

> Long have I wandered, tossed by stormy tides,
>   Benumbed in calms—but here, how sure the sea!
> Furl the worn sails—the ship at anchor rides—
>   Leave me with these! Leave me to these and Thee!

Ina kept the poem to herself for over a year. But it was the press of events rather than sentiment that prevented her from sending it to the *Overland Monthly* until the autumn of 1914.[4]

These events included her anxiety over the last days of Joaquin Miller, her memorial program for him at her club, and her contribution to the Bohemian Club's service in May, as related on previous pages. On 13 March 1913 her preparations for the coming Congress were formally launched at a luncheon given by James D. Phelan at the Bohemian Club for Miss Coolbrith and some of the members of her committee. Those present, in addition to Ina Coolbrith, were President Benjamin Ide Wheeler of the University of California; David Starr Jordan, chancellor of Stanford University; Dr. Edward Robeson Taylor, head of Hastings School of Law; William C. Morrow; the *Chronicle's* literary editor, George Hamlin Fitch; the Exposition manager, James A. Barr; and officers from the Women's Press Association, Mrs. Atherton, Mrs. Lowenberg, and Mrs. Pinney. The group at lunch that day formed the nucleus of what would be a larger committee on the Congress.[5]

Miss Coolbrith was aware that her strength might not be equal to the amount and variety of paper work and planning that she was assuming. She had assurances on all sides, however, that she would have the clerical help she needed. She had already asked Herman Whitaker to serve as secretary to the Congress, but he declined because such voluminous correspondence would interfere with the novel he had to finish.[6] Later in the year she asked Mrs. Phoebe Apperson Hearst to be the honorary president of the Congress, but Mrs. Hearst, too, declined because of other claims on her time and strength.[7] Mrs. Atherton and the poet Herman Scheffauer both offered to help obtain lists of English and European authors to be invited to the Congress.[8] Scheffauer had gone to England, had married an English girl, and was writing plays for the London stage.[9] Mrs. Atherton expected to be in England and France for an indefinite stay. Miss Coolbrith probably accepted the offers of both these friends to supply a mailing list of authors abroad. She herself obtained similar lists from writers' associations and press clubs of the states and leading cities in the United States. It was not long before she had an impressive card file of prospective delegates to the Authors' Congress. Her friends were alarmed that so much clerical work had devolved upon her.[10] Charles Phillips, who lived in San Francisco and was still editor of the archdiocesan paper, the *Monitor,* may have aided her when he could. He was busy at that time, however, completing the requirements for his Master of Arts degree from St. Mary's College in Oakland. It is safe to assume that James D. Phelan, who was as deeply interested in the success of the coming meeting as any other person, would have provided helpers when they were needed. An attack of rheumatism struck Ina early in December and she spent that month and half of the next in bed.

Two Thousand Invitations

In January 1914, the invalid was cheered by the gift of a handsome, lively, long-haired white cat, two years old.[11] This was Popcorn, who came to keep Moona company, and to become a faithful and pampered companion of his mistress. In spite of the illness of December and January, the mailing lists were ready early in the year. So, too, were the addressed envelopes and a form letter, printed on the letterhead of the Panama-Pacific International Exposition Congress of Authors and Journalists. Each guest was told:

> Our congress of Authors and Journalists extends greeting to you, and invites you to be with us in our great year of rejoicing over the coming closer together of the Nations by the completion of the Panama Canal, 1915.

There followed a longer paragraph that would have done credit to any California Chamber of Commerce for florid description of the state's wonders, and then the prospective visitor was told that the Exposition would open on 20 February 1915 and that the Congress would be held in May or June, the exact date to be sent later. Each one of an estimated two thousand letters was signed by Ina Coolbrith herself.[12]

If the aging poet's friends were concerned about this sudden deluge of work on her, she herself found the correspondence stimulating. In a list of British authors she came across the name of Albert Brecknock, the author of a biography of Byron. He was, moreover, the city librarian of Hucknall Torkard, where Byron was buried and where she had sent a laurel wreath by Joaquin Miller in 1870. She wrote Brecknock about the incident and told him how she had longed in vain to see Hucknall Torkard Church and Newstead Abbey. She told him that she herself had owned a fine engraved reproduction of the Phillips portrait of Byron, the original of which hung in the Abbey. Her picture had

been lost in the San Francisco fire and she had never been able to secure another. She suggested that he might know where a copy could be obtained. With this letter the two librarians began a correspondence that was to continue to the end of Ina's life.[13]

It was not long before replies were coming to her from many distant points. Mary Eileen Ahern said she would be there. She asked Miss Coolbrith if she remembered the 1891 library convention in San Francisco. Miss Ahern had never forgotten the Oakland librarian who was also a poet.[14] Louise Imogene Guiney, who could not come, said she was "glad of this chance to pay my respects to you whose name is familiar to me this long while."[15] Out-of-state authors who had had any California experience were inspired, by her invitation, to write at length about such experiences. One octogenarian described in hair-raising detail a Sierran stage ride by night when the driver was thrown from his seat under the coach from where he pulled his teams to a stop; in spite of broken ribs he brought his passengers to their destination.[16] Another recipient of an invitation, LaSalle Corbell Pickett, the beautiful widow of General George Edward Pickett, sent regrets.[17] So, too, did General George Goethals, chief engineer of the Panama Canal and governor of the Canal Zone, whose obligation to attend a meeting of engineers at the Exposition would prevent his presence in the Congress of Authors.[18] The daughter of Richard Henry Dana wrote sorrowfully that she was unable to come; she had never seen the California coast, but had always longed to because of the descriptions in *Two Years before the Mast*.[19] Anthony Comstock, notorious censor, was invited, but said he was so busy "heading off the Devil's printing press" that he could not come; he gloated over the one hundred-seventy tons of contraband matters and the thirty thousand pictures seized during the first seven months of 1914.[20] A letter came from Albert Kinross, the London editor who had long before introduced Ina Coolbrith to the British reading public. He would come and he would meet her in person after all the years. She, too, was elated at the prospect. Then, suddenly, in August, began the tragic conflict later named World War I. Albert Kinross was called to military duty.[21] Another letter came from a mother who said she was writing for her son, then at the front.[22] The innocent cheerfulness of Ina's invitation and the follow-up reminder were irritating to some of the British who said sarcastically that Cali-

---

Ina Coolbrith and Her Cat, Popcorn. Portrait by Ansel Adams in 1925. Reproduced with the permission of the photographer. Courtesy of Mrs. Delpha Stevens de Timofeev, Librarian, Ina Coolbrith Branch, Oakland Free Library.

fornia must be so far away that it was unaware of the seriousness of life across the Atlantic. Romain Rolland, writing from the Geneva office of the International Red Cross, thanked her for the *"aimable invitation,"* but regretted that *"les dures nécessités de l'heure present en Europe"* would prevent him from taking part.[23] Herman Scheffauer, San Francisco writer then in London, chose this time to express his pride in his Teutonic ancestry and his admiration for true *kultur*, was annoyed by what he termed the excesses of the British wartime press, talked of leaving, and actually went later to Berlin, to the dismay of his friends in England and America.[24]

Ina Coolbrith, President, Congress of Authors

This correspondence with authors at home and abroad was an exhilarating experience that stirred Ina to a surprising variety of activities. It even roused her sleeping Muse. Several new lyrics published in 1914 received praise. In May appeared "On a Fly-leaf of Omar," written in Fitzgerald's *Rubaiyat* verse form, published in the *Catholic World*, and copied by the *Literary Digest* with comment by Joyce Kilmer. The *Overland* printed her "Point Bonita" that month, too, a dozen evocative lines that pleased George Hamlin Fitch and any reader who has known danger points on the California coast. The next month Edward O'Day published this piece as the one hundred forty-eighth in his *Town Talk* series of poems about San Francisco. Miss Coolbrith's poem, "War and Peace," was written for recitation at a spectacular outdoor peace meeting in Golden Gate Park, in September 1914. One hundred thousand persons crowded the band concert area under the plane trees. They heard the poem read, then gasped with surprise as the school-girl chorus on the platform released a flock of white doves into the air. Peace demonstrations of half a century later could have been more effective as irritants to the *status quo,* but could not surpass the Golden Gate Park event as pure spectacle. The lyric read at the meeting disappeared as newspaper verse ephemera, for it was not included in Miss Coolbrith's last published volume. In November her verse to Stoddard, printed in the *Overland*, though written a year before, was followed the next month by "A Tribute," published in the *California Outlook*, a lyric for Caroline M. Severance.[25]

Miss Coolbrith's lyric mood in 1914 may have been inspired by her contact with other authors. But it was also the result of better health. She seemed to be less afflicted than usual with her chronic trouble, for she was singularly active and was optimistic about her potential energy. When she was seventy-three in March, her doctor congratulated her on her sixteenth birthday.[26] She was persuaded that spring to accept

306

the presidency of the Women's Press Association again, this time to serve only until the close of the Exposition, a necessary formality, since she was expected to preside at the coming Congress.[27] In May she gave a lecture on Stoddard for the Ebell Club in Oakland.[28] All spring and summer she was in correspondence with the Houghton Mifflin Company to arrange for a reprint of her *Songs from the Golden Gate*. The book was again out of print, and her own supply was exhausted. She knew that there would be some demand for her poems during the Congress. In August the publishers issued a fourth printing of five hundred copies, bound in five colors, a different color for each one hundred.[29] This was the month that the poet entertained in her home the members of the old Board of Directors of the Mercantile Library.[30] The same month she gave to the local press her whole-hearted endorsement of James Duval Phelan, Democratic candidate for the United States Senate.[31] This political commitment surprised even herself, not only because she was a Republican, but because she had seldom been involved in any political movements. Though not personally active in the Woman Suffrage Party of California, her support was acknowledged by them in their publications. The ballot for women was new in California, having been granted as recently as 1911.[32] Miss Coolbrith joined Mrs. Atherton in endorsing Phelan, and probably agreed with her that this was an opportunity to use their new power. Had James Phelan not been a friend of many years' standing, had he not been a patron of art and literature, she might not have given her public endorsement. He was not friendly to labor, and he was an exclusionist on the Oriental question, taking the position of many other California native sons. Whatever Miss Coolbrith may have felt about these matters, she did not let them bother her. To her he was a gentleman of culture, a poet, a man with civic interests. Though rich, he was honest, so honest, indeed, that President Roosevelt had sent federal relief funds directly to Phelan after the earthquake and fire, not trusting the notorious Abe Ruef administration of the city.[33]

Miss Coolbrith had no press agents and certainly needed none. The papers were full of stories about the plans for the coming exposition, including the Authors' Congress. But the poet herself was the subject of several interesting press accounts during the year, and had her poem to Bret Harte used on the dedicatory page of a new collection of Harte's poems and stories compiled by Charles Kozley, and published by Houghton Mifflin that spring.[34] The articles about her were all noteworthy, a story in the *San Francisco Examiner* in May, one in the June issue of *Everywoman*, and a long biographical account in the *Overland Monthly*. The *Examiner* story was by Redfern Mason, music critic for that paper. It concerned Mason's predecessor, Edward Stillman Kelley, a composer who had lived abroad for years. Mason told how Ina Coolbrith came to write her lyric, "Lines on Hearing Kelley's Music to 'Macbeth.'" In the 1880s, when she was Oakland's librarian, she listened to Kelley playing his "Macbeth" composition for her on the piano in her home. She was deeply stirred by the wild and haunting music and succeeded in carrying its qualities over into her poem which the *Overland* published in January 1886.[35] The *Everywoman* article, concerning the preparations for the Congress, giving names of committee members, and quoting from some of the letters received by Ina Coolbrith, is notable for one anecdote concerning her. It is a story that has been related often enough, and without source, to give it the character of a legend. If it be legend or fact, it is repeated here, with the name of the California woman who first told it. When Mrs. D. O. Murphy, wife of a California judge, was in England, she met George Meredith, and they conversed a while.

"Your great western country," he commented, "has introduced some remarkable writers—virile, forcible and original." Then he asked her, "Do you know Ina Coolbrith? A true poetess," he went on, "she has genius; she is foremost among your writers; keenly alive to every mood of nature; in touch with every human emotion; she has suffered; an echo of sadness rings in her work. If I go to your California I must meet her; why doesn't she come to London? We have no such women writers with us now. When you go home tell her she is one of the very few lyric writers that has impressed me." Meredith never came to California. He died six years before the Authors' Congress was to take place. One can imagine with what pleasure he might have received one of those two thousand invitations Miss Coolbrith signed, and how he would have responded, had he lived. Meredith, a nature poet too, had been impressed by the California poet's precision in choice of the right word to convey an emotion or an image. As he could put the note of a blackbird into English words, so could she the song of a meadowlark.[36]

The Meredith anecdote was repeated by Mrs. Marian Taylor in her article entitled "Ina Coolbrith, California Poet," thirteen biographical pages in the October 1914 *Overland Monthly*. This account, by a mem-

---

Ina Coolbrith, President, Congress of Authors and Journalists, Panama-Pacific International Exposition, San Francisco, 1915. (Left to right: Charles Phillips, Ina Coolbrith, Edward Robeson Taylor). Detail of group photograph by Cardinell Vincent Co., San Francisco. Courtesy of Mrs. Alice Bashford Wallace, Sidney, B.C., Canada.

...onal Exposition San Francisco Cal

ber of the Women's Press Association who wrote in worshipful vein, served as attractive advance publicity for one who would take a prominent position in the affairs of the Exposition in 1915. In spite of errors and some exaggerations, the article has been used by generations of school children and others in search of information on the state's first woman poet. Mrs. Taylor illustrated her material with portraits of the poet and her literary colleagues, and with views of the poet's home. She quoted some of Miss Coolbrith's verse and many tributes to her.[37] In October, when this sketch was published, Charles Phillips took a leave of absence from the *Monitor,* to arrange for the production of his first play. This was *The Divine Friend,* produced in New York City in 1915, with Margaret Anglin.[38] He kept Ina informed of his progress and promised to be in San Francisco in time to assist her and to take part in the anticipated Congress of Authors. For Ina, an unusually stimulating and exciting year closed benignly with the Bohemian Club singing her "Hymn to the Nativity" at their annual Christmas festivities.[39]

The Crown of Laurel

Not long after the beginning of the important year 1915, three men met at night in the office of the *San Francisco Chronicle* to hatch a plot. To the office of the night editor, George Hamlin Fitch, had come two other writers, Richard Edward White, known as the "Mission Poet," and Zoeth Skinner Eldredge, historian. Eldredge and Fitch were both members of the Congress committee, but White was one with them in this conspiracy. They agreed that the coming Congress should be climaxed by making Miss Coolbrith the state's poet laureate. She should, of course, receive the traditional wreath of laurel, and the gesture should have Governor Johnson's sponsorship. The three were united in the opinion that either Senator Phelan or President Wheeler should make the presentation. But the senator was in Washington, so they decided to discuss their plan with the university president. The conspirators parted. They kept the secret well. They knew, however, that as soon as the program schedule was taking shape they must present their plan. By then, with all arrangements completed, Miss Coolbrith would be informed, and she would be obliged to allow time on the program for the ceremony.[40]

The program, the Committee was beginning to feel, would be a disappointment. Its balance and scope would be affected by the war. No one from England or the continent could participate. European subjects would have to be presented by non-Europeans. While the Committee as a whole was working on the preliminary plans for the events to take place, Miss Coolbrith was plagued by a number of minor worries, not the least of which was a two-week spell of rheumatism in April.[41] There had been some discussion of an Exposition ode, for which a prize would be given, and George Sterling was urged to write it. He did so, in the fall of 1914, and then discovered that a little group had hoped Miss Coolbrith would write the ode. Sterling was embarrassed, and begged his friends to say nothing about his work which he would simply sell to a newspaper. Lorenzo Sosso had backed Sterling, and he told Ina he had, and why. Ina, commenting on Sosso's frankness and his opinion that Sterling's style was better suited to the subject, said she took off her "bonnet to him" for his honesty.[42] She was fully occupied in a dozen other directions. She would have written an ode only on command, and then would have been dissatisfied. Her greatest annoyance during the spring was a lack of cooperation from one of the club officers. The woman, clever, attractive, and competent in presiding, failed to carry out certain responsibilities to which she had agreed. She may have been governed by petty jealousy, especially of Mrs. Atherton. The trouble seemed to be a matter of protocol. Miss Coolbrith could not overlook what she regarded as an insult to California's foremost woman writer. She did not forgive the woman yet gave her the presidency of two of the six sessions of the Congress.[43]

By early June Ina Coolbrith had been told of the plan to present her with the laureate's crown. She had known nothing of it, of course.[44] The program was taking shape, and it was decided to place the presentation of the laureateship on the agenda for the second afternoon session. Senator Phelan was back from Washington and he would be asked to participate. A reception for the senator by the Women's Press Association, on the evening of 15 June, was arranged to coincide with the opening of the downtown headquarters of the Congress of Authors and Journalists at the Forum Club rooms, 525 Sutter Street.[45] Here the local and visiting writers were invited to make themselves at home. All meetings of the Congress, from 29 June through 2 July, would be held at the Exposition Auditorium in the Civic Center, at Hayes and Larkin Streets.[46] Miss Coolbrith, herself, had been so occupied with the details of calling the Congress that she had little time to enjoy the fair. Her dear friend Mrs. Boalt had come in April. She had taken a room at the Inside Inn, the only hotel on the Exposition grounds, and begged Ina to come see her there, as her heart would permit no more climbing of the city's hills.[47] It may be supposed that the two old friends saw part of the Jewel City together, if only by carriage or car, or even wheelchairs side by side. Their age and ills made full enjoyment of the spectacle impossible. But they may have seen some of the beauties, the Tower of

311

Jewels, the fountains and reflecting pools, the sculptures, the colonnades and the dreamlike perfection of Bernard Maybeck's Palace of the Fine Arts. It is known that Miss Coolbrith was on the grounds on Saturday evening, 26 June, at a Spanish-California fiesta in the Cuban Pavilion. This program of Spanish music and dances was given in honor of the Congress of Authors and Journalists, with Miss Coolbrith as hostess and Commissioner General Enrique del Castillo of Cuba as host, a gentleman who showed the California poet many courtesies during the Exposition.[48]

At last the great day arrived. The Panama-Pacific International Exposition Congress of Authors and Journalists was called to order on Tuesday morning, 29 June, at ten o'clock, by Miss Ina Coolbrith. After greetings by Miss Coolbrith and James A. Barr, director of the Exposition congresses, the session turned to the serious business of literature. Mrs. M. E. North-Whitcomb of San Francisco gave a talk on Norse literature. Her remarks were followed by a paper on the influence of Chinese literature on the politics of that country. Sent by Sin Lun, exspeaker of the Chinese Senate, it was read by his friend Robert Norman, United States Consul at Canton, and long before, an impecunious student roomer in Miss Coolbrith's house.[49] The last speaker, Dr. Edward Robeson Taylor, a good mayor, a good law school administrator, but a decidedly prosaic sonneteer, spoke on the value of poetry. The local press found much to praise and blame in the addresses by Gertrude Atherton, Charles Lummis, and William Dallam Armes. These three were reported with a good deal of distortion. Mrs. Atherton was still in New York, and Senator Phelan read her paper.[50] Under the title "Literary Merchandise" she discussed the American magazine article as purely commercial writing, an opinion that was challenged by the local press. The papers also took issue with Professor Armes's idea that the older California writers were more honest than those of 1915. They reported that he regarded the writings of Mrs. Atherton and Jack London as mere potboilers.[51] Charles Lummis, in his usual iconoclastic style, asked "What's the Matter with California Literature?"[52] The newspapers gave space to the more controversial addresses and had little room for comment on such themes as Irish folk songs, free verse, Medieval Jewish poets, and the Shakespeare festival in Stratford-on-Avon. Miss Coolbrith presided again at the Wednesday morning session when talks were given on California history and literature, and the sonnet in American literature, all given by personal friends of hers: Zoeth Eldredge, Professor Armes, Charles Phillips, and Herbert Bashford.

The auditorium was crowded Wednesday afternoon. Miss Coolbrith's old friend, Mrs. Josephine Clifford McCrackin, had come from Santa

312

Cruz. She had only a few hours in the city and had gone directly to the auditorium to be present at that one session, then to take the train home at the close of the day. She walked in hesitantly, but was greeted by several women whom she knew but had not seen for many years. They found a place for her near the platform. And they found her unchanged except that the heavy dark hair was now white, though the dark eyes were as brilliant as ever. Mrs. McCrackin's eyes sought Ina's face, but they did not find Ina among those on the stage. Up there were President Wheeler, Senator Phelan, Arthur Arlett from the governor's office, also Edwin Markham, Zoeth Eldredge, and Charles Murdock. Mrs. McCrackin decided that Charles Phillips must have been the one she did not know—the youngest in the group. In the audience were many who had come to this session especially to see Miss Coolbrith invested with the poet's crown. Mrs. Boalt had not been well enough, to her sorrow and Ina's. Herbert and Mrs. Bashford and their daughter Alice were there. So were Ina Peterson Cook and her young daughter Ina. Miss Coolbrith had not yet come in. Mrs. McCrackin, intent on the paper being read, felt a hand on her shoulder, and heard Ina say, "Jo!" She could only say, "Ina, oh Ina!" as they clasped hands. Ina moved on to take a place nearer the stage, and, as Josephine McCrackin fought back the tears, the words of Ina's lyric, "The Years," came back to her. The years—the years! What had they done to these two women? She turned her attention to the stage and heard Governor Johnson's message. Edwin Markham, representing the Poetry Society of America, then spoke on "The Saving of Poetry." He was followed by Senator Phelan on the golden era of California letters and the group who made it golden, Harte and Stoddard, Twain and Miller, and their sister writer, Ina Coolbrith. He discussed the quality and finish of her poetry, and its small quantity. He then turned to President Wheeler and asked him to present the poet's crown to Miss Coolbrith.

The poet rose and was escorted to the stage. She moved slowly, dressed in black and wearing a sash embroidered in a design of California poppies, the insignia of the Women's Press Association. She had removed her black-plumed hat to be ready to receive the crown of bay.[53] President Wheeler greeted her. He closed his short speech with the words, "therefore upon thee so worthy do I confer this laurel crown and name thee Poet Laureate of California." He then handed her the crown, instead of placing it on her head as she had expected, and the room burst into applause and a wild waving of white handkerchiefs. She began to reply before the clapping died down, and some of her words were lost, but the room soon grew still. It was an intensely emotional experience for those present. Many were on the verge of tears, and the laureate's words were lost to them. Mrs. McCrackin, taking notes for her paper and for an *Overland* article, failed to catch the words. And all that Mrs. Mighels heard was something about "a labor of love."[54] The moment was tumultous with feeling that seemed to stop the ears. Nevertheless Ina Coolbrith did make a formal acceptance speech, facing President Wheeler at first, then turning to the audience. With the wreath in her hands she said:

> While with pride and gratitude I feel the magnitude of the honor you would confer upon me, I cannot but voice my own realization of my own unworthiness. Senator Phelan has spoken justly of the little I have published. By me poetry has been regarded not only as supremest of the arts, but as a divine gift, for the best use of which its recipient should be fitted by education, time, opportunity. None of these have been mine. The "higher education" was not open to my sex in my youth, although, singularly, I was the first woman to furnish a commencement poem to any university, which I did at the request of the faculty of the University of California; and in a life of unremitting labor, "time and opportunity" have been denied. So my meagre output of verse is the result of odd moments, and only done at all because so wholly a labor of love.
>
> I feel that the honor extended me today is meant not so much because of any special merit of my own, as in memory of that wonderful group of early California writers with which it was my fortune to be affiliated, and of which I am the sole survivor; and for that reason—for those who are passed away and for my sister women—I accept this laurel, with deep gratitude and deeper humility.[55]

So speaking, she stepped forward to the edge of the flower-banked stage and asked Mrs. McCrackin to come forward. In something like a dream, Jo said afterward, she was escorted to the platform where she stood beside Ina. Taking her friend's hand, Ina said, "There is one woman here with whom I want to share these honors, Josephine Clifford McCrackin; for we are linked together, the last two living members of Bret Harte's staff of *Overland* writers." Back in her seat once more and deeply stirred by the incident, Mrs. McCrackin listened to

---

Mrs. Finlay Cook (Ina Lillian Peterson) and Daughter Ina; Niece and Grandniece of Ina Coolbrith, at Congress of Authors and Journalists, San Francisco, 1915. Detail of group photograph by P. Cardinell Vincent Co., San Francisco. Courtesy of Mrs. Alice Bashford Wallace, Sidney, B.C., Canada.

the rest of a rather long program, during which Charles Murdock gave a talk about Bret Harte, Zoeth Eldredge spoke, and Charles Phillips read Miss Coolbrith's poem, "Bret Harte."[56]

While the Congress was formally closed on Thursday, the Exposition officials had set aside the next afternoon as a "special day" for the entertainment of guests of the Congress and for the awarding of a medal to the Congress Committee. James Barr asked Miss Coolbrith to preside at this affair. It was held in the Recital Hall on the Exposition grounds, and began with the presentation of a bronze medal to Miss Coolbrith for the Pacific Coast Women's Press Association's successful Congress. Miss Coolbrith's acceptance of the medal was followed by a talk by Mrs. North-Whitcomb about the Press Association itself. Two of the poet's songs were sung, "Quest," as a solo, and "In Blossom Time," by a local boys' choir, "accompanied with great expression by Herbert Bashford's gifted daughter." By this time the chairman must have been quite uncomfortable, having to preside at a program consisting mostly of compliments to herself. But she had one more participant to introduce, Charles Phillips, whose reading of her long ode, "California," brought the session to a close in a way that convinced those who had heard the poem that its author's new title belonged to her indeed.[57]

Legislative Recognition of the Laureateship

The Authors' Congress and the bestowal of the laureateship upon Miss Coolbrith both had their aftermaths. Congratulations were heaped upon her by letter and by the press, even as far away as New York City, where the *Times*'s comment was, "There was no lack of enthusiasm in the crowning of the laureate. To the cold and 'effete East' it (the West) may even seem a little overwrought at times. That, however, is probably due to envy. New York has no Poet Laureate—and California has."[58] James Barr was sincere in his praise of her work, requested a summary of the proceedings, a copy of each paper read, and asked to borrow her card file of authors and journalists. All these were needed, he said, for use in the comprehensive history of the exposition to be published.[59] Ina Coolbrith complied with these requests. But she was tired, "Very tired," she told one friend, "and aware that the years are upon me."[60] And to Mrs. Torrey Connor she remarked, "I just want to go somewhere and sit down!" To sit down in her Russian Hill home, to look out over the Bay and city, to relax and dream, now that the long, hard task was finished. The August *Sunset* carried her first poem printed after she received her title. This was "From Russian Hill." She had sent it to the periodical early in the summer, perhaps hoping

316

that the July issue would contain it. Lillian Gatlin of the *Sunset* staff told her that the lines had been singing in her head ever since she had sent them to be set.[62]

Although Miss Coolbrith was addressed and referred to as the Poet Laureate, her title was not official for several years. On 26 April 1919 there was filed with the California Secretary of State the following:

> Senate concurrent resolution no. 24—Relative to Ina Coolbrith of San Francisco, California, being given the honorary title of the Loved Laurel-Crowned Poet of California.
>
> WHEREAS, Ina Coolbrith of San Francisco, California, has brought prominently to the attention of the world the glories and beauties of California's fruits and flowers, its climate, its scenery, its wealth and possibilities, through her many brilliant poems, and has contributed to the high standing of our literature, thereby winning the admiration and gratitude of all loyal Californians, and is truly deserving of our most favorable recognition and mention, therefore, be it
>
> RESOLVED BY THE SENATE, THE ASSEMBLY CONCURRING, That Ina Coolbrith be hereby recognized and given the honorary title of the Loved Laurel-Crowned Poet of California.[63]

The laureateship, though officially sanctioned, is honorary only. It is accompanied by no stipend, though statements to the contrary have been made.[64] Ina Coolbrith was the first woman poet laureate in the United States. In September 1965 four brass plaques honoring the poets laureate of California were placed in the foyer of the California State Library in Sacramento. They will be seen on the wall opposite the entrance. Ina Coolbrith's plaque reads:

> Ina Donna Coolbrith. California Poet Laureate
> from 1915 to 1928.
>
> Child of the earth yet kindred to the stars
> He walks in dreams with angels face to face
> And God Himself speaks in his voice of song.
>
> From "With the Laurel."
> In tribute to a fellow poet.[65]

317

28
Disenchantment

As grows the rose,
The thistle grows.

Ina Coolbrith, from
"Rose and Thistle"
(ca. 1920)

The California Literature Society

"How many honors you are getting now-a-days!" wrote Elizabeth
Boalt to Ina Coolbrith, and added, "But you deserve them all." The
note was written to congratulate the poet specifically for having a
newly hybridized poppy named for her. Luther Burbank had developed
a flower which he named "crimson eschscholtzia Ina Coolbrith." Ina
in thanking him, said that when she wrote her "Copa de Oro" she did
not know she would ever be a member of the family. This happened in
the fall of 1915.[1] During that autumn, too, the College of the Holy
Names in Oakland put on a "Coolbrith program," where she gave a talk,
Charles Phillips read some of her verse, and the girls sang her lyric,
"The Poet," which had been set to music by one of the sisters for the
occasion.[2] In March 1916 her friends, about fifty of them, gave her a
surprise birthday party in her home with the gleeful aid of Josie who
kept the secret well. Ina, seventy-five that month, said that the surprise party was her "first ever," and she was as pleased as a child. One
friend, masculine, said that she was dressed in white: another, feminine,
noted that Miss Coolbrith wore a lavender silk gown with white acces-
sories.[3] The white in her costume, impressing them both, was probably
a white lace mantilla worn over the thinning white hair. About this
time she adopted this headdress for wear at home and when she went
out in company. The last time she had been photographed in a hat

319

had been at the close of the Congress of Authors and Journalists, when a group portrait had been made, with a very tired-faced, unsmiling Miss Coolbrith sitting in the middle of the front row. The lace mantilla, always white, which she wore from 1916 on, was a distinctive part of her costume, whether she was at home in an invalid's dressing gown, or abroad, giving a talk in her best afternoon dress. Her friends said that the mantilla was a reminder of her girlhood days when she was the belle of the ball in old Los Angeles. The graceful head covering enhanced Miss Coolbrith's always queenly bearing, and made her dark gray eyes shine in contrast to the white. The lace fluttered and moved as she spoke, and it softened the lines of her aging face. It was partly out of feminine vanity that this beautiful woman adopted such an accessory of dress. Few of the newspaper photographs during these years pleased her. She pasted the clippings in her scrapbook, but erased the face in each one she could not bear to see. At the birthday party in 1916, Ina was effervescent, and she related anecdotes out of her long life in her wittiest style.

One can imagine the woman, her hair covered with the pretty mantilla, sitting like a queen at the next memorable event in her life, the outdoor commencement exercises of Dominican College in San Rafael, on Tuesday afternoon, 30 May 1916. Indeed, on this occasion, dressed in black satin, she sat on a dais beside Archbishop Hanna, his Eminence splendid in purple vestments. The archbishop was present to distribute the diplomas, but the poet laureate was the guest of honor. Her ode, "California," written forty-five years before for another college graduation program, was to be presented as a pageant by the girls of Dominican College. As a reading by the Reverend Horatio Stebbins, long before, in Oakland, the poem's ringing lines had been inspiring. But in the sun and shade of the oak-dotted lawn in front of the main college hall, spoken by beautifully costumed young girls, the lines had a vibrant, exultant quality that was enhanced by musical accompaniment and interpretative dancing. The performance gave the ode new meaning, just as the poem itself gave new significance to Miss Coolbrith's crown of laurel. Those present must have wondered, "Why did they wait so long to name her the state poet?" Charles Phillips congratulated her, "Never before did you so completely come into your own as the Laureate of California as when your great ode was performed as a pageant." Miss Coolbrith's companion, Miss Zeller, went with her that day. Their escorts were Richard E. White and Nathan Newmark.[4]

Both Newmark and White had been guests in her home the Sunday before at the regular monthly meeting of the California Literature Society. This was an informal organization, without by-laws or dues, though the nature of the meetings required minutes. The group met usually on the third Sunday of the month, or sometimes on the fourth, as it had in May 1916. The members gathered in Miss Coolbrith's home because she herself was not often able to go out. The organization, however, was not hers. It had been started by Mrs. Ella Sterling Cummins Mighels, as an outgrowth of a neighborhood club of young people. Miss Coolbrith tried not to interfere in program planning for these afternoons.

"Why it makes no difference to me about *our* day, whether the third or fourth day," she said to Mrs. Mighels. "And don't you defer to me, dear," she continued. "It is *your* club, and you are very kind to me to bring the folks to my home. It is all the pleasure I have."[5]

Among those who came to these meetings, besides Richard White and Nathan Newmark, were her old friends the Eldredges, Charles Turrill, and Charles Murdock. Sometimes Brother Leo, the popular English professor and lecturer in St. Mary's College, would be there; and so would Clarence Urmy, troubadour from San Jose. Henry Kirk would come from Oakland. Young people—Carleton Kendall; Robin Lampson, Berkeley poet then in his teens; Joan London, Jack London's older daughter—were some who climbed the hill to Ina's house. And one afternoon a special guest was Richard Bret Harte, grandson of the writer. He spent the summer in San Francisco and contributed travel articles to the *Overland Monthly*. California writers were usually the subject of discussion: John Rollin Ridge, on one occasion; Stoddard, Webb; and Jack London, late in the year of his death. The California Literature Society continued to meet monthly for several years, and those who went up to the top of Russian Hill to 1067 Broadway did so as pilgrims to a shrine.[6]

The year 1916 brought other recognition. Fremont High School in Oakland unveiled a framed portrait of her for their assembly room, and gave a Coolbrith evening program at which she herself spoke.[7] She asked Herbert Bashford and his wife to come to the annual breakfast meeting of the Press Club on 20 May, when, she said, "I go out of office forever." She regretted that she could not invite them as her guests, and signed herself, "Your bankrupt Ina Coolbrith." At that affair Dr. Edward Robeson Taylor read some of her lyrics, fairly shouting the gentle lines.[8] On 2 November the city of San Diego observed an Ina Coolbrith Day, as one of the events on the calendar of its Panama-California Exposition.[9] In August Herman Whitaker went to Europe as a war correspondent with a good letter from Senator Phelan.[10] That month there began a slight rift between Miss Coolbrith and Mrs. Mighels. Ina was hurt when she detected a deliberate coolness in Ella's attitude, which must have been explained soon, for a friendly relationship continued. It is obvious, however, from Mrs. Mighel's annotations on Miss Coolbrith's notes to her, that Ella was inhibited by her friend.

"She gets off jokes at my expense all the time," Mrs. Mighels wrote defensively on the back of the very letter asking for an explanation of the coolness. "She says, 'Look at Mrs. Mighels going to open our society with prayer!' in derision! When I am doing the best I can to jot down some names and nothing but a chair is handy for me to write on!" Mrs. Mighels wrote on, her indignation and self-righteousness swelling, "She covers me with mortification by deriding what I am saying to the boys (members of her neighborhood club, the Arkadians) about their needing a guardian angel, 'They don't need one!' she says. 'They are young and innocent, but if anyone needs them, it is us because we are old sinners, and I can see the flicker of demonism in the eye of one of them who is old for his 21 years.'" She thought of Ina's frequent complaints about her troubles and her aches, "And she has no more troubles and sorrows than the rest of us," she went on writing; "but she has no philosophy to help her bear them."[11]

Mrs. Mighels hid her resentment. The two women continued to plan programs together and to write hasty notes. Ella was at that time preparing for publication a volume which she called *Literary California*, and Ina was aiding her when she could by supplying photographs, or data from her own good memory.[12] All summer Ina had been doing what she could to further the collection of Stoddard's poems. She had learned through Mrs. Atherton that Mrs. Morton Mitchell was anxious to see such a volume published and wanted to finance it. An old friend of Stoddard, she was also a friend of Thomas Walsh, one of Stoddard's former students. Walsh was a poet, a prominent Catholic layman, one of the associate editors of *Commonweal*. Ina Coolbrith was impressed by his enthusiasm, his own verse writing, and his editorial experience. The two carried on a correspondence all summer, as she built up her collection of Charlie's scattered verse and Walsh made his own.[13]

In late September Ina received a letter from Mrs. Boalt in Connecticut. She was going into New York City to consult a heart specialist, and then she planned to go with a nurse to Santa Barbara. With the letter was a fresh-plucked fringed gentian, its fragility a touching reminder to Ina of Mrs. Boalt's frail health. This may have been her last letter to the poet whom she loved and respected and always addressed formally as "Miss Coolbrith."[14] Ina was cast down, literally, by the news of her friend's death shortly after. She spent the last two months of the year in bed.[15] In January 1917 she learned that Mrs. Boalt had left a trust fund of $10,000 for her, the interest to be paid Ina as long as she lived. This was not unexpected; the two had discussed the arrangements in 1915 when Mrs. Boalt was in San Francisco. Painful as the subject had been for Ina, Mrs. Boalt was practical. She said that this trust would also provide for Josie, if the latter should outlive Ina. A number of other persons were remembered in the will, but the largest amount, $100,000, was bequeathed to the University of California for the construction of a law school building on the Berkeley campus.[16] This became the Boalt Hall of Law, housing classes and library until these were transferred to the present large law building still known as Boalt Hall. The old building has been named for Henry Durant, the university's first president. Mrs. Boalt's friendship for Ina and this recent material aid gave her courage for the year just beginning. At last she would be free to edit Stoddard's poems, some of which had been trickling in to her as the result of an advertisement she had placed in 1913:

WANTED

Published or unpublished
poems of the late Charles
Warren Stoddard; also a
valuable autograph album
belonging to the deceased.
Send to Ina Coolbrith,
1067 Broadway, San Francisco.[17]

Disappointment with Stoddard's *Poems*

The year 1917 was a frustrating one for Ina Coolbrith. How she became involved with Thomas Walsh on the Stoddard volume is uncertain. Back in 1909 she and Alexander Robertson had planned to collaborate on the publication, with Charles Phillips as a willing third. Robertson may have felt that the project was hopeless when he learned that Stoddard had destroyed his manuscripts. In 1914 Miss Coolbrith became acquainted with Mrs. Morton Mitchell. As a young woman Elizabeth Mitchell had met Stoddard when both were traveling in the British Isles in the 1870s.[18] She told Ina that she wanted to finance the publication of Charlie's poems. The book would be her memorial, if a sentimental one, to Stoddard. She then proposed that Thomas Walsh, an experienced anthologist and editor, assist in preparing the material for publication. Mrs. Mitchell bought a copy of *Songs from the Golden Gate*, as a Christmas gift for Walsh, and asked the author to inscribe it for him. Walsh was so impressed with the gift and the verse that he wrote an extremely flattering letter to Miss Coolbrith, saying that he hoped to meet her the following year.[19] If he realized his hope, he was present at the Authors' Congress in 1915. At that time he may have agreed to collaborate with Miss Coolbrith on the Stoddard book in order to take advantage of Mrs. Mitchell's offer. Ina Coolbrith, feeling her years at the close of her duties connected with the Exposition, and missing the aid and advice of Charles Phillips who had gone East, may have been grateful for Walsh's interest, and may have decided on an impulse to work with him.

Her decision was unfortunate. Too late, she found herself committed. The two were soon in disagreement about the scope and content of the book. All during 1916 they quarreled by letter over details.[20] Miss Coolbrith wanted the volume to be as inclusive and as representative as possible. She had hoped the book might be a definitive edition, containing all the poems in the 1867 collection as well as later verse, and furnished with a good memoir, written, preferably, by Charles Phillips. But Walsh deferred always to Mrs. Mitchell who had the pocketbook, and, in the long run, that lady decided that Miss Coolbrith might collect the poems, but that Walsh should make the final selection and edit the volume. The memoir would be omitted altogether, for economy, but Miss Coolbrith would be allowed a brief foreword. The book came out in mid-summer, 1917, "selected to death," Miss Coolbrith said.[21] Walsh had omitted all but thirteen of the pieces in the 1867 edition. Ina was humiliated with the whole business, especially when reviewers, who did not know the circumstances, lauded the book and ascribed its editorship to her. But among the friends who knew what had happened and who were in a position to discuss the inadequate Stoddard book in the press, the story came out. Some of these were Burton Kline, book editor of the *Boston Transcript*, and such California reviewers as Charles Shinn, Clarence Urmy, Edward F. O'Day, and Brother Leo.[22] Miss Coolbrith begged Herbert Bashford to wait until she could see him, but for some reason he went ahead and reviewed the book in the *Bulletin*.

"Charlie's book has been such a grief to me," she told him. "I needed a word to set both him and me an atom toward the right." She made a helpless gesture, "Well, the one God's blessing is that it can't last much longer."[23] If she felt disheartened, she did not hold his review against him, and was soon urging him and Mrs. Bashford to come to the next meeting of the Literature Society at her house.[24]

Charles Phillips was indignant and let Walsh know how he felt. So did Father Francis O'Neill of San Francisco, who that fall published an article on Stoddard in the *Catholic World*.[25] Walsh himself was angry with Miss Coolbrith and all her friends. He told her that the foreword—one and one-half pages—in which he had humored her, was an impertinence and out of place in the volume. In what was probably the most ungracious letter she ever received from anyone, he remarked, "What a collection of friends dear Charlie left after him. I have been saying it and thinking it for years. A jealous, cantankerous, venomous lot of people who use his dead body as a tool and a shield."[26] Miss Coolbrith was sick with disappointment and sorry her name was associated with the book. But Edward F. O'Day in his *Town Talk* did much to cheer her in an article entitled "What an Editor Has Done with Stoddard's Poems." Like Ina he regretted the omission of many, many pieces, but more than anything else, he missed a biographical introduction to the book, and proceeded to relate in a pleasant, unhurried manner, a few of the fascinating facts that he knew of Stoddard's career as writer, traveler, and friend. Some of Charlie's own charm invades the pages of *Town Talk* here. Phillips read O'Day's article. "Bless his fiery red head!" he exclaimed. The loyalty of O'Day, Phillips, and other friends mitigated but could not end the sorrow Ina felt about the book.[27]

She was despondent all year long. She thanked the school children who serenaded her, singing her own songs under her window on her birthday, and bringing her bouquets.[28] She appreciated Marguerite Wilkinson's heartening words in a letter thanking her for permission to include some of Ina's poems in her new anthology. Miss Wilkinson had said, in answer to Ina's remark that she no longer had any illusions, "Somehow I think you are one of the people brave enough and big enough to do without any and look all the truth full in the face. . . . Most people need illusions because they are not big enough to do without them, but that is not true of you. . . . Bless you."[29] Shortly before this letter came, Miss Coolbrith had a request for her *Songs* from Annie Florence Brown in Oakland. Miss Brown, then a high school English teacher, later the city's most prominent woman civic leader and founder of the Oakland Forum, wrote humbly. She recalled gratefully that many a time, when she was a girl in high school and college, Miss Coolbrith had given her helpful service in the Oakland library.[30]

The library subject came up again during the summer when Mrs. Marian Taylor said that a group of club women wanted to have Ina Coolbrith's portrait in the central library, as it was already in two schools, Fremont High School and Durant Elementary. Miss Coolbrith hesitated. Still deeply sensitive, she felt that there were some on the library staff who would not want it. She wrote to Charles S. Greene, then the librarian, presenting what was to her a delicate matter. "You might not wish it," she wrote, "and I beg you to be perfectly frank in

325

saying so. Others in the library I know would not, that I could name, and in this world to right, or partly right a wrong, is difficult indeed."[31] She was referring to three staff members who had worked with and liked Henry Peterson. Unknown to her, Mrs. Taylor and her friends asked to talk to the librarian, and he waited until after his conference with them before he answered Miss Coolbrith's letter. Ten days elapsed before his answer came, and that was time enough for Ina to imagine that he and his staff were embarrassed about the idea and would not want the portrait. It was time enough for her to decide against having her picture placed in the library. The librarian's reply apparently did not shake her decision, though he did say, "So far as the Library is concerned, there is nobody here who would not be glad to have the picture in the Library. Indeed, there is nobody here who has been longer in the service than I, except Miss Fenton, Mr. Bamford, and Mrs. Louderback. I have talked to each of these and find that all will be glad to have a suitable picture in a suitable place."[32] She must have imagined the lack of enthusiasm back of the stiff sentences. Nothing came of the proposition. Charles Greene had been one of the editors of the *Overland Monthly* before he succeeded Peterson as Oakland City Librarian in 1899. He was a poet himself and a contributor of verse and prose to Bay Area periodicals. Warm and friendly, he was fond of people, and he had a good sense of humor. But he was diffident about Miss Coolbrith. He did not want to intrude himself upon her for fear that his very presence would remind her of some of the darkest days of her life. And this total lack of communication on his part may have convinced her that he agreed with her "enemies." He was always very sorry about this, for he admired her even if he hesitated to tell her so. Moreover their common interest in poetry and in associations with the *Overland* would have been a basis for friendship, if Librarian Greene had tried it.

The gloom of the year was relieved in November by a long appreciative analysis of the poetry of Ina Coolbrith, by Edward F. O'Day in *The Lantern*, a San Francisco journal.[33] But even that highly complimentary judgment of her work failed to ease her heart that autumn. For some reason connected with her club she and some of her longtime associates became estranged. She was accused, falsely, of preventing the election to the board of one of her dearest friends. The

---

327

hurt was so deep on each side that the wounds were never healed. Though she made copies of her letters and retained those received, and these are to be found in the Coolbrith papers, there are not enough of them to establish the facts. And nothing would be gained by so doing. The matter was trivial, though the heartbreak was real. Ina closed one of her letters with this postscript, "One thing more: How must we appear before God in this causeless, senseless bickering in the midst of the awful World Tragedy being enacted before His eyes!"[34]

The Decision to Leave San Francisco

By the time the United States had declared war on Germany on 6 April 1917 Miss Coolbrith, though an advocate of peace all her life, was convinced that this country should become involved. Her only poem published in 1917 was "In the Midst of War."[35] That fall, because her autograph had value, she had written her name a hundred times for the benefit of the Red Cross.[36] And in May 1918 the manuscript of her poem "Soldiers of Freedom" was auctioned off at a giant Red Cross benefit in the Oakland Auditorium.[37] Her friends and the children of friends were "over there" as service men or war correspondents. In December 1918 Herman Whitaker was in Paris and Charles Phillips was in Coblenz.[38] Phillips later went to Poland for the Red Cross, became interested in the country and its government, and wrote *The New Poland*. While there, he met Ignace Paderewski and gave him a copy of Miss Coolbrith's sonnet to him.[39]

Phillips had found it necessary to sell his piano to pay family medical bills.[40] Miss Coolbrith felt the deprivation of piano and companionship. Alice Bashford came before the piano was taken for one last afternoon of music. Carl Gunderson seemed to have disappeared. Actually he was with his parents in San Francisco, writing plays under a pseudonym, Carl G. Seyfforth. He gave a farewell public piano recital, then departed for New York. Before he left he came to tell Miss Coolbrith good-bye and to take from her a letter of introduction to Gertrude Atherton. Carl, an engaging young man, adopted Seyfforth as his name when he reached New York City, and continued to write. He showed Mrs. Atherton his plays and she was impressed. She found a friend who offered Carl the use of a piano. But the better she came to know him, the more she was convinced that he was attaching himself to her

for her patronage in his music and writing. She wrote to Ina that she liked the "infant," but that she had "not that form of vanity that welcomes adoration." She said she could tide him over, but could not finance his trip to Europe.[41] While Mrs. Atherton went on to the Paris Peace Conference as a correspondent for the *New York Times,* young Carl remained in New York at work on a novel and playing for his friends there. Almost without funds he spent a miserable winter in an unheated, unventilated room. His health was damaged and he was despondent, as he let Ina know by letter or telegram.[42] To her concern for Carl was added her grief for the death of three good friends during 1918, Richard W. White, Zoeth Skinner Eldredge, and William Dallam Armes.[43] "Close the ranks," said Ina in a kind of desperation.[44]

The year 1918 was not all despair for her, however. In July she had become acquainted with Albert Bender, San Francisco's Maecenas. He persuaded her to write an introduction to her poem "California," to be published in a limited edition of five hundred copies for the Book Club of California. The book, designed and printed by John Henry Nash with a profile portrait of the author drawn by Dan Sweeney, was out in November, a beautiful production.[45] In August and September she carried on an agreeable correspondence with Albert Brecknock, librarian of Hucknall Torkard, England. He was planning to give a lecture on Byron and he wanted to use the incident of her wreath and poem sent with Joaquin Miller in 1870. Brecknock wanted a slide of her portrait, pictures of Sausalito, where the laurel grew, and, if possible, a sprig of bay. It took her a month to assemble all the items, but she did so in time for his lecture. She told him that Sausalito was "now a town, when at that time, 1870, it was a beautiful wildwood."[46] There were other amenities during the year. The school children again serenaded her on her birthday.[47] She was the guest of honor at an important luncheon at the Palace Hotel where the Home Industries League entertained the local writers, and it was discovered that poets and manufacturers got along very well when the food was bountiful and good. Miss Coolbrith was not present, but at the close of the affair the principal floral decoration on the speakers' table was taken to her at her home.[48] During 1918 she wrote but two poems, "Soldiers of Freedom" for the Red Cross and "Tribute to the Convent and College of the Holy Names, Oakland."[49]

In 1919, the year that Ina Coolbrith was officially proclaimed the state poet laureate, she was deeply troubled. Carl, in New York, had contracted tuberculosis and had threatened to take his own life, because he did not have the means for proper medical care and rest.[50] Miss Coolbrith sent him money in February, having arranged to borrow it through Albert Bender's insurance firm.[51] Matters at home were difficult. Her rental flat was vacant, and there were bills for repairs to be met. Josie was becoming hard to live with. Fanatically loyal as always, concerned for Miss Coolbrith's health and well-being, she tried to guard the poet from callers until Ina felt like a prisoner in her own home. Alice Bashford and her parents called at 1067 Broadway less frequently because of Josie's persistent hovering.[52] Her housekeeping too began to irk Ina. Josie was too meticulous, especially with Ina's papers, and the poet could not find letters and notes when she needed them. Ina came to speak of her companion, half seriously, as "the fourth dimension."[53] About this time a permanent break with Ella Mighels occurred. When Ina read Ella's absurd poem, "Broken Friendship," in the *San Francisco Bulletin* in July, she knew the end of their relationship had come.[54] This meant, too, the end of the California Literature Society, Ella's organization, that met in Ina's flat. She told Robert Norman, "I cannot endure my shut-in, lonely existence longer, accompanied by such almost constant physical suffering."[55]

She said that there was a famous physician in New York who offered her his services if she would make the change of climate. Her own San Francisco physician, Dr. H. Staats Moore, had been urging her for months to make a change. He believed that New York would be the right place.[56] In the late summer of 1919, therefore, she decided to leave San Francisco for an indefinite period. She would stay for a few months to give the change of climate and the specialist a chance. She would rent her own flat and ask Josie to take Popcorn, by then her only pet. She would share her small income with Josie who could go to live with her sister, Mary Zeller, in Oakland. She knew that this would mean deprivation for both of them, and perhaps hurt feelings too. The uprooting of the aged from the security expected to last until death is a cruel experience. Miss Zeller was an old woman by then. She had taken for granted that she would share Miss Coolbrith's home until the end of her days. She knew, too, that the poet had made some provision for her in her will. The problem of the single, aged woman was not the concern of the state in the late 1910s. Mrs. Josephine McCrackin, Ina's old friend in Santa Cruz, wrote about her own circumstances not long before this. A talented writer, an indefatigable conservationist, she said,

> The world has not used us well, Ina; California has been ungrateful to us. Of all the hundred thousands the state pays out in pensions of one kind and another, don't you think you should be at the head of the pensioners, and I somewhere down below? Ina Coolbrith has always been called "the sweetest note in California

331

literature"; and though I hate the word "uplift," no one will dispute that your poems, your writings, have been the uplift in California literature. No later writer has ever approached you, and still you are not an independent woman. As for me, I claim to have done more for the preservation of the Redwoods of California, for the conservation of birds and game, than any Native Daughter of California, but who thanks me for it?

I have worked faithfully while I was able; and I am still working when I am no longer able; but working principally for the few dollars it brings me.

It is dreadful that you are confined to the house, though I should be glad many a time to stay at home when I have to go out. I am out almost every night of the week, lucky to get the last street car for home. But the Beach Company pays me 10 dollars a month for the three summer months which means a great deal to me.

Her evening work was the collection of resort news for her paper, the *Santa Cruz Sentinel*, thereby adding ten important dollars to her small monthly pay. She said, further, that the owner of the company paid for her treatments at a sanatorium, which she could not have afforded. She suffered from heart trouble. "I pray the Lord I may drop dead before I become helpless," she said fervently. This letter, though a diversion from the narrative, is quoted as a poignant comment on the life and times, not only of Josephine Clifford McCrackin, daughter of a baroness, widow of a wealthy landowner whose estate was destroyed by a forest fire, but of all poor, single, aged women before old age pensions and Medicare were realities.[57]

Ina pondered about Jo's pluck. She compared Jo's circumstances with her own and with Josie's. All three women were approaching their eighties. Ina, at times, regretted that she had not married again, for companionship and for the protection for which she now yearned. In making arrangements for her departure, she gave Robert Norman power of attorney, asking him to transact all business matters for her, saying that her "years, feeble health, and rather peculiar conditions of life, will require a man's hand, experience and wisdom to cope with them." She asked him to look after the rentals of her two flats, and, if necessary, the sale of the house. She wanted him to make an investment for her to insure Josie's care in the event of her own death. And she begged him to try to make Josie understand, as she had been unable to do.[58] Miss Zeller's resentment became angry and menacing; Ina feared physical violence.[59] The poet made her will and asked Senator Phelan to be the executor of her estate.[60] Though she still hoped to do some writing in New York, she was preparing for the end.

29
Sojourn
in
New York

As one, of all the stars un-kinned,
Apart and lone as I.

Ina Coolbrith, from
"Alone" (ca. 1920)

New Friends

Miss Coolbrith's experience had led her to expect the worst whenever she began a new venture. So she had rewritten her will, appointed
an executor of her estate, made provision for her former companion,
Josie Zeller, and turned the care of her house over to her lawyer. She
was, indeed, preparing for the end. She found it not an end, however,
but a beginning. Late in September 1919, with good-byes said, letters of
introduction in her purse, away from Josie's hysterical threats, she
settled back to enjoy her five days' journey across the country. She was
not alone. A young acquaintance, Kenneth Sultzer, a friend of Carl
Seyfforth, made the trip at the same time, going home to Yonkers. He
took charge of tickets and baggage checks and cabs. He was, she said,
"a perfect cavalier, thinking wholly of my comfort." She arrived well
and rested and felt like a fraud when she said she had been an invalid.
She was met at the station by Carl and Mrs. Jeanne Francoeur, who took
her to the St. James Hotel at 109 West Forty-fifth Street.[1] She had expected to find another place to stay but found this hotel warm and
safe; so she decided to remain for the year.

Her first days in a hotel room were cheered by letters from California. Robert Norman assured her that Popcorn was well cared for
and that Josie was calming down, though she refused to accept a cent
from Miss Coolbrith.[2] Charles Lummis wondered how she would ad-

333

just to a "horizon of those who scratch it with their elbows every time they turn around."[3] She was informed about a new literary club just organized in San Francisco. It was called the Ina Coolbrith Circle. It was to be a continuation of the old California Literature Society meetings on Russian Hill and a reminder of her while she was away. Its first meeting took place in the St. Francis Hotel.[4] She was surprised and moved by this demonstration of loyalty by her old friends. Answering her letters helped to pass the time in the strange quiet and lonely peace of this impersonal room, far from Josie's bustling, far from her books and other treasures.

In November Edwin and Anna Markham called on her, coming from their home in Staten Island. Ina was glad to see them, but she found that Edwin had grown too "bulky," she said, to give him the impulsive hug that would have expressed her feelings.[5] He was the honorary president of the American Poetry Society and he insisted that she speak before the group at their Christmas meeting. He told her that she ought to be interviewed for one of the Sunday newspaper book sections, and he promptly made an appointment with her for Benjamin De Casseres of the *New York Sun*. De Casseres came to her hotel with his wife, Bio, and, as often happened with Ina Coolbrith, this brief meeting developed into a strong and lasting friendship. He gave her a full page, with her portrait, in the *Sun's* book supplement of December 7—singular notice of a newcomer in a New York City daily. She told the old stories of Beckwourth, of the *Overland* days and the "Golden Gate Trinity," recited some of the limericks that she and Bret Harte made up, told how she had given Joaquin Miller his nom-de-plume, and showed him Jack London's 1906 fan letter to her. The account was pleasantly gossipy, but Ina, on reading it, was amused to see how many errors could be found on a single page based on an interview.[6]

Young Ben and Bio De Casseres kept their promise to look in on her now and then. And she had other friends in New York whom she had known by letter and would soon meet in person, among them two poets, Edna Dean Proctor, ninety-three years old at the time, and Edith Thomas, whom she knew through Iza Hardy. There were the Markhams and Mrs. Francoeur. And there were Carl and Kenneth. She was not wholly alone. But as winter came on, and she knew that the icy streets were unsafe, she put off until spring some of the calls she intended to make. Sometimes the silence in the room became almost a tangible thing, as she sat long hours reading or writing. As Christmas approached, and the messages began coming to her from California and elsewhere, she was overcome by homesickness in the still room. A light fall of snow in the street and on her window sill increased the stillness. What was it like on Russian Hill? she wondered. There was a rhythm in her thought of the winter rains at home. She sat at her desk and wrote some lines that she named, "Listening Back."

> There are no comrade roses at my window,
>   No green things in the lane;
> Upon the roof no sibilant soft patter—
>   The lullaby of rain;
> Without is silence, and within is silence,
>   Till silence grows a pain.
>
> Within is silence, and without is silence,
>   The snow is on the sill,
> In snow the window wreath'd instead of roses,
>   And snow is very still . . .
> I wonder is it singing in the grasses,
>   The rain, on Russian Hill?[7]

The words satisfied her. They expressed her mood. And they had come with a rush. She was surprised that they had come effortlessly as the lyrics did when she was a young poet. At the end of the year she took heart. Perhaps the leisure, the freedom from pain and from interruptions would put her pen hand to work again. Perhaps even the stillness would be a boon to her.

On the evening of 26 December Mrs. Francoeur and Carl Seyfforth called for Ina to escort her to the National Arts Club in Gramercy Park where the Poetry Society members were to assemble. The Society's small newsletter had already announced that Miss Ina Coolbrith of California would be the guest of the evening, and had reprinted with apparent awe the text of the California legislative resolution that had conferred the laureateship in 1919.[8] To Ina's surprise she was met at the door of the club by Miss Clara McChesney, the daughter of a member of the old Oakland Library Board when Miss Coolbrith was librarian. Both the Markhams were present, and both participated in the evening's program, Anna reading the laureate's "California," and Edwin describing Ina's place in California literature and giving an account of the bestowal of the crown of bay during the Congress of Authors and Journalists in 1915. The honored guest, in her black satin gown and white lace mantilla, spoke for an hour in her usual conversational style, drawing on her full store of literary anecdotes of San Francisco.[9]

With the new year, 1920, there was an increase in the great influenza

335

epidemic that had struck the country months before. Ina wrote her friends in California, who were experiencing the same thing, that nearly every family had its crepe on the door.[10] Ina, who left her room only for dinner in the dining room, did not contract the flu. Carl was ill in January, from influenza or the chronic respiratory ailment. That month Ina sent her lyric, "Listening Back," to the *Sunset Magazine*, thinking it appropriate for winter publication and knowing that it would serve as a message to her friends. The snow-inspired lyric had suggested another that was fairly dancing in her brain, and it was not long before she had it down on paper, a delicate thing she called "The Dancers." It was prompted by the swirling snowflakes that seemed like a ballet by little girls in full white skirts, dusted with glitter, and even more than the image, a hint of the transcience of beauty and joy:

> They were so light, the little dancing feet,
> The little feet, such little dancing feet!
>   Snow-white, snow-soft, snow-light;
> First feather-flakes of snow, that only play
>   To fall, then disappear.
>   Lighter than gossamer;
>   Lighter than dew at dawn;
> Lighter than thistle-down upon the wind,
>   Or humming-bird in flight—
> Poised—then a dazzling flash of jeweled light;
>   Flower-fair, flower-soft, flower-sweet,
>   The little dancing feet.[11]

There were two more stanzas, each as buoyant as the first. The poem was original and graceful, and may have surprised even herself into a belief that with the coming of spring she would know a renascence of writing. She sent a copy of the lyric to Charles Phillips in Poland. He was entranced by this airy interruption to his duties of piloting refugee trains through the heavy dark misery of the Polish winter.[12]

Ina was writing again. Once more she was listening back, far back, as she wrote, trying to recapture the soft Spanish speech she had heard as a girl. She had begun a long narrative poem, "Concha," a composition that was reminiscent of the old Los Angeles. The idea may have come to her a few years before as she read a novel entitled *The Dons*

Ina Coolbrith about 1919. Portrait by Bianca Conti, San Francisco. Courtesy of the Bancroft Library, University of California, Berkeley.

of the Old Pueblo. A friend who had called on her one day in San Francisco found her engrossed in the story and charmed by its fidelity to the atmosphere of the pueblo as she remembered it. An illustration in the book, Charles Koppel's view of Los Angeles in 1853, delighted her.[13]

"Look," she told her friend, "there is the house where we lived." She pointed to one of the low brea-roofed adobes not far from the plaza. So, writing in New York in 1920 and 1921, Ina went back to old Los Angeles for the setting of some of her new poems, "Felipe," "Pancho," and "Concha." "Concha" is a simple tale of the love of a Mexican girl and boy, with an aspect of coeducation as its theme. In gentle, colloquial Mexican-English speech, the poem's iambic trimeter lines give it a quiet liveliness, like Concha's smile and her uncontrollable dark eyes.[14] Immersed in the mood of the story, Ina recalled her own lost yesterdays, the boys with whom she danced, the girls with whom she shared secrets. When she told Charles Lummis a little later about this poem, she remarked that she would love a Spanish flirtation again; Don Carlos, as she often called him, responded gallantly in a letter that closed with "*Alma de mi alma, adorada y idolatrada,* Ina *tus ojos divinos me encienden la alma,* likewise *labios de rubí, cuello de marfil, mi bien, mi tesoro, mi cielo tus brazos*—&c."[15] Ina's poem "Concha," of nine hundred lines, was probably completed that spring. She did not think of selling it. Her pleasure was in the writing, and it had not tired her in any way.

Free, moreover, from rheumatic pains for the first time in fourteen years, she forgot herself in this new spurt of writing. When she saw that spring was coming on, she made some of the calls she had promised herself. She called on Margaret Anglin first of all, to give her a copy of the Book Club edition of her *California.* Miss Anglin read the poem at the next meeting of the Browning Society, and Miss Coolbrith, listening, wished fervently that she might someday hear the actress read the ode in the Greek Theatre in Berkeley.[16] In April she attended a testimonial dinner given Edwin Markham.[17] As May advanced and the days grew warmer, Miss Coolbrith knew that she must return to San Francisco, though she dreaded the effect on her health.

She returned by way of Los Angeles for a visit with her old friend, Mrs. Perry. Ina probably sought her friend's advice in her dilemma. Should she give up her home on Russian Hill and make a permanent removal to New York City? Her New York sojourn had given her health and mental stimulation. Or should she return to the California she loved, her friends and family—and her bed of invalidism? She must have been encouraged to return to New York, for, shortly after she reached San

Francisco, where she went at once to her brother William's home on Clay Street, she decided to sell her furniture and some of her books. Robert Norman, her lawyer, had gone back to China; so Ina turned to Albert Bender for advice on disposing of some of her best period pieces, the pier glass given her by Judge and Mrs. Boalt, and a fine little Victorian divan.[18] Her flat was vacant; so she occupied it while disposing of her larger possessions.[19] Albert Bender called on her now and then and brought her little gifts, such as a package of her favorite Kona coffee. During one of their conversations he persuaded her to make copies of some of her best-known lyrics and send them to him. She assented gladly. In August and September she attended two affairs that were actually farewell parties for her. One was a meeting of the Ina Coolbrith Circle, and the other a California Writers Club dinner.[20] Maynard Dixon, artist, gave her a small oil landscape to place on her hotel room wall and be reminded of California's sun.[21] After disposing of her furniture she had her few remaining possessions, including the unsold pier glass, moved to her niece's home in Berkeley. Near the end of September she asked Bender to secure her reservations for her journey east, saying that she now had some cash, and was eager to get off and to rest—"if it will be rest, with so sad a heart."[22] She was weary and disconsolate, believing that she was leaving her beloved California forever.

New Urges to Write

Her railroad journey in October 1920 was not a restful one. She was so tired when she boarded the train that, she said, she ached all the way. She returned to the St. James Hotel where her room was offered her again at reduced rates, for former good conduct, she said laughingly.[23] Thus began her second of four winters in New York City. Her San Francisco friends said that she had become a regular commuter. For the winter seasons of October 1920 until June 1922 she lived at the St. James. Her last winter in New York she spent at the Latham Hotel on East Twenty-eighth Street. Except for the autumn of 1920 she found her overland journeys pleasant and restful and even enjoyed the anonymity of travel alone. Once, on arrival in New York, she told a friend that she was not fatigued in the least, in fact she was "just sweet sixteen."[24] That was the year she was eighty-one. Except for one illness and an accident, both of which occurred early in 1923, she enjoyed good health. The illness had been an attack of influenza. Friends looked after her but she missed her dear Dr. Moore and even Josie's ministrations. The accident occurred as she stepped out of the elevator on the way to her room on the fifth floor. The elevator started up as she was leav-

339

ing it, and she was thrown to the floor. She was shaken and bruised but she broke no bones. She wondered what she was made of.[25]

The poet's good health gave her ambition to write. So did the long, uninterrupted hours she had in her quiet room. Though lonely at times, and knowing periods of black despondency, she found her sudden wealth of time a cherished luxury. She wrote more during the four winters in New York than she had in the previous twenty-five years.[26] After "Listening Back," "The Dancers," and "Concha," there came "In the Orchard," "With the Caravan," "Sahara," "Foch," "Alien," "Lucifer," "Alone," and some of her clean-cut quatrains. Some were published in periodicals, "Listening Back" and "In the Orchard" in *Sunset Magazine* after a wait of many months in each case, and poor pay as well. (The *Overland Monthly* had paid her twice as much in the 1870s). "With the Caravan" appeared in the *University of California Chronicle*, "Alien" in the *Overland*, and "Foch" in the *San Francisco Bulletin*. The last named she did not like, but she wrote it to satisfy a request from Bailey Millard to write a greeting to the famous French general when he visited San Francisco in 1921. Her poem shared the paper's front-page story, headlined, " 'The Bulletin' *Souhaite la Bienvenue au Maréchal Foch*." The text of the poem was decorated with sketches of parades, *fleurs-de-lis,* and the flags of both countries, so that the poet shared the honors with the general. "Foch" was Miss Coolbrith's only poem of occasion written during her New York period.[27]

At this time she was embarrassed because there was no really good Western literary magazine. She said she was twitted about it good naturedly in New York. She wrote at length to Albert Bender about the subject, asking that he bring up the matter discreetly in the Bohemian Club and the Book Club of California. The West, she said, had many first-rate writers—original, productive, competent—but they all sent their work to Eastern periodicals. She was still mourning the lost old *Overland,* and wished that the current journal that still bore the name could be taken over and revamped into something like its ancestor.[28] Nothing came of this suggestion of hers, but the subject was discussed with her by George Douglas of the *Bulletin,* and others, during her summers in the Bay Area. From time to time she wrote out copies of her lyrics, old and new, to send Albert Bender. She apologized for them, saying that she wrote "such a fist."[29] She wrote to the Houghton Mifflin Company concerning a new printing of her *Songs from the Golden Gate,* but was urged to prepare her reminiscences first. The company promised to publish them and follow with a collection of verse, either new, or a reprint of the *Songs.*[30] With this incentive she set to work on her memoirs, but complained that the work went slowly. Shortly before she had begun her autobiographical writing, she read a letter that disturbed her. She knew that she was a traditionalist, though she had experimented a little with free verse forms, that she was a Victorian poet, and that even the prose she was now writing linked her to a period that was now past. She could not change, nor would she, but she knew that what she wrote would suffer by comparison with current literary fashions. [31]

Her fears grew out of the fine print of the letter quoted by John Farrar in his "Gossip Shop" pages of the November 1922 *Bookman*, a letter that was copied and vigorously manhandled by the literati of San Francisco. It had been written by Witter Bynner to an English woman, in answer to a request for information on the California poets. Written in New Mexico, from memory and without access to reference books, Bynner's comments were little more than the expression of his own prejudices. Joaquin Miller was dead, in both a literary and a literal sense; Stoddard and Bierce were boring; Markham and Mary Austin wrote a few things of interest; Sterling maintained a traditional style with dignity; Clark Ashton Smith imitated Sterling; it was said that Arthur Ryder's translations from the Sanscrit were excellent. Bynner's praises went to three "California" poets whose major work was done elsewhere, Edward Rowland Sill, Charles Erskine Scott Wood, and Yone Noguchi. He admired the work of Gelett Burgess, Wallace Irwin, Bruce Porter, and Ruth Comfort Mitchell, but, more than any others, the poetry of four students of his during his brief period as an instructor in verse writing at the University of California in Berkeley. These were Eda Lou Walton, Hildegarde Flanner, David Greenhood, and Genevieve Taggard, all certainly gifted. Bynner's random thrusts angered writers in the San Francisco area, more because of his three sentences about Miss Coolbrith than anything else in his letter. He had written of her, "Ina Coolbrith has been voted by the California legislature the Poet Laureate of the state. I am told that she is an admirable old lady. What I have seen of her work is commonplace but gentle."[32] Ina would have been the first to admit that her work was "commonplace." Not so her friends in the Bay Area. Edward F. O'Day shamed Bynner for his lack of gallantry, at the same time calling attention to the fact that though Bynner had been on the faculty at Berkeley he had not bothered to read any of the translations from the Sanscrit made by his very distinguished colleague, Arthur Ryder.[33] Sterling, in a letter to Ina about the incident, expressed his own dislike of Bynner and referred unflatteringly to certain aspects of that poet's private life.[34] Miss Coolbrith, when asked for a statement, merely sent a newspaper clipping that quoted Bynner's free verse portrait of Carl Sandburg. Ina's marginal note and

341

only comment was, "a delicate example of the modern Muse."[35] Writing to Albert Bender, however, she was less restrained in her opinion of the young poet who would destroy California's literary past with a few blasé strokes of a pen.[36]

While Miss Coolbrith, writing of her part in that past, was jealous of the golden moments left to her, she was not a recluse in her room. She accepted a number of interesting invitations in New York. She had met Miles Menander Dawson, treasurer of the Poetry Society of America, **when she was introduced** to the Society in 1919. Thereafter she was frequently a guest in the Dawson home. It was there that she met May Riley Smith and Edith Thomas for the first time.[37] On 27 January 1921 she was one of many authors to speak briefly at the Authors' Matinée at the Waldorf Astoria. It was a prestige affair with as many prominent authors as could be persuaded to come together at one time, Edna Ferber, Zona Gale, Amy Lowell, and Clement Wood being among the speakers. Before the event Anna Markham fussed nervously, telling Ina that her black silk gown, worn at the Poetry Society meeting two years before, would be suitable. Anna arranged for a conveyance to take Ina to the Waldorf.[38] That same day the Poetry Society had a dinner meeting at the Astor Hotel which Miss Coolbrith attended, though Mrs. Markham feared that two events in one day might be too much for Ina's strength.[39] About a week later, 7 February, she was a guest of the Dickens Fellowship at the Astor Hotel, and was persuaded to recite Bret Harte's "Dickens in Camp." She was introduced by Miles Dawson.[40] In March 1921 John Farrar, editor of the *Bookman,* called on her. In fact he was there on her eightieth birthday, and he described her and his meeting with her in his "Gossip Shop" in the April *Bookman.*[41] She had frequent callers, but none was ever more welcome than her San Francisco physician, Dr. H. Staats Moore, who made a surprise appearance one December day.[42] She met Fanny Bandelier while in New York, an encounter that pleased Charles Lummis who wrote her that Mrs. Bandelier was "one God made on purpose."[43] Ina saw Michael and Peggy Williams whom she had known from the Authors' Congress in 1915. Williams was an editor of the *Commonweal.* Ina and Peggy went together to see Margaret Anglin in "Joan of Arc."[44] And of course Carl Seyfforth called on her frequently. He had adopted another pseudonym, Ulv Youff. Carl's friend, Kenneth Sultzer, was also an occasional visitor.

Loneliness and Financial Worries

In spite of callers and letters Ina Coolbrith went through periods of despondency. She had lost two dear friends within the year, Mrs. Mc-

Crackin in December 1920, and Mary E. Hart in March 1921.[45] Josephine McCrackin had lost the sight of her fine dark eyes but had continued to write for her paper to the very end. Mrs. Hart, an Alaskan newspaperwoman, fearing an operation, took her own life by gas. In December 1921 a "Christmas tree" of greetings sent her by the members of the Ina Coolbrith Circle cheered her somewhat. Each one had written a note, a letter, or a bit of verse, and one had sent a snapshot of Popcorn. Ina was surprised and diverted. She was proud of what she referred to as "my Christmas tree."[46] But she could not shake off a feeling of despair that month. On Christmas Eve, overcome by loneliness, she was writing to Lena Simons in San Francisco, saying that she had neglected writing sooner, because she had "been worried and troubled in all ways." She was writing, too, in gentle self-mockery:

> I have made up my mind that a woman in the world without a man has no right to be in it, for she is without comfort or protection. But when one does not find a man she could marry, or cannot marry because of the great responsibilities thrust upon her during her marrying years, why, what is she to do? Just be the victim that she is and find herself in age alone, unprotected and uncared for. Selah! and *blast* it!![47]

Earlier in the year she had expressed her loneliness in a lyric she named "Alien." It was her mood in December, too, a black mood:

> The great world has not known me,
>   Nor I the world have known;
> The great world will not own me
>   Altho' I am her own.
>
> I walk with her a stranger
>   Who am of her a child—
> A vagrant, and a ranger
>   Of ways forlorn and wild.
>
> Clear unto other vision,
>   Blind ever unto me,
> My soul is as a prison
>   Whereof none holds the key.
>
> My Mother-World, I wonder
>   When no more of life a part—
> A clod your bosom under—
>   Will you take me to your heart?[48]

Ina had told Mrs. Simons that she had been "worried and troubled in all ways." One of the ways was the knowledge that had recently come to her that an annuity she had expected for life had failed the previous July. What it was, she did not say, but it is reasonable to assume that she was referring to Mrs. Boalt's trust fund. She hesitated to tell Albert Bender of this disaster to her fortunes, but finally confided in him in a long letter in January 1922. Her loss of income would compel her to return to California and the "rack of inflammatory rheumatism," since the cost of living was lower in San Francisco. She said that she had tried to economize. She told him

> You see, when the expenses of taxes (so enormous), insurance, water-rates, dues on the house debt, repairs and incidentals are met, it leaves a sum inadequate to meet the cost of living at the present after-the-war rates, tho' the most restricted. I have the cheapest room I can get in a safe and *warm* house. I make my own morning coffee, and then take only the 6 p.m. most reasonable dinner. Clothes I buy none. I indulge in *no* luxuries.

She spoke of trying to get correspondence to do to help out, knowing that she could no longer do the manual labor she once did, and added, "and no one would have an old woman around anyway!" She spoke of seeing the Markhams and the Dawsons, lightening the tenor of her letter somewhat, but could not overcome her black mood. "I wonder how it feels," she wrote, "to be 'taken care of'—as most women are. I never was."[49]

The next month she copied some more of her poems for Bender. She had a letter from her grandniece scolding her playfully for her gloomy letters.[50] In March 1922 she received word that the Bohemian Club wanted to help her through this emergency so that she could remain in New York. They wanted to send her fifty dollars a month. This was done through Albert Bender and Dr. Moore, the two in whom she had confided her financial circumstances. No word came from the club officially, and her thanks to them went through the two men. She told Bender that the Bohemian Club had come to her assistance in three separate crises in her life, and she had expected nothing more from them than the flowers for her funeral.[51] The gift was made with the consideration for her feelings and the lack of ostentation that were characteristic of the Bohemians in all their relations with Miss Coolbrith, at that time their only, and revered, woman member. The monthly gift of money enabled her to stay on in New York City until late spring in 1922, and to return for the following winter season.

Before the end of the year 1922 Carl and Kenneth were making plans for a European tour. Ina was saddened, for her boy was sick, and she wondered if she would see him again. Carl left in January 1923, in spite of his doctor's advice to seek rest and quiet in Arizona. The boy had tuberculosis which might be checked with proper care. But he went off cheerfully, saying that if he needed desert air he preferred Egypt. Ina had given him a letter of introduction to Albert Kinross in London, and Kinross wrote her that he liked young Mr. Youff, but that he looked ill and should be in Italy instead of England.[52] In farewell Carl had given Miss Coolbrith a thick address book, bound in black leather, with an inscription on the front flyleaf, in clear, upright script, "A Record of your Friends, but I come first—for I love you more than any—and that love could only be first, from Carl, 6 Jan. 1923, N. Y."[53] To protect the book, Ina made a jacket of the patterned paper in which it had been wrapped as a gift, then she carefully filled the pages with the names and addresses of all her friends and of some business acquaintances. Even Popcorn's name was entered, in proper alphabetic position, as living with Miss Josie Zeller at 780 Seventeenth Street, Oakland. If it seems surprising to find the names of such rich men as William Randolph Hearst, J. Pierpont Morgan, and Dr. A. S. W. Rosenbach, it is because Ina Coolbrith made an attempt when she was in New York to sell some of her autographed books, to help meet her own expenses and to help Carl, just as she had written to foundations in an attempt to secure a music scholarship for him.[54]

In the spring of 1923 she did not want to return to California, but was unsuccessful in finding a summer place that came within her budget.[55] Before she left, however, a beautiful thing happened to her. Bio De Casseres invited her to go with her to see the spectacular new film, *The Covered Wagon*, then showing in New York. Ina was lost in the picture which she found true to her own experience. She became a child again, smelling the dust, suffering with the oxen, afraid to cross the rivers. She was crying before the movie was over. Mrs. De Casseres was moved by Ina's tearful enjoyment, and said afterwards, "If you want to appreciate *The Covered Wagon*, take a pioneer with you!"[56]

30
This
Receding
World

I turn to the few left me in this receding
world with even stronger clinging.

Ina Coolbrith, to
Albert Bender in 1927

Last Westward Journey

As Ina Coolbrith crossed the prairies on her westward journey the
first week of June 1923, she reflected that this was probably her last
overland trip. She wanted to reach out and hold the landscape to her,
as she had felt about the *Covered Wagon* film. But the train sped on.
It was too fast. She thought of her first journey—seven months behind
the plodding oxen from St. Joseph to Spanish Ranch.[1] And in 1923—five
days from New York City to Berkeley. Berkeley. She dreaded what lay
ahead. She would be ill, she knew. She would be housebound, unable to
see her friends unless they came to her. Why must California, the place
she loved, always "whack" her every time she came back to it?[2] She
remembered how it was the last summer, and the summer before that.
In June 1921 she had gone to Hotel Robins in San Francisco, thinking,
mistakenly, that she could copy her situation in New York, and have
the solitude of a hotel room where she could write and also make a
collection of her recent verse.[3] But the old rheumatic pains had seized
her and she had been persuaded to accept her niece's invitation to come
to Berkeley. She had resisted what she thought was a loss of independence and she had feared the effect on her work.

As she leaned back in the car seat in June of 1923, she recalled the
events of those two summers in the Ward Street house in Berkeley.
Much of the time she had been confined to her bed, or had sat in her

347

dressing gown in a big arm chair when callers were present. Though often invited, she seldom left the house, except to attend the monthly meetings of the Ina Coolbrith Circle in the St. Francis Hotel in San Francisco. On these cherished occasions she had been chauffeured by a San Francisco friend, Mrs. O. G. Beverly, who had made the round trip twice as she took the poet to the city and back on the fourth Sunday of every month.[4] She had had many callers in the summer of 1921; Albert Bender had come once in a while, bringing sweets or fruit or a book; Nancy Barr Mavity had called to interview her for the *San Francisco Chronicle*.[5] Miss Coolbrith remembered that she had liked what young Mrs. Mavity had put in the paper about her. She had been less pleased with a story published in the *Oakland Tribune* one Sunday that summer, a full page with pictures, and a story by Henry Meade Bland in his florid style.[6] That was the year, too, she recalled, when she had been elected to the English Club at the University of California, as an honorary member with Margaret Anglin, Blanche Bates, and two others.[7] She had been pleased about that, and a little amused, since she possessed none of the academic prerequisites for such select society. She had been in no better health the following summer; yet she had attended some of the Circle affairs and she had gone to Mrs. Lawrence's grand party for her.[8] But those two summers in Berkeley, she said, were wasted.[9] She had done no writing. She had done nothing to advance her own business, whereas she had really worked in New York. She recalled warning Mrs. Mavity of the temptation to play in California's easy climate, warning her that the spirit of *mañana* would get her, too. Miss Coolbrith's homecoming, that early June day in 1923, filled her with dread.

Honorary Degree, Mills College, 1923

The Cook family had moved from Ward Street to 2731 Hillegass Avenue, a few blocks south of the campus of the University of California. Miss Coolbrith arrived on 7 June and found the climate colder than she had remembered it. By the middle of July she knew that she would not return East, saying that the cost of living there was more than she could command.[10] She was depressed by her news of Carl, who had gone to Switzerland for medical treatment. Moreover, within a month from her arrival, three old friends died, Clarence Urmy, C. W. Carruth, and Dr. Edward R. Taylor, and then a small great-grandnephew was killed in an automobile accident. To a friend in the Midwest she wrote, "Only death seems in the world, yet *youth* does not realize it, and under my present roof only *youth* is manifest. I wonder was I similar in *my* youth? . . . California is so changed. Or am *I*? Anyway, the *Planet* seems different." She received a few letters, more than she was able to answer. Charles Phillips was in Missoula, Montana, but his letters did not reach her. Robert Norman was still in China. Herman Whitaker had never come back to California. He had died in New York, in 1919, on his return from Paris. The summer of 1923, the poet said, she felt lonely beyond words. Her loneliness was lessened, however, by autumn, when several social events in her honor took place. Receptions were given by the California Poetry Society and the Pacific Coast Women's Press Association; also by the Business and Professional Women's Association in Oakland, with a luncheon where she gave a talk. On 14 September she was invited to a special preview of the film she had seen in New York, *The Covered Wagon.* Her niece accompanied her and so did her twin brothers, William and Don Carlos Pickett, who were there with a number of other "covered wagon babies." The showing, arranged by Mrs. Gertrude Atherton, was given in the St. Francis Hotel. Miss Coolbrith enjoyed it all over again, perhaps as tearfully, in the presence of family and friends.[12]

Three days after that pleasant event, without warning, disaster struck Berkeley. A grass fire in the hills northeast of the city was carried by a strong north wind into the residence area north of the campus. By two o'clock the air on the campus, and south, past the Oakland line, was gray with smoke and bits of charred leaves and debris. Students rushed out of classes to fight the fire. The campus lay directly in its path. For two anxious hours it seemed as if all of Berkeley and perhaps all of Oakland would be burned. Most of the dwellings of these cities were of frame construction, many with shingle exteriors and nearly all with shingle roofs. Bits of blazing shingles carried the wind-driven fire from roof to roof. Then suddenly the wind died down, and the fire stopped almost as quickly as it had begun, the precise point where it burned itself out being Hearst Avenue, the north boundary line of the university campus. But within those two frantic hours the fire had turned all the northern area of the city of Berkeley into a desolate smoldering ruin of blackened chimneys. Martial law was declared, and some order was brought out of the chaos; and Ina was soon to learn of the many losses sustained by some of her friends, both students and faculty members. Some had lost valuable collections of books, others their notes or the uncompleted manuscripts of books. Benjamin Ide Wheeler, by then president emeritus of the university, found his personal losses difficult to bear.[13]

A few days before the Berkeley fire Ina Coolbrith had received a humble little note from Dr. Aurelia Henry Reinhardt, president of Mills College, an exclusive school for women, situated in the Oakland hills.

She invited the poet to come and spend the rest of the summer as a guest of the college; or, if she could not do that, to come and have tea with her. If the latter, too, were impossible, could she, Aurelia Reinhardt, call on Miss Coolbrith in her home in Berkeley?[14] Dr. Reinhardt probably came to the Hillegass Avenue house. She invited Miss Coolbrith to be present at the coming Founders' Day ceremony in October when the college wanted to confer an honorary degree on her.

On Saturday, 6 October 1923, the morning sun shone on the open lawn in front of Mills Hall, and brightened the white walls of the handsome Victorian building. The pungence of sun-warmed eucalyptus scented the air, and clear chimes from the bell tower opposite Mills Hall sounded the hour when the academic procession began to move toward Lisser Hall for the Founders' Day program. The principal address was given by David Starr Jordan, by then Emeritus Chancellor of Stanford University. As an old friend of Susan Tolman Mills, founder of the college, he gave a history of the fifty-two-year-old school. Four persons received honorary degrees, Lou Henry Hoover, wife of Herbert Hoover, then United States Secretary of Commerce; Melville Best Anderson, Dante scholar; Ina Coolbrith, Poet Laureate; and Bernard Maybeck, architect, designer of the Palace of Fine Arts in San Francisco. Miss Coolbrith was presented to Dr. Reinhardt by Professor Elias Olan James of the English Department. As the two women faced each other, the poet, stately in her white mantilla, waited while Dr. Reinhardt, a tall, beautiful woman, spoke these words:

> Ina Coolbrith, Poet Laureate of California. You answered the call of the meadowlark in California's sunrise; you followed the song of the mockingbird under her fragrant moon; flower and melody, love of man and worship of God, you have wrought them into imperishable loveliness in the fabric of your song.[15]

The Poet Laureate of California was awarded the honorary degree of Master of Arts. When the impressive ceremonies came to an end, teachers, students, alumnae, and guests all gathered for a picnic lunch beside Lake Aliso, a sylvan spot on the campus. It was a day to remember. It was reported in the local dailies with an excellent photograph of Ina Coolbrith, one of the few she could tolerate in those years. And

---

Ina Coolbrith, October 1923, on Occasion of Receiving an Honorary Degree, Mills College, Oakland. Photograph by **Oakland Post-Enquirer.** Courtesy of the Oakland Free Library.

Robert Shaw, of the *Oakland Post-Enquirer* staff, wrote an appreciative editorial, a combined biography and tribute, occupying half a page in large type. Shaw reminded his readers:

> The years fly past so swiftly. It is strange to remember that this woman, not yet very old in years, crossed the plains in a covered wagon before the railroad was built; saw San Francisco in its beginnings, Los Angeles when it was an adobe settlement in a desert, and who was for twenty years of her life the only librarian Oakland had.[16]

Carl Seyfforth and Other Friends

The next four years, 1924 through 1927, were eventful ones for the poet, by then heavier of figure and slower of movement, her mouth unsmiling in repose, but ready to laugh in animated conversation, her eyes still brilliant whether she were lost in thought or engaging in repartée with friends. These years were a kaleidoscope focused on bright and dark pieces moving into a pattern through which ran a thick gray thread, sometimes hidden by the bright or the dark, but never broken. This thread was Ina's agony for Carl Seyfforth, fighting for his life in far away Norway. He was dear to her, she said, "as an own and only son."[17] He was a lad in his teens when she first knew him, about the time of the Authors' Congress, blond and good-looking, musically gifted, poised, and charming. When she learned that his parents discouraged his interest in music, she had offered him the use of the piano in her home, and through the years had developed a motherly relationship with him. He had ignored his New York physician's advice to go to Arizona, but had gone abroad, instead, with the intention of giving piano recitals. While there his condition became serious and he began a long series of treatments, first in Switzerland, then with a specialist in Oslo. Ina Coolbrith helped him with her meager funds and sought further aid frantically from her own and Carl's friends.[18] They responded, though some were unwilling, for they believed that the young man was taking advantage of an aged woman, herself in need of money and care. Ina wrote to Carl's New York physician who said that he could not help a patient determined to "burn himself out," and she carried on a correspondence with Carl's nurse in Oslo and with a Norwegian concert pianist who had befriended him.[19] Carl, while a convalescent, made two hurried trips to America but had to be rushed back to the sanatorium each time. His disregard of early medical advice, his hectic moving about, and his frequent cablegrams to Miss Coolbrith were resented by her friends and family. They could see that she was greatly agitated by a situation in which she was help-less.[20]

In helping Carl, Ina was fighting for life. Carl represented youth and life and song. Would his going mean the end of all these for her? Was she, in seeking to prolong his life, seeking to fight death itself? "Only death seems in the world," she had said. And for her it was true in those years. She could see them all departing, the old and the young. Edna Dean Proctor, Mrs. Perry in Los Angeles, Emma ("Old Glory") Dawson in Palo Alto, Luther Burbank, Charles Turrill—all were gone, and she mourned their passing.[21] But when death took the gifted young, she was stricken. The suicides of George Sterling in November 1926 and Herman Scheffauer in October 1927 were devastating to her spirit.

"What dew before the dawn we are!" she exclaimed when she learned of Sterling's death, "I loved the dear Singer above his kind."[22] Carl Seyfforth's death, a month before Scheffauer's, though expected for years, was the greatest blow of all to her.

"How did you bear it?" she asked a friend, "when you lost the ones you loved? Do you ever question God and His purposes and the meaning of it all? Oh! these are heavy days!"[23]

Heavy days, indeed, brought by her losses, but there were many bright days in those four years. It was as though all who knew her were seeking to prolong their contact with her. She was interviewed for local dailies.[24] She was the subject of articles in national magazines, one of which, however, enraged her by its false statements and its emphasis on her old age and feebleness. The author, a young man she had met in New York, applied the word "venerable" to her, a word she detested; but, worse than that were his absurd statements that Stoddard had died in her arms, and that she, Ina Coolbrith, alone knew the fate of Ambrose Bierce. When she asked the author "Why?" he replied lamely that he had expressed his feelings, not historical accuracy. Lummis may have twitted her about the article, for she wrote him "from the depths," a reply so filled with resentment against her own frustrated life, that she did not mail the letter. Six months later, after two other letters which she destroyed, she told him, she was still seething about this "inane article," as she called it.[25]

There were, nevertheless, many days during this period that were lightened by the thoughtfulness of her friends, or by her own desire to participate—not to give up to despair. She was entertained at breakfasts, luncheons and dinners, large affairs arranged by organizations, and small ones by personal friends.[26] A crown was placed upon her head by a small school girl, representing five hundred others, in the San Francisco Civic Auditorium.[27] She went to see Max Reinhardt's

353

The Miracle, in the city, escorted by Albert Bender.[28] She continued to attend the Coolbrith Circle meetings every month, even arranging all the details of the Sterling memorial program of the Circle in February 1927, though she said she could not take part, and would do well simply to be there.[29] She gave more than one talk during the period, wrote, as Poet Laureate, the official jubilee poem for the state Diamond Jubilee in 1925, and was appointed by Governor C. C. Young to represent California at the Women's World's Fair in Chicago in 1927, when she was eighty-six years of age, at which time her biography and a poem by her were broadcast on a national radio program.[30] This idea pleased her, for she had been interested in Marconi's invention of the wireless from its beginning. A poem of hers had been broadcast over KPO in San Francisco in 1924, but when she was given a radio for her eighty-fourth birthday, she said "It is a wonder, and a joy—but I'd rather talk with my friends than with it."[31]

She saw old friends, she knowing and they knowing that it would be the last time; Charles Lummis in 1925, and Edwin Markham in 1927. Lummis spent the last three months of 1925 in the Bay Area. Ina enjoyed several long afternoons with "Don Carlos," who played the guitar and sang his Spanish songs for her. Harry Noyes Pratt photographed the two one afternoon, and there were sparkles in Ina's eyes and adoration in those of Don Carlos.[32] Their parting was touching. Mrs. Cook said she had to rush from the room, blinded by tears.[33] And Ina may have reminded Don Carlos then, as she did later in one of her brief letters, "Remember, you're not to go and leave me behind!" If she failed to write promptly, she would offer age as her excuse, and say "and so I defer writing and the things I should do—tho' God He knows I love you, Señor, Don Carlos!"[34] Her last meeting with Markham was on 24 April 1927. That day the Circle held a luncheon for him with Ina Coolbrith sharing the congratulations that came by letter and telegram to the two white-haired poets. It was on this occasion that Miss Coolbrith told once more the story of her entry into the state by way of Beckwourth Pass seventy-five years before.[35]

Her letters were becoming fewer and briefer, though she continued to write to Albert Bender and Charles Phillips. She was kept busy answering requests from strangers for permission to quote her lyrics or set them to music. She had requests for information on Joaquin Miller and others, and audacious pleas for autographed poems. One un-

---

Ina Coolbrith and Charles Fletcher Lummis, 1925. Photograph by Harry Noyes Pratt. Courtesy of the Bancroft Library, University of California, Berkeley.

lettered enquirer even asked her to make two copies for her of "your little poem, 'California.'" She complained that she needed a secretary.[36] Up to the time of his death George Sterling saw Miss Coolbrith occasionally; he was a dinner guest at her home less than a month before his suicide. Many younger people came to call during the period, among them Lionel Stevenson, professor of English at the University of California, and his colleague Derrick Norman Lehmer, professor of mathematics. Professor Lehmer and his wife, Eunice Mitchell Lehmer, were both poets, and they preferred to call their favorite poet "Donna" instead of "Ina." To her, the Lehmers were loyal and unfailing. To them, she was a mountain of strength and inspiration.[37] Harry Noyes Pratt and his wife were frequent callers.[38] He too was a poet, and an editor of the *Overland Monthly* for a brief period before its sale to a Chicago publishing house. Another poet friend among Miss Coolbrith's frequent visitors was Ruth Harwood, a young woman, gifted in art as well as poetics.

One sunny December afternoon in 1927 Miss Harwood brought three of her friends, Oakland library staff members, to meet Miss Coolbrith, who was living then at 2906 Wheeler Street in Berkeley. As they came into the room, those who saw Miss Coolbrith for the first time took in the picture that she made. The Poet Laureate was seated in a large armchair in a bay window. Sunlight streamed in from the south, illuminating her violet gown and lacy white headdress. At her feet lay the beautiful fifteen-year-old white Persian cat, Popcorn. The poet made a few casual remarks about the library, saying that for her it had meant twenty years in prison, for the hours were long—ten hours a day. Her poet friends, Eunice and Derrick Lehmer, came in and were warmly greeted. She was persuaded to tell the story of her wreath for Byron and to read the poem she had sent with it. She read it from Albert Brecknock's new edition of his *Byron*, published the year before. Her voice was rich and strong as she read those lines from her young days. Her eyes shone. Seeing her thus and hearing her read was an experience never forgotten by those who were present that winter afternoon.[39]

Reunion with an Old Friend, Charles Phillips

During the four-year period, 1924 through 1927, in spite of concern for Carl, in spite of frequent changes of residence (two in San Francisco, two in Berkeley) Miss Coolbrith was busy with some literary activities.[40] She finally, and sorrowfully, gave up her hope to finish the memoirs, though the services of an amanuensis were offered. For that she said she needed solitude, such as she had had in her four winters in New York.[41] In 1924 she was persuaded to write an introduction to

Bret Harte's *The Heathen Chinee,* to be printed in a limited edition for Christmas giving. She was glad to do so, for it gave her an opportunity to express Harte's own views on the poem he was sorry he wrote. John Henry Nash printed the poem and the five-page introduction on hand-made paper—a handsome folio.[42] A year later Nash printed Miss Coolbrith's evocative lyric, "Retrospect," with an introduction by the author, one of her best statements on her childhood in Los Angeles. A profile portrait of the poet, from a drawing by Dan Sweeney, made the frontispiece to the large folio. This collector's item was printed for Ernest Dawson of Los Angeles as a Christmas gift to his friends.[43] On 28 June 1924 Ina Coolbrith's first poem written for and read over radio was broadcast on KPO from Hale's department store in San Francisco. This was "The Call of the Forests," her free verse contribution to Fire Prevention Week.[44]

In 1925 California observed its Diamond Jubilee, and the state's Poet Laureate was requested to write a poem for this occasion. And so the poet who, as a young woman in her twenties, had written a lyric celebrating the state's eighteenth birthday, was commissioned to write one for the seventy-fifth. It is doubted that on this occasion five ten-dollar gold pieces were put into her hand as had been done in 1868. Not even a more mundane check was given her. The office of state poet was strictly honorary, uncontaminated by money. Her "California Jubilee Poem," an unrhymed ode of forty-four lines was read by Mrs. Rita I. Hayden at the banquet for Vice-President Charles G. Dawes on 10 September at the Fairmont Hotel. The poem was published in the dailies the next day and before the week was out had been requested for quoting in two books.[45]

The same month Miss Coolbrith arranged for a new printing of her *Songs from the Golden Gate,* ordering the entire printing of five hundred copies sent to her for her own resale.[46] This was necessary, not only because the book was again out of print, but because Albert Brecknock of Hucknall Torkard had asked to use the plate made for the frontispiece in her *Songs.* He was about to bring out a new edition of his *Byron* and wanted to tell the story of the wreath, quote Miss Coolbrith's poem, and use her portrait in the volume. The poet acceded, saying that when Houghton Mifflin had used it for this last printing of her book, they could forward the plate to him. She had no further use for it. This was done and the Brecknock book on Byron published the following year, 1926.[47]

In 1925 another poem by Miss Coolbrith appeared, this too on request. Charles Phillips, after several years of wandering over Europe and taking an ill-advised trip to Mexico, had settled down to teach

English at the University of Notre Dame. His department was planning to issue a little poetry magazine, and he, as editor, asked Ina to write for it. She responded, and the verses were published in the second issue of *Pan, Poetry and Youth.* The piece was a whimsical lyric that took its name from that of the periodical.[48] Phillips, his colleagues, and his students were all pleased. In 1926 three poems by the laureate were printed, "With the Caravan," which had been written in New York and was now published by the University of California, "Portolá Speaks," and a memorial sonnet for Luther Burbank who had died in April, all fresh in imagery and measure, yet written when her concern for Carl was deepest. Her "Mexico" was written this year too.[49] One other, "Robin," not published during her lifetime, seems to have been written for Carl. She had sent a copy of it to Phillips, as she often did with her short lyrics.[50] He had not seen Miss Coolbrith since shortly after the Authors' Congress in 1915. He wrote long, affectionate letters to her and was always planning to see her, but did not actually achieve a visit until late in 1927.

In September that year Phillips asked Brother Leo at St. Mary's College to get him some lecture engagements if he could between 20 December 1927 and the following 4 January.[51] He wanted to spend his Christmas vacation in the San Francisco area, he said, and needed added funds to pay his expenses. His real reason, however, was to visit Miss Coolbrith and help her make a selection from her later unpublished poems for a volume to be issued in 1928 if possible. They had only two weeks in which to accomplish a desire of years. Charlie, with his years of editorial experience, and of teaching English, gave her exactly the help she needed. They decided to include very few lyrics that had appeared in the two previous volumes. Ina insisted that her poem, "my wretched Sterling verse," written in September 1927 and printed in the November *Overland* be omitted, but did want one, written only a month before Phillips came, to be included. This was "The Vision of St. Francis."[52] Remembering the sad failure of the 1917 Stoddard collection, Phillips urged that the book now being prepared have a biographical introduction. He wanted to write it, and Ina gladly supplied the answers to his questions about the major events in her life. She had never told her story herself and had dismissed pleas to do so with, "were I to write what I know, the book would be too sensational to print; but were I to write what I think proper, the book would be too dull to read."[53] When asked to specify the city of her birth, she had put off the curious by saying, "I've been told I was born in Springfield. I have no personal memory, but I wish you'd say Illinois. That's near enough and gives me the whole state!"[54] Phillips promised to write a brief biography and send it to her for her approval as soon after the first of the coming year as his duties at the university would permit. They decided to call the new book *Wings of Sunset,* and Ina pencilled the title inside the front cover of her address book—the one Carl had given her. And to Carl, she said, she would dedicate the new book. She wrote out the dedication in her firm hand and handed it to Charlie, "to the boy Carl whose song begun on Earth is finished in Heaven."[55] Reading it, Charles felt a twinge of jealousy, that of an older son for his young brother.[56] He dismissed the guilty thought immediately and humored Ina gently in her earnest need to link these poems with the memory of the boy she could not save. Charlie did not expect to see his own name on the dedication page. His one concern was to put the collection into publishable form before he left. Mrs. Cook helped him tirelessly, and he came to appreciate this sensitive and gracious woman whose affection for her aunt had never wavered through all the years.

Phillips' presence gave Ina strength. They went together to the December meeting of the Ina Coolbrith Circle, the last one she was able to attend.[57] And she gave him new strength, as she used to in what he thought were the old days when he first knew her. That year, 1927, he had published a volume of verse entitled *High in her Tower,* and had sent her six copies for her to use as gifts.[58] It was dedicated to her, and its title poem was about her as he always thought of her, high in her hilltop home. She had taken the place of a mother to him when he lived in San Francisco, and he said later that she was next to his mother in his affections.[59] As a writer he owed much to her, as had all the others—all the long line—from Stoddard and Miller down to the younger generation, London and Lummis, Bashford and the Lehmers, Sterling, and young Ruth Harwood. Ina did not guide them or instruct them in the arts of prosody. But her encouragement and personality compelled them to go forth and interpret life as they saw it, simply and honestly. In this way she had inspired Charles Phillips, too, a lonely writing man of some success, living austerely as a monk, his only emotional release in his letters to her. His final gift of love was made plain in his help with her last book.

31
Wings
of
Sunset

Housed for a litle space
In how infinitesimal a star.

Ina Coolbrith, from
"The Unsolvable"
(*Wings of Sunset*, 1929)

Mind and Heart of the Poet

By the time Charles Phillips left Berkeley on 3 January 1928, the new book, *Wings of Sunset*, promised to be a reality. To both author and editor this assurance was partial compensation for their painful leavetaking. After Phillips' departure, Ina was depressed and weary. Making the selection of verse for the volume had been physically and emotionally exhausting. As she leaned back against the cushions of her big armchair, she closed her eyes and felt a rush of self-pity. Her book was ready at last, she mused. Ready—in time for the funeral. More than thirty years since her last book. Why had her achievements been so few and far between, and her frustrations so numerous? she asked herself. She thought back to some lines she had written long ago. She murmured a fragment to herself,

What do I owe the years . . .
What have they brought to me, these many years?
Silence and bitter tears.[1]

"These many years," she thought. How many years had they been? Seventy? Eighty? Yes, more than eighty years since the incidents of violence and sudden death in Nauvoo had impinged themselves so indelibly onto the subconscious mind of her earliest infancy.

361

Her father had died when she was only five months old, and her mother, partly to compensate for her loss, held her youngest child to her with a special closeness. Two years later Ina's next older sister died of scarlet fever, and Ina was frightened when she saw her mother weeping. Her sister's passing was Ina's first conscious memory, and the event made such a strong impression on her mind that she described it later as "the bloody couch of death." Perhaps she was confusing the incident with the murders, a year later, of her uncles, Joseph and Hyrum, and the death of another uncle, Samuel, or perhaps with subsequent acts of violence that took place in Nauvoo's streets. Life in Nauvoo at that time would have been traumatic to any child, and especially so to a child as impressionable as Ina was. To protect her children Agnes Smith kept them near her at all times, often in the home of her mother-in-law Lucy Smith. In later years Ina recalled some of the "scenes of desolation" in Nauvoo, in one of her very few autobiographical poems, lines written for her mother's fiftieth birthday in 1861. These scenes, witnessed and described by her elders, terrified the little girl and her oldest sister Agnes. Indeed they frightened all those in the enlarged Smith household, where the Smith widows and their children gathered together in the evenings for prayers and despairing conversation. The fear of another Far West haunted them all, and that fear reached Ina and her cousins even as they romped at games in the twilight. Ina's one poem about Nauvoo is a series of vignettes, some pleasant, some painful. Those pictures of her childhood were shadowy, run-together memories, confused with her mother's stories. She recalled the pleasant woodlands, the wide river, her grandmother Smith's home, and the cemetery where her father and sister lay. The desolation, too, was part of the whole picture, and Ina called herself in the poem "the child of sorrow and of song." *Child of sorrow* was a phrase used more than once in her early verse, a conscious reminder of what she and her family had suffered.[2]

Ina Coolbrith suppressed these early childhood fears and others she experienced later. From the time she was five years of age she was trained by her mother to hide the Nauvoo background. The Mormon connections of the Smith girls and their mother were kept as a family secret in the Pickett household, not from lack of faith in the church, but as practical protection from harm. This discipline of silence had unforeseen effects on Ina. It was humiliating to be forbidden to tell who

---

Ina Coolbrith and Popcorn, 1925. Photo by the poet's niece, Mrs. Finlay Cook. Courtesy of the Oakland Free Library.

her father was and even where she was born. She could say that her father had died when she was an infant, that she was born in Illinois. But Ina was naturally a candid, outspoken girl as she grew up in Los Angeles. And it pained her to be unable to boast of the gifted, unselfish young man with the romantic name, Don Carlos, who was her father, or to say that her birthplace was Nauvoo, a unique and tragic city on the banks of the Mississippi River. But the family was still close to their part in the tragedy, and the sect to which they belonged was misunderstood in that time and place. So it was common sense to be still. And no one thought of the harmful consequences of such severe restraint on the child Ina.

Sharing the family secret kept the girl close to her mother as long as her mother lived. Ina came to trust few others, and, after her own personal tragedy in marriage and divorce, her long practice of reticence about her past served her well when she went to San Francisco and changed her name to Ina Coolbrith. Why her mother's maiden name? It had a pleasing sound, but more than that, it erased the Smith and Carsley connections and enabled her to hide her true identity. She continued to confide in her mother and hesitated to form other close relationships. Her mother was her only intimate. Ina respected her mother's wishes, and kept the family secret, adding to it her own, and guarding them both to her dying day. Suppression of the facts of her past was not too hard while her mother lived. Only after Mrs. Pickett's death did Ina's loneliness become oppressive. Her friends found her aloof at times, even austere as she grew older.

The above may, in some measure, explain why Ina Coolbrith's personal life was incomplete as we look back at her today. Much of her melancholy verse is evidence. It seems regrettable that she did not seek to enrich her own life and that of another by remarriage. Her one brief experience had been devastating, and she was afraid to try again. She said once, in expressing her regret that she had not married, that she had not found a suitable partner. According to her family she had numerous suitors. Though her beauty and brains drew many to her, her reticence, caused by fear and repression, prevented closeness, prevented love affairs, prevented remarriage. In the Coolbrith papers, in the sedate Bancroft Library, are two tiny packets, each labeled in Ina's handwriting, and each containing a lock of hair. One was from Bret Harte's head, the other from Charles Warren Stoddard's. The surprised reader, coming across the sentimental keepsakes, might attach some significance to them and assume that Ina was in love with one or both of the men. But probably they are nothing more than tokens of a girl's playful use of her scissors back in the 1860s when it was a fad to collect locks of friends' hair and to make hair wreaths and bouquets and chains. Ina (who seldom discarded letters or cards or small souvenirs) kept them, and they even survived the San Francisco fire. It is true that her name has been linked romantically with those of Bret Harte and Charlie Stoddard, as well as with those of other San Francisco men, chiefly writers. But Harte was a married man, devoted to his home and children. Stoddard was near her own age, single, and they had known each other always, Ina at some time said. They were "pals"—to use Ina's and Charlie's word—never lovers. They tramped along the beach at San Francisco on Sundays, like children, collecting seaweeds and shells; they read poetry together on these outings, or in her family home. They were often together, but she never went to his rooms, as she made clear to another woman writer who did so. Joaquin Miller, when he met Ina, thought that she was Charlie's "girl," and never trespassed. Stoddard was charming, effeminate, lazy. Ina loved him as a sister would, but she would not have married him.

Other names linked romantically with Ina include those of William Keith, Mark Twain, and especially Joseph C. Duncan, who was the father of the famous dancer, Isadora Duncan. One close friend of Miss Coolbrith's once remarked, "You know, of course, that she was madly in love with Keith." If there was any evidence of this, it was kept discreetly out of Ina's letters and her poems to Keith, who, like Harte, was married, and whose wife was one of Ina's friends. Mark Twain was in San Francisco only during the 1860s, and Ina knew him merely as an acquaintance. Duncan was said to be in love with a lady who lived on Russian Hill at the time his wife obtained a divorce from him. There are those who believe that Ina was the lady, but there is no evidence for the belief. It is true that Duncan admired Miss Coolbrith, that his daughter was sure her father was in love with the poet, and that Ina's eyes had a special brilliance in them when his name was mentioned.

Besides these Californians, she was courted by a high official in The Church of Jesus Christ of Latter-day Saints in Salt Lake City, but she declined the honor of marriage. John Carmany, also a Californian, loved Ina Coolbrith, as has been related elsewhere. He was unattached, except to a set of puritanical principles as rigid as Ina was reserved. He backed out, at the urging of his even more puritanical sister, and Ina's pride turned her away from him. She later regretted her decision. At least she regretted that she had not married again. But by that time, it was security she wanted, not the sweet sharing of intimacies.

In her last years she was attracted to young men. She surrounded herself with them, embarrassing other friends and her family. She loved one especially, the talented youth, Carl Seyfforth, and her passion for him was more than that of a mother for a son. Carl evaded her, not intentionally, but by going recklessly to an early death. Charles Phillips, forty years her junior, adored her, and once begged her to come with him to England where they would live and see the places of interest to them both. But he delayed putting his proposal into practice until it was too late. When he saw her next, as 1927 was fading into 1928, it was to saw good-bye.[3]

Ina Coolbrith was despondent as the year 1928 dawned. She felt that her end was near, but did not regret it, for many of her "own dear, dear ones," as she called them, were gone. Yet she begged for a bit of comfort in the few letters she wrote. She was "sick of science" she told one friend, and wanted something of "unquestioning faith" to sustain her. She was heartened by the friend's reply that faith was strengthened by science, and that scientific development inspired belief in immortality and continuous growth, that our only word of certainty is in ourselves and humanity; and, if she asks for something to cling to, she will find the answers in her own poetry, saying that as "one who has made for herself so secure a place in the romance, history and poetry of the fairest spot on earth, you should sing a song of thanks and joyfulness, not one of lamentation," and added, "Let us sit up on the front seat of the go-cart and 'face the wind.'" This was tonic to Ina, the reassurance she needed.[4]

She was a skeptic, a doubter, an enquirer. "God help us all," she said once to Albert Bender, "I don't know what we are here for, nor the meaning of the trials, nor the end—but someday we shall know—or rest in oblivion."[5] But she never swerved from her belief in God. "And God—the Supreme—in whom I do believe . . ." she said.[6] She believed in him as easily and simply as she believed in sunshine. Her verse shows love of Christ, not as a divine being, but as a man, humble and compassionate. Her skepticism extended to her thoughts on immorality. To Charles Lummis she said, "Wonder will we meet some place *Over There?* O, Don Carlos! to meet and know the ones I have cared for would be Heaven enough for me. I don't want things too new!"[7] She questioned the comfortable, orthodox acceptance of life after death. None of her poems describe the hope of joyful reunions with loved ones. Death brings bitter grief to the mourner, and release from pain and labor to the dead. The dead are not gone if they remain with us in our thought and memory. If her imagination strayed to a hereafter, she made a gloomy picture, suggestive of the scenes wherein Homeric heroes wandered, seeking the shades of their dead. Her poems, "A Meeting" (for Robert Carsley?), "Return," and the tomblike "Oblivion," are examples.

If her images of life after death were dismal, this was precisely be-

366

cause she loved living things with an almost pagan intensity and joy. She loved "earth's dear brown bosom," all creation, the sea, the sun, the rain. Though the years brought tragedy, pain, loss of friends, disillusionment, she never lost her sensuous delight in life and beauty. She suffered the loss of love, but never escaped from the wonder of love. There was beauty in the world before her eyes, and beauty, too, in the unsolvable,

> What use the questioning? this thing we are:
>   A breath called life, housed for a little space
> In how infinitesimal a star;
>   Then vanished, leaving neither sound nor trace.[8]

While Ina Coolbrith disliked "religiosity," many of her poems are sincerely religious. Yet she was a member of no church.[9] She who had been "endowed" in the Mormon temple at Nauvoo, married by a Methodist minister in the shadow of a Franciscan mission, and buried by a funeral service held in an Episcopalian church, belonged to no denomination. It is characteristic that a hymn of hers could be sung in Catholic and Protestant churches on the same Sunday.[10] She was influenced more by Thomas Starr King of the Unitarian church in San Francisco than by any other preacher. His humanity, his concern for Civil War sufferers, and his literary taste impressed her as a young woman and never left her memory. She numbered many prominent clergymen among her friends, Henry Durant, Laurentine Hamilton, Archbishop Hanna, and many others.

She herself was neither saint nor optimist. She never looked on the bright side of a coming event. She expected the worst. She never seemed to be truly happy.[11] Her experience had made her a pessimist. In her contact with people, through her work and clubs, she had made enemies, some of whom she never forgave. She once remarked, after a night of fitful rest, "I dreamed of all my enemies, what time I slept."[12] Miss Coolbrith had strong convictions, a stern conception of right and wrong, a compulsive sense of irony, and a ready tongue, agile in repartee. These qualities made trouble for her. Like many witty people, she was quick to feel a slight or an imagined injury to herself. Failure to receive an answer to a letter could throw her into despair for days. While capable of expressing righteous wrath in the most uncompromising terms, without losing anything of her dignity, she could, at times, stoop to pettiness. An occasional letter, not mailed, but kept, or a letter mailed to or about an "enemy," reminds us that there was some ordinary clay in her makeup.

Character flaws, however, are part of the whole person. She was high-spirited and articulate, and she could be high-tempered and sharp-tongued. She had no patience with small talk; and if her callers indulged in it, she was known to excuse herself and leave the room. But in most of her relationships, she was understanding, ready to listen, seeking always to bring out the best in every person whom she knew, and to minimize his faults. Those who idealized her tended to give extravagant praise that approached flattery, or they attributed a cold perfection to her which was not inherent in her true personality. George Sterling once said she was like a "sibyl of stone," a cruel simile for a truly human woman. And Herbert Bashford, before he knew her well, put her name among the distant stars, in an often-quoted quatrain he wrote in 1907:

> A clear white flame illumes her song,
> The love of Truth, the hate of Wrong;
> 'Tis like a star wherein we see
> The fire of Immortality.[13]

Death of Ina Coolbrith

February 1928 was Ina Coolbrith's last month. She was living at that time in the Cook home at 2906 Wheeler Street, Berkeley. Her niece was a devoted nurse who observed that her aunt's mind and humor were as keen as ever. Near the end of the month the aged poet lapsed into a coma. When the doctor called, he believed that his patient was asleep and he remarked aloud to Mrs. Cook that she might expect her aunt to live two more days. Miss Coolbrith stirred and murmured, "Today and tomorrow! Today . . . and . . . tomorrow!" Those were her last words.[14] Her death came just after midnight, at 12:40 a.m., Wednesday, 29 February 1928, only ten days before her eighty-seventh birthday.[15]

On Friday, 2 March, two hundred friends of the Poet Laureate gathered in St. Mark's Episcopal Church in Berkeley to pay their last homage. The light, coming through stained glass windows, was mellow, but the air in the church was heavy with the scent of lilies-of-the-valley, the poet's favorite flower, which blanketed the casket. This was the last of the Bohemian Club's many gifts to their cherished lady member.[16] Words of affection and consolation were spoken by her dear friend, the rector of All Souls Church, the Reverend Hugh Montgomery. George

Facsimile of Manuscript, "When the Grass Shall Cover Me," Copied by Ina Coolbrith for Her Friend Herbert Bashford. Courtesy of Mrs. Alice Bashford Wallace, Sidney, B.C., Canada.

When the Grass Shall Cover Me.

When the grass shall cover me,
Head to foot where I am lying;
  When not any wind that blows,
  Summer blooms, nor winter snows,
Shall awake me to your sighing, –
Close above me as you pass,
  You will say, "How kind she was,"
  You will say, "How true she was" –
When the grass grows over me.

When the grass shall cover me,
Holden close to earth's warm bosom, –
  While I laugh, or weep, or sing,
  Nevermore for anything,
You will find in blade and blossom,
  Sweet small voices, odorous,
  Tender pleaders in my cause,
  That will speak me as I was,
When the grass grows over me.

When the grass shall cover me!
Ah! beloved, in my sorrows
  Very patient, I can wait,
  Knowing that, or soon or late,
There will dawn a clearer morrow:
  When your heart will moan, "Alas!
  Now I know how true she was,
  Now I know how dear she was"; –
When the grass grows over me!
                    – Ina Coolbrith –

Sterling's "Holy River of Sleep," set to music by Rose Travis, was sung by Alphonse Rosa, baritone. Miss Beatrice Sherwood, a mezzo-soprano, sang Miss Coolbrith's favorite hymns, "Nearer, my God, to Thee," and "Softly, Now, the Light of Day." Lionel Stevenson, from the English Department of the University of California, read the most fitting of all the Laureate's poems, her beautiful sonnet, "Beside the Dead," written for her sister in 1873. It began,

> It must be sweet, O thou, my dead, to lie
>   With hands that folded are from every task;
> Sealed with the seal of the great mystery,
>   With lips that nothing answer, nothing ask . . .

and ended with,

> Past all the hours, or slow of wing or fleet—
> It must be sweet, it must be very sweet![17]

Only a year before, at the Circle's memorial poem for Sterling, Professor Stevenson had read a group of Sterling's poems at Ina's request, for she thought his reading of verse the best she had heard in those years. Eight men she had known long and well were her pallbearers, Professor Derrick Norman Lehmer, Albert Bender, George Beach Brady, ex-Senator James D. Phelan, Dr. John T. Grant, president of the Coolbrith Circle, Charles B. Weikel, University of California chimes master, Dr. H. Staats Moore, and Harry Francis.[18] Ina Coolbrith was buried beside her mother in Mountain View Cemetery in Oakland. Her grave is unmarked.[19] Perhaps, in years to come, a simple stone may be placed there, engraved with a passage from the most poignant of all her lyrics, "When the Grass Shall Cover Me." A passer-by, reading, will be set to wondering about the woman who wrote the lines, the woman who said that in her poems was the whole story of her life.[20]

> When the grass shall cover me,
> Head to foot where I am lying—
>   When not any wind that blows,
>   Summer-blooms nor winter-snows,
> Shall awake me to your sighing:
>   Close above me as you pass,
>   You will say, 'How kind she was,'
>   You will say, 'How true she was,'
> When the grass grows over me.

When the grass shall cover me,
Holden close to earth's warm bosom—
While I laugh, or weep, or sing,
Nevermore, for anything,
You will find in blade and blossom,
Sweet small voices, odorous,
Tender pleaders in my cause,
That shall speak me as I was—
When the grass grows over me.

When the grass shall cover me!
Ah, beloved, in my sorrow
Very patient, I can wait,
Knowing that, or soon or late,
There will dawn a clearer morrow;
When your heart will moan: 'Alas!
Now I know how true she was;
Now I know how dear she was'—
When the grass grows over me!"[21]

Ruth Harwood, going home from St. Mark's that March afternoon, found herself saying, over and over, two lines from the poem, "While I laugh, or weep, or sing, / Nevermore, for anything." She put her own thoughts into words as she went along, and when the Laureate's friends read them later in the *University of California Chronicle*, they felt that Miss Harwood spoke for them, too:

Two lines that I have read before
With poignancy, yet how much more
They cut the heart for being true
Now that the earth has covered you.

Two lines in simplest music told,
Yet what infinity of pain they hold
For those who still can sing and weep,
And mourn the silence that you keep.[22]

Mormon Background Revealed

Among the mourners at Ina Coolbrith's funeral were Henry Meade Bland and Jesse Winter Smith, one from San Jose, the other at that time from the San Joaquin Valley. They happened to be seated in the same pew though they were strangers to each other. After the services

371

they introduced themselves. As Smith handed his card to Bland, he told him that Ina Coolbrith was a relative of his. Bland was surprised, but gave the statement little thought. After he had returned to his office at the Normal School, Dr. Bland received a telephone call from a reporter on one of the San Francisco dailies asking if the professor could verify statements in an Associated Press story about Ina Coolbrith's Mormon background. Professor Bland was puzzled and unbelieving. Then he remembered Jesse Winter Smith, and he suggested that the reporter get in touch with him, as he was a relative of the poet. The startling news first appeared in the *New York Sun* on 6 March in an article by Robert H. Davis and was soon copied by Bay Area newspapers. When Bland read the press accounts, he himself telephoned J. Winter Smith and was surprised to learn that it was all true. Smith told him of the promise made by Ina's mother and kept as a family secret for eighty years. He also related how Ina had said to him, "When I am gone, you may tell the world, if you care to."[23] In Berkeley, Mrs. Cook was interviewed by reporters from several papers. She told, simply and frankly, partly to correct errors that had appeared, the story of her aunt's long life, beginning with her birth in Nauvoo, as Josephine Donna Smith, daughter of Don Carlos Smith, niece of Joseph Smith the Prophet. She told about Don Carlos's death, and about Ina's mother's hardships and remarriage. She told the story of crossing the plains, the sojourn in Los Angeles, Josephine's marriage and divorce, and the subsequent move to San Francisco where Josephine Smith Carsley took a pen name which became her own name for the rest of her life.[24]

Mrs. Cook was asked by Robert Norman to be the executrix of her aunt's estate, modest though it was. After payment of a small legacy to Miss Josie Zeller, there was barely enough cash left to pay the spring installment of taxes and the interest on the mortgage of the San Francisco house. Miss Coolbrith's library and paintings had been willed to Robert Norman. What was left included a large collection of autographed photographs of distinguished people, hundreds of letters, and an old diary kept by Joaquin Miller in 1856. This latter had been requested years before by George Miller for deposit in the Oregon Historical Society's library. It had considerable value, Mrs. Cook said. True to Joaquin's trust in her, Ina had never let the manuscript out of her possession. She, too, had known its value in money and as primary literary source material.[25] The only jewelry of any value was a small diamond ring.[26]

Mrs. Cook and the poet's friends made the March meeting of the Ina Coolbrith Circle a memorial to her. Only three months before she herself had been present and had urged that the Circle not die with her.

She had hoped that it would keep alive the memory of California's literary pioneers, many of whom were being forgotten or misunderstood.[27] The members followed her suggestion, and the Circle has continued ever since. It has sponsored, throughout its more than fifty years, many interesting programs and speakers, its own library, and an annual poetry contest. Both of Miss Coolbrith's namesakes—Mrs. Ina Cook and her daughter, Mrs. Ina Graham—have served as officers of the Circle. So, too, has their relative, Jesse Winter Smith. A number of distinguished authors have been elected to honorary membership. When space in the St. Francis Hotel was no longer available, the Circle met in the Assembly room of the San Francisco Public Library, and now holds its monthly meetings in the Western Women's Club at Sutter and Mason Streets, San Francisco.[28]

Wings of Sunset

During the year following the death of Ina Coolbrith, her collection of verse, *Wings of Sunset,* was published by Houghton Mifflin Company, with a twenty-six-page, rather disappointing biographical memoir by Charles Phillips. The one hundred poems composing the volume contain only ten that were published in her two previous books. Phillips grouped the contents carefully under six topics, beginning with the California local verse. These are followed by a selection of nature lyrics, and these in turn by a small group of story poems, including the long narrative poem "Concha." The next group presents verse written for fellow artists, writers, painters, musicians. Religious and philosophical verse makes up the next subdivision, and the last, her poems of love and death. The arrangement is thus from the very general to the very personal. The volume, a delight to read, closes appropriately with "When the Grass Shall Cover Me."

The book was reviewed by Laura Bell Everett in the *University of California Chronicle* in January 1930, and Professor Lionel Stevenson in an April issue of the *Saturday Review of Literature.*[29] Of Ina Coolbrith's literary output, the latter critic wrote, "A strictness of self-criticism rare in woman poets kept her from prodigality. That there was no failure of inspiration is proved by the fact that the poems written in her eighty-seventh year, as well as being fresh as those of seventy years earlier, showed experimentation in new themes and verse forms."[30] In May 1930 Lionel Stevenson used the posthumous book as the basis for a critical essay which he titled, "The Mind of Ina Coolbrith," and which appears in full as an appendix at the end of this volume.[31]

Though the essay is a concise statement, it does not imply that the mind, the spirit of this great woman could be analyzed, reduced to a

373

formula, and synthesized into a few pages of print. Professor Stevenson emphasizes her "critical austerity which limited her production"; he speaks of her being accepted by Bret Harte and his associates as "a colleague on an equal footing with experienced men"; and he states that the most significant element in her poetry is "her clear perception of tragedy and suffering, of disappointment and frustration." The poet is brought into sharp focus in this essay, but it is difficult in either one page or many to describe the complex spirit of Ina Coolbrith.

For the total spirit of Ina Coolbrith is probably beyond our power to encompass it. One person cannot hope to analyze even in a full-length book all the nuances of her character, the subtilties of her spirit, the lights and shadows, depths and passions of her mind and heart. No one can attempt to comprehend her total life: the tragedies of her early years, the sorrow of her lost love, the drudgery of her daily routine of earning a living for herself and her dependents, or the bitterness of her later life, as friend after friend was taken from her by death.

Ina Coolbrith was, to quote or paraphrase some lines selected at random from her own poetry,

> A light that shone with clear, unswerving flame . . . [32]

She was, again in her own words,

> Poet of songs unsung,
> Dreamer, clear-eyed;
> Slave not to gain or greed;
> Bound by no narrow creed . . . [33]

Her only creed was love of God, and love of all God's creation. In her own words she praised

> . . . this simple creed:
> "Love thou thy God; thy neighbor as thyself;
> Forgive, as thou dost hope to be forgiven!"
> And lo! we have sweet Heaven
> About us on the earth. [34]

Despite her firm belief in God, and her joy in the wonders of His creation, Ina's life was not full of happiness. Even as a young woman she could write,

> What have they brought to me, these many years?
> Silence and bitter tears. [35]

374

Yet her vision never dimmed. She knew, as she approached her eighty-eighth year, that her life was coming to an end. Perhaps she then recalled those lines she had written, years before, as part of a commencement poem for the University of California in 1876:

> All these mysteries shall open, though to surer
>   hands than mine;
> All these doubts of our discerning, to the peace of
>   knowledge turning,
> All our darkness, which is human, to the light,
>   which is divine![36]

Ina Coolbrith was herself a dazzling particle of that light which is divine.

Epilogue:
The Naming
of the
Mountain

Two of Ina Coolbirth's dearest friends, during the last years of her life, were Derrick and Eunice Lehmer, a mathematics professor and his wife. Both were poets and both found Miss Coolbrith's friendship an inspiration in their own living and writing. In May 1927 they went to Bozeman, Montana, to attend a Crow Indian pageant where Professor Lehmer hoped to record Crow songs for his collection of Indian music. On their way north they stopped for a brief holiday in the Siskiyou Mountains where the mariposa lilies reminded them of Ina Coolbrith. From the highway, as they drove on, they could see matchless Mount Shasta for many miles. It was white almost to the foot, and, from one point, suggested Miss Coolbrith's profile with the white headdress. They remarked about the likeness, and instantly thought that one of California's peaks should be named for the state's first poet laureate. It was a pleasant, almost idle thought.[1]

Mrs. Lehmer was a member of the Ina Coolbrith Circle. At one of the meetings in 1928, not long after Miss Coolbrith's death, Mrs. Lehmer proposed that the Circle launch a movement to have a mountain named for the poet. The group was enthusiastic, and Mrs. Lehmer, Mrs. Nellie Van de Grift Sanchez, Mrs. Ina L. Cook, and Leo Shenstone Robinson were asked to serve on a committee to learn if such a thing could be done. A petition, prepared by the committee to present to the state and national geographic boards, was endorsed by the Native Sons of the Golden West, as well as the California Writers Club and other literary societies. It urged that Reconnaissance Peak in Plumas County be changed to Mount Ina Coolbrith, but this choice was not practical. Summit Peak in Sierra County was suggested instead, and by action of the United States Geographic Board in 1932, was named "Mount Ina Coolbrith," and so appears on the topographic maps of the area.[2] It is a peak of eight thousand fifty-nine feet elevation in Section 1, Township 21 North, Range 16 East, Mount Diablo Meridian of the public lands surveys. It is visible from Beckwourth Pass where Ina Coolbrith as a child of ten saw it as she rode in front of Jim Beckwourth on his horse. She was the first white child to enter California by way of this pass, a tired little girl, but "the happiest little girl in the whole world," she said as she told the story for the last time in her life, at a Circle luncheon in San Francisco on 24 April 1927.[3]

The Circle made one pilgrimage to Mount Ina Coolbrith. And Mrs. Cook, who worked tirelessly to accomplish the naming of the mountain, said to Mrs. Sanchez, "What a pity beloved Grandie is not here to enjoy this honor, the greatest that was ever bestowed upon her."[4]

Appendices

Appendix A
The Mind of Ina Coolbrith°
Lionel Stevenson

Although Ina Coolbrith has a particular importance for Californians as the poet most completely identified with the literary life of the state, her place in literature must not be determined on merely local grounds. Her importance in California resides in the fact that her life spanned nearly eighty years of the state's history, that she was closely associated with all the leading writers who sojourned here, and that she became the state's first poet laureate. She did, moreover, what every poet should do for his own locality—she invested its scenes and history with that permanent imaginative significance which will affect future generations.

Her work, however, was not restricted by the fact that she seldom traveled out of the state or had leisure for study. From her library desk her imagination and emotion winged out freely into the ageless ether of poetry. In view of the place accorded her by such men as Whittier and Stedman, one might expect to find her name occurring more frequently than it does in anthologies; the neglect may be partly due to her isolation from the centers of literary log-rolling, but it is due in a larger degree to her own critical austerity which limited her production. Her poetical output during her lifetime was practically restricted to *Songs from the Golden Gate*, and that one moderately-sized volume was apt to be overlooked by critics who measure literary importance by the yard and the pound. Now *Wings of Sunset*, containing the poems of her last thirty years, permits a juster estimate of her work; but a posthumous volume is always at a disadvantage, and many readers, on learning that she was born in 1840, will ignore the book without reading a page of it.

Throughout the history of literature, women poets have been particularly endowed with musical gifts, shown in graceful fluency of meter and melodious sweetness of word-sounds. Their ease in these respects, however, too often becomes diffuseness and banality. They tend to echo established meters and phrases so facilely that individuality vanishes from their poems, or else they record every passing mood and trivial episode of their own lives, in which the reader finds little interest. Ina Coolbrith had the musical gift and spontaneity, but never committed either of the excesses just named, for the simple reason that she had always something to say. The personal emotion was always present, as well as the technical skill, but dominating it was the restraint of a vig-

---

°This essay, which first appeared in the pages of the *Overland Monthly* in May 1930, is reproduced here by the author's permission.

orous intellect. For this reason every poem, no matter how brief and apparently slight, is individual and genuine. The simplicity and brevity may be deceptive at first glance, until one finds that the poems linger in the mind as clean-edged as sculpture, and that repeated reading only makes them the more precious. One then realizes that the simplicity is not weakness but the strength, needing no ornament or novelty of phrase, which speaks straight from poet to reader, mind to mind and heart to heart.

It was the keen intellectual force of Ina Coolbrith that made her the comrade of three generations of writers. When Bret Harte and his *Overland Monthly* associates first accepted her into their circle, it was not as a youthful prodigy, a pretty girl who happened to have literary aspirations, but as a colleague on an equal footing with experienced men. In middle life she was the chosen counsellor of such men as Joaquin Miller and Charles Warren Stoddard, who consulted her about their personal affairs as well as their writings, and respected the vigorous advice that she gave. And later, the younger writers, from Jack London and George Sterling onward to those who were sixty years or more her juniors, never regarded her as a condescending patroness or an antiquated survival; to them, too, she was an equal, mentally, of their own age. The evidence of this agelessness is in *Wings of Sunset,* in the poems of her later years which expertly employ the freer forms evolved within the last twenty years.

Accordingly, the estimate of her poetic stature must be based on the quality of the thought which her poems express. The most significant element in it is her clear perception of tragedy and suffering, of disappointment and frustration. There is bitter pathos in some of her poems on the transience of love and happiness, such as "A Meeting" and "Return," the poignance of ephemeral beauty in "The Dancers," stoic acceptance of the soul's isolation in "Alone" and "Alien." The lyric fragility and conciseness of these poems make their pathos all the more intense.

Regret and tragedy are not her predominant themes, but their presence in a number of her best poems proves that she honestly confronted the darker side of life; and by contrast her poems of faith and joy carry all the more conviction. She reveals two particular sources of confidence and strength—religion and nature. To her the Christian religion seems to have meant infinite love and fortitude surviving infinite pain and grief. Her two magnificent poems in Miltonic blank verse, showing what she could do in the "grand style," "God's Gethsemane," and "Lucifer," present that concept, as do "The Crucifixion, Still," "Redemption," "The Chosen Hour," and others. On the other hand, nature was to her overflowing with carefree rapture. The infectious joy of living expressed actually in the meter as well as the words and images, in such poems as "Flower o' the World," "In the Orchard," and "Opportunity," cannot but brighten the eye and speed the heart of any reader.

She is anything but a didactic poet, showing no trace of the egotism which leads many poets to fancy themselves prophets and teachers; yet a few of her lyrics reveal glimpses of a personal creed of universal brotherhood and spiritual evolution, based on man's unity with nature, which links her with those who are seeking a faith consistent with the modern scientific revelations. Such poems as "One," "Reincarnation," "Renewal," "After the Battles," and "Pan," display the insight and serene assurance of the elect to whom poetry has shown her face unveiled—the perfect harmony of emotion, beauty, and wisdom.

Appendix B
*Chronological List of Ina Coolbrith's Verse**

1856

August 30	My Childhood's Home
November 8	Ally

1857

January 31	Lines on the Recent Massacre
May 2	Lines to the Unknown
June 27	To M**tb*r
July 11	To Nelly
July 25	To *******
August 22	My Ideal Home
September 12	We Miss Thee at Home
November 7	One on Earth, and One in Heaven

All from *Los Angeles Star*

*Date indicates when the poem was composed or when it first appeared in print. Not all the poems can be dated exactly. Those noted under 1860, for example, are cited as they appear on early pages of Miss Coolbrith's *Scrapbooks* with titles of periodicals given but dates omitted. Approximate dates are followed by question marks. In some cases the first appearance in print occurred when a collection was published, 1881 for *A Perfect Day*, 1895 for *Songs from the Golden Gate*, and 1929 for the posthumous *Wings of Sunset*. There is thus a group of lyrics under each of these years. Most of the pieces listed under 1929 were actually composed between 1920 and 1923.

Editor's note: To avoid repeating references, we have given the names of the publications in which the poems appeared in the right hand column following the lists of poems, e.g., all from *Overland Monthly*.

1858

April 8	Little Elsie	*Southern Vineyard*
May 8	To "Harry Quillem"	
July 17	Ida Lee (written 1 June)	
August 21	One More Loved One Had Departed	
November 27	Little Fred (written 21 October)	

1859

June 4   How I Came to Be a Poet (written
                  3 May)

All from Los Angeles Star

1860?

Bring Music
Doubting
Embroidery
Leonore
A Moonlight Search for the Fairies
The Sleeping Maid
Stanzas (Down by the shores of
    the moonlit sea—first line)
To May

1861

July 11?   In the Night. To My Mother
All from California Home Journal

December 21   In Memoriam. Dr. T. J. White,
                  Died, December 17th, 1861

1862

November 22   Unrest (written in September)
From Los Angeles Star

1863

June 7	June
December 20	December
December 27	Christmas Eve, 1863

1864

March 13   Starr King

All from Golden Era

August 13	Cupid Kissed Me
November 5	Mists
November 19	Fragment from an Unfinished Poem
December 31	A Lost Day

1865

February 11	"In the Pouts"
March 25	The Mother's Grief
April	The Blossom of the South
	[Abraham Lincoln] (not published)
June 3	Hereafter
Undated	Spiders (in *Scrapbooks;* not published)

1866

February 23	Sunset
March 10	A Poet's Grave on Lone Mountain
April 14	The Sweetest Sound
June 16	Love in Little

All from *Californian*
San Francisco Alta

Undated   Daisies (in *Scrapbooks*)

1867

January 12	Heliotrope	*Californian*
February 15	Who Knoweth?	
April	At Peace	
June	Among the Daisies	
July	Wearisome	

All from *New York Galaxy*

1868

July	Longing
July	Heart of Our Hearts (written at this time; published in 1881 as The Faded Flower)
August	In Blossom Time
September	Siesta
September 9	The City by the Golden Gate (read at the eighteenth annual Admission Day celebration)
October	October
November	When the Grass Shall Cover Me

All from *Overland Monthly*

| December | December |

1869

January	Under the Christmas Snow
February	Rebuke
March	My "Cloth of Gold"
April	To-day (same as To-morrow Is Too Far Away)
May	Fulfillment
August	The Coming
September	Sufficient
October	I Cannot Count My Life a Loss
November	Ungathered
Undated	Invitation (in *Scrapbooks*)

1870

January	La Flor del Salvador
February	The Years
March	Not Yet
April	Dead
May	"While Lilies Bud and Blow"
July	Two Pictures (written this month; not published until 1881)
July	If Only
August	An Answer
September	With a Wreath of Laurel (written in July)
November	A Hope

1871

January	Just for a Day
February	An Emblem
April	Sometime
May	Oblivion
July 19	California (University of California Commencement Ode; read in Oakland)
August	In Adversity
September	Summons
October	From Year to Year
	Telling a Secret (not published)

All from *Overland Monthly*

1872

January	At the Hill's Base
February	The Road to School
March	The Brook
May	An Ending
July	Love-song
September	Loneliness
November	A Perfect Day

1873

January	Christmas Eve, 1872
February	After the Winter Rains
March	Two
June	Marah
August	Leaf and Blade
September	The Sea Shell
October	A Fancy
November	"One Touch of Nature"
December	Withheld

1874

January	How Looked the Earth?
March	Question and Answer
May	Respite
June	Hope (not the same as A Hope)
July	A Song of the Summer Wind
August	A Prayer for Strength (also with title A Prayer)
November	"Unto the Day"

1875

March	Discipline
May	Beside the Dead
June	Meadow-larks
July	No More
August	Ownership
October	In Time of Storm
November	Regret (also with title Freedom)
December	In Memoriam (To Benjamin P. Avery) (also with title At Rest)

All from *Overland Monthly*

1876

June 7	From Living Waters (University of California Commencement Ode; read in Berkeley)
December 26	When Spring Shall Come (not published until March 1882, in *Californian*)

1877

May 24	To .... (not published)
October 14	The Poet (dictated to J. H. Carmany; first published December 1885, in *Century*)
December 19	Fruitionless (not published until 1881)
1877?	To John Muir. Self Explanatory (in *Scrapbooks*)

1878

January 12	Renewed	*Argonaut*
May 24	A Birthday Rhyme. To .... (not published)	
May 24	Written for *** (Translation from Horace, Book I, Ode 38) (not published)	

1879

May 24	To .. .. (not published)

1880

March 20	Retrospect (not published until February 1886, in *Century*)
September	Forgotten

1881

March	A Night of Storm
April 1	Spring in the Desert (read at the Bohemian Club High Jinks)
May 30	Memorial Poem: Decoration Day (read in San Francisco, Decoration Day, 1881)
September	Be Happy, Happy, Little Maid

All from *Californian*

At Set of Sun
In Time of Falling Leaves
Sailed

Summer Past
To the Memory of My Mother

All from *A Perfect Day*

1881?   A Riddle (not published)

1882

July   James P. Bowman, Died April 29th, 1882   *Californian*
December 22 Our Poets (read at the *Overland Monthly*
            revival dinner; first published
            26 December 1882)   *San Francisco Daily Report*
            Peace (in *Scrapbooks;* not published until
            1929, in collection *Wings of Sunset*)

1883

January   Unattained   *Overland Monthly*
March   February   *Century Magazine*
March 31   Rev. Laurentine Hamilton (also with
            title The Truth Seeker)   *Oakland Tribune*
December 24 Poem to Jacob Milliken   Portland, Maine, *Press*

1884

February 21 Longfellow   *Oakland Tribune*
1884?   Rosemary, That's for Remembrance.
            To W. W. Crane
            (in *Scrapbooks;* not published)

1885

September   Helen Hunt Jackson   *Overland Monthly*
October   Mrs. Amila H. Lemmon (published in
            John Gill Lemmon, *In Memoriam*:
            Amila Hudson Lemmon, Oakland, 1885)
1885?   Woman in Age (in *Scrapbooks;* not
            published)

1886

January   Lines on Hearing Kelley's Music
            of "Macbeth"
March   March (By the Pacific)

From *Overland Monthly*

July   A Welcome to the Grand Army
            (in *Scrapbooks*)

December	The Colonel's Toast (for the Bohemian Club Christmas Jinks, 1886; printed as a pamphlet by Bosqui)	
	The Mariposa Lily (published in H. R. Chamberlain, *A Christmas Greeting*, San Francisco, 1886)	
	"The Soul of One Whose Creed Was Love" (published in Chamberlain, *A Christmas Greeting*)	
1886?	The Light in the Cottage at Stratford-on-Avon (in *Scrapbooks*; not published)	
1886?	A Question (in *Scrapbooks*)	

1887

April 10	Edwin Booth	*San Francisco Call*
June	Edward Rowland Sill	*Overland Monthly*
1887?	Julia Ward Howe (in *Scrapbooks*)	
1887?	On Reading Mrs. Burnett's "Little Lord Fauntleroy" (in *Scrapbooks*)	
1887?	To E. J. B. (Elizabeth J. Boalt) (in *Scrapbooks*)	

1888

January	A Birthday Rhyme	*Overland Monthly*
January	California Rain	*Oakland Tribune*
November	Frederick III of Germany	*Century Magazine*

1899

| April | A Leaf for Memory (M. E. P.) (Martha E. Powell) | |

1891

January	A New Leaf	
		From *Overland Monthly*
May	In Memoriam—John LeConte	
		California Educational Review
July	Elizabeth Wood, Arrived July 19th, 1891 (in *Scrapbooks*; not published)	
October	In the Library (read October 15; published in December 1891)	*Library Journal*
November 9	Just After Death (in *Scrapbooks*; unpublished)	

December 19	The Day of Our Lord	*Oakland Tribune*
December 25	Hymn of the Nativity	*San Francisco Examiner*
December	A Christmas Jingle	*San Francisco Wasp*

1892

April 14	"Sorrow Is Better than Laughter" (read at Bohemian Club breakfast for George Bromley's seventy-fifth birthday; published in G. T. Bromley, *The Long Ago and the Later On,* San Francisco, 1914)	
September	In the Grand Cañon	*Lippincott's Magazine*
December 25	The Millennium	*San Francisco Examiner*

1893

January 9	Lines Written on the Fly-leaf of My First Book of Verse (in J. H. Carmany's copy of *A Perfect Day;* not published)	
May 24	Copa de Oro (California Poppy)	*San Francisco Bulletin*
August	Bohemia (not published until 1929, in *Wings of Sunset*)	
Autumn	The Captive of the White City (published two years later in *Songs from the Golden Gate*)	
Autumn	Isabella of Spain (in *Scrapbooks*)	
December 25	Mid Winter East and West	*San Francisco Examiner*

1894

| October | The Flight of Song | *Century Magazine* |
| December | The Singer of the Sea (published as a booklet by the Century Club of San Francisco) | |

1895

March	Memory	*Scribner's*
November 2	To William Keith (presentation inscription)	*Songs from the Golden Gate*
November 3	A Last Word (To My Mother)	*San Francisco Examiner*
December	One (presentation inscription for Charles Lummis in *Songs from the Golden Gate,* not published until 1929)	
December 25	The Vision of Sir Francis Drake	*San Francisco Call*
	The Art of William Keith	
	At the Close	

At the Dawn
A Good-bye
The Lost Note
Quest
To a New Beatrice (B. A.)
The Unknown Great

All from Songs from the Golden Gate

1896

June 12	The Gold Seekers	*Oakland Enquirer*
July?	Heroes of '76 (in *Scrapbooks*)	
September 8	A Paper for the Convention	*Oakland Enquirer*
November 23	In Memoriam (for Kate Marshall Field; read at memorial services)	
December 20	The Crucifixion, Still	

1897

December 19   Redemption

From San Francisco Examiner

1897?   Poem in Memory of Helen Cornwall (read at Ebell Club meeting in Oakland)

1898

December   The California Year   *Land of Sunshine*

December 18   A Christmas Song (music by Oscar Weil)

San Francisco Call

The Blood of a Nation   California Club *War Poems, 1898*, San Francisco

1899

January 31   The Dead Artist, J. H. E. Partington

San Francisco Examiner

June 5   Thomas Moore   *San Francisco Star*

December 25   The Lay of the Lost Picture, Painfully Dedicated to William Keith (in *Scrapbooks*)

1899?   Calla (undated manuscript; published in 1929)

1899?   The "Juliet" of Miss Mather (in *Scrapbooks*)

1900

April   When Love Is Dead   *Current Literature*

April 6   Paderewski   *San Francisco Examiner*

1901

September   Joseph Le Conte   *University of California Magazine*

1902

June 29	A Page of Herrick	*San Francisco Call*
September	Bret Harte	*Overland Monthly*
October	The Cactus Hedge	

1903

April   William Keith, Artist

           From *Out West*

October 8   With the Laurel to Edmund Clarence Stedman on His Seventieth Birthday (not published
until August 1908, in *Atlantic Monthly*)

1903?   Loma Alta (in *Scrapbooks;* published in
1929 in *Wings of Sunset*)

1904

June 30   Rose and Thistle (not published until 1929)

September 3   In Memoriam of Fanny DeC. Miller Who
Died in Florence, Italy, March 22, 1903

       San Francisco Monitor

October   The Wind's Word   *Sunset Magazine*

L'Envoi   C. P. Nettleton, *A Voice from the Silence*,
San Francisco, 1904

The Lot of Christ   *San Jose Normal Pennant*

1905

July   Wood-call   *Sunset Magazine*

California (a Prophecy)   A. E. Krebs, *La Copa de
Oro*, San Francisco, 1905

1906

February	Henry Holmes	*Sunset Magazine*
October	San Francisco, April 18, 1906	*Putnam's Magazine*
October 27	The Sea	
October 27	The Sea's Answer	

       From *Once a Week*

1906?   The Gardens of God (in *Scrapbooks*)

1906?   My Brother's Keeper (in *Scrapbooks*)

1907

December	Alcatraz	*Overland Monthly*
December	Whittier, 1807-1907 (written for Whittier program in Palo Alto)	

1908

February	George Washington	*Philopolis*

1909

May	Renewal	*Century Magazine*
August	Opportunity	*Munsey's Magazine*
August 22	At Carmel (also with title Carmel-by-the-Sea)	*Oakland Tribune*
December	Evenfall at the Gate	*Sunset Magazine*
December	Harriet M. Skidmore	*Notre Dame Quarterly*

1910

March 15	Santa Clara Valley	*Santa Clara News*
November 9	Woman	*San Francisco Post*

1911

May	Mount Hamilton	*Sunset Magazine*

1912

June	After	
June	Birthday Verses (For Mrs. Elizabeth Lightner)	
June	Carrie Stevens Walter	
June	Who	
		All from *Notre Dame Quarterly*
June 26	Greeting	*San Francisco Call*
September	To Gertrude Atherton (not published; read at a dinner party for Mrs. Atherton)	

1913

May 26	Vale, Joaquin	*San Francisco Call;* also *San Francisco Examiner*
June	At Anchor (not published until November 1914 in *Overland Monthly*)	
1913	The Garden's Story	*Green Star Magazine*

394

1914

May	On a Fly-leaf of Omar	*Catholic World*
May	Point Bonita	*Overland Monthly*
September 21	War and Peace	*San Francisco Examiner*
December 12	A Tribute (to Caroline M. Severance)	*California Outlook*

1915

February 28	To Edwin Markham (not published)	
August	From Russian Hill	*Sunset Magazine*

1917

January	A Prayer for the Year	*St. Ignatius Church Calendar*
1917?	In the Midst of War	*Everywoman*

1918

June 1   Tribute to the Convent and College of
the Holy Names   *San Francisco Monitor*
Friendship   (in E. S. Mighels, *Literary California*,
San Francisco, 1918)
Soldiers of Freedom (manuscript auctioned
at Red Cross benefit in Oakland Auditorium)

1919

December 2   Love's Worth (not published until 1929)
Love's Age (not published until 1929)

1920

January?   The Dancers (not published until 1929, in
Wings of Sunset)
January   Listening Back (published in December
of 1920)   *Sunset Magazine*
April   Return (not published until 1929)
April 10   "They Shall Be Satisfied" (not
published until 1929)

1921

March	Alien	*Overland Monthly*
Spring	Felipe (not published until 1929 in *Wings of Sunset*)	

Spring	Pancho (not published until 1929 in *Wings of Sunset*)	
December 3	Foch: California's Greeting	*San Francisco Bulletin*

1922

November	Concha (completed this month; not published until 1929 in *Wings of Sunset*)
	To the Bohemian Club (manuscript on flyleaf of *Songs from the Golden Gate*, presented to the Bohemian Club)

1923

February	March Hares (birthday poem for Charles Lummis; published in *Overland Monthly*, June 1924)	
April	In the Orchard	*Sunset Magazine*
November	Twenty-two (not published; manuscript in Mrs. Ina Graham's collection, Berkeley, California)	

1924

July 12	The Call of the Forests	*San Francisco Wasp*
1924?	To Frances (manuscript in Bancroft Library, University of California, Berkeley)	

1925

July	Pan	*Pan, Poetry and Youth*
September 10	California Jubilee Poem	*San Francisco Examiner*

1926

April 17	Luther Burbank	*Argonaut*
July	With the Caravan	*University of California Chronicle*
October	Mexico (published in 1929 in *Wings of Sunset*)	
October 12	Portolá Speaks (under title Quest of the Bay)	
		San Francisco Examiner
1926?	Robin (published in 1929 in *Wings of Sunset*)	

November	George Sterling	*Overland Monthly*

November   The Vision of St. Francis (published
                   in 1929 in *Wings of Sunset*)

Undated   **1929***

Across the Chasm
After the Battles
All
Alone
Atom
The Birds
The Birth of Love
The Bribe
Came to My Side
The Chosen Hour
Christmas Roses
Ecce Homo
Flower o' the World
The Funeral
God's Gethsemane
The Green Coverlet
Haunted
Honey-throats
'Hope Deferred'
If I Have Never Loved Before
Immortals
Lady Moon
Life's Purpose
Lost Love
Lucifer
A Meeting
My House
My Kindred
The Night Watch
The Night Wind
'One Little Song'

All from *Wings of Sunset*

---

*Published in Miss Coolbrith's posthumous collection, *Wings of Sunset,* many of these lyrics were written, but not dated, during her winters in New York City from the autumn of 1919 to the spring of 1923.

1929

Only a Rose
Passed (H. C.)
Reincarnation
Sahara
The Shadowed Room
Songs of Content
To San Francisco
Unheeded
The Unsolvable
The Watcher
With a La France Rose

All from *Wings of Sunset*

Appendix C

*Ina Coolbrith's Lyrics Set to Music**

Beach, Amy M. C. *In Blossom Time*. New York, Schirmer, 1917.
—————. *Meadow-larks*. New York, Schirmer, 1917.
Bullock, Flora. *In Blossom Time*. Undated manuscript.
Cahill, August M. *At the Dawn*.
    This and the following song, mentioned by Mrs. Ina L. Cook
in a list in the Bancroft Library, were lent by her but were apparently not returned.
—————. *When the Grass Shall Cover Me*.
Cator, Thomas V. *Quest*. Undated manuscript.
Emerson, Mabel Day. *Beside the Dead*. Undated manuscript.
Foerster, Adolph M. *Among Flowers; Songs for a Soprano or Tenor Voice*. Pittsburgh, Kleber, 1889.
    "In Blossom Time," by Ina Coolbrith, pp. 24-25.
Haines-Kuester, Edith. *Daisies* . . . 11 March 1916. Manuscript.
Hausmann, Rosalia L. *Love Song*. San Francisco, 1913. Manuscript.
Henschel, George. *No More*. London, Boosey, 1900.
Needham, Alicia Adelaide. *In Blossom Time*. New York, Schirmer, 1898.
Pasmore, Henry Bickford. *Eight Songs*. Berkeley, Pasmore Studio, 1931.
    "Daisies," by Ina Coolbrith, pp. 3-5.
Pendleton, Emmet. *Eight Songs from the Sunny Shores of the Golden Gate*, Opus eight, "No More," words by Ina Coolbrith. Red Bluff, California, n.d.

---

*Listed by composer. Items in Bancroft Library, University of California, Berkeley, unless otherwise noted. Most of them were the gift of Mrs. Ina L. Cook, the poet's niece.

On the title page of this manuscript seven other lyrics by Ina Coolbrith are listed but not included: "A Hope," "Tomorrow Is Too Far Away," "A Memory," "A Good-by," "Who Knoweth?" "Respite," and "If Only."

Powell, Mrs. Watkin A. *Cupid Kissed Me.* Philadelphia, Hatch, 1897.

Proctor, David. *How Long Ago, My Love!* 1922. Manuscript.

Stewart, H. J. *Hymn of the Nativity.* Boston, Ditson, 1900.

Trace, Gertrude. *In Blossom Time,* as sung by Miss Nella Rogers on Ina Coolbrith Day at the Women's Club, San Jose, California, 1907. Manuscript.

Weil, Oscar. "Christmas Song," *San Francisco Call,* 25 December 1898. Newspaper on file in Bancroft Library, Berkeley; also in California state Library, Sacramento. A clipping of the song is in Miss Coolbrith's *Scrapbooks,* Oakland Free Library.

Genealogical Chart of the Smith and Coolbrith Families

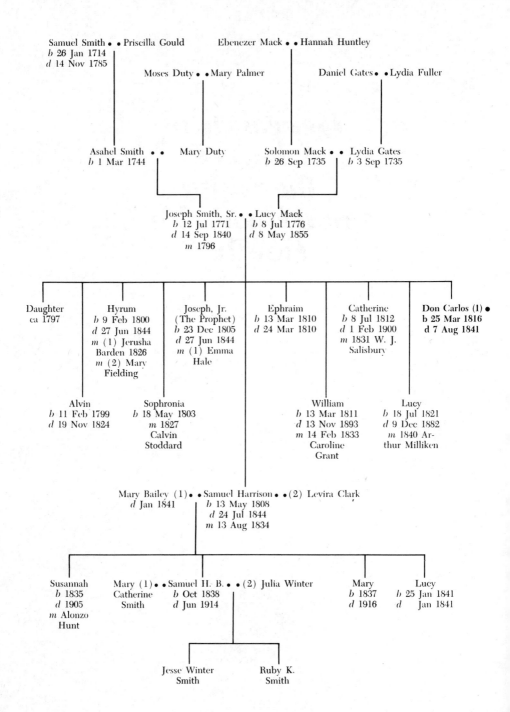

Samuel Smith • • Priscilla Gould
b 26 Jan 1714
d 14 Nov 1785

Ebenezer Mack • • Hannah Huntley

Moses Duty • • Mary Palmer

Daniel Gates • • Lydia Fuller

Asahel Smith • •   Mary Duty
b 1 Mar 1744

Solomon Mack • • Lydia Gates
b 26 Sep 1735   b 3 Sep 1735

Joseph Smith, Sr. • • Lucy Mack
b 12 Jul 1771   b 8 Jul 1776
d 14 Sep 1840   d 8 May 1855
m 1796

Daughter
ca 1797

Hyrum
b 9 Feb 1800
d 27 Jun 1844
m (1) Jerusha
Barden 1826
m (2) Mary
Fielding

Joseph, Jr.
(The Prophet)
b 23 Dec 1805
d 27 Jun 1844
m (1) Emma
Hale

Ephraim
b 13 Mar 1810
d 24 Mar 1810

Catherine
b 8 Jul 1812
d 1 Feb 1900
m 1831 W. J.
Salisbury

Don Carlos (1) •
b 25 Mar 1816
d 7 Aug 1841

Alvin
b 11 Feb 1799
d 19 Nov 1824

Sophronia
b 18 May 1803
m 1827
Calvin
Stoddard

William
b 13 Mar 1811
d 13 Nov 1893
m 14 Feb 1833
Caroline
Grant

Lucy
b 18 Jul 1821
d 9 Dec 1882
m 1840 Ar-
thur Milliken

Mary Bailey (1) • • Samuel Harrison • • (2) Levira Clark
d Jan 1841   b 13 May 1808
                   d 24 Jul 1844
                   m 13 Aug 1834

Susannah
b 1835
d 1905
m Alonzo
Hunt

Mary (1) • • Samuel H. B. • • (2) Julia Winter
Catherine   b Oct 1838
Smith   d Jun 1914

Mary
b 1837
d 1916

Lucy
b 25 Jan 1841
d   Jan 1841

Jesse Winter
Smith

Ruby K.
Smith

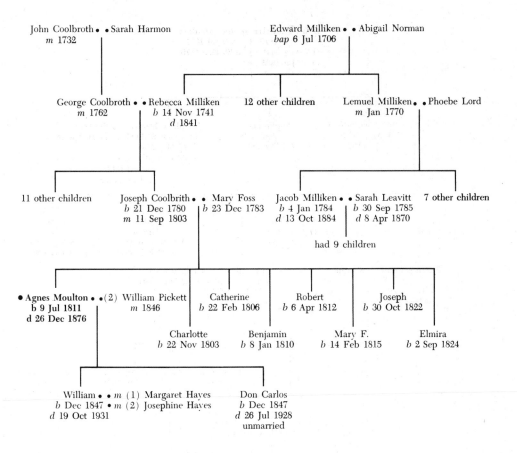

John Coolbroth • • Sarah Harmon
m 1732

Edward Milliken • • Abigail Norman
bap 6 Jul 1706

George Coolbroth • • Rebecca Milliken
m 1762
b 14 Nov 1741
d 1841

12 other children

Lemuel Milliken • • Phoebe Lord
m Jan 1770

11 other children

Joseph Coolbrith • • Mary Foss
b 21 Dec 1780
m 11 Sep 1803
b 23 Dec 1783

Jacob Milliken • • Sarah Leavitt
b 4 Jan 1784
d 13 Oct 1884
b 30 Sep 1785
d 8 Apr 1870

7 other children

had 9 children

• Agnes Moulton • •(2) William Pickett
b 9 Jul 1811
d 26 Dec 1876
m 1846

Catherine
b 22 Feb 1806

Robert
b 6 Apr 1812

Joseph
b 30 Oct 1822

Charlotte
b 22 Nov 1803

Benjamin
b 8 Jan 1810

Mary F.
b 14 Feb 1815

Elmira
b 2 Sep 1824

William • • m (1) Margaret Hayes
b Dec 1847 • m (2) Josephine Hayes
d 19 Oct 1931

Don Carlos
b Dec 1847
d 26 Jul 1928
unmarried

DAR of California, *Collections*, vols. 12, 17 (Los Angeles, 1942, 1953).

G. T. Ridlon, *Saco Valley Settlements and Families* (Portland, Me., 1895).

Saco, Maine, City Council, *First Book of Records of the Town of Pepperrellborough, now the City of Saco* (Saco, 1895).

E. M. Skinner, *Joseph Smith, Sr., First Patriarch of the Church.* (Provo, Utah, 1948).

Lucy Mack Smith, *Biographical Sketches of Joseph Smith, the Prophet and his Progenitors* (Lamoni, Iowa, 1912).

403

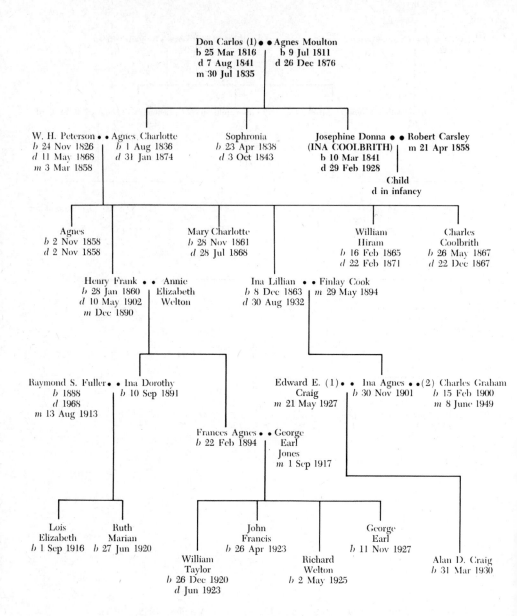

Don Carlos (1) ● ● Agnes Moulton
b 25 Mar 1816 | b 9 Jul 1811
d 7 Aug 1841 | d 26 Dec 1876
m 30 Jul 1835

W. H. Peterson ● ● Agnes Charlotte
b 24 Nov 1826 | b 1 Aug 1836
d 11 May 1868 | d 31 Jan 1874
m 3 Mar 1858

Sophronia
b 23 Apr 1838
d 3 Oct 1843

Josephine Donna ● ● Robert Carsley
(INA COOLBRITH) | m 21 Apr 1858
b 10 Mar 1841
d 29 Feb 1928

Child
d in infancy

Agnes
b 2 Nov 1858
d 2 Nov 1858

Mary Charlotte
b 28 Nov 1861
d 28 Jul 1868

William
Hiram
b 16 Feb 1865
d 22 Feb 1871

Charles
Coolbrith
b 26 May 1867
d 22 Dec 1867

Henry Frank ● ● Annie
b 28 Jan 1860 | Elizabeth
d 10 May 1902 | Welton
m Dec 1890

Ina Lillian ● ● Finlay Cook
b 8 Dec 1863 | m 29 May 1894
d 30 Aug 1932

Raymond S. Fuller ● ● Ina Dorothy
b 1888 | b 10 Sep 1891
d 1968
m 13 Aug 1913

Edward E. (1) ● ● Ina Agnes ● ●(2) Charles Graham
Craig | b 30 Nov 1901 | b 15 Feb 1900
m 21 May 1927 | m 8 June 1949

Frances Agnes ● ● George
b 22 Feb 1894 | Earl
Jones
m 1 Sep 1917

Lois
Elizabeth
b 1 Sep 1916

Ruth
Marian
b 27 Jun 1920

John
Francis
b 26 Apr 1923

George
Earl
b 11 Nov 1927

Alan D. Craig
b 31 Mar 1930

William
Taylor
b 26 Dec 1920
d Jun 1923

Richard
Welton
b 2 May 1925

404

Notes
and
Sources

Prologue: The Crossing of the Mountains

1. James P. Beckwourth, *Life and Adventures*, pp. 355-58; Mildred B. Hoover, *Historic Spots in California*, pp. 137-38, 142. The latter source quotes Ina Coolbrith's own account of Beckwourth and his mountain pass, as related by her in 1927.

Part One: Nauvoo to the Western Sea

Chapter 1: Roads to Nauvoo

The quotation at the beginning of the chapter is from Ina Coolbrith's lyric, "Sorrow is Better than Laughter," written for George Bromley's seventy-fifth birthday, 14 April 1892, and read at a Bohemian Club breakfast by Daniel O'Connell. The poem was published in George T. Bromley, *The Long Ago and the Later On* (San Francisco, 1904), also in Ina Coolbrith, *Wings of Sunset*, pp. 32-33.

1. For the date of her birth see note 6, chapter 3, *infra.*
2. Ina Coolbrith was christened Josephine Donna Smith, but was called "Ina" by her mother and, later on, by her stepbrothers. Her namesakes, relatives named in her honor, were all "Ina," not "Josephine." In the Los Angeles County District Court, Case #853, Ina was used in the mother's testimony. Ina was her *nom de plume* in Los Angeles; in San Francisco she adopted the name "Ina Donna Coolbrith," using her mother's maiden name as a surname. She herself would have regarded "Josephine Smith" a poor name for a poet. Ina was pronounced *Eye-na*, not *Ee-na*, according to her grandniece, Mrs. Ina Graham, of Berkeley, California.
3. She was born 8 July 1776.
4. Lucy Mack Smith, *Biographical Sketches of Joseph Smith the Prophet and His Progenitors for Many Generations;* the first edition (Liverpool, 1853) was condemned in 1865 by the Mormon Church in Salt Lake City as unauthorized, and an edition based on corrections made in 1865 appeared in Salt Lake City in 1900. The Reorganized Church of Jesus Christ of Latter Day Saints of Lamoni, Iowa, published editions in 1908 and 1912; the 1912 edition is the one cited in these notes. For the ancestry of Don Carlos Smith, father of Ina Coolbrith, see also Stanford J. Robinson, *Mormon Genealogy*, and *Utah Genealogical and Historical Magazine* 20:8-11; 26:101-2.
5. Lucy Mack Smith.
6. Fawn M. Brodie, *No Man Knows My History*, p. 87; Alma P. Burton, *Mormon Trail from Vermont to Utah*, p. 28; Joseph Smith, *History of The Church of Jesus Christ of Latter-day Saints.* The question of church revivals is a controversial one, especially in western New York state; see Milton V. Backman, *American Religions and the Rise of Mormonism* (Salt Lake City, 1965), pp. 290, 302, 311. The literature of the Mormon Church is extensive. Of the many works consulted, those of most use in the preparation of this volume will be found in the bibliography.
7. Brodie, p. 98; Robert Mullen, *The Latter-day Saints* (New York, 1966), p. 31; Joseph Smith, 1:139-40, 142, 145-46; Lucy Mack Smith, pp. 209-33.
8. Brodie, pp. 122-24.
9. Ruby K. Smith, *Mary Bailey*, p. 26.
10. Ibid.
11. Dorothy S. Libbey, *Scarborough Becomes a Town;* G. T. Ridlon, *Saco Valley Settlements and Families.*
12. DAR of California, *Collections*, 17:101; Ridlon, pp. 584-90; Saco, Maine, City Council, *First Book of Records of the Town of Pepperellborough*, pp. 16-19. The date of the birth of Agnes Moulton Coolbrith is given variously. Her granddaughter, Ina Lillian Cook (Mrs. Finlay Cook), used 11 July 1811 from a Bible, letters,

and other sources in the family. This is the date given in the records of the Mountain View Cemetery in Oakland, also in the *Utah Genealogical and Historical Magazine* 26:105. G. T. Ridlon, in consulting Saco town records, found 9 July 1808 as Agnes Coolbrith's birth date. She herself in December 1861, in the Los Angeles District Court Case #853, stated that she was fifty-one years of age, making her birth year 1810. In the text of this book we have preferred to use 11 July 1811.

13. Ruby K. Smith, p. 10. Also from personal interview with Jesse Winter Smith of San Jose, California. Ruby K. Smith and Jesse Winter Smith, sister and brother, are grandchildren of Mary Bailey Smith. Ruby K. and J. Winter Smith were thus first cousins once removed of Ina Coolbrith.

14. Ruby K. Smith, pp. 29-30.

15. Ruby K. Smith, pp. 32-35; Lucy Mack Smith, p. 249.

Chapter 2: Kirtland to Nauvoo

The quotation at the beginning of the chapter is from Ina Coolbrith's "Memorial Poem," read in San Francisco on 31 May 1881. It is included in her collection, *Songs from the Golden Gate*, pp. 99-103.

1. Ruby K. Smith, *Mary Bailey*, pp. 32-35; Lucy Mack Smith, *Biographical Sketches of Joseph Smith the Prophet and His Progenitors for Many Generations*, p. 249.

2. Joseph Smith, *History of The Church of Jesus Christ of Latter-day Saints*, 1:446, 4:393-97.

3. Based on photograph, also on description given to Mrs. Ina Graham by her mother, Agnes Smith's granddaughter.

4. DAR of California, *Collections*, 17:101; *Utah Genealogical and Historical Magazine* 26(July 1935):105. See also family group sheet in E. M. Skinner, *Joseph Smith, Sr.* (Provo, Utah, 1948).

5. DAR of California, 17:101; *Utah Genealogical and Historical Magazine* 26:105.

6. Fawn Brodie, *No Man Knows My History*, p. 205.

7. *Utah Genealogical and Historical Magazine* 26:105, gives 24 May 1838 but this is incorrect. A letter from Don Carlos Smith to his brother Joseph states that the baby was two weeks old on 7 May 1838, the day the family left Norton, Ohio, for Missouri. A copy of this letter is on file in the LDS Church Historical Department in Salt Lake City. It is reproduced in Ruby K. Smith, p. 65, and in Joseph Smith, 3:443.

8. Ruby K. Smith, pp. 65-66.

9. Joseph Smith, 3:443, 4:393-99.

10. Joseph Smith, 3:39.

11. Ruby K. Smith, pp. 70-71.

12. Joseph Smith, 3:84-85.

13. U. S. 26th Congress, 2d Session, House of Representatives. *Petition of the Latter-day Saints . . . December 21, 1840*, House Document 22, p. 9; Joseph Smith 3:163-64; Ruby K. Smith, pp. 69-70; *Times and Seasons*, 1:98. Also recorded in *Notes on the Church History* on file in the Church Historical Department in Salt Lake City. The incident of Agnes Smith taking her infants across the Grand River is related in most of the histories of the Mormon Church.

14. *Petition*, pp. 1-13; Brodie, pp. 234-35; Joseph Smith, 3:189.

15. Lucy Mack Smith, pp. 364-65, quotation from a journal of Don Carlos Smith.

16. *Notes on the Church History*, Joseph Smith, 3:164.

17. Joseph Smith, 3:261; Lucy Mack Smith, p. 322.

18. Joseph Smith, 3:273. Copies of letters from Don Carlos and Agnes Smith, in Quincy, Illinois, 6 March and 11 April 1839 to Joseph and Hyrum Smith in Liberty Jail, Missouri, are on file in *Notes on the Church History*, in the Church Historical Department, Salt Lake City.

19. Joseph Smith, 3:375.

Chapter 3: Birth and Death in Nauvoo

The quotation at the beginning of this chapter is from Ina Coolbrith's "Memorial Poem," read in San Francisco on 31 May 1881. It is included in her collection, *Songs From the Golden Gate*, pp. 99-103.

1. Lucy Mack Smith, *Biographical Sketches of Joseph Smith the Prophet and His Progenitors for Many Generations*, p. 369.
2. Lucy Mack Smith, pp. 369-71, quotes a letter in full from Don C. Smith, in Commerce, 25 July 1839, to his wife in Macomb, Illinois; *Nauvoo Times and Seasons*, 1:1-2, editorial by E. Robinson and D. C. Smith on the buried type. *Times and Seasons* was a monthly newspaper, subscription one dollar a year. (A complete file, originally the property of Newel K. Whitney and bearing his signature, is in the library of the Utah Historical Society in Salt Lake City.) The first *Times and Seasons* building was one of the three original frame houses in Commerce, when the land was acquired by Joseph Smith (as related in his *History of The Church of Jesus Christ of Latter-day Saints*, 3:375), and is no longer standing. The site of the second building was at Bain and Water streets, and of the third, now restored, on Main Street at Kimball. (Based on a visit to the site and information from Mr. and Mrs. C. Dewey Hale, officials of Nauvoo Restoration, Inc., Nauvoo, Illinois.)
3. Federal Writers' Project, *Nauvoo Guide;* Robert B. Flanders, *Nauvoo;* Gustavus Hill, *Map of the City of Nauvoo,* [published during Joseph Smith's lifetime]; Elmer C. McGavin, *Nauvoo the Beautiful;* Lucy Mack Smith, pp. 335-43.
4. Hubert H. Bancroft, *History of Utah*, p. 143; Thomas Ford, *A History of Illinois,* 1:61, note; *Times and Seasons*, 15 January 1841; U. S. 26th Congress, 2d Session, *Petition of the Latter-day Saints . . . December 21, 1840,* House Document 22, p. 9.
5. Ruby K. Smith, *Mary Bailey*, pp. 87-88; *Times and Seasons*, 2:324, (Obituary of Mary Bailey Smith, by Don Carlos Smith).
6. For the correct date of Ina Coolbrith's birth, 10 March 1841, the following authorities are cited: Ina L. Cook, "Ina Donna Coolbrith," *Westward* 1:3-5; Cook, *Oakland Tribune*, 20 May 1928; DAR of California, *Collections*, 17:101; *Utah Genealogical and Historical Magazine*, 26(July 1935):105, Franklin Walker, *San Francisco's Literary Frontier*, p. 59. The Library of Congress and the *Dictionary of American Biography*, in error, give 1842, though this was later corrected in the *Concise Dictionary* (1964), p. 187. It is well known that Ina Coolbrith was five months old when her father died on 7 August 1841.
7. Joseph Smith, *History*, 4:399.
8. *Notes on the Church History,* in the Church Historical Department, Salt Lake City; *Quincy Whig*, Vol. 4, no. 19, p. 2; B. H. Roberts, *A Comprehensive History of the Church*, 2:42-43; Joseph Smith, *History*, 4:393-99; Lucy Mack Smith, pp. 345-71; *Times and Seasons*, 2:503-4, *Utah Genealogical and Historical Magazine* 26 (July 1935):105.
9. Letter from Don Carlos Smith in Commerce 25 July 1839 to his wife in Macomb, Illinois, quoted by Lucy Mack Smith, p. 370.
10. Advertisements and editorials in *Times and Seasons* after 7 August 1841; McGavin, p. 201.
11. Lucy Mack Smith, p. 348; *Utah Genealogical and Historical Magazine*, 26 (July 1935):105. Population estimates of Nauvoo vary, see *Times and Seasons*, 3 (1 April 1842):750, also Flanders, pp. 51, note; 56, note.
12. Bancroft, pp. 170-76; Alma P. Burton, *Mormon Trail from Vermont to Utah*, pp. 52-57; John S. Fullmer, *Assassination of Joseph and Hyrum Smith*. This event is described in detail in all histories of the church and biographies of Joseph and Hyrum Smith.
13. Bancroft, p. 215; Ruby K. Smith, p. 105; *Times and Seasons* 1:1018.
14. Bancroft, p. 218.

15. Letter from Agnes M. Smith to George A. Smith (Spring, 1846) quoted by McGavin, p. 201. "Emma's garden" is the family cemetery, back of the Joseph Smith Homestead, at Main and Water streets in Nauvoo.

16. Fawn Brodie, *No Man Knows My History*, p. 342; Federal Writers Project, *Nauvoo Guide*, p. 12; Lucy Mack Smith, p. 96, note; Ruby K. Smith, p. 97.

17. Bancroft, pp. 225-31; Ina Coolbrith, Memo in her *Scrapbooks*, 1:131.

18. Bancroft, pp. 225-31.

19. DAR of California, *Collections*, 12:296, 17:101; McGavin, p. 202. Whether they were married in Nauvoo or St. Louis is not known. No certificates are on file in either Hancock County, Illinois, or St. Louis County, Missouri (according to letters in our files from R. L. McDaniel, Hancock County Clerk and Recorder, 18 June 1968 and from E. J. Pung, St. Louis County Recorder, 17 June 1968).

20. Cook, *Westward*, 1(May 1928):3. In an interview in 1953, a relative of Ina Coolbrith, Jesse Winter Smith, stated that Agnes Pickett made this promise to her husband and persuaded her children to keep it as long as they lived.

21. Interview between Miss Coolbrith and Mira Maclay, *Oakland Tribune*, 2 March 1924; Cook, 1:4.

22. The twins were born 11 December 1847; letter in Huntington Library, San Marino, California, dated 15 December 1926 from Don C. Pickett to Ina Coolbrith. In the Los Angeles County District Court, in December 1861 (Case #853) Don Carlos and William, Junior, gave their ages as fourteen, on pp. 5 and 7 of the testimony. *San Francisco Chronicle*, 28 July 1928, states that Don Carlos Pickett was seventy when he died July 26; he would have been seventy-one in December of that year. St. Louis birth records go back to 1870 only (according to letter in our files from D. R. Patterson of the Bureau of Vital Statistics, St. Louis, Mo., July 1968).

23. "The blood-stained couch of death"; from her autobiographical poem, "In the Night," written in Los Angeles when she was twenty; one stanza:

> For mid scenes of desolation
> Drew I first life's feeble breath,
> And my earliest recollection
> Is the blood-stained couch of death.

The verse, written for her mother's fiftieth birthday, mentioned her father's and sister's graves, "side by side." Miss Coolbrith told Mira Maclay (*Oakland Tribune*, 2 March 1924) that her first memory was of her sister's funeral. "In the Night" appears in Ina Coolbrith, *Scrapbooks*, 1:7.

24. Ernest Kirschten, *Catfish and Crystal*, pp. 156-61; M. Quigley, *St. Louis, the First Two Hundred Years;* John T. Scharf, *History of St. Louis, City and County*, vol. 1.

25. Kirschten; Quigley; Scharf.

26. Joseph E. Ware, *The Emigrants' Guide to California.*

27. *St. Louis Republican* [Information about the California Emigrants and California of the Gold Rush Era; Correspondence from St. Joseph, Mo., and Independence, Mo., by the Correspondent, "California."]. Bancroft Library, Berkeley, has photocopy of *St. Louis Republican* of the pages in this series from 7 April to 17 May 1849. Ina Coolbrith, in a letter to her niece, dated 17 March 1914 (in possession of Mrs. Ina Graham, Berkeley, California), said that her stepfather went to California in 1849 and returned in the fall of 1851 to take his family west in the spring of 1852(actually 1851).

Chapter 4: Overland to California

The quotation is from "Portolá Speaks," a lyric by Ina Coolbrith, which was published in the *San Francisco Examiner* of 12 October 1926 with the title "Quest of the Bay." In Ina Coolbrith, *Wings of Sunset*, pp. 6-7, the former title is used.

1. Documentation for this chapter is meager, because information on the part the Pickett family played on the Overland Trail is slight. While the literature of the Overland is rich and informative, and there are minute and on-the-spot descriptions of nearly every point of interest passed on the various trails and cutoffs to California, the family itself did not keep a journal. Moreover neither the Pickett family nor the Smith girls appear to have been mentioned in diaries kept by other migrants. We thus do not know with which party they traveled. Ina Coolbrith was a child of ten when the journey was made. She remembered what she herself felt, terror of the fords, anquish for starved and drowning oxen, delight in the beauty of the plains and the mountains, fear of possible Indian attack, fright when lost in the desert, elation when selected by Jim Beckwourth to ride with him and be "the first white child" to cross the Sierra by his newly opened pass. These feelings she later expressed many times. But for the dates, the routes followed, the names of places, she was dependent on what she was told by her elders. And with the passage of time these "facts" could have become vague or distorted. Thus she, her family, and her friends all have said that the trip was made in 1852, but the year was actually 1851, the year the Beckwourth Pass was opened. Other contradictions cloud the account, with Miss Coolbrith having added as much to the confusion as anyone else. In 1914 she told her niece that the family made the trip in three months, arriving at Spanish Ranch on 4 July 1852 thus leaving Beckwourth quite out of the picture. Her usual version gave seven and one-half months to the journey and brought the travelers to Spanish Ranch in September (Mildred B. Hoover, *Historic Spots in California*, pp. 137-38). She once reported that they came through Salt Lake City and were even met there by Beckwourth, though she usually agreed with his account that the meeting took place at the Truckee River (*Oakland Tribune*, 2 March 1924). Some others stated that the Mormon city was on the itinerary (Annaleone D. Patton, *California Mormons*, pp. 149-72); and others implied that the family did not come that way (Ruby K. Smith, *Mary Bailey*, p. 106). Since the route by way of Salt Lake City would have increased the travel time and difficulty, it seems unlikely that William Pickett would have come that way, only to bring his wife again into the Mormon relationship that he had urged her to forget. Whatever the route they chose, it is true that they were on the Beckwourth Pass in the autumn of 1851. Chapter 4, then, is an account of what *might* have been, as a setting for what little we actually know.
2. *St. Louis Republican* [Information about the California emigrants and California of the Gold Rush era; correspondence from St. Joseph, Mo., and Independence, Mo., by the correspondent, "California."]
3. George R. Stewart, *The California Trail*, pp. 302-3.
4. James P. Beckwourth, *Life and Adventures*, p. 358.
5. Beckwourth, pp. 355-58.
6. Hoover, pp. 137-38, 142; this gives Miss Coolbrith's own account of the incident as related by her in 1927. See also Stewart, pp. 302-3; also May Dornin, "The Emigrant Trails into California."

Chapter 5: *The Glittering Lure*

The quotation is from Miss Coolbrith's poem, "The Gold Seekers," published in the *Oakland Enquirer*, 12 June 1896, also in Ina Coolbrith, *Wings of Sunset*, pp. 40-43.

1. James Beckwourth, *Life and Adventures of James P. Beckwourth*, p. 359.
2. Information from J. Winter Smith of San Jose, California, in a personal interview in 1953.
3. Farris and Smith, *Illustrated History of Plumas, Lassen and Sierra Counties*, with view of Spanish Ranch in the fifties, pp. 137, 250.
4. James P. Beckwourth, *Life and Adventures*, pp. 358-59; May Dornin, "The Emigrant Trails into California," pp. 165-69.

5. California. State Mining Bureau, *Mines and Mineral Resources of Sierra County*, p. 92; California. Division of Mines, *Mining in California*, April 1929, p. 178; U. S. Forest Service, [*Map*] *Plumas National Forest*, shows Howland Flat in relation to Spanish Ranch, also shows Beckwourth Pass and Mt. Ina Coolbrith.

6. Jeanne E. Francoeur, "Ina Coolbrith, Our Poet, in the Past and Present," *Woman Citizen* 1(1913):106-7. This is the account as dictated to her by Miss Coolbrith.

7. Thompson and West, *History of Yuba County, California*, pp. 44-46; Ina Coolbrith, *Memo* (in Coolbrith Papers, California Room, Oakland Free Library).

8. Mrs. D. B. Bates, *Four Years on the Pacific Coast*, chapters 12-25 on Marysville, California, 1851-54.

9. Thompson and West, p. 44-46, 75.

10. Francoeur, pp. 106-7.

11. Francoeur.

12. Ina Coolbrith in a letter to her niece, Mrs. Ina L. Cook, 17 March 1914, in possession of Mrs. Ina Graham of Berkeley, Calif.; Coolbrith, *Memo*.

13. There is some confusion about this story. Ina Coolbrith and her little brothers were lost one night in the forest. But when? There are two accounts, one by Henry Meade Bland in the *Oakland Tribune*, 31 July 1921, and the other by George Wharton James in "Ina Donna Coolbrith," *National Magazine* 26(June 1907): 315-22. Bland said she was lost while the family was still on the Overland Trail; James placed the setting in the mining camp a year later. Both these authors were inclined to exaggerate and embroider the facts. The article by James was pasted in full in Miss Coolbrith's *Scrapbooks*, 2:10-11, without comment by her, and may be presumed to be correct in the main. It is the version used in these pages.

14. Hale and Emory, *Marysville City Directory*, August, 1853.

15. Thompson and West, pp. 67-68.

16. Hale and Emory, p. 37; Ina Coolbrith, letter to her niece, 17 March 1914, also Coolbrith, *Memo*; J. Winter Smith, a relative, in a personal interview in 1953, said that the Pickett family remained in Marysville during the summer of 1853.

17. Frank Soulé, *The Annals of San Francisco*.

18. "In the Mission," that is, in the large area south of Market Street, not literally in or very near Mission Dolores.

19. Ina L. Cook, "Ina Donna Coolbrith," *Westward* 1(May 1928):4.

20. First few lines from her lyric, "San Francisco, April 18, 1906," in her collection, *Wings of Sunset*, p. 9.

21. Horace Davis, "How I Got into the Library Business," in Joyce Backus, "History of the San Francisco Mercantile Library Association," pp. 155-62.

22. James, pp. 315-22; Marian Taylor, "Ina Coolbrith, California Poet," *Overland Monthly*, n.s. 64(October 1914):327-39.

Chapter 6: Los Angeles in the Fifties

The quotation is line four of Miss Coolbrith's "In Blossom Time," first published in the second number of the *Overland Monthly*, August 1868; it also appears in her three collections. Among the many sources used in preparing chapters 6 and 7, the following were especially helpful: George W. Beattie, *Heritage of the Valley*; Horace Bell, *Reminiscences of a Ranger*; Benjamin Hayes, *Scrapbooks*; files of the *Los Angeles Star*; Harris Newmark, *Sixty Years in Southern California*; William B. Rice, *The Los Angeles Star*; and Franklin Walker, *Literary History of Southern California*. These and other references to the Los Angeles period are cited in the bibliography.

1. "In 1855 we went to Los Angeles," Ina Coolbrith in a letter to her niece, Mrs. Ina L. Cook, 17 March 1914, in possession of Mrs. Ina Graham, Berkeley, California. For Miss Coolbrith's recollections of Los Angeles as a Mexican pueblo see her

Retrospect and her long narrative poem, "Concha," in Ina Coolbrith, *Wings of Sunset*, pp. 87-125.

2. J. M. Guinn, "Los Angeles in the Adobe Age," Historical Society of Southern California, *Annual Publications* 4(1898):49-55. Mrs. Ina Graham of Berkeley relates that her mother, as a small child in the Los Angeles of the 1860s and early 1870s, remembered the pepper trees.

3. J. M. Guinn, "The Old-time Schools and School-masters of Los Angeles," reprinted in Historical Society of Southern California, *Annual Publications* (1896) p. 11; Newmark, pp. 162-63. There was a family legend that Ina Coolbrith attended the Benicia Seminary, in Benicia, California (forerunner of Mills College in Oakland) for a while, but she herself stated, in a letter to her niece, "the very little [education] I had, I got from home study at night, and reading," Ina Coolbrith to Mrs. Ina L. Cook, 17 March 1914; in private collection of Mrs. Ina Graham.

4. Luther A. Ingersoll, *Century Annals of San Bernardino County*, p. 304; Beattie, p. 304.

5. *California Blue Book*, 1907; Ina Coolbrith in a letter to Mrs. Cook, 17 March 1914; DAR of California, *Collections*, 12:294-97; Freemasons, Los Angeles Lodge #42, *Historical Review*, pp. 42, 45, with excellent portrait of William Peterson on p. 42; Ingersol, p. 305.

6. Newmark, pp. 48-49, 315, 344, 397.

7. Hayes, in Bancroft Library; Ingersol, p. 306, with portrait of Benjamin Hayes.

8. Rice, *The Los Angeles Star, 1851-1864*, p. 240.

9. *California Blue Book*, 1907; Robert G. Cleland, *El Molino Viejo*, p. 26; George Cosgrove, *Early California Justice*, pp. 46-47; *Los Angeles Star*, 8 November 1856; Newmark, pp. 54, 189 (with portrait of E. J. C. Kewen); 351; *Sacramento Illustrated*, pp. 35, 46-47.

10. El Molino Viejo is near the present Huntington Hotel in Pasadena. Cleland. Glenn S. Dumke, "The Masters of San Gabriel Mission's Old Mill," *California Historical Society Quarterly* 45(September 1966):259-65; Oscar Lewes, *Here Lived the Californians*, pp. 37-40, with illus.; *Los Angeles Times*, 16 October 1955 part 7:3; Emily G. Mayberry, "El Molino Viejo," *Land of Sunshine* 3(July 1895): 59-62; Newmark, p. 54; Lawrence C. Powell, "Books of the West," *Westways* 58(October 1966):62.

11. For Dr. White's personality see Ina Coolbrith's memorial poem on his death, *Los Angeles Star*, 17 December 1861; this is in her *Scrapbooks*, 1:7.

12. *California Blue Book*, 1907; Newmark, p. 185.

13. *Los Angeles Star*, 12 October 1861 (military camps in Los Angeles); Newmark, pp. 296, 321; Rice, p. 217.

14. Marian Taylor, "Ina Coolbrith, California Poet," *Overland Monthly* n.s. 64 (October 1914):327-39.

15. Coolbrith, *Retrospect*, see introduction.

16. Nathan Newmark, in *San Francisco Hebrew* [a weekly in English and German] (v. 1-53? 1863-1916?) This reference is to a dated clipping in Ina Coolbrith's *Scrapbooks*, 2:175. E. J. C. Kewen [Harry Quillem] *Idealina*.

17. Her first published poem appeared in the *Los Angeles Star*, 30 August 1856. She was thus fifteen when her first verse was published, not ten or eleven, as most accounts state. The second poem, "Ally," was printed in the issue of November 8 of the same year.

18. *Los Angeles Star*, 31 January 1857; Rice, p. 124.

19. *Los Angeles Star*, 2 May, 13 June 1857.

20. *Los Angeles Star*, 27 June 1857.

21. *Los Angeles Star*, 11 July 1857.

22. *Los Angeles Star*, 25 July 1857.

23. Newmark, pp. 186, 226.

24. Advertisement, *Los Angeles Star*, 26 March 1859.

25. Beattie, p. 304.

26. DAR of California, *Collections*, 12:294.
27. Published in the *Los Angeles Star*: "My Ideal Home," 27 August 1857; "We Miss Thee at Home," 12 September 1857; "One on Earth and One in Heaven," 7 November 1857; "Little Elsie," 17 April 1858.

Chapter 7: Marriage and Divorce

Quotation from "Summons," by Ina Coolbrith, *Overland Monthly,* (September 1871); also in her two collections, *A Perfect Day,* pp. 157-58, and *Songs from the Golden Gate,* p. 143.

1. "In Blossom Time," first published in the *Overland Monthly,* 1(August 1868):2, and included in Miss Coolbrith's three collections.
2. Los Angeles County Recorder, *Marriage Register* 1:22-23; *Los Angeles Star,* 24 April 1858 news item. The "Act of Secularization" of the California missions, promulgated by the Republic of Mexico, 17 August 1833, in theory provided for the gradual removal of the missionary padres (Franciscans), and their replacement by members of the secular, diocesan clergy, as well as for the dissolution of the paternalistic mission system in favor of a system of partly self-governing pueblos, whenever it was believed that the Indians at each existing mission were ready for the change. Unfortunately, by prematurely insisting on this secularization, and by turning the responsibility for the secularization over to local "administrators," many of whom were unworthy of their responsibility, the Mexican government ruined almost all the missions within a decade; Pio Pico, the last Mexican governor, was especially anxious to sell, or even to give away, the last of the mission lands before the invading American armies could halt this wholesale robbery. San Gabriel Mission, near Los Angeles, differed in no way from the others. In June 1846 Pico sold the remaining 16,000 acres of mission land, including the "principal edifices"—the mission buildings themselves—to Julian (William) Workman and Hugo Reid. These two men did not occupy all of the land or all of the buildings, but permitted other settlers to move in; they were in fact powerless to prevent it, since Fremont, acting as Civil Governor of California after the Cahuenga Capitulation in 1847, refused to recognize Pico's right to sell the property, a decision finally recorded some years later in Lincoln's presidential Letters Patent of 18 March 1865 which restored some of the lands and the partly ruined buildings to the jurisdiction of the Catholic church. During the intervening years, however, there were many immigrants who built homes on the fertile mission lands, and the home of David F. Hall, scene of the 1858 wedding of Josephine Smith and Robert Carsley, was one of these. See Zephyrin Engelhardt, *San Gabriel Mission and the Beginnings of Los Angeles;* Robert G. Cleland, *El Molino Viejo,* pp. 15-20.
3. Coolbrith, "In Blossom Time."
4. *Los Angeles Star,* 24 April 1858 editorial.
5. E. J. C. Kewen [Harry Quillem], *Idealina.*
6. Advertisement, *Los Angeles Star,* 26 March 1859 indicates that the move to the New High Street shop was made on 16 October 1868.
7. *Los Angeles Star,* 8 May 1858.
8. Published in *Los Angeles Star:* "Ida Lee," 7 July; "One More Loved One Had Departed," 21 August; "Little Fred," (written 21 October), 27 November; all 1858.
9. *Los Angeles Star,* 4 June 1859.
10. Edward C. Kemble, *A History of California Newspapers* ed. by Helen Harding Bretnor, p. 327.
11. These poems were clipped from the *California Home Journal* and were pasted without dates, in Ina Coolbrith, *Scrapbooks,* 1:6-7.
12. California Supreme Court, *Reports,* 1959, 14:390-95.
13. *Los Angeles Star,* 21 July 1860.
14. DAR of California, *Collections,* 17:101.

15. *Los Angeles Star,* 18 February 1860.
16. Benjamin F. Hayes, *Scrapbooks,* 50:1; *Los Angeles Star,* 28 April 1860.
17. U. S. Bureau of the Census, *Population,* 1860.
18. *Los Angeles Star,* 28 April, 14 July 1860.
19. Hayes, *Scrapbooks,* 49.
20. Hayes, 50:1.
21. *Los Angeles Star,* 14 April 1860.
22. William B. Rice, *The Los Angeles Star, 1851-1864,* p. 217; *Los Angeles Star,* 12 October 1861.
23. Los Angeles County, District Court, Case #853. All incidents in the text, relating to the accusations and threats of Robert Carsley against his wife, are drawn from the court proceedings as recorded in this case.
24. *Los Angeles Star,* 19 October 1861.
25. *Los Angeles Star,* 30 November 1861.
26. *Los Angeles Star,* 21, 28 December 1861.
27. District Court, Case #853.
28. Hayes, 50:2; Harris Newmark, *Sixty Years in Southern California,* p. 309; *Los Angeles Star,* 4, 11 January 1862.
29. Mrs. Ina (Cook) Graham said, in a personal interview, 23 June 1956, that her grandaunt, Miss Coolbrith, lost her baby before the divorce. She believes he may have lived about a year. Mrs. Graham had this information from her mother, not from Miss Coolbrith herself. Mrs. Graham's statement coincided with that of Mrs. Eunice Mitchell Lehmer, a close friend of Ina Coolbrith, in a conversation following an Ina Coolbrith program at the Oakland Free Library, during the Oakland Centennial in 1952. A cousin of the poet, Dr. Harrison Salisbury of San Rafael, in an article in the *Improvement Era,* January 1950, said "she lost . . . her only child." Franklin Walker, in his *San Francisco Literary Frontier,* surmises that Miss Coolbrith's "The Mother's Grief," might have been a personal experience.
30. Both these poems appear in her collections, *A Perfect Day* and *Songs from the Golden Gate.*
31. "The Mother's Grief," signed in full, was printed on the first page of the *San Francisco Californian,* 25 March 1865; it also appeared in Bret Harte, *Out-croppings,* pp. 48-49; and in Miss Coolbrith's collections.

Part Two: City of Mists and of Dreams

Chapter 8: Literary San Francisco in the Sixties

The title of Part Two and the quotation at the beginning of this chapter are taken from Ina Coolbrith's eight-line lyric "To San Francisco," (ca. 1922) written during a winter in New York City, and published in *Wings of Sunset,* p. 8.

1. "When I was twenty, just,/ Life seemed crumbled into dust," from an unpublished poem, entitled "Twenty-two," written by Miss Coolbrith for the twenty-second birthday of her grandniece, Ina Cook (later Mrs. Graham of Berkeley).
2. The date for Ina Coolbrith's arrival in San Francisco is determined by her poem "Unrest" ("I cannot sleep" . . .) datelined San Francisco, September 1862, and sent to the *Los Angeles Star* where it was printed 22 November; William B. Rice, *The Los Angeles Star,* p. 285.
3. Gertrude Atherton, many years later, with library assistance from Ina Coolbrith, made this California romance the theme of her novel, *Rezánov.* Gertrude F. Atherton, *Rezánov* [a novel] (New York: Authors and Newspapers Association, 1906).
4. John S. Hittell, *A History of San Francisco,* pp. 339-498.
5. Franklin Walker, *San Francisco's Literary Frontier,* the most important history of San Francisco literature, followed by a companion volume, *A Literary History of Southern California. San Francisco's Literary Frontier* is of value to students and

general readers; it is well documented, has abundant notes, a bibliography and an excellent index. But it is much more than a reference book; it is witty, rich in incident and personality, and has a narrative pace that makes it absorbing reading. For this chapter the files of the *San Francisco Golden Era* and the *San Francisco Californian,* consulted in the Bancroft and Huntington Libraries, have been essential sources. Ella Sterling Mighels, *Story of the Files,* has been useful. Its compiler was still close to the literary beginnings of San Francisco, and her volume is brimful of surprising little personal notes. Other helpful books, general histories of San Francisco and biographies of prominent persons who appear in this chapter, are listed in the bibliography.

6. Julia C. Altrocchi, *The Spectacular San Franciscans.*

7. *San Francisco Golden Era,* 12 October 1862, p. 3; Walker, p. 178.

8. *San Francisco Californian,* 19 November 1864.

9. *San Francisco Californian,* 3 September 1864.

10. Mira Maclay, "A Talk with Ina Coolbrith"; interview, *Oakland Tribune,* 2 March 1924, p. 13.

11. Henry G. Langley, *San Francisco Directory,* 1867-68; 1868-69.

12. Langley, 1867-68.

13. Ina Coolbrith, in a letter to her niece, Mrs. Ina L. Cook, 17 March 1914, in private collection of Mrs. Ina Graham of Berkeley; George W. James, "Ina Coolbrith," *National Magazine* 26(June 1907):315-22; Langley, 1860, p. 226; Mabel W. Thomas, *History and Description of Ina Donna Coolbrith,* pp. 2-3, manuscript in California Room, Oakland Free Library; Walker, p. 224.

14. Langley, 1867-68.

15. Walker, p. 81; Evelyn Wells, "Last of Group Mourns at San Francisco Poet's Death;" interview with Mrs. Mary Tingley Lawrence, *San Francisco Call,* 5 March 1928.

16. "Unrest" ("I cannot sleep" . . .) *Los Angeles Star,* 22 November 1862; also in Ina Coolbrith, *Scrapbooks,* 1:7.

17. Ina L. Cook, "Ina Coolbrith," *Wasp-News Letter,* 22-29 December 1928, p. 50; Wells, interview *San Francisco Call,* 5 March 1928.

18. "June," *San Francisco Golden Era,* 7 June 1863, p. 1; "December," *San Francisco Golden Era,* 4(20 December 1863):3.

19. *San Francisco Golden Era,* 27 December 1863, p. 7.

20. Cook, p. 49.

21. *San Francisco Golden Era,* 5, 11 March 1864.

22. *San Francisco Californian,* 13 August 1864, p. 4.

23. Benjamin De Casseres, "Ina Coolbrith of California's 'Overland Trinity,'" *New York Sun,* 7 December 1919.

24. *San Francisco Californian:* "Mists," 5 November; "A Lost Day," 31 December; "Fragment from an Unfinished Poem," 19 November; all 1864. The last named was one of the poems Ina later offered Harte for inclusion in his *Outcroppings,* but he rejected it, giving his reasons in a letter to her dated 3 June 1865, in the Bancroft Library, University of California. Quotation from letter: "My reasons for not preferring the 'Fragment' are these: To the general public, one of the evidences of genius is *completeness.* People have an idea that anyone can write occasional good lines, and that it is quite easy to achieve 'fragments' which imply that the rest of their poems are unfit for publication. Every man has sometime in his life said something good: it is the *habit* of being smart that makes the good writer a poet, and the power of carrying a thought or fancy to completeness that makes the article or poem. I do not know as I have expressed myself clearly; so perhaps this note is an evidence that I am not a writer or poet. Excuse my prosiness and believe me. . . . "

25. Walker, p. 272.

26. *San Francisco Californian,* 4 February 1865, p. 1; 4 March 1865, p. 9.

27. *San Francisco Californian*, 25 March 1865, p. 1.
28. "Hereafter," 3 June, p. 5; "The Blossom of the South," Ina Coolbrith, *Scrapbooks*, 1:10.
29. Advertisement, *San Francisco Californian*, 7 December 1867.
30. *San Francisco Californian*, 15 December 1865, p. 1.
31. Walker, p. 217.
32. *San Francisco Californian*, 9 December 1865, p. 8.
33. *San Francisco Californian*, 20 January 1866, pp. 4-5.
34. Ina Coolbrith, in a talk at the monthly meeting of the California Literature Society in her home on 24 June 1917, stated that John Rollin Ridge was "her earliest literary friend who recognized her poetic gift while she was still a school girl." Gist of her talk reported in *Richmond Banner* 8 July 1917 over her signature. A clipping of the report appears in her *Scrapbooks*, 2:200.
35. See Joseph Henry Jackson's introduction to John R. Ridge, *Life and Adventures of Joaquin Murieta* (Norman, Oklahoma, 1944).
36. Mary Wentworth Newman (Mrs. Mary Doliver) [May Wentworth] ed., *Poetry of the Pacific*, pp. 343-46; Walker, pp 218-19.
37. Mighels, pp. 426-28.
38. In the *San Francisco Californian*: "Sunset," 23 February, p. 9; "A Poet's Grave on Lone Mountain," 10 March, p. 1; "The Sweetest Sound," 14 April, p. 1, "Love in Little," 16 June, p. 1; all these in 1866. "Heliotrope," 12 January 1867, p. 2. "Love in Little" was later included in her collections, *A Perfect Day*, pp. 63-64, and *Songs from the Golden* Gate, p. 30.
39. Amelia R. Neville, *The Fantastic City*, p. 257; Walker, p. 238.
40. Francis Bret Harte, *Last Galleon, and Other Tales* (San Francisco, 1867); *Condensed Novels, and Other Papers* (New York, 1867).
41. Charles Warren Stoddard, *Poems* (San Francisco, 1867).
42. Walker, pp. 230-32.
43. John Rollin Ridge, *Poems* (San Francisco, 1868); Edward Rowland Sill, *The Hermitage and Other Poems* (San Francisco, 1868).
44. Charles W. Stoddard, "Ina D. Coolbrith," *The Magazine of Poetry* 1(1889): 313 ff. Stoddard was romancing about Ina's hair. She was, as her grandniece, Mrs. Ina Graham, said, probably a "honey blonde," or had light brown hair as a young woman.

Chapter 9: Golden Gate Trinity

Bret Harte's impromptu limerick was recalled by Miss Coolbrith when she was interviewed by a reporter for the *New York Sun* in 1919.

1. See files of the *Overland Monthly*, vols. 1-15, July 1868—December 1875; W. C. Bartlett, "*Overland* Reminiscences," *Overland Monthly*, n.s. 32(July 1898):41-46; Noah Brooks, "Early Days of the *Overland*," *Overland Monthly*, n.s. 32(July 1898):1-11; John H. Carmany, "The Publishers of the *Overland*," *Overland Monthly*, n.s. 1(February 1883):Supp. 1-16; Charles S. Greene, "Magazine Publishing in California," California Library Association, *Publications* #2, 1 May 1898; Ella S. Mighels, *Story of the Files*; Frank L. Mott, *A History of American Magazines*, 3:402-09; Anton Roman, "Beginnings of the *Overland*," *Overland Monthly*, n.s. 32(July 1898):72-75; George R. Stewart, *Bret Harte, Argonaut and Exile*, chapters 20-23; Franklin Walker, *San Francisco's Literary Frontier*, pp. 256-83.
2. *California Blue Book*, 1907.
3. DAR of California, *Collections*, 12:294; 17:101-2.
4. Ina Coolbrith, *Some of Ina D. Coolbrith's Poems Published in the Overland Monthly from 1869 to 1875* . . . (manuscripts collected by John H. Carmany) p. 6, in Coolbrith Papers, Bancroft Library, University of California, Berkeley. Published

with title "A Faded Flower" in Miss Coolbrith's collections, *A Perfect Day,* pp. 137-38, and *Songs from the Golden Gate,* p. 149.

5. *Overland Monthly,* 1(July 1868):17.

6. Carmany, "The Publishers of the *Overland.*"

7. Bret Harte in a letter to Ina Coolbrith, Tuesday, a.m. [August ? 1868] in Bancroft Library.

8. Verse on a letter to Ina Coolbrith from Bret Harte, 6 July 1868, Bancroft Library.

9. Bret Harte to Ina Coolbrith, letter, 22 July 1868. The lyric, "In Blossom Time," *Overland Monthly* 1(August 1868):145, in later years was the most often reprinted of all of Ina Coolbrith's verse. It is included in her three collections.

10. Letters of Ina Coolbrith to Ella S. Mighels 28 August 1916, California State Library, Sacramento, and to Albert Bender 18 May 1927 in Bender Room, Margaret Carnegie Library, Mills College, Oakland, California.

11. Bret Harte, in a letter to Ina Coolbrith, Tuesday a.m. [August ? 1868]; "Siesta," *Overland Monthly* 1(September 1868):220; included also in Coolbrith, *A Perfect Day,* pp. 92-93, and Coolbrith, *Songs from the Golden Gate,* p. 84.

12. Ina Coolbrith in a letter to Mrs. Lannie Haynes Martin, 9 February 1912 in Huntington Library, San Marino, California; George W. James, "Ina Donna Coolbrith," *National Magazine,* (June 1907); Marian Taylor, "Ina Coolbrith, California Poet," *Overland Monthly,* n.s. 64(October 1914):331-32. The poem, "The City by the Golden Gate," appeared in the following: Albert S. Evans, *A la California* (San Francisco, 1873), pp. 16-17; Oscar T. Shuck, *The California Scrapbook* (San Francisco, 1869); Society of California Pioneers, *Eighteenth Anniversary* (San Francisco, 1868), 1:18-20; *San Francisco Wasp,* Christmas, 1902; also in Ina Coolbrith, *Scrapbooks,* 1:174.

13. "October," 1(October):331; "When the Grass Shall Cover Me," 1(November): 473; "December," 1(December):552, *Overland Monthly,* (1868). "When the Grass Shall Cover Me," published anonymously in John Greenleaf Whittier, comp., *Songs of Three Centuries,* led to a friendship between Whittier and Miss Coolbrith; the lyric appears in her three collections.

14. *Overland Monthly* 1(December 1868):6.

15. Benjamin De Casseres, "Ina Coolbrith of California's 'Overland Trinity,'" *New York Sun,* 7 December 1919; James, "Ina Donna Coolbrith"; Josephine C. McCrackin, "Ina Coolbrith Invested with Poet's Crown," *Overland Monthly,* n.s. 66(November 1915):449; Walker, pp. 268-69.

16. Amelia R. Neville, *The Fantastic City,* pp. 167-68.

17. Ina Coolbrith, in letter to Mrs. L. H. Martin, 9 February 1912; Henry C. Merwin, *Life of Bret Harte,* p. 49.

18. De Casseres.

19. With Harte Papers in the Bancroft Library.

20. Ada K. Lynch, "Stories from the Files," *Overland Monthly* n.s. 75(November 1920):66.

21. Files of the *Overland Monthly,* vols. 1-2, (July 1868—June 1869).

22. Letters of Bret Harte to Ina Coolbrith, 1868-71, in Bancroft Library.

23. McCrackin.

24. George W. James, "The Romantic History of Josephine Clifford McCrackin"; introduction to Mrs. McCrackin's novel, *The Woman Who Lost Him,* pp. 1-44.

25. Josephine C. McCrackin, "Reminiscences of Bret Harte and Pioneer Days in the West," *Overland Monthly,* n.s. 66(November 1915):366-68; "Ina Coolbrith," p. 449.

26. Some letters were saved when Mrs. McCrackin lost her home in the Santa Cruz Mountains forest fire of 1899. (See her article in the *Overland Monthly,* "Reminiscences.") Ina Coolbrith's letters from Harte were rescued from her burning house (April 1906) by Robert Norman, a student rooming there. (See Ina L. Cook, "Ina Donna Coolbrith," *Westward* 1(May 1928):4.

418

27. The eight lyrics in the *Overland Monthly*: "Under the Christmas Snow," 2(January):56; "Rebuke," 2(February):110 (also *A Perfect Day*, pp. 114-15, and *Songs from the Golden Gate*, p. 104); "My 'Cloth of Gold,'" 2(March):255-56 (*Perfect Day*, pp. 25-29; *Songs*, pp. 18-20); "To-day," 2(April):386; "Fulfillment," 2(May):468 (*Perfect Day*, pp. 172-73; *Songs*, p. 158); "The Coming," 3(August):177 (*Perfect Day*, pp. 111-13; *Songs*, pp. 97-98); "I Cannot Count My Life a Loss," 3(October):354 (*Perfect Day*, pp. 144-45; *Songs*, p. 41); "Ungathered," 3(November) (*Perfect Day*, pp. 119-21; *Songs*, pp. 109-10).

Chapter 10: A Wreath of Laurel

Quotation from Ina Coolbrith's "With a Wreath of Laurel," *Overland Monthly*, 5:256-57; Ina Coolbrith, *A Perfect Day*, pp. 84-87; *Songs from the Golden Gate*, pp. 61-62; *Wings of Sunset*, pp. 140-42.

1. Julia C. Altrocchi, *The Spectacular San Franciscans*.
2. U. S. Bureau of the Census, *Population*, 1870.
3. Julia C. Altrocchi, *The Spectacular San Franciscans;* John S. Hittell, *A History of San Francisco*, pp. 382-498; Amelia R. Neville, *The Fantastic City*.
4. Neville, p. 167-68.
5. *Dictionary of American Biography*, 17:158-60, also Supplement 2:428-30; Isobel Field, *This Life I've Loved*, pp. 72-79; Louis Filler, *The Unknown Edwin Markham;* Edward R. Sill, *Poems* (Boston, 1887), introductory note, p. vii; William L. Stidger, *Edwin Markham;* Franklin Walker, *San Francisco's Literary Frontier*, pp. 233-35.
6. Altrocchi, pp. 158-60.
7. *Overland Monthly*, 4(February 1870):161; Coolbrith, *A Perfect Day*, pp. 38-39; Coolbrith, *Songs from the Golden Gate*, p. 64.
8. *Overland Monthly*, (February 1870); Coolbrith, *A Perfect Day;* Coolbrith, *Songs from the Golden Gate*.
9. *Overland Monthly*, 4(January 1870):88.
10. Joaquin Miller, *Joaquin et al.*
11. Bret Harte, "Etc.," *Overland Monthly*, 4(January 1870):104.
12. Harriet Beecher Stowe, *Lady Byron Vindicated* (Boston, 1870).
13. *Overland Monthly*, 4(April 1870):385-86.
14. *Overland Monthly*, 4(February 1870):161.
15. In *Overland Monthly*, vols. 4 and 5(1870): "Not Yet," 4(March):213; "Dead," 4(April):345; "While Lilies Bud and Blow," 4(May):436; "If Only," 5 (July):60. All but the poem "Dead" were later included in Miss Coolbrith's collections, *A Perfect Day* and *Songs from the Golden Gate*.
16. Letter from Bret Harte to Ina Coolbrith 28 July 1870 in Coolbrith Papers, Bancroft Library, University of California, Berkeley. Harte refers to Edward Pollock.
17. "Two Pictures"; not published until 1881 when it was included in *A Perfect Day*, pp. 96-99; also in *Songs*, p. 75-77.
18. *Overland Monthly*, 5(August 1870):162; "With a Wreath of Laurel," 5 (September 1870):256-57; "A Hope," 5(November 1870):474. "With a Wreath of Laurel" later appeared in all three of Miss Coolbrith's collections; the other two in *A Perfect Day* and *Songs* only.
19. Ina Coolbrith, ["A Tribute to Joaquin Miller," 1913]; manuscript in Coolbrith Papers, Bancroft Library.
20. Joaquin Miller, in a letter to Charles W. Stoddard 22 July 1870, in Huntington Library, San Marino, California.
21. Cincinnatus Hiner Miller's given names honored his father's birthplace, Cincinnati, Ohio, and Dr. Hiner, the physician in attendance at the poet's birth. Ina Coolbrith, in July 1870, suggested the pen name "Joaquin." See her "Tribute." See

also letters: Ina Coolbrith to Mrs. Lannie H. Martin 9 February 1912 in Huntington Library, and to Joaquin Miller, same date, in Bancroft Library, also Miller's reply, Bancroft. A letter from George Miller (Joaquin's brother) to Ina Coolbrith 4 October 1916 concerns the family physician for whom Joaquin Miller was named. George Miller said that his brother, "after reaching popularity, concluded he was named for the poet Heine." (This letter in Bancroft Library.) Joaquin Miller used "C. H. Miller," or "Cincinnatus Heine Miller," as a signature on legal documents. (See William W. Winn, "Joaquin Miller's 'Real Name,'" *California Historical Society Quarterly* 33(June 1954):143-46. James D. Fountain, friend and neighbor of Joaquin Miller in Oregon and near The Hights in Oakland, always called him "Hiner." The Library of Congress gives the real name as Cincinnatus Hiner Miller.
22. Coolbrith, "Tribute."
23. Coolbrith, "Tribute"; Joaquin Miller, "California's Fair Poet," *San Francisco Call*, 12 August 1892; Miller's letter to Stoddard, 22 July 1870; C. W. Stoddard, *Exits and Entrances*, p. 26; C. W. Stoddard, "Ina D. Coolbrith," *The Magazine of Poetry* 1(1889):313 ff.; Walker, pp. 277-78.
24. Miller's letter to Stoddard. Miss Coolbrith's photograph, small and delicately tinted, is now owned by her grandniece, Mrs. Ina Graham. In 1879 the poet had the San Francisco photographer, Thors, make an enlargement of this portrait, a likeness often used in magazine articles about her.
25. Coolbrith, "Tribute."
26. Ina Coolbrith, in a letter to Mrs. Laura Drum, 8 February 1927; Coolbrith Papers, California Room, Oakland Free Library. For other accounts of the wreath see the following: Albert Brecknock, *Byron*; Miss Coolbrith's letter to Brecknock, 24 September 1918 in Oakland Free Library; Coolbrith, "Tribute"; Joaquin Miller, *Memorie and Rime*, p. 15; Joaquin Miller, *Songs of the Sierras*; Charles Phillips, "Memoir," the introduction to Miss Coolbrith's posthumous *Wings of Sunset*, pp. xxviii-xxxii. In the summer of 1952, Oakland's centennial year, another wreath (in memory of that of Miss Coolbrith, eighty-two years before) was placed on Lord Byron's tomb by a group representing the Ina Coolbrith Circle and the Friends of the Oakland Library, with C. Jones Tyler of Oakland as leader of the group. Byron memorial services were held in Hucknall Torkard church. Among those present was the retired city librarian, Albert Brecknock, then eighty years of age, and for many years a friend of Miss Coolbrith by letter.
27. *Overland Monthly*, 5(September 1870):256-57; also appears in Miss Coolbrith's collection, *A Perfect Day*, pp. 84-87; *Songs from the Golden Gate*, pp. 61-62; *Wings of Sunset*, pp. 140-42.

Chapter 11: The University Poet

The quotation at the beginning of the chapter is from Ina Coolbrith's "Memorial Poem," (1881). It appears in her *Songs from the Golden Gate*, pp. 99-103.

1. Charles Warren Stoddard, *South Sea Idyls* (Boston, 1873); Franklin Walker, *San Francisco's Literary Frontier*, pp. 271-73.
2. John H. Carmany, "The Publishers of the *Overland*," *Overland Monthly*, n.s. 1(February 1883):Supp. 1-16; Ina Coolbrith's letter to Mrs. Lannie H. Martin, 9 February 1912 in Huntington Library, San Marino, California; Walker, p. 267.
3. Carmany.
4. F. B. Harte's letter to Ina Coolbrith, Tuesday, P.M. [31 January 1871] in Coolbrith Papers, in Bancroft Library, University of California; Walker, p. 267.
5. Carmany; Ina Coolbrith's letter to Mrs. Martin, 9 February 1912; Walker, p. 267.
6. Frank L. Mott, *A History of American Magazines*, 2:493.
7. Empty envelope with directions, Bancroft Library. Harte had requested her poems to send to Osgood as early as 16 April 1870 according to his letter to her, 16 April P.M. [1870?] in Bancroft Library.

8. Miss Coolbrith's letter to Mrs. Martin, 9 February 1912.

9. Letter from F. B. Harte to John H. Carmany 18 December 1878 in Bancroft Library; letter from Harte to Nan (his wife, Mrs. Anna G. Harte) 5 July 1879 (in which he asks to have "Miss Coolbrith's pacquet" forwarded) in William Andrews Clark Library, University of California at Los Angeles. The same letter to Nan Harte is included in F. B. Harte, *Letters*, ed. by G. B. Harte (Boston, 1926), p. 147.

10. Alice K. Cooley's letters to Ina Coolbrith, 1906-10, in Coolbrith Papers, Bancroft and Huntington Libraries; Josephine C. McCrackin, letter to Ina Coolbrith, 11 August 1917, Huntington Library.

11. Letter from Ina Coolbrith to Laura Y. Pinney, undated [28 November 1910] in Huntington Library; with this letter is a brief memorial of Alice K. Cooley which Miss Coolbrith, who was ill, wrote and asked Mrs. Pinney to read at the Pacific Coast Women's Press Association meeting in memory of Mrs. Cooley 28 November 1910. Alice Cooley died 3 November 1910.

12. Ina L. Cook, "Ina Coolbrith," *Wasp-News Letter*, (22-29 December 1928), p. 50.

13. *California Blue Book*, 1907; *Dictionary of American Biography* 1:443-44; Edward C. Kemble, *A History of California Newspapers*, 1846-58.

14. John S. Hittell, *The Resources of California* (San Francisco, 1863, and six subsequent editions, 1866-79); *History of the City of San Francisco*. Theodore H. Hittell, *History of California*, 4 vols. (San Francisco, 1885-97).

15. Mary Austin, *Earth Horizon*, p. 297.

16. William C. Morrow, *The Ape, the Idiot, and Other People* (Philadelphia, 1897); *Blood Money* (San Francisco, 1882); *Lentala of the South Seas* (New York, 1908).

17. *San Jose Mercury-Herald*, 14 February 1907; also clipping of this in Ina Coolbrith, *Scrapbooks*.

18. "James F. Bowman; died April 29, 1882," *The Californian* 6(July 1882):5. (*The Californian; a Western Monthly* [San Francisco], 6[July 1882]:5. A short-lived magazine [1880-82] that became in January 1883 the *Overland Monthly*, 2d ser. This *Californian* is not to be confused with the *San Francisco Californian* [a San Francisco literary weekly of the 1860s]. See F. L. Mott, *A History of American Magazines*, vol. 4, p. 406.) Poem was later published with title, "Unbound," in Ina Coolbrith, *Songs from the Golden Gate*, pp. 91-93. References to James F. Bowman in Walker, and to both James and Margaret Bowman in Bohemian Club *Annals*, 1880-95, vol. 1.

19. Ina Coolbrith, *Some of Ina D. Coolbrith's Poems Published in the Overland Monthly from 1869 to 1875* (manuscripts collected by John H. Carmany while he was publisher of the Overland Monthly, with some additional unpublished poems) in Coolbrith Papers, Bancroft Library; letter from Ina Coolbrith to Albert Bender, 10 February 1922. "Of course I have no 'first drafts' of any old ones; they were all burned" (in the fire of 1906). This letter is in the Bender Room, Margaret Carnegie Library, Mills College, California.

20. *Overland Monthly*, 6(January 1871):33, "Just for a Day"; (February) p. 187, "Emblem"; (April p. 319, "Sometime"; (May) p. 148, "Oblivion"; 7(August):190, "In Adversity"; (September), p. 258, "Summons"; (October), p. 385, "From Year to Year." "From Year to Year" was not included in her collections, but the other six were published in *Songs from the Golden Gate*, and four ("Emblem," "Oblivion," "In Adversity," and "Summons") in *A Perfect Day*.

21. William W. Ferrier, *Origin and Development of the University of California*, pp. 327-28; William C. Jones, *Illustrated History of the University of California*, pp. 334, 347.

22. Jones, pp. 36-40; *San Francisco Call*, 20 July 1871; also clipping of *Call* article in Coolbrith, *Scrapbooks*, 1:17.

23. Ferrier, p. 332.

24. *San Francisco Call,* 20 July 1871; Edith M. Coulter, "Horatio Stebbins," *California Historical Society Quarterly,* 34:180.
25. "California" appears in full in *A Perfect Day,* pp. 49-59, and *Songs from the Golden Gate,* pp. 1-6.

Chapter 12: The Bohemian Club

Quotation from "Bohemia," written in August 1893 as an expression of Ina Coolbrith's gratitude to the Bohemian Club and published in her posthumous collection, *Wings of Sunset,* p. 28.

1. Susan Brownell Anthony, 1820-1906, an American leader in the woman suffrage movement.
2. San Francisco *News-Letter,* 22 July 1871; also clipping of same in Ina Coolbrith, *Scrapbooks,* 1:17.
3. Ina Coolbrith, *California;* Paul Elder, *California the Beautiful* (San Francisco, 1911); *San Francisco Examiner,* Sunday, 3 November 1895, 29:1-5.
4. Presented 30 May 1916; program in Coolbrith Papers, Bancroft Library, University of California, Berkeley. Second presentation 4 May 1940; program in California State Library, Sacramento.
5. Bohemian Club, San Francisco, *Annals.*
6. Bohemian Club, *Annals;* Charles W. Stoddard, "In Old Bohemia," *The Pacific Monthly* 18(December 1907):639-50, 19(March 1908):261-73.
7. Raymund F. Wood, "Ina Coolbrith, Librarian," *California Librarian* 19(April 1958):101-4.
8. Ina Coolbrith, in a letter to Mrs. Jeannie Peet, undated [January 1918?] in Bancroft Library.
9. Bohemian Club, San Francisco, *Bohemian Club Certificate of Incorporation, Constitution . . . Officers and Committees, Members, in Memoriam.*
10. "At the Hill's Base," *Overland Monthly,* 8(January 1872):60; *Songs from the Golden Gate,* p. ix. "Le Chemin de l'Ecole, *Overland Monthly,* 8(February 1872):155; with title "The Road to School," *A Perfect Day,* pp. 102-6, also *Songs from the Golden Gate,* pp. 81-83. "The Brook," *Overland Monthly,* 8 (March 1872):285; *A Perfect Day,* pp. 164-66; *Songs from the Golden Gate,* pp. 116-17. "An Ending," *Overland Monthly,* 8(May 1872):465.
11. Of the various spellings, the one preferred for these pages is "Calli-Shasta," Miller's own spelling of his daughter's name in his romanticised *Unwritten History.* Both Ina Coolbrith and Lischen Miller (Mrs. George Miller) called her "Callie," a diminutive from Miller's form of the name. George W. James spelled it "Calle-Shasta," and Franklin Walker used "Cali-Shasta," as did all of Miller's biographers. Ina Coolbrith's letter to Herbert Bashford, 25 February 1913 and Lischen Miller's to her, March and April 1913, all in Bancroft Library; George W. James, "Ina Donna Coolbrith," *National Magazine,* (June 1907); Joaquin Miller, *Unwritten History,* pp. 438, 440; M. M. Marberry, *Splendid Poseur* (New York, 1953), pp. 32, 34, 111, 265; Martin S. Peterson, *Joaquin Miller, Literary Frontiersman,* pp. 36, 95; Harr Wagner, *Joaquin Miller and his Other Self,* pp. 238-41; Franklin Walker, *San Francisco's Literary Frontier,* pp. 333, 354.
12. Charlotte P. Stetson Gilman, *The Living of Charlotte Perkins Stetson,* p. 142; Miller, p. 440; also information from personal interview with Mrs. Ina Cook Graham of Berkeley, California, 23 June 1956.
13. The three lyrics were published in volume 9: "Love Song" in July, p. 90, "Loneliness" in September, p. 255, and "A Perfect Day" in November, p. 467. All three were included in her *Songs from the Golden Gate,* and the last two in *A Perfect Day.*
14. DAR of California, *Collections,* 17:101-2.

15. *Overland Monthly*, 10:247; also in *A Perfect Day* and *Songs from the Golden Gate*.

16. *Overland Monthly*, 10:82, 183; both in *A Perfect Day* and *Songs from the Golden Gate*.

17. The address was 1139½ Folsom Street, the upper flat. The Pickett twins later lived in the lower flat, 1139 Folsom Street. Langley, *San Francisco Directory*, 1873-74, 1874-75. Ina L. Cook mentions this house in her unpublished article, "Charles Warren Stoddard" (1908?), pp. 1-2; a manuscript in the collection of her daughter, Mrs. Ina Graham, in Berkeley, California.

18. Personal interview with Mrs. Ina Cook Graham on 23 June 1956, narrating these events of more than eighty years before from the recollections of her mother.

19. *Overland Monthly*, 10(June 1873):545; also *A Perfect Day*, pp. 108-10, and *Songs from the Golden Gate*, pp. 95-96.

20. "Sea Shell," "A Fancy," "One Touch of Nature," "Withheld," *Overland Monthly*, 11(September—December, 1873):272, 368, 457, 565-66. All were later published in *Songs from the Golden Gate*, and all but "Sea Shell" in *A Perfect Day*.

21. *San Francisco Bulletin*, 31 January and 2 February 1874.

22. "Beside the Dead," *Overland Monthly*, 14(May 1875):464. Also appears in all three collections of Ina Coolbrith's poems. The sonnet was thought by some to have been written for Ina Coolbrith's mother, but it was published the year before Mrs. Pickett's death. The statement that Miss Coolbrith took her sister's body to Los Angeles for burial is based on an undated letter to Mrs. Ina Cook in Mrs. Ina Graham's files.

23. Langley, *San Francisco Directory*, 1869-70.

24. Langley, 1873-74.

25. Both Mrs. Ina Cook Graham and Jesse Winter Smith were in agreement on this, as stated in separate personal interviews with each of them.

26. Don C. Pickett, letters to Ina Coolbrith, 31 March and 6 April 1913; 2 December 1919, in Huntington Library; obituary of D. C. Pickett, San Francisco *Chronicle*, 28 July 1928.

27. Once, in the 1870s, "Joaquin Miller asked for a scribbling pad and I gave him an old blank ledger, once the property of the 'Ina Ledge.' One might be sure that a mine with that name would not 'pan out' well." From Ina Coolbrith "A Tribute to Joaquin Miller," 1913, manuscript in Coolbrith Papers, Bancroft Library.

28. California. State Mining Bureau, *Mines and Mineral Resources*, December 1918, p. 92.

29. *Overland Monthly*, 1869-75, *Account of Money Paid for Contributions*, manuscript in Bancroft Library.

30. *San Francisco Call*, 15-16 January 1874; clippings of this, also program, in Coolbrith, *Scrapbooks*, 1:22.

31. *San Francisco Alta*, 16 January 1874; also in Coolbrith, *Scrapbooks*, 1:22.

32. Wood.

33. Letter from Ina Coolbrith to Frank Deering, 18 March 1917, quoted by Dan Gilson in his manuscript, "Ina Donna Coolbrith, 1841-1928," in our files. Mr. Gilson quotes Charles Josselyn on the statement about the curtains.

34. *Overland Monthly* 12:159, 280. Both lyrics appear in her collections, *A Perfect Day* and *Songs from the Golden Gate*.

35. *Overland Monthly* 12:477; *San Francisco Call*, undated clipping in Coolbrith, *Scrapbooks*, 1:23. "Respite" included in *Songs from the Golden Gate*.

36. *Overland Monthly* 12(June 1874):559; also in *Wings of Sunset*, pp. 177-78. Not to be confused with "A Hope," *Overland Monthly* 5(November 1870):474, published in her two earlier collections.

37. *Overland Monthly* 13(July 1874):84-85; also in *A Perfect Day* and *Songs from the Golden Gate*.

38. *Overland Monthly* 13(August 1874):121; also in *A Perfect Day* and *Songs from the Golden Gate*.

39. Miss Willard's resignation as librarian of the Oakland Library Association was accepted 4 September 1874; Oakland Library Association, *Minutes*, 4 September 1874, p. 119; in Oakland Free Library.

Part Three: The Librarian

Chapter 13: Oakland in the Seventies

Quotation at head of chapter from Ina L. Cook, "Ina Coolbrith," *Wasp-News Letter*, 22-29 December 1928, p. 49.

1. Sergeant Luis María Peralta and his four sons. Rancho San Antonio was granted to the father in 1820 and willed to the sons in 1842. It became the site of Oakland, Berkeley, Alameda, Piedmont, Emeryville, Albany and part of San Leandro. J. N. Bowman, "The Peraltas and Their Houses," *California Historical Society Quarterly*, 30(September 1951):217-31.
2. Important sources for the history and description of Oakland, California, before the turn of the century are the following: Joseph E. Baker, *Past and Present of Alameda County*; William Halley, *The Centennial Yearbook of Alameda County, California*; Frank C. Merritt, *History of Alameda County*; Myron W. Wood, *History of Alameda County*.
3. William C. Jones, *Illustrated History of the University of California*, pp. 36-43.
4. Jones, p. 30; William W. Ferrier, *Origin and Development of the University of California*, pp. 327-28.
5. California, *Statutes*, 1877-78, Chapter 266, p. 2; Oakland. Free Library. *Minutes* 1:3-4, 27, 1 June and 18 October 1878; in Oakland Free Library.
6. Statement by Ina Coolbrith in an interview for the *San Francisco Daily News*, 8 September 1925. Also Ray E. Held, *Public Libraries in California*, 1849-1878, pp. 85-87.
7. *Minutes* of the Oakland Library Association, 5 March 1868, p. 1; in office of city librarian, Oakland Free Library.
8. *Minutes* of the Oakland Library Association, 27 April 1868, pp. 4-10.
9. *Minutes* of the Oakland Library Association, 18 May 1868, p. 17.
10. Oakland. Free Library. Board of Library Directors, *1st Annual Report, 1880-1881*, in *Minutes* of the Library Board, 5 July 1881, pp. 161-66.
11. Ibid.
12. California Library Association, *Libraries of California*, p. 11; *Minutes* of the Oakland Library Association, 13 March 1869, p. 21.
13. California Library Association, p. 11; *Minutes* of the Oakland Library Association, 2 June 1871, p. 56.
14. *Minutes* of the Oakland Library Association, 4, 8 September 1874, pp. 119-22.
15. *Minutes* of the Oakland Library Association, 8 September 1874, p. 121.
16. Ibid.
17. *Minutes* of the Oakland Library Association, 23 September 1874, pp. 123-25.
18. Ibid.
19. *Minutes* of the Oakland Library Association, 8 September 1874, p. 120.
20. Henry G. Langley, *Oakland City Directory*, 1875; Bishop, *Oakland City Directory*, 1880-81.
21. Henry G. Langley, *San Francisco Directory*, 1874-75.
22. Georgia L. Bamford, *The Mystery of Jack London*, p. 37.
23. Map of the Oakland campus of the University of California drawn by Joseph C. Rowell. Photograph in Oakland Free Library, original in Bancroft Library.
24. Jacob N. Bowman, "The Peraltas and Their Houses," *California Historical Society Quarterly*, 30(September 1951):217-31.
25. U. S. Bureau of the Census, *Population*, in 1870, 10,500.
26. *Oakland Tribune*, 15 January 1967, pp. 15-16.

27. Bishop, *Oakland City Directory*, 1889-99.
28. Edward R. Sill, *Poems* (Boston, 1888), p. vii; *Dictionary of American Biography* 17:158-60.
29. Harr Wagner, *Joaquin Miller and his Other Self*, pp. 118-27.
30. *Dictionary of American Biography, Supplement* (New York, 1944) 2:428-30.
31. William F. Badé, *The Life and Letters of John Muir*, 2:27.
32. Ina Coolbrith, *Scrapbooks*, 1:26.
33. From personal interview with his niece, Mrs. Ina Cook Graham of Berkeley, California, 23 June 1956.
34. Calli-Shasta Miller was a maid in Miss Coolbrith's household, according to Mrs. Charlotte Perkins Stetson, who lived across the street. See Charlotte P. Stetson Gilman, *The Living of Charlotte Perkins Stetson*, p. 142.
35. *San Francisco Alta*, 17 December 1874, 1:1; also undated clippings from the *Oakland Transcript*, *San Francisco Call*, and *San Francisco Bulletin*, in Miss Coolbrith's *Scrapbooks*, 1:24.
36. *Overland Monthly* 13:416; also Ina Coolbrith, *Songs from the Golden Gate*, p. 90.
37. From personal interview with Mrs. Ina C. Graham, 23 June 1956.
38. Letter from Ina Coolbrith to Mrs. Benton, 21 December 1874, in Coolbrith Papers, California State Library.
39. Cook, "Ina Coolbrith," p. 49.
40. Marian Taylor, "Ina Coolbrith, California Poet," *Overland Monthly*, n.s. 64 (October 1914):330.
41. Cook; also letter from Ina Coolbrith to Ina Lillian Cook, 17 March 1914, in private collection of Mrs. Ina Cook Graham of Berkeley.
42. *Overland Monthly*, 14(May 1875):464; included in her three collections, *A Perfect Day, Songs from the Golden Gate*, and *Wings of Sunset*.
43. "Meadow Larks," *Overland Monthly*, 14(June 1875):524; "Discipline," 14 (March):250; "Ownership," 15(August):180; "In Time of Storm," 15(October): 386; "Regret," 15:482-83. All but one, "In Time of Storm," appeared later in her collections, "Meadow Larks" and "Ownership" in both *A Perfect Day* and *Songs from the Golden Gate;* "Discipline" in *A Perfect Day*, and "Regret" in *Songs from the Golden Gate*, with title "Freedom."
44. Ina Coolbrith, *Some of Ina D. Coolbrith's Poems Published in the Overland Monthly from 1869 to 1875;* [manuscripts collected by John H. Carmany] p. 40, in Coolbrith Papers, Bancroft Library.
45. See his name in San Francisco city directories, 1868-83, for his periodical publications.
46. Some of Ina Coolbrith's unpublished verse appears in print in her *Scrapbooks*. These were set up for her by J. H. Carmany, and later, C. W. Carruth, Oakland printer, poet, and personal friend.
47. After 1891 J. H. Carmany was listed in the Oakland city directories as a farmer living on Thirteenth Avenue, near Millbury, in East Oakland.
48. *Dictionary of American Biography*, 1:443-44.
49. *Overland Monthly* 15(December 1875):585; the lyric appears in *A Perfect Day* and *Songs from the Golden Gate*, with the title changed to "At Rest" in the latter volume.
50. Letter from Henry Edwards to Ina Coolbrith, 20 October 1875, in Bancroft Library.
51. John Greenleaf Whittier, ed., *Songs of Three Centuries*.
52. *Minutes* of the Oakland Library Association, 3 April 1876, p. 149.
53. *San Francisco Bulletin*, 8 June 1876; *Oakland Transcript*, undated clipping in Coolbrith, *Scrapbooks*, 1:25.
54. Jones, p. 348-49.
55. DAR of California, *Collections*, 1953, 17:101.
56. Undated clipping in *Scrapbooks*, 1:28.

57. *The Californian; a Western Monthly* (March 1882).

Chapter 14: A Free Library

Quotation at beginning of chapter from a statement by Ina Coolbrith in the *San Francisco Daily News*, 8 September 1925.

1. Carrie K. Louderback, *Reminiscences*, 1943, manuscript in California Room, Oakland Free Library.
2. *Minutes* of the Oakland Library Association, 1874-78, passim, office of the librarian, Oakland Free Library.
3. *Minutes* of the Oakland Library Association, 1874-78.
4. *Minutes* of the Oakland Library Association, 4 December 1874, p. 128.
5. Ibid.
6. *Minutes* of the Oakland Library Association, 4 January 1877, p. 164.
7. *Minutes* of the Oakland Library Association, 5 May 1877, p. 163.
8. California, *Statutes*, 1877-78, chapter 266:2.
9. *Minutes* of the Oakland Library Association, 1 April 1878, p. 177.
10. *Minutes* of the Oakland Library Association, 1 April 1878, pp. 177-78; *Oakland Times*, 8 July 1883.
11. *Minutes* of the Oakland Library Association, 9 May 1878, p. 179.
12. Ibid.
13. *Minutes* of the Board, 1 June 1878, pp. 3-4.
14. *Minutes* of the Board, 5 August, 18 October 1878, pp. 7, 25.
15. *Minutes* of the Board, 24 August 1878, pp. 10-15.
16. *Minutes* of the Board, 6, 20 September 1878, pp. 16-21. The encyclopedia here referred to was not the well-known *Encyclopedia Americana* of today.
17. *Minutes* of the Board, 18 October 1878, pp. 25-26.
18. *Minutes* of the Board, 18 October 1878, p. 26.
19. Ibid, p. 27.
20. Louderback; *Minutes* of the Board, 28 November 1879, p. 71.
21. Louderback.
22. From personal experience of staff members; only one branch librarian was on duty at a time, so lunch or supper was consumed hastily in the workroom from where the desk and front door could be watched.
23. Miss Coolbrith, in a letter to the Board of Library Directors, 5 June 1883, "Add to the thorough training of my two assistants the fact that they were in the library a long time without remuneration in order to get that training as well as to assist me with my too numerous duties." This letter was entered in the *Minutes* of the Board, 5 June 1883, p. 256.
24. *Minutes* of the Board, 27 December 1878, 3, 31 January 1879, pp. 35, 38, 41.
25. Miss Coolbrith, in letter to Board of Library Directors, 5 June 1883.
26. *Minutes* of the Board, 6 December 1878, p. 30.
27. *Minutes* of the Board, 11 July 1879, p. 56.
28. *Minutes* of the Board, 28 February 1879, p. 44.
29. Ibid.
30. *Minutes* of the Board, 28 November 1879, p. 69.
31. *Minutes* of the Board, 30 July 1880, p. 76.
32. California, *Statutes*, 1880. An act to establish free public libraries and reading rooms, approved, 26 April 1880, pp. 231-33.
33. *Oakland Times*, 8 July 1883.
34. *Minutes* of the Board, 4, 11 June 1880, pp. 100, 104.
35. *Minutes* of the Board, 11 June 1880, p. 104.
36. *Minutes* of the Board, 6 July 1880, p. 105.
37. *Minutes* of the Board, 3 August 1880, pp. 109-11.
38. Ibid, p. 112.

39. *Minutes* of the Board, 7 December 1880, p. 134.
40. *Minutes* of the Board, 5 July 1881, pp. 161-66.
41. *Minutes* of the Board, 13 September 1881, pp. 175-76.
42. Personal interview with Miss Amy Rinehart, 28 September 1947.
43. Mabel W. Thomas, "The Memory of a Smile," Oakland Free Library, *Staff Bulletin*, August 1925, p. 5.
44. Georgia L. Bamford, *The Mystery of Jack London*, p. 41.
45. Isadora Duncan, *My Life*, pp. 22-23.
46. From conversation with Henry Kirk, Oakland, 3 June 1952.
47. Jack London, in a letter to Ina Coolbrith, 13 December 1906; *Oakland Enquirer*, 10 January 1920, p. 4.
48. Mary Austin, *Earth Horizon* (Boston, 1832), p. 231.
49. Mabel W. Thomas, *History and Description of Ina Donna Coolbrith, 1932-42*, manuscript in Oakland Free Library.
50. Thomas, "The Memory of a Smile."

Chapter 15: A Perfect Day

The chapter takes its title from that of Miss Coolbrith's first book of verse; the quotation is from an unpublished poem, "A Riddle," composed about 1881, which appears as a clipping in her *Scrapbooks*, 1:27.

1. *Overland Monthly*, vol. 1, no. 1 (July 1868)—vol. 15, no. 12 (December 1875).
2. John Carmany's own set of the *Overland*, in fine calf bindings, is now in the library of his grandnephew, Robert M. Carmany of Walnut Grove, California. The manuscript portfolio in the Bancroft Library of the University of California in Berkeley is entitled "Some of Ina D. Coolbrith's Poems Published in the *Overland Monthly* from 1869 to 1875."
3. Biographical data in letter to California State Library, Sacramento, 3 June 1956, from Mrs. Robert H. Carmany; J. H. Carmany's birth certificate, property of Mr. Robert Carmany; Bailey Millard, *History of the San Francisco Bay Region* 2:107; San Francisco County Clerk, *Great Register*, 1867; San Francisco and Oakland city directories.
4. Mrs. Carmany's letter; Millard, p. 107.
5. W. C. Bartlett, "*Overland* Reminiscences," *Overland Monthly*, n.s. 32(July 1898):41-46; Noah Brooks, "Early Days of the *Overland*," *Overland Monthly*, n.s. 32(July 1898):1-11; John H. Carmany, "The Publishers of the *Overland*," *Overland Monthly*, n.s. 1(February 1883):Supp. 1-16; Charles S. Greene, "Magazine Publishing in California," California Library Association, *Publications*, #2, 1 May 1898; Frank L. Mott, *A History of American Magazines* 3:402-9; George R. Stewart, *Bret Harte, Argonaut and Exile*, chapters 20-23; Franklin Walker, *San Francisco's Literary Frontier*, pp. 256-83.
6. Bret Harte's letter to John H. Carmany, 18 December 1878, in Bancroft Library.
7. Edward R. Sill's letter to Ina Coolbrith, 12 January 1881, in her *Scrapbooks*, 1:28.
8. Ina D. Coolbrith, *A Perfect Day, and Other Poems*.
9. Prices in publisher's announcement in the manuscript portfolio, *Some of Ina D. Coolbrith's Poems . . . 1869 to 1875*, in Bancroft Library. The dedication: To the memory of my mother in whose living hands I once hoped to place this little volume, I now dedicate whatever of worth it may contain, with all reverence and love.
10. Sill's letter, 31 July 1881, *Scrapbooks*, 1:33.
11. *San Francisco News Letter*; undated clipping, *Scrapbooks*, 1:35.
12. Stoddard's letter to Miss Coolbrith, 6 May 1881, Bancroft Library.
13. *San Francisco Bulletin*, 30 May 1881; the poem is included in Ina Coolbrith, *Songs from the Golden Gate*, p. 99.

14. *The Californian; a Western Monthly*, 4(September 1881):250; included in her posthumous collection, *Wings of Sunset*, p. 191.

15. In conversation with Mr. and Mrs. Robert M. Carmany, Walnut Grove, California, 28 May 1967; also letter in State Library from Mrs. Carmany, 3 June 1956.

16. This beautiful book is in the library of Robert M. Carmany. A printed copy of the inscription, with title "Lines Written on the Fly-Leaf of my First Book of Verses," January 1893, in Coolbrith, *Scrapbooks*, 1:27.

17. *Scrapbooks*, 1:27.

18. *Scrapbooks*, 1:26.

19. *Scrapbooks*, 1:26.

20. Berkeleyan Stock Company, comp., *College Verses*, pp. 91-92, 96-97; copy in Bancroft Library.

21. Isobel Field, *This Life I've Loved*.

22. *Who Was Who in America*, 1897-1942, p. 552; *New York Times*, 9 June 1929; *San Francisco Chronicle*, 9 June 1929, p. 1, 10 June 1929, pp. 8, 10; William C. Jones, *Illustrated History of the University of California*, p. 350.

23. *Scrapbooks*, 1:26; all three lyrics in manuscript in *Some of Ina D. Coolbrith's Poems . . . 1869 to 1875*, in Bancroft Library.

24. Portrait as an adult, *Men of California, 1900-1902* (San Francisco, 1901), p. 83; Polk-Husted, *Oakland, Alameda and Berkeley Directory*, 1910-17.

25. *Californian* 3(March 1881):220-21; complete lyric has twelve stanzas.

26. Georgia L. Bamford, *The Mystery of Jack London*, p. 42.

27. From personal conversation with Miss Coolbrith, 1 December 1927, Berkeley, California.

28. Ina Coolbrith's letters to Albert Bender, 20 November 1926 and 27 September 1927, in Bender Room, Margaret Carnegie Library, Mills College, Oakland, California.

29. Letter to Bender, 8 October 1927, Mills College.

30. Letter to Bender, 27 August 1918, Mills College.

31. Letter to Bender, 30 November 1926, Mills College; also personal interview with Mrs. Ina Cook Graham, Berkeley, California, 23 June 1956.

32. Conversation with Mrs. Lehmer in Oakland Free Library, May 1952.

33. Ruth Harwood's letters to Ina Coolbrith, 28 November 1926 and 2 March 1927, Bancroft Library.

34. Full account, with invitation, seating diagram, etc., in *Overland Monthly*, n.s. 1(February 1883):Supp. 1-16; Frank L. Mott, *A History of American Magazines*, 3:402-9.

35. *San Francisco News Letter*, (January 1883), undated clipping in *Scrapbooks*, 1:39.

36. *Wasp*, (February 1883); undated clipping in *Scrapbooks*, 1:39.

37. Mott, 2:407.

38. "Unattained," and "Our Poets," *Overland Monthly*, n.s. 1(January, February 1883):68, Supp. 13; "February," *Century Magazine*, 25(March 1883):670. The third of these was the only one included in any of her collections, *Songs from the Golden Gate*, p. 17.

39. *Wasp*, (February 1883); clipping in *Scrapbooks*, 1:39.

40. *Oakland Tribune*, 31 March 1883.

Chapter 16: An Elected Board of Library Directors

Quotation at beginning of chapter from Miss Coolbrith's lyric "Withheld," first published in the *Overland Monthly*, 11:565, December 1873, and later included in her collections, *A Perfect Day* and *Songs from the Golden Gate*.

1. *Minutes* of the Oakland Library Board, 3 April 1883, pp. 238-41; Husted, *Oakland, Alameda and Berkeley Directory*, 1884.

2. *San Francisco Daily Evening Star*, 12 April 1884; clipping of this in Ina Coolbrith, *Scrapbooks*, 1:42.
3. *Wasp*, (July 1884); undated clipping in Coolbrith, *Scrapbooks*, 1:42.
4. *Oakland Times*, 8 July 1883.
5. This incident, Miss Coolbrith's letter, and Board conversation in *Minutes* of the Board, 5 June 1883, pp. 255-58.
6. *Minutes* of the Board, 26 June 1883, pp. 259-62.
7. Incidents, communications, and petition with all names, in *Minutes* of the Board, 3 July 1883, pp. 263-72.
8. *Minutes* of the Board, 1883, passim.
9. *Oakland Times*, 8 July 1883.
10. *San Francisco Daily Evening Star*, 12 April 1884.
11. Oakland Free Library, *Catalogue of the Oakland Free Library*, 10 July 1879.
12. *Minutes* of the Board, 6 November and 4 December 1883, pp. 292-303.
13. Melvil Dewey (1851-1931), *A Classification and Subject Index for Cataloguing and Arranging the Books and Pamphlets of a Library* (Amherst, Mass., 1876). He was an organizer of the American Library Association, 1876; editor of the first professional library periodical in the United States, *Library Journal*, for its first five years, 1876-81; and founder of the first school of library economy, 1884. See biographical sketch by H. M. Lydenberg, *Dictionary of American Biography*, Supplement 1:241-43.
14. *Minutes* of the Board, 4 December 1883, pp. 296-302; also Ina Coolbrith's letter to the Board, *Minutes* of the Board, 1 April 1884, pp. 316-17.
15. Perkins's letter quoted by Ina Coolbrith in her letter of 1 April 1884.
16. *Minutes* of the Board, 1 April 1884, pp. 316-17.
17. *Minutes* of the Board, 3 June 1884, pp. 326-28.
18. *Minutes* of the Board, 3 June 1884, p. 330; also Carrie K. Louderback, *Reminiscences;* manuscript in California Room, Oakland Free Library.
19. *Minutes* of the Board, 5 August 1884, p. 339.
20. Note by Ina Coolbrith on a letter to her from Miss Rose Brier, Santa Barbara, 15 October 1911: The Daughter of one of the Trustees of the Oakland library—a Man who knew how I was wronged (I.D.C.), in Huntington Library, San Marino, California.
21. *Minutes* of the Board, 10 September 1884, p. 343.
22. *Minutes* of the Board, 1 October 1884—7 April 1885, passim.; Oakland Free Library, *Catalogue* April 1885.

Chapter 17: A Leave of Absence

Quotation at beginning of chapter from "From Living Waters," Ina Coolbrith's second University of California commencement ode, June 1876; appears in full in her collections, *A Perfect Day* and *Songs from the Golden Gate*.

1. "Poem to Jacob Milliken," by Ina Coolbrith.
2. *Portland Press*, 24 December 1883; clipping of this in Ina Coolbrith, *Scrapbooks*, 1:40. For family relationships see G. T. Ridlon, *Saco Valley Settlements and Families*, pp. 567-68; also genealogical chart in this volume.
3. McKenney, *Oakland, Alameda and Berkeley Directory*, 1884-85, 1886-87, 1887-88; also Ina Cook Graham, *Ina Lillian Peterson (Mrs. Finlay Cook) . . . Memories by Her Daughter;* a mimeographed pamphlet for private circulation.
4. McKenney, 1884-85.
5. From photographic view of house, in California Room, Oakland Free Library.
6. Charlotte P. Stetson Gilman, *The Living of Charlotte Perkins Stetson*, p. 142.
7. George W. James, "Ina Donna Coolbrith," *National Magazine* 26(June 1907): 315-22; M. M. Marberry, *Splendid Poseur* (New York, 1953), pp. 32, 34, 111, 265; Joaquin Miller, *Unwritten History*, pp. 438, 440; M. S. Peterson, *Joaquin Mil-*

ler, *Literary Frontiersman*, pp. 36, 95; Harr Wagner, *Joaquin Miller and his Other Self*, pp. 238-41; Franklin Walker, *San Francisco's Literary Frontier*, pp. 333, 354.

8. Story told by Mrs. Ina Cook Graham, as told her by her mother.

9. Mrs. Ina Graham, 23 June 1956, in an interview; also her mimeographed pamphlet cited above.

10. "The Poet" was first written in October 1877, and "Retrospect" in March 1880. See Ina Coolbrith, *Some of Ina D. Coolbrith's Poems Published in the Overland Monthly from 1869 to 1875* [manuscripts collected by John H. Carmany]; in Coolbrith Papers, Bancroft Library.

11. *Oakland Tribune*, 21 February 1884; clipping of this in Coolbrith, *Scrapbooks*, 1:41; also *Overland Monthly*, n.s. 3 (April 1884):416.

12. "Rosemary, That's for Remembrance, To W. W. Crane," poem in Coolbrith, *Scrapbooks*, 1:40.

13. *Oakland Tribune*, 24 September 1884; clipping also in Coolbrith, *Scrapbooks*, 1:42.

14. *Lippincott's Magazine* 50(September 1892):406-7; clippings of the poem, Coolbrith, *Scrapbooks*, 1:72.

15. We are indebted to Mrs. Dorothy Shaw Libbey, author of *Scarborough Becomes a Town*, who made us a map to show locations of the two Coolbrith homesteads.

16. He lacked two months of being twenty-one when he voted for Jefferson; see Libbey, p. 225.

17. Ridlon; *Portland Press*, 18 October 1884; clipping of this in Coolbrith, *Scrapbooks*, 1:40.

18. Ina Lillian Cook, "Ina Coolbrith," *Wasp-News Letter*, 22-29(December 1928), p. 50.

19. Letter from Ina Coolbrith to Henry Peterson, 1 December 1884, in personal files of Mrs. Ina Graham of Berkeley, California.

20. Ina Coolbrith, "John Greenleaf Whittier," 1909, manuscript in library of Mrs. Ina Graham.

21. Ina Coolbrith to Henry Peterson, 28 October 1884; letter in Mrs. Graham's files.

22. Edmund C. Stedman, *An American Anthology, 1787-1900* (Cambridge, Mass., 1900), 2 vols.

23. Ina Coolbrith, *Songs from the Golden Gate*.

24. *Cleveland Leader and Herald*, Sunday, 10 May 1885; clipping in Coolbrith, *Scrapbooks*, 1:43.

25. Letters from Ina Coolbrith to her nephew, Henry Peterson, 28 October and 1 December 1884, and to her half-brothers, William and D. C. Pickett, 23 December 1884; in Mrs. Graham's files.

26. *Minutes* of the Oakland Library Board, 3 June 1885, p. 390; first mention of book repairing in Oakland Free Library.

27. *Boston Evening Transcript*, 6 December 1884; clipping in Coolbrith, *Scrapbooks*, 1:42.

Chapter 18: The Library in the Eighties

The autograph album with Jack London's inscription is in the private library of Mrs. Ina Graham, Berkeley, California.

1. Boalt Hall, University of California, Berkeley, is named in honor of Judge Boalt.

2. *Minutes* of the Oakland Library Board, 1(10 April 1885):382-83.

3. *Minutes* of the Board, 1(4 August 1885):398-400.

4. Ibid.

5. *Minutes* of the Board, 1(13 July 1886):427-30.

6. *Minutes* of the Board, 1(2 November 1886):439.

7. Ina Coolbrith, in a letter to Judge John H. Boalt, 31 August 1886, in Bancroft Library.

8. Letter in Coolbrith Papers, Bancroft Library.

9. *Minutes* of the Board, 1(2 November 1886):439. This was the *Charter* adopted by the Board of Freeholders in 1888, and approved by the State Legislature 14 February 1889.

10. *Minutes* of the Board, 2(8 January 1887):6.

11. *Minutes* of the Board, passim.

12. *Minutes* of the Board, 2(4 December 1888):77.

13. Jack London, *Letters from Jack London* (New York, 1965), pp. 438-39.

14. Jack London's letter to Ina Coolbrith, 13 December 1906, in *Oakland Post-Enquirer*, 10 January 1920, p. 40.

15. Carrie Knapp Louderback, *Reminiscences*, manuscript in California Room, Oakland Free Library.

16. Isadora Duncan, *My Life* (New York, 1927), pp. 15-16. Other references to Joseph Duncan: Edward C. Kemble, *A History of California Newspapers, 1846-1858*, pp. 124-29, 337; Allan R. Macdougall, *Isadora*, pp. 18-22, 26.

17. Bret Harte, ed., *Outcroppings* (San Francisco, 1866), "The Intaglio," pp. 138-42.

18. Duncan, pp. 22-23.

19. Samuel Dickson, *San Francisco Kaleidescope*, pp. 183-84; letter from Victoria M. Shadburne to Ina Coolbrith, October [13, 1926?] in Bancroft Library.

20. *Minutes* of the Board, passim.

21. *Minutes* of the Board, vol. 2, passim.

22. *San Francisco Call*, 3 December 1892.

23. Harr Wagner, *Joaquin Miller and his Other Self*, pp. 112-17; William W. Winn, "The Joaquin Miller Foundation," *California Historical Society Quarterly* 32(September 1953):231-41. See also clippings in Ina Coolbrith, *Scrapbooks*, 1:48.

24. Wagner, p. 117.

25. Mabel W. Thomas, "History and Description of Ina Donna Coolbrith," p. 5, manuscript in California Room, Oakland Free Library.

26. Thomas W. Higginson, *American Sonnets* (Boston, 1890), p. 52; also undated clippings in Ina Coolbrith, *Scrapbooks*, 1:61-62.

27. Helen R. Chamberlain, *A Christmas Greeting Expressed in Paintings and Poems of California Wild Flowers* (San Francisco, 1886); Irene E. Jerome, comp., *Nature's Hallelujah* (Boston, 1886).

28. Letter from E. C. Stedman to Ina Coolbrith, 27 July 1889; in Bancroft Library.

29. Charles W. Stoddard, "Ina D. Coolbrith," *The Magazine of Poetry* 1(1889): 313 ff.

30. Ina D. Coolbrith, *The Colonel's Toast*, Bohemian Club Christmas Jinks, 1886.

31. Undated clippings in Coolbrith, *Scrapbooks*, 1:60-61.

32. "Lines on Hearing Mr. Edgar S. Kelley's Music of 'Macbeth,'" *Overland Monthly*, n.s. 7(January 1886):68 appears with slightly changed titles in her collections, *Songs from the Golden Gate* and *Wings of Sunset*. "March (by the Pacific)," *Overland*, n.s. 7(March 1886):316, appears as "March" in *Songs from the Golden Gate*. "Edward Rowland Sill," *Overland*, n.s. 9(June 1887):658; Sill died on 27 February 1887. *Dictionary of American Biography*, 17:158-60.

33. "The Poet," *Century Magazine*, 31(December 1885):228; "Retrospect," *Century Magazine*, 31(February 1886):356; "Frederick III of Germany," *Century Magazine*, 37(November 1888):80. All are included in *Songs from the Golden Gate*. "The Poet," reprinted, *Magazine of Poetry*, 1(January 1889):105 and *Current Literature* 28(April 1900):16-17. "Retrospect" printed as a folio in 1925 by John Henry Nash with an introduction by Ina Coolbrith.

34. Ina Coolbrith, *Some of Ina D. Coolbrith's Poems Published in the Overland Monthly from 1869 to 1875* [manuscripts collected by John H. Carmany], "The

Poet," with comment by John H. Carmany, p. 1, "Retrospect," with note by Ina Coolbrith to J. H. C., p. 24.

Chapter 19: Dawn of the Nineties

The quotation at the beginning of the chapter is from a statement by Ina Coolbrith in the *Oakland Times*, 4 September 1892.

1. U. S. Bureau of the Census, *Population*, 1890.
2. *Oakland Times*, 22 November 1890; *Oakland Tribune*, 17 January 1891; *San Francisco Chronicle*, 5 November 1890. The *Oakland Times* reported that the building was "steadily settling toward the east," as the foundation on that side was only one brick thick. City Engineer T. E. Morgan, according to the *San Francisco Chronicle*, said that the library might "topple over."
3. *Minutes* of the Oakland Library Board, 2(7 October 1890):159-60.
4. *Minutes* of the Board, 2(1 July 1890):139-40.
5. *Minutes* of the Board, 2(1 April 1890):128.
6. *Minutes* of the Board, 2(4 April 1890):129, (Special meeting of Book Committee).
7. *Minutes* of the Board, 2(1 July 1890):141.
8. Oakland Free Library, *Oak Leaves*, 20(1 January 1967):2.
9. *Minutes* of the Board, 2(7 October 1890):161.
10. *Minutes* of the Board, 2(2 September 1890):157.
11. The Brown charging system remained in use until after John Boynton Kaiser became City Librarian in 1927.
12. Oakland Free Library, *Bulletin*, 1890-93.
13. *Minutes* of the Board, 2(2 December 1890):167.
14. Ibid.
15. *Oakland Times*, 8 October 1890; *Oakland Tribune*, 28 September 1890; *San Francisco Chronicle*, 29 September 1890; *San Francisco Examiner*, 29 September 1890.
16. Letter from Elizabeth J. Boalt to Elizabeth Bonney Wills, 6 February, year not given, but probably 1887; in California Historical Society Library, San Francisco, California. Miss Coolbrith's sonnet "Calla" appears in *Wings of Sunset*, p. 79. A manuscript of the poem and a photograph of the cat are framed together; Coolbrith Collection, California Room, Oakland Free Library.
17. DAR of California, *Collections*, 17:101; Husted, *Oakland, Alameda and Berkeley Directory*, 1892-93.
18. *Minutes* of the Board, 2(31 March and 5 May 1891):180, 184.
19. *Minutes* of the Board, 2(2 June 1891):185-86.
20. *Minutes* of the Board, 2(31 March 1891):180; Husted, 1892-93.
21. *Minutes* of the Board, 2(6 January and 1 September 1891):171, 198.
22. *Minutes* of the Board, 2(6 October 1891):200-201.
23. *Minutes* of the Board, 2(4 August 1891):194-95.
24. F. H. Clark, "Libraries and Librarians of the Pacific Coast," *Overland Monthly*, n.s. 18(November 1891):449-64.
25. Clark, editor's note, p. 464.
26. Program for the East Bay reception of the ALA, Coolbrith, *Scrapbooks*, 1:65.
27. DAR of California, *Collections*, 17:101.
28. Letter from Mary Eileen Ahern to Ina Coolbrith, 11 May 1914, in Huntington Library, San Marino, California. Miss Ahern was founder and editor of *Public Libraries*, a monthly; see *Who Was Who in America*, 1(1897-1942):10.
29. Oakland Free Library, *Scrapbook, ALA in Oakland*, 15 October 1891; in California Room.
30. Miss Ahern's letter cited above.

31. Oakland Free Library, *Scrapbook;* "Reception at Oakland," *Library Journal,* 16(December 1891):138-40.

32. Text of poem is that of copy in Miss Coolbrith's *Scrapbooks,* 1:65, where corrections were made by the author; "In the Library," *Library Journal,* 16(December 1891):139; Oakland Free Library, *Staff Bulletin,* July—August 1932; California Writer's Club, *The Monthly Letter,* (October 1932), p. 8. In all these printings the error in line 28 is repeated, "Of all of human life the strain," corrected by Miss Coolbrith to read, "The all of human life, the strain."

33. Of the one hundred-forty persons attending the Palace Hotel banquet, fifty-nine were women. Both Miss Coolbrith and her nephew were present; others at the dinner were R. R. Bowker, Professor Eliot Coues, Charles A. Cutter, John Cotton Dana, Samuel S. Greene, Martin Kellogg, Joseph C. Rowell, and Adolph Sutro. A full account of professional and social activities, "San Francisco Conference Number," *Library Journal,* 16(December 1891):1-154. Dr. Poole's strange encounter is described in an undated clipping in the Oakland Free Library, *Scrapbook: ALA in Oakland.* Was the animal a gila monster, rather than a tarantula?

34. Director Burnham expressed this view as early as 1883, *Minutes* of the Board, 1(3 May 1883):248.

35. *Minutes* of the Board, 2(3 November 1891):203-5.

36. *Minutes* of the Board, 2(December 1891—February 1892):206-15, passim.

37. *Minutes* of the Board, 2(1 March 1892):217-19.

38. Mary Austin, *Earth Horizon,* pp. 229-32, 297-98.

39. Joaquin Miller, "California's Fair Poet," *San Francisco Call,* 12 August 1892; clipping of this in Coolbrith, *Scrapbooks,* 1:73.

40. *Overland Monthly,* n.s. 20(September 1892):246-47.

41. *Lippincott's* 50(September 1892):406-7; also appears in Ina Coolbrith, *Songs from the Golden Gate,* p. 44.

42. Clippings in Coolbrith, *Scrapbooks,* 1:72.

43. "Sorrow Is Better Than Laughter (To 'Uncle' George Bromley)," Ina Coolbrith, *Wings of Sunset,* pp. 32-33; "In Memoriam—John Le Conte," *California Educational Review* 1(May 1891):193-94; "The Day of Our Lord," *Oakland Tribune,* 19 December 1891, p. 1, also in Coolbrith, *Songs from the Golden Gate,* pp. 85-87; "Hymn of the Nativity," *San Francisco Examiner,* 25 December 1891, p. 12.

44. *Oakland Tribune,* September 1892, undated clipping in Coolbrith, *Scrapbooks,* 1:72.

45. *Oakland Times,* 4 September 1892; also clipping in Coolbrith, *Scrapbooks,* 1:78.

46. *Oakland Times,* 4 September 1892; Coolbrith, *Scrapbooks,* 1:78.

OAKLAND FREE LIBRARY

Oakland Free Library: Interview with Miss Ina Coolbrith, Librarian.

The Council's Action Regretted

The Amount Asked for Was Not in Excess of the Actual Needs—The Estimate Reduced by About $9,000—The Building Considered Very Unsafe—Suffering from Want of Funds.

Miss Ina D. Coolbrith, the efficient librarian of the Oakland Free Library, is probably the busiest woman in this city. Yesterday she was interrupted in her arduous labors by a TIMES representative, but cheerfully granted him an interview relative to the estimate for the public library for the coming year.

"What is your opinion concerning the estimate, Miss Coolbrith?" asked the reporter.

"I regret the action of the Council in cutting down the estimate for the library and reading rooms greatly. The estimate called for $22,152.57. The amount asked for—inclusive of the fund for a new building of $5,000—was not in excess of actual needs. In fact I do not see the possibility of properly maintaining the library and reading room [sic] with a less amount. You know the Council reduced the estimate by about $8,800 or $9,000, which will leave us only about $13,000 for all expenses."

"Will there be anything for new books and a new building?"

"The amount will give nothing for book purchases and nothing toward a new building, which is needed more than any other public building in Oakland, as the present one is the worst public building in this city."

"There is a rumor about that the building is very unsafe. Is there any foundation for the rumor?"

"Yes, I consider the building very unsafe, and even if it were not, it affords no space for the proper arrangement of the books. We can maintain no definite order or system of shelving, being obliged to locate the volumes where we can best find room for them and giving no room for needed accessions. If we could have a certain sum set apart each year for a building fund, for say two or three years, this want could be readily met I think and be comparatively little felt by the taxpayers."

"Are you able to satisfy the demands of the readers at the library?"

"No, we cannot keep up with the demands of our readers in the current literature of the day. We cannot even meet the demand for standard works. Our reference department—one of the most important—needs to be largely increased. The school children, who visit us daily in large numbers, are not supplied with a sufficient number of books called for to supplement their studies. We need many duplicates of these to meet this demand which is not met in the school libraries themselves. Of course, the children are the losers."

"Is the musical library well patronized?"

"Our musical library, recently added, is very small and deficient. Yes, we find it very popular."

"Are reading rooms furnished with all the periodicals and other literature needed?"

"Periodical literature should be more largely represented in the reading rooms. For purposes of economy the lists have been cut down from past years, so that the reading rooms, as well as the library, suffer from want of funds. There are books to the number of about two thousand sent to us by leading book-dealers, awaiting our inspection and selection at the present time, and a private library in San Francisco offers us at less than a tenth of their value some rare books of incalculable value in any library. But we will have to forego these opportunities unless we can buy without money and without price, and we are hardly near enough the millenium for that."

"Have you sufficient assistance in the library?"

"No, we need more assistance in the library. I have but two assistants and two attendants—the latter are young boys. The Los Angeles library furnishes its librarian with twenty assistants and she does not find that number too great. I should like to see the library placed upon a better basis before I pass out of it. I should like to have the satisfaction of seeing it well and safely housed at least. I can but feel an abiding interest in an institution that has claimed my care and labor for so many years."

At this point several ladies claimed the attention of the obliging librarian, and the scribe withdrew.

434

47. *Minutes* of the Board, 2(6 September 1892):235-36.

Chapter 20: Loss of Position

The lines at the head of the chapter are from "The Years," first published in the *Overland Monthly*, 4(February 1870):161, and later included Miss Coolbrith's collections, *A Perfect Day* and *Songs from the Golden Gate*.

1. *Oakland Tribune*, 27 September 1892.
2. The original letter is no longer extant. The text as printed in the *Oakland Times*, 30 September 1892, is presumed to be a true copy.
3. *Oakland Times*, 30 September 1892.
4.-8. *Oakland Tribune*, 27 September 1892.
9. *Oakland Times*, 29 September 1892.
10. *Oakland Enquirer*, 27 September 1892.
11. *Oakland Times*, 30 September 1892; *Oakland Enquirer*, 27 September 1892.
12. Oakland City Council, *Minutes*, 27 September 1892, p. 53.
13. *Oakland Tribune*, 28 September 1892.
14. *Oakland Tribune*, 28 September 1892; *Alameda Argus*, 29 September 1892; DAR of California, *Collections*, 1953, 17:101.
15. *Oakland Enquirer*, 27 September 1892.
16. Ibid.
17. With title, "A Prayer," Coolbrith, *A Perfect Day*, pp. 162-63; Coolbrith, *Songs from the Golden Gate*, p. 118.
18. Coolbrith, *Scrapbooks*, 1:76-80.
19. *Oakland Times*, 29 September 1892.
20. *Oakland Enquirer*, 30 September 1892.
21. Oakland City Council, *Minutes*, 25 August—19 December 1892.
22. A remark by John F. Hassler, in conversation with Josephine DeWitt, Oakland City Hall, 31 December 1940.
23. Oakland City Council, *Minutes*, 5 December 1892, p. 119.
24. Oakland Board of Library Trustees, *Minutes* of the Board, 2(4 October 1892): 239.

> *To the Honorable, the Board of Trustees of the Oakland Free Library. Gentlemen: I hereby agreeably to your request tender my resignation as Librarian of the Free Public Library, said resignation to take effect January 1st 1893. Inasmuch as no charges of incompetency upon my part have been made and I am ignorant of the causes which have led you to make this request, I therefore tender my resignation under protest. While I am aware that your actions as a board are not governed by the provisions of the Oakland Charter, still I think the principles enunciated there should govern your board in this matter. The Charter guarantees to all holding positions under the city government a fair and impartial hearing and permits those accused the privilege of making their defense. Had this course been pursued, myself and the general public, who are presumed to have some interest in the matter, would not have been left in ignorance of the causes which determined your action. During the time that I have acted as Librarian of the Free Library, I have sought faithfully and diligently to discharge the duties of the trust reposed in me, and it seems to me that I should have been heard before summary action was taken against me. I am, Gentlemen, Very Respectfully yours, Ina D. Coolbrith, Librarian, Oakland Free Library.*

25. Ibid.; also San Francisco *Examiner*, 5 October 1892.
26. *Minutes* of the Board, 2(4 October 1892):240.
27. *Minutes* of the Oakland City Council, 18 October 1892, p. 75.
28. *Minutes* of the Board, 2(1 November 1892):243.
29. *Minutes* of the Oakland City Council, 21 November 1892, p. 108.

30. Ralph J. Roske, *Everyman's Eden* (New York, 1968), pp. 394, 397-412, 417-21.

31. James M. Guinn, *Historical and Biographical Record of Los Angeles and Vicinity*, pp. 181, 183; Frank C. Merritt, *History of Alameda County*, 1:216; Paul G. Vigness, *Alameda Community Book* (Alameda, 1952), pp. 62-64.

32. *Minutes* of the Board, 1893, passim; Mrs. Carrie K. Louderback mentioned Peterson's popularity in her *Reminiscences*, a manuscript in the California Room, Oakland Free Library; Charles Samuel Greene, Oakland City Librarian, 1899-1926, spoke of his predecessor as a competent and progressive administrator.

Chapter 21: Songs from the Golden Gate

Quotation at beginning of chapter by San Francisco columnist, Henry James, in *San Francisco Call*, 30 October 1898.

1. *San Francisco Daily News*, 8 September 1925. Miss Coolbrith believed that Oakland was the first, though it was actually the second established under the Rogers Free Library Act of 1878. See Ray E. Held, *Public Libraries in California, 1849-1878*, pp. 85-87.

2. Oakland is now a city of 361,561; U. S. Bureau of the Census, *Population*, 1970.

3. Henry Peterson, in a report of comparative data on Pacific Coast libraries in 1895, in Oakland Free Library, *Scrapbook, 1890-1895*, p. 1, an undated clipping in California Room, Oakland Free Library.

4. Ina Coolbrith in a letter to "Dear Don Carlos" (Charles Lummis), 14 June 1926, in Huntington Library, San Marino, California. This letter was never sent to Lummis.

5. Coolbrith's letter to Lummis.

6. The lines, so dated, in Coolbrith, *Scrapbooks*, 1:88; in California Room, Oakland Free Library.

7. Front flyleaf, Coolbrith, *A Perfect Day*, limited edition, specially bound for John H. Carmany and now in the possession of Robert Carmany of Walnut Grove, California.

8. "Millennium," *San Francisco Examiner*, 25 December 1892; also in Miss Coolbrith's collection, *Songs from the Golden Gate*, pp. 150-51.

9. "Hymn of the Nativity," *San Francisco Examiner*, 25 December 1891.

10. "The Day of Our Lord," *Oakland Tribune*, 19 December 1891.

11. Ella Sterling Cummins Mighels, *The Story of the Files*, p. 212.

12. *Oakland Tribune*, 30 January 1893; *San Francisco Chronicle*, 30 January 1893. Numerous clippings on the event in Coolbrith, *Scrapbooks*, 1:89-90.

13. Mighels.

14. California. Columbia World's Fair Commission, *Final Report* (Sacramento, 1894).

15. *California Illustrated Magazine* 4(July 1893):141.

16. George Sterling quoted by Edward F. O'Day, *Town Talk*, 27 April 1918.

17. *San Francisco Chronicle*, 1 September 1893; this and other clippings in Coolbrith, *Scrapbooks*, 1:95-96. *San Francisco Examiner*, 27 November 1892, comments on the trustee's query, "What has she done?"

18. *San Francisco Chronicle*, 1 September 1893; Bohemian Club, *Annals* 3(San Francisco, 1880-95):226.

19. "Bohemia," Coolbrith, *Wings of Sunset*, pp. 28-29.

20. *San Francisco Bulletin*, 22 September 1893.

21. *Chicago Post*, 18 November 1893; clipping in Coolbrith, *Scrapbooks*, 1:99-100.

22. "Isabella of Spain," Coolbrith, *Scrapbooks*, 1:97.

23. Undated clipping in Coolbrith, *Scrapbooks*, 1:97, quotes letter by Ina Coolbrith dated 2 November 1893.

24. "The Captive of the White City," Coolbrith, *Songs from the Golden Gate*, pp. 57-60.

25. "Two Pictures," *San Francisco Examiner*, 25 December 1893, p. 13. Published with title "Midwinter East and West" in *Songs from the Golden Gate*, pp. 146-48.
26. *Boston Herald*, 20 January 1894; this and other clippings in Coolbrith, *Scrapbooks*, 1:100-101.
27. Undated clipping from *New York Evening Telegram*, February 1894; excerpts printed in *Oakland Enquirer*, 26 February 1894; both in Coolbrith, *Scrapbooks*, 1:101-2.
28. From a prose sketch by Ina Coolbrith entitled "Some Wild Flowers of California," in Coolbrith, *Scrapbooks*, 1:183.
29. *San Francisco Examiner*, 22 April 1894.
30. DAR of California, *Collections*, 1953, 17:101.
31. *San Francisco Chronicle*, 25 June 1893.
32. *Century Magazine* 48(October 1894):914; also in Coolbrith, *Songs from the Golden Gate*, p. 154.
33. *San Francisco Call*, 27 November 1894.
34. Coolbrith, *The Singer of the Sea*.
35. E. C. Alexander, *A Collection of California Wild Flowers*.
36. *San Francisco Call*, 7, 22 July 1895.
37. *Eureka Standard*, 27 July 1895.
38. *San Francisco Post*, 27 July 1895; this and other clippings, Coolbrith, *Scrapbooks*, 1:113.
39. Coolbrith, *Songs from the Golden Gate*.
40. Coolbrith, *Scrapbooks*, 1:116-28.
41. Albert Kinross, "Views and Reviews," *London Outlook*, 20 August 1898. Poster in Coolbrith, *Scrapbooks*, 1:152-53.
42. Letters from Albert Kinross to Ina Coolbrith, 20 August, 28 September 1898. The Kinross article inspired letters to the *Outlook*, and comment in the following United States periodicals of 1898: *New York Times*, 3 September; *San Francisco Chronicle*, 18 September; *San Francisco Wave*, 24 September, 29 October; *Oakland Enquirer*, 29 September; *St. Louis Republican*, 9 October; *San Francisco Call*, 22 October; *Los Angeles Times*, 29 October. These and others appear as clippings in Coolbrith, *Scrapbooks*, 1:154-55.
43. *San Francisco Wave*, 24 September, 29 October 1898; clippings in Coolbrith, *Scrapbooks*, 1:155.
44. *San Francisco Call*, 22 October 1898.
45. *Scribner's Monthly* 17(March 1895):315, "Songs from the Golden Gate," p. 157.
46. *Oakland Tribune*, 4 July 1895; Ina Coolbrith, "Mr. Miller and His Muse," prose, *San Francisco Examiner*, 21 April 1895; *San Francisco Call*, 25 December 1895; also Coolbrith, *Scrapbooks*, 1:110-11, 123.
47. Undated clippings in Coolbrith, *Scrapbooks*, 1:121.
48. *Los Angeles Times*, 6 December 1895; *Los Angeles Capital*, 7 December 1895, and other clippings in Coolbrith, *Scrapbooks*, 1:121.
49. "One," Coolbrith, *Wings of Sunset*, p. 158.
50. *San Diego Union*, 13 December 1895.
51. *Oakland Enquirer*, 16 March 1896.
52. *San Francisco Call*, 6 January 1897.
53. *Berkeley Advocate*, 9 November 1897; *Berkeley Gazette*, 17, 31 March, 10 April 1897.
54. *San Francisco Examiner*, 29 April 1897; *Oakland Tribune*, 2 May 1897.
55. *Oakland Enquirer*, 12, 20 November 1897; *Berkeley World*, 12 December 1897; *Oakland Tribune*, 14 December 1897.
56. *Oakland Tribune*, 22 December 1897; this and other clippings in Coolbrith, *Scrapbooks*, 1:146-48.
57. *Oakland Enquirer*, 12 June 1896; Coolbrith, *Wings of Sunset*, pp. 40-43.
58. *Oakland Enquirer*, 8 September 1896; *San Francisco Bulletin*, 19 September 1896; "Paper" in full in Coolbrith, *Scrapbooks*, 1:135.

59. Letter from Adeline Knapp to Ina Coolbrith, 27 February 1909, in Huntington Library.
60. The memorial service was held 23 November 1896, at 2:30 P.M., in the Native Sons Building in San Francisco. See letter from Joaquin Miller to Ina Coolbrith, 22 November 1896, in Coolbrith Papers, California Room, Oakland Free Library. "The Crucifixion, Still," 25 December 1896, and "Redemption," 19 December 1897. Both were included in her collection *Wings of Sunset*.
61. *St. Louis Mirror*, 6 July 1896; *St. Louis Republican*, 26 July 1896; *Hesperian*, (August-October, 1896); *Leslie's Weekly*, (15 October 1896), *Munsey's Magazine* (April 1896); Cora M. Older, "One of California's Sweet Singers," *San Francisco Bulletin*, April 1896, date incomplete on clipping in Coolbrith, *Scrapbooks*, where other clippings cited also appear.
62. *Pacific Ensign*, 12 August 1897; clipping in Coolbrith, *Scrapbooks*, 1:144.
63. *Los Angeles Capital*, June 1897, date incomplete on clipping in Coolbrith, *Scrapbooks*, 1:142.
64. Anecdote told by Nathan Newmark, *San Francisco Star*, 25 March 1916; clipping in Coolbrith, *Scrapbooks*, 2:145.

Chapter 22: Librarian, Mercantile Library

The quotation at the beginning of the chapter is from a statement by Ina Coolbrith in the *San Francisco Call*, 9 January 1898.

1. This vacancy was brought about by the announcement of the forthcoming resignation of Mrs. Clara B. Fowler, which she tendered to the Board of Directors early in the spring of 1897. Despite the excellent recommendations which accompanied Miss Coolbrith's application for the position, she was found not acceptable for technical reasons, and the position was given to Mrs. Harriet Child Wadleigh, who assumed her post on 16 June 1897. (Los Angeles. Public Library. *Annual Report*, 1897, pp. 3, 15, 24).
2. *San Francisco Call*, 7 May 1897; *Oakland Enquirer*, 6 May 1897.
3. *Oakland Enquirer*, 11 January 1898; *Oakland Tribune*, 11 January 1898; these and other clippings in Ina Coolbrith, *Scrapbooks*, 1:145-49.
4. Joyce Backus, *A History of the San Francisco Mercantile Library Association;* Hugh S. Baker, "Rational Amusement in Our Midst," *California Historical Society Quarterly*, 38(December 1959):295-320. Both include views of the Mercantile Library.
5. Mercantile Library Association, *Annual Report*, 44th-45th, 1896-97 (San Francisco, 1897-98); California Library Association, *Libraries of California in 1899* (San Francisco, 1900).
6. Mercantile Library Association, *Annual Report*, 44th-45th.
7. Letter from Miss Coolbrith to T. R. Bannerman, undated, Coolbrith Papers, Bancroft Library, University of California, Berkeley.
8. Two letters from Ina Coolbrith, to T. R. Bannerman, one undated, the other 10 October 1898; Bancroft Library.
9. Coolbrith, *Scrapbooks*, 1:150.
10. Letter to Bannerman from C. J. King, per I.D.C., 17 January 1898, Bancroft Library.
11. Backus.
12. Letter, Coolbrith to Bannerman, 1 February 1898; Bancroft Library.
13. *San Francisco Chronicle*, 8 March 1899; *Oakland Tribune*, 10 April 1899; *San Francisco Call*, 10, 15 April 1899; *San Francisco Examiner*, 23 April 1899; also Coolbrith, *Scrapbooks*, 1:161-62.
14. *San Francisco Call*, 18 December 1898, p. 16.
15. *Land of Sunshine* 10(December 1898):3; also in Ina Coolbrith, *Wings of Sunset*, p. 27.

16. California Club, *War Poems, 1898* (San Francisco, 1898); undated clipping of poem in Coolbrith, *Scrapbooks,* 1:155.

17. "General Gossip of Authors and Writers," *Current Literature,* 23(June 1898): 500.

18. *San Francisco Examiner,* 15 January 1898, p. 30.

19. *San Francisco Call,* 9 January 1898.

20. Crocker-Langley, *San Francisco Directory, 1898.*

21. *Oakland Tribune,* 13 August 1898; *San Francisco Bulletin,* 13 August 1898.

22. *San Francisco Examiner,* 18 January 1899.

23. "The Dead Artist, J. H. E. Partington," *San Francisco Examiner,* 31 January 1899; "Thomas Moore," *San Francisco Chronicle,* 30 May 1899; "The Lay of the Lost Picture, Painfully Dedicated to William Keith"; "The 'Juliet' of Miss Mather." The last two appear in Coolbrith, *Scrapbooks,* 1:167.

Part Four: "Lost City"

Chapter 23: On Russian Hill Again

The quotation at the beginning of the chapter is stanza seven of Ina Coolbrith's lyric, "From Russian Hill," *Sunset Magazine* 35(August 1915):270-71; also in her collection, *Wings of Sunset.*

1. These attacks of rheumatism (or perhaps it would be called arthritis today) were a constant problem for her to the end of her life.

2. Crocker-Langley, *San Francisco Directory,* 1900-1901.

3. Crocker-Langley, 1901-1902.

4. Letter from Ina Coolbrith to Herbert Bashford, 8 April 1901; Coolbrith Papers, Bancroft Library, University of California, Berkeley.

5. Crocker-Langley, 1902-1906.

6. Letter from Ina Coolbrith to Lorenzo Sosso, undated, gives in heading, "1604 Taylor St., 2d house north of Broadway, upper flat"; in library of Society of California Pioneers, San Francisco.

7. Personal interview with Miss Anna DeMartini, 22 July 1958, on Miss Zeller as companion to Ina Coolbrith.

8. "From Russian Hill," Coolbrith, *Wings of Sunset,* pp. 14-16.

9. Description of room based on photograph by G. W. James used in his article, "Ina Donna Coolbrith," *National Magazine* 26(June 1907):315-22.

10. *San Diego Union,* 10 April 1900; *San Francisco Chronicle,* 12 April 1900.

11. Daniel O'Connell, *Songs from Bohemia* (San Francisco, 1900).

12. Henry Herman Behr, *The Hoot of the Owl* (San Francisco, 1904).

13. Charles Philip Nettleton, *A Voice from the Silence* (San Francisco, 1904).

14. Letters by Ina Coolbrith, 2 September 1904; 17 March 1905; in Society of California Pioneers library.

15. An entry in the Bohemian Club Board of Directors *Minutes,* 11 January 1899, reads, "On motion, it was resolved that the Bohemian Club, recognizing the effort of its only living Honorary member of the gentler sex, does, through its directory, appoint Miss Ina D. Coolbrith its librarian, at a salary of $50 monthly, payable to her order, as a slight testimonial of the affectionate esteem in which she is held by her fellow members." This statement is quoted in a letter from Dan Gilson, Bohemian Club Historiographer, to Josephine Rhodehamel, 29 January 1968; letter in our files. Additional comment in Daniel Gilson, "Ina Donna Coolbrith, 1841-1928," manuscript, 1968, also in our files; Raymund Wood, "Ina Coolbrith, Librarian," *California Librarian* 19(April 1958):102-4, 132.

16. Letter from Bohemian Club member, Ferdinand Burgdorff, to Josephine Rhodehamel, 19 December 1967; in our files.

17. Gilson, "Ina Coolbrith," manuscript; also Bohemian Club, *Annals* and its *A Brief Catalog of the Published Works of Bohemian Club Authors.*
18. Ina Coolbrith, in a letter to Frank Deering, 18 March 1917, in Bohemian Club files; quoted by Gilson in "Ina Coolbrith" manuscript.
19. Letter, Ferdinand Burgdorff to Josephine Rhodehamel, 19 December 1967.
20. "A Page of Herrick," *San Francisco Call,* 29 June 1902, also Coolbrith, *Wings of Sunset,* p. 133; "The Wind's Word," *Sunset Magazine* 13(October 1904):554; "Wood-call," *Sunset Magazine* 15(July 1905):276, also Coolbrith, *Wings of Sunset,* pp. 55-56; "The Cactus Hedge," *Out West Magazine* 17(October 1902):429.
21. Ina Coolbrith, *Scrapbooks,* 1:177.
22. "The Lot of Christ," *Normal Pennant* 7:4(1904); "Paderewski," *San Francisco Examiner,* 6 April 1900; "Joseph Le Conte," *University of California Magazine* 7(September 1901):213; "William Keith, Artist," *Out West Magazine* 18(April 1903):432; "Henry Holmes," *Sunset Magazine* 16(February 1906):370; "With the Laurel to Edmund Clarence Stedman, on his Seventieth Birthday, October 8, 1903," *Atlantic Monthly* 102(August 1908):202; "Bret Harte," *Overland Monthly,* n.s. 40(September 1902):208. All but two, "Joseph Le Conte" and "Henry Holmes," are included in *Wings of Sunset.*
23. E. C. Stedman, in a letter to Miss Coolbrith, 17 November 1903, Bancroft Library.
24. *Atlantic Monthly* 102(August 1908):202.
25. "Bret Harte," stanzas 11 and 12; *Wings of Sunset,* pp. 34-37.
26. DAR of California, *Collections,* 1953, 17:101; DAR of California, *Records from Tombstones in Laurel Hill Cemetery, San Francisco, California, 1853-1937,* p. 95, in Sutro Branch, California State Library, San Francisco.
27. Personal interview with Mrs. Ina (Cook) Graham, Berkeley.
28. Ibid.
29. DAR of California, *Collections,* 1953, 17:102.
30. Crocker-Langley, *San Francisco Directory,* 1896-1928.
31. Letters from D. C. Pickett to Ina Coolbrith, Coolbrith Papers, Huntington Library, San Marino, California.
32. Letter of Ina Coolbrith, 18 July 1904, in library of the Society of California Pioneers, San Francisco.
33. *San Francisco Chronicle,* 24 October 1904.
34. *San Francisco Examiner,* 13 October 1904.
35. *San Francisco Call,* 15 May 1905; also letter from Lydia Morrow to C. W. Stoddard, 29 April 1905, in Stoddard Papers, Bancroft Library.
36. Coolbrith, *Scrapbooks,* 1:222.
37. Letter, E. C. Stedman to Ina Coolbrith, 17 November 1903; Bancroft Library.
38. *San Francisco Bulletin,* 22 October 1903.
39. "American Poets of Today," *Current Literature* 28(April 1900):16-17.
40. *Appleton's Annual Cyclopedia and Register of Important Events of the Year 1900,* 5:331-35.
41. Flora H. Loughead, "Books and Writers," *Sunset Magazine* 9(July 1902):217-19; G. W. James, "Ina D. Coolbrith," *Impressions Quarterly* 4(June 1903):45-48.
42. G. W. James, "Ina D. Coolbrith," *National Magazine* 26(June 1907):315-22.
43. T. W. Higginson, "Butterflies in Poetry," *Atlantic Monthly* 93(June 1904):746-54.
44. Coolbrith, *Scrapbooks,* 1:185.
45. Charles Warren Stoddard, *For the Pleasure of His Company, an Affair of the Misty City, Thrice Told.*
46. Letter from Ina Coolbrith to Mrs. Jeanie Peet, undated, about 1918, Bancroft Library; also a manuscript in Mrs. Graham's files wherein the prototype of "Little Mama" complains that Stoddard had betrayed her confidences, and that the novel had defamed her character.

47. *San Francisco News-Letter*, 17 April 1906; clipping of this in Coolbrith, *Scrapbooks*, 1:189.
48. Based on personal interview with Jesse Winter Smith in San Jose, California, summer 1953.
49. Last stanza of lyric, "From Russian Hill," *Sunset Magazine* 35(August 1915): 270-71; Coolbrith, *Wings of Sunset*, pp. 14-16.

Chapter 24: Toppling Wall and Ruined Hearth

Quotation at beginning of chapter is the fifth stanza of Ina Coolbrith's lyric, "San Francisco—April 18, 1906," *Putnam's Magazine*, October 1906; also in her collection, *Wings of Sunset*.

1. The literature of the San Francisco earthquake and fire of 18 April 1906, is extensive. Helpful sources for this chapter: typewritten statement by Ina Coolbrith in her *Scrapbooks*, 1:190, California Room, Oakland Free Library; William Bronson, *The Earth Shook, the Sky Burned*, pp. 50, 77, 79; John C. Kennedy, *The Great Earthquake and Fire, San Francisco, 1906*, pp. 165-66; Oscar Lewis, *This was San Francisco*, pp. 259-84; *San Francisco Call-Chronicle-Examiner*, 19 April 1906; James B. Stetson, *San Francisco During the Eventful Days of April 1906;* Monica Sutherland, *The Damndest Finest Ruins*.
2. Sutherland, pp. 94-95.
3. *San Francisco Call-Chronicle-Examiner*, 19 April 1906.
4. Miss Coolbrith's statement, *Scrapbooks*, 1:190; Harr Wagner, *Joaquin Miller and His Other Self*, p. 228; also letter from Harriet Howe to Ina Coolbrith, 1 May 1906, in Coolbrith Papers, Huntington Library, San Marino, California.
5. Information from Mrs. Ina Graham, Berkeley, California.
6. Ina Coolbrith in an undated letter in answer to one from Eleanor Davenport of 9 April 1907. Miss Coolbrith's very frank letter may not have been mailed, for Miss Davenport made no reference to it in subsequent correspondence, in Coolbrith Papers, Bancroft Library, University of California, Berkeley.
7. Letters from Harriet Howe to Ina Coolbrith, 19 April and 1 May 1906, Huntington Library.
8. Mary Huff's letter to Ina Coolbrith, 20 April 1906, Huntington Library.
9. Letters to Ina Coolbrith from M. Perry, 22 April, and S. G. Darling, 10 May 1906, Huntington Library.
10. Alice Cooley's letter to Miss Coolbrith, 4 May 1906, in Huntington Library.
11. Letter, Stedman to Coolbrith, 31 July 1906, Huntington Library.
12. Gertrude Atherton's letter to Mrs. W. C. Morrow, 13 June [1906], in Bancroft Library.
13. Bronson, p. 50.
14. Oakland Free Library, *Annual Report*, 1907 (Oakland, 1907) pp. 16-17; Josephine DeWitt, *The Murals in the Oakland Free Library*, 1931, manuscript in California Room, Oakland Free Library.
15. Undated (April 1907) letter from Ina Coolbrith to Eleanor Davenport.
16. Ina Lillian Cook, "Ina Donna Coolbrith," *Westward* 1(May 1928):4.
17. Bronson, p. 77.
18. Bronson, p. 79.
19. Letter of Eleanor Davenport to Mrs. E. J. Boalt, 4 June 1906, Bancroft Library.
20. Letters from Mary Austin to Ina Coolbrith, 29 May and 14 June 1906, Bancroft Library.
21. Ina Coolbrith, "A Letter from Ina Coolbrith," *Town Talk*, 28 November 1908.
22. Torrey Connor to Ina Coolbrith, 16 May 1906, letter in Huntington Library.
23. Letters from E. C. Stedman to Ina Coolbrith, 8, 14 July, 4 October 1906, Huntington Library.
24. Address given by Miss Coolbrith in an advertisement in *Oakland Enquirer*,

30 October 1906. Letters were addressed to her there from August to November 1906.

25. Letters from Ina Coolbrith to J. L. Gillis, 6 July 1906, Coolbrith Papers, California State Library, Sacramento.

26. Undated (April 1907) letter from Ina Coolbrith to Eleanor Davenport.

27. Letter from J. L. Gillis to Ina Coolbrith, 13 December 1906, with Miss Coolbrith's reply on verso, Coolbrith Papers, California State Library.

28. Letters, G. W. James to Ina Coolbrith, 25, 30 June 1906, Huntington Library.

29. James to Coolbrith, 25 June 1906, letter.

30. G. W. James to Ina Coolbrith, 4 July 1906, letter in Huntington Library.

31. Coolbrith, "A Letter from Ina Coolbrith"; also *San Francisco Chronicle*, 11 December 1906, and other clippings on the gift of a Corte Madera lot to Ina Coolbrith by Frank Pixley's widow, *Scrapbooks*, 1:194.

32. *San Francisco Examiner*, 1 August 1906.

33. Registered letter from Eleanor Davenport to Ina Coolbrith, 10 August 1906, with letter carrier's memo on envelope, Bancroft Library.

34. Letter from Miss Davenport to Miss Coolbrith, 11 August 1906, describes James's plan to cooperate with Spinners, Bancroft Library.

35. Anna Pratt Simpson, "The Spinners' Book of Fiction," review, *San Francisco Call*, Sunday Magazine Section, Part 1, 27 October 1907. This full-page, illustrated article by the wife of the *Call's* managing editor, Ernest S. Simpson, gives a history of the club and an account of the benefit proposed. See also Eleanor Davenport's letters to Ina Coolbrith in Bancroft Library.

36. Coolbrith, *Scrapbooks*, 1:197, 199.

37. Coolbrith, *Scrapbooks*, 1:199.

38. Letter from Irving Richman to Ina Coolbrith, 20 March 1914, Huntington Library.

39. *Putnam's Magazine* 1(October 1906):108; also in *Wings of Sunset*, pp. 9-10.

40. Edward F. O'Day, "A Neglected Poet," *Town Talk* 15(22 September 1906): 10-11.

41. Letter from Josephine Zeller to Ina Coolbrith, dated only Wednesday [26 September 1906], in Huntington Library.

42. Coolbrith, "A Letter from Ina Coolbrith."

43. Letter from Ferdinand Burgdorff to Josephine Rhodehamel, 19 December 1967, in our files.

44. *Oakland Enquirer*, 30 October 1906.

45. 15 Lincoln Street is used in letters Ina Coolbrith wrote to J. L. Gillis in December 1906, California State Library. Eleanor Davenport addressed one to her there on 10 December 1906, Bancroft Library.

46. "A small flat was found in the artist Cadenasso's home on Russian Hill," Lydia Morrow, "Ina Donna Coolbrith," *Clubwoman*, (June 1916). The house is described as a green and white Victorian by Margot Patterson Doss, *San Francisco at Your Feet* (New York, 1964), p. 70. The artist was Giuseppi Cadenasso who lived in the upper flat, no. 17. Miss Coolbrith's occupancy of no. 15 from 1907 through 1909 confirmed by her next-door neighbor, Miss Anna De Martini of 1809 Taylor Street, in a personal interview, 22 July 1958.

47. *San Jose Mercury*, 14 February 1907; Coolbrith, *Scrapbooks*, 1:217-19.

48. Letter from Mrs. E. J. Boalt to Ina Coolbrith, 12 April 1908; Bancroft Library.

49. Letter from Joyce Jansen, San Francisco Recreation and Park Department, 31 July 1968, to Josephine Rhodehamel, gives location and size of park; in our files. In the upper right corner of the bronze plaque is a bas relief profile portrait of Ina Coolbrith. The text is as follows:

Ina Donna Coolbrith. First white child to enter California by Beckwourth Pass, in first covered wagon train traveling that route, September, 1852. Thirty-two years a librarian, friend and counselor to three generations of California writers. Inscribed on roll of honor Native Daughters of the Golden West, June

11, 1915. Given the honorary title 'Loved Laurel-Crowned Poet of California,' April 21, 1919, by act of State Legislature. First Poet-Laureate in America. Presented to the City of San Francisco, June 15, 1947, by the San Francisco Parlors, Native Daughters of the Golden West.

50. Letter, 13 December 1906, published in full in *Oakland Enquirer*, 10 January 1920.

Chapter 25: The Home Funds

The lines quoted at the beginning of the chapter are from Ina Coolbrith's lyric "Hope," first published in the *Overland Monthly* of June 1874 and later included in her *Wings of Sunset*.

1. Grace Hibberd, Emma Dawson, Anna Shaw, and Mrs. B. W. Cook are some of the names mentioned by Miss Coolbrith as persons offered homes or lots; statement in undated letter (April 1907) from Ina Coolbrith to Eleanor Davenport, in Coolbrith Papers, Bancroft Library, University of California, Berkeley.
2. "Also, I am supposed to be 'supported' (I ought to be able to *stand!*) by Mrs. Boalt and other rich friends, and when I make denial they look at me with pained incredulity." From undated letter to Eleanor Davenport cited above.
3. Letter, Ina Coolbrith to Eleanor Davenport, 5 November 1908, Bancroft Library.
4. Ina Coolbrith, "A Letter from Ina Coolbrith," *Town Talk*, 28 November 1908.
5. Letters between Miss Coolbrith and Miss Davenport, Bancroft Library.
6. The two undated broadsides are in the Coolbrith Papers, Bancroft Library. She did not see them before they were distributed.
7. Brief letter from Ina Coolbrith to Eleanor Davenport (undated, but probably 8 April 1907) and reply from Miss Davenport, 9 April 1907, both in Bancroft Library.
8. *San Francisco Examiner*, 4 August 1907.
9. Gertrude Atherton in a letter to Ina Coolbrith, 18 September 1907, Bancroft Library.
10. Letters from Herman Whitaker to Ina Coolbrith, 1908-10, also letters to him from the following, all in 1909: Mary Hallock Foote, 24 March; W. C. Morrow, 24 March; Miriam Michelson, 25 March; Henry Rideout, 26 March; Bailey Millard, 27 March; Isobel Field, 6 April; and James Hopper, 9 April. All in Coolbrith Papers, Bancroft Library.
11. Spinners Club, *The Spinners' Book of Fiction*, by Gertrude Atherton and others.
12. Anna Pratt Simpson, "The Spinners' Book of Fiction," review, *San Francisco Call*, Sunday Magazine Section, Part 1, 27 October 1907.
13. *San Francisco Call*, Sunday, 3 September 1908.
14. Letters from Ina Coolbrith to Eleanor Davenport (undated, probably 5 November 1908) and Ednah Robinson Aiken, 6 January 1909; both in Bancroft Library; also a letter to Mrs. Aiken, 9 November 1908, in Coolbrith Papers, California Room, Oakland Free Library.
15. Ina Coolbrith to the Spinners Club, letter of resignation, 5 November 1908, also her letter to Eleanor Davenport, sent with the money, and with a receipt in Miss Coolbrith's hand, dated 5 November 1908, and signed by Miss Davenport, Bancroft Library.
16. Ina Coolbrith, *Scrapbooks*, 2:35-38.
17. Letter from C. W. Stoddard to Ina Coolbrith, 16 October 1908, Coolbrith Papers, Bancroft Library.
18. Letters of Herman Whitaker to Ina Coolbrith in 1909, Bancroft Library.
19. Note by Miss Coolbrith at bottom of letter to her from G. W. James, 30 June 1906, Coolbrith Papers, Huntington Library, San Marino, California.
20. Letter, G. W. James to Ina Coolbrith, 25 June 1906, Huntington Library.

21. Gertrude Atherton, in a letter to Ina Coolbrith, 11 December 1907, Huntington Library.
22. Letter from James to Coolbrith, 11 March 1907, Huntington Library.
23. Authors' Club, *Liber Scriptorum*, first book of the Authors' Club (New York, 1893). The book is described in the *Los Angeles Times*, 18 April 1907, as a gift to the Home Fund for Ina Coolbrith; also clippings in Coolbrith, *Scrapbooks*, 1:222.
24. Ina Coolbrith's letter to James, 7 August 1908, Huntington Library.
25. Letter, James to Coolbrith, 31 May 1907, Huntington Library.
26. Coolbrith, *Scrapbooks*, 1:190-99, 203-8, 220-22; 2:5-9, 12-25, 35-38.
27. James to Coolbrith, 4 August 1908, letter in Huntington Library.
28. Letters: Ina Coolbrith to American Bank and Trust Co., Pasadena, 9 June; American Bank and Trust Co. to Miss Coolbrith, 12 June; Ina Coolbrith to Mrs. M. H. Lewis, 14 June; all 1908, all in Huntington Library.
29. Ina Coolbrith to G. W. James, undated letter [14 June 1908?] in Huntington Library.
30. Coolbrith to James, 7 August 1908, letter in Huntington Library.
31. Letter from G. W. James to Ina Coolbrith, 6 August 1908, Huntington Library.
32. ["A Collection of Poems Dedicated to Ina Coolbrith"], 1907, manuscript in Bancroft Library.
33. Letter from C. W. Stoddard to Miss Coolbrith, 16 February 1907, Bancroft Library.
34. Citation in *American Catalog*, 1905-7 (New York, 1908); see also *San Francisco Chronicle*, 19 June 1907.
35. Letter from James D. Phelan to Ina Coolbrith, 5 May 1925, Bancroft Library.
36. *San Jose Mercury*, 24 November 1907.
37. Copies of the program in both Bancroft Library and Oakland Free Library.
38. Ibid.
39. Letter from Gertrude Atherton to Ina Coolbrith, 30 November 1907, Bancroft Library.
40. *San Francisco Chronicle*, 28 November 1907; *San Francisco Bulletin*, 16 December 1907.
41. Letter from Herman Whitaker to Ina Coolbrith, 9 January 1908, Bancroft Library.
42. Gertrude Atherton to Ina Coolbrith, 11 December 1907, letter in Huntington Library.
43. *Redwood City Gazette*, 4 December 1907.
44. Letter from Ina Coolbrith to Mrs. Lena Simon, 26 November 1907, Coolbrith Papers, California Historical Society, San Francisco.
45. Letter to Mrs. Simon, 16 December 1907, California Historical Society Library.
46. Based on interview, 22 July 1958, with Miss Anna De Martini, San Francisco, Miss Coolbrith's next door neighbor from 1907 to 1909.

Chapter 26: A Home of Her Own

The quotation at the beginning of the chapter is from Ina Coolbrith's lyric, "Opportunity," published in *Munsey's Magazine*, (August 1909), and later included in her collection, *Wings of Sunset*.

1. Letters to Ina Coolbrith from Gertrude Atherton, 30 November and 1 December 1907, and Eleanor Davenport, 10, 15 August 1906, all in Coolbrith Papers, Bancroft Library, University of California, Berkeley.
2. Memorandum by Ina Coolbrith enclosed with her letter to Herman Whitaker, 17 September 1909, in Bancroft Library; also letter to Miss Coolbrith from Johannah L. Neall, 21 January 1908, in Coolbrith Papers, Huntington Library, San Marino, California.

3. Letter from G. W. James to J. G. and Sara [Lemmon] 2 March 1908, Huntington Library.
4. Ibid.; also letter to unnamed correspondent, 28 February 1908, Huntington Library.
5. Ina Coolbrith to Mrs. M. H. Lewis, 14 June 1908, letter in Huntington Library.
6. Letters from Ina Coolbrith to American Bank and Trust Co., Pasadena, 17 March, 9 June 1908, Huntington Library.
7. *San Francisco Call*, 6, 7, 17 May 1908; post card from Kate Kennedy to Ina Coolbrith, 17 April 1908, Bancroft Library.
8. E. C. Stedman died 18 January 1908; *Dictionary of American Biography* 17:552-53; letter from Bliss Perry to Ina Coolbrith, 21 April 1908, in Bancroft Library.
9. *Atlantic Monthly* 102(August 1908):202.
10. *San Francisco Call*, 24, 25 April 1909; *San Francisco Chronicle*, 25 April 1909.
11. *San Francisco Chronicle*, 27 April 1909.
12. Letter by Ina Coolbrith read at the Stoddard Memorial meeting held by the Pacific Short Story Club in Berkeley; Ina Coolbrith, *Scrapbooks*, 2:42.
13. Letter from Ina Coolbrith to Charles Lummis, 14 June 1926, Huntington Library.
14. Letter from Ferdinand Burgdorff to Josephine Rhodehamel, 19 December 1967, in our files.
15. Ina L. Cook, "Ina Coolbrith," *Wasp-News Letter*, (22-29 December 1928), p. 50.
16. "Ina Coolbrith came down to the funeral, looking like a sibyl of stone." From a letter of George Sterling to Ambrose Bierce, 6 July 1909, in the Berg Collection, New York Public Library; quoted by M. E. Grenander, "Ambrose Bierce and Charles Warren Stoddard: some unpublished correspondence," *Huntington Library Quarterly* 23(May 1960):261-92.
17. Cook, "Ina Coolbrith."
18. Charles Warren Stoddard, *Poems* (San Francisco, 1867).
19. Letters from Sara Makee to Ina Coolbrith in July 1909, Huntington Library.
20. C. W. Stoddard, *For the Pleasure of his Company*, p. 91.
21. Sara Makee to Ina Coolbrith, 15 October [1909?] Huntington Library.
22. Letters to Ina Coolbrith from D. E. Hudson (incorrectly dated 13 February 1909) and Ellen G. Moriarty, 18 November 1909, both in Huntington Library.
23. Letter from J. C. McCrackin to Ina Coolbrith, 21 November 1909, Huntington Library.
24. *San Francisco Bulletin*, 9 October 1909.
25. Letter from Mrs. Makee to Miss Coolbrith, 15 October [1909?].
26. Letters to Ina Coolbrith, from William Woodworth, 9 November 1909, 16 February 1910, and from Burton Kline, one undated, another 22 May 1913, all in Bancroft Library. Letters to her from C. M. Kozley, 25 May 1913, and from Sara Makee, 15 October [1909?], both in Huntington Library.
27. Sara Makee's letter to Ina Coolbrith, 15 October [1909?].
28. Sara Makee to Ina Coolbrith, 17 February 1910, letter in Huntington Library.
29. Death of Adeline Knapp, 6 June 1909, *San Francisco Call*, 7 June 1909; also letter from Mary C. Richardson to Ina Coolbrith, 18 June 1909, in Huntington Library.
30. *San Francisco Call*, 25 May 1909, program in Coolbrith Papers, California Room, Oakland Free Library.
31. *San Francisco Bulletin*, 14 December 1909.
32. Letter from Alice K. Cooley to Ina Coolbrith, 28 December 1909, in Huntington Library.
33. Description of facade and interior based on photographic illustrations in Marian Taylor, "Ina Coolbrith, California Poet," *Overland Monthly*, n.s. 64(October 1914): 327-39. Miss Coolbrith's small account book for building expenditures is in Bancroft Library.

34. Letter from Ferdinand Burgdorff to Josephine Rhodehamel, 19 December 1967, in our files. Bohemian Club at Post and Leavenworth, 1907-1908; at Post and Taylor thereafter; Crocker-Langley, *San Francisco Directory,* 1907 and after.

35. Letters to Ina Coolbrith: Sara Makee, 17, 26 February, 2 March 1910, and William Woodworth, 8 May 1910, all in Huntington Library; from Burton Kline, undated, William Woodworth, 16 February 1910, and Gertrude Atherton, 9 May 1910, all in Bancroft Library.

36. Letters from Alice Cooley to Ina Coolbrith, 16 May and 7 July 1910, in Huntington Library.

37. Letter from Ina Coolbrith to James L. Gillis, undated, Coolbrith Papers, California State Library, Sacramento.

38. Abbie E. Krebs, ed., *La Copa de Oro,* pp. 113-18.

39. Letter, Alice Cooley to Ina Coolbrith, 16 May 1910, Huntington Library.

40. Undated letter from Augusta Borle to Ina Coolbrith, Huntington Library.

41. Letters from Leon Blum to Ina Coolbrith, 22 August and 10 October 1910, Huntington Library.

42. *San Francisco Call,* 1 March 1910, p. 5.

43. Letters from Mrs. Leslie to Ina Coolbrith, 15 December 1911, 31 March 1912, in Bancroft Library.

44. Madeleine B. Stern, *Purple Passage, the Life of Mrs. Frank Leslie,* pp. 71-76, 179, 264.

45. Letter from W. W. Cooley to Ina Coolbrith, 25 November 1910, Huntington Library.

46. Letter from Ina Coolbrith to Laura Y. Pinney, undated [28 November 1910], Huntington Library.

47. City of Berkeley, California, Health Dept., Bureau of Vital Statistics. *Death Certificate #144.*

48. *San Francisco Call,* 10 January 1911.

49. Letter from Ina Coolbrith to Herbert Bashford, 19 December 1910, in Bancroft Library.

50. *Who Was Who in America, 1897-1942,* p. 66. Letters from Ina Coolbrith to Herbert Bashford, 8 April 1901, 4 March 1911; also personal conversations with Mrs. Alice Bashford Wallace, Sidney, B. C., Canada.

51. Letter from Frank Unger to Ina Coolbrith, 28 January 1911, in Bancroft Library.

52. *San Francisco Call,* 14 March 1911.

53. *Oakland Enquirer,* 3 April 1911; *Alameda Argus,* 28 March 1911; Ina Coolbrith, *Scrapbooks,* 2:59-61. Description of the Connor home and grounds from a relative of the family, Mrs. Frances Sadler McFall of Berkeley, 17 February 1968. Miscellaneous letters to Ina Coolbrith from Torrey Connor and June Nahl in Huntington Library. Letter from Warren Cheney to Ina Coolbrith, 6 April 1911, Bancroft Library.

54. Letters to Miss Coolbrith from L. Y. Pinney, 14 March 1911, and George H. Fitch, 11 March 1911, Huntington Library.

55. H. M. Bland to Ina Coolbrith, 11 April 1911, letter in Bancroft Library.

56. Letter from Mary Burbank to Ina Coolbrith, 10 April 1911, Huntington Library.

57. Letter, L. Y. Pinney to Ina Coolbrith, 30 September 1911, Huntington Library.

58. Letter from Ina Coolbrith to J. L. Gillis, 2 May 1911, California State Library.

59. "Renewal," *Century Magazine* 78(May 1909):81; "Opportunity," *Munsey's Magazine* 41(August 1909):659; "Evenfall at the Gate," *Sunset Magazine* 23(December 1909):558; "Harriet M. Skidmore," *Notre Dame Quarterly* 2(December 1909):30; "At Carmel," *Oakland Tribune,* 22 August 1909. All but "Harriet M. Skidmore" are included in Ina Coolbrith's collection, *Wings of Sunset,* with "At Carmel," renamed "Carmel-by-the-Sea."

60. "Santa Clara Valley," *Santa Clara News,* 15 March 1910; "Woman," *San Francisco Post,* 9 November 1910; both in *Wings of Sunset.*

446

61. "Mt. Hamilton," *Sunset Magazine* 26(May 1911):536; *Wings of Sunset,* p. 23.
62. Letters to Ina Coolbrith: Gertrude Atherton, 9, 22 January 1911; Jessie B. Rittenhouse, 6 June 1911, all in Bancroft Library.
63. Letter from Ina Coolbrith to Panama-Pacific International Exposition Company, 29 April 1911, in her *Scrapbooks,* 2:62-63.
64. *San Francisco Chronicle,* 30 April 1911.
65. Ina Coolbrith Circle, *Letter and Enclosure,* 9 November 1946, in Atherton Papers, Bancroft Library.
66. Letters from E. F. O'Day to Ina Coolbrith, 20 September 1911, in Huntington Library; *Town Talk,* 30 September 1911.
67. H. M. Bland, "Sketch of the First Western Literary Period," *Pacific Short Story Club Magazine* (July 1911).
68. H. M. Bland, "Where Some California Writers Live," *San Francisco Call,* 19 November 1911, Magazine Section, part. 1, p. [5].
69. Letters to Ina Coolbrith from C. W. Carruth, 28 November 1911, and Herman Whitaker, undated, both in Bancroft Library.
70. Mrs. L. H. Martin, "The Literature of California," *Out West Magazine* 3(January 1912):62-64, 98-100.
71. Letter, Mrs. L. H. Martin to Ina Coolbrith, 2 February 1912, in Huntington Library.
72. Mrs. Martin to Miss Coolbrith, 9 February 1912, letter in Huntington Library.
73. Ina Coolbrith's letter to G. W. James, 9 February 1912, Huntington Library.
74. Letter, Ina Coolbrith to J. Miller, 9 February 1912, Huntington Library.
75. Reply, Miller to Coolbrith, 14 February 1912, Bancroft Library.
76. W. D. Armes in a letter to Miss Coolbrith, 23 May 1913, Bancroft Library.
77. Ina Coolbrith in a letter to Mrs. Anna B. Games, 30 April 1912, California Room, Oakland Free Library.
78. Letter from Ina Coolbrith to Mrs. Lena Simons, 20 December 1912, Coolbrith Papers, California Historical Society Library.
79. Postcard to Ina Coolbrith from Ina Lillian Cook, 7 June 1912, Bancroft Library.
80. Letters to Ina Coolbrith from Charles Lummis, 1 November 1912, Huntington Library, and 18 November 1912, Bancroft Library.
81. Letter to Ina Coolbrith from Mary Zeller, 1 June 1912, Huntington Library.
82. Letter from J. Miller to Ina Coolbrith, 11 October 1912 (postmarked 12 November), in Bancroft Library.
83. Letters to Ina Coolbrith from Florence de Bazus, 31 March 1912, and from Iza Hardy, 5 April 1911, both in Bancroft Library.
84. Miller's letter, 11 October 1912.
85. Joaquin Miller to Ina Coolbrith, 17 October 1912 (postmarked 18 November), in Bancroft Library.
86. Coolbrith, *Scrapbooks,* 2:108.
87. Letters to Ina Coolbrith from James D. Phelan, 12 September 1912, Huntington Library, and Gertrude Atherton, 14 September 1912, Bancroft Library.
88. *San Francisco Call,* 26 June 1912.
89. *Notre Dame Quarterly* 4(June 1912):3.
90. From Charles Phillips to Ina Coolbrith, a postcard from Rome, 12 November 1912, and a letter, 13 June 1916, both in Huntington Library; also interview with Mrs. Ina Graham of Berkeley, 23 June 1956.
91. Mrs. Graham, in interview; also letters from Ina Coolbrith to Mrs. L. Simons, 11 October 1912, California Historical Society, and to Herbert Bashford, 25 February 1913, Bancroft Library.
92. From personal conversation with Mrs. Alice Bashford Wallace from time to time.
93. Ina Coolbrith in an undated letter to Herbert Bashford [? February 1913], in Bancroft Library.
94. Letter from Ina Coolbrith to Joaquin Miller, 9 February 1913, Bancroft Library.

95. Undated letter from Herman Whitaker to Ina Coolbrith, Bancroft Library.
96. Date of birth 8 September 1837, according to *Joaquin Miller's California Diary, 1855-1857*, ed. by John S. Richards (Seattle, 1936).
97. *San Francisco Examiner*, 18 February 1913.
98. "Joaquin Miller Day at Pacific Coast Women's Press Association, 14 April 1913, meeting," *Town Talk* 19 April 1913.
99. Jeanne E. Francoeur, "Classic Day of Women's Press Association," *Woman Citizen*, (May 1913). Ina Coolbrith, "A Tribute to Joaquin Miller," autographed manuscript in Bancroft Library. The "personal notebook" in her possession was a diary kept by Miller from 1855 to 1857. It was later edited by John S. Richards as *Joaquin Miller's California Diary*. It establishes Miller's birth date as 8 September 1837, instead of 10 November 1841. Miller, in a letter to Ina Coolbrith, dated 10 November 1907, said he was "sixty-six today!" In Bancroft Library.
100. Letter from Mrs. S. A. Darling to Ina Coolbrith, 8 April 1912, Huntington Library. Mrs. Darling was the wife of Miller's caretaker at The Hights.
101. Undated letter from Lischen Miller to Ina Coolbrith, Bancroft Library.
102. Letter from Ina Coolbrith to Herbert Bashford, 25 February 1913, Bancroft Library. A map of The Hights in the files of the Oakland Park Department shows the cemetery back of the pyre. There were no markers when the estate became a city park, and the burial plot has become obliterated.
103. *San Francisco Examiner*, 26 May 1913; "Vale, Joaquin!" *San Francisco Star*, 31 May 1913; also in Coolbrith, *Scrapbooks*, 2:94.

Part Five: The Laureate

Chapter 27: The Laureate

The quotation at the beginning of the chapter is from Ina Coolbrith's acceptance speech, 30 June 1915.

1. Letter from George Sterling to Ina Coolbrith, 27 May 1913, Bancroft Library, University of California, Berkeley.
2. Josephine C. McCrackin in a letter to Miss Coolbrith, 9 June 1913, Bancroft Library.
3. Iza Hardy in a letter to Ina Coolbrith, 15 August 1913, Bancroft Library.
4. "At Anchor," *Overland Monthly*, n.s. 64(November 1914):442; also in Ina Coolbrith, *Wings of Sunset*, p. 38-39.
5. *San Francisco Chronicle*, 14 March 1913.
6. Letter from Herman Whitaker to Ina Coolbrith, 2 December 1912, Bancroft Library.
7. Letter from Mrs. Hearst to Miss Coolbrith, 15 September 1913, in Bancroft Library.
8. Letters to Ina Coolbrith: Herman Scheffauer, 17 June and 3 August 1913, 16 March 1914, all in Bancroft Library; Gertrude Atherton, 28 February and 1 March 1914, in Huntington Library, San Marino, California.
9. Scheffauer's wedding announcement, 25 June 1912, Bancroft Library.
10. Letters to Ina Coolbrith: Gertrude Atherton, 14 June 1915; Sara Lemmon, 7 June 1914, both in Huntington Library.
11. Popcorn born 15 June 1912. The cat's pedigree is among the Coolbrith Papers in the California Room, Oakland Free Library.
12. Ina Coolbrith, *Scrapbooks*, 2:112.
13. Letter from Ina Coolbrith to Albert Brecknock, 19 February 1914, Oakland Free Library. In 1952 Albert Brecknock presented to the Oakland Library his file of letters from Miss Coolbrith.
14. Letter, Mary E. Ahern to Miss Coolbrith, 11 May 1914, Huntington Library.
15. Miss Guiney to Miss Coolbrith, 16 March 1914, Bancroft Library.

16. Tracy Robinson to Ina Coolbrith, 22 November 1914, Bancroft Library.
17. La Salle Pickett to Ina Coolbrith, 7 June 1915, Bancroft Library.
18. General Goethals to Miss Coolbrith, 27 August 1914, Huntington Library.
19. Henrietta Dana Skinner to Ina Coolbrith, 15 June 1915, Bancroft Library.
20. Comstock to Miss Coolbrith, 25 August 1914, Huntington Library.
21. Kinross to Coolbrith, 12 May 1914 and 30 May 1915, Huntington Library.
22. Kate H. Prichard to Ina Coolbrith, 8 June 1915, Bancroft Library.
23. Romain Rolland to Miss Coolbrith, 17 June 1915, Bancroft Library.
24. Herman Scheffauer to Ina Coolbrith, 6 January 1915, Bancroft Library.
25. "On a Fly-leaf of Omar," *Catholic World* 99(May 1914):381; *Literary Digest* 48(30 May 1914):1321; "Point Bonita," *Overland Monthly*, n.s. 63(May 1914):427; "War and Peace," *San Francisco Examiner*, 4(21 September 1914):4, also in Coolbrith, *Scrapbooks*, 2:120; "At Anchor," *Overland Monthly*, n.s. 64(November 1914):442; "A Tribute" (to Caroline M. Severance), *California Outlook*, 17(12 December 1914):8. All but "War and Peace" and "A Tribute" are included in Miss Coolbrith's collection, *Wings of Sunset*.
26. Letter to Ina Coolbrith from Dr. H. Staats Moore, 20 March 1914, Huntington Library.
27. *Everywoman* (June 1914).
28. Two letters to Ina Coolbrith from H. Isabel Kinsey, 31 March 1914, and undated [April 1914], both in Huntington Library.
29. Houghton Mifflin to Ina Coolbrith, 16 May, 11, 26 June, 23 July, 17 August 1914, all in Bancroft Library.
30. Letter from T. R. Bannerman to Ina Coolbrith, 29 July 1914, Huntington Library.
31. Coolbrith, *Scrapbooks*, 2:108.
32. Selina Solomon, *How We Won the Vote in California* (San Francisco, 1912); also letter from Rose Brier to Ina Coolbrith, 15 October 1911, in Huntington Library.
33. *Dictionary of American Biography*, 14:523-24; Walton Bean, *Boss Ruef's San Francisco* (Berkeley, 1952), p. 10.
34. Bret Harte, *Stories and Poems and Other Uncollected Writings;* comp. by Charles Meeker Kozlay (Boston, 1914).
35. Coolbrith, *Scrapbooks*, 2:114.
36. *Everywoman* (June 1914).
37. Marian Taylor, "Ina Coolbrith, California Poet," *Overland Monthly*, n.s. 64 (October 1914):327-99.
38. Letter from Charles Phillips to Ina Coolbrith, 18 October 1914, Huntington Library.
39. Zoeth S. Eldredge in a letter to Miss Coolbrith, 21 December 1914, Huntington Library.
40. Richard E. White in a letter to Ina Coolbrith, 27 July 1915, Huntington Library.
41. Letter from Ina Coolbrith to Mrs. North-Whitcomb, 10 April 1915, Sutro Library, San Francisco.
42. Letter from Ina Coolbrith to Mrs. Richard E. White, 1 March 1915, Bancroft Library; Richard E. White to Ina Coolbrith, 4 March 1915, Huntington Library.
43. Letters, Ina Coolbrith to Mrs. I. Lowenberg, 17 March, 19, 20 May 1915; Mrs. Lowenberg to Miss Coolbrith, 20, 22 May 1915; all in Huntington Library. Letter from Ina Coolbrith to Herbert Bashford, 20 May 1915, in Bancroft Library.
44. Letter, Ina Coolbrith to Herbert Bashford, 25 June 1915, Bancroft Library.
45. *San Francisco Examiner*, 16 June 1915.
46. Congress program, Coolbrith Papers, Bancroft Library.
47. Letter from Elizabeth J. Boalt to Ina Coolbrith, 30 April 1915, Bancroft Library.
48. *Everywoman* (July 1915); letters to Ina Coolbrith from Enrique del Castillo,

449

22, 27 November and 10 December 1915, in Bancroft Library.
49. Letter, Robert S. Norman to Ina Coolbrith, undated, in Huntington Library.
50. Manuscript of Mrs. Atherton's paper, "Literary Merchandise," and a letter from her to Senator Phelan, 12 June 1915, in Bancroft Library; also, concerning the paper, an undated telegram to Senator Phelan and a letter from her to Ina Coolbrith, 14 June [1915] in Huntington Library.
51. Coolbrith, *Scrapbooks*, 2:143.
52. Coolbrith, *Scrapbooks*, 2:143.
53. Interview with Mrs. Ina Cook Graham, 23 June 1956.
54. Ella S. Mighels, "Crowned Poet Laureate," *Grizzly Bear* 17(August 1915):4.
55. As none of the published accounts of the event included Miss Coolbrith's speech of acceptance, she had the text printed to give her friends; *Scrapbooks*, 2:148.
56. Josephine C. McCrackin, "Ina Coolbrith Invested with Poet's Crown," *Overland Monthly*, n.s. 66(November 1915):448-50.
57. Coolbrith, *Scrapbooks*, 2:144, program and clippings.
58. *New York Times Book Review*, 18 July 1915, p. 260.
59. Letters, Ina Coolbrith to Mrs. North-Whitcomb, 4 July 1915, Sutro Library; to Herbert Bashford, 7 July 1915, in Bancroft Library; Frank M. Todd to Ina Coolbrith, 15 August 1915, in Huntington Library. Material was requested by F. M. Todd for his history, *The Story of the Exposition*, 5 vols. (New York, 1921). Miss Coolbrith's summary and the papers did not appear in the volumes, since there were nearly a thousand "congresses" at the Exposition.
60. Letter from Ina Coolbrith to Mrs. Wills, 8 July 1915, in California Historical Society Library.
61. Letter from Torrey Connor to Ina Coolbrith, 26 October 1915, Huntington Library.
62. Letter, Lillian Gatlin to Ina Coolbrith, 9 June 1915; Bancroft Library.
63. California. Laws, Statutes, etc. *Statutes, 1919*, chapter 15, p. 1537.
64. Letter from Ina Coolbrith to Albert Bender, 1 March 1922, in Bender Room, Margaret Carnegie Library, Mills College, Oakland, California. She said, "What a mockery is all human honor! *A poet laureate of the Golden State of great America*, with *only the title*. That is, I confess, a pleasant sound but entails difficulties, as the *people* seem to think it is not an empty one." (Her italics.)
65. Letter from Allan R. Ottley to Josephine Rhodehamel, 8 July 1968, in our files. The quotation used comes from Miss Coolbrith's sonnet, "With the Laurel to Edmund Clarence Stedman on His Seventieth Birthday, October 8, 1903," *Atlantic Monthly* 102(August 1908):202; also in Miss Coolbrith's collection, *Wings of Sunset*, p. 149.

Chapter 28: Disenchantment

The chapter begins with a quotation from Ina Coolbrith's brief song, "Rose and Thistle," probably written at some time during her New York sojourn in the early 1920s, and published in her *Wings of Sunset*.

1. Elizabeth J. Boalt to Ina Coolbrith, undated [1915?], in Coolbrith Papers, Bancroft Library, University of California, Berkeley; Ina Coolbrith to Luther Burbank, 3 December 1915, and other letters on the naming of the crimson poppy, Ina Coolbrith, *Scrapbooks*, 2:172.
2. *San Francisco Examiner*, 17 October 1915.
3. Coolbrith, *Scrapbooks*, 2:175.
4. Program for the event, Coolbrith Papers, Bancroft Library, California State Library, and Oakland Free Library; also clippings in *Scrapbooks*, 2:178-83. Letters: Sister Mary Rosalie to Ina Coolbrith, 26 April 1916, in Bancroft Library; Charles

Phillips to Miss Coolbrith, 13 June 1916, Huntington Library, San Marino, California.

5. Ina Coolbrith to Ella S. Mighels, 30 November 1917, California State Library, Sacramento.

6. "At Home Days of Ina Coolbrith," *Wasp*, 2 March 1918; Nathan Newmark, "Literature Society Hears Fine Program," *Hebrew*, 4 January 1918; Ina Coolbrith, "An Afternoon with John Rollin Ridge," *Richmond Banner*, 8 July 1917; Coolbrith, *Scrapbooks*, 2:175-222. Letters, Richard Bret Harte to Ina Coolbrith, 17, 18 July 1916, in Huntington Library.

7. *Oakland Tribune*, 28 April 1916.

8. Ina Coolbrith to Herbert Bashford, 12 May 1916, Bancroft Library; Eufina Tompkins to Ina Coolbrith, 24 May 1916, Huntington Library.

9. *San Diego Union*, 28 October and 2 November 1916; Coolbrith, *Scrapbooks*, 2:189.

10. Herman Whitaker to Ina Coolbrith, 1 August 1916, Bancroft Library.

11. Ina Coolbrith to Mrs. Mighels, 28 August 1916, in California State Library.

12. Ella S. Mighels, *Literary California* (San Francisco, 1918).

13. Thomas Walsh to Ina Coolbrith, 6 September 1917, refers to their correspondence during 1916, letter in Bancroft Library.

14. Elizabeth Boalt to Ina Coolbrith, 29 September 1916, in Bancroft Library.

15. Letter from Ina Coolbrith to Marian Taylor, 14 January 1917 in Bancroft Library.

16. *Oakland Tribune*, 2 January 1917.

17. Coolbrith, *Scrapbooks*, 2:104.

18. M. E. Grenander, "Ambrose Bierce and Charles Warren Stoddard: Some Unpublished Correspondence," *Huntington Library Quarterly* 23(May 1960):261-92.

19. Thomas Walsh to Ina Coolbrith, 19 December 1914, in Bancroft Library.

20. Thomas Walsh to Ina Coolbrith, 6 September and 1 October 1917, letters in Bancroft Library.

21. Charles Warren Stoddard, *Poems*, collected by Ina Coolbrith.

22. *San Francisco Monitor*, 15 September 1917; *Fresno Republican*, 25 October 1917; *San Jose Mercury*, 16 September 1917; *Town Talk*, 25 August 1917; clippings of all these in Coolbrith, *Scrapbooks*, 2:200-205, 207. Letters, Burton Kline to Ina Coolbrith, 6 September 1917, Bancroft Library; Charles Shinn to Ina Coolbrith, 24 September and 26 October 1917, Huntington Library.

23. Ina Coolbrith to Herbert Bashford, 8, 14 August 1917, Bancroft Library.

24. Coolbrith to Bashford, 22 August 1917, letter in Bancroft Library.

25. Francis O'Neill, "Stoddard, Psalmist of the South Seas," *Catholic World*, 105(July 1917):511-16; Walsh to Ina Coolbrith, 1 October 1917, in Bancroft Library; Charles Phillips to Ina Coolbrith, 15 October 1917, in Huntington Library.

26. Walsh's letter to Ina Coolbrith, 6 September 1917, Bancroft Library.

27. *Town Talk*, 25 August 1917.

28. *San Francisco Chronicle*, 22 March 1917.

29. Letter from Marguerite Wilkinson to Ina Coolbrith, 26 February 1917, in Bancroft Library.

30. Annie F. Brown to Ina Coolbrith, 13 January 1917, in Bancroft Library.

31. Ina Coolbrith to Charles S. Greene, 30 June 1917, in Oakland Free Library.

32. Greene to Coolbrith, 10 July 1917, in Oakland Free Library.

33. Edward F. O'Day, "The Laureate of California," *The Lantern* 2(November 1917):227-41.

34. Ina Coolbrith in a letter to Marian Taylor, 26 October 1917, Bancroft Library.

35. Ina Coolbrith, "In the Midst of War," undated clipping from *Everywoman*, in Coolbrith Papers, Oakland Free Library.

36. Letter from Torrey Connor to Ina Coolbrith, 10 August 1917, Huntington Library.

37. *Oakland Tribune*, 8 May 1918.

38. Herman Whitaker to Ina Coolbrith, 10 December 1918; Charles Phillips to Miss Coolbrith, 30 December 1918, both letters in Bancroft Library.

39. Phillips to Coolbrith, 28 January 1920, letter in Bancroft Library.

40. Letter from Charles Phillips to Ina Coolbrith, 13 June 1916, in Huntington Library; Ina Coolbrith to Herbert Bashford, 24 March 1917; letter in Bancroft Library.

41. Letters from Gertrude Atherton in Ina Coolbrith, 12 October and 3 December 1918, in Bancroft Library.

42. Carl Gunderson [Carl Seyfforth, Ulv Youff] *Ulven; Written during Retirement in Switzerland,* pp. 70, 75.

43. *San Francisco Examiner,* 17 March 1918; *San Francisco Call,* 9 July 1918.

44. In a letter to Mrs. Mighels, 19 August 1918, California State Library.

45. Ina Coolbrith, *California.*

46. Ina Coolbrith to Albert Brecknock, 7, 24, September 1918, letters in Oakland Free Library.

47. *San Francisco Examiner,* 9 March 1918.

48. Edward F. O'Day, "The Value to California of Her Poets," *Town Talk,* 22 June 1918.

49. *San Francisco Monitor,* 1 June 1918.

50. Ina Coolbrith's letter to Albert Bender [4? February] 1919, Coolbrith Papers, Bender Room, Margaret Carnegie Library, Mills College, Oakland, California; also her long letter to James D. Phelan, 25 December 1925, in Huntington Library.

51. Bender's letter to Coolbrith, 4 February 1919, and her answer, same date, both in Mills College.

52. Personal interview with Mrs. Alice Bashford Wallace.

53. " . . . and I get wild hunting for things. . . ." Ina Coolbrith in an undated letter to Mrs. Mighels, California State Library.

54. *San Francisco Bulletin,* 15 July 1919.

55. Ina Coolbrith's copy of an undated letter to Robert Norman, in Bancroft Library.

56. Ibid.

57. A letter from Josephine C. McCrackin to Ina Coolbrith, 11 August 1917, in Huntington Library.

58. Ina Coolbrith's undated letter to Robert Norman.

59. It was thought by Miss Coolbrith's physician, friends, and family that faithful Josie "had lost her mind."

60. Letter from James D. Phelan to Miss Coolbrith, 21 June 1919, in Bancroft Library.

Chapter 29: Sojourn in New York

Quoted at the beginning of this chapter are the last two lines of Miss Coolbrith's twelve-line lyric, "Alone," written during her New York period, probably about 1920; it is included in her volume, *Wings of Sunset.*

1. Letter from Ina Coolbrith to Albert Bender, 26 October 1919, in Coolbrith Papers, Bender Room, Margaret Carnegie Library, Mills College, Oakland, California.

2. Letters from Robert Norman to Ina Coolbrith, 31 October, 4, 17, 21 November, 9, 29 December 1919, all in Coolbrith Papers, Bancroft Library, University of California, Berkeley.

3. Charles Lummis in a letter to Ina Coolbrith, 29 September 1919, in Huntington Library, San Marino, California.

4. Ina L. Cook, "Ina Coolbrith and her Circle," *Wasp-News Letter,* (20-27 December 1930), p. 38.

5. Ina Coolbrith in a letter to Albert Bender, 16 December 1919; Mills College.

6. Benjamin De Casseres, "Ina Coolbrith of California's 'Overland Trinity,' " *New York Sun, Books and the Book World,* 7 December 1919, p. 15.
7. "Listening Back," *Sunset Magazine* 45(December 1920):41; also in Coolbrith, *Wings of Sunset,* p. 46.
8. *Poetry Society of America,* November-December 1919, p. 1.
9. *San Francisco Bulletin,* 6 January 1920.
10. Ina Coolbrith to Albert Bender, 20 February 1920, Mills College.
11. "The Dancers," Coolbrith, *Wings of Sunset,* pp. 131-32.
12. Letter from Charles Phillips to Miss Coolbrith, 10 May 1920, Bancroft Library.
13. Percival J. Cooney, *The Dons of the Old Pueblo.*
14. Coolbrith, *Wings of Sunset,* "Felipe," p. 85; "Pancho," p. 86; "Concha," pp. 87-125. Manuscript of "Concha" in Oakland Free Library.
15. Charles Lummis to Ina Coolbrith, 29 July 1921, in Huntington Library.
16. Letters: Ina Coolbrith to Albert Bender, 23 March 1920, Mills College; Josephine H. Phelps to Miss Coolbrith, 25 January 1922, Bancroft Library.
17. *Invitation,* Pleiades Club, Sunday, 18 April 1920 . . . a birthday testimonial to Edwin Markham, Bancroft Library.
18. Letter from Ina Coolbrith to Albert Bender, 12 August 1920, Mills College.
19. Miss Coolbrith to Lena Simons, 13 July 1920, California Historical Society, San Francisco.
20. Letters: Coolbrith to Bender, 19 August 1920, Mills College; Charles Keeler to Coolbrith, 2 September 1920, Bancroft Library.
21. Maynard Dixon in a letter to Ina Coolbrith, 26 August 1920, Bancroft Library.
22-25. Letters from Ina Coolbrith to Albert Bender, 27 September, 30 October 1920, 28 September 1922, 26 March 1923, all in Mills College.
26. *San Francisco Chronicle,* 11 September 1921.
27. Those published in periodicals were "In the Orchard, *Sunset Magazine* 50 (April 1923):50; "With the Caravan," *University of California Chronicle* (July 1926), also a reprint of this with a portrait; "Alien," *Overland Monthly,* n.s. 77(March 1921):41; "Foch: California's Greeting," *San Francisco Bulletin,* 3 December 1921, p. 1. "Foch" was omitted from her collection *Wings of Sunset,* but the first three listed above and the others mentioned in the text were included. For payment for contributions to the *Overland Monthly,* see account book in the Bancroft Library, *Overland Monthly,* 1869-75, *Account of moneys paid contributors.*
28. Miss Coolbrith's letters to Albert Bender, 14 March and 13 April 1921, Mills College.
29. In her letter to Albert Bender, 10 February 1922, Mills College.
30. Letters from Houghton Mifflin Company to Ina Coolbrith, 20 December 1922, 10 January 1923, Bancroft Library.
31. Coolbrith to Bender, 16 December 1922; letter, Mills College.
32. *Bookman* 56(November 1922):379-81.
33. *Oakland Post-Enquirer,* 11 November 1922.
34. George Sterling to Ina Coolbrith, 11 January 1923, Bancroft Library.
35. *Oakland Post-Enquirer.*
36. Letter to Albert Bender, 16 December 1922, Mills College.
37. Miss Coolbrith, in a letter to Albert Bender, 30 December 1920, Mills College.
38. Letter from Anna Markham to Ina Coolbrith [? January 1921], Bancroft Library.
39. Anna Markham in letter to Ina Coolbrith, 18 January 1921, Bancroft Library.
40. Lyman Whitney Allen to Ina Coolbrith, 12 January and 6 February 1921, letters in Bancroft Library.
41. Undated letter from John Farrar to Ina Coolbrith in Bancroft Library; *Bookman* 53(April 1921):185.
42. Letter to Albert Bender from Ina Coolbrith, 30 December 1920, Mills College.
43. Charles Lummis to Ina Coolbrith, 29 July 1921, Huntington Library.
44. Peggy Williams to Ina Coolbrith, 29 April 1927, Bancroft Library.

45. Etta L. Aydelotte's letter to Ina Coolbrith, 6 January 1921, Bancroft Library; letters from Esther B. Darling, 6 July 1921, and Eugene A. Hart, 12 April 1921, to Ina Coolbrith, both in Huntington Library.

46. Christmas messages, 1921, to Ina Coolbrith from Charles Turrill, Mrs. Nellie Sanchez, Nancy B. Mavity, A. M. Robertson, Emily Page, and others, in Bancroft Library.

47. Letter to Mrs. Lena Simons, 24 December 1921, in library of California Historical Society.

48. *Overland Monthly,* n.s. 77(March 1921):41; Coolbrith, *Wings of Sunset,* p. 139. When she sent the poem to the *Overland Monthly,* she changed the final stanza to read,

> No light, revealing, o'er me
> Until from her I go—
> There, where I stand before Thee,
> I trust Thee, God, to know!

In 1927, when she chose the lyric for inclusion in her last collection, she preferred the less optimistic form.

49. Miss Coolbrith's letter to Albert Bender, 4 January 1922, Mills College.

50. Ina Agnes Cook to Ina Coolbrith, 8 February 1922, Bancroft Library.

51. Coolbrith to Bender, 1 March 1922, Mills College.

52. Albert Kinross to Ina Coolbrith, 25 January 1923, Bancroft Library.

53. Address book with Coolbrith Papers, California Room, Oakland Free Library.

54. Edwin and Anna Markham's letters to Ina Coolbrith, 20, 30 March 1922, both in Bancroft Library.

55. Ina Coolbrith in a letter to Albert Bender, 8 June 1923, Mills College.

56. Bio De Casseras, "Pioneer Relives Girlhood Scenes at 'Covered Wagon,' Ina Coolbrith, Poet Laureate of California, Finds James Cruze's Paramount Picture True to Life." An unidentified clipping in Coolbrith Papers, Oakland Free Library.

Chapter 30: This Receding World

Chapter title and quotation from a letter Ina Coolbrith wrote to Albert Bender 18 May 1927.

1. The journey was made from March to September, 1851. "The Covered Wagon" story is supposed to have taken place at about the same period.

2. Her expression in a letter to Albert Bender, 24 June 1921, in Coolbrith Papers, Bender Room, Margaret Carnegie Library, Mills College, Oakland, California.

3. She stayed at Hotel Robins, 711 Post Street, San Francisco, from the last week of May to the end of July 1921; postcard to Ina Coolbrith from Albert Bender, 30 May 1921, in Bancroft Library; letter, Ina Coolbrith to Albert Bender, 27 July 1921, Mills College.

4. Ina L. Cook, "Ina Coolbrith and Her Circle," *Wasp-News Letter,* 20-27 December 1930, p. 38.

5. *San Francisco Chronicle,* 11 September 1921; also Nancy B. Mavity to Ina Coolbrith, 4 November 1921, in Bancroft Library.

6. *Oakland Tribune,* 31 July 1921.

7. *Berkeley Gazette,* 24 October 1921.

8. *San Francisco Call,* 27 August 1922; also letter, Ina Coolbrith to Mrs. Wills, 18 August 1922, California Historical Society, San Francisco.

9. Ina Coolbrith's letter to Albert Bender, 4 September 1921, Mills College.

10. Miss Coolbrith to Mrs. Laura Drum, 17 July 1923, letter in Coolbrith Papers, California Room, Oakland Free Library.

11. Ibid.

12. *San Francisco Chronicle,* 9, 15 September 1923; *San Francisco Examiner,* 28 August 1923; *Business Women's Herald* 1(29 October 1923):1; *San Francisco Call,*

23 September 1923; also letter, Ida M. Ziebe to Ina Coolbrith, 10 September 1923, in Coolbrith Papers, Bancroft Library, University of California, Berkeley.
13. *Oakland Tribune*, 18 September 1923, pp. 1A-10A.
14. Dr. Reinhardt to Miss Coolbrith, 15 September 1923, Huntington Library, San Marino, California.
15. *San Francisco Chronicle*, 6 October 1923.
16. *San Francisco Chronicle*, 6 October 1923; Robert Shaw, "Oakland Honors Its Most Distinguished Woman," *Oakland Post-Enquirer*, 13 October 1923.
17. Ina Coolbrith, in a letter to Albert Bender, 22 November 1923, Mills College; C. F. Lewis to Ina Coolbrith, 20 April 1925, a letter in Huntington Library.
18. Letter from Ina Coolbrith to James D. Phelan, 25 December 1925, Huntington Library.
19. Dr. James A. Miller to Carl Gunderson [Carl Seyfforth, Ulv Youff] 6 February 1926, and to Ina Coolbrith 16 February and 9 March 1926. Letters from Norway: Sister Hanna Dahl to Ina Coolbrith, 25 January, 25 August, 23 November 1925, 9 May 1926, and from Dagmar Walle-Hanson to Miss Coolbrith, 12 January and 9 March 1925, all in Bancroft Library.
20. Information from Mrs. Ina Graham in an interview, 23 June 1956; also Ulv Youff (pseudonym of Carl [Seyfforth] Gunderson) *Ulven; Written during Retirement in Switzerland.* Autobiography of a self-styled egomaniac. Miss Coolbrith did not like the book, though it both lauded her and apologized for his neglect of her.
21. Emma Frances Dawson died in February and Luther Burbank in April 1926.
22. Letter from Ina Coolbrith to Albert Bender, 20 November 1926, Mills College. Sterling's suicide, 17 November 1926; Carey McWilliams in *Dictionary of American Biography*, 17:586-87.
23. Ina Coolbrith's letter to Mrs. Laura Drum, 13 November 1927, Oakland Free Library.
24. Mira Maclay, "A Talk with Ina Coolbrith," *Oakland Tribune*, 2 March 1924; Evelyn Wells, "Ina Coolbrith Spurns Birthday," *San Francisco Call*, 8 March 1924; also letter, Evelyn Wells to Miss Coolbrith, 19 March 1924, Huntington Library.
25. Maurice T. Andrews, "California's Venerable Woman Laureate," *Literary Digest International Book Review*, 4:443, 445; letters: M. T. Andrews to Ina Coolbrith, 29 June 1926, Bancroft Library; Ina Coolbrith to Charles Lummis, 14 June 1926, Huntington Library, and 2 January 1927, Southwest Museum Library, Los Angeles, California.
26. Reception by California Poetry Society, 25 September 1926, in the home of N. Laurence Nelson, 1814 Vallejo Street, San Francisco, invitation in Oakland Free Library; letter from Tracy Beverly to Ina Coolbrith, 21 September 1926, in Huntington Library; telegram to her from Miles M. Dawson, 25 September 1926, Bancroft Library. Large dinner party given by the Brewster W. Ameses, 1019 Pacific Avenue, San Francisco, October 1926. On this occasion Miss Coolbrith read two of her recent poems, "Portolá Speaks," and "Mexico"; among the guests was Samuel Dickson, whose charming vignette of Ina Coolbrith that evening appears in his *San Francisco Kaleidoscope*, pp. 183-86. Also undated letter and a telegram, 15 October 1926, from Victoria M. Shadburne to Ina Coolbrith, in Bancroft Library. "Portolá Speaks" was published in the *San Francisco Examiner*, 12 October 1926, with title, "Quest of the Bay." Both it and "Mexico" are included in Ina Coolbrith, *Wings of Sunset*, pp. 6-7 and 44-45.
27. *San Francisco Chronicle*, 30 October 1925.
28. Mentioned by Mrs. Ina Graham in interview, 23 June 1956.
29. Letters: Ina Coolbrith to Albert Bender, 4, 7, 23 February 1927, Mills College; Edward F. O'Day to Miss Coolbrith, 13 January 1927, Huntington Library, 5 February and 23 March, Bancroft Library; Rose Travis to Ina Coolbrith, 9 February 1927, Bancroft Library.
30. *Oakland Times*, 11 March 1927; letters to Ina Coolbrith: Governor C. C.

Young, 28 May 1927, Oakland Free Library; Charles Phillips, 20 March 1927, and Louis Block, 14 April and 21 June, in Bancroft Library.

31. Letter from Ina Coolbrith to Albert Bender, 1 May 1925, Mills College.

32. Letters to Ina Coolbrith from Harry N. Pratt, 2, 23 October 1925, and from Torrey Connor, 3 October and December 1925, also Pratt's photograph, all in Bancroft Library.

33. Ina L. Cook, "Ina Coolbrith," *Wasp-News Letter,* 22-29 December 1928, p. 50.

34. Letters from Ina Coolbrith to Charles Lummis, 7 January 1924, 2 January 1927, in Southwest Museum Library.

35. Letters from Edith Daley to Ina Coolbrith, 21, 28 April and to Mrs. I. B. Weston, 18 April; Ruth Comfort Mitchell to Ina Coolbrith (telegram) 24 April; James D. Phelan to Miss Coolbrith, 26 April; all 1927, all in Bancroft Library. For this telling of the Beckwourth Pass story, see Thomas P. Brown's press release on the naming of Mt. Ina Coolbrith, in Coolbrith Papers, Oakland Free Library.

36. Ina Coolbrith, letter to Mrs. Laura Drum, 8 February 1927, Oakland Free Library.

37. Postcard from Eunice Lehmer to Miss Coolbrith, 16 May 1927, Bancroft Library.

38. Letters, Harry N. Pratt to Ina Coolbrith, 23 October 1925, 10 March 1926.

39. Albert Brecknock, *Byron;* Josephine DeWitt, "A Visit with Ina Coolbrith," *Oakland Free Library Staff Bulletin,* 21(April-June 1928):1, 4. The librarians with Miss Harwood: Leona Alexander, Clara Bishop, Josephine DeWitt.

40. Miss Coolbrith's residences from June 1923 to February 1928: 2731 Hillegass Avenue, Berkeley; 56 Taraval Street and 112 Lyon Street, San Francisco; then 2906 Wheeler Street, Berkeley.

41. Ina Coolbrith in a letter to Albert Bender, 30 November 1925, Mills College.

42. Bret Harte, *The Heathen Chinee,* with an introduction by Ina Coolbrith.

43. Ina Coolbrith, *Retrospect: in Los Angeles.*

44. San Francisco *Wasp,* 12 July 1924; text of poem and comment.

45. Letters to Ina Coolbrith: Rita I. Hayden, 11 September, Josephine Wilson, 12 September, Nellie V. Sanchez, 10, 25 September, J. W. Ryckman, 15 September; all 1925, all in Bancroft Library; also letter from Miss Coolbrith to Mrs. Sanchez, 23 September 1925, in private files of Louis A. Sanchez, Oakland, California.

46. Letters from Houghton Mifflin Company to Ina Coolbrith, 2, 12, 15, 19 September 1925, in Bancroft Library.

47. Letters: Ina Coolbrith to Albert Brecknock, 23 September and 24 December 1926, 28 March 1927, Oakland Free Library, and from Houghton Mifflin Company to Albert Brecknock, 6 July 1925, in Huntington Library. The portrait plate sent by the publishers to Brecknock is now in the Oakland Free Library.

48. "Pan," *Pan Poetry and Youth,* 1(July 1925):11; *Westward* 1(May 1928):8; Coolbrith, *Wings of Sunset,* p. 70.

49. "Luther Burbank," *Argonaut* (17 April 1926), *Literary Digest* 89(8 May 1926): 34; "With the Caravan," *University of California Chronicle* 28(July 1926):245-46; *Westward* 1(May 1928):6-7; "Portolá Speaks," *San Francisco Examiner,* 12 October 1926, with new title, "Quest of the Bay," H. M. Bland, ed. *A Day in the Hills,* pp. 23-24. All three included in Coolbrith, *Wings of Sunset.*

50. "Robin," Coolbrith, *Wings of Sunset,* p. 212.

51. Letter from Charles Phillips to Brother Leo, St. Mary's College, 26 September 1927, Bancroft Library.

52. "George Sterling," *Overland Monthly,* n.s. 85(November 1927):328; "The Vision of St. Francis," Coolbrith, *Wings of Sunset,* pp. 3-5.

53. Carlton Waldo Kendall, "California's Pioneer Poetess," *Overland Monthly,* n.s. 87(August 1929):229-30.

54. Ina Coolbrith in a letter to Mrs. Ella S. Mighels, 30 May [1917?], Coolbrith Papers, California State Library, Sacramento.

55. Dedication in Coolbrith, *Wings of Sunset.*

56. Charles Phillips, in a letter to Ina Coolbrith, 2 October 1927, explains his feelings about Carl Seyfforth whom he never saw; Bancroft Library.
57. 23 December 1927; Ina L. Cook, "Ina Coolbrith and Her Circle," *Wasp-News Letter*, 22-29 December 1928, p. 38.
58. Charles Phillips, *High in Her Tower* (privately printed, 1927).
59. Charles Phillips in a letter to Robert S. Norman, 10 November 1919, in Bancroft Library.

Chapter 31: Wings of Sunset

The chapter begins with a quotation from "The Unsolvable," a quatrain written by Ina Coolbrith during her New York days.
1. "The Years," Ina Coolbrith, *Songs from the Golden Gate*, p. 64.
2. The quotations, "the bloody couch of death," "scenes of desolation," and "the child of sorrow and of song," are from Ina Coolbrith's 128-line autobiographical poem, "In the Night. To My Mother," written in July 1861 and published in the *San Francisco Home Journal;* an undated clipping of this appears in Ina Coolbrith, *Scrapbooks,* 1:7.
3. Sources for information on the love interest in Miss Coolbrith's life include the following: Raine Bennett, "Sappho of the Western Sea," *Touring Topics* 28(November 1933):22-23, 36-37; Samuel Dickson, *San Francisco Kaleidoscope*, pp. 183-86; Isadora Duncan, *My Life,* pp. 15-16; Allan R. Macdougall, *Isadora*, pp. 18-22; undated (ca. 1918) letter from Ina Coolbrith to Jeanie Peet, and letters from Charles Phillips to Ina Coolbrith, all in Bancroft Library; letter from Ina Coolbrith to Lena Simons, 24 December 1921, in California Historical Society library; personal interviews with the following: Mr. and Mrs. Robert Carmany, Walnut Grove, California; Mrs. Ina Graham, Berkeley; Mr. Carlton Kendall, Oakland; Mrs. June Nahl, Berkeley, now deceased.
4. Letter from Eufina Tompkins to Ina Coolbrith, 28 February 1927, Coolbrith Papers, Bancroft Library.
5. Ina Coolbrith to Albert Bender, 28 October 1921, Mills College Library, Oakland, California.
6. Miss Coolbrith to Bender, 18 May 1927, Mills College Library.
7. Letter from Ina Coolbrith to Charles Lummis, 7 January 1925, Southwest Museum, Los Angeles.
8. "The Unsolvable," Ina Coolbrith, *Wings of Sunset*, p. 201.
9. Information from Mrs. Ina Graham of Berkeley.
10. "Hymn of the Nativity," *San Francisco Examiner*, 25 December 1891, p. 12; also Ina Coolbrith, *Scrapbooks,* 1:68-70.
11. Ina L. Cook, "Ina Coolbrith," *Wasp-News Letter*, 22-29 December 1928, p. 49.
12. Ina Coolbrith in a letter to Mrs. Richard E. White, 1 March 1915, Coolbrith Papers, Bancroft Library.
13. "Sibyl of stone," *Huntington Library Quarterly*, 23(May 1960):291; Bashford's quatrain, San Jose Women's Club, San Jose, California, "Collection of Poems Dedicated to Ina D. Coolbrith" 1907, manuscript in the Bancroft Library.
14. Mrs. Graham, interview 16 May 1968.
15. City of Berkeley, California, Health Department, Bureau of Vital Statistics, *Death Certificate #132, Ina Coolbrith,* gives cause of death as arteriosclerosis. Parents of deceased are given as Agnes Moulton and C. Coolbrith.
16. The Bohemian Club also asked to be permitted to share funeral costs.
17. "Beside the Dead," *Overland Monthly,* 14(May 1875):464; also in all three of Ina Coolbrith's verse collections.
18. Obituaries: *Oakland Tribune*, 29 February; *San Francisco Call*, 29 February (with headline: "The most honored woman California has ever known"); *New York Times*, 1 March, p. 5 Editorials: *Oakland Tribune*, 1 March, p. 4, *New York Times*, 2 March, p. 8. Account of funeral, *Oakland Times*, 2 March, all 1928.

19. Buried in plot number 11, lot 84, Mountain View Cemetery, Oakland. Buried beside her are her mother, her two half-brothers, her niece, and her niece's husband.

20. Charles Phillips in his "Memoir," introduction to Coolbrith, *Wings of Sunset,* p. xv.

21. "When the Grass Shall Cover Me," *Overland Monthly* 1(November 1868):473; also in all three of her collections.

22. "Ina Donna Coolbrith," *University of California Chronicle,* April 1929, p. 156.

23. *San Francisco Chronicle,* 7 March 1928; *San Francisco Call,* 10 March 1928; Annaleone D. Patton, *The California Mormons,* pp. 149-72. Mrs. Patton, in a personal interview in Berkeley, in 1968, stated that she had been an assistant in Dr. Bland's office and was present when he received the news of Miss Coolbrith's Mormon background. Also personal interview with Jesse Winter Smith in San Jose, in 1953.

24. *San Francisco Bulletin,* 6 March 1928; *San Francisco Call,* 10 March 1928; *San Francisco Chronicle,* 7 March 1928.

25. Information on Ina Coolbrith's estate in letter to Albert Bender from Mrs. Ina L. Cook, 10 January 1929, Mills College; will filed for probate in San Francisco Superior Court, 3 March 1928, *Oakland Tribune,* 4 March 1928. The manuscript mentioned, later published as *Joaquin Miller: His California Diary,* edited by John S. Richards was acquired by Willard Morse and subsequently sold to the Claremont Colleges Library; letter from John S. Richards to Josephine Rhodehamel, 13 May 1968, in our files.

26. Ina L. Cook to Bender, letter cited above.

27. Ina L. Cook, "Ina Coolbrith and Her Circle," *Wasp-News Letter,* 20-27 December 1930, p. 38.

28. Ina Cook Graham, *History of the Ina Coolbrith Circle* (Berkeley, 1969), pp. 100, 117.

29. Laura B. Everett, "Ina Coolbrith's Poems; Review of *Wings of Sunset,*" *University of California Chronicle* 32(January 1930):145-47; Lionel Stevenson, "Ina Coolbrith," *Saturday Review of Literature* 6(26 April 1930):992.

30. Lionel Stevenson, "Ina Coolbrith."

31. Lionel Stevenson, "The Mind of Ina Coolbrith," *Overland Monthly,* n.s. 88 (May 1930):150. This essay is reproduced in full, with permission, in the appendix.

32. "To a New Beatrice," Ina Coolbrith, *Songs from the Golden Gate,* p. 138.

33. "Unbound," Coolbrith, *Songs from the Golden Gate,* pp. 91-93.

34. "The Day of Our Lord," Coolbrith, *Songs from the Golden Gate,* pp. 85-87.

35. "The Years," Coolbrith, *Songs from the Golden Gate,* p. 64.

36. "From Living Waters," Coolbrith, *Songs from the Golden Gate,* pp. 65-69.

Epilogue: The Naming of The Mountain

1. Letters from Mrs. Lehmer to Ina Coolbrith, 16 May 1927, Bancroft Library, University of California; this idea for the naming of the mountain was also mentioned by Mrs. Lehmer at an Ina Coolbrith program in the Oakland Free Library in May 1952.

2. United States Geological Survey, *Loyalton Quadrangle, California-Nevada* (Washington, 1955).

3. Thomas P. Brown, "Press Release." San Francisco, 15 February 1932, mimeographed. Copy with Coolbrith Papers, California Room, Oakland Free Library; material for this release was prepared by Ina L. and Finlay Cook. Letters: Frank Bond, chairman of the United States Geographic Board, to Ina L. Cook, 26 January 1932; Ina L. Cook to Mrs. Nellie Sanchez, 15 February 1932, both in the files of Louis Adolfo Sanchez, Oakland, California, now deceased; quotation permitted by his widow, Mrs. L. A. Sanchez.

4. Ina L. Cook to Mrs. Sanchez.

Bibliography

In preparing to write the life of Ina Coolbrith we found that the richest supplies of recorded information are located in three major sources: Miss Coolbrith's two large scrapbooks in the Oakland Free Library, the collections of Coolbrith Papers housed in the Bancroft, Huntington, Mills College and other libraries, and the files of periodicals to which she contributed, especially the *Los Angeles Star,* and San Francisco's three important pioneer literary magazines, the *Golden Era,* the *Californian,* and the *Overland Monthly.* These materials and others are cited in the bibliography which follows. The valuable assistance provided by some persons who knew Miss Coolbrith personally is acknowledged elsewhere.

The bibliography is divided into two major parts: the writings of Ina Coolbrith herself and materials relating to her life and works. The specific subdivisions of the bibliography are as follows:

Part One: The Writings of Ina Coolbrith

Books Written by Ina Coolbrith
Books Containing Introductions, Forewords, or Special Contributions Written by Ina Coolbrith, and Books Edited by Her
Manuscripts
Periodical Articles
Anthologies Containing Poems by Ina Coolbrith

Part Two: Materials Relating to Ina Coolbrith and Her Times

Bibliographies
General Works
Periodical Articles
Official Documents
Newspapers
City Directories
Maps
Letters, Manuscripts, Scrapbooks

Part One: The Writings of Ina Coolbrith

*Books Written by Ina Coolbrith**

Coolbrith, Ina. *California.* San Francisco: The Book Club of California, 1918.
9 p. front. (mounted port.) 26 cm.

---

*A chronological list of the individual poems of Ina Coolbrith will be found in Appendix B.

500 copies printed by John Henry Nash, San Francisco, decorations by Lawrence B. Haste, portrait by Dan Sweeney.

——. *The Colonel's Toast.* S[an] F[rancisco]: Bosqui Eng[raving] Company [1886].
Cover title, [3] p. 26 cm.
Toast by Miss Ina Coolbrith, Honorary Member; Bohemian Club Christmas Jinks, 1886.

——. *A Perfect Day, and Other Poems.* San Francisco: [John H. Carmany and Company, Printers], 1881. Author's Special Subscription Edition.
173 p. 18 cm.
Also a limited, large-paper edition of fifty copies printed at the same time, identical except for size (36 cm.) and a red line border on each page.

——. *Retrospect: "in Los Angeles."* San Francisco: Printed for Ernest Dawson of Los Angeles by John Henry Nash, December 1925.
Cover title, [2] l. 50 cm.

——. *Retrospect: in Los Angeles.* Los Angeles: Ampersand Press, 1930.
Cover title, [4] l. 22 cm.
Colophon: Sixty copies printed by Arthur M. Ellis at the Ampersand Press, 1930.

——. *The Singer of the Sea.* [San Francisco]: Century Club of California, December 1894.
[8] p. 12½ cm.
C. A. Murdock and Company, Printers.
On cover: In Memory of Celia Thaxter.

——. *Songs from the Golden Gate.* Boston: Houghton Mifflin Company, [c 1895].
159 p. front. (port.), 4 pl. 18½ cm.
Illustrations by William Keith.

——. *Wings of Sunset.* Boston: Houghton Mifflin Company, 1929.
xxxvii, [i], 214 p. 19½ cm.
With a memoir.

Books Containing Introductions, Forewords, or Special Contributions Written by Ina Coolbrith, and Books Edited by Her.
Alexander, E. C. *A Collection of California Wild Flowers* with Appropriate Sonnets Specially Written by Miss Ina D. Coolbrith, of Oakland, California. San Francisco: The Popular Bookstore, [1894].
12 l. 15½ cm.

Behr, Henry Herman. *The Hoot of the Owl.* San Francisco: Robertson, 1904.
227 p. 20 cm.
Ina Coolbrith assisted A. M. Robertson in compiling this volume for publication.

California Writers Club. *West Winds, an Anthology of Verse.* San Francisco: Harr Wagner, [c 1925].
196 p. 21 cm.
Foreword by Ina Donna Coolbrith, pp. v-vii.

Chamberlain, Helen R. *A Christmas Greeting Expressed in Paintings and Poems of California Wild Flowers*, Hand-painted from Nature by Miss Helen R. Chamberlain, with Appropriate Sonnets Specially Written by Miss Ina D. Coolbrith, of Oakland, California. San Francisco: Roberts [c 1886].
[8] p. 23 cm.

Harte, Bret. *The Heathen Chinee: Plain Language from Truthful James.* San Francisco: Printed by John Henry Nash for His Friends, 1924.
23 p. 44 cm.
Table Mountain, 1870, by Bret Harte; with an Introduction by Ina Coolbrith . . . also a Note Concerning the History of the Manuscript, by J. C. Rowell, and a Bibliography with Notes, by Robert Ernest Cowan.

Nettleton, Charles Philip. *A Voice from the Silence*, edited by Ina Coolbrith. San Francisco: Robertson, 1904.
113 p. front. (port.) 20 cm.
Biographical Sketch and Poem by Isabel Darling, Appreciation by Rev. Hamilton Lee.

O'Connell, Daniel. *Songs from Bohemia*, edited by Ina D. Coolbrith. San Francisco: Robertson, 1900.
232 p. front. (port.) 19½ cm.
Biographical Sketch by William Greer Harrison.

Stoddard, Charles Warren. *Poems of Charles Warren Stoddard*, collected by Ina Coolbrith. New York: Lane, 1917.
144 p. front. (port.) 19½ cm.

*Manuscripts**
The Alchemist.
1 1. 12½ cm. AMS in ink. San Francisco Public Library.

*Titles are of poems unless otherwise indicated.

At Evenfall.

1 1. 13 cm. AMS in ink. Bender Collection, Mills College Library, Oakland.

[California].

3 1. 28 cm. AMS in ink. Mills College, Oakland.

The manuscript, without title, of the prose introduction to Ina Coolbrith's poem, "California," published as a book in 1918, by the Book Club of California.

Calla.

1 1. 15 cm. AMS in ink. Oakland Free Library.

Manuscript mounted between two photographs of a favorite cat, Calla, and framed.

Concha.

38, [1] 1. 28 cm. AMS in ink. Oakland Free Library.

Copa de Oro.

1 1. 25 cm. AMS in ink. Mills College Library, Oakland.

"Gertrude Franklin Atherton," in Ina Coolbrith Circle, *Letter and Enclosure,* 9 November 1946.

6 1. 28 cm. Typewritten. Atherton Collection, Bancroft Library, University of California, Berkeley.

Text of an address given by Ina Coolbrith in 1911.

In the Orchard.

1 1. 25 cm. AMS in ink. Mills College Library, Oakland.

["*Later Poems*"].

[209] 1. 37 cm. Bancroft Library, Berkeley.

Two folders of loose leaves with poems from which a selection was made for Ina Coolbrith's last collection, *Wings of Sunset* (Boston, 1929). Most of the poems in the folders are typewritten, but a few are holograph manuscripts by Miss Coolbrith. The latter are as follows:

At the Funeral (published as "The Funeral")
For You One Little Song to Sing (first line of an untitled poem)
Francis d'Assisi, Gentlest Saint of Saints (published as "The Vision of Saint Francis")
Immortals
The Laurel (published as "With the Laurel to Edmund Clarence Stedman on His Seventieth Birthday")
Mañana
Mexico
Monterey

464

Robin
Song
Telling a Secret
To Frances
A Yellow Rose
Youth

[Lines Written on the Fly-leaf of My First Book of Verse], March 10, 1893.
Front flyleaf of John Henry Carmany's copy of the limited edition of *A Perfect Day*. The full-page inscription was written without a title in the book, but a broadside of the poem uses this title. In Robert Carmany's private library, Walnut Grove, California.

Longing.
2 1. 25 cm. AMS in ink. Mills College Library, Oakland.

March Hares [birthday rhymes for Charles Fletcher Lummis].
2 1. 18 cm. AMS in ink. Mrs. Ina Graham's files, Berkeley.

[Memorial to Alice K. Cooley] with a letter to Laura Y. Pinney, 28 November 1910. Prose. In Coolbrith Papers, Henry E. Huntington Library, San Marino, California.

No More.
1 1. 17 cm. AMS in ink. Mills College Library, Oakland.

The Poet.
1 1. 21 cm. AMS in ink. Mills College, Oakland.

[Reminiscences] Charles Warren Stoddard, [1923? prose].
24 p. 21½ cm. AMS in ink. Personal library, Mrs. Ina Graham of Berkeley.
Text of an address given by Ina Coolbrith in Oakland.

[Reminiscences] Early California Writers [1911; prose].
73, [3] p. 23 cm. AMS in ink. Mrs. Graham's collection.
Text of an address given 10 April 1911, before the Pacific Coast Women's Press Association in San Francisco.

[Reminiscences] John Greenleaf Whittier, 1909. [prose].
22 1. 15 cm. AMS in ink. Mrs. Graham's collection.

[Small Notebook, undated; prose].
50 p. 17 cm. AMS in ink and pencil. Mrs. Graham's collection.
Memoranda relating to books.

Some of Ina D. Coolbrith's Poems Published in the Overland Monthly *from 1869 to 1875 and Other Poems, etc.*
96 p. front. (port.) 30 cm. Bancroft Library, Berkeley.

Hand-decorated title page; frontispiece: photograph of a bas relief portrait of Ina Coolbrith, by W. C. Coffin, 1878.

Manuscripts and broadsides collected by John Carmany, and pasted on numbered pages of a scrapbook. Poems in manuscript are as follows:

After the Winter Rain
An Answer
Benjamin P. Avery
Beside the Dead
Le Chemin de l' Ecole
The Coming
Cupid Kissed Me
Daisies
Dead
Discipline
An Emblem
From Year to Year
Fruitionless
Hope
A Hope
How Looked the Earth?
I Cannot Count My Life a Loss
If Only
In Adversity
In Blossom Time
In Time of Storm
Just for a Day
Loneliness
Love in Little
Love Song
Meadow-larks
No More
Not Yet
Oblivion
"One Touch of Nature"
Ownership
A Perfect Day
The Poet (This poem is in the hand of J. H. Carmany as it was dictated to him by the author on 17 October 1877)
Question and Answer

466

Regret

Respite

Retrospect

Sailed

The Savior's Flower (also entitled La Flor del Salvador)

The Sea Shell

A Song of the Summer Wind

Spring in the Desert

Sufficient (two versions)

Summons

To the Memory of My Mother

True Love

Two

Two Pictures

Ungathered

Unto the Day

"While Lillies Bud and Blow"

With a Wreath of Laurel

Withheld

The Years

[Statement About the Day of the Earthquake and Fire in San Francisco, 18 April 1906; prose].
  1 1. 18 cm. Typewritten. Oakland Free Library.
  Pasted in Ina Coolbrith, *Scrapbooks*, 1:190.

[Statement Concerning the Pickett Family in Marysville. Undated; prose].
  1 1. 10 cm. AMS in ink. Oakland Free Library.

[Statement Concerning the "Relief Fund" and the "Home Fund," 1909? prose].
  2 p. 30 cm. AMS in ink. Bancroft Library, Berkeley.

To the Bohemian Club.
  AMS, 1922, on front flyleaf of *Songs from the Golden Gate*, presented to the Bohemian Club. Bohemian Club, San Francisco.

["A Tribute to Joaquin Miller"].
  29 1. 21 cm. AMS in ink. Coolbrith Papers, Bancroft Library, Berkeley.
  Prose: text of an address given by Ina Coolbrith on 14 April 1913, before the Pacific Coast Women's Press Association.

Twenty-two. [Berkeley, California, 1923].
  Written for her grandniece, Ina Agnes Cook (Mrs. Charles E. Graham) of Berkeley. In Mrs. Graham's files.

467

When the Grass Shall Cover Me.
2 1. 21 cm. AMS in ink.
Copied as a gift for Herbert Bashford. In the authors' files; facsimile in this volume.

Periodical Articles

"An Afternoon with John Rollin Ridge," *Richmond* [California] *Banner*, 8 July 1917.

["Comments on Mary Austin's Articles on the Caminetti-Diggs Trial."] *San Francisco Examiner*, 11 December 1913. In Ina Coolbrith, *Scrapbooks*, 2:108. Oakland Free Library.

"Great Poem; I'd Like to Have Written It." [Review of George Sterling's *Wine of Wizardry*], *San Francisco Examiner*, 12 September 1907. Also in Ina Coolbrith, *Scrapbooks*, 2:15, in Oakland Free Library.

"How Best to Beautify San Francisco?" *San Francisco Examiner*, 18 January 1899. Also in Ina Coolbrith, *Scrapbooks*, 1:155, in Oakland Free Library.

"If I Had a Million Dollars to Distribute." *San Francisco Call*, 9 January 1898.

"Joaquin Miller." *Woman Citizen*, February 1913.
Clipping in Ina Coolbrith, *Scrapbooks*, 2:94, Oakland Free Library.

"A Letter from Ina Coolbrith." *Town Talk*, 28 November 1908.
Clipping in Ina Coolbrith, *Scrapbooks*, 2:37, Oakland Free Library.

Merrill, Meg [pseud.] "Meg Merrilliana, a Declaration of First Love." *Californian* 2:9, (4 March 1865).

———. "Not an Intercepted Letter." *Californian* 2:1, (4 February 1865).

Anthologies Containing Poems by Ina Coolbrith

Bland, Henry Meade, ed. *A Day in the Hills*. [San Francisco]: Privately Printed, 1926.
Portolá Speaks, pp. 23-24.

California Writers Club. *West Winds*. San Francisco: Wagner, 1925.
From Russian Hill, pp. 31-32.
A Song of the Summer Wind, pp. 29-30.
Summer Past, p. 28.

Coblentz, Stanton A., comp. *Modern American Lyrics*. New York: Minton, 1924.
Loneliness, p. 26.
The Unknown Great, p. 116.

Cooper, Alice C., ed. *Poems of Today*. Boston: Ginn, 1924.
The Poet, p. 245.

———. *Poems of Youth*. Boston: Ginn, 1928.
In Blossom Time, pp. 199-200.

Davis, Franklyn P., comp. *Davis' Anthology of Newspaper Verse for 1926*. Enid, Oklahoma: Davis, 1927.
Luther Burbank, p. 19.

DeMille, Alban B., comp. *American Poetry*. New York: Allyn, 1923.
Helen Hunt Jackson, p. 204.

Elder, Paul, comp. *California the Beautiful*. San Francisco: Elder, 1911.
At Carmel, p. 30.
California (excerpt) p. v.
Copa de Oro, p. 52.

Evans, Albert S. *A la California*. San Francisco: Bancroft, 1873.
The City by the Golden Gate, pp. 16-17.

Ford, James L., comp. *Every Day in the Year*. New York: Dodd, 1914.
Frederick III, p. 202.
Helen Hunt Jackson, p. 274.

Gaines, Nettie V., comp. *Pathway to Western Literature*. Stockton, California: Author, 1910.
In Blossom Time, pp. 40-41.
Leaf and Blade, pp. 45-46.
The Mariposa Lily, p. 148.

Harte, Bret, ed. *Outcroppings*. San Francisco: Roman, 1866.
Cupid Kissed Me, pp. 45-47.
"In the Pouts," pp. 53-54.
A Lost Day, pp. 50-52.
The Mother's Grief, pp. 48-49.

Higginson, Thomas W., ed. *American Sonnets*. Boston: Houghton, 1890.
Beside the Dead, p. 52.

Horder, William G., comp. *Treasury of American Sacred Song*. London: Frowde, 1896.
In Blossom Time, pp. 308-9.
A Prayer, p. 309.

Macdonald, Augustin S., comp. *A Collection of Verse by California Poets from 1849 to 1915*. San Francisco: Robertson, 1914.
In Blossom Time, p. 24.
The Poet, p. 85.

Markham, Edwin, comp. *The Book of American Poetry.* New York: Wise, 1934.
A Memory, p. 343.
With the Caravan, pp. 344-45.

———, comp. *Songs and Stories.* San Francisco: Powell, 1931.
California (abridged), p. 243.
From Russian Hill, pp. 241-42.
A Memory, p. 242.
When the Grass Shall Cover Me, p. 246.
With the Caravan, pp. 244-46.

Mighels, Ella S. *Literary California.* San Francisco: Wagner, 1918.
Edwin Booth, p. 286-87.
Friendship, p. 342.
Helen Hunt Jackson, pp. 284-85.
Lines on Hearing Mr. Edgar S. Kelley's Music of "Macbeth," p. 74.
Meadow Larks, p. 113.
A Perfect Day, p. 238.
William Keith, pp. 57-58.

Newman, Mary Wentworth, [May Wentworth] ed. *Poetry of the Pacific.* San Francisco: Pacific, 1867.
Fragment from an Unfinished Poem, pp. 343-44.
Love in Little, p. 345.
Sunset, p. 346.

Persall, Robert, ed. *The Californians: Writings of the Past and Present,* 2 vols., San Francisco: Hesperian House, [1961].
Christmas Eve, 1:408.
Helen Hunt Jackson, 1:407.
Sailed, 1:405.
Siesta, 1:406.

Press Club of Alameda County, California. *A Book of Verses.* [Oakland], 1910.
Renewal, p. [1].

Richert, Edith, comp. *American Lyrics.* Garden City: Doubleday, 1912.
Meadow Larks, p. 347.

Rittenhouse, Jessie B., ed. *The Little Book of American Poets.* Boston: Houghton, 1929.
Fruitionless, pp. 210-11.
When the Grass Shall Cover Me, pp. 211-12.

Shurter, Edwin DuBois, comp. *Masterpieces of Modern Verse*. New York: Noble, 1926.

In Blossom Time, pp. 151-52.

———, comp. *New Poems That Will Take Prizes in Speaking Contests*. New York: Noble, 1926.

In Blossom Time, p. 151.

Stedman, Edmund Clarence, ed. *An American Anthology, 1787-1900*. Boston: Houghton, 1906.

Fruitionless, p. 495.
Helen Hunt Jackson, p. 495.
The Mariposa Lily, p. 495.
When the Grass Shall Cover Me, pp. 494-95.

Sterling, George, and others, ed. *Continent's End; an Anthology of Contemporary California Poets*. San Francisco: Printed for the Book Club of California by John Henry Nash, 1925.

Beside the Dead, p. 101.
The California Poppy: Copa de Oro, p. 15.
In Blossom Time, p. 14.
When the Grass Shall Cover Me, p. 102.

Stevenson, Burton Egbert, ed. *The Home Book of Verse*. 2 vols., 8th edition. New York: Holt, 1949.

When the Grass Shall Cover Me, 1:1114-15.

Waterman, S. D., comp. *Graded Memory Selections*. New York: Educational Publishing Co., 1903.

In Blossom Time, pp. 93-94.
Meadow Larks, pp. 98-99.

Whittier, John Greenleaf, comp. *Songs of Three Centuries*. Revised Edition. Boston: Houghton, 1890.

When the Grass Shall Cover Me, p. 357. This poem appeared anonymously in the first edition (Boston: Osgood, 1875), pp. 273-74.

Wilkinson, Marguerite, ed. *Contemporary Poetry*. New York: Macmillan, 1923.

When the Grass Shall Cover Me, pp. 41-42.

———, comp. *Golden Songs of the Golden State*. Chicago: McClurg, 1917.

California, pp. 29-35.
When the Grass Shall Cover Me, pp. 35-36.

Part Two: Materials Relating to Ina Coolbrith and Her Times

Bibliographies

Bellamy, Richard C. *Ina Donna Coolbrith: a Subject Bibliography.* [Oakland?] Spring, 1966.
20 1. Mimeographed.

Stevens, Ivalu Delpha. *A Bibliography of Ina Donna Coolbrith.* Sacramento: California State Printing Office, 1932.
Cover title, [19] p.
Reprinted from *News Notes of California Libraries,* 27: [105]-123, April 1932.

Individual manuscript poems are here described in detail; an alphabetical list of poems indicates appearance in Ina Coolbrith's published collections, and in anthologies and periodicals.
Contents: Manuscripts, Books, Books with an Introduction or edited by Ina Donna Coolbrith, Alphabetical list of poems.

[Thomas, Mabel W., comp.] Inventory of Ina Coolbrith Material Purchased from Mrs. Ina Craig, April 10, 1945, and Additional Items Obtained from Other Sources at Various Times. Oakland Free Library. Reference Department. 1947.
9 1. Typewritten.

Zamorano Club. *The Zamorano 80; a Selection of Distinguished California Books.* Los Angeles: Zamorano Club, 1945.
66 p.
No. 21, p. 15: Coolbrith, Ina, *Songs from the Golden Gate.*

General Works°

Altrocchi, Julia (Cooley). *The Spectacular San Franciscans.* New York: Dutton, 1949.

Appleton's Annual Cyclopaedia and Register of Important Events of the Year 1900. New York: Appleton, 1901.

Austin, Mary (Hunter). *Earth Horizon.* Boston: Houghton, 1932.

Backus, Joyce. "A History of the San Francisco Mercantile Library Association." Master's thesis, University of California, Berkeley, 1931.

Badé, William F. *The Life and Letters of John Muir.* 2 vols. Boston: Houghton, 1923.

°A list of publications of major usefulness in the preparation of this volume. Included are general reference works, as well as books in the fields of biography, local history and description, Mormon history, library history, and literature.

Baker, Joseph Eugene. *Past and Present of Alameda County.* 2 vols. Chicago: Clarke, 1914.

Bamford, Georgia (Loring). *The Mystery of Jack London.* Oakland: Author, 1931.

Bancroft, Hubert Howe. *History of Utah, 1540-1886.* San Francisco: History Company, 1889.

Bates, Mrs. D. B. *Four Years on the Pacific Coast.* Boston: Author, 1860.

Bean, Walton, *Boss Ruef's San Francisco.* Berkeley: University of California Press, 1952.

Beattie, George William. *Heritage of the Valley; San Bernardino's First Century.* Pasadena: San Pasqual Press, 1939.

Beckwourth, James P. *Life and Adventures* . . . T. D. Bonner, ed., New York: Knopf, 1931.

Bell, Horace. *Reminiscences of a Ranger; or, Early Times in Southern California.* Santa Barbara: Hebberd, 1927.

Berkeleyan Stock Company, comp. *College Verses.* San Francisco: California Publishing Company, 1882.

Berrett, William E. and Burton, Alma P., *Readings in L.D.S. Church History from Original Manuscripts.* 3 vols. Salt Lake City: Deseret Book Company, 1953-58.

Bohemian Club, San Francisco. *Annals* . . . 3 vols. San Francisco, 1880-95.

————. *Bohemian Club Certificate of Incorporation, Constitution, By-laws and Rules, Officers and Committees, Members, in Memoriam.* San Francisco, 1939.

————. *A Brief Catalog of the Published Works of Bohemian Club Authors.* San Francisco, 1937.

Brecknock, Albert. *Byron; a Study of the Poet in the Light of New Discoveries.* London: Palmer, 1926.

Brodie, Fawn M. *No Man Knows My History; the Life of Joseph Smith, the Mormon Prophet.* New York: Knopf, 1946.

Bronson, William. *The Earth Shook, the Sky Burned.* New York: Doubleday, 1959.

Brown, Thomas P. *Western Pacific News Service [Press Release on the Naming of Mount Ina Coolbrith].* San Francisco, 1932.

Burton, Alma P. *Mormon Trail from Vermont to Utah.* Salt Lake City: Deseret Book Company, 1960.

California Library Association. *Libraries of California in 1899.* San Francisco: The Association, 1900.

473

Cleland, Robert Glass. *El Molino Viejo*. Los Angeles: Ward Ritchie, 1950.

Conmy, Peter Thomas. *The Dismissal of Ina Coolbrith as Head Librarian of Oakland Free Public Library and a Discussion of the Tenure Status of Head Librarians*. Oakland: Oakland Public Library, 1969.

———. *Oakland Library Association, 1868-1878*. Oakland: Oakland Public Library, 1968.

Cooney, Percival J. *The Dons of the Old Pueblo* (novel). Chicago: Rand, 1914.

Cornelius, Fidelis, Brother. *Keith, Old Master of California*. 2 vols. New York: Putnam, 1942-56. (vol. 2, published by Academy Library Guild, Fresno, California, is called A Supplement).

Cowan, Robert Ernest. *Booksellers of Early San Francisco* . . . Los Angeles: Ward Ritchie, 1953.

Daughters of the American Revolution, California. *Collections*. vols. 12, 17. Los Angeles, 1942, 1953.

———. Genealogical Records Committee. *Vital Records from the Daily Evening Bulletin, San Francisco, California*. vol. 15. San Francisco, 1943-49.

———. San Francisco Chapter. *Pioneer Obituaries from the San Francisco Chronicle, 1911-28*. San Francisco, 1932.

———. San Francisco Chapter. *Records from Tombstones in Laurel Hill Cemetery, San Francisco, California, 1853-1937*. San Francisco, 1938.

Dickson, Samuel. *San Francisco Kaleidoscope*. Stanford: Stanford University Press, 1949.

Dictionary of American Biography, vol. 4. 20 vols. New York: Scribner, 1928-37.

Dornin, May. "The Emigrant Trails into California." Master's thesis, University of California, Berkeley, 1921.

Duncan, Isadora. *My Life*. New York: Liveright, 1927.

Engelhardt, Zephyrin, Father. *San Gabriel Mission and the Beginnings of Los Angeles*. San Gabriel: Mission San Gabriel, 1927.

Farris and Smith. *Illustrated History of Plumas, Lassen and Sierra Counties*. San Francisco: Farris and Smith, 1882.

Federal Writers' Project. *Nauvoo Guide*. Chicago: McClurg, 1939.

Ferrier, William Warren. *Origin and Development of the University of California*. Berkeley: Sather Gate Book Shop, 1930.

Field, Isobel (Osbourn). *This Life I've Loved*. New York: Longmans, 1937.

Filler, Louis. *The Unknown Edwin Markham*. Yellow Springs, Ohio: Antioch College, 1966.

Flanders, Robert Bruce. *Nauvoo*. Urbana: University of Illinois Press, 1965.

Ford, Thomas. *A History of Illinois from Its Commencement as a State in 1818 to 1847*. 2 vols. Chicago: Lakeside Press, 1945.

Freemasons. Los Angeles Lodge No. 42. *Historical Review*. Los Angeles: Author, 1929.

Fullmer, John S. *Assassination of Joseph and Hyrum Smith . . . Also a Condensed History of the Expulsion of the Saints from Nauvoo*. Liverpool: Richards, 1855.

Gilman, Charlotte (Perkins) Stetson. *The Living of Charlotte Perkins Stetson*. New York: Appleton-Century, 1935.

Graham, Ina Cook. *History of the Ina Coolbrith Circle*. Berkeley, California, Wuerth, 1969.

Guinn, James Miller. *Historical and Biographical Record of Los Angeles and Vicinity*. Chicago: Chapman, 1901.

Gunderson, Carl, [Carl Seyfforth, Ulv Youff]. Ulven; *Written during Retirement in Switzerland*, London: Lane, 1925.

Halley, William. *The Centennial Yearbook of Alameda County, California*. Oakland: Author, 1876.

Harte, Bret, comp. *Outcroppings; Being Selections of California Verse*. San Francisco: Roman, 1866.

Held, Ray E. *Public Libraries in California, 1849-1878*. Berkeley: University of California Press, 1963.

Hill, Laurence L. *La Reina; Los Angeles in Three Centuries*. Los Angeles: Security Trust and Savings Bank, 1929.

Hittell, John Shertzer. *A History of San Francisco and Incidentally of the State of California*. San Francisco: Bancroft, 1878.

Hoover, Mildred B. et al. *Historic Spots in California*. 3rd ed., rev. William N. Abeloe. Stanford: Stanford University Press, 1966.

Hunt, Rockwell Dennis. *California's Stately Hall of Fame*. Stockton: College of the Pacific, 1950.

Ingersoll, Luther A. *Ingersoll's Century Annals of San Bernardino County, 1769 to 1904*. Los Angeles: Author, 1904.

Jones, William Carey. *Illustrated History of the University of California*. San Francisco: Dukesmith, 1895.

Kemble, Edward Cleveland. *A History of California Newspapers, 1846-1858.* Edited with a Foreword by Helen Harding Bretnor. Los Gatos: Talisman Press, 1962.

Kennedy, John Castillo. *The Great Earthquake and Fire, San Francisco, 1906.* New York: Morrow, 1963.

Kewen, Edward John Case [Harry Quillem]. *Idealina; and Other Poems.* San Francisco: Cooke, 1853.

Krebs, Abbie E., ed. *La Copa de Oro.* San Francisco: George Spaulding, 1905.

Lewis, Oscar. *Bay Window Bohemia.* Garden City: Doubleday, 1956.

———. *Here Lived the Californians.* New York: Rinehart, 1957.

———. *This Was San Francisco.* New York: McKay, 1962.

Libbey, Dorothy Shaw. *Scarborough Becomes a Town.* [Portland, Maine]: Bond Wheelwright Company, 1955.

McCrackin, Josephine Clifford. *The Woman Who Lost Him* (novel). Pasadena: James, 1913.

Macdougall, Allan Ross. *Isadora.* New York: Nelson, 1960.

McGavin, Elmer Cecil. *The Family of Joseph Smith.* Salt Lake City: Bookcraft, 1963.

———. *Nauvoo the Beautiful.* Salt Lake City: Stevens and Wallis, 1946.

Marberry, M. M. *Splendid Poseur, Joaquin Miller—American Poet.* New York: Crowell, 1953.

Merritt, Frank Clinton. *History of Alameda County.* 2 vols. Chicago: Clarke, 1928.

Merwin, Henry Childs. *The Life of Bret Harte.* Boston: Houghton, 1911.

Mighels, Ella Sterling Cummins. *The Story of the Files.* [San Francisco]: World's Fair Commission of California, 1893.

Millard, Bailey. *History of the San Francisco Bay Region.* 3 vols. San Francisco: American Historical Society, 1924.

Miller, Joaquin. *Joaquin Miller: His California Diary, Beginning in 1855 and Ending in 1857.* Edited and with an Introduction by John S. Richards. Seattle: McCaffrey, 1936.

———. *Memorie and Rime.* New York: Funk and Wagnalls, 1884.

———. *Songs of the Sierras.* London: Longmans, 1871.

———. *Unwritten History: Life Amongst the Modocs.* Hartford: American, 1874.

476

Miller, Juanita Joaquina. *About "The Hights."* Oakland: Tooley-Towne, 1933.

Mitchell, Ruth Comfort. *Curtain (the Sixties).* New York: Appleton, 1933.

A novel in which Ina Coolbrith is a character.

Mott, Frank Luther. *A History of American Magazines.* 4 vols. Cambridge: Harvard University Press, 1938-57.

National Cyclopedia of American Biography. vol. 13. New York: James T. White and Company, 1906.

Neville, Amelia (Ransome). *The Fantastic City; Memoirs of the Social and Romantic Life of Old San Francisco.* Boston: Houghton, 1932.

Newman, Mary Wentworth [May Wentworth], ed. *Poetry of the Pacific.* San Francisco: Pacific, 1867.

Newmark, Harris. *Sixty Years in Southern California, 1853-1913.* New York: Knickerbocker Press, 1916.

Pacific Coast Women's Press Association, San Francisco, Calif. *Year Book, 1916-1917.* San Francisco: Author, 1916.

Paden, Irene D. *The Wake of the Prairie Schooner.* New York: Macmillan, 1947.

Patton, Annaleone D. *California Mormons.* Salt Lake City: Deseret Book Company, 1961.

Peterson, Martin Severin. *Joaquin Miller, Literary Frontiersman.* Stanford: Stanford University Press, 1937.

Phillips, Charles. *High in Her Tower.* Privately Printed, 1927.

———. *Memoir.* (In Ina Coolbrith, *Wings of Sunset.* Boston: Houghton, 1929).

Poets Laureate Memorial Plaque Dedication Program, 11 September 1965, California State Library, Sacramento, Calif. Illustrated folder.

Rice, William Broadhead. *The Los Angeles Star, 1851-1864.* Berkeley: University of California Press, 1947.

Ridlon, G. T. *Saco Valley Settlements and Families.* Portland, Maine: Author, 1895.

Robison, Stanford J. *Mormon Genealogies.* Salt Lake City: Deseret Book Company, 1946.

Roske, Ralph Joseph. *Everyman's Eden; a History of California.* New York: Macmillan, 1962.

San Francisco. Mercantile Library Association. *Forty-fifth Annual Report of the President, Treasurer, and Librarian.* San Francisco: The Association, 1897.

477

Scharf, John Thomas. *History of Saint Louis City and County*. 2 vols. Philadelphia: Everets, 1883.

Seyfforth, Carl. *See* Gunderson, Carl.

Smith, Joseph. *History of the Church of Jesus Christ of Latter-day Saints*. 7 vols. Salt Lake City: Deseret Book Company, 1902-1912.

Smith, Lucy Mack. *Biographical Sketches of Joseph Smith the Prophet and His Progenitors for Many Generations*. Lamoni, Iowa: Herald Publishing House, Reorganized Church of Jesus Christ of Latter-day Saints, 1912.

Smith, Ruby K. *Mary Bailey*. Salt Lake City: Deseret Book Company, 1954.

Soulé, Frank. *The Annals of San Francisco*. New York: Appleton, 1855.

The Spinners' Club, San Francisco. *The Spinners' Book of Fiction . . .* San Francisco: Paul Elder and Company, 1907.

Stern, Madeleine B. *Purple Passage, the Life of Mrs. Frank Leslie*. Norman: University of Oklahoma Press, 1953.

Stetson, James Burgess. *San Francisco During the Eventful Days of April, 1906*. San Francisco: Murdock [1906?].

Stewart, George Rippy. *Bret Harte, Argonaut and Exile*. Boston: Houghton, 1931.

–––. *The California Trail*. New York: McGraw-Hill, 1962.

Stidger, William LeRoy. *Edwin Markham*. New York: Abingdon Press, 1933.

Stoddard, Charles Warren. *Exits and Entrances*. Boston: Lothrop, 1903.

–––. *For the Pleasure of His Company, an Affair of the Misty City, Thrice Told*. San Francisco: Robertson, 1903.
A novel in which Ina Coolbrith is a character.

Sutherland, Monica. *The Damndest Finest Ruins*. New York: Coward-McCann, 1959.

Thompson and West. *History of Yuba County, California*. Oakland: Authors, 1879.

Vigness, Paul G. *Alameda Community Book*. Alameda, California: Cawston, 1952 .

Wagner, Harr. *Joaquin Miller and His Other Self*. San Francisco: Author, 1929.

Walker, Franklin. *A Literary History of Southern California*. Berkeley: University of California Press, 1950.

–––. *San Francisco's Literary Frontier*. New York: Knopf, 1939.

Ware, Joseph E. *The Emigrant's Guide to California* . . . Reprinted from the 1849 Edition with Introduction and Notes by John Caughey. Princeton: Princeton University Press, 1932.

Wentworth, May. *See* Newman, Mary Wentworth.

Wheeler, Edwin. *18th Anniversary of the Corporate Society of California Pioneers* . . . Poem by Ina D. Coolbrith. San Francisco: Author, 1868.

Who Was Who in America, 1897-1942. Chicago: Marquis, 1942.

Wood, Myron W., ed. *History of Alameda County, California.* Oakland: Author, 1883.

Youff, Ulv. *See* Gunderson, Carl.

Periodical Articles

American Library Association. "San Francisco Conference Number." *Library Journal* 16(December 1891):1-154.

"American Poets of Today: Ina Coolbrith." *Current Literature* 28(April 1900):16-17.

Anderson, W. H. "California's First Poet Laureate." *Historical Society of Southern California Quarterly* 32(June 1950):105-7.

Andrews, Maurice T. "California's Venerable Woman Poet." *Literary Digest International Book Review* 4(June 1926):443, 445.

Armes, William Dallam. "Beginnings of California Literature." *University of California Chronicle* 17(July 1915):261 ff.

Baker, Hugh S. "Rational Amusement in Our Midst" (Mercantile Library) *California Historical Society Quarterly* 38(December 1959): 295-320.

Bartlett, W. C. "*Overland* Reminiscences," *Overland Monthly*, n.s. 32(July 1898):41-46.

Bashford, Herbert. "To Ina Coolbrith" (poem). *Sunset Magazine* 20(December 1907):163.

Bennett, Raine. "Sappho of the Western Sea," *Touring Topics* 28(November 1933):22-23, 36-37.

Biven, Millie S. "Ina D. Coolbrith." *Once a Week*, 11 August 1906.

Bland, Henry Meade. "Ina Coolbrith Crosses the Plains Again." *Oakland Tribune*, 31 July 1921, p. 3.

———. "Ode in Memory of Ina Coolbrith," *Overland Monthly*, n.s. 86 (June 1928):185.

———. "A Sketch of the First Western Literary Period." *Pacific Short Story Club Magazine* 4(July 1911):2.

479

———. "Where Some California Writers Live." *San Francisco Call*, 19 November 1911, part 1, p. [5].

Bowman, Jacob N. "The Peraltas and Their Houses." *California Historical Society Quarterly* 30(September 1951):217-31.

Bowman, James F. "The Singer" (poem to Ina Coolbrith). *Argonaut* 15 January 1874.

"Brief Genealogy of Don Carlos Smith (1816-1841); His Wife, Agnes Moulton Coolbrith, and Their Children." *Utah Genealogical and Historical Magazine* 26(July 1935):105.

Brooks, Jacqueline. "The Feather River Gateway to a Poet's Kingdom." *National Motorist* (August 1940):8-9.

Brooks, Noah. "Early Days of the *Overland*." *Overland Monthly*, n.s. 32 (July 1898):1-11.

Carmany, John Henry. "The Publishers of the *Overland*." *Overland Monthly*, n.s. 1(February 1883):Supp. 1-16.

Clark, F. H. "Libraries and Librarians of the Pacific Coast." *Overland Monthly*, n.s. 18(November 1891):449-64.

Colburn, Frona Eunice Wait. "The Passing of Ina Coolbrith." *Overland Monthly*, n.s. 86(April 1928):106.

Conmy, Peter Thomas. "Centennial of Oakland Public Library," *California Librarian* 30(January 1969):42-47.

Connell, Sarah. "Ina Coolbrith." *Grizzly Bear* 17(June 1915):1-2.

Connor, Torrey. "Long Distance Interviews; Poet Beloved." *Overland Monthly*, n.s. 82(June 1924):270.

Cook, Ina Lillian (Peterson). "Ina Coolbrith and Her Circle." *Wasp-News Letter*, 20-27 December 1930, p. 38.

———. "Ina Coolbrith, Some Impressions and Recollections." *Wasp-News Letter*, 22-29 December 1928, pp. 49-50.

———. "Ina Donna Coolbrith: A Short Account of Her Life." *Westward* 1(May 1928):3-5.

Coulter, Edith M. "Horatio Stebbins." *California Historical Society Quarterly* 34(June 1955):180.

DeCasseras, Benjamin. "Ina Coolbrith of California's 'Overland Trinity.'" *New York Sun, Books and the Book World*, 7 December 1919.

DeWitt, Josephine. "A Visit with Ina Coolbrith," *Oakland Free Library Staff Bulletin*, April-June 1928, pp. 1-4.

Dumke, Glenn S. "The Masters of San Gabriel Mission's Old Mill." *California Historical Society Quarterly* 45(September 1966):259-65.

480

Everett, Laura Bell. "*High in Her Tower*, by Charles Phillips," (a review, and appreciation of Ina Coolbrith). *Overland Monthly*, n.s. 86(April 1928):121.

———. "Ina Coolbrith's Poems; Review of *Wings of Sunset*." *University of California Chronicle* 32(January 1930):145-47.

Everywoman, July 1915. [Ina Coolbrith Number].

Fee, Harry T. "Ina Coolbrith" (poem). *Overland Monthly*, n.s. 86(April 1928):106.

Francoeur, Jeanne E. "Classic Day of Women's Press Association." *Woman Citizen* May 1913.

———. "Ina Coolbrith, Our Poet—in the Past and Present." *Women Citizen* 1(1913):106-7.

Franklin, Viola Price. "In Memoriam: Ina Coolbrith" (poem). *Overland Monthly*, n.s. 87(August 1929):253.

Graham, Ina Agnes (Cook). "Ina Coolbrith." *Pony Express* 14(July 1947):8-9.

———. "The Ina Coolbrith Circle." *The Poet* 4(Spring-Summer 1944):12-13.

Greene, Charles Samuel. "Library History in Oakland," *Oakland Free Library Staff Bulletin* December 1923—May 1925.

———. "Magazine Publishing in California." California Library Association, *Publications* 2 (1 May 1898).

Grenander, M. E. "Ambrose Bierce and Charles Warren Stoddard: Some Unpublished Correspondence." *Huntington Library Quarterly* 23(May 1960):261-92.

Guinn, James Miller. "Los Angeles in the Adobe Age." Historical Society of Southern California, *Annual Publications* 4(1897):49-55.

———. "The Old-time Schools and Schoolmasters of Los Angeles." Historical Society of Southern California, *Annual Publications* 3(1896):11.

Harwood, Ruth. "Ina Donna Coolbrith" (poem). *University of California Chronicle* 31(April 1929):156.

———. "To Ina Coolbrith" (poem). *Overland Monthly*, n.s. 83(February 1925):79.

Haverland, Stella E. "Ina Donna Coolbrith." *Pacific Bindery Talk* 8(April 1936):131-34.

Herby, N. J. "Ina Donna Coolbrith" (poem). *Overland Monthly*, n.s. 86 (April 1928):106.

Higginson, Ella. "To Ina Coolbrith" (poem). *Overland Monthly*, n.s. 20 (September 1892):246-47.

Howe, Harriet. "Sailed; for Ina Donna Coolbrith, February 29th, 1928" (poem). *Westward* 1(May 1928):5.

"Ina Coolbrith Evening." Book Club of California, *Quarterly Newsletter* 12(Spring 1947):30-31.

"Ina Coolbrith's Recollections of Bret Harte." *California Historical Society Quarterly* 4(March 1925):91.

James, George Wharton. "Ina D. Coolbrith." *Impressions Quarterly* 4(June 1903):45-48.

———. "Ina Donna Coolbrith." *National Magazine* 26(June 1907):315-22.

———. "Ina Donna Coolbrith and Her Poetry." *Fellowship*, Los Angeles, August 1906.

———. "The Spiritual Life of a Great Woman: Ina Donna Coolbrith." *P. E. Topics*, Los Angeles, December 1906, pp. 11-14.

James, Henry. "With Entire Frankness." *San Francisco Call*, 30 October 1898, p. 32.

Jones, Idwal. "She Knew the Giants of Her Time." *Westways* 51(March 1959):24-25.

Keeler, Ormeida. "She Dwelt Among Us Like a Star" (poem). *Oakland Tribune*, 1 March 1928.

Kendall, Carlton Waldo. "California's Pioneer Poetess." *Overland Monthly*, n.s. 87(August 1929):229-30.

Kennedy, Kate M. "Ina Coolbrith Day." *Overland Monthly*, n.s. 49(April 1907):339-48.

———. "Ina Coolbrith—Poet, Friend; an Appreciation." *Pacific Short Story Club Magazine*, January 1912, pp. 25-33.

Kinross, Albert. "The *Outlook* Views and Reviews: Ina Coolbrith." *London Outlook*, 20 August 1898.

London, Jack. ["Letter to Ina Coolbrith, December 13, 1906"]. *Oakland Enquirer*, 10 January 1920.

Loughead, Flora Haines. "Books and Writers: Miss Ina D. Coolbrith." *Sunset Magazine* 9(July 1902):217-19.

Lynch, Ada Kyle. "Stories from the Files; Ina D. Coolbrith as the Associate of Bret Harte." *Overland Monthly*, n.s. 76(November 1920):66-67.

McCarthy, John Russell. "Here is California—Here is Your Kingdom." *California History Nugget* 6(February 1939):131-34.

Maclay, Mira. "A Talk with Ina Coolbrith." *Oakland Tribune Magazine* 2 March 1924, p. 13.

McCrackin, Josephine Clifford. "Ina Coolbrith Invested with Poet's Crown." *Overland Monthly,* n.s. 66(November 1915):448-50.

———. "Reminiscences of Bret Harte and Pioneer Days in the West." *Overland Monthly,* n.s. 66(December 1915):463-68.

Markham, Edwin. "Tribute to Ina Coolbrith." *Everywoman* 10(July 1915):11.

"Marriages and Marriage Intentions from Pepperrellborough (Now Saco), Maine, from 1768," *New England Historical and Genealogical Register* 50:13-14; 71:123, 211.

Martin, Lannie Haynes. "The Literature of California," *Out West* 3(January 1912):62-64, 98-100.

Mayberry, Emily Gray. "El Molino Viejo." *Land of Sunshine* 3(July 1895):59-62.

Mighels, Ella Sterling Cummins. "Broken Friendship" (poem). *San Francisco Bulletin,* 15 July 1919.

———. "Crowned Poet Laureate," *Grizzly Bear* 17(August 1915):4.

Miller, Joaquin. "California's Fair Poet." *San Francisco Call,* 12 August 1892.

Mitchell, Ruth Comfort. "Dirge for Ina Coolbrith." *Overland Monthly,* n.s. 86(June 1928):164.

Notre Dame Quarterly, San Jose, California, 12(June 1912):3. [Ina Coolbrith Number].

"Obituary." *Library Journal* 53(15 March 1928):265.

O'Day, Edward F. "Ina Coolbrith's Poetry." *Town Talk,* 30 November 1907.

———. "The Laureate of California." *Lantern* 3(November 1917):227-41.

———. "A Neglected Poet." *Town Talk* 15(22 September 1906):10-11.

———. "The Poems of Charles Warren Stoddard." *Town Talk,* 25 August 1917.

———. "Some Poets of San Francisco." Society of California Pioneers, *Quarterly* 10(1933):45-52.

———. "The Value to California of Her Poets." *Town Talk,* 22 June 1918.

———. "Varied Types, XLI: Ina Coolbrith." *Town Talk,* 30 September 1911.

Once a Week. Oakland, California, 2(27 October 1906):23. ["Coolbrith Edition"].

Phillips, Charles. "The Laureate of California." *The Magnificat,* (Manchester, N. H.) 21(March 1918):250-52.

Purdy, Helen Throop. "Ina Donna Coolbrith, 1841-1928." *California Historical Society Quarterly* 7(March 1928):78.

"Record of Deaths in the First Parish of Scarborough, Maine, 1795-1899." *New England Historical and Genealogical Register* 103:188-97, 254-70.

Reid, M. J. "Four Women Writers of the West." *Overland Monthly*, n.s. 24(August 1894):138-44.

Roman, Anton. "Beginnings of the *Overland*." *Overland Monthly*, n.s. 32 (July 1898):72-75.

Salisbury, H. S. "Josephine Donna Smith—Ina Coolbrith." *Improvement Era*, Salt Lake City, January 1950, p. 27, 73-74.

Shaw, Robert. "Oakland Honors Its Most Distinguished Woman." *Oakland Post-Enquirer*, 13 October 1923.

"Songs from the Golden Gate. Review." *Dial* 20(16 February 1896):112-13.

Stevenson, Lionel. "Ina Coolbrith, *Wings of Sunset*." *Saturday Review of Literature*, 6(26 April 1930):992.

———. "The Mind of Ina Coolbrith." *Overland Monthly*, n.s. 88(May 1930):150.

Stoddard, Charles Warren. "In Old Bohemia." *The Pacific Monthly* 18(December 1907):639-50; 19(March 1908):261-73.

———. "Ina D. Coolbrith." *The Magazine of Poetry* 1(1898):313 ff.

Sullivan, Albert E. "California's Poet Laureate, Miss Ina Coolbrith." *Every Child's Magazine* April 1917, p. 56.

Taylor, Marian. "California's Poet Laureate Honored." *Grizzly Bear* 19 (June 1916):1, 32.

———. "Congress of Authors and Journalists at the Panama-Pacific International Exposition." *Overland Monthly*, n.s. 66(November 1915):439-46.

———. "Ina Coolbrith, California Poet." *Overland Monthly*, n.s. 64(October 1914): 327-39.

———. "Poet-Laureate Hostess." *Sunset Magazine* 34(January 1915):135-38.

Thomas, Mabel Winifred. "The Memory of a Smile." *Oakland Free Library Staff Bulletin* August 1925, p. 5.

Tompkins, Eufina C. "The Crowning of Ina Coolbrith." *San Francisco Star*, 3 July 1915.

———. "The Laurel Wreath" (poem). *San Francisco Monitor*, 10 July 1915.

True, Eliot C. "To Ina Coolbrith" (poem). *San Francisco Chronicle,* 23 June 1918.

Urmy, Clarence. "To Ina Coolbrith" (poem). *Oakland Enquirer,* 28 August 1920.

Winn, William W. "The Joaquin Miller Foundation." *California Historical Society Quarterly* 32(September 1953)23--41.

———. "Joaquin Miller's 'Real Name.'" *California Historical Society Quarterly* 33(June 1954):143-46.

Wood, Raymund Francis. "Ina Coolbrith, Librarian." *California Librarian* 19(April 1958):102-4, 132.

Official Documents

California. Laws, Statutes, etc. *Statutes, 1877-1878.*
Chapter 266: An Act to establish and maintain free public libraries and reading rooms, approved 18 March 1878.

———. Laws, Statutes, etc. *Statutes 1880.*
An Act to establish free public libraries and reading rooms, approved 26 April 1880, pp. 231-33.

———. Laws, Statutes, etc. *Statutes, 1919.*
Chapter 15: Senate Concurrent Resolution no. 24—relative to Ina Coolbrith of San Francisco, California, being given the honorary title of the Loved and Laurel Crowned Poet of California.

———. Secretary of State. *California Blue Book; or, State Roster, 1907.* Sacramento, 1907.

———. State Mining Bureau. *Mines and Mineral Resources of Sierra County.* Sacramento, 1919. (State Mineralogist's Report, 16:92, December 1918).

———. Supreme Court. *Reports, October Term, 1859.* 14:390-95, *Carsley v. Lindsay.*

Los Angeles (City). Public Library. *Annual Report, 1897.* Los Angeles, 1897.

Los Angeles County. District Court. *Case #853: Josephine D. Carsley v. Robert B. Carsley,* 26 December 1861.

———. Recorder. *Marriage Certificates,* 1:22-23.

Oakland. City Council. *Minutes,* 25 August to 31 December 1892.

———. Free Library. *Annual Report* no. 1, 1880-81. In *Minutes* of the Board of Directors, 5 July 1881, pp. 161-66.

———. Free Library. *Bulletin* 3 vols. 1890-92.

———. Free Library. *Catalogue* of the Oakland Free Library comp. by Charles Miel, April, 1885. *Oakland Tribune*, 1885.

———. Free Library. *Minutes* of the Board of Directors, 1 June 1878 to 1 February 1898. 2 vols. manuscript; Librarian's office, Oakland Free Library.

———. Oakland Library Association. *Minutes,* 5 March 1868 to 28 May 1878, 183 pages of manuscript; Librarian's office, Oakland Free Library.

Saco, Maine. City Council. *First Book of Records of the Town of Pepperrellborough, Now the City of Saco.* Saco, 1895.

San Francisco County. Clerk. *Great Register, 1867.*

U.S. Bureau of the Census. *Population,* 1850, 1860, 1870, 1880, 1890.

U.S., Congress, House, *The Petition of the Latter-day Saints, Commonly Known as Mormons . . . December 21, 1840,* 26th Cong., 2d sess., 1841, (House Document 22).

Newspapers

The files of the newspapers listed below were consulted in the following libraries: California State Library, the libraries of the University of California at Berkeley and at Los Angeles, the Henry E. Huntington Library in San Marino, California, Los Angeles Public Library, Oakland Free Library, and the library of the Utah Historical Society in Salt Lake City. Some other newspaper references are cited in the "Notes and Sources" in this volume; these are chiefly single items to be found as clippings in Ina Coolbrith's scrapbooks. The dates following titles indicate inclusive years consulted, not publication dates.

Berkeley Gazette (1897-1928)
Chicago Evening Post (1893)
Los Angeles Star (1855-62)
Los Angeles Times (1895-1907)
Missouri Republican, April 23, 1849. Photostat in Bancroft Library, University of California, Berkeley.
Nauvoo Times and Seasons (1839-1846)
New York Times (1898-1928)
Oakland Enquirer (1892-1921)
Oakland Post-Enquirer (1922-23)
Oakland Times (1883-1928)
Oakland Tribune (1874-1928)
St. Louis Republican, April 7 to May 17, 1849. Photostat in Bancroft Library.

San Diego Union (1895-1916)
San Francisco Alta (1874)
San Francisco Bulletin (1876-1928)
San Francisco Californian (1864-67)
San Francisco Call (1871-1928)
San Francisco Call-Chronicle-Examiner, April 19, 1906.
San Francisco Chronicle (1890-1928)
San Francisco Daily News (1925)
San Francisco Examiner (1890-1928)
San Francisco Golden Era (1862-68)
San Jose Mercury Herald (1907)

City Directories

Marysville City Directory. 1853. (Hale and Emory)
Oakland City Directory. 1874-75. (Langley)
Oakland City Directory. 1874-90. (Bishop)
Oakland, Alameda and Berkeley Directory. 1883-90. (McKenney)
Oakland, Alameda and Berkeley Directory. 1891-1909. (Husted)
Oakland, Alameda and Berkeley Directory. 1910-17. (Polk-Husted)
San Francisco Directory. 1860-95. (Langley)
San Francisco Directory. 1879. (Bishop)
San Francisco Directory. 1896-1933. (Crocker-Langley)

Maps

Hill, Gustavus. Map of the City of Nauvoo . . . [Salt Lake City]: Nauvoo
  Restoration, Incorporated, 1965.
  Facsimile of a map published in Joseph Smith's lifetime.
Miller, Juanita Joaquina. [Map of "The Hights"] in her About "The
  Hights." Oakland: Tooley-Towne, 1933.
  Mimeographed copy of this map in files of Oakland Park Department.
Nauvoo Restoration, Incorporated. Historic Nauvoo. [Springfield, Ill.:
  State Division of Tourism, 1964].
  Map shows location of principal buildings during Mormon period.
Rowell, Joseph C. "Map of the Buildings of the College of California
  and the College School in Oakland." Drawn by Joseph C. Rowell, July
  1938.
  Photostat of manuscript map, Bancroft Library, Berkeley.
U.S. Forest Service. Plumas National Forest. Washington, 1950.
U.S. Geological Survey. Loyalton Quadrangle, California-Nevada. Wash-
  ington, 1955.

Letters, Manuscripts, Scrapbooks

[Address Book]. Presented to Ina Coolbrith by Carl Seyfforth, New York, 6 January 1923. In Oakland Free Library.

Cook, Ina Lillian (Peterson). "Charles Warren Stoddard." [1908?] 15 1., 4 plates (photographs).
Typewritten; in files of Mrs. Ina Graham, Berkeley, Calif.

Coolbrith, Ina. Letters and Papers in the following libraries and private collections:
Bancroft Library, University of California, Berkeley.
California Historical Society, San Francisco.
California State Library, California Section, Sacramento.
California State Library, Sutro Branch, San Francisco.
Graham Family Collection, Berkeley.
Henry E. Huntington Library, San Marino, California.
Mills College Library, Oakland.
Oakland Free Library, Oakland.
Sanchez Family Collection, Oakland.
Society of California Pioneers, San Francisco.
Southwest Museum, Los Angeles.

Coolbrith, Ina, comp. *Scrapbooks.* 2 vols. in Oakland Free Library.

Gilson, Daniel. "Ina Donna Coolbrith, 1841-1928." Oakland, 1968. 6 1. Typewritten. In authors' files.

Graham, Ina Agnes (Cook). "Ina Lillian Peterson . . . Memories by Her Daughter."
27 1. Mimeographed; for limited distribution.
pp. 6-27, Poems by Ina Lillian Cook.

Hayes, Benjamin I., comp. *Scrapbooks.* 138 vols. in Bancroft Library, Berkeley.

Louderback, Carrie (Knapp). "Reminiscences." Oakland, 1943. 5 1. Typewritten. In Oakland Free Library.

Mountain View Cemetery, Oakland. "Burial Records." 1877-1932.

"Notes on the Church History." On file in the Church Historical Department, Salt Lake City, Utah.

Oakland. Free Library, comp. *Scrapbook, ALA in Oakland, 1891.*

Oakland. Free Library. Reference Dept., comp. *Ina Donna Coolbrith; a Scrapbook of Clippings from the San Francisco and Oakland Newspapers.* Oakland, 1917-45.
37 pp.

488

Minutes. See Oakland Free Library and Oakland Library Association in Part Two: Official Documents.

Overland Monthly, 1869-75. *Account of Moneys Paid Contributors.* Manuscript in Bancroft Library, Berkeley.

San Jose Women's Club, San Jose, California. ["Collection of Poems Dedicated to Ina D. Coolbrith"] 1907.
Mounted in scrapbook. Ina Coolbrith Papers, Bancroft Library, Berkeley.

Schaufler, Elsie T. "Trustees and Directors of the Oakland Free Library, 1868-1949." Oakland, 1949.
19 l. Typewritten. Oakland Free Library.

Thomas, Mabel Winifred, comp. "History and Description of Ina Donna Coolbrith" . . . Comp. for the Historical Marker Committee, Oakland Chamber of Commerce, 21 March 1932; with corrections and additions made January, 1942.
8 l. Typewritten. Oakland Free Library .

Index

494

City, 344; IDC poems to, 117, 119, 224, 391, 396; at IDC's funeral, 368
Bonney, Frank, 160
Book Club of California, 330, 340
Book of Mormon, 5, 7
The Bookman, 341, 342
Booth, Edwin, actor, 79, 119, 185, 288; IDC's sonnet to, 227-28, 390
Borle, Augusta, 287
Bosqui, Edward, printer of IDC's poem "The Colonel's Toast," 190
Boston, Mass., 7, 8; IDC's visits, 180-82, 226
Boston Transcript, 182, 324
Bowers, Mrs. D. P., honorary member, Bohemian Club, 119
Bowman, James F., "Jimmy", friend and literary associate of IDC, 87, 88, 91, 113-14, 249; editor, *Californian*, 88; IDC's memorial poem to, 113-14; influence on IDC, 88, 113; Bohemian Club's beginnings in Bowman home, 118; character in Stoddard's novel, *For the Pleasure of His Company*, 253
Bowman, Margaret, wife of James Bowman, friend of IDC, 88, 113, 119; honorary member Bohemian Club, 119; curtains for club, 118
Bradley's Ranch, Calif., 41
Brady, George Beach, 370
Bragg, Elizabeth, 141
Brecknock, Albert, city librarian, Hucknall Torkard, England, 303, 305, 330, 356, 357; *Byron*, 356, 357
"Bret." *See* Harte, Bret
Brier, Columbus, Oakland Free Library board, 170, 173; friendly to IDC, 173
Briggs, Annie, pupil of William Keith, 232
Brock, Amanda, "Sutatot", mother of Calle Shasta Miller, 178
Bromley, George, "Uncle George," master of ceremonies at Bohemian Club initiation of IDC and Margaret Bowman: 119, 202, 249; IDC's birthday poem for, 391; *The Long Ago and the Later On*, 391
Brooks, Noah, 91
Brother Leo. *See* Leo, Brother, "Thomas Meehan"
Brown, Annie Florence, 325
Browne, J. Ross, 290
Browning, Robert, 287
Browning Society, New York City, 338
Brule, Nebr., 32
Buck's Lake, Calif., 43

Bunker Hill Monument, Boston, Mass., IDC at, 181
Burbank, Luther, 119, 276, 353; names crimson poppy for IDC, 319, memorial poem by IDC, 396
Burbank, Mary, 291
Burgess, Gelett, 341
Burnett, Frances Hodgson, *Little Lord Fauntleroy*, 390
Burnham, O. H., Oakland Free Library board, 145, 167-69
Business and Professional Women's Association, Oakland, Calif., luncheon for IDC, 349
Bynner, Witter, sarcastic comments on California writers including IDC, 341-342
Byron, George Gordon, Lord, poems in William Pickett's library, 27, 57-58; influence on IDC, 101; laurel wreath and poem for Byron's tomb in Hucknall Torkard church, 102-3, 105-7, 330, 386; Phillips's portrait of, in IDC's home, 246, 303
Byron (Brecknock), 303, 356, 357

Cadenasso, Giuseppi, artist, IDC's landlord, 1907-8, 264
California. Legislature, official laureate status for IDC, 317, 330, 335
California. State Library, plaques honoring state poets laureate, 317
California. University. *See* University of California
"California" (Coolbrith), 117, 330
"California" (series of articles in *Missouri Republican*), 29
California Academy of Sciences, 247, 253
California Club, 276; *War Poems*, 239, 392
California Diamond Jubilee, IDC the official poet for, 354, 357
California Educational Review, 390
California Federation of Women's Clubs, 291
California Floral Society, IDC a member, 253
California Home Journal, San Francisco, 81-82, 384; poems by IDC, 1858-61, 65-66
California Illustrated, 222, 224
California Literature Society, meetings in home of IDC, 319, 320-21, 331, 334
California Outlook, 306, 395
California Poetry Society, reception for IDC, 349

California Publishing Company, 163
California Room, Oakland Free Library. *See* Oakland Free Library. California Room
California the Beautiful (Elder), IDC's commencement ode, 1871, reprinted in, 117
California Writers' Club, 290-91, 339, 377
Californian, literary weekly, 81, 85, 87, 88, 89, 91, 110, 113, 275, 385; editors: Charles Henry Webb, 85, James F. Bowman, 88; C. W. Stoddard a contributor, 86, 275; prose by IDC, 86; IDC's files lost in fire of 1906, 261; verse by IDC: Cupid Kissed Me, Mists, A Lost Day, Fragment from an Unfinished Poem, 85; In the Pouts, Hereafter, 86; The Mother's Grief, 73, 74, 86; Sunset, A Poet's Grave on Lone Mountain, The Sweetest Sound, Love in Little, Heliotrope, 88
The Californian, a Western Monthly, 163, 388, 389
The Californian and Overland Monthly, 163
"California's Early Distinguished Writers," lecture by IDC, 232
"California's Fair Poet," article by Joaquin Miller, 201-2
Call-Chronicle-Examiner, 256
Calla, pet cat, 193, 240, 392
"Callie." *See* Miller, Calle Shasta
Calle Shasta. *See* Miller, Calle Shasta
Cameron, Alice Marsh, daughter of Dr. John Marsh, 133
Cameron, William, 133
Camp Drum, Wilmington and Los Angeles, Calif., 69
Camp Fitzgerald, Los Angeles, 69
Camp Latham, Los Angeles, 69
Campbell, Fred M., 142, 170, 188, 202; secretary, Oakland Library Association, 130; on Oakland Free Library's first board, 145; petition, Peterson case, 169; public reading of poem by IDC, 190
Carleton, James M., 57, 69, 97
Carmany, Cyrus, brother of J. H. Carmany, 139, 154
Carmany, John Henry, publisher, 119, 139, 142; biographical sketch, 154, 157; and IDC, 114, 138-39, 153-54, 157-59, 190, 220-21; and Bret Harte, 154, 156, 164; publisher, *Overland Monthly*, 1869-75, 109, 114, 139, 141;

pay for contributions to *Overland*, 125; right to use *Overland* title given to Warren Cheney, 163; address at *Overland* revival dinner, 164; publisher of IDC's *A Perfect Day*, 156; "The Poet," by IDC, dictated to him, 190; IDC's manuscripts preserved by him, 114; death, 288
Carmel, Calif., 260, 271, 281
"Carmen Sylva Day," 287
Carpentier, Horace, 129, 133
Carr, Jeanne, Mrs. Ezra Carr, 202-3, 287; board member, Oakland Library Association, 132
Carruth, C. W., printer, friend of IDC, 348
Carsley, Josephine Donna Smith. *See* Coolbrith, Ina Donna
Carsley, Robert, husband of IDC, minstrel player and ironmonger, 60, 102, 141, 364, 366; and IDC, 60-72; partner of Daniel B. Lindsay in Salamander Iron Works, 60; partnership dissolved, 66; workshop, 64, 66, 68; San Bernardino jail casing, 66, 68; engagement and marriage, 61, 63, 64; minstrel show in San Francisco, 69; threats against wife, 69-71; hand wounded and amputated, 70; divorce, 72
Carsley, Mrs. Robert. *See* Coolbrith, Ina Donna
Carson, Kit, 97
Carson Sink, Nev., 36
Carthage, Ill.: jail, 22; assassination of Joseph and Hyrum Smith, 22, 24
Castillo, Enrique del, 312
Catholic World, 306, 324, 395
Cator, Thomas B., music for IDC's "Quest," 274, 398
Cats: IDC's many cats, 193; Calla, 193, 240, 392; Beauty, 193; Titian, 256, 257, 261, 284, 294; Moona, 256, 257, 261, 284, 303; Popcorn, 303, 331, 333, 343, 345, 356
Censorship, 170
Centennial Yearbook of Alameda County (Halley), 144
Century Club, San Francisco, 231, 232, 235, 276
Century Dictionary, 193
Century Magazine, 190, 227, 284, 389, 390, 391, 394
Chabot, Anthony, petition, Peterson case, 169

See Pickett, Agnes Moulton Coolbrith Smith

Coolbrith, Catherine, aunt of IDC, sister of Agnes Moulton Coolbrith Smith Pickett, 7

Coolbrith, Charlotte, aunt of IDC, sister of Agnes Moulton Coolbrith Smith Pickett, 7

COOLBRITH, INA DONNA. (Note: Entries under this heading are classified into four groups: I, Personal; II, Literary Career; III, Career in Librarianship; and IV, Relationships with others)

I Personal

a) ancestry, 3-4, 7-8; Mormon background, 5-26, 254; promise to mother to keep secret, 80, 254, 363
b) birth, 3, 21, 358
c) childhood experiences: in Nauvoo, 22, 363; in St. Louis, 27-28; first white child to cross Beckwourth Pass, xxiii-xxiv, 39, 378; walk from Spanish Ranch to Marysville, 43-44; summer in the mines, 45-47; lost in the woods, 46-47; Marysville flood, 44-45; San Francisco in 1853-54, 48-49
d) education, 53; in Los Angeles's first public school, 53; first school composition in verse, 57
e) family: marriage of parents, Agnes Coolbrith and Don Carlos Smith, 12; births of sisters Agnes and Sophronia, 12; death of father, 21; death of sister Sophronia, 22; remarriage of mother to William Pickett, 25; birth of twin stepbrothers, William and Don Carlos Pickett, 27; sickness and death of sister Agnes, 120-21, 122; disappearance of stepfather, 125; IDC gives home to orphaned niece and nephew, Ina and Henry Peterson, 126, 135, 136, 138, 211; family circle in Oakland home, 136, 138; death of IDC's mother, 141-42; affection for mother, 364; quarrel with nephew, 193, 195; death of nephew, 250, 251; devotion to grandnieces and stepbrothers, 251
f) friendships: many friends, 87, 110, 112-14, 162-63, 312-14, and *passim;* Valentine, 1907, 274-75; surprise 75th birthday party, 319-20;

entertain IDC in last years, 339, 353; Golden Gate Trinity, 94-95; New York friends, 334-45; William D. Armes, 298, 312, 330; Gertrude Atherton, 251, 269, 276, 278, 292, 293, 295; Herbert Bashford family, 288-90, 296, 313, 321, 324, 328, 331; Albert Bender, 119, 330-31, 339, 344, 348, 354; Mrs. O. G. Beverly, 348; Judge John and Elizabeth Boalt, 183-84, 193, 257-58, 286, 390, 322-23; James and Margaret Bowman, 88, 112, 113-14, 119; John H. Carmany, 114, 125, 138-39, 142, 153-54, 157-59, 190, 220-21; Torrey Connor, 162, 260, 290-91; Alice Kingsbury Cooley, 112, 190, 286; Miles M. Dawson, 342, 344; Benjamin and Bio De Casseras, 334, 345; Anna De Martini, 278, 294; Joseph C. Duncan, 82-83, 186, 365; Henry and Minnie Edwards, 112, 119; Zoeth Skinner Eldredge, 316, 321, 330; Jeanne Francouer, 333, 334, 335; Charlotte P. S. Gilman, 176, Iza Hardy, 287, 294, 301, 334; Bret Harte: meets, 85, *Outcroppings,* 86-87, 88, Admission Day poem, 94, *Overland,* 91-95, 97-98, Golden Gate Trinity, 94-95, 98, friend, critic, and editor, 102, 110, 365, shelling peas, 275, letters, 93-94, 247, 258, 260, his farewell call, 109, IDC's memorial poem to him, 250; Ruth Harwood, 163, 356, 371; Frederick W. Henshaw, 159-63; John S. Hittell, 112; Theodore Hittell, 112-13, 201; Harriet Howe, 228, 258; George W. James, 252-53, 261-63, 272-74, 280; Charles Keeler, 162, 274, 276; William Keith, 112, 113, 119, 227, 228, 246, 250, 276, 365; Adeline Knapp, 228, 232, 284; Robin Lampson, 321; Mary V. T. Lawrence, 82-83, 112, 348; Derrick and Eunice Lehmer, 162-63, 356, 370, 377; Jack London, 119, 150-51, 162, 183, 185-86, 266, 269, 334; Joan London, 321; Charles F. Lummis, 162, 272, 338, 354; Josephine C. McCrackin, 97-98, 112, 312-14, 316, 331-32; Anna and Edwin Markham, 239, 272, 334, 335, 354; Ella S. Mighels, 320-22, 331; Joaquin Miller: laurel wreath for Byron's tomb, 103, 106, 297, 330,

498

502

504

507

509

510

Fort Sumter, Charleston, S. C., 69
Foss, Mary, IDC's grandmother. *See* Coolbroth, Mary Foss
Foster, William F., Providence, R. I., librarian in Oakland, 198
Francis, Harry; pallbearer, IDC funeral, 370
Francis of Assisi, Saint, 358, 397
Francoeur, Jeanne, 333, 334, 335
Frederick III, emperor of Germany, IDC's poem on, 190, 390
Fremont, Jessie Benton, 287
Fremont High School, Oakland, Calif.; IDC's portrait unveiled, 321
French College, San Francisco: John Mibiele, principal, 81; IDC teacher of English, 81
Friday Morning Club, Los Angeles, reception for IDC, 230
Frost, Robert, 202
Fuller, Ina Dorothy Peterson, IDC's grandniece, daughter of Henry and Elizabeth Peterson: birth, 197; named for IDC, 211

Gale, Zona, 342
Gallatin, Mo., 13
Garcia, bandit, 54
Gates, Eleanor, 269
Gates, Lydia, IDC's great-grandmother. *See* Mack, Lydia Gates
Gatlin, Lillian, 317
"Geewhillican," 272, 276
Gentiles in Nauvoo, 24-26
Gibsonville mining district. Calif., 42, 45
Gibsonville Ridge, Calif., 42
Gillis, James, California state librarian, 261; requests IDC's talk on early writers of the state, 291
Gilman, Charlotte Perkins Stetson, writer, 203, 226, 287; IDC's neighbor and friend, 176
Glascock, William H., charter member, Oakland Library Association, 130
Goat Island. Calif. *See* Yerba Buena Island, Calif.
Goddaughter of IDC, Mary Lee Nahl, 291
"The Goddess" (Harte), 83
Goethals, George, 305
Gold Canyon, Calif., 45
Gold discovered in California, 28
Golden Era, 80, 81, 83, 85, 87, 101, 110, 156, 384; poems of IDC published in: "June," 83, "December," 83, "Christmas Eve, 1863," 83, "Starr King," 85; IDC's files destroyed in fire of 1906, 261
Golden Gate, 78, 116, 246, 280
"Golden Gate Trinity," 85, 94-98, 101, 109, 112, 119, 272, 281; limericks exchanged, 95, 334; scattered, 109, 245. *See also* Coolbrith, Ina Donna II, Literary Career, b) in San Francisco
Golden Plates. *See* Book of Mormon
Graham, Ina Agnes Cook Craig, 313, 396; officer of Ina Coolbrith Circle, 373
Graham, R. H., Oakland Free Library board, 183
Grand Canyon, Ariz., IDC visit and poem, 179-80
Grand River, Mo.: Adam-ondi-Ahman on bank, 13; crossed by Agnes Smith Pickett, 15
Grant, John T., president, Ina Coolbrith Circle, pallbearer IDC funeral, 370
Grant, Ulysses S., 97
Grass Valley (on Feather River), Calif., 44
"Great White Fleet," 280
Green, Harriet F., librarian, at ALA in Oakland, 198
Green. Horace, 196
Green River, Wyo., 34-35
Green Star Magazine, 394
Greene, Charles S., Oakland librarian (1899-1926), former editor of *Overland Monthly,* 327; on portrait of IDC, 325, 327
Greene, Clay M., 119
Greene, Samuel S., librarian, at ALA in Oakland, 198
Greenhood, David, 341
Guiney, Louise I., 305
Gunderson, Carl. *See* Seyfforth, Carl

Haight, Henry H., California governor, 115
Hale's department store, San Francisco. 357
Hall. D. F., 64
Halley, William, *Centennial Year Book of Alameda County,* 144
Hamilton, Henry, editor, *Los Angeles Star,* 56. 64, 72
Hamilton. Laurentine, Oakland clergyman, 142; IDC's memorial poem, 165, 389
Hanna, Edward J., archbishop, 320, 367

Hardy, Iza, 287, 294, 301, 334

Hardy, W. B., charter member, Oakland Library Association, 130, 144; petition, Peterson case, 169

Harmon, A. K. P., charter member, Oakland Library Association, 130; petition, Peterson case, 169

Harper's Weekly, 88, 89, 156

Harris, Martin, 7

Harrison, William Greer, 224

Hart, Mary E., Alaskan journalist, suicide, 342-43

Harte, Bret, writer, editor, 79, 83, 85-88, 91-95, 97-98, 101-2, 114, 115, 119, 139, 154, 164, 186, 250, 293, 307, 313, 316, 342, 374, 382; assistant editor, *Californian*, 85; meets IDC, 85; criticism of verse by IDC, 85-86, 102; in IDC's home, 89, 109, 245, 275; anecdotes: the little asp, 93-94, gold coins, 94, shelling peas, 275; asks IDC to write Admission Day poem, 94; "Frank," IDC's name for Harte, 95; farewell call on IDC, 109; takes IDC's poems to have published in Boston, 110, 154, 156; IDC's tribute to Harte as friend, critic, and editor, 110, 365; IDC's introduction to *Heathen Chinee* (Harte), 356-57; IDC's lecture on, 231; IDC's memorial poem to, 250, 393

Harte, Francis Bret. *See* Harte, Bret

Harte, Frank. *See* Harte, Bret

Harte, Richard Bret, grandson of Bret Harte, 321

Harwood, Ruth, artist, poet: IDC an inspiration to, 163, 356; her poem to IDC, 371

Hastings School of Law, San Francisco, 302

Haun's Mill massacre, Mo., 15, 20

Hayden, Mrs. Rita I., 357

Hayes, Benjamin, judge, lawyer, antiquarian, 54-55; divorce decree in Carsley v. Carsley case, 72

Hayes, Josephine. *See* Pickett, Josephine Hayes

Hayes, Louisa, Los Angeles teacher, 53, 57

Hayes, Margaret. *See* Pickett, Margaret Hayes

Hearst, George, and Yerba Buena Island tree planting, 188

Hearst, Phoebe Apperson, declines honorary presidency, Congress of Authors and Journalists, 302

Hearst, William Randolph, 345

The Heathen Chinee (Harte), 356-57

"Heights." *See* "Hights"

Henshaw, Frederick William: judge, 160, 162-63; IDC aids in a translation from Horace, 159; IDC's birthday poems to, 159-61, 388; as subject of her poems "A Night of Storm," 161-62, "Dreams and Reality," and "Enter June," 159

The Hermitage and Other Poems (Sill), 88

Herrick, Robert, 250, 393

"Hesperia," E. C. Stedman's sobriquet for IDC, 181, 189

Hesperian, 232

Higbee, Elias, petition to Congress concerning Mormon persecutions in Missouri, 20

Higginson, Ella Mae, Washington poet: "To Ina Coolbrith," 202; her goddaughter, Alice Bashford, 290

Higginson, Thomas Wentworth, writer: includes IDC's "Beside the Dead" in his *American Sonnets*, 189; praise for IDC's "The Mariposa Lily," 253

High in Her Tower (Phillips), 359

"Hights," 178, 189, 296, 298, 301

Hittell, John Shertzer, historian and publisher, 97, 105, 112; friend of IDC, 112

Hittell, Theodore, historian, 112; friend of IDC, 112, 201; *Overland* revival dinner, 164

Hobart, J. A., charter member, Oakland Library Association, 130

Holbrook, Nellie, 157

Holcomb Valley, Calif., 69

Holmes, Henry, 250, 393

Holmes, Oliver Wendell, author: *Atlantic Monthly*, 109; IDC's visit to, 181

Holy Names College. *See* College of the Holy Names, Oakland

Home Industries League, San Francisco, 330

Home Journal. See California Home Journal

The Hoot of the Owl (Behr), edited by IDC, 247

Hoover, Herbert, 350

Hoover, Lou Henry, 350

Hopper, James, 276

Horace, 159, 388

Horn, William, 64

Horton, Mrs. S. W., public reading of poem by IDC, 190

512

Hotaling, Richard D., 298
Houghton Mifflin Company, Boston, Mass., publishers of books by IDC: *Songs from the Golden Gate*, 228, 275, 307, 357; *Wings of Sunset*, 373; urges IDC to write her reminiscences, 340
Howard, Mrs. Charles Webb; reception for Pacific Coast educators, 202
Howe, Harriet, 258; at IDC's sick bed, 228
Howe, Julia Ward: reception for, 190; IDC's verse tribute to, 190, 390
Howells, William Dean, editor, *Atlantic Monthly*, 109
Howland Flat, Calif., 42, 45
Hucknall Torkard, England, 330, 357; Byron's tomb, 106, 303
Hudspeth's Cutoff, Idaho, 36
Huff, Mary, 258
Humboldt River, Nev., 36
Humphreys, C. T., 276
Hyde, Orson, mission to Boston, 7, 8-9
Hymns by IDC, 202

Impressions Quarterly, 252-53
In Memoriam: Amila Hudson Lemmon (Lemmon), 389
Ina. *See* Coolbrith, Ina Donna I. Personal, j) name
"Ina Coolbrith, California Poet" (Taylor), 308, 310
Ina Coolbrith, Mount. *See* Mount Ina Coolbrith
Ina Coolbrith Circle, 348, 354; organized, 334; IDC attends for first time, 339; "Christmas tree" for IDC, 343; IDC attends for last time, 359; memorial to IDC, 372-73; instrumental in having a Sierra peak named for IDC, 377-78
Ina Coolbrith Day: San Diego, 321; San Francisco, 284; San Jose, 274
Ina Coolbrith Park, San Francisco, 266
Ina D. Coolbrith Branch Library, Oakland, 192
Ina D. Coolbrith Home Fund Committee, Pasadena, Calif., 261-62, 279-80
Ina Ledge, Gibsonville mining district, Calif., 42, 45, 125
Independence, Mo., 13, 28, 29
Independence Rock, Wyo., 34
"Indian Callie." *See* Miller, Calle Shasta
"The Indian of Romance," lecture by IDC, 231
Indians: on the Overland Trail, 32, 33,

34; saved by Indian guide, 36
Ingersoll, Robert, 144
"Inigo." *See* Webb, Charles Henry
"The Intaglio" (Duncan), 186
Irish, John P., editor: *Oakland Times*, 148; *San Francisco Alta*, 188; editorial on Oakland Free Library board irregularities, 170; and Yerba Buena Island tree planting, 188; eulogy for Joaquin Miller, 298
Irwin, Wallace, 341
Isabella, Queen of Spain, statue, poem by IDC, 224, 225, 391

"Jack" (Constance Fletcher), 253
Jackson, Helen Hunt, IDC's tribute to 189, 227, 389
James, Elias Olan, 350
James, George Wharton, writer, editor, 268, 272, 275, 279; articles on IDC, 252-53; meets Joaquin Miller and daughter, 252; his "home fund" as benefit for IDC, 261-62, 272-74, 293; reception for IDC in Pasadena, 263; fund building methods, 272-73; "Geewhillican," 272, 276; contributor to "Valentine" for IDC, 274; at Authors' Reading, 276; guest of IDC, 280
James, Henry, San Francisco newspaperman, praise of IDC, 219, 230
"Jeems Pipes of Pipesville." *See* Massett, Stephen
Jefferson, Thomas. Jacob Milliken's first vote for, 180
Jewish poets, 312
"Joan of Arc," IDC attends play, 342
Joaquin et al (Miller), 101, 105, 293
Joaquin Miller Park, 298
"John Paul." *See* Webb, Charles Henry
Johnson, Edmund, uncle of John Greenleaf Whittier, 180
Johnson, Hiram, 310, 313
Jordan, David Starr, president, Stanford University, 202, 239, 302, 350; endorses IDC for position of Los Angeles city librarian, 235
Jordan, Mrs. David Starr, 276

KPO, Hale's department store, San Francisco, 357
Kaw River, Kans., Mormon missionaries near, 6
Kean, Charles, actor in San Francisco, 79, 185, 288; as Lear and Hamlet, 80
Keeler, Charles: IDC's friend, 162, 228;

513

contributor to "Valentine" for IDC, 274; at Authors' Reading, 276

Keith, William, artist 79, 119, 142, 203, 228, 232, 258; IDC's friend, 112, 113, 365; at *Overland* revival dinner, 164; his landscapes in IDC's home, 246; IDC's poems to, 227, 250, 391, 392, 393; illustrations for IDC, *Songs from the Golden Gate*, 228; large landscape raffled off at Authors' Reading, 276

Keith, Mrs. William, 276

Kelley, Edward Stillman, 190, 308, 389

Kellogg, Charles W., board member, Oakland Free Library, 167-69, 170, 183; on ALA reception committee, 193

Kellogg, Martin, president, University of California, 202, 239; at *Overland* revival dinner, 164

Kendall, Carleton, IDC's friend, 321

Kendall, W. A., contributor to *Outcroppings*, 87

Kennedy, Kate, IDC's guest, 280; describes IDC's Lincoln Street flat, 264; presents "Valentine" to IDC in San Francisco, 274-75

Kennedy, W. G., 280

Kewen, Edward John Case, pseud., "Harry Quillem," lawyer, politician, poet, 54, 55-56, 58, 68-69, 71, 73, 80, 94; his home, *El Molino Viejo*, 56, 64; *Idealina*, 58, 64, 65; IDC's verses "To 'Harry Quillem,' " 65, 384; answer by Kewen, 65; reprimands Robert Carsley, 70; advises divorce, 71; counsel for IDC in divorce proceedings, 72

Kewen, Jennie White, at *El Molino Viejo*, 56, 64, 68

Kibbe, Minora, physician, 271

Kilmer, Joyce, poet, 306

Kimball, Heber, leader in exodus of Mormons from Missouri, 15

King, Andrew J., deputy sheriff, Los Angeles County, 54-55; arrest and jailing of Robert Carsley, 71; witness against Carsley in court, 72

King, Thomas Starr, 83; influence on IDC, 83, 85; Sanitary Fund, 83, 85; death, 85; poetic tributes by IDC, Harte, and Stoddard, 85, 384

Kingsbury, Alice. *See* Cooley, Alice Kingsbury

Kinross, Albert, editor, *London Outlook*, 230, 239, 345; discovers IDC, 230, 239; war prevents his coming to Con-

gress of Authors and Journalists, 305

Kirk, Henry: beauty of IDC, 150; California Literature Society, 321

Kirkham, R. W., charter member, Oakland Library Association, 130

Kirtland, Ohio, 7, 8, 11-12; arrival of Joseph and Emma Smith, 6; arrival of Smith family, 6; arrival of converts, 7

Kirtland Company, in Far West, Mo., 12, 13

Kline, Burton, 286, 324

Knapp, Adeline, 228, 232, 284

Kohler, William, purchaser of IDC's Webster Street, Oakland, house, 240

Koppel, Charles, 338

Kozley, Charles, 307

Krebs, A. E., *La Copa de Oro*, 393

Krefeld, Germany, Bret Harte, American consul, 119, 154

Krout, Mary H., article concerning IDC, *Chicago Post*, 224

LDS Church. *See* Church of Jesus Christ of Latter-day Saints, The

Ladies' Patriotic Fund benefit program, Bret Harte's poem "The Goddess," read by Thomas Starr King, 83

Lady Byron Vindicated (Stowe), review by Harte in *Overland*, 101

Lampson, Robin, IDC's friend, 321

Land of Little Rain (Austin), 251

Land of Sunshine, 239, 291, 392

The Lantern, 327

Laramie Peak, 33

Latham, Camp. *See* Camp Latham

Latham Hotel, New York City, IDC a resident of, 339

Latter-day Saints, The Church of. *See* Church of Jesus Christ of Latter-day Saints, The

Lawrence, James Henry, state senator, husband of Mary V. Tingley Lawrence, 83

Lawrence, Mary V. Tingley, IDC's first friend in San Francisco, 83, 86; introduced by Joseph C. Duncan, 82-83; friend of many years, 112, 348; reception for IDC, 348

Lawson, Emilie, contributor to *Outcroppings*, 87

Le Conte, John: present at *Overland* revival dinner, 164; memorial poem by IDC, 202, 390

Le Conte, Joseph, 165; at *Overland* revival dinner, endorses IDC for posi-

514

Loughead, Laura Haines, article on IDC, 252

Lowell, Amy, 342

Lowell, James Russell, editor, *Atlantic Monthly*, 109

Lowenberg, Mrs. Isadore: proposes an "authors' congress," 292; on committee for "congress," 302

Lummis, Charles Fletcher, "Don Carlos," writer, editor, *Land of Sunshine*, librarian, IDC's friend, 262, 312, 333-34, 342, 353; Los Angeles city librarian, 260, 261; IDC inscribes and presents copy of *Songs from the Golden Gate* to, 230; tells Markham of Spinners' Club, 272; temporary blindness, 294; his Spanish love letter to IDC, 338; "March Hares," IDC's poem to, 396; last meeting with IDC, 354; portrait with IDC, 354; IDC an inspiration to, 359

"Macbeth" (Shakespeare), 190, 308

McChesney, Clara, 335

McChesney, J. B., charter member, Oakland Library Association, 130; on board of Oakland Library Association and later of Oakland Free Library, 132, 145, 183; helps save Oakland Free Library from city hall fire, 143; on committee for ALA day in Oakland, 197

McCrackin, Jackson, husband of Josephine Clifford McCrackin, 112

McCrackin, Josephine Clifford, "Jo," writer and conservationist: IDC's friend, 112, 287, 301; Bret Harte's secretary, 97; meets IDC in *Overland* office, 97-98; sketch of life, 97-98; her photograph, 283; honored by IDC at Congress of Authors and Journalists, 312-14, 316; on old age, 331-32; conservation, 332; death; 342-43

Mack, Lucy, IDC's grandmother. *See* Smith, Lucy Mack

Mack, Lydia Gates, IDC's great-grandmother, 4

Mack, Solomon, IDC's great-grandfather, 4

McKinnon, John A., 204, 209; board member, Oakland Free Library, 195; on committee for ALA day in Oakland, 197; letter requesting resignation of IDC, 205-6, 207

McLean, D. D., speaker at Oakland Free Library opening, 145

McLean, J. K., petition, Peterson case, 169

Macomb, Ill., 16

Macondray Lane, San Francisco. *See* Lincoln Street

Magazine of Poetry, 190

Maguire's Opera House, San Francisco, Adah Menken in "Black-Eyed Susan," 83

Makee, Ada, daughter of Sara Makee, Stoddard's Boston papers in her keeping, 283

Makee, Sara Stoddard, sister of Charles Warren Stoddard, 86, 281, 282, 283, 286; turns over Stoddard's effects to IDC, 282-83; sells brother's library, 283

"Man with the Hoe" (Markham), 134, 239, 272

Mantilla of white lace worn by IDC in later years, 319, 320, 377

Marconi, Guglielmo, 354

Markham, Anne, wife of Edwin Markham, 334, 342, 344; reads IDC's "California" at Poetry Society meeting, 335

Markham, Edwin, poet, 99, 134, 228, 247, 290, 313, 338, 344; "Man with the Hoe," 134, 239, 272; autographed books and manuscripts for benefit of IDC, 272; "To Edwin Markham," by IDC, 395; calls on IDC in New York City, 334; introduces IDC to Poetry Society, 335; last meeting with IDC, 354

Marrowbone, Mo., 13

Marsh, Alice. *See* Cameron, Alice Marsh

Marsh, John, 133

Marsh, L. L., Miss, assistant, Oakland Free Library, 183

Marsh, Thomas, 7

Martin, J. W., mayor, Oakland, letter to Oakland Free Library board urging reinstatement of Miss Peterson, 169

Martin, Lannie Haynes, article on California literature, 293-94; errors, 293

Martinez, Xavier, artist, 290

Marysville, Calif.: fire, August 1851, 42; description, 44-45; floods, 44-45, 47; first public library in California, 130

Marysville Express, poem by Montbar in answer to one by IDC, 59

Marysville Herald, prints poem by IDC, 59

Mason, Redfern, anecdote about E. S. Kelley and IDC, 307-8

516

Miller, 79, 80, 83; children, 120; is character in Stoddard's novel, *For the Pleasure of His Company*, 253

Milliken, Arthur, husband of Lucy Smith, IDC's uncle, 25

Milliken, Edward, IDC's great-great-grandfather, 180

Milliken, Jacob, a cousin of IDC's grandfather: 100th birthday, 175; IDC's poem to, 175; IDC visits, 180

Milliken, Lemuel, father of Jacob Milliken, 175

Milliken, Lucy Smith, youngest child of Lucy Mack and Joseph Smith, Sr., 6; decision to remain in Nauvoo, 25

Milliken, Rebecca. *See* Coolbroth, Rebecca Milliken

Millport, Mo., arrival of Don Carlos Smith and family, 13

Mills, Susan Tolman, 350

Mills College, Oakland, 130, confers honorary degree on IDC, 350, 352

"The Mind of Ina Coolbrith" (Stevenson), 373-74, 381-83

"Minnie Myrtle." *See* Miller, Minnie Myrtle Dyer

"The Miracle" (Reinhardt), 353-54

"Miss Juno" (Constance Fletcher), 253

"Mission Poet." *See* White, Richard Edward

Missouri Republican: foreman, William Pickett, 25, 232; "California" series, 29

Mrs. Blake's Seminary, Oakland, 130

Mitchell, Elizabeth, 322, 323-24

Mitchell, Mrs. Morton. *See* Mitchell, Elizabeth

Mitchell, Ruth Comfort, 287, 341

Mohave Desert. Calif., flowers described by IDC, 226

Montbar, Marysville poet, 59

Monterey, Calif., 271, 281, 282, 283

Montez, Lola, 79

Montgomery, Hugh, 368

Moona, pet cat, 256, 257, 261, 284, 303

Moore, H. Staats, IDC's physician, 331, 339, 342, 344, 370

Moore, J. Preston, board member, Oakland Library Association and Oakland Free Library, 145

Moore, Thomas, poet, 392

Morgan, J. Pierpont, 345

Mormon Church. *See* Church of Jesus Christ of Latter-day Saints, The

Mormons: IDC's Mormon background, 5-26; persecution in Missouri, 13-15, 20; petition to Congress for redress of grievances, 20; assassination of leaders, Joseph and Hyrum Smith, 22, 24; driven from Nauvoo, 24, 25; IDC's mother pledges to keep her Mormon background hidden, 26; in San Bernardino, 68; IDC promises to keep her mother's pledge, 254

Moroni, angel, in a vision of Joseph Smith, the Prophet, 5

Morrow, Lydia, IDC's close friend, 112, 113, 274, 280

Morrow, William C., writer, IDC's friend, 112, 113, 119, 280, 292, 302; word portrait of IDC, 113; contributor to *Spinners' Book of Fiction*, 269; to "Valentine" for IDC, 274

Mount Ina Coolbrith, 378

Mount Shasta, 377

Mountain View Cemetery, Oakland, 142, 370

Muir, John, writer, IDC's friend, 112, 113, 134-35, 140, 142, 192-93, 203, 253; matchmaking, 154; "To John Muir," by IDC, 134-35, 388

Muir, Louise Strenzel, wife of John Muir, 134

Mulford, Prentice, pseud., "Dogberry," 80

Municipal Library Act, 1880. *See* Rogers Free Library Act

Munsey's Magazine, 232, 394

Murdock, Charles, 313, 316, 321

Murieta, Joaquin, 87

Murphy, Mrs. D. O., 308

Murray, John, reading of IDC's poem "Our Poets," at *Overland* revival dinner, 164

Nahl, June Connor, wife of Perham Nahl and IDC's friend, 162, 291

Nahl, Mary Lee, IDC's godchild, 291

Nahl, Perham, artist, 291

Nash, John Henry, San Francisco art printer: *California*, by IDC, 117, 330; *Retrospect*, by IDC, 357; *The Heathen Chinee*, by Bret Harte, introduction by IDC, 356-57; *Spinners' Book of Fiction*, 269

Native Sons of the Golden West, 377

Nauvoo, Ill.: named by Joseph Smith, 17; history and description, 16-26, 363, 364; charters, 20; citizens congratulated by Abraham Lincoln, 20; temple, 24, 25, 26; gentiles in city, 24-26; "new citizens," 25; exodus of Saints from Nauvoo, 24, 25

IDC's resignation accepted, 214; considers closing branches, 214; protests from citizens and City Council, 214-16; Henry Peterson appointed new librarian, 217

Oakland. Free Library. California Room, collection of works of local authors begun by IDC, 185

Oakland. High School, 134, 144, 160

Oakland Enquirer, 209, 392; opposed to City Council in 1892, 212

Oakland Library Association, Oakland, Calif.: vacancy in position of librarian, 126; organization, 130; building site and funding, 130-31; librarians, 131; IDC appointed librarian, 131; finances, 131; removal of building to city hall grounds, 131-32; policies, regulations, salaries, 130, 143-44; lectures sponsored, 141, 144; members save building from fire, 143; interest in library legislation, 132, 143, 219; transfers property to city under Rogers Act, 144, 145; organization dissolved, 145; former members petition to reinstate Ina Peterson, 169

Oakland Post-Enquirer, 352

Oakland Times, 148, 193, 209; editorial on Oakland Free Library, 170; reporter interviews IDC on needs of library, 203-4, 208, 429-30; on star chamber sessions, 212

Oakland Tribune, 160, 193, 222, 256, 291, 348, 389-91, 394; interviews board members and librarian on dismissal of IDC, 205, 206-11

Oakland vs. Carpentier, 129

Oakland vs. Waterfront Company, 129

O'Connell, Daniel, 119; reads poem by IDC at Bohemian Club breakfast, 202; on program, IDC testimonial, 224; *Songs from Bohemia*, edited by IDC, 247

O'Day, Edward F., 306, 324, 325; asks IDC for key to Stoddard's novel, *For the Pleasure of His Company*, 253; articles on IDC, 263, 293, 306, 327; criticism of Witter Bynner, 341; criticism of Stoddard's *Poems* as edited by Thomas Walsh, 324, 325

Old age, 258, 261, 286, 316, 320, 331-32, 343, 344, 353

"Old Block," pseud. of Alonzo Delano, 80

"Old Glory" Dawson, nickname of Emma Dawson, 227, 353

Old South Church, Boston, Mass., IDC's mother in choir, 8, 9

Old Thompson, ex-slave aids Pickett family in flood, 44-45

Older, Cora, Mrs. Fremont Older: interview with IDC for *San Francisco Bulletin*, 232; at Authors' Reading, 276

Omar Khayyam, *Rubaiyat*, 306

Once a Week, 393

The One Fair Woman (Miller), 287

O'Neill, Francis, Father, on the Stoddard *Poems*, 1917, 324

Oregon Historical Society, 372

Osbourne, Isobel. *See* Field, Isobel Osbourne Strong

Osgood, F. S., board member, Oakland Free Library, 195, 204, 214; letter requesting IDC's resignation, 205-6; his reasons for IDC's resignation, 206, 207; admits star chamber session, 207-8; does not rescind action, 210

Osgood, James R., Harte's publisher, 110, 141, 156

Oslo, Norway, Carl Seyfforth's illness and death in, 352

Out West, published by George W. James, 293, 393

Outcroppings (Harte, comp.), 86, 89, 91, 97; cause of literary civil war in California, 86-87; review in the *Nation* gives IDC first national recognition, 87

Overland Monthly, 89, *passim*; publishers: Anton Roman, 91, 114, 154; J. H. Carmany, 109, 114, 154, 288; editors: Bret Harte, 91-98, 114, 154; W. C. Bartlett, 109, 114, 154; B. P. Avery, 112, 139, 154; Walter M. Fisher, 138, 154; payment for contributions, 125, 340; discontinued 1875, 139, 141; new series proposed, 163-65; published by Warren Cheney and edited by Milicent Shinn, 163; IDC's files destroyed by fire of 1906, 261; contributions by IDC:

   After the Winter Rain, 121
   Alcatraz, 394
   Alien, 340
   An Answer, 102
   At Anchor, 306
   At the Hill's Base, 119
   Beside the Dead, 138
   A Birthday Rhyme, 190
   Bret Harte, 250
   The Brook, 120
   Le Chemin de l'Ecole, 120

520

Saints, 9; in Kirtland, Ohio, 11-12; appearance, 12; marriage to Don Carlos Smith, 12; daughters, 12, 21; in Missouri, house burned by mob, 13-15, 20; in Nauvoo, 19-25; death of husband and second child, 21, 22; sells husband's printing shop, 24; marriage to William Pickett, 25, 372; pledge to keep Mormon background secret, 26, 80, 372; in St. Louis, 25-29; twin sons, 27; overland to California, 31-41; Marysville flood, 44-45; in Los Angeles and San Bernardino, 54-57, 60; and son-in-law, Robert Carsley, 69-72; in San Francisco, 78, 81, 120-22; death of oldest daughter, 122; disappearance of husband, 124-25; in Oakland with IDC, 134, 135-36, 138, 141; death, 142

Pickett, Don Carlos, IDC's stepbrother: birth, 27; lost in forest, 46-47; and Robert Carsley, 70, 72; to San Francisco, 77-78; clerk for wine merchant and book dealer, 81, 132; mining interests, 125, 251; did not marry, 251; *The Covered Wagon*, 349

Pickett, George Edward, general, Civil War, 305

Pickett, Josephine Hayes, "Josie," second wife of William Pickett, Jr., 251

Pickett, La Salle Corbell, wife of General Pickett, 305

Pickett, Margaret Hayes, first wife of William Pickett, Jr., 251

Pickett, William, IDC's stepfather; printer and lawyer, 25, 232; "new citizen" of Nauvoo, 25; marriage to Agnes Coolbrith Smith, 25; in St. Louis, employed by *Missouri Republican*, 25, 27, 232; his library, 27, 31, 43, 49; birth of twin sons, 27; overland to California, 31-41, 31 n 40; mining experiences, 42-47; printer in Marysville, 47; lawyer in San Francisco, 48, 49, 232; house burned, 49; takes family to Los Angeles, 49; practices law, 54-57, 68-70; returns to San Francisco, 78; employed as printer for the *Californian*, 81, 85; whereabouts in 1874 unknown, 124-25

Pickett, William, Jr., IDC's stepbrother: birth, 27; lost in forest, 46-47, hunting accident, 68; and Robert Carsley, 70, 72; to San Francisco with parents, 77-78; apprentice printer for *Californian*, 81; compositor, *New Age*, 125,

132; prospector, 125; at IDC's sick bed, 228; marriages, 251; IDC's visit to, 338-39; *The Covered Wagon*, 349

Pico, Pio, last Mexican governor of California, IDC dances with, 57

Pinney, Laura Y., member, Press Club, IDC's friend, 288, 302

Pioneers, Society of. *See* Corporate Society of Pioneers

"Pip Pepperpod." *See* Stoddard, Charles Warren

"Pipes of Pipesville, Jeems." *See* Massett, Stephen

Pixley, Frank, lot in Corte Madera to IDC, 262

Plummer, Mrs. J. L., sister of E. A. Trefethen, board member, Oakland Free Library: appointed to replace Ina Peterson, 168; cataloging, 173; resignation, 183

Poems (Ridge), 87

Poems, 1868 (Stoddard), 88, 97, 291

Poems, 1917 (Stoddard), 322-25

"Poetry as a Factor in Education," lecture (IDC), 232

Poetry of the Pacific (Doliver), 87-88

Poetry Society of America, 313, 342; IDC elected to, 292; guest speaker, 335

Pollock, Edward, 88; "Evening," 102

Poole, William Frederick, librarian: IDC's conference with, 181; and tarantula, 200

Popcorn, pet cat, 303, 331, 333, 343, 345, 356

Pope, Alexander, poetry in William Pickett's library, 27

Port Wine, Calif., 42

Porter, Bruce, poet, 341

Portland, Maine, IDC visits relatives, 225-26

Portland, Maine, *Press*, 389

Portolá, Gaspar de, poem on by IDC, 358, 396

Powell, Martha E., 390

Powers, Frank, invites IDC to spend a month at his Pine Inn in Carmel, Calif., 260

Pratt, Harry Noyes, editor, *Overland Monthly*, n.s., IDC's friend, 354, 356

Presidio, San Francisco, 78, 189

Press League, Chicago, Ill., meeting attended by IDC, 224

Proctor, Edna Dean, poet, IDC's friend, 334, 353

Prosit (Spinners' Club), 263

Pseudonyms in San Francisco journals, 80, 81, 89
Putnam's Magazine, 263, 393

"Quillem, Harry." *See* Kewen, Edward John Case
Quincy, Calif., 41, 42
Quincy, Ill., 16

Rabe, B. A., board member, Oakland Free Library, 195; committee, ALA in Oakland, 197; on dismissal of librarian, IDC, 205-8; presents library's financial needs to City Council, 209-10, 214, 216
Raft River, Idaho, 36
Rain-in-the-Face, poem about by IDC, 225
Ralston, William, 256
Ramirez, Conchita, and Yerba Buena Island tree planting, 188
Rancho San Antonio, Calif., 129, 133
Readers' Guide to Periodical Literature, 200
Reading Room Association, Oakland, beginning of, 131
Realf, Richard, poet, memorial program, poems by IDC, 222
Reconnaisance Peak, Calif., 377
Red Cross, check to IDC, 262, 279; IDC's autographs for, 328
Reinhardt, Aurelia Henry, president, Mills College, Oakland, 349-50
Reinhart, Max, "The Miracle," 353-54
"Relieving Guard" (Harte), 85
Religious revivals in America, 5, 8
Reorganized Church of Jesus Christ of Latter Day Saints, 25
Resources of California (Hittell), 97, 112
Retrospect (IDC), 357
Rezanov (Atherton), 269, 293
Richards, John E., judge, San Jose, 274, 275
Richman, Irving, historian, meets IDC, 263
Ridge, John Rollin, in Marysville, 44; pseud., "Yellow Bird," 44, 80; *The Life and Adventures of Joaquin Murieta,* 87; *Poems,* 87; IDC's indebtedness to him, 87
Rigdon, Sidney, in Kirtland, Ohio, 5-6
Rinehart, Amy, and IDC in library, 149
Robertson, Alexander M.: publisher of books edited by IDC, 247; and IDC learn that Stoddard burned his manu-

scripts, 283, 323
Robins Hotel, San Francisco, 347
Robinson, Ebenezer, printer: partner of Don Carlos Smith, 19; tribute to D. C. Smith, 21; editor, *Times and Seasons* after death of D. C. Smith, 22
Robinson, Ednah. *See* Aiken, Ednah Robinson
Robinson, Leo Shenstone, member, Mount Ina Coolbrith committee, 377
Rogers, Robert, major in Indian Wars, 4
Rogers Free Library Act, approved 18 March 1878, 130, 144; revised 1880, 148, 167
Rolfe, Horace, lawyer, reading law in William Pickett's office, 54
Rolland, Romain, letter to IDC, 306
Roman, Anton, publisher: *Outcroppings,* 86, 97; *Overland Monthly,* 91, 114, 154; *Californian, a Western Monthly,* 163; sale of *Overland* to J. H. Carmany, 109, 114, 154, 288; sale of *Californian* to C. Phelps, 163; book store, 97
Roosevelt, Theodore, 280, 307
Rosa, Alphonse, singer, 370
Rosenbach, A. S. W., book collector, 345
Rowell, Joseph, librarian, University of California, 171, 196; committee, ALA in Oakland, 197
Rubaiyat (Omar Khayyam), 306
Ruef, Abe, politician, 307
Rumanian folklore, 287
Rumanian folk songs, lecture on by IDC, 231
Russell, Edmund: recites IDC's "California," 226; calls on IDC, 227
Russian Hill, San Francisco: legends, 78; IDC homes on: 1302 Taylor Street, 81, 89, 245; 1604 Taylor Street, 245-47, 256-58, 260; 15 Lincoln Street (Macondray Lane), 264-66; 1067 Broadway, 150, 279-80, 284, 286, 293, 321, 334; one block spared by fire, 260; IDC's poem, "From Russian Hill," 316, 395
Ryder, Arthur, Sanscrit scholar, poet, 341

Saco (f o r m e r l y Pepperellborough), Maine, birthplace of Mary Foss Coolbroth, 7; IDC's visit, 180
"Sailor Dick," rescues lost children, 46-47
St. Francis Hotel, San Francisco, meeting place of Ina Coolbrith Circle, 334, 348, 349, 373

St. Ignatius Church, San Francisco, *Calendar,* poem by IDC, 395
St. James Hotel, New York City, residence of IDC, 333, 339
St. Joseph, Mo., 28, 29, 31, 32, 347
St. Louis, Mo., home of William Pickett and family, 25, 26-29
St. Louis Mirror, 232
St. Mark's Episcopal Church, Berkeley, Calif., IDC's funeral, 368, 371
St. Mary's College, Moraga, Calif., 130, 321, 358
Salamander Iron Works, Los Angeles: Carsley and Lindsay, partners, 60; quarters on New High Street, 64, 66, 68; Carsley, sole owner, 66; iron casting for jail, 68
Salisbury, Catherine Smith, IDC's aunt: daughter of Joseph and Lucy Mack Smith, 6; birth of daughter, 13
Salisbury, Wilkins, husband of Catherine Smith, 6
Sanchez, Nellie Van de Grift, writer, IDC's friend, 290, 377-78
San Bernardino, Calif.: Pickett family in, 54, 60; Mormons, 68; jail, 66, 68; southern sympathy, 69
Sandburg, Carl, poet, 341-42
San Diego, Calif.: IDC visit, 231; IDC on building advisory committee for public library, 247; Ina Coolbrith Day, 321
San Francisco, Calif.: in 1853-54, 48-49; in 1862, 78-79; cultural life, 79-80, 81, 89, 99-100; IDC's suggestions for beautifying the city, 240-41; earthquake and fire, 18 April 1906, 255-57, 260; "Great White Fleet," 280; IDC's poems on, 94, 263, 291, 306, 316, 358
San Francisco. Public Library, 252, 373
San Francisco Alta, 105, 112, 125, 156, 188, 385
San Francisco Bulletin, 105, 112, 232, 391, 396; "Copa de Oro" (IDC), 224; anonymous tribute to IDC, 252; Herbert Bashford, literary editor, 290; "Foch" (IDC), front page feature, 340
San Francisco Call, 126, 228, 230, 293, 390-94; IDC on how to spend a million dollars, 239-40; review of *Spinners' Books of Fiction,* 269; IDC accused of ingratitude by Spinners, 271
San Francisco Chronicle, 160, 193, 302, 310, 348
San Francisco Daily Report, Overland

revival dinner, 164, 389
San Francisco Examiner, 117, 193, 222, 226, 232, 307, 308, 391-92, 394-96; "Man with the Hoe" first printed, 239; IDC on how best to beautify San Francisco, 240-41; on Spinners' benefit for IDC, 268-69
San Francisco Monitor, 282, 295, 303, 310, 393, 395
San Francisco Post, 394
San Francisco Star, 392
San Francisco Wasp, 391, 396
San Gabriel, Calif.: IDC's marriage, 63; in Civil War, 69
San Gabriel Mission, 56, 64
Sanitary Fund, 83, 85
San Jose, Calif., 100, 280, 371
San Jose Normal, San Jose, Calif., 274, 372
San Jose Normal Pennant, 393
San Jose Short Story Club, IDC a guest, 275, 278
San Jose Women's Club, Ina Coolbrith Day, 274, 275
San Rafael, Calif., home of Bret Harte, 95, 99
Santa Clara News, 394
Santa Cruz, Calif., 100
Santa Cruz Sentinel, employs Josephine Clifford McCrackin, 332
"Sappho of the Western Sea," one of Stedman's sobriquets for IDC, 181
Saturday Review of Literature, 373
Sausalito, Calif.: bay leaves gathered by IDC and Joaquin Miller for wreath for Byron's tomb, 103, 330; town in 1918, 330
"The Saving of Poetry," lecture (Markham), 313
Scarborough, Maine: birthplace of Agnes Moulton Coolbrith Smith Pickett, 7; IDC visit, 1884, 175, 180
Scheffauer, Herman, playwright, IDC's friend, 98, 276, 302; pro-German sympathy, 306; suicide, 162, 353
Scott, Irving M., host, *Overland* revival dinner, 163, 164
Scott, Mrs. Irving M., hostess, *Overland* revival dinner, 164
Scott's Bluff, Nebr., 33
Scribner's Monthly, 230, 391
Sequoia Club, San Francisco, 276; IDC meets Gertrude Atherton, 251
Sessions, E. C., charter member, Oakland Library Association, 130

Severance, Caroline M., IDC's friend, 306, 395

"Seyfforth, Carl," pseud. of Carl Gunderson, musician: IDC's friend, 162, 296, 333, 356, 358; biographical sketch, 328, 352-53; tuberculosis, 330, 345; leaves for Europe though ill, 345; in Switzerland, 348; in Norway, 352-53; sees IDC in New York City, 334, 335, 336, 342; financial aid from IDC, 330-31, 352; gives address book to IDC, 345; final illness and death, 353; *Wings of Sunset* (IDC) dedicated to him, 359

Shafter, O. L., judge, charter member, Oakland Library Association, 130

Shakespeare, William, 27, 312, 390; influence on IDC, 57-58; IDC at plays, 80; "Macbeth," music for, 190, 308

Shasta, Calle. *See* Miller, Calle Shasta

Shattuck, F. K., charter member, Oakland Library Association, 130

Shaw, Robert, on IDC, 350, 352

Sheppard home, San Francisco, saved in fire, 260

Sheridan, Philip H., 97

Sherman, William T., 97

Sherwood, Beatrice, 370

Shinn, Charles H., writer, IDC's friend: Congress of Literature, San Francisco, 226; review of *Poems*, 1917 (Stoddard), 324

Shinn, Milicent, 160; editor, *Overland Monthly*, new series, 163-64, 196, 201

Shuey, Sarah, 141

Sill, Edward Rowland, poet, IDC's friend, 79, 99, 117, 134, 156, 160, 341; *The Hermitage, and Other Poems*, 88; review of IDC's *A Perfect Day* in *Atlantic*, 156; at *Overland* revival dinner, 164; IDC visits in Cuyahoga Falls, Ohio, 181; memorial poem by IDC, 190, 390

Simons, Lena, IDC's friend, 343, 344

Simpson, Anne Pratt: review of *The Spinners' Book of Fiction*, 269; IDC embarrassed by, 269

Sin Lun, on Chinese literature, 312

The Singer of the Sea (IDC), 227

Skidmore, Harriet M., IDC poem to, 394

Smith, Agnes Charlotte, IDC's sister. *See* Peterson, Agnes Charlotte Smith

Smith, Agnes Moulton Coolbrith, IDC's mother. *See* Pickett, Agnes Moulton Coolbrith Smith

Smith, Catherine, IDC's aunt. *See* Salisbury, Catherine Smith

Smith, Clarke Ashton, poet, IDC's friend, 162, 341

Smith, Don Carlos, IDC's father: son of Lucy Mack and Joseph Smith, Sr., 3; birth, 4; in Kirtland, Ohio, 6, 11-12; appearance, 11-12; printer, 12; marriage, 12; children, 12, 21; journey to Missouri, 12-13; Millport, Mo., 13; goes south to seek aid for persecuted Mormons, 14; sees Cherokees on death march, 16; departure with family from Missouri, 16; McDonough County, Ill., 16; *Times and Seasons* printing shop, Nauvoo, 19; member, City Council and Nauvoo Legion, 20; death and tributes, 21, 22, 363, 364, 372; last letter to wife quoted, 21-22; buried in Smith family cemetery, 24

Smith, Emma Hale: wife of Joseph Smith the Prophet, 5-6; journey to Kirtland, Ohio, 6; assassination of husband, 22, 24; Smith family cemetery, 24; remains in Nauvoo, 25; marriage to Major L. C. Bidamon, 25

Smith, George A.: cousin of Don Carlos Smith, 14; journey south to seek funds, 14; Cherokees on death march, 16; letter from widow of Don Carlos quoted, 24

Smith, Hyrum, IDC's uncle, son of Joseph and Lucy Mack Smith, 6; at Kirtland, Ohio, 6; imprisoned 15-16; assassination, 22, 24

Smith, Ina. *See* Coolbrith, Ina Donna

Smith, Jesse Winter, grandnephew of Don Carlos Smith, son of Samuel H. B. and Julia Winter Smith: calls on IDC and sees her manuscript of literary history of California, 254; they discuss her Mormon background, 254, 372; at funeral of IDC, 371-72; officer of Ina Coolbrith Circle, 373

Smith, Joseph, Sr., IDC's grandfather: marriage to Lucy Mack, 4; in Palmyra, N. Y., 4-5; family's conversion, 5; in Kirtland, Ohio, 11, 12; and creditors, 12; with family in Nauvoo, 19

Smith, Joseph, the Prophet, IDC's uncle: fourth child of Joseph and Lucy Mack Smith, 4; vision at Palmyra, 5; personality, 5; and The Church of Jesus Christ of Latter-day Saints, 4-6; arrival in Kirtland, Ohio, 6; tarred and feathered by mob, 6; business activities, failure of bank in Kirtland, 12;

526

in Missouri, 6, 12-16; imprisoned, 15-16; in Commerce, Ill., 16-17; tribute to brother Don Carlos quoted, 21; assassination, 24

Smith, Josephine Donna. *See* Coolbrith, Ina Donna

Smith, Lucy, IDC's aunt. *See* Milliken, Lucy Smith

Smith, Lucy, IDC's cousin, infant daughter of Samuel and Mary Bailey Smith, birth and death, 20

Smith, Lucy Mack, IDC's grandmother, daughter of Lydia and Solomon Mack: birth, 4; marriage to Joseph Smith, 4; in Palmyra, N. Y., 4; in Kirtland, Ohio, 6-11; decision to remain in Nauvoo, 25; connection with Reorganized Church of Jesus Christ of Latter Day Saints, 25; last years and death, 25

Smith, Mary Bailey, wife of Samuel Smith, from Andover, Mass.: in Boston, Mass., 7; meets Agnes Moulton Coolbrith, 7-9; Old South Church, 8-9; converted to Mormon faith, 9; in Kirtland, 11; marriage, 11; in Marrowbone, Mo., 13; birth of son Samuel, 14; death in childbirth, 20; death of infant, Lucy, 20; her grandson, Jesse Winter Smith, 254

Smith, Mary Bailey, daughter of Samuel and Mary Bailey Smith. *See* Norman, Mary Bailey Smith

Smith, May Riley, poet, IDC's friend, 342

Smith, Samuel H. B., IDC's cousin, son of Samuel Harrison and Mary Bailey Smith, birth, 14

Smith, Samuel Harrison, IDC's uncle, son of Lucy Mack and Joseph Smith, Sr., 6; mission to Boston, 7, 8-9; marriage to Mary Bailey, 11; in Marrowbone, Mo., 13, 14; death of wife and infant daughter, 20; death, 22

Smith, Sophronia, IDC's aunt, daughter of Lucy Mack and Joseph Smith, Sr. *See* Stoddard, Sophronia Smith

Smith, Sophronia, IDC's sister, second daughter of Don Carlos and Agnes Smith: birth, 12; death of scarlet fever, 22

Smith, William, IDC's uncle: son of Lucy Mack and Joseph Smith, Sr., 6; marriage, 11

Snow, Eliza, poetic tribute to Don Carlos Smith, 21

Soda Springs, Idaho, 36

"Some California Wild Flowers," essay (IDC), 253

Songs from Bohemia (O'Connell), edited by IDC, 247

Songs from the Golden Gate (IDC), 181, 228, 230-31, 261, 275, 307, 323, 325, 340, 357, 381

Songs of Three Centuries (Whittier), 139

Sosso, Lorenzo, 311

Soulé, Frank, committee ALA day in Oakland, 197

South Pass, Wyo., 34

South Platte River, 32

South Sea Idyls (Stoddard), 105-6

Southern California Women's Press Association, Los Angeles, IDC a guest, 263

Southern Vineyard, 384; local verse, 58

Spanish-American War, IDC's poem on, 239

Spanish Ranch, Calif., Pickett family's stay, 41-43, 347

The Spinners' Book of Fiction (Spinners' Club), 269, 271-72

Spinners' Club, San Francisco, Calif., 263, 276, 278; *Prosit*, 263; to furnish home for IDC, 262-63; to publish a book as benefit, 263, 268; "Coolbrith Fund," name changed to "Spinners' Benefit Fund," 268; circulars advertising fund, 268; financing, 268-69, 271-72; *The Spinners' Book of Fiction*, 269, 271-72; review of *Spinners' Book* humiliating to IDC, 269-71; Gertrude Atherton's indignation, 269; Spinners' fear of being sued, 271; accuse IDC of ingratitude in *Call* article, 271; criticism of club by Stoddard and Lummis, 271, 272; all royalties finally paid IDC, 272

Spreckels, Mrs. Rudolph, 276

Springfield, Ill., 358

"Squibob, John P." *See* Derby, George H.

Stadfelt family, with IDC during San Francisco fire, 256

Stanford, Josiah, brother of Leland Stanford, 133

Stanford University, 235, 239, 276, 350

"Star Chamber" meeting of Oakland Free Library board, 207-8, 212

Stark, Father, 281

Staten Island, N. Y., home of Edwin Markham, 334

Stearns, Abel, 54, 69

Stebbins, Horatio: reads IDC's first commencement ode, 115-16, 320; funeral oration for Laurentine Hamilton, 165

Stedman, Edmund Clarence: IDC's visit, 181; his sobriquets for IDC, 181; *American Anthology*, 189, 381; dedication of *Songs from the Golden Gate* (IDC) to, 228; birthday sonnet by IDC, 250, 280-81, 393; his sister's loss of home in fire of 1906, 258; letters to IDC, 247, 260, 266; Newberry Library, Chicago, 260-61; death, 250, 280-81

Sterling, Ella. *See* Mighels, Ella Sterling Cummins

Sterling, George, poet, IDC's friend, 119, 301, 341, 356, 382; when IDC first saw him, 162; praise for IDC's sonnet, "La Copa de Oro," 224; contributor to *Spinners' Book of Fiction*, "Valentine," and Authors' Reading, 269, 271, 274, 276; dislike of Witter Bynner, 341; suicide, 162, 353; memorial service arranged by IDC, 354, 370; IDC's memorial poem for, 162, 358, 397; his song, "Holy River of Sleep," sung at IDC's funeral, 368, 370

Stern, Mrs. Sigmund, 276

Stetson, Charlotte Perkins. *See* Gilman, Charlotte Perkins Stetson

Stevenson, Lionel, 356, 370, 373-74; "The Mind of Ina Coolbrith," 373-74, 381-83

Stevenson, Robert Louis, 290; his physician's daughter, Mary Bamford, 185

Stiles Hall, Berkeley, Calif., IDC's lectures, 232

Stillman, John, 203

Stock Circular, published by J. H. Carmany, 154

Stoddard, Calvin, husband of Sophronia Smith, 6

Stoddard, Charles Warren, writer, IDC's friend, 79, 83, 85, 86, 92, 97-98, 101-2, 112-13, 118-19, 162, 228, 246, 251-52, 313, 321, 341, 353; pseud., "Pip Pepperpod," 80; contributor to *Californian*, 86; student at College of California, 86; *Outcroppings*, 87; *Poems*, 1867, 88, 97; IDC's salon, 89, 91, 189-90; Golden Gate Trinity, 94-95; introduces Joaquin Miller to IDC, 105, 196-97; South Seas, 105, 106, 109; praise for IDC's verse, 156, 252; lock of hair, 156; praise of Ina Cook's

writing, 179; his autobiographical novel, *For the Pleasure of His Company*, 251, 253, 269; his letters to IDC, 247, 260, 271; contributor to *Spinners' Book of Fiction* and to "Valentine," 269, 274, 275; criticism of Spinners, 271; death and funeral, 281-82; grave, 281, 301; verse manuscripts burned, 283; memorial program, 290; memorial poem, "At Anchor" (IDC), 301-2, 306; lecture on, by IDC, 307; *Poems*, 1917, collected by IDC, 282, 283-84, 322-25, 358; influence and affection of IDC, 359, 364-65, 381

Stoddard, Fred, brother of Charles W. Stoddard, 281

Stoddard, Sara. *See* Makee, Sara Stoddard

Stoddard, Sophronia Smith, IDC's aunt, daughter of Lucy Mack and Joseph Smith, Sr., 6; wife of Calvin Stoddard, 6

The Story of the Files (Mighels), 222, 238

Stowe, Harriet Beecher, *Lady Byron Vindicated*: review by Harte in *Overland*, 101; IDC's dislike of book, 101, 103

Stratton, James, charter member, Oakland Library Association, 130

Strenzel, Louise. *See* Muir, Louise Strenzel

Strong, Dwight, curator, reading room, Oakland Free Library: agreement to take board minutes in Henry Peterson's absence, 203, 204, 210; close friend of Peterson, 251

Strong, Isobel Osbourne. *See* Field, Isobel Osbourne Strong

Sublette's Cut-off, Wyo., 34-35

Suburbs of San Francisco, 99

Sultzer, Kenneth, IDC's friend, 333, 334, 342, 345

Summit Peak, Calif., renamed Mount Ina Coolbrith, 377-78

Sunset Magazine, 252, 263, 291, 316, 336, 340, 393-96

Sutatot, Mrs. Amanda Brock, mother of Calle Shasta Miller, 178

Sutro, Adolph: and Yerba Buena Island tree planting, 188; private library, 196; at ALA session in Oakland, 197

Sweeney, Dan, artist, portrait of IDC, 330, 357

Sweetwater River, Wyo., 34

528

Tacoma, Wash., rose carnival, IDC attends, 232

Taggard, Genevieve, poet, 341

Tamalpais, Mt., Pacific Coast Women's Press Association outing, 232

Taylor, Edward Robeson, poet, IDC's friend, 119, 280, 302, 312, 321; mayor of San Francisco, 275; at Authors' Reading for IDC, 276; death, 348

Taylor, Marian, 325, 327; biographical sketch of IDC, 308, 310

Telegraph Hill, San Francisco: in 1862, 78; how to beautify, 240-41; viewed from IDC's home, 246

Temperance books, 184

Tennyson, Alfred, "Ulysses," 261

Tenure, Oakland Free Library: Ina Peterson, 167-69; IDC, 148-49, 213, 205-17

Tewksbury, Lucio M., reads IDC's poem at Admission Day program, 94

Thaxter, Celia: memorial by IDC, 227; lecture on by IDC, 231

This Life I've Loved (Field), 160

Thomas, Edith, poet, 334, 342

Thomas, Mabel, librarian, IDC's service in Oakland Free Library, 189

Thompson, John, speaker at Oakland Free Library opening, 145

Thompson, Robert B., petition to Congress for redress of wrongs against Mormons in Missouri, 20

Thorpe, Rose Hartwick, 287

Times and Seasons, first issue, 19; edited by Don Carlos Smith, 19; obituary of D. C. Smith, 21; share of profits to widow of D. C. Smith, 22

Tingley, Mary V. See Lawrence, Mary V. Tingley

Titian, pet cat, 256, 257, 261, 284, 294

"To Ina Coolbrith" (Higginson), 202

Tompkins, Edward, gift of lot to Oakland Library Association, 130

Tompkins School, Oakland, Calif., Edwin Markham, principal, 134

Town and Country Club, San Francisco, 276

Town Talk, 263, 293, 306, 325

Travis, Rose, composer, friend of George Sterling, 370

Trefethen, Eugene A., board member, Oakland Free Library, 167, 174; has Ina Peterson dismissed to make way for his sister, 167-69; sarcasm of Ambrose Bierce, 167; book committee,

168-74; library catalog, 170-74

"Trefethenization," word coined by Ambrose Bierce, 167

Truckee River, Nev., 36, 38

Tubbs, Hiram, petition, Peterson case, 169

Tubbs sisters, friends of Isobel Osbourne Field, 160

Tully, Richard Walton, contributor to Spinners' Book of Fiction, 271

Tunbridge, Vt., marriage of Lucy Mack and Joseph Smith, Sr., 4

Twain, Mark, 83, 119, 313, 365; IDC meets in Overland office, 97; his portrait in IDC's home, 246

Two Years Before the Mast (Dana), 305

Turrill, Charles, historian, IDC's friend, 321, 353

Tyrrel, Jeremiah, member, Oakland Free Library board: letter requesting resignation of IDC as librarian, 205-6; interviewed on dismissal, 209

"Ulysses" (Tennyson), 261

United States. Army, Union Army camps in Southern California, 69

United States. Geographic Board, Mount Ina Coolbrith, 378

United States. Navy: permission to plant trees on Yerba Buena Island, 188; "Great White Fleet," 280

University of California, Berkeley, 235, 239, 298, 302; charter, 99, 115, 129; Oakland campus, 115; coeducation, 115-16, 141; commencement odes by IDC, 115-16, 141, 156; J. C. Rowell, university librarian, 171, 196, 197; Mrs. Boalt's bequest, 323

University of California Chronicle, 340, 371, 373, 396

University of California Magazine, 247, 393

University of Notre Dame, 358, 359

Unrest in the 1830s, 8

Urmy, Clarence, poet, IDC's friend, 321, 324, 348

Urso, Camilla, musical festival, San Francisco, 79, 100

"Vale, Joaquin" (IDC), 297-98

"Valentine," booklet of tributes to IDC by her writer friends, 274-75

Vallejo, Mariano Guadalupe, and Yerba Buena Island tree planting, 188

Villa, Pancho, 288

WCTU convention, IDC recites poems, 232

Wadleigh, Mrs. Harriet C., librarian, Los Angeles Public Library, 237

Wagner, Harr, writer: and Yerba Buena Island tree planting, 188, finds IDC among refugees from fire, 257

Waldorf Astoria Hotel, New York City, 342

Walker, Wilbur, board member, Oakland Free Library, 167-74

Walker, William, E. J. C. Kewen with in Nicaragua, 56, 58

Wallace, Alice, Bashford, musician: IDC's friend, 313, 328; daughter of Herbert and Kinnie Cole Bashford, 288, 290; goddaughter of Joaquin Miller and Ella Mae Higginson, 290; plays Beethoven for IDC, 296; accompanist for IDC's songs, 316

Wallace, William A., Los Angeles teacher, 53

Walsh, Thomas, help with Stoddard's Poems, 1917, 322, 323-25

Walter, Carrie Stevens, 394

Walton, Eda Lou, poet, 341

War Poems (California Club), 239, 392

Ware, Joseph, The Emigrants' Guide to California, 28, 29

Warner, J. J., 69

Washington, George, 394

Washington Heights Literary Circle, Pasadena, 262, 272, 273, 279

Webb, Charles Henry: editor and publisher, 79, 85, 291; publisher, The Californian, 85; review of Outcroppings, 86, 87; departure for New York, 88, 91; in IDC's home, 89

Weikel, Charles B., university chimes master, pallbearer at IDC's funeral, 370

Weil, Oscar, writes music for IDC's lyric, "A Christmas Song," 239, 392, 399

Weill, Raphael, 260

Welton, Elizabeth. See Peterson, Elizabeth Welton

Wendte, Charles W., clergyman, 197; ALA meeting in Oakland, 197-99; welcome to delegates, 197; reads IDC's poem "In the Library," at evening session, 198; gives IDC sprig of yew from Wordsworth's grave, 222

Wentworth, May. See Doliver, Mary Wentworth

Western Women's Club, San Francisco, meeting place of Ina Coolbrith Circle, 373

Westward movement, 28, 29

"What an Editor Has Done with Stoddard's Poems" (O'Day), 325

"What's the Matter with California Literature?" lecture (Lummis), 312

Wheeler, Benjamin Ide, president, University of California at Berkeley, 276, 302, 310, 313, 349; confers laurel crown on IDC, 313-14

Wheeler, Mrs. Benjamin Ide, 276

Whiskey Diggings, Calif., 42

Whitaker, Herman, novelist, IDC's friend, 119, 286, 288, 290, 321, 328; contributor to Spinners' Book of Fiction, 269; obtains full royalties for IDC from Spinners' Club, 271-72; at Authors' Reading, 276; Joaquin Miller's last illness, 296; declines to serve as secretary of Congress of Authors and Journalists, 302; death, 349

White, Jennie. See Kewen, Jennie (White)

White, Richard Edward, the "Mission Poet," IDC's friend, 310, 320, 330

White, Thomas J., physician, IDC's friend, 56, 64; El Molino Viejo, 56, 68; first speaker of the California State Assembly, 56; death, memorial poem by IDC, 71-72, 384

White Cloud (ship), cause of waterfront fire in St. Louis, 27

Whitney, Newel K., greets Joseph and Emma Smith in Kirtland, Ohio, 6

Whittaker, A. E: librarian, Mercantile Library, 196; at ALA meeting in Oakland, 197

Whittier, John Greenleaf, poet, IDC's friend, 224, 227-28, 381, 394; Songs of Three Centuries, 139, 141; visit of IDC in 1884, 180-81, 284; praise of IDC's verse, 189, 224; "Whittier, 1807-1907" (IDC), 394

Wiggin, Kate Douglas, 287

Wight, Lyman: at Adam-ondi-Ahman, Mo., 15; Agnes Smith and children seek shelter from mob, 15; permission to call troops to protect Mormons, 15

Wilkinson, Marguerite, poet, 325

Willard, L. C., Miss, third librarian, Oakland Library Association, 131

Willey, S. H., 202

Williams, Michael, editor, Commonweal, IDC's friend, 342

Williams, Peggy, IDC's friend, 342

Williams, Mrs. Virgil, 276
Wilmington, Calif., Camp Drum, 69
Wilson, Benjamin, 54
Wilson, Regina, president, Spinners' Club, 271-72
Wings of Sunset (IDC), 359, 361, 373, 381-83, 397-98
Winter Quarters, Nebr., 24
"The Woman He Married," play (Bashford), 288
Woman Suffrage Party of California, 307
Women, employment of, 148-49, 235, 237, 240, 258, 261
Women, prejudice against: women attend ALA banquet for first time, 200; employment challenged in Oakland, 148-49; dismissal of IDC, 213; Mercantile Library, 235, 237
Women's Christian Temperance Union, 232
Women's Congress, San Francisco, 231-32
Women's World's Fair, Chicago, 354
Wood, Charles Erskine Scott, poet, 341
Wood, Clement, poet, 342
Wood, Elizabeth, 390
Woodruff, E. H., librarian, Stanford University, 196
Woods, Viona, paper at Congress of Literature, San Francisco, 226
Woodworth, William, 286; angered at sale of Stoddard's books, 283
Wordsworth, William, 222
World's Columbian Exposition, Chicago:

California literary exhibit, 222; IDC attends, 224-25

"Yellow Bird." *See* Ridge, John Rollin
Yerba Buena Island, Calif., 78; tree planting, 188-89
Youff, Carl. *See* Seyfforth, Carl
Youff, Ulv. *See* Seyfforth, Carl
Young, Brigham: leader in exodus from Missouri, 15; successor to Joseph Smith, 24, 25; call to San Bernardino Mormons to return to Salt Lake City, 68
Young, C. C., governor, California, 354
Yuba River, Calif., 41, 44

Zeller, Josephine, "Josie," IDC's companion and housekeeper: at IDC's sick bed in Oakland, 228, 246; IDC's housekeeper in San Francisco, 246; with IDC during earthquake and fire of 1906, 255-57; temporary homes with IDC, 257, 261, 263; shares Lincoln Street flat with IDC, 264; injury in fall from street car, 278; with IDC at 1067 Broadway, 284-86, 290; illness, 294; with IDC at pageant, 320; eccentricities, 331-32, 334; hysteria, 333; cares for Popcorn, the cat, 333, 345; IDC's bequest to, 372
Zeller, Mary, sister of Josephine Zeller, 331
Zola, Emile: novels ordered removed from shelves of Oakland Free Library by board members of 1883-85, 170; ordered replaced by next board, 185